Linux Application Development

Second Edition

▲▲▲

Linux Application Development

Second Edition

▼

Michael K. Johnson

Erik W. Troan

✦Addison-Wesley

Boston

The authors and publisher have taken care in the preparation of this book, but make no expressed or implied warranty of any kind and assume no responsibility for errors or omissions. No liability is assumed for incidental or consequential damages in connection with or arising out of the use of the information or programs contained herein.

The publisher offers excellent discounts on this book when ordered in quantity for bulk purchases or special sales, which may include electronic versions and/or custom covers and content particular to your business, training goals, marketing focus, and branding interests. For more information, please contact:

U. S. Corporate and Government Sales
(800) 382-3419
corpsales@pearsontechgroup.com

For sales outside the U. S., please contact:

International Sales
international@pearsoned.com

Visit us on the Web: www.informit.com/aw

Library of Congress Cataloging-in-Publication Data

Johnson, Michael K.
    Linux application development / Michael K. Johnson, Erik W. Troan.-- 2nd ed.
        p. cm.
    Includes bibliographical references and index.
    ISBN 0-321-56322-0 (hardback : alk. paper)
    1. Linux. 2. Application software--Development.   I. Troan, Erik W. II. Title.

QA76.76.O63J635   2004
005.1--dc22   2004017882

ISBN 0-321-56322-0
Text printed in the United States on recycled paper at OPM in Laflin, PA.
This product is printed digitally on demand.

*To Loren and Ian, for providing constant distractions
and a steady stream of better things to do.*

—Erik

*To the memory of my grandmother, Eleanor Johnson,
who taught faith in God by example,
and who believed that I could write a book.*

Soli Deo Gloria.

—Michael

Abbreviated Contents

Contents

List of Tables

Code Examples

Preface

We wrote this book for experienced (or not-so-experienced, but eager-to-learn) programmers who want to develop Linux software or to port software from other platforms to Linux. This is the book we wish we had when we were learning to program for Linux, and the book we now keep on our desks for reference. As soon as we wrote the first three chapters of the first edition, we were using the drafts as reference material while we worked.

This second edition removes outdated information, adds new information, and introduces an online version. You can now browse and search the entire content of this book at http://ladweb.net/ to make this book even more useful to you.

Linux is designed to be similar to Unix. This book gives you a good background in Unix programming basics and style. Linux is not fundamentally different from Unix; it differs in some details, but no more than one Unix version typically differs from another Unix version. This book is very much a Unix programming guide that is written from a Linux viewpoint and with specific Linux information.

Linux also has unique extensions, such as its direct screen access capabilities (see Chapter 21), and it has features that are used more often on it than on other systems, such as the popt library (see Chapter 26). This book covers many of those extensions and features so that you can write programs that truly take advantage of Linux.

- If you are a C programmer, but you know neither Unix nor Linux, reading this book cover-to-cover and working with the examples should put you well on the road to being a competent Linux programmer. With the aid of system-specific documentation, you should find the transition to any version of Unix easy.

- If you are already a proficient Unix programmer, you will find that this book makes your transition to Linux easier. We have tried very hard to make it easy for you to find precisely the information you need to know. We also carefully and clearly cover topics that sometimes trip up even experienced Unix programmers, such as process and session groups, job control, and tty handling.

• If you are already a Linux programmer, this book covers confusing topics clearly and will make many of your programming tasks easier. Nearly every chapter will stand alone for you, because you already possess the essential knowledge of Linux on which they are based. No matter how experienced you are, you will find material here that you will appreciate having at your elbow.

This book is different from typical Unix programming texts because it is unabashedly specific to a particular operating system. We do not try to cover all the differences between different Unix-like systems; to do so would not be useful to Linux programmers, Unix programmers, or C programmers unfamiliar with Linux or Unix. We know from our own experience that once you learn how to program well for any Unix-like system, the others are easy to learn.

This book does not cover *all* the details of Linux programming. It does not explain the basic interface specified by ANSI/ISO C—other books do that quite well. It does not cover the wealth of other programming languages available for Linux, and it does not cover the graphical programming libraries that are identical no matter what system you are using. Instead, we point you to books that specialize in those areas. Without extraordinary verbosity, we cover the information you need to know to go from being a C programmer for another system, such as Windows, Macintosh, or even DOS, to being a C programmer for Linux.

Linux Application Development is written in four parts:

• The first part introduces you to Linux—the operating system, license terms, and online system documentation.

• The second part covers the most important facets of the development environment—the compilers, linker and loader, and some debugging tools that are not widely used on other platforms.

- The third part is the heart of the book—it describes the interface to the kernel and to system libraries that are meant primarily as an interface to the kernel. In this section, only Chapters 19, 20, and 21 are very Linux-specific; most of this section covers general Unix programming from a Linux perspective. A new chapter in this second edition, Chapter 22, covers the basics of writing secure programs.

- The fourth part rounds out your knowledge—it includes descriptions of some important libraries that provide interfaces that are more independent of the kernel. These libraries are, properly speaking, not Linux-specific, but several are used more often on Linux systems than on other systems.

If you are already familiar with Linux or Unix programming, you will be able to read the chapters in this book in any order, skipping any that do not interest you. If you are not familiar with either Linux or Unix, most of the chapters will stand alone, but you will probably want to read Chapters 1, 2, 4, 5, 9, 10, 11, and 14 first, as they give you most of what you need to know to read the other chapters. In particular, Chapters 10, 11, and 14 form the core of the Unix and Linux programming model.

The following books, although they may overlap a little here and there, mostly complement this book by being simpler, more advanced, or on related topics.

- *The C Programming Language, second edition* [Kernighan, 1988] concisely teaches ANSI standard C programming, with scant reference to the operating system. It recommends that readers have either some programming knowledge or "access to a more knowledgeable colleague."

- *Practical C Programming* [Oualline, 1993] teaches C programming and style in a step-by-step, easy-to-follow manner that is designed for people with no prior programming experience.

- *Programming with GNU Software* [Loukides, 1997] is an introduction to the GNU programming environment, including chapters on running the C compiler, the debugger, the make utility, and the RCS source code control system.

- *Advanced Programming in the UNIX Environment* [Stevens, 1992] covers most important Unix and Unix-like systems, although it predates Linux. It covers similar material to the final two parts of *Linux Application Development*: system calls and shared libraries. It also provides many examples and explains the difference between various Unix versions.

- *UNIX Network Programming* [Stevens, 2004] thoroughly covers network programming, including legacy types of networking that are not available on Linux, at least as we write this. While reading this book, stick to the Berkeley socket interface (see Chapter 17) to maintain maximum portability. This book may be useful if you need to make a few slight changes to port your Linux network program to some brand of Unix.

- *A Practical Guide to Red Hat Linux 8* [Sobell, 2002] is a 1,500-page tome that contains introductions to using Linux, shell programming, and system administration. While this book does mention Red Hat Linux 8, most of the information it contains applies to all flavors of Linux. It also contains a summary reference to many of the utilities that are included with a Linux system.

- *Linux in a Nutshell* [Siever, 2003] is smaller and shorter and concentrates on a summary utility reference derived from O'Reilly's earlier nutshell references.

- *Linux Device Drivers, second edition* [Rubini, 1998] teaches those who have never touched operating system code, as well as those who have, how to write Linux device drivers.

See the bibliography on page 679 for an extensive list of related titles.

All the source code in this book comes from working examples that we have tested while writing. All of the source code in this book is available in electronic format at http://ladweb.net/ In the interest of clarity, some short source code segments check only for likely errors that document how the system works rather than check for all possible errors. However, in the full programs in the book and on our Web site, we have made an attempt (we are not perfect) to check for all reasonable errors.

This book will teach you which functions to use and how they fit together; we encourage you to learn also how to use the reference documentation, the great majority of which was included with your system. Chapter 3 discusses how to find online information on your Linux system.

Linux is a rapidly developing operating system, and by the time you read this book, some facts (although we hope little substance) will no doubt have changed. We wrote this book in reference to the Linux 2.6 kernel and the GNU C library version 2.3.

With your help, we will maintain a list of errata and changes on the World Wide Web at http://ladweb.net/errata.html

We welcome your comments sent to lad-comments@ladweb.net. We will read your comments, although we cannot promise to respond to them individually.

Second Edition

Additions to and modifications from the first to the second edition include:

- The whole book has been updated to take into account the new Single Unix Specification, issue 6; the updated version of the POSIX standard.

- A table of example source code has been added to make it easier to find sample programs.

- Small segments of example source code now are listed with line numbers printed, making it easier for you to orient yourself in respect to each entire soure code example.

- Chapter 1 has an updated and expanded history of Linux development.

- Chapter 4 now discusses the strace and ltrace utilities.

- Chapter 6 is a new chapter that discusses the GNU C library (glibc) and the standards on which it is based. Of particular interest, it explains how (and why) to use feature test macros. It also describes some basic types used by system calls discussed throughout the book, how to discover the capabilities of your system at run time, covers some miscellaneous system interfaces glibc provides, and describes glibc's approach to backward compatibility.

- Chapter 7 has significantly expanded information on memory debugging tools, including new memory debugging facilities in the GNU C Library, a new version of mpr, and the new Valgrind tool.

- Chapter 12 discusses real-time signals and signal contexts.

- Chapter 13 documents the `poll()` and `epoll` system calls, which provide recommended alternatives to `select()`.

- Chapter 16 now discusses and recommends the newer mechanism for allocating Pseudo TTYs, and covers the modification of the utmp and wtmp system databases.

- Chapter 17 now covers IPv6 as well as IPv4, including new system library interfaces for writing programs that can use both IPv6 and IPv4 interchangeably. It still explains the older interfaces covered in the first edition, in order to enable you to maintain code that uses those interfaces and to port that older code to the newer interfaces. It also discusses more functionality that is required of many network server programs, such as non-blocking `accept()`.

- Chapter 22 is a new chapter that discusses the basic requirements of writing secure programs, and explains why security concerns apply to all programs, not just system daemons and utilities.

- Chapter 23 has much-improved discussion of using regular expressions, including a simple version of the grep utility as an example.

- Chapter 26 covers the latest improvements to the popt library and has better example source code, more than doubling the length of the chapter.

- Chapter 28 has useful coverage of the Linux-PAM implementation of PAM added.

- Chapter 25 now documents the qdbm library rather than Berkeley db, as the qdbm license is less restrictive.

- The index and glossary have been greatly improved in scope and quality. In particular, canonical entries in the index are now flagged in **bold** to make it obvious where to look first.

- There are smaller changes throughout the book, with nearly every chapter having important updates.

Subtractions include:

- How to find generic Linux information on mailing lists, Web sites, and newsgroups; this information changes too rapidly to be part of a book that should otherwise be useful for many years.

- Discussion of manipulating I/O ports; this facility is generally deprecated because it conflicts with Linux's device and power management structure.

- Verbatim copies of the GNU General Public License and GNU Library General Public License. While these two licenses are as important as ever, it will not increase public awareness of their contents to print them again. Also, several other licenses have become more important since the first edition was published.

- The Checker tool for memory debugging is no longer maintained, so the second edition no longer discusses it.

Acknowledgments

We would like to thank each of our technical reviewers for their time and careful thought. Their suggestions have made this book stronger. Particular thanks go to Linus Torvalds, Alan Cox, Ted Ts'o, and Arjan van de Ven, who took time to answer our questions.

After supporting us through writing the first edition, our wives, Kim Johnson and Brigid Troan, were so brave and generous that they encouraged us to write this second edition. Without their help, this book would never have been written, let alone updated.

Part 1

Getting Started

CHAPTER 1

History of Linux Development

People use **Linux** to mean different things. A technically accurate definition is this:

> Linux is a freely distributable, Unix-like operating system kernel.

However, most people use **Linux** to mean an entire operating system based on the Linux kernel:

> Linux is a freely distributable, Unix-like operating system that includes a kernel, system tools, applications, and a complete development environment.

In this book, we use the second definition, as you will be programming for the entire operating system, not just the kernel.

Linux (by the second definition) provides a good platform from which to port programs, because its recommended interfaces (the ones we discuss in this book) are supported by nearly every version of Unix available, as well as by most Unix clones. After you learn the contents of this book, you should be able to port your programs to nearly every Unix and Unix-like system, with little extra work.

On the other hand, after working with Linux, you may prefer to use only Linux and not bother porting.

Linux is not just another Unix. It is more than a good platform from which to port programs—it is also a good platform on which to build and run applications. It is widely used around the world, and has become a household name. It has helped to popularize the concept of **Open Source** or **Free Software**. A brief history lesson will help explain how, and why, this has happened.

1.1   A Short History of Free Unix Software

This history is simplified and biased toward the most important elements in a Linux system. For longer, more even coverage, you can read an entire book, *A Quarter Century of UNIX* [Salus, 1994].

In the earliest days of computing, software was seen as little more than a feature of the hardware. It was the hardware that people were trying to sell, so companies gave away the software with their systems. Enhancements, new algorithms, and new ideas flowed freely among students, professors, and corporate researchers.

It did not take long for companies to recognize the value of software as intellectual property. They began enforcing copyrights on their software technologies and restricting distribution of their source code and binaries. The innovations that had been seen as public property became fiercely protected corporate assets, and the culture of computer software development changed.

Richard Stallman, at the Massachusetts Institute of Technology (MIT), did not want any part of a world in which software innovation was controlled by corporate ambitions. His answer to this development was to found the Free Software Foundation (FSF). The goal of the FSF is to encourage the development and use of freely redistributable software.

The use of the word *free* in this context has created great confusion, however. Richard Stallman meant *free* as in freedom, not *free* as in zero cost. He strongly believes that software and its associated documentation should be available with source code, with no restrictions placed on additional redistribution. More recently, others coined the term **Open Source** in an attempt to describe the same goals, without the confusion over the word *free*. The terms **Open Source** and **Free Software** are generally treated synonymously.

To promote his ideal, Richard Stallman, with help from others, created the General Public License (GPL). This license has been so influential that *GPL* has entered the developers' jargon lexicon as a verb; to apply the terms of the GPL to software you write is *to GPL* it.

The GPL has three major points:

1. Anyone who receives GPLed software has the right to obtain the source code to the software at no additional charge (beyond the cost of delivery).

2. Any software derived from GPLed software must retain the GPL as its license terms for redistribution.

3. Anyone in possession of GPLed software has the right to redistribute that software under terms that do not conflict with the GPL.

An important point to notice about these licensing terms is that they do not mention price (except that source is not allowed to be an extra-cost item). GPLed software may be sold to customers at any price. However, those customers then have the right to redistribute the software, including the source code, as they please. With the advent of the Internet, this right has the effect of keeping the price of GPLed software low—generally zero—while still allowing companies to sell GPLed software and services, such as support, designed to complement the software.

The part of the GPL that generates the most controversy is the second point: that software derived from GPLed software also must be GPLed. Although detractors refer to the GPL as a virus because of this clause, supporters insist that this clause is one of the GPL's greatest strengths. It prevents companies from taking GPLed software, adding features, and turning the result into a proprietary package.

The major project the FSF sponsors is the GNU's Not Unix (GNU) project, whose goal is to create a freely distributable Unix-like operating system. There was little high-quality freely distributable software available for the GNU project when it was started, so project contributors began by creating the applications and tools for the system rather than the operating system itself. As the GPL was also produced by the FSF, many of the key components of the GNU operating system are GPLed, but through the years the GNU project has adopted many other software packages, such as the X Window System, the TEX typesetting system, and the Perl language, that are freely redistributable under other licenses.

Several major packages, and a multitude of minor ones, have been produced as a result of the GNU project. Major ones include the Emacs editor, the GNU C library, the GNU Compiler Collection (gcc, which originally stood for GNU C Compiler before C++ was added), the bash shell, and gawk (GNU's awk). Minor ones include the high-quality shell utilities and text-manipulation programs that users expect to find on a Unix system.

1.2 Development of Linux

In 1991, Linus Torvalds, at that time a student at the University of Helsinki, started a project to teach himself about low-level Intel 80386 programming. At the time, he was running the Minix operating system, designed by Andrew Tanenbaum, so he initially kept his project compatible with the Minix system calls and on-disk file-system layout to make his work much easier. Although he released the first version of the Linux kernel to the Internet under a fairly restrictive license, he was soon convinced to change his license to the GPL.

The combination of the GPL and the early functionality of the Linux kernel convinced other developers to help develop the kernel. A C library implementation, derived from the then-dormant GNU C library project, was released, allowing developers to build native user applications. Native versions of gcc, Emacs, and bash quickly followed. In early 1992, a moderately skilled developer could install and boot Linux 0.95 on most Intel 80386 machines.

The Linux project was closely associated with the GNU project from the beginning. The GNU project's source base became an extremely important resource for the Linux community from which to build a complete system. Although significant portions of Linux-based systems are derived from sources that include freely available Unix code from the University of California at Berkeley and the X Consortium, many important parts of a functional Linux system come directly from the GNU project.

As Linux matured, some individuals, and later, companies, focused on easing the installation and usability of Linux systems for new users by creating packages, called **distributions,** of the Linux kernel and a reasonably complete set of utilities that together constituted a full operating system.

In addition to the Linux kernel, a Linux distribution contains development libraries, compilers, interpreters, shells, applications, utilities, graphical operating environments, and configuration tools, along with many other components. When a Linux system is built, distribution developers collect the components from a variety of places to create a complete collection of all the software components that are necessary for a functional Linux system. Most distributions also contain custom components that ease the installation and maintenance of Linux systems.

Many Linux distributions are available. Each has its own advantages and disadvantages; however, they all share the common kernel and development libraries that distinguish Linux systems from other operating systems. This book is intended to help developers build programs for any Linux system. Because all Linux distributions use the same code to provide system services, program binaries and source code are highly compatible across distributions.

One project that has contributed to this compatibility is the **Filesystem Hierarchy Standard** (FHS), previously called the **Linux Filesystem Standard** (FSSTND), which specifies where many files should be kept and explains, in general terms, how the rest of the file system should be organized. More recently, a project called **Linux Standard Base** (LSB) has expanded beyond the file system layout, defining Application Program Interfaces (APIs) and Application Binary Interfaces (ABIs) intended to make it possible to compile an application once and deploy it on any system that complies with the LSB definition for that CPU architecture. These documents are available, with others, at http://freestandards.org/.

1.3 Notional Lineage of Unix Systems

Although the major portions of Linux comprise code developed independently of traditional Unix source bases, the interfaces that Linux provides were influenced heavily by existing Unix systems.

In the early 1980s, Unix development split into two camps, one at the University of California at Berkeley, the other at AT&T's Bell Laboratories. Each institution developed and maintained Unix operating systems that were derived from the original Unix implementation done by Bell Laboratories.

The Berkeley version of Unix became known as the **Berkeley Software Distribution** (BSD) and was popular in academia. The BSD system was the first to include TCP/IP networking, which contributed to its success and helped to convince Sun Microsystems to base Sun's first operating system, SunOS, on BSD.

Bell Laboratories also worked on enhancing Unix, but, unfortunately, it did so in ways slightly different from those of the Berkeley group. The various releases from Bell Laboratories were denoted by the word *System* followed by a roman numeral. The final major release of Unix from Bell Laboratories was **System V** (or SysV); **UNIX System V Release 4** (SVR4) provides the code base for most commercial Unix operating systems today. The standard document describing System V is the **System V Interface Definition** (SVID).

This forked development of Unix caused major differentiation in the system calls, system libraries, and basic commands of Unix systems. One of the best examples of this split is in the networking interfaces that each operating system provided to applications. BSD systems used an interface known as **sockets** to allow programs to talk to one another over a network. By contrast, System V provided the **Transport Layer Interface** (TLI), which is completely incompatible with sockets, and is officially defined in the X/Open Transport Interface (XTI). This divergent development greatly diminished the portability of programs across versions of Unix, increasing the cost and decreasing the availability of third-party products for all versions of Unix.

Another example of the incompatibilities among Unix systems is the `ps` command, which allows users to query the operating system's process information. On BSD systems, `ps aux` gives a complete listing of all the processes running on a machine; on System V, that command is invalid, and `ps -ef` can be used instead. The output formats are as incompatible as the command-line arguments. (The Linux `ps` command attempts to recognize both styles.)

In an attempt to standardize all the aspects of Unix that had diverged because of the split development in this period (affectionately known as the Unix Wars), the Unix industry sponsored a set of standards that would define the interfaces Unix provides. The portion of the standards that deals with programming and system-tool interfaces was known as **POSIX** (technically, this is the IEEE Std 1003 series, comprised of many separate standards and draft standards), and was issued by the **Institute for Electrical and Electronic Engineers** (IEEE).

The original POSIX series of standards, however, were insufficiently complete. For example, basic UNIX concepts such as processes were considered optional. A more complete standard went through several versions and names (such as the **X/Open Portability Guide** [XPG] series of standards) before being named the **Single Unix Specification** (SUS), released by **The Open Group** (the owner of the UNIX trademark). The SUS has gone through several revisions and now also has been adopted by the IEEE as the latest version of the POSIX standard, currently IEEE Std 1003.1-2004 [Open Group, 2002], and updated occasionally by corrigenda. IEEE Std 1003.1-2003 was also adopted as an ISO/IEC standard as ISO/IEC 9945-2003. You can read the latest version of the standard online at http://www.unix-systems.org/.

Older standards from which this newer unified standard was created include all the older IEEE Std 1003.1 (POSIX.1—the C programming interface), IEEE Std 1003.2 (POSIX.2—the shell interface), and all related POSIX standards, such as the real-time extensions specified as POSIX.4, later renamed POSIX.1b, and several draft standards.

Since "POSIX" is pronounceable and "POSIX" and "SUS" are now synonymous, we refer to the combined work as POSIX throughout this book.

1.4 Linux Lineage

"The best thing about standards is that there are so many to choose from."[1] Linux developers had 20 years of Unix history to examine when they designed Linux, and, more important, they had high-quality standards to reference. Linux was designed primarily according to POSIX; where POSIX

---

1. Andrew Tanenbaum, Computer Networks, Prentice Hall, 1981, page 168.

left off, Linux generally followed System V practice, except in networking, where both the system calls and networking utilities followed the far more popular BSD model. Now that the joint SUS/POSIX standard exists, further development is normally compatible with the newer POSIX standard, and past deviations have been largely corrected when possible.

The biggest difference between SVR4 and Linux, from a programming perspective, is that Linux does not provide quite as many duplicate programming interfaces. For example, even programmers who coded exclusively for SVR4 systems generally preferred Berkeley sockets to SysV TLI; Linux eschews the overhead of TLI and provides only sockets.

When there are insufficient available standards (formal, *de jure*, and informal, *de facto*) for an implementation, Linux sometimes has to provide its own extensions beyond POSIX. For example, the POSIX asynchronous I/O specification is widely judged as inadequate for many real applications, so Linux implements the POSIX standard by means of a wrapper around a more general, more useful implementation. Also, there is no general specification for a highly scalable I/O polling interface, so an entirely new interface called `epoll` was devised and added. We call out these nonstandard interfaces as such when we document them.

CHAPTER 2

Licenses and Copyright

Newcomers to the free-software world are often confused by the variety of licensing terms attached to free software. Some free-software devotees twist normal words into jargon and then expect you to understand every nuance they have attached to each piece of jargon.

To write and distribute software that runs on a free platform such as Linux, you must understand licenses and copyright. These matters are regularly confused by intelligent and informed people, free-software devotees among them. Whether you intend to write free or commercial software, you will be working with tools that come with a variety of license terms. A general understanding of the field of copyright and licensing will help you to avoid common errors.

In these litigious times, it is vitally important that we warn you that **we are not lawyers**. This chapter reflects our understanding of the matters that we discuss, but it does not offer legal advice. Before you make any decisions regarding your own or anyone else's intellectual property, you should study the subject further and, unless you think it unnecessary, consult an attorney.

2.1 Copyright

We deal with the simpler subject first. A **copyright** is the simple assertion of ownership of certain types of intellectual property. Under the latest international copyright conventions, you do not even need to claim copyright for material you create. Unless you explicitly disclaim ownership, other people are allowed to use your intellectual property only in strictly defined ways, called **fair use**, unless you explicitly give them permission, called **license**, to do otherwise. So if you write a book or a piece of software, you do not need to put "Copyright c *year*" on it to own it. However, if you do not put this phrase on your writing, you may find it much more difficult to claim ownership in court if someone violates either your copyright (by claiming that, or acting as if, you do not own the copyright) or your license terms. The Berne copyright convention,[1] an international treaty covering international copyright conventions and enforcement, requires participating nations to enforce copyright only

> ... if from the time of the first publication all the copies of the work published with the authority of the author or other copyright proprietor bear the symbol of a lower case "c" inside of a circle accompanied by the name of the copyright proprietor and the year of first publication placed in such manner and location as to give reasonable notice of claim of copyright.

The sequence (c) has been generally used as a replacement for the lower case "c" inside of a circle, but courts have not upheld that. Always use the word *Copyright* (in addition to the sequence (c), if you choose), when asserting your copyright. If a c character is available to you, it is best also to make use of that character, but do not neglect the word *Copyright*.

Copyright is not perpetual. All intellectual property eventually passes into the **public domain**; that is, the public eventually owns the copyright to the property, and any person can do anything with the property. No license terms are binding once the property is in the public domain. There is one twist: If you create a **derived work** based on public-domain work, then you own the copyright to your **modifications**. Therefore, although many old books are now **out of copyright**, their copyright having passed into the public domain, editors often make small changes here and there, correcting mistakes made in the original. They often then claim copyright ownership of the derived work that includes their changes. This copyright prevents you from legally copying the edited version, although you can freely copy the public-domain, out-of-copyright original.

---

1. http://www.wipo.org/

Note that there are limits on what can be copyrighted. You cannot publish a book containing only the word *the* and then attempt to extort license fees from everyone using the word *the* in their books. However, if you create a sufficiently stylized painting of the word *the*, you would own the copyright to that particular representation, as long as it was sufficiently identifiable for you to show that prior art did not exist with the same representation. Although we are free to use the word *the* in this sentence, we would not be allowed to sell reproductions of your work without getting a license from you.

These limitations apply to software as well. If you are licensed to alter someone else's software and you make a trivial, one-word change, it would be absurd for you to claim copyright to that change. You would not be able to defend a copyright claim to that change in court; your contribution would be as much in the public domain as the word *the* is. However, if you add significantly to the software, you would own the copyright to your modification, unless, for instance, the copyright owners of the original licensed the software for modification with the license restriction that copyright ownership of all modifications revert to them.

2.2 Licensing

Copyright owners have wide latitude in determining license terms. Common areas of restriction (or permission) include use, copying, distribution, and modification. As a concrete example, the GNU General Public License (GPL, commonly called the *copyleft*) explicitly does not limit use. It limits only "copying, distribution, and modification."

Here is an example of free-software jargon with which you want to be familiar. In the free-software world, *public domain* is used almost exclusively in terms of ownership. In other circles, it is often applied to use, as well. Magazine articles that refer to the GPL as a "public-domain copyright" are clearly wrong because the GPL does not give ownership of the copyright to the public domain; articles that refer to it as a "public-domain license" are in one sense correct, because the GPL explicitly places no license restrictions on use. Free-software fanatics, however, often cringe at this use of *public domain*, and many believe it to be completely incorrect.

Certain license restrictions may not be legal in certain localities. Most governing bodies prevent you from restricting what they consider **fair use** in a license agreement. For example, many European countries explicitly allow reverse engineering of software and hardware for certain purposes, license terms restricting such activities notwithstanding. For this reason, most license agreements include a **separability clause** something like the following one, from the GPL:

> If any portion of this section is held invalid or unenforceable under any particular circumstance, the balance of the section is intended to apply and the section as a whole is intended to apply in other circumstances.

Most license agreements use less comprehensible language to say the same thing.

Many people who attempt to write their own license terms without legal help write licenses with terms that have no legal force, and few of those licenses include a separability clause. If you wish to write your own license terms for your software, and if you care whether people comply with the license terms, have an intellectual-property lawyer vet your license terms.

2.3   Free Software Licenses

As described in Chapter 1, the term **Open Source** was coined in an attempt to resolve the confusion surrounding the word *free* in "free software." The **Open Source Initiative** (OSI) was created in order to administer the term **Open Source**, and although its attempts to trademark the term (to protect its meaning) were rejected by the US Patent and Trademark Office, the OSI does hold the certification mark **OSI Certified Open Source Software**. (There are no legal constraints on the use of the term **Open Source**, but there are on the **OSI Certified Open Source Software** certification mark.)

The OSI maintains the **Open Source Definition** (OSD), a description of the rights provided by Open Source licenses; it also maintains a complete list of all licenses that it certifies to have met the requirements of the OSD, among which are: Source code must be available; the product must be freely redistributable; derived works must be allowed; and discrimination against persons, groups, or fields of endeavor must not be allowed. The complete OSD, along with a list of licenses certified as OSI Certified Open Source Software, is available at http://opensource.org/.

2.3.1 The GNU General Public License

The GPL is one of the more restrictive free-software licenses. If you include source code that is licensed under the terms of the GPL in another program, that program must also be licensed under the terms of the GPL.[2] The Free Software Foundation (FSF; author of the GPL) considers linking with a library to be "creating a derivative work"; some others believe it to be a "work of mere aggregation." Therefore, the FSF holds that you are not allowed to link with a library covered under the terms of the GPL unless the program being linked also is covered by the terms of the GPL. However, some people hold that linking is "mere aggregation," and the GPL says:

> In addition, mere aggregation of another work not based on the Program with the Program (or with a work based on the Program) on a volume of a storage or distribution medium does not bring the other work under the scope of this License.

If you consider an executable to be a "volume of storage," you could consider linking mere aggregation.

To the best of our knowledge, this distinction has not yet been tested in court. In the fairly unlikely case that you wish to link a program not licensed under the terms of the GPL with a library that is, ask the authors of the library in question for their interpretation.

2.3.2 The GNU Library General Public License

The GNU Library General Public License (LGPL) was designed to make libraries more generally useful. The point of the LGPL is to allow users to upgrade or improve their libraries without having to get new versions of programs linked against those libraries. To that end, the LGPL does not attempt to place any licensing restrictions on programs linked against the library, as long as those programs are linked against shared versions of libraries licensed under the LGPL or are provided with the object files

---

2. Some people call the GPL a virus for this reason.

for the application, allowing the user to relink the application with new or altered versions of the library.

In practice, this restriction is not significant; it would be unreasonable not to link against shared libraries where they are available.

Few libraries are licensed under the terms of the GPL; most are licensed under the terms of the LGPL. Libraries licensed under the terms of the GPL are usually that way simply because the author did not know about or consider the LGPL. In response to a polite request, many authors will relicense their libraries under the terms of the LGPL.

2.3.3 MIT/X/BSD-Style Licenses

MIT/X-style licenses are much simpler than the GPL or LGPL; their only restrictions are (stated simply) to keep all existing copyright notices and license terms intact in source and binary distributions, and not to use the name of any author to endorse or promote derived works without prior written permission.

2.3.4 Old BSD-Style Licenses

Old BSD-style licenses essentially add to the conditions of the MIT/X-style licenses the restriction that advertising materials that mention features or use of the software include an acknowledgment. The BSD license itself has been changed to removed this restriction, but some software continues to use licenses modeled after the old BSD license.

2.3.5 Artistic License

The Perl language source code is distributed with a license that allows you to follow either the terms of the GPL or of an alternative license, whimsically called the **Artistic License.** The main goals of the Artistic License are to preserve redistribution rights and to prevent users from selling altered, proprietary modifications that masquerade as the official version. Other software authors have adopted Perl's convention of allowing users to follow the terms of either the GPL or the Artistic License; a few are licensed only under the terms of the Artistic License.

2.3.6 License Incompatibilities

Different free-software license terms allow various types of commercial use, modification, and distribution. It is often desirable to reuse existing code in your own projects. To some extent, it is inevitable that you do so—almost any program that you write will be linked with the C library, so you need to be aware of the licensing terms of the C library, as well as the terms of other libraries that you link with your program. You may often wish to include fragments of other programs' source code in your own programs, as well.

Mixing code from software with different licenses can sometimes be a problem. The problem does not occur when linking with shared libraries, but it definitely applies to creating derived works. If you are modifying someone else's software, you have to understand their licensing terms. If you are trying to combine in one derived work two pieces of software that have different licenses, you have to determine if their licenses conflict. Again, this does not apply when you are writing your own code from scratch.

If you are working with code licensed under the terms of the GPL or LGPL, you cannot include in it code licensed under an old BSD-style license, because the GPL and LGPL forbid "additional restrictions," and the old BSD license contains additional restrictions (that is, beyond any in the GPL or LGPL) in regard to advertising and endorsement. Because of this conflict, some pieces of software are licensed under alternative terms—both the GPL and an old BSD-style license terms are offered; you can choose with which licensing terms to comply.

If the code licensed under the GPL or LGPL is included in a work derived from a BSD/MIT/X-style license, the entire derived work (for all practical purposes) must be licensed under the terms of the GPL or LGPL, respectively.

There are many other potential incompatibilities. If you are in doubt about what you are allowed to do with particular pieces of free software, do not be shy—ask the copyright owners. Remember that they can give you license to use the software in any way they wish.

Online System Documentation

The *Linux Application Development* Web site, http://ladweb.net, has updates to this book's text, detailed information beyond this book's scope, and pointers to more information on the Internet.

3.1 The man Pages

Access the system reference manual pages (man pages) through the `man` command. To read the reference page on the `man` command itself, run the command line `man man`. Man pages generally contain reference documentation, not tutorial information, and are renowned for being so succinct that they are barely understandable at times. Nevertheless, when you need reference material, they can be exactly what you want.

Three programs provide access to man pages. The man program displays individual man pages, and the `apropos` and `whatis` commands search for a keyword in the set of man pages. The `apropos` and `whatis` commands search the same database; the difference is that `whatis` displays only lines that match exactly the word you are searching for, and `apropos` displays any line that contains the word you are searching for. That is, if you are looking for `man`, `apropos` matches `manager` and `manipulation`, whereas `whatis` matches only `man` separated from other letters by white space or by punctuation, as in `man.config`. Try the commands `whatis man` and `apropos man` to see the difference.

Many of the man pages on a Linux system are part of a large package assembled by the LDP. In particular, the section 2 (system calls), section 3 (libraries), section 4 (special, or device, files), and section 5 (file formats) pages are mainly from the LDP's man-pages collection and are generally the pages most useful for programming. If you want to specify which section to look in, give the number of that section before the name of the man page you want to read. For example, `man man` gives the man page for the `man` command from section 1; if you want to see the specification for how to write man pages, you need to specify section 7 with `man 7 man`.

While you are reading man pages, remember that many system calls and library functions use the same names. In most cases, you want to know about the library functions to which you will be linking, not about the system calls that those library functions eventually call. Remember to use `man 3 function` to get the descriptions of library functions, because some library functions have the same names as system calls in section 2.

Also, be particularly aware that the C library man pages are maintained separately from the C library itself. Since the C library does not usually change behavior, that is not usually a problem. All the Linux distributions now use the GNU C library, introduced in Chapter 6. The GNU C library comes with full documentation, which is maintained with the library. This information is available in Texinfo form.

3.2 The Info Pages

The GNU project has adopted the Texinfo format for its documentation. Texinfo documentation can be printed (using a conversion to $\text{T}_{\text{E}}\text{X}$) or read online (in the "info" format, a very early hypertext format that preceded the World Wide Web). There are many programs for reading the info documentation in Linux. Here is a small selection.

- The Emacs editor has an info reading mode; type `[ESC] X info` to enter this mode.

- The `info` and `pinfo` programs are small text-mode programs for browsing info pages.

- Most system documentation programs (such as the GNOME `yelp` and KDE `khelpcenter` programs) are capable of displaying info pages. We recommend these tools, as they generally provide a hypertext interface to the info pages that is more familiar to anyone who is comfortable using a Web browser than the interface presented by Emacs, `info`, or `pinfo`. (These tools also present other system documentation such as man pages and documentation for the system they are part of.)

3.3 Other Documentation

The `/usr/share/doc` directory provides a catch-all location for otherwise uncollected documentation. Most packages installed on your system install "README" files, documentation in various formats (including plain text, PostScript, PDF, and HTML), and examples under the /usr/share/doc directory. Each package has its own directory, which is named for the package and generally carries the package version number as well.

Part 2

Development Tools and Environment

CHAPTER 4

Development Tools

An amazing variety of development tools is available for Linux. Everyone should be familiar with a few of the important ones.

Linux distributions include many solid, proven development tools; most of the same tools have been included in Unix development systems for years. These tools are neither flashy nor fancy; most of them are command-line tools without a GUI. They have proved themselves through years of use, and it will be worth your while to learn them.

If you are already familiar with Emacs, vi, make, gdb, strace, and ltrace, you are not likely to learn anything new here. However, in the remainder of the book, we assume that you are comfortable with a text editor. Also, nearly all free Unix and Linux source code is built with make, and gdb is one of the most common debuggers available on Linux and Unix. The strace utility (or a similar utility called trace or truss) is available on most Unix systems; the ltrace utility was originally written for Linux and is not available on many systems (as of this writing).

This should not be taken to mean that there are no GUI development tools available for Linux; in fact, quite the reverse is true. There are so many available that the variety can be overwhelming.

At the time of writing, two **integrated development environments** (IDEs) you might want to consider (and that are likely to be included with your distribution) are KDevelop (http://kdevelop.org/), a part of the KDE desktop environment, and Eclipse (http://eclipse.org/), a Java-based cross-platform environment originally developed by IBM and now maintained by a large consortium. However, using these tools is beyond the scope of this book, and both come with full documentation.

Even though multiple IDEs are available for Linux, they have not been as popular as IDEs have been on other platforms. Even when IDEs are in use, a common rule of thumb when writing Open Source software is that your project should build without the IDE in order to make it possible for developers not comfortable with your choice of IDE to contribute to the project. KDevelop supports this by helping you build projects that use the standard Automake, Autoconf, and Libtool tools used to build many Open Source software projects.

The standard Automake, Autoconf, and Libtool tools themselves are important development tools. They were created to allow you to design your application in such a way that it can be mostly automatically ported to many operating systems. Because these tools are so complex, they are beyond the scope of this book. Also, these tools are changed regularly, and an electronic version of *GNU Autoconf, Automake, and Libtool* [Vaughan, 2000] is maintained online at http://sources.redhat.com/autobook/.

4.1 Editors

Unix developers have traditionally held strong and diverse preferences, especially about editors.

Many programmers' editors are available for you to try; the two most common are vi and Emacs. Both have more power than they appear to have at first glance, both have a relatively steep learning curve—and they are radically different. Emacs is large; it is really an operating environment of its own. vi is small and is designed to be one piece of the Unix environment. Many clones and alternative versions of each editor have been written, and each has its own following.

Tutorials on vi and Emacs would take far too much space to include in this book. The excellent *A Practical Guide to Red Hat*ᴿ *Linux*ᴿ *8* [Sobell, 2002] includes a detailed chapter on each editor. O'Reilly has published an entire book on each editor: *Learning GNU Emacs* [Cameron, 1996] and *Learning the vi Editor* [Lamb, 1990]. Here, we compare only Emacs and vi and tell you how to get online help for each.

Emacs includes a comprehensive set of manuals that explains not only how to use Emacs as an editor, but also how to use Emacs to read and send email and Usenet news, to play games (its gomoku game is not bad), and to run shell commands. In Emacs, you can always execute internal Emacs commands, even those commands that are not bound to keys, by typing the entire name of the command.

In contrast, the documentation available for vi is less generous and less well known. It is exclusively an editor, and many powerful commands are bound to single keystrokes. You switch back and forth between a mode in which typing standard alphabetic characters causes them to be inserted in your document and a mode in which those alphabetic characters are commands; for example, you can use the h, j, k, and l keys as arrow keys to navigate your document.

Both editors allow you to create macros to make your work easier, but their macro languages could hardly be more different. Emacs has a complete programming language called elisp (Emacs Lisp), which is closely related to the Common Lisp programming language. The original vi has a more spartan, stack-based language. Most users merely map keys to simple, one-line vi commands, but those commands often execute programs outside vi to manipulate data within vi. Emacs Lisp is documented in a huge manual that includes a tutorial; documentation for the original vi's language is relatively sparse.

Some editors allow you to mix and match functionality. You can use Emacs in a vi mode (called **viper**) that allows you to use the standard vi commands, and one of the vi clones is called **vile**—"vi like Emacs."

4.1.1 Emacs

Emacs comes in several flavors. The original Emacs editor was written by Richard Stallman, of Free Software Foundation fame. For years, his GNU Emacs has been the most popular version. Recently, a more graphic-environment-aware variant of GNU Emacs, called XEmacs, has also become popular. XEmacs started life as Lucid Emacs, a set of enhancements to GNU Emacs managed by the now-defunct Lucid Technologies that was intended to be folded back into the official GNU Emacs. Technical differences prevented the teams from merging their code. The two editors remain highly compatible, however, and programmers on both teams regularly borrow code from each other. Because these versions are so similar, we refer to both of them as Emacs.

The best way to become comfortable with the Emacs editor is to follow its tutorial. Run `emacs` and type ^h t (think "control-help, tutorial"). Type ^x^c to exit Emacs. The tutorial will teach you how to get more information on Emacs. It will not teach you how to get at the Emacs manual that is distributed with Emacs. For that, use ^h i (control-help, info).

Although its user interface may not be as flashy as those of a graphical IDE, Emacs does have powerful features that many programmers want. When you use Emacs to edit C code, for example, Emacs recognizes the file type and enters "C mode," in which it recognizes C's syntax and helps you to recognize typos. When you run the compiler from within Emacs, it will recognize error and warning messages, and take you straight to the line at which each error was found when you type a single command, even if it has to read in a new file. It also provides a debugging mode that keeps the debugger in one window and follows the code you are debugging in another window.

4.1.2 vi

If you are a touch typist and like to keep your fingers on the home row,[1] you may appreciate vi, because its command set was designed to minimize finger movement for touch typists. It was also designed for Unix users; if you are familiar with sed or awk or other Unix programs that use standard regular expressions, using ^ to go to the beginning of a line and $ to go to the end of one will feel perfectly natural.

Unfortunately, vi can be harder to learn than Emacs because, although there are vi tutorials similar to the standard Emacs tutorial available, there is no standard way to execute the tutorial from any version of vi. However, most versions, including versions shipped with common Linux distributions, support the `:help` command.

The most common version of vi, vim ("Vi IMproved"), has many of the features integrating development tools provided by Emacs, including syntax highlighting, automatic indentation, an expressive scripting language, and compiler error parsing.

---

1. If you are a qwerty touch typist, that is. Dvorak touch typists who use vi generally use lots of vi macros to make vi comfortable for them.

4.2 Make

A mainstay of Unix development is make, a tool that makes it easy for you to describe how to compile programs. Although small programs may need only one command to compile their one source code file into one executable file, it is still easier to type make than to type gcc -O2 -ggdb -DSOME_DEFINE -o foo foo.c. Furthermore, when you have lots of files to compile, and you have changed only a few source files, make will create new object files only when the relevant source files have been modified.

For make to perform this magic, you need to describe all the files in a **Makefile**. Here is an example:

```
 1: # Makefile
 2:
 3: OBJS = foo.o bar.o baz.o
 4: LDLIBS = -L/usr/local/lib/ -lbar
 5:
 6: foo: $(OBJS)
 7:         gcc -o foo $(OBJS) $(LDLIBS)
 8:
 9: install: foo
10:         install -m 644 foo /usr/bin
11: .PHONY: install
```

- Line 1 is a comment; make follows the common Unix tradition of delimiting comments with a # character.

- Line 3 defines a variable called OBJS as foo.o bar.o baz.o.

- Line 4 defines another variable, LDLIBS.

- Line 6 starts the definition of a **rule**, which states that the file foo depends on (in this case, is built from) the files whose names are contained in the variable OBJS. foo is called the **target**, and $(OBJS) is called the **dependency** list. Note the syntax for variable expansion: You wrap the variable name in $(...).

- Line 7 is a command line that tells you how to build the target from the dependency list. There may be multiple command lines, and the *first* character in the command line *must* be a tab.

- Line 9 is an interesting target. It does not actually try to make a file called `install`; instead (as you can see in line 10), it installs `foo` in `/usr/bin` using the standard `install` program. But this line brings up an ambiguity in make: What if a file named `install` exists and it is newer than `foo`? In that case, when you run the command `make install`, make says, "`'install' is up to date`" and quits.

- Line 11 tells make that `install` is not a file, and that it should ignore any file named "install" when computing the `install` dependency. Thus, if the `install` dependency is invoked (we shall see how to do that later), the command in line 10 will always be invoked. `.PHONY` is a **directive**, which alters make's operation; it tells make, in this case, that the `install` target is not the name of a file. `PHONY` targets are often used to take actions such as installation or making a single target name that relies on several other targets all being built, like this:

```
all: foo bar baz
.PHONY: all
```

Unfortunately, `.PHONY` is not supported by some versions of make. A less obvious, less efficient, but more portable way of doing the same things is

```
all: foo bar baz FORCE
FORCE:
```

This works only if there is no file named "FORCE".

Items in dependency lists may be file names, but, as far as make is concerned, they are other targets. The `foo` item in the `install` dependency list is a target. When make attempts to resolve the `install` dependency, it sees that it first has to resolve the `foo` dependency. To resolve the `foo` dependency, it has to resolve the `foo.o`, `bar.o`, and `baz.o` dependencies.

Note that there are no lines that explicitly tell make how to build `foo.o`, `bar.o`, or `baz.o`. You certainly do not create these files directly in your editor of choice! make provides implied dependencies that you do not have to write. If you have a dependency on a file that ends in .o and you have a file that has the same name except that it ends in .c, make assumes that the object file depends on the source file. Built-in **suffix rules** provided with make allow you to greatly simplify many Makefiles, and you can write your own suffix rules (explained on page 34) when the built-in rules do not meet your needs.

By default, make exits as soon as any command it runs fails (returns an error). There are two ways to get around this, if you wish to.

The -k argument causes make to build as much as possible, without stopping as soon as a command invocation returns an error. It is useful, for example, when porting; you can build as many object files as possible, then port the files that failed to build without having to wait for intermediary files to build in the meantime.

If you know that one command will always return an error, but you wish to ignore the error condition, you can use some shell magic. The /bin/false command always returns an error, so the command

    /bin/false

will always cause make to abort its current run unless the -k option is in use. However,

    any_command || /bin/true

will never cause make to abort its current run; if any_command returns false, then the shell will run /bin/true and return its exit code, which is guaranteed to be success.

Make interprets unrecognized command-line arguments that do not start with a dash (-)[2] as targets to build. So make install will cause make to try to satisfy the install target. If the foo target is not up to date, make will first satisfy the foo dependency by building it, and then it will install it. If you need to build a target that starts with a dash, you will need to precede the target name with a separate double-dash (- -) argument.

---

2. The combined minus and hyphen character is often called a *dash*.

4.2.1 Complex Command Lines

Each command line is executed in its own subshell, so cd commands in a command line affect only the line on which they are written. You can extend any line in a Makefile over multiple lines by using backslash extension: If you put a \ as the final character on a line, the line after it will be considered to be part of it, joined to it by a space. Command lines often look like this:

```
 1:        cd some_directory ; \
 2:          do this to file $(FOO); \
 3:          do that
 4:        cd another_directory ; \
 5:          if [ -f some_file ] ; then \
 6:            do something else ; \
 7:          done ; \
 8:          for i in * ; do \
 9:            echo $$i >> some_file ; \
10:          done
```

There are only two lines in that fragment, as far as make is concerned. The first command line starts on line 1 and continues through line 3; the second command line starts on line 4 and continues through line 10. There are several points to note here.

- another_directory is relative not to some_directory, but rather to the directory in which make was run, because they are executed in different subshells.

- The lines that constitute each command line are passed to the shell as a single line, so all the ; characters that the shell needs must be there, including the ones that are usually omitted in a shell script because the presence of newline characters implies them. For more information on shell programming, see *Learning the bash Shell* [Newham, 1995].

- When you need to dereference a make variable, you can just dereference it normally (that is, $(VAR)), but when you need to dereference a shell variable, you need to escape the $ character by including it twice: $$i.

4.2.2 Variables

It often happens that you want to define a variable one component at a time. You might want to write something like this:

```
OBJS = foo.o
OBJS = $(OBJS) bar.o
OBJS = $(OBJS) baz.o
```

At this point, you expect OBJS to be defined as foo.o bar.o baz.o—but it is actually defined as $(OBJS) baz.o, because make does not expand variables until they are used.[3] If you do this, as soon as you reference OBJS in a rule, make will enter an infinite loop.[4] For this reason, many Makefiles have sections that look like this:

```
OBJS1 = foo.o
OBJS2 = bar.o
OBJS3 = baz.o
OBJS = $(OBJS1) $(OBJS2) $(OBJS3)
```

You will most often see variable declarations like the preceding one when a variable declaration would otherwise be too long for the programmer's comfort.

Variable expansion brings up a typical issue that a Linux programmer is called on to decide. The GNU tools distributed with Linux are generally more capable than the versions of the tools included with other systems, and GNU make is no exception. The authors of GNU make created another way to do variable assignment that avoids this problem, but not every version of make understands GNU make's alternative forms of variable assignment. Fortunately, GNU make can be built for any system to which you could easily port source code written on Linux, but do you want to force the people porting your code to other systems to use GNU make? If you do, you can use **simple variable assignment**:

---

3. Although this behavior may seem inconvenient, it is an important feature and not a bug. Not expanding variables is critically important for writing the generic suffix rules that create implied dependencies.
4. Most versions of make, including the GNU version, which is distributed with Linux, will detect that they are in an infinite loop and quit with an error message.

```
OBJS := foo.o
OBJS := $(OBJS) bar.o
OBJS := $(OBJS) baz.o
```

The := operator causes GNU make to evaluate the variable expression at assignment time, rather than wait to evaluate the expression when it is used in a rule. With this code, OBJS does indeed contain foo.o bar.o baz.o.

Simple variable assignment is often useful, but GNU make also has another assignment syntax that deals specifically with this problem, one straight from the C language:

```
OBJS := foo.o
OBJS += bar.o
OBJS += baz.o
```

4.2.3 Suffix Rules

This is another context in which you have to decide whether to write standard Makefiles or to use useful GNU extensions. Standard suffix rules are more limited than are the GNU pattern rules, but most situations can be handled sufficiently well by the standard suffix rules, and pattern rules are not supported by many other versions of make.

Suffix rules look like this:

```
.c.o:
        $(CC) -c $(CFLAGS) $(CPPFLAGS) -o $@ $<
.SUFFIXES: .c .o
```

This rule says (we sweep the details under the carpet) that make should, *unless it is otherwise explicitly instructed*, turn a .c file into a .o file by running the attached command line. Each .c file will be treated as though it were explicitly listed as a dependency of the respective .o file in your Makefile.

That suffix rule introduces another of make's features: automatic variables. It is clear that you need a way to substitute the dependency and target into the command line. The automatic variable $@ stands for the target, $< stands for the first dependency, and $^ stands for all the dependencies.

Several other automatic variables are available and documented in the make manual. All automatic variables can be used in normal rules, as well as in suffix and pattern rules.

The final line of the example introduces another directive. `.SUFFIXES` tells make that `.c` and `.o` are suffixes that make should use to find a way to turn the existing source files into the desired targets.

Pattern rules are more powerful and, therefore, slightly more complex than suffix rules; it would take too long to cover them in detail here. The equivalent pattern rule to the preceding suffix rule is

```
%.o : %.c
        $(CC) -c $(CFLAGS) $(CPPFLAGS) -o $@ $<
```

If you want to know more about make, see *Managing Projects with make* [Oram, 1993]. GNU make also includes an excellent and easy-to-read manual in Texinfo format, which you can read online, print out, or order as a book from the Free Software Foundation.

Most large Open Source projects use the Automake, Autoconf, and Libtool tools. These tools are essentially collections of knowledge about the peculiarities of different systems and of community standards for how to build projects, so that you have to write only the bits that are actually specific to your project. For example, Automake writes "install" and "uninstall" targets, Autoconf automatically determines the capabilities of the system and configures the software to match the system, and Libtool deals with differences in how shared libraries are managed between different systems. Documenting these three tools is an entire book of its own, *GNU Autoconf, Automake, and Libtool* [Vaughan, 2000]; *Linux Application Development* provides the background you need in order to read and use *GNU Autoconf, Automake, and Libtool*.

4.3 The GNU Debugger

Gdb is the Free Software Foundation's debugger. It is a good command-line debugger, on which several tools have been built, including Emacs' gdb mode, the graphical Data Display Debugger (DDD),[5] and built-in debuggers in several graphical IDEs. We cover only gdb in this section.

Start gdb by running `gdb progname`. Gdb will not search the `PATH` looking for the executable file. Gdb will load the executable's symbols and then prompt you for what to do next.

There are three ways to inspect a process with gdb:

- Use the `run` command to start the program normally.

- Use the `attach` command to start inspecting an already-running process. When you attach to a process, the process will be stopped.

- Inspect an existing core file to determine the state of the process when it was killed. To inspect a core file, start gdb with the command `gdb progname corefile`.

Before you run a program or attach to an already-running program, you can set breakpoints, list source code, and do anything else that does not necessarily involve a running process.

Gdb does not require that you type entire command names; `r` suffices for `run`, `n` for `next`, `s` for `step`. Furthermore, to repeat the most recent command, simply hit Return. This makes single-stepping easy.

A short selection of useful gdb commands is included here; gdb includes a comprehensive online manual in GNU info format (run `info gdb`) that explains all of gdb's options in detail in a tutorial format. *Programming with GNU Software* [Loukides, 1997] contains a good detailed tutorial on using gdb. Gdb also includes extensive online help available from within gdb; access it with the `help` command. Specific help on each command is available with `help commandname` or `help topic`.

Just like shell commands, gdb commands may take arguments. We use "call `help` with an argument of `command`" to mean the same as "type `help command`".

---

5. http://www.gnu.org/software/ddd/

Some gdb commands also take format identifiers to identify how to print values. Format identifiers immediately follow the command name and are separated from the command name by a slash. Once you have chosen a format, you do not have to use it each time you repeat the command; gdb will remember the format you chose as the default.

Format identifiers are separated from commands by a / character and are composed of three elements: a count, a format letter, and a size letter. The count and size letters are optional; count defaults to 1, and the size has reasonable defaults based on the format letter.

The format letters are o for octal, x for hexadecimal, d for decimal, u for unsigned decimal, t for binary, f for floating-point, a for address, i for instruction, c for character, and s for string.

The size letters are b for byte, h for half word (2 bytes), w for word (4 bytes), and g for giant (8 bytes).

attach, at   Attach to an already-running process. The only argument is the pid of the process to which to attach. This stops the processes to which you attach, interrupting any sleep or other interruptible system call in progress. See detach.

backtrace, bt, where, w
        Print a stack trace.

break, b   Set a breakpoint. You can specify a function name, a line number of the *current* file (the file containing the currently executing code), a filename:linenumber pair, or even an arbitrary address with *address. Gdb assigns and tells you a unique number for each breakpoint. See condition, clear, and delete.

clear   Clear a breakpoint. Takes the same arguments as break. See delete.

condition   Changes a breakpoint specified by number (see break) to break only if a condition is true. The condition is expressed as an arbitrary expression.

```
(gdb) b 664
Breakpoint 3 at 0x804a5c0: file ladsh4.c, line 664.
(gdb) condition 3 status == 0
```

delete   Clear a breakpoint by number.

detach   Detach from the currently attached process.

display   Display the value of an expression every time execution
            stops. Takes the same arguments (including format mod-
            ifiers) as print. Prints a display number that can be used
            later to cancel the display. See undisplay.

help   Get help. Called with no argument, provides a summary
            of the help available. Called with another command as an
            argument, provides help on that command. Extensively
            cross-referenced.

jump   Jump to an arbitrary address and continue execution there.
            The address is the only argument, and it can be specified ei-
            ther as a line number or as an address specified as *address.

list,l   With no argument, list first lists the 10 lines surrounding
            the current address. Subsequent calls to list list subsequent
            sections of 10 lines. With an argument of -, lists the previous
            10 lines.

            With a line number, lists the 10 lines surrounding that line.
            With a filename:linenumber pair, lists the 10 lines sur-
            rounding that line. With a function name, lists the 10 lines
            surrounding the beginning of the function. With an address
            specified as *address, specifies the 10 lines surrounding the
            code found at that address.

            With two line specifications separated by commas, lists all
            the lines between the two specified lines.

next,n   Step to the next line of source code in the current function;
            make function calls without stepping. See step.

nexti   Step to the next machine language instruction; make function calls without stepping. See stepi.

print,p   Print the value of an expression in a comprehensible representation. If you have a char *c, the command print c will print the address of the string, and print *c will print the string itself. Printing structures will expand the structures. You can include casts in your expressions, and gdb will honor them. If the code was compiled with the -ggdb option, enumerated values and preprocessor definitions will be available for you to use in your expressions. See display.

The print command takes format identifiers, although with proper types and with typecasts, the format identifiers are rarely necessary. See x.

run,r   Run the current program from the beginning. The arguments to the run command are the arguments that would be used to run the program on the command line. Gdb will do shell-style globbing with * and [], and it will do shell-style redirection with <, >, and >>, but it will not do pipes or here documents.

With no arguments, run uses the arguments that were specified in the most recent run command, or in the most recent set args command. To run with no arguments after running with arguments, use the set args command with no extra arguments.

set   Gdb allows you to change the values of variables, like this:

```
(gdb) set a = argv[5]
```

Also, whenever you print an expression, gdb gives you a shorthand variable, like $1, that you can use to refer to it later. So if you had previously printed argv[5] and gdb had told you that it was $6, you could write the previous assignment as

```
(gdb) set a = $6
```

The set command also has many subcommands, far too numerous to list here. Use help set for more information.

step, s   Step the program instruction by instruction until it reaches a new line of source code. See next.

stepi   Execute exactly one machine language instruction; traces into function calls. See nexti.

undisplay   Without any argument, cancels all displays. Otherwise, cancels the displays whose numbers are given as arguments. See display.

whatis   Prints the data type of an expression given as its argument.

where, w   See backtrace.

x   The x command is like the print command, except that it is explicitly limited to printing the contents of an address in some arbitrary format. If you do not use a format identifier, gdb will use the most recently specified format identifier.

4.4 Tracing Program Actions

Two programs help you trace the actions that an executable is taking. Neither requires the source code; in fact, neither can make use of the source code. Both print out in symbolic, textual form a log of the actions being taken by a program.

The first, strace, prints out a record of each system call that the program makes. The second, ltrace, prints out a record of each library function that the program makes (and can optionally also trace system calls). These tools can be particularly useful for determining "what went wrong" in obvious failure cases.

For example, consider a system daemon that has been working for quite a while, but then starts exhibiting segmentation faults when you try to start it up. It is likely that the bug has been triggered by a change in some data files, but you do not know which one. The first step might be to run the system daemon under strace and look for the last few files that it opens before taking the segmentation fault, and examining those files to look for likely causes. Or consider another daemon that is unexpectedly taking lots of CPU time; you can run it under strace first, and then ltrace if strace doesn't show clearly what it is doing, to understand what input or conditions are causing it to take an unexpected amount of CPU time.

Like gdb, strace and ltrace can either be used to run a program from beginning to end, or can attach to running programs. By default, both programs send their output to standard out. Both programs require that their own options come first, followed by the executable to run (when applicable), and if an executable is specified, any options to pass to that executable follow next.

Both programs provide a similar set of options:

-C or --demangle
> In ltrace only, decode (or "demangle") the names of library symbols into recognizable names. This strips leading underscore characters (many glibc functions are internally implemented with versions with leading underscores) and makes C++ library functions readable (C++ encodes type information into symbol names).

-e
> In strace only, specify a subset of actions to print. There are many possible specifications described in the strace man page; the most commonly useful specification is -e trace=file, which traces only system calls involved in file I/O and manipulation.

-f
> Attempt to "follow fork()," trace child processes as well as possible. Note that the child process may run without being traced for a short time before strace or ltrace is able to attach to it and trace its actions.

-o filename
> Instead of sending the output to standard out, store it in the file named filename.

-p *pid*   Instead of starting a new instance of a program, attach to the process ID specified in *pid*.

-S   In ltrace only, report system calls as well as library calls.

-v   In strace only, do not abbreviate large structures in system calls such as the `stat()` family of calls, `termios` calls, and others with large structures.

The manual pages for each of the utilities cover these options and others not mentioned here.

gcc Options and Extensions

To use gcc, the standard C compiler used with Linux, you need to know the command-line options. Also, gcc extends the C language in several ways. Even if you intend to write only ANSI-C-compliant source code, you will need to know some of the extensions to understand the Linux header files.

Most of gcc's command-line options are normal, as C compilers go. For a few options, there do not appear to be any standards. We cover the most important options, options that are used on a day-to-day basis.

Standard—ISO-standard—C is a useful goal, but as low-level as C is, there are situations in which it is not expressive enough. There are two areas in Linux in which gcc's extensions get particular use: interfacing with assembly-language code (covered in *Brennan's Guide to Inline Assembly*[1]) and building shared libraries (covered in Chapter 8). Because header files are parts of those shared libraries, some of the extensions show through in the system header files, as well.

Of course, there are also lots of extensions that are useful in all sorts of other everyday coding, as long as you do not mind being gratuitously nonstandard. For more documentation about these extensions, see the gcc Texinfo documentation.

---

1. http://www.delorie.com/djgpp/doc/brennan/

5.1 gcc Options

gcc has a multitude of command-line options. Fortunately, the set you usually need to know about is much smaller, and we cover those options here. Most of the options are generally the same or similar on other compilers, as well. gcc has voluminous documentation on its options available with `info gcc`.[2]

`-o filename`   Specify the output file name. This is not usually needed if you are compiling to an object file because the default is to substitute filename.o for filename.c. However, if you are creating an executable, the default (for historical reasons) is to create an executable named a.out. It is also useful if you wish to put output files in another directory.

`-c`   Compile, without linking, the source files specified on the command line, creating an object file for each source file. When using make, it is common to use one invocation of gcc per object file, because it is easy to see which file failed to compile if an error occurs. However, when you are typing commands by hand, it is commonly useful to specify many files in one invocation of gcc. In cases in which specifying many input files on the command line would be ambiguous, specify only one, or gcc may get confused. For instance, `gcc -c -o a.o a.c b.c` is equivalent to `gcc -c -o a.o b.c`.

`-Dfoo`   Define a preprocessor macro on the command line. You may need to escape characters that are special to the shell. For instance, if you want to define a string, you will have to escape the " characters that delimit the string. Two common ways to do this are `'-Dfoo="bar"'` and `-Dfoo=\"bar\"`. Note that the first works much better if there are any spaces in the string, because spaces are treated specially by the shell.

---

2. `man gcc` has them too, but the man page is not updated as often as the Texinfo documentation.

-I*dir*	Prepend *dir* to the list of directories in which to search for include files.
-L*dir*	Prepend *dir* to the list of directories in which to search for libraries. Unless otherwise instructed, gcc uses shared libraries in preference to static libraries.
-l*foo*	Link against lib*foo*. Unless otherwise instructed, gcc links against shared libraries (lib*foo*.so) in preference to static libraries (lib*foo*.a). The linker searches for functions in all the libraries listed, in the order in which they are listed, until each function is found.
-static	Link against static libraries only. See Chapter 8 for details.
-g, -ggdb	Include debugging information. The -g option instructs gcc to include standard debugging information. The -ggdb option instructs gcc to include a large amount of information that only the gdb debugger is capable of understanding. Use -g if you have limited disk space, expect to use a debugger other than gdb, or are willing to trade away some functionality in gdb for linking speed. Use -ggdb if you need all the help you can get debugging, and gcc will pass more information to gdb.
	Note that unlike most compilers, gcc is willing to include debugging information in optimized code. However, following the debugger as it traces through optimized code can be challenging—the code path may jump around and completely miss sections of code you expected to be executed. It can also give you a better understanding of your code, and of how optimizing compilers change the way your code executes.
-O, -O*n*	Instruct gcc to optimize your code. By default, gcc does a few optimizations; specifying a number (*n*) instructs gcc to optimize to a certain level. The most common optimization level is 2; with the standard version of gcc, 3 is currently the highest optimization level. Unless you wish to compile quickly at the expense of run-time speed, you expect to use a debugger on the output file, or you

have found a bug in the optimizer, we recommend using -O2 or -O3 when compiling; -O3 may increase the size of your application, so if this is a concern, we recommend that you test both ways. You may also consider -Os, which optimizes for minimum code size instead of for speed, if memory or disk space is at a premium for your application.

gcc does not implement inline functions unless at least minimal optimization (-O) has been enabled.

-ansi   Support all standard ANSI (X3.159-1989) or the technically equivalent ISO (ISO/IEC 9899:1990) C programs (often abbreviated C89 or occasionally C90). Note that this does not enforce complete ANSI/ISO compliance. The -ansi option turns off gcc extensions that officially conflict with the ANSI/ISO standard. (Because many of these extensions are also supported by other C compilers, this is rarely a problem in practice.) It also defines the __STRICT_ANSI__ feature macro (as described on page 49), which the header files use to provide an ANSI/ISO-compliant environment.

-pedantic   Give all warnings and errors *required* by the ANSI/ISO C standard. This does not enforce absolute ANSI/ISO compliance.

-Wall   Turn on all the *generally useful* warning messages that gcc can provide. It does not turn on options that are useful only in specific cases. This provides a similar level of detail to running the lint syntax checker on your source code. gcc allows you to turn each warning message on or off individually. The gcc manual lists all the warning messages.

5.2   **Header Files**

You may, from time to time, find yourself browsing the Linux header files. You are likely to find some constructs there that go beyond ANSI/ISO-compliant C code. A few, at least, are worth understanding. All of the constructs documented here are more fully documented in the gcc info documentation.

5.2.1 `long long`

The `long long` type denotes a storage unit at least as large as a `long`. On Intel i86 and other 32-bit platforms, `long` is 32 bits wide, and `long long` is 64 bits wide. On 64-bit platforms, pointers and `long long` are 64 bits wide, and `long` may be 32 or 64 bits wide depending on the platform. The `long long` type is supported in the "C99" dialect of C (ISO/IEC 9899:1999), and has been a long-standing extension to C provided by gcc.

5.2.2 **Inline Functions**

In certain parts of the Linux header files (system-specific ones, in particular), inline functions are used pervasively. They are as fast as macros (no function call overhead is incurred) but provide all the type checking available with a normal function call. Code that calls inline functions must be compiled with at least minimal optimization on (`-O`).

5.2.3 **Alternative Extended Keywords**

In gcc, every extended keyword (keywords not covered by the ANSI/ISO standards) has two versions: the keyword itself and the keyword surrounded by two underscore characters on each side. When the compiler is used in standard-compliant mode (usually, because the `-ansi` argument was used), the normal extended keywords are not recognized. So, for example, the `attribute` keyword is written as `__attribute__` in the header files.

5.2.4 Attributes

The attribute extended keyword is used to tell gcc more about a function, variable, or declared type than is possible in ANSI/ISO-compliant C code. For example, the aligned attribute tells gcc exactly how to align a variable or type; the packed attribute specifies that padding not be used; and noreturn specifies that a function never returns, which allows gcc to optimize better and avoid spurious warnings.

Function attributes are declared by adding them to the function declaration, like this:

```
void die_die_die(int, char *) __attribute__ ((__noreturn__));
```

The attribute declaration is placed between the closing parenthesis and the semicolon of the declaration and consists of the attribute keyword followed by the attributes in double parentheses. If there are multiple attributes, use a comma-separated list.

```
int printm(char *, ...)
  __attribute__ ((const,
                 format (printf, 1, 2)))
  ;
```

This says that printm does not examine any values other than its arguments and has no side effects related to code generation (const), that gcc should check the arguments given to it as it checks the arguments to printf(), and that the first argument is the format string and the second argument is the first substituted parameter (format).

We cover some attributes in context (for instance, building shared libraries in Chapter 8), and you can find all the documentation on attributes in the gcc Texinfo documentation.

CHAPTER 6

The GNU C Library

The GNU C Library (**glibc**) is the standard C library on Linux systems. Other C libraries exist and are sometimes used for special purposes (such as very small subsets of the standard C libraries used for embedded systems and bootstrapping), but glibc is the standard C library on all Linux distributions. It provides a significant portion of the functionality documented in *Linux Application Development*—in fact, this book might more accurately but less concisely have been titled *Linux and glibc Application Development*.

6.1 Feature Selection

In glibc, there are a set of feature selection macros that are used to select which standards you wish glibc to comply with. Standards sometimes conflict, and so glibc allows you to select exactly which set of standards (formal, *de jure*, and informal, *de facto*) with which to comply, fully or partially. These macros are technically called *feature test macros*.

You need to be aware of these macros because the default set of macros defined does not provide all the functionality of glibc. A few mechanisms discussed in this book are not available with the default feature set selected; we document the required feature macros to use each of these mechanisms.

The feature test macros are designed to specify with what standards (*de jure* or *de facto*), and in some cases precisely which versions of those standards, glibc should comply. This compliance often includes not defining functions and macros beyond what is specified by a standard for header files that are themselves defined by that standard. That means that an application written to conform with a standard can define its own functions and macros without conflicting with extensions not defined by that standard.

The feature test macros do not guarantee that your application is fully compatible with the set of standards specified by the set of macros you define. Setting the feature test macros may find some use of nonportable extensions, but it will not show, for example, use of header files that are entirely unspecified by the standard.

The macros are defined in the system header file feature.h, which you should not include directly. Instead, all other header files that might be affected by the contents of feature.h include it.

The default set of feature macros if none are defined is `_SVID_SOURCE=1`, `_BSD_SOURCE=1`, `_POSIX_SOURCE=1`, and `_POSIX_C_SOURCE=199506L`. Each option is described in more detail below, but this essentially translates into "support the capabilities of the 1995 POSIX standard (see page 8; this is from before POSIX and the Single Unix Standard were combined), all standard System V features, and all BSD features that do not conflict with System V features." This default set of feature macros suffices for most programs.

When you give gcc the `-ansi` option, as documented on page 46, it automatically defines the internal `__STRICT_ANSI__` macro, which turns off all the default feature macros.

With the exception of the `__STRICT_ANSI__` macro, which is special (and which should be set only by the compiler in the context of the `-ansi` command line option), these feature macros are cumulative; you can define any combination of them. The exact definition of `_BSD_SOURCE` changes depending on which other feature macros are set (as documented below); the rest are purely cumulative.

Some of the feature test macros are defined by various versions of POSIX or other standards, some are common in the industry, and others are strictly limited to glibc.

`_POSIX_SOURCE`
> If this macro is defined, all the interfaces defined as part of the original POSIX.1 specification are made available.

This macro was defined by the original POSIX.1-1990 standard.

`_POSIX_C_SOURCE`

This macro supersedes `_POSIX_SOURCE`. If it is set to 1, it is equivalent to `_POSIX_SOURCE`. If it is `>=2`, then it also includes C interfaces defined by POSIX.2, including regular expressions. If it is `>=199309L`, then it also includes additional C interfaces defined in the 1993 revision of POSIX, particularly including the soft real-time functionality; if it is `>=199506L` (the default), it also includes additional C interfaces defined in the 1995 revision of POSIX, particularly including POSIX threads. This macro was defined by versions of POSIX released after 1990 in order to differentiate support for various versions of the POSIX (and now also Single Unix) standards. It is largely superseded by `_XOPEN_SOURCE`.

`_XOPEN_SOURCE`

The `_XOPEN_SOURCE` macro is defined by the XSI portion of the Single Unix Standard, and defines a logical superset of the interfaces included by `_POSIX_C_SOURCE`. It was also defined by XPG. If it is defined at all, base-level conformance with XPG4 (Unix95) is included. If it is defined as `500`, then base-level conformance with XPG5 (Unix98, SuS version 2) is included. If it is defined as `600`, base-level conformance with IEEE Std 1003.1-2003 (the combined POSIX and SuS document) is included.

`_ISOC99_SOURCE`

This feature test macro exports the interfaces defined by the new ISO/IEC C99 standard.

`_SVID_SOURCE` This feature test macro makes functionality specified by the System V Interface Definition (SVID) available. This does not imply that glibc provides a complete implementation of the SVID standard; it merely exposes the SVID-specified functionality that exists in glibc.

_BSD_SOURCE   BSD features can conflict with other features, and the conflicts are always resolved in favor of System V or standard-compliant behavior if any POSIX, X/Open, or System V feature macro is defined or implied—so the only feature macro that allows BSD behavior to be asserted is _ISOC99_SOURCE. (The exact definition of this feature test macro has changed from time to time, and may change again, since it is not specified by any standard.)

_GNU_SOURCE   _GNU_SOURCE turns on everything possible, favoring System V interfaces to BSD interfaces in cases of conflict. It also adds some GNU- and Linux-specific interfaces, such as file leases.

When the standard set of feature test macros will not suffice, the most commonly useful feature macros to define are _GNU_SOURCE (turn everything on—the easiest solution), _XOPEN_SOURCE=600 (most things you are likely to care about, a subset of _GNU_SOURCE), or _ISOC99_SOURCE (use features from the most recent C standard, a subset of _XOPEN_SOURCE=600).

6.2   POSIX Interfaces

6.2.1 POSIX Required Types

POSIX defines several typedefs defined in the header file <sys/types.h> and used for many arguments and return values. These typedefs are important because the standard C types can vary from machine to machine and are loosely defined by the C standard. The C language is more useful on a wide range of hardware because of this loose definition—a 16-bit machine does not have the same native word size as a 64-bit machine, and a low-level programming language should not pretend it does—but POSIX needs more guarantees, and so requires that the C library's <sys/types.h> header file define a set of consistent types for each machine that implements POSIX. Each of these typedefs can be easily distinguished from a native C type because it ends in _t.

The subset used for interfaces described in this book is:

dev_t   An arithmetic type holding the major and minor numbers corresponding to device special files, normally found in the /dev subdirectory. In Linux, a dev_t can be manipulated using the major(), minor(), and makedev() macros found in <sys/sysmacros.h>. It is normally used only for system programming, and is described on page 189.

uid_t,gid_t

     Integer types holding a unique user ID number or group ID number, respectively. The user ID and group ID credentials are described on page 108.

pid_t   An integer type providing a unique value for a process on a system, described on page 107.

id_t   An integer type capable of holding, without truncation, any pid_t, uid_t, or gid_t.

off_t   A signed integer type measuring a file size in bytes.

size_t   An unsigned integer type measuring an in-memory object, such as a character string, array, or buffer.

ssize_t   A signed integer type that holds a count of bytes (positive) or an error return code (negative).

time_t   An integer (on all normal systems) or real floating point (so that VMS can be considered a POSIX operating system) type giving the time in seconds, as described on page 484.

The type descriptions are intentionally vague. There is no guarantee that the types will be the same on two different Linux platforms, or even two different environments running on the same platform. It is quite likely that a 64-bit machine that supports both 64-bit and 32-bit environments will have different values in each environment for some of these types. Also, these types may change in future versions of Linux, within the scope allowed by POSIX.

6.2.2 Discovering Run-Time Capabilities

Many system capabilities have limits, others are optional, and some may have information associated with them. A limit on the length of the string of arguments passed to a new program protects the system from arbitrary demands for memory that could otherwise bring the system to a standstill. Not all POSIX systems implement job control. A program may wish to know the most recent version of the POSIX standard the currently running system claims to implement.

The sysconf() function provides this type of system-specific information that may differ from system to system for a single executable, information that cannot be known at the time the executable is compiled.

```
#include <unistd.h>

long sysconf(int);
```

The integer argument to sysconf() is one of a set of macros prefixed with _SC_. Here are the ones that are most likely to be useful to you:

_SC_CLK_TCK   Return the number of kernel internal clock ticks per second, as made visible to programs. Note that the kernel may have one or more clocks that run at a higher rate; _SC_CLK_TCK provides the accounting clock tick unit used to report information from the kernel and is not an indicator of system latency.

_SC_STREAM_MAX

      Return the maximum number of C standard I/O streams that a process can have open at once.

_SC_ARG_MAX   Return the maximum length, in bytes, of the command-line arguments and environment variables used by any of the exec() functions. If this limit is exceeded, E2BIG is returned by the exec() call.

_SC_OPEN_MAX   Returns the maximum number of files that a process can have open at once; it is the same as the RLIMIT_NOFILE soft limit that can be queried by getrlimit() and set by setrlimit(). This is the only sysconf() value that can change value during the execution of a program; when setrlimit() is called to change the RLIMIT_NOFILE soft limit, _SC_OPEN_MAX follows the new soft limit.

_SC_PAGESIZE or _SC_PAGE_SIZE

Returns the size of a single page in bytes. On systems that can support multiple page sizes, returns the size of a single normal page as allocated to resolve a normal user-space request for memory, which is considered the native page size for the system.

_SC_LINE_MAX   Returns the length in bytes of the maximum line length that text-processing utilities on the system are required to handle, including the trailing newline character. Note that many of the GNU utilities used on Linux systems actually have no hard-coded maximum length and can take arbitrarily long input lines. However, a portable program must not provide text-processing utilities with text with line lengths longer than _SC_LINE_MAX; many Unix systems have utilities with fixed maximum line lengths, and exceeding this line length may produce undefined output.

_SC_NGROUPS_MAX

Returns the number of supplemental groups (as discussed in Chapter 10) a process can have.

6.2.3 Finding and Setting Basic System Information

There are a few pieces of information about the system on which a program is running that can be useful. The operating system name and version, for example, can be used to change what features system programs provide. The uname() system call allow a program to discover this run-time information.

```
#include <sys/utsname.h>

int uname(struct utsname * unameBuf);
```

The function returns nonzero on error, which occurs only if unameBuf is invalid. Otherwise, the structure it points to is filled in with NULL

Table 6.1 Members of `struct utsname`

Member	Description
`sysname`	The name of the operating system running (`Linux` for the purposes of this book).
`release`	The version number of the kernel that is running. This is the full version, such as 2.6.2. This number can be easily changed by whoever builds a kernel, and it is common for more than these three numbers to appear. Many distributions use an additional number to describe what patches they have applied, leading to release numbers like 2.4.17-23.
`version`	Under Linux, this contains a time stamp describing when the kernel was built.
`machine`	A short string specifying the type of microprocessor on which the operating system is running. This could be `i686` for a Pentium Pro or later processor, `alpha` for an Alpha-class processor, or `ppc64` for a 64-bit PowerPC processor.
`nodename`	The host name of the machine, which is often the machine's primary Internet host name.
`domainname`	The NIS (or YP) domain the machine is part of, if any.

terminated strings describing the system the program is running on. Table 6.1 describes the members of `struct utsname`.

The `nodename` member is what is commonly called the system host name (it is what the `hostname` command displays), but it should not be confused with an Internet host name. While these are the same on many systems, they are not necessarily the same thing. A system with multiple Internet addresses has multiple Internet host names, but only a single node name, so there is not a one-to-one equivalence.

A more common situation is home computers on broadband Internet connections. They normally have Internet host names something like `host127-56.raleigh.myisp.com`, and their Internet host names change whenever they have disconnected their broadband modem for an extended period of time.[1] People who own those machines give them node names

---

1. Most, but not all, home Internet services assign dynamic IP addresses rather than static ones.

that better suit their personalities, along the lines of loren or eleanor, which are not proper Internet addresses at all. If they have multiple machines behind a home gateway device, all of those machines will share a single Internet address (and a single Internet host name), but may have names like linux.mynetwork.org and freebsd.mynetwork.org, which are still not Internet host names. For all of these reasons, assuming that the system's node name is a valid Internet host name for the machine is not a good idea.

The system's node name is set using the sethostname() system call,[2] and its NIS (YP) domain name[3] is set by the setdomainname() system call.

```
#include <unistd.h>

int sethostname(const char * name, size_t len);
int setdomainname(const char * name, size_t len);
```

Both of these system calls take a pointer to a string (not necessarily NULL terminated) containing the appropriate name and the length of the string.

6.3 **Compatibility**

Applications that are compiled with header files from and linked to one version of glibc are intended to continue to work with later versions of glibc. This **backward compatibility** generally means that you do not have to rebuild applications just because a new version of glibc has been released.

There are practical limitations to this backward compatibility. First, mixing objects linked against different versions of glibc in a single executable may sometimes accidentally work, but not by intentional design. Note that this includes dynamically loaded objects as well as statically linked objects. Second, the application should be standard-conforming; an application

---

2. Despite the misleading name, this system call sets the node name, not the machine's Internet host name.
3. Network Information Service, or NIS, is a mechanism for machines on a network to share information such as user names and passwords. It used to be called Yellow Pages, or YP, but was renamed. The NIS domain name is part of this mechanism, which is implemented outside of the kernel with the exception of the domain name being stored in struct utsname.

that depends on side effects of bugs or on unspecified behavior in one version of glibc may not continue to work with later versions of glibc, and an application that links to private symbols in glibc (generally speaking, symbols prefixed with a _ character) is also very unlikely to work with later versions of glibc.

One way that this backward compatibility is maintained is with versioned symbols. When the authors of glibc wish to introduce an incompatible change in glibc, they preserve the original implementation or write a compatible implementation of the interface in question and mark it with the older glibc version number. They then implement the newer, different interface (which may differ in semantics, signature, or both) and mark it with the new glibc version number. Applications built against the older glibc version use the older interface; applications built against the newer glibc version use the new interface.

Most other libraries maintain compatibility by including the version number in the library name and having multiple different versions installed at the same time if necessary; for example, GTK+ 1.2 and GTK+ 2.0 might both be installed on the same system, each with its own set of header and library files and with the version name embedded in the path to the header files and in the names of the library files.

Part of the standard for naming shared libraries on Linux includes a major version number, in order to provide multiple versions of a library on a system. This is not much used for its intended purpose, because it does not allow you to link new applications against multiple versions of a library on a single system; it merely allows backward compatibility to be maintained for already-built applications built on older systems. In practice, developers have found that they have needed to build applications against multiple versions of the same library on the system, and therefore most major libraries have migrated to providing the version number of the library as part of the name of the library.

CHAPTER 7

Memory Debugging Tools

Although C is undisputedly the standard programming language on Linux systems, C has a number of features that lead programmers into writing code with subtle bugs that can be very hard to debug. **Memory leaks** (in which `malloc()`ed memory is never `free()`ed) and **buffer overflows** (writing past the end of an array, for example) are two of the most common and difficult-to-detect program bugs; **buffer underruns** (writing before the beginning of an array, for example) are much less common but usually even harder to track down. This chapter presents a few debugging tools that greatly simplify the detection and isolation of such problems.

7.1 Buggy Code

```
 1: /* broken.c */
 2:
 3: #include <stdlib.h>
 4: #include <stdio.h>
 5: #include <string.h>
 6:
 7: char global[5];
 8:
 9: int broken(void) {
10:     char * dyn;
11:     char local[5];
12:
13:     /* First, overwrite a buffer just a little bit */
14:     dyn = malloc(5);
```

```
15:        strcpy(dyn, "12345");
16:        printf("1: %s\n", dyn);
17:        free(dyn);
18:
19:        /* Now overwrite the buffer a lot */
20:        dyn = malloc(5);
21:        strcpy(dyn, "12345678");
22:        printf("2: %s\n", dyn);
23:
24:        /* Walk past the beginning of a malloced local buffer */
25:        *(dyn - 1) = '\0';
26:        printf("3: %s\n", dyn);
27:        /* note we didn't free the pointer! */
28:
29:        /* Now go after a local variable */
30:        strcpy(local, "12345");
31:        printf("4: %s\n", local);
32:        local[-1] = '\0';
33:        printf("5: %s\n", local);
34:
35:        /* Finally, attack global data space */
36:        strcpy(global, "12345");
37:        printf("6: %s\n", global);
38:
39:        /* And write over the space before the global buffer */
40:        global[-1] = '\0';
41:        printf("7: %s\n", global);
42:
43:        return 0;
44: }
45:
46: int main(void) {
47:        return broken();
48: }
```

Throughout this chapter, we look for the problems in this code segment.
This code corrupts three types of memory regions: memory allocated from
the dynamic memory pool (the **heap**) via malloc(); local variables allocated on the program's stack; and global variables, which are stored in
a separate area of memory that is statically allocated when the program

starts.[1] For each of these memory classes, this test program writes over the end of the reserved area of memory (usually, by a single byte) and stores a byte immediately before the allocated area as well. In addition, the code includes a memory leak to show how various tools can help track down leaks.

Although this code has many problems, it actually runs just fine. Does that mean these problems are not important? Not by any means. Buffer overflows tend to cause a program to misbehave long after the actual overflow, and memory leaks in programs that run for a length of time waste a computer's resources. Furthermore, buffer overflows are a classic source of security vulnerabilities, as discussed in Chapter 22. For reference, here is what the program looks like when it is executed.

```
$ gcc -Wall -o broken broken.c
$ ./broken
1: 12345
2: 12345678
3: 12345678
4: 12345
5: 12345
6: 12345
7: 12345
```

---

1. Unfortunately, none of the tools discussed in this chapter is capable of tracking memory errors with global variables; this requires help from the compiler. In the first edition of *Linux Application Development,* we discussed a tool called Checker that was a modified version of the gcc compiler, but it is no longer maintained. A new technology called "mudflap" is in the process of being added to the official gcc compiler, but it is not yet integrated as we write this. If you are looking for errors involving global variables, you may wish to check the current state of mudflap technology in gcc by reading the current gcc manual. However, since overuse of global variables tends to be a sign of bad program design, you might also consider design changes that eliminate or reduce your use of global variables, which might give other benefits as well.

7.2 Memory-Checking Tools Included in glibc

The GNU C Library (glibc) includes three simple memory-checking tools. The first two, mcheck() and MALLOC_CHECK_, enforce heap data structure consistency checking, and the third, mtrace(), traces memory allocation and deallocation for later processing.

7.2.1 Finding Memory Heap Corruption

When memory is allocated from the heap, the memory management functions need someplace to store information about the allocations. That place is the heap itself; this means that the heap is composed of alternating areas of memory that are used by the program and by the memory management functions themselves. This means that buffer overflows or underruns can actually damage the data structures that the memory management functions use to keep track of what memory has been allocated. When this happens, all bets are off, except that it is a pretty good bet that the memory management functions will eventually cause the program to crash.

If you set the MALLOC_CHECK_ environment variable, a different and somewhat slower set of memory management functions is chosen that is more tolerant of errors and can check for calling free() more than once on the same pointer and for single-byte buffer overflows. If MALLOC_CHECK_ is set to 0, the memory management functions are simply more tolerant of error but do not give warnings. If MALLOC_CHECK_ is set to 1, the memory management functions print out warning messages on standard error when they notice problems. If MALLOC_CHECK_ is set to 2, the memory management functions call abort() when they notice problems.

Setting MALLOC_CHECK_ to 0 may be useful if you are prevented from finding one memory bug by another that is not convenient to fix at the moment; it might allow you to use other tools to chase down the other memory bug. It may also be useful if you are running code that works on another system but not on Linux and you want a quick workaround that may allow the code to function temporarily, before you have a chance to resolve the error.

Setting MALLOC_CHECK_ to 1 is useful if you are not aware of any problems and just want to be notified if any problems exist.

Setting MALLOC_CHECK_ to 2 is most useful from inside the debugger, because it allows you to get a backtrace as soon as the memory management functions discover the error, which will get you closest to the point at which the error has happened.

```
$ MALLOC_CHECK_=1 ./broken
malloc: using debugging hooks
1: 12345
free(): invalid pointer 0x80ac008!
2: 12345678
3: 12345678
4: 12345
5: 12345
6: 12345
7: 12345
$ MALLOC_CHECK_=2 gdb ./broken
...
(gdb) run
Starting program: /usr/src/lad/code/broken
1: 12345
Program received signal SIGABRT, Aborted.
0x00c64c32 in _dl_sysinfo_int80 () from /lib/ld-linux.so.2
(gdb) where
#0  0x00c64c32 in _dl_sysinfo_int80 () from /lib/ld-linux.so.2
#1  0x00322969 in raise () from /lib/tls/libc.so.6
#2  0x00324322 in abort () from /lib/tls/libc.so.6
#3  0x0036d9af in free_check () from /lib/tls/libc.so.6
#4  0x0036afa5 in free () from /lib/tls/libc.so.6
#5  0x0804842b in broken () at broken.c:17
#6  0x08048520 in main () at broken.c:47
```

Another way to ask glibc to do heap consistency checking is with the mcheck() function:

```
typedef void (*mcheckCallback)(enum mcheck_status status);
void mcheck(mcheckCallback cb);
```

When the mcheck() function has been called, malloc() places known byte sequences before and after the returned memory region in order to make it possible to spot buffer overflow and buffer underrun conditions. free() looks for those signatures, and if they have been disturbed, it calls the function pointed to by the cb parameter. If cb is NULL, the library exits instead. Running a program linked against mcheck() through gdb can show you exactly which memory regions have been corrupted, as long as those regions are properly free()ed. However, the mcheck() method does not pinpoint exactly where the corruption occurred; it is up to the programmer to figure that out based on an understanding of the program flow.

Linking our test program against the mcheck library yields the following results:

```
$ gcc -ggdb -o broken broken.c -lmcheck
$ ./broken
1: 12345
memory clobbered past end of allocated block
```

Because mcheck merely complains and exits, this does not really pinpoint the error. To pinpoint the error, you need to run the program inside gdb and tell mcheck to abort() when it notices a problem. You can simply call mcheck() from within gdb, or you can call mcheck(1) as the first line of your program (before you ever call malloc()). (Note that you can call mcheck() from within gdb without linking your program against the mcheck library!)

```
$ rm -f broken; make broken
$ gdb broken
...
(gdb) break main
Breakpoint 1 at 0x80483f4: file broken.c, line 14.
(gdb) command 1
Type commands for when breakpoint 1 is hit, one per line.
End with a line saying just "end".
>call mcheck(&abort)
>continue
>end
(gdb) run
Starting program: /usr/src/lad/code/broken
Breakpoint 1, main () at broken.c:14
47              return broken();
$1 = 0
1: 12345
Program received signal SIGABRT, Aborted.
```

```
0x00e12c32 in _dl_sysinfo_int80 () from /lib/ld-linux.so.2
(gdb) where
#0  0x00e12c32 in _dl_sysinfo_int80 () from /lib/ld-linux.so.2
#1  0x0072c969 in raise () from /lib/tls/libc.so.6
#2  0x0072e322 in abort () from /lib/tls/libc.so.6
#3  0x007792c4 in freehook () from /lib/tls/libc.so.6
#4  0x00774fa5 in free () from /lib/tls/libc.so.6
#5  0x0804842b in broken () at broken.c:17
#6  0x08048520 in main () at broken.c:47
```

The important part of this is where it tells you that the problem was detected in broken.c at line 17. That lets you see that the error was detected during the first free() call, which indicates the problem was in (or more precisely, bordering) the dyn memory region. (freehook() is just the hook that mcheck uses to do its consistency checks.)

mcheck does not help you to find overflows or underruns in local or global variables, only in malloc()ed memory regions.

7.2.2 Using mtrace() to Track Allocations

A simple way to find all of a program's memory leaks is to log all its calls to malloc() and free(). When the program has completed, it is straightforward to match each malloc()ed block with the point at which it was free()ed, or report a leak if it was never free()ed.

Unlike mcheck(), mtrace() has no library against which you can link to enable mtrace(). This is no great loss; you can use the same technique with gdb to start tracing. However, for mtrace() to enable tracing, the environment variable MALLOC_TRACE must be set to a valid filename; either an existing file that the process can write to (in which case it is truncated) or a filename that the process can create and write to.

```
$ MALLOC_TRACE=mtrace.log gdb broken
...
(gdb) break main
Breakpoint 1 at 0x80483f4: file broken.c, line 14.
(gdb) command 1
Type commands for when breakpoint 1 is hit, one per line.
End with a line saying just "end".
```

```
>call mtrace()
>continue
>end
(gdb) run
Starting program: /usr/src/lad/code/broken
Breakpoint 1, main () at broken.c:47
47              return broken();
$1 = 0
1: 12345
2: 12345678
3: 12345678
4: 12345
5: 12345
6: 12345
7: 12345
Program exited normally.
(gdb) quit
$ ls -l mtrace.log
-rw-rw-r--   1 ewt       ewt            220 Dec 27 23:41 mtrace.log
$ mtrace ./broken mtrace.log
Memory not freed:
-----------------
   Address      Size    Caller
0x09211378       0x5  at /usr/src/lad/code/broken.c:20
```

Note that the mtrace program has found the memory leak exactly. The mtrace program can also find memory that is free()ed that was never allocated in the first place if this case shows up in the log file, but in practice it will not find it there because the program should crash immediately when attempting to free() the unallocated memory.

7.3 Finding Memory Leaks with mpr

The mtrace() facility in glibc is good, but the mpr memory allocation profiler[2] is in some ways easier to use and has some more sophisticated scripts for processing its logfile output.

---

2. Available from http://www3.telus.net/taj_khattra/mpr.html as well as with many Linux distributions.

The first step in using mpr (after building the code with debug information enabled[3]) is to set an environment variable, MPRFI, that tells mpr what command it should pipe the log through (if it is not set, no log is generated). For small programs, MPRFI should be set to something like cat > mpr.log. For larger programs, it can save a significant amount of space to compress the log file while writing it by setting MPRFI to gzip -1 >mpr.log.gz.

The easiest way to do this is to use the mpr script to run your program; if MPRFI is not already set, it sets MPRFI to gzip -1 >log.%p.gz, which creates a logfile with the process ID of the program being debugged and preloads the mpr library so that you do not have to rebuild your program at all. Here is what we did to create a log file for a fixed version of our test program:

```
$ MPRFI="cat >mpr.log" mpr ./broken
1: 12345
2: 12345678
3: 12345678
4: 12345
5: 12345
6: 12345
7: 12345
$ ls -l mpr.log
-rw-rw-r--   1 ewt       ewt              142 May 17 16:22 mpr.log
```

Once the log file has been created, there are a number of tools available for analyzing it. All of these programs expect an mpr log on standard input. If the output from these tools has numbers where you expect function names (probably with a warning like "cannot map pc to name"), the problem may be the version of the awk utility that mpr is using. The mpr documentation suggests exporting the MPRAWK environment variable to choose the mawk version of awk for best results: export MPRAWK='mawk -W sprintf=4096'. In addition, the stack randomization provided by the kernel "Exec-shield" functionality can confuse mpr; you can ameliorate this by using the setarch command to disable Exec-shield while running the program under investigation and while running the mpr filters: for example, setarch i386 mpr *program* and setarch i386 mprmap ....

---

3. For portability, most of the mpr log analysis tools use gdb to relate addresses to their location in the source code. For this to work, the program must include debugging information.

You may still end up with a few stack frames that mpr cannot find a textual symbol name for; you can generally ignore them.

`mprmap program`

This converts the program addresses in an mpr log into function names and source code locations. The executable file name that generated the log must be given as an argument. To see all the allocations that occurred in a program, along with the function call chain that led to the allocations, you could use `mprmap program < mpr.log`. By default, this program displays the function name. Using the `-f` flag causes it to display the file names, as well, and `-l` displays the line number within the file. The `-l` argument implies the `-f` argument.

The output of this program is considered a valid mpr log file, and as such it can be piped through any of the other mpr utility programs.

`mprchain`   This converts the log into output grouped by call chain. A function call chain is a list of all the functions that are currently active at some point in a program. For example, if `main()` calls `getargs()`, which then calls `parsearg()`, the active call chain while `parsearg()` is running is displayed as `main:getargs:parsearg`. For each unique call chain that allocated memory during a program's execution, `mprchain` displays the number of allocations made by that chain[4] and the total bytes allocated by that chain.

`mprleak`   This filter examines the log file for all of the allocated regions that were never freed. A new log file, which consists of only those allocations that caused leaks, is generated on standard out.

The output of this program is considered a valid mpr log file, and as such it can be piped through any of the other mpr utility programs.

---

4. More specifically, it is the sum of all the allocations made by the final function in the chain when it was invoked through that particular chain.

mprsize   This filter sorts memory allocations by size. To see memory leaks by size, use the output from mprleak as the input to mprsize.

mprhisto   Displays a memory allocation histogram.

Now that we know about the log analyzers, it is easy to find the memory leak in our test program: Merely use the command mprleak mpr.log | mprmap -l ./broken (which is equivalent to mprmap -l ./broken mpr.log | mprleak) to find the memory leak on line 20.

```
$ mprleak mpr.log | mprmap -l ./broken
m:broken(broken.c,20):main(broken.c,47):5:134518624
```

7.4 Investigating Memory Errors with Valgrind

Valgrind[5] is an Intel x86-specific tool that emulates an x86-class CPU to watch all memory accesses directly and analyze data flow (for example, it can recognize reads of uninitialized memory, but it also recognizes that moving one uninitialized value into another location that is never read does not actually constitute an uninitialized read). It has many other capabilities, including investigating cache use and looking for race conditions in threaded programs, and in fact has a general facility for adding more capabilities based on its CPU emulator. However, for our purposes, we merely briefly introduce its aggressive memory error checking, which is its default behavior.

Valgrind does not require that a program be recompiled, although its analysis, like all debugging tools, is enhanced by compiling the program with debugging information included.

```
$ valgrind ./broken
==30882== Memcheck, a.k.a. Valgrind, a memory error detector for x86-linux.
==30882== Copyright (C) 2002-2003, and GNU GPL'd, by Julian Seward.
==30882== Using valgrind-2.0.0, a program supervision framework for x86-linux.
==30882== Copyright (C) 2000-2003, and GNU GPL'd, by Julian Seward.
==30882== Estimated CPU clock rate is 1547 MHz
```

---

5. Available from http://valgrind.kde.org/

```
==30882== For more details, rerun with: -v
==30882==
==30882== Invalid write of size 1
==30882==    at 0xC030DB: strcpy (mac_replace_strmem.c:174)
==30882==    by 0x8048409: broken (broken.c:15)
==30882==    by 0x804851F: main (broken.c:47)
==30882==    by 0x802BAE: __libc_start_main (in /lib/libc-2.3.2.so)
==30882==  Address 0x650F029 is 0 bytes after a block of size 5 alloc'd
==30882==    at 0xC0C28B: malloc (vg_replace_malloc.c:153)
==30882==    by 0x80483F3: broken (broken.c:14)
==30882==    by 0x804851F: main (broken.c:47)
==30882==    by 0x802BAE: __libc_start_main (in /lib/libc-2.3.2.so)
==30882==
==30882== Conditional jump or move depends on uninitialised value(s)
==30882==    at 0x863D8E: __GI_strlen (in /lib/libc-2.3.2.so)
==30882==    by 0x83BC31: _IO_printf (in /lib/libc-2.3.2.so)
==30882==    by 0x804841C: broken (broken.c:16)
==30882==    by 0x804851F: main (broken.c:47)
1: 12345
==30882==
==30882== Invalid write of size 1
==30882==    at 0xC030D0: strcpy (mac_replace_strmem.c:173)
==30882==    by 0x804844D: broken (broken.c:21)
==30882==    by 0x804851F: main (broken.c:47)
==30882==    by 0x802BAE: __libc_start_main (in /lib/libc-2.3.2.so)
==30882==  Address 0x650F061 is 0 bytes after a block of size 5 alloc'd
==30882==    at 0xC0C28B: malloc (vg replace_malloc.c:153)
==30882==    by 0x8048437: broken (broken.c:20)
==30882==    by 0x804851F: main (broken.c:47)
==30882==    by 0x802BAE: __libc_start_main (in /lib/libc-2.3.2.so)
==30882==
==30882== Invalid write of size 1
==30882==    at 0xC030DB: strcpy (mac_replace_strmem.c:174)
==30882==    by 0x804844D: broken (broken.c:21)
==30882==    by 0x804851F: main (broken.c:47)
==30882==    by 0x802BAE: __libc_start_main (in /lib/libc-2.3.2.so)
==30882==  Address 0x650F064 is 3 bytes after a block of size 5 alloc'd
==30882==    at 0xC0C28B: malloc (vg_replace_malloc.c:153)
==30882==    by 0x8048437: broken (broken.c:20)
==30882==    by 0x804851F: main (broken.c:47)
==30882==    by 0x802BAE: __libc_start_main (in /lib/libc-2.3.2.so)
```

```
==30882==
==30882== Invalid read of size 4
==30882==    at 0x863D50: __GI_strlen (in /lib/libc-2.3.2.so)
==30882==    by 0x83BC31: _IO_printf (in /lib/libc-2.3.2.so)
==30882==    by 0x8048460: broken (broken.c:22)
==30882==    by 0x804851F: main (broken.c:47)
==30882==  Address 0x650F064 is 3 bytes after a block of size 5 alloc'd
==30882==    at 0xC0C28B: malloc (vg_replace_malloc.c:153)
==30882==    by 0x8048437: broken (broken.c:20)
==30882==    by 0x804851F: main (broken.c:47)
==30882==    by 0x802BAE: __libc_start_main (in /lib/libc-2.3.2.so)
==30882==
==30882== Invalid read of size 1
==30882==    at 0x857A21: _IO_file_xsputn@@GLIBC_2.1 (in /lib/libc-2.3.2.so)
==30882==    by 0x835309: _IO_vfprintf_internal (in /lib/libc-2.3.2.so)
==30882==    by 0x83BC31: _IO_printf (in /lib/libc-2.3.2.so)
==30882==    by 0x8048460: broken (broken.c:22)
==30882==  Address 0x650F063 is 2 bytes after a block of size 5 alloc'd
==30882==    at 0xC0C28B: malloc (vg_replace_malloc.c:153)
==30882==    by 0x8048437: broken (broken.c:20)
==30882==    by 0x804851F: main (broken.c:47)
==30882==    by 0x802BAE: __libc_start_main (in /lib/libc-2.3.2.so)
==30882==
==30882== Invalid read of size 1
==30882==    at 0x857910: _IO_file_xsputn@@GLIBC_2.1 (in /lib/libc-2.3.2.so)
==30882==    by 0x835309: _IO_vfprintf_internal (in /lib/libc-2.3.2.so)
==30882==    by 0x83BC31: _IO_printf (in /lib/libc-2.3.2.so)
==30882==    by 0x8048460: broken (broken.c:22)
==30882==  Address 0x650F061 is 0 bytes after a block of size 5 alloc'd
==30882==    at 0xC0C28B: malloc (vg_replace_malloc.c:153)
==30882==    by 0x8048437: broken (broken.c:20)
==30882==    by 0x804851F: main (broken.c:47)
==30882==    by 0x802BAE: __libc_start_main (in /lib/libc-2.3.2.so)
2: 12345678
==30882==
==30882== Invalid write of size 1
==30882==    at 0x8048468: broken (broken.c:25)
==30882==    by 0x804851F: main (broken.c:47)
==30882==    by 0x802BAE: __libc_start_main (in /lib/libc-2.3.2.so)
==30882==    by 0x8048354: (within /usr/src/d/lad2/code/broken)
==30882==  Address 0x650F05B is 1 bytes before a block of size 5 alloc'd
```

```
==30882==     at 0xC0C28B: malloc (vg_replace_malloc.c:153)
==30882==     by 0x8048437: broken (broken.c:20)
==30882==     by 0x804851F: main (broken.c:47)
==30882==     by 0x802BAE: __libc_start_main (in /lib/libc-2.3.2.so)
==30882==
==30882== Invalid read of size 4
==30882==     at 0x863D50: __GI_strlen (in /lib/libc-2.3.2.so)
==30882==     by 0x83BC31: _IO_printf (in /lib/libc-2.3.2.so)
==30882==     by 0x804847A: broken (broken.c:26)
==30882==     by 0x804851F: main (broken.c:47)
==30882==   Address 0x650F064 is 3 bytes after a block of size 5 alloc'd
==30882==     at 0xC0C28B: malloc (vg_replace_malloc.c:153)
==30882==     by 0x8048437: broken (broken.c:20)
==30882==     by 0x804851F: main (broken.c:47)
==30882==     by 0x802BAE: __libc_start_main (in /lib/libc-2.3.2.so)
==30882==
==30882== Invalid read of size 1
==30882==     at 0x857A21: _IO_file_xsputn@@GLIBC_2.1 (in /lib/libc-2.3.2.so)
==30882==     by 0x835309: _IO_vfprintf_internal (in /lib/libc-2.3.2.so)
==30882==     by 0x83BC31: _IO_printf (in /lib/libc-2.3.2.so)
==30882==     by 0x804847A: broken (broken.c:26)
==30882==   Address 0x650F063 is 2 bytes after a block of size 5 alloc'd
==30882==     at 0xC0C28B: malloc (vg_replace_malloc.c:153)
==30882==     by 0x8048437: broken (broken.c:20)
==30882==     by 0x804851F: main (broken.c:47)
==30882==     by 0x802BAE: __libc_start_main (in /lib/libc-2.3.2.so)
==30882==
==30882== Invalid read of size 1
==30882==     at 0x857910: _IO_file_xsputn@@GLIBC_2.1 (in /lib/libc-2.3.2.so)
==30882==     by 0x835309: _IO_vfprintf_internal (in /lib/libc-2.3.2.so)
==30882==     by 0x83BC31: _IO_printf (in /lib/libc-2.3.2.so)
==30882==     by 0x804847A: broken (broken.c:26)
==30882==   Address 0x650F061 is 0 bytes after a block of size 5 alloc'd
==30882==     at 0xC0C28B: malloc (vg_replace_malloc.c:153)
==30882==     by 0x8048437: broken (broken.c:20)
==30882==     by 0x804851F: main (broken.c:47)
==30882==     by 0x802BAE: __libc_start_main (in /lib/libc-2.3.2.so)
3: 12345678
4: 12345
==30882==
==30882== Invalid write of size 1
```

```
==30882==     at 0x80484A6: broken (broken.c:32)
==30882==     by 0x804851F: main (broken.c:47)
==30882==     by 0x802BAE: __libc_start_main (in /lib/libc-2.3.2.so)
==30882==     by 0x8048354: (within /usr/src/d/lad2/code/broken)
==30882==     Address 0xBFF2D0FF is just below %esp.  Possibly a bug in GCC/G++
==30882==     v 2.96 or 3.0.X.  To suppress, use: --workaround-gcc296-bugs=yes
5: 12345
6: 12345
7: 12345
==30882==
==30882== ERROR SUMMARY: 22 errors from 12 contexts (suppressed: 0 from 0)
==30882== malloc/free: in use at exit: 5 bytes in 1 blocks.
==30882== malloc/free: 2 allocs, 1 frees, 10 bytes allocated.
==30882== For a detailed leak analysis,  rerun with: --leak-check=yes
==30882== For counts of detected errors, rerun with: -v
```

Note that Valgrind found everything but the global overflow and underrun, and it pinpointed the errors more specifically than any other tool we have described here.

One option allows you to turn on an aggressive form of leak checking in which the program is searched to determine for each memory allocation whether any accessible pointers still hold a reference to that memory. This is more accurate than simply asking whether memory has been free()ed because it is reasonably common to allocate some memory that is held for the lifetime of the program, and not to free() it because it returns to the operating system when the program exits anyway.

```
$ valgrind --leak-check=yes ./broken
...
==2292== searching for pointers to 1 not-freed blocks.
==2292== checked 5318724 bytes.
==2292==
==2292== 5 bytes in 1 blocks are definitely lost in loss record 1 of 1
==2292==     at 0xEC528B: malloc (vg_replace_malloc.c:153)
==2292==     by 0x8048437: broken (broken.c:20)
==2292==     by 0x804851F: main (broken.c:47)
==2292==     by 0x126BAE: __libc_start_main (in /lib/libc-2.3.2.so)
==2292==
==2292== LEAK SUMMARY:
==2292==     definitely lost: 5 bytes in 1 blocks.
```

```
==2292==      possibly lost:   0 bytes in 0 blocks.
==2292==    still reachable: 0 bytes in 0 blocks.
==2292==         suppressed: 0 bytes in 0 blocks.
==2292== Reachable blocks (those to which a pointer was found) are not shown.
==2292== To see them, rerun with: --show-reachable=yes
```

Valgrind includes fairly detailed information on its capabilities, called skins, and has many command-line options for modifying its behavior.

Because Valgrind uses a CPU emulator, it runs many times slower than a program running natively on the system. Exactly how much slower depends on the program, but Valgrind is intended to be at least usable for running interactive programs.

There are occasional subtle issues that can confuse Valgrind when you compile with high levels of optimization. If you get a report of a memory error that does not seem to make sense, try compiling with -O rather than -O2 (or higher) and see if the report changes.

7.5   Electric Fence

The next tool we look at is **Electric Fence**.[6] While it makes no attempt to find memory leaks, it does a nice job of helping programmers isolate buffer overflows. Every modern computer (including all the computers that Linux runs on) provides hardware memory protection. Linux takes advantage of this to isolate programs from each other (your vi session can not access the memory of my gcc invocation, for example) and to share code safely among processes by making it read-only. Linux's mmap()[7] system call allows processes to take advantage of hardware memory protection, as well.

Electric Fence replaces the C library's normal malloc() function with a version that allocates the requested memory and (usually) allocates a section of memory immediately after this, which the process is not allowed to access! Although it may seem odd for a process to allocate memory

---

6. Available from ftp://sunsite.unc.edu/pub/Linux/devel/lang/c as well as with many distributions.
7. See Chapter 13 for details on mmap().

that it is not allowed to access, doing so causes the kernel to halt the process immediately with a segmentation fault if the program tries to access the memory. By allocating the memory in this manner, Electric Fence has arranged things so that your program will be killed whenever it tries to read or write past the end of a `malloc()`ed buffer. For full details on using Electric Fence, consult its man page (`man libefence`), which is detailed.

7.5.1 Using Electric Fence

One of the nicest things about Electric Fence is that it is easy to use. Simply link a program against `libefence.a` by running the final link step with `-lefence` as the final argument, and the code is ready to be debugged. Let's see what happens when we run our test program against Electric Fence:

```
$ ./broken
  Electric Fence 2.2.0 Copyright (C) 1987-1999 Bruce Perens.
1: 12345
Segmentation fault (core dumped)
```

Although Electric Fence does not tell us exactly where the problem occurred, it does make the problem itself *much* more obvious. Pinpointing where the problem occurred is easily done by running the program under a debugger, such as gdb. To use gdb to pinpoint the problem, build the program with debugging information by using gcc's `-g` flag, run gdb and tell it the name of the executable to debug, and run the program. When the program is killed, gdb shows you exactly what line caused the problem. Here is what this procedure looks like:

```
$ gcc -ggdb -Wall -o broken broken.c -lefence
$ gdb broken
...
(gdb) run
Starting program: /usr/src/lad/code/broken
  Electric Fence 2.2.0 Copyright (C) 1987-1999 Bruce Perens.
1: 12345
Program received signal SIGSEGV, Segmentation fault.
0x007948c6 in strcpy () from /lib/tls/libc.so.6
(gdb) where
#0  0x007948c6 in strcpy () from /lib/tls/libc.so.6
```

```
#1  0x08048566 in broken () at broken.c:21
#2  0x08048638 in main () at broken.c:47
(gdb)
```

Thanks to Electric Fence and gdb, we know there is a problem in file broken.c code at line 21, which is the second time strcpy() is called.

7.5.2 Memory Alignment

While Electric Fence did a fine job of finding the second problem in the code—namely, the strcpy() that overwrote its buffer by a large amount—it did not help us at all in finding the first buffer overflow.

The problem here has to do with memory alignment. Most modern CPUs require multibyte objects to start at particular offsets in the system's RAM. For example, Alpha processors require that an 8-byte long begin at an address that is evenly divisible by eight. This means that a long may appear at address 0x1000 or 0x1008, but not at 0x1005.[8]

Because of this consideration, malloc() implementations normally return memory whose first byte is aligned on the processor's word size (4 bytes on 32-bit processors and 8 bytes on 64-bit processors) to ensure the caller can store whatever data it likes into the memory. By default, Electric Fence attempts to mimic this behavior by providing a malloc() that returns only addresses that are an even multiple of sizeof(int).

In most programs, such alignment is not all that important, because memory allocations are done in increments that are already based on the machine's word size, or of simple character strings, which do not have any alignment requirements (as each element is only one byte long).

In the case of our test program, the first malloc() call allocated five bytes. For Electric Fence to meet its alignment restrictions, it must treat the allocation as a request for eight bytes and set up the memory with an extra three bytes of accessible space after the malloc()ed region! Small buffer overflows in this region are not caught because of this.

---

8. Most traditional Unix systems deliver a bus error (SIGBUS) to a process that attempts to use misaligned data. The Linux kernel actually handles unaligned accesses so that the process can continue normally, but at a large performance penalty.

As malloc() alignment concerns can normally be ignored and the alignment can allow buffer overflows to remain undetected, Electric Fence lets you control how alignment works through the EF_ALIGNMENT environment variable. If it is set, all malloc() results are aligned according to its value. For example, if it is set to 5, all malloc() results will be addresses evenly divisible by 5 (this probably is not a very useful value, however). To turn off memory alignment, set EF_ALIGNMENT to 1 before running your program. Under Linux, improperly aligned accesses are fixed in the kernel anyway, so although this may slow your program down substantially, it should function properly—unless it has slight buffer overflows!

Here is how our test program linked against Electric Fence behaved when we set EF_ALIGNMENT to 1:

```
$ export EF_ALIGNMENT=1
$ gdb broken
...
(gdb) run
Starting program: /usr/src/lad/code/broken
  Electric Fence 2.2.0 Copyright (C) 1987-1999 Bruce Perens.
Program received signal SIGSEGV, Segmentation fault.
0x002a78c6 in strcpy () from /lib/tls/libc.so.6
(gdb) where
#0  0x002a78c6 in strcpy () from /lib/tls/libc.so.6
#1  0x08048522 in broken () at broken.c:15
#2  0x08048638 in main () at broken.c:47
```

This time it found the first buffer overflow that occurred.

7.5.3 Other Features

Not only does Electric Fence help detect buffer overflows, but it also can detect buffer underruns (accessing the memory before the start of a malloc()ed buffer) and accesses to memory that has already been free()ed. If the EF_PROTECT_BELOW environment variable is set to 1, Electric Fence traps buffer underruns instead of overflows. It does this by placing an inaccessible memory region immediately before the valid memory region returned by malloc(). When it does this, it can no longer detect overflows because of the memory paging layout of most processors. The memory alignment concerns that make overflows tricky do not affect underruns, however, as in this mode, Electric Fence's `malloc()` always returns a memory address at the beginning of a page, which is always aligned on a word boundary.

If `EF_PROTECT_FREE` is set to 1, `free()` makes the memory region passed to it inaccessible rather than return it to the free memory pool. If the program tries to access that memory at any point in the future, the kernel will detect the illegal access. Setting `EF_PROTECT_FREE` makes it easy to ensure that your code is not using `free()`ed memory at any point.

7.5.4 Limitations

While Electric Fence does a nice job of finding overflows of `malloc()`ed buffers, it does not help at all with tracking down problems with either global or locally allocated data. It also does not make any attempt to find memory leaks, so you have to look elsewhere for help with those problems.

7.5.5 Resource Consumption

Although Electric Fence is powerful, easy to use, and fast (because all the access checks are done in hardware), it does exact a price. Most processors allow the system to control access to memory only in units of a **page** at a time. On Intel 80x86 processors, for example, each page is 4,096 bytes in size. Because Electric Fence wants `malloc()` to set up two different regions for each call (one allowing access, the other allowing no access), each call to `malloc()` consumes a page of memory, or 4K![9] If the code being tested allocates a lot of small areas, linking the code against Electric Fence can easily increase the program's memory usage by two or three orders of magnitude! Of course, using `EF_PROTECT_FREE` makes this even worse because that memory is never freed.

For systems with lots of memory relative to the size of the program you are debugging, when you are looking to find the source of a specific instance of corruption, Electric Fence may be faster than Valgrind. However, if you need to enable a gigabyte of swap space just to make Electric Fence work, then Valgrind will probably be much faster even though it is using a CPU emulator instead of the native CPU.

---

9. On Linux/Intel and Linux/SPARC systems anyway. The page size depends on the underlying hardware architecture, and may be 16K or even larger on some systems.

CHAPTER 8

Creating and Using Libraries

Executable binaries can get functions from libraries in one of two ways: The functions can be copied from a static library directly into the executable binary image, or they can be indirectly referenced in a shared library file that is read when the executable is run. This chapter teaches you how to use and create both types of archives.

8.1 Static Libraries

Static libraries are simply collections of object files arranged by the **ar** (archiver) utility. ar collects object files into one archive file and adds a table that tells which object files in the archive define what symbols. The linker, **ld**, then binds references to a symbol in one object file to the definition of that symbol in an object file in the archive. Static libraries use the suffix .a.

You can convert a group of object files into a static library with a command like

```
ar rcs libname.a foo.o bar.o baz.o
```

You can also add one object file at a time to an existing archive.

```
ar rcs libname.a foo.o
ar rcs libname.a bar.o
ar rcs libname.a baz.o
```

In either case, `libname.a` will be the same. The options used here are:

r   Includes the object files in the library, *replacing* any object files already in the archive that have the same names.

c   Silently create the library if it does not already exist.

s   Maintain the table mapping symbol names to object file names.

There is rarely any need to use other options when building static libraries. However, ar has other options and other capabilities; the ar man page describes them in detail.

8.2 Shared Libraries

Shared libraries have several advantages over static libraries:

- Linux shares the memory used for executable code among all the processes that use the shared library, so whenever you have more than one program using the same code, it is to your advantage, and to your users' advantage, to put the code in a shared library.

- Because shared libraries save system memory, they can make the whole system work faster, especially in situations in which memory is not plentiful.

- Because code in a shared library is not copied into the executable, only one copy of the library code resides on disk, saving both disk space and the computer's time spent copying the code from disk to memory when programs are run.

- When bugs are found in a library, a shared library can be replaced by a version that has the bugs fixed, instead of having to recompile every program that uses the library.

The cost exacted by these advantages is primarily complexity. The executable consists of several interdependent parts, and if you give a binary executable to someone who does not have a shared library that the executable requires, it will not run. A secondary cost is the time it takes when the program starts to find and load the shared libraries; this is generally negated because the shared libraries usually have already been loaded into memory for other processes, and so they do not have to be loaded from disk again when the new process is started.

Linux originally used a simplistic binary file format (actually, three variations on a simplistic binary file format) that made the process of creating shared libraries difficult and time-consuming. Once created, the libraries could not be easily extended in a backward-compatible way. The author of the library had to leave space for data structure expansion by hand-editing tables, and even that did not always work.

Now, the standard binary file format on almost every Linux platform is the modern, extensible **Executable and Linking Format (ELF)** file format.[1] This means that on practically all Linux platforms, the steps you take to create and use shared libraries are exactly the same.

8.3 Designing Shared Libraries

Building shared libraries is only marginally harder than building normal static libraries. There are a few constraints, all of which are easy to manage. There is also one major feature, designed to manage binary compatibility across library versions, that is unique to shared libraries.

Shared libraries are intended to preserve backward compatibility. That is, a binary built against an older version of the library still works when run against a newer version of the library. However, there needs to be a way to mark libraries as incompatible with each other for cases in which developers find it necessary to modify interfaces in a non-backward-compatible manner.

---

1. See *Understanding ELF Object Files and Debugging Tools* [Nohr, 1994] or ftp://tsx-11.mit.edu/pub/linux/packages/GCC/ELF.doc.tar.gz for detailed information on the ELF format. The Linux-specifix details are covered in the document ftp://tsx-11.mit.edu/pub/linux/packages/GCC/elf.ps.gz.

8.3.1 Managing Compatibility

Every Linux shared library is assigned a special name, called a **soname**, that includes the name of the library and a version number. When developers change interfaces, they increment the version number, altering the name. Some libraries do not have stable interfaces; developers may change their interface in an incompatible way when a new version is released that has changed only a minor number. Most library developers attempt to maintain stable interfaces that change in an incompatible manner only when they release a new major version of the library.

For example, the developers and maintainers of the Linux C library attempt to maintain backward compatibility for all releases of the C library with the same major number. Version 5 of the C library has gone through five minor revisions, and with few exceptions, programs that worked with the first minor revision work with the fifth. (The exceptions have been poorly coded programs that took advantage of C library behavior that was not specified or that was buggy in older versions and fixed in newer versions.)

Because all version 5 C libraries are intended to be backward compatible with older versions, they all use the same soname—libc.so.5—which is related to the name of the file in which it is stored, /lib/libc.so.5.*m.r*, where *m* is the minor version number and *r* is the release number.

Applications that link against a shared library do not link directly against /lib/libc.so.6 (for instance), even though that file exists. The **ldconfig** program, a standard Linux system utility, creates a symbolic link from /lib/libc.so.6 (the soname) to /lib/libc-2.3.2.so, the real name of the library. This makes upgrading shared libraries easy. To upgrade from 2.3.2 to 2.3.3, it is necessary only to put the new libc-2.3.3.so into the /lib directory and run ldconfig. The ldconfig looks at all the libraries that provide the libc.so.6 soname and makes the symbolic link from the soname to the latest library that provides the soname. Then all the applications linked against /lib/libc.so.6 automatically use the new library the next time they are run, and /lib/libc-2.3.2.so can be removed immediately, since it is no longer in use.[2]

---

2. That is, you can use the `rm` command to remove it from the directory structure immediately; programs that are still using it keep it on the disk automatically until they exit. See page 194 for an explanation of how this works.

Unless you have a particular reason to do so, do not link against a specific version of a library. Always use the standard -*llibname* option to the C compiler or the linker, and you will never accidentally link against the wrong version. The linker will look for the file lib*libname*.so, which will be a symlink to the correct version of the library.

So, for linking against the C library, the linker finds /usr/lib/libc.so, which tells the linker to use /lib/libc.so.6, which is a link to the /lib/libc-2.3.2.so file. The application is linked against libc-2.3.2.so's soname, libc.so.6, so when the application is run, it finds /lib/libc.so.6 and links to libc-2.3.2.so, because libc.so.6 is a symlink to libc-2.3.2.so.

8.3.2 Incompatible Libraries

When a new version of a library needs to be incompatible with an old version, it should be given a different soname. For instance, to release a new version of the C library that is incompatible with the old one, developers used the soname libc.so.6 instead of libc.so.5, which shows that it is incompatible and also allows applications linked against either version to coexist on the same system. Applications linked against some version of libc.so.5 will continue to use the latest library version that provides the libc.so.5 soname, and applications linked against some version of libc.so.6 will use the latest library version that provides the libc.so.6 soname.

8.3.3 Designing Compatible Libraries

When you are designing your own libraries, you need to know what makes a library incompatible. There are three main causes of incompatibilities:

1. Changing or removing exported function interfaces

2. Changing exported data items, except adding optional items to the ends of structures that are allocated within the library

3. Changing the behavior of functions to something outside the original specification

To keep new versions of your libraries compatible, you can:

- Add new functions with different names rather than change the definitions or interfaces of existing functions.

- When changing exported structure definitions, add items only to the end of the structures, and make the extra items optional or filled in by the library itself. Do not expand structures unless they are allocated within the library. Otherwise, applications will not allocate the right amount of data. Do not expand structures that are used in arrays.

8.4 Building Shared Libraries

Once you have grasped the concept of sonames, the rest is easy. Just follow a few simple rules.

- Build your sources with gcc's `-fPIC` flag. This generates position-independent code that can be linked and loaded at any address.[3]

- Do not use the `-fomit-frame-pointer` compiler option. The libraries will still work, but debuggers will be useless. When you need a user to provide you with a traceback because of a bug in your code (or a savvy user wants a traceback to do his or her own debugging), it will not work.

- When linking the library, use gcc rather than ld. The C compiler knows how to call the loader in order to link properly, and there is no guarantee that the interface to ld will remain constant.

- When linking the library, do not forget to provide the soname. You use a special compiler option: `-Wl` passes options on to ld, with commas replaced with spaces. Use

```
gcc -shared -Wl,-soname,soname -o libname filelist liblist
```

---

3. The difference between `-fPIC` and `-fpic` relates to how the position-independent code is generated. On some architectures, only relatively small shared libraries can be built with `-fpic` while on others they do exactly the same thing. Unless you have a very good reason to use `-fpic`, just use `-fPIC` and things will work properly on every architecture.

to build your library, where *soname* is the soname; *libname* is the name of the library, including the whole version number, such as libc.so.5.3.12; *filelist* is the list of object files that you want to put in the library; and *liblist* is the list of other libraries that provide symbols that will be accessed by this library. The last item is easy to overlook, because the library will still work without it on the system on which it was created, but it may not work in all other situations, such as when multiple libraries are available. For nearly every library, the C library should be included in that list, so explicitly place -lc at the end of this list.

To create the file libfoo.so.1.0.1, with a soname of libfoo.so.1, from the object files foo.o and bar.o, use this invocation:

```
gcc -shared -Wl,-soname,libfoo.so.1 -o libfoo.so.1.0.1 foo.o bar.o \
    -lc
```

- Do not strip the library unless you are in a particularly space-hungry environment. Shared libraries that have been stripped will still work, but they have the same general disadvantages as libraries built from object files compiled with -fomit-frame-pointer.

8.5 Installing Shared Libraries

The ldconfig program does all the hard work of installing a shared library. You just need to put the files in place and run ldconfig. Follow these steps:

1. Copy the shared library to the directory in which you want to keep it.

2. If you want the linker to be able to find the library without giving it a -L*directory* flag, install the library in /usr/lib, or make a symlink in /usr/lib named *libname*.so that points to the shared library file. You should use a relative symlink (with /usr/lib/libc.so pointing to ../../lib/libc.so.5.3.12), instead of an absolute symlink (/usr/lib/libc.so would not point to /lib/libc.so.5.3.12).

3. If you want the linker to be able to find the library without installing it on the system (or before installing it on the system), create a `lib-name.so` link in the current directory just like the system-wide one. Then use `-L.` to tell gcc to look in the current directory for libraries.

4. If the full pathname of the directory in which you installed the shared library file is not listed in /etc/ld.so.conf, add it, one directory path per line of the file.

5. Run the ldconfig program, which will make another symlink in the directory in which you installed the shared library file from the soname to the file you installed. It will then make an entry in the dynamic loader cache so that the dynamic loader finds your library when you run programs linked with it, without having to search many directories in an attempt to find it.[4]

You need to create entries in /etc/ld.so.conf and run ldconfig only if you are installing the libraries as system libraries—if you expect that programs linked against the library will automatically work. Other ways to use shared libraries are explained in the next section.

8.5.1 Example

As an extremely simple but still instructive example, we have created a library that contains one short function. Here, in its entirety, is libhello.c:

```
1: /* libhello.c */
2:
3: #include <stdio.h>
4:
5: void print_hello(void) {
6:     printf("Hello, library.\n");
7: }
```

Of course, we need a program that makes use of libhello:

```
1: /* usehello.c */
```

---

4. If you remove /etc/ld.so.cache, you may be able to detect the slowdown in your system. Run ldconfig to regenerate /etc/ld.so.cache.

```
2:
3: #include "libhello.h"
4:
5: int main (void) {
6:     print_hello();
7:     return 0;
8: }
```

The contents of libhello.h are left as an exercise for the reader.

In order to compile and use this library without installing it in the system, we take the following steps:

1. Use -fPIC to build an object file for a shared library:

   ```
   gcc -fPIC -Wall -g -c libhello.c
   ```

2. Link libhello against the C library for best results on all systems:

   ```
   gcc -g -shared -Wl,-soname,libhello.so.0 -o libhello.so.0.0 \
           libhello.o -lc
   ```

3. Create a pointer from the soname to the library:

   ```
   ln -sf libhello.so.0.0 libhello.so.0
   ```

4. Create a pointer for the linker to use when linking applications against -lhello:

   ```
   ln -sf libhello.so.0 libhello.so
   ```

5. Use -L. to cause the linker to look in the current directory for libraries, and use -lhello to tell it what library to link against:

   ```
   gcc -Wall -g -c usehello.c -o usehello.o
   gcc -g -o usehello usehello.o -L. -lhello
   ```

   (This way, if you install the library on the system instead of leaving it in the current directory, your application will still link with the same command line.)

6. Now run usehello like this:

```
LD_LIBRARY_PATH=$(pwd) ./usehello
```

The LD_LIBRARY_PATH environment variable tells the system where to look for libraries (see the next section for details). Of course, you can install libhello.so.* in the /usr/lib directory and avoid setting the LD_LIBRARY_PATH environment variable, if you like.

8.6 Using Shared Libraries

The easiest way to use a shared library is to ignore the fact that it is a shared library. The C compiler automatically uses shared libraries instead of static ones unless it is explicitly told to link with static libraries. However, there are three other ways to use shared libraries. One, explicitly loading and unloading them from within a program while the program runs, is called dynamic loading, and is described in Chapter 27. The other two are explained here.

8.6.1 Using Noninstalled Libraries

When you run a program, the dynamic loader usually looks in a cache (/etc/ld.so.cache, created by ldconfig) of libraries that are in directories mentioned in /etc/ld.so.conf to find libraries that the program needs. However, if the LD_LIBRARY_PATH environment variable is set, it first dynamically scans the directories mentioned in LD_LIBRARY_PATH (which has the same format as the PATH environment variable) and loads all the directories it finds in the path, before it looks in its cache.

This means that if you want to use an altered version of the C library when running one specific program, you can put that library in a directory somewhere and run the program with the appropriate LD_LIBRARY_PATH to access that library. As an example, a few versions of the Netscape browser that were linked against the 5.2.18 version of the C library would die with a segmentation fault when run with the standard 5.3.12 C library because of a more stringent enforcement of malloc() policies. Many people put a copy of the 5.2.18 C library in a separate directory, such as

/usr/local/netscape/lib/, move the Netscape binary there, and replace /usr/local/bin/netscape with a shell script that looks something like this:

```
#!/bin/sh
export LD_LIBRARY_PATH=/usr/local/netscape/lib:$LD_LIBRARY_PATH
exec /usr/local/netscape/lib/netscape $*
```

8.6.2 Preloading Libraries

Sometimes, rather than replacing an entire shared library, you wish to replace only a few functions. Because the dynamic loader searches for functions starting with the first loaded library and proceeds through the stack of libraries in order, it would be convenient to be able to tack an alternative library on top of the stack to replace only the functions you need.

An example is **zlibc**. This library replaces file functions in the C library with functions that deal with compressed files. When a file is opened, zlibc looks for both the requested file and a gzipped version of the file. If the requested file exists, zlibc mimics the C library functions exactly, but if it does not exist, and a gzipped version exists instead, it transparently uncompresses the gzipped file without the application knowing. There are limitations, which are described in the library's documentation, but it can trade off speed for a considerable amount of space.

There are two ways to preload a library. To affect only certain programs, you can set an environment variable for the cases you wish to affect:

```
LD_PRELOAD=/lib/libsomething.o exec /bin/someprogram $*
```

However, as with zlibc, you might want to preload a library for every program on the system. The easiest way to do that is to add a line to the /etc/ld.so.preload file specifying which library to preload. In the case of zlibc, it would look something like this:

```
/lib/uncompress.o
```

CHAPTER 9

Linux System Environment

This chapter explains how to request system services, including low-level kernel facilities and higher-level library facilities.

9.1 The Process Environment

As described in more detail in Chapter 10, each running process has **environment variables**. Environment variables are name/value pairs, and a few of the variable names have meaning that is important to C programmers. (Many are used primarily for shell programming as quick alternatives to running programs that call library functions; those we do not describe here.)

`EDITOR` or `VISUAL`

> `EDITOR`, or `VISUAL` if it is set, provides the user's preference for which text editor to use to edit text files, if your program requires asking the user to edit a text file. The reason for having two different variables comes from the days when `EDITOR` would be used on a paper teletype machine and `VISUAL` on a full-screen terminal.

`LD_LIBRARY_PATH`

> Provides a colon-separated path of directories to search through to look for libraries. It should normally not be set, because the system file /etc/ld.so.conf provides the default path. You are unlikely to have to modify it in your programs; it provides

information for the system run-time linker, ld.so. However, as documented in Chapter 8, it can be useful while developing shared libraries.

LD_PRELOAD

Lists libraries to load in order to override symbols in system libraries. LD_PRELOAD, like LD_LIBRARY_PATH, is described in more detail in Chapter 8.

PATH

Provides a colon-separated path of directories to search through to look for binary programs to run. Note that unlike some operating systems, Linux (like all variants of Unix) does not automatically search the current working directory for binaries; for an automatic search, the path must include the directory ".". Chapter 10, pages 125–127, describes how this works in detail.

TERM

Provides information on which type of terminal the user is using; this determines how to position characters on the screen. Chapter 24 and Chapter 21 describe this in more detail.

9.2   Understanding System Calls

This book mentions system calls (syscalls, for short) repeatedly because they are fundamental to the programming environment. At first glance, they look just like normal C function calls. That is no accident; they are function calls, just a special variety. To understand the difference, you need to have a basic understanding of the structure of the operating system.

Although there are many pieces of code that make up the Linux operating system (utility programs, applications, programming libraries, device drivers, file systems, memory management, and so on), all those pieces run in one of two contexts: user mode or kernel mode.

When you write a program, the code that you write runs in **user mode**. Device drivers and file systems, by contrast, run in **kernel mode**. In user mode, programs are strictly protected from damaging each other or the rest of the system. Code that runs in kernel mode has full access to the machine to do, and break, anything.

For a device driver to manipulate the hardware device it is designed to control, it needs full access to it. The device needs to be protected from arbitrary programs so that programs cannot damage themselves or each other by damaging or confusing the device. The memory it runs in is also protected from the ravages of arbitrary programs.

All this code running in kernel mode exists solely to provide services to code running in user mode. A **system call** is how application code running in user mode requests protected code running in kernel mode to provide a service.

Take allocating memory, for instance. It is protected, kernel-mode code that must allocate the physical memory for the process, but it is the process itself that must ask for the memory. As another example, take file systems, which need to be protected to maintain coherent data on disk (or over the network), but it is your everyday, run-of-the-mill process that actually needs to read files from the file system.

The ugly details of calling through the user/kernel space barrier are mostly hidden in the C library. Calling through that barrier does not use normal function calls; it uses an ugly interface that is optimized for speed and has significant restrictions. The C library hides most of the interface from you by providing you with normal C functions wrapped around the system calls. However, you will be able to use the functions better if you have some idea what is going on underneath.

9.2.1 System Call Limitations

Kernel mode is protected from the rampages of user mode. One of those protections is that the kind of data that can be passed back and forth between kernel mode and user mode is limited to what can be easily verified, and it follows strict conventions.

- Each argument that is passed from user mode to kernel mode is the same length, which is almost always the native word size used by the machine for pointers. This size is big enough to pass long integer arguments, as well as pointers. `char` and `short` variables will be promoted to a larger type by C before being passed in.

- The return type is limited to a signed word. The first few hundred small negative integers are reserved as error codes and have a common meaning across system calls. This means that system calls that return a pointer cannot return a few pointers to the top of available virtual memory. Fortunately, those addresses are in reserved space and would never be returned anyway, so the signed words that are returned can be cast to pointers without a problem.

Unlike the C calling convention, in which C structures can be passed by value on the stack, you cannot pass a structure by value from user mode to kernel mode, nor can the kernel return a structure to user mode. You can pass large data items only by reference. Pass pointers to structures, just as you always pass pointers to anything that may be modified.

9.2.2 System Call Return Codes

The return codes that are reserved across all system calls are universal error return codes, which are all small negative numbers. The C library checks for errors whenever a system call returns. If an error has occurred, the library stuffs the value of the error in the global variable errno.[1] Most of the time, to check for errors, all you have to do is see if the return code was negative. The error codes are defined in <errno.h>, and you can compare errno to any error number defined there that you want to handle in a special way.

The errno variable has another use. The C library provides three ways to get at strings designed to describe the error you have just encountered:

perror()
> Prints an error message. Pass it a string with information about what the code in question was trying to do.
>
> ```
> if ( (file = open(DB_PATH, O_RDONLY)) < 0) {
>     perror("could not open database file");
> }
> ```

---

1. If you are using threads, the library actually keeps the error where an errno() function that knows what thread is current can get at it, because different threads might have different current error return codes. But you can ignore that because it ends up working the same way as an errno variable.

This causes `perror()` to print an error describing the error that just occurred, along with the explanation of what it was trying to do, like this:

```
could not open database file: No such file or directory
```

It is generally a good idea to make your arguments to `perror()` unique throughout your program so that when you get bug reports with a report from `perror()`, you know exactly where to start looking. Note that there is no newline character in the string passed to `perror()`. You are passing it only one part of a line, and it prints the newline itself.

`strerror()`

Returns a statically allocated string describing the error passed as the only argument. Use this when building your own version of `perror()`, for instance. If you want to save a copy of the string, use `strdup()` to do so; the string returned by `strerror()` will be overwritten on the next call to `strerror()`.

```
if ( (file = open(DB_PATH, O_RDONLY)) < 0) {
    fprintf(stderr,
            "could not open database file %s, %s\n",
            DB_PATH, strerror(errno));
}
```

`sys_errlist`

A poor alternative to `strerror()`. `sys_errlist` is an array of size `sys_nerr` pointers to static, read-only character strings that describe errors. An attempt to write to those strings causes a segmentation violation and a core dump.

```
if ( (file = open(DB_PATH, O_RDONLY)) < 0) {
    if (errno < sys_nerr) {
        fprintf(stderr, "could not open database file %s, %s\n",
                DB_PATH, sys_errlist[errno]);
    }
}
```

This is neither standard nor portable, and it is mentioned here only because you are likely to find code that relies on it. Convert each such instance to use `strerror()` and you will do the world a service.

If you are not going to use `errno` immediately after generating the error, you must save a copy. Any library function might reset it to any value, because it may make system calls that you do not know are being made, and some library functions may set `errno` without making any system calls.

9.2.3 Using System Calls

The interface that you as a programmer are expected to work with is the set of C library wrappers for the system calls. Therefore, we use *system call* through the rest of this book to mean the C wrapper function that you call to perform a system call, rather than the ugly interface that the C library kindly hides from you.

Most, but not all, system calls are declared in `<unistd.h>`. The `<unistd.h>` file is really a catch-all for system calls that do not seem to fit anywhere else. In order to determine which include files to use, you will generally need to use the system man pages. Although the function descriptions in the man pages are often terse, the man pages do accurately state, right at the top, which include files need to be included to use the function.

There is one snag here that is endemic to Unix systems. The system calls are documented in a separate manual page section from the library functions, and you will be using library functions to access system calls. Where the library functions differ from the system calls, there are separate man pages for the library functions and the system calls. This would not be so bad except that if there are two man pages for a function, you will nearly always want to read the one describing the library function with that name. But the system calls are documented in section 2, and the library functions in section 3, and because man gives lower numbers precedence, you will consistently be shown the wrong function.

You should not simply just specify the section number, however. System calls that use the most minimal wrappers in the C library are not documented as part of the C library, so `man 3 function` will not find them. In order to make sure you have read all the information you need, first look up the man page without specifying the section. If it is a section 2 man page, check to see if there is a section 3 man page by the same name. If, as happens with `open()`, you get a section 1 man page, look explicitly in sections 2 and 3.

There is, fortunately, another way around this problem. Many versions of the man program, including the one on most Linux systems, allow you to specify an alternate search path for man pages. Read the `man man` man page to determine if your version of man supports the `MANSECT` environment variable and the `-S` argument to the `man` command. If so, you can set `MANSECT` to something like `3:2:1:4:5:6:7:8:tcl:n:l:p:o`. Look at your man configuration file (/etc/man.config on most Linux systems) to determine the current setting of `MANSECT`.

Most system calls return 0 to indicate success, and they return a negative value to indicate an error. Because of this, in many cases, a simple form of error handling is appropriate.

```
if (ioctl(fd, FN, data)) {
  /* error handling based on errno */
}
```

Also common is the following form.

```
if (ioctl(fd, FN, data) < 0) {
  /* error handling based on errno */
}
```

For the system calls that return 0 on success, these two cases are identical. In your own code, choose what suits you best. Be aware that you will see all sorts of conventions in others' code.

9.2.4 Common Error Return Codes

There are many commonly occurring error codes that you likely have seen error messages from before. Some of these explanations may seem confusing. Without knowing what you can do on a Linux system, it is hard to understand the errors you might get while you are working on one. Read this list now to get a sense of what errors exist, and then read it again after you have read this whole book, to gain a more thorough understanding.

For many of the error return codes, we give a sample system call or two likely to trigger the error message in common circumstances. This does not mean that those system calls are the only ones that trigger those errors. Consider them examples to elucidate the output of `perror()`, the brief descriptions in `<asm/errno.h>`, or `man 3 errno`.

Use the man pages to determine which errors to expect from a specific system call. In particular, use `man 3 errno` to get a list of error codes defined by POSIX. However, understand that this sometimes changes, and the man pages may not be completely up to date. If a system call returns an error code that you do not expect, presume that the man page is out of date rather than that the system call is broken. The Linux source code is maintained more carefully than the documentation.

E2BIG	The argument list is too long. When trying to `exec()` a new process, there is a limit to the length of the argument list you can give. See Chapter 10.
EACCES	Access *would be* denied. This is returned by the `access()` system call, explained in Chapter 11, and is more an informational return code than a true error condition.
EAGAIN	Returned when you attempt to do nonblocking I/O and no data is available. `EWOULDBLOCK` is a synonym for `EAGAIN`. If you had been doing blocking I/O, the system call would have blocked and waited for data.
EBADF	Bad file number. You have passed a file number that does not reference an open file to `read()`, `close()`, `ioctl()`, or another system call that takes a file number argument.
EBUSY	The `mount()` system call returns this error if you attempt to mount a file system that is already mounted or unmount a file system that is currently in use.
ECHILD	No child processes. Returned by the `wait()` family of system calls. See Chapter 10.
EDOM	Not a system call error, but an error from the system's C library. `EDOM` is set by math functions if an argument is

out of range. (This is `EINVAL` for the function's domain.) For example, the `sqrt()` function does not know about complex numbers and therefore does not approve of a negative argument.

`EEXIST`   Returned by `creat()`, `mknod()`, or `mkdir()` if the file already exists, or by `open()` in the same case if you specified `O_CREAT` and `O_EXCL`.

`EFAULT`   A bad pointer (one that points to inaccessible memory) was passed as an argument to a system call. Accessing the same pointer from within the user-space program that made the system call would result in a segmentation fault.

`EFBIG`   Returned by `write()` if you attempt to write a file longer than the file system can logically handle (this does not include simple physical space restrictions).[2]

`EINTR`   System call was interrupted. Interruptible system calls are explained in Chapter 12.

`EINVAL`   Returned if the system call received an invalid argument.

`EIO`   I/O error. This is usually generated by a device driver to indicate a hardware error or unrecoverable problem communicating with the device.

`EISDIR`   Returned by system calls that require a file name, such as `unlink()`, if the final pathname component is a directory rather than a file and the operation in question cannot be applied to a directory.

`ELOOP`   Returned by system calls that take a path if too many symbolic links in a row (that is, symbolic links pointing to symbolic links pointing to symbolic links pointing to...) were encountered while parsing the path. The current limit is 16 symbolic links in a row.

---

2. It also occurs if you write a file longer than your soft resource limit for file size and have changed the default disposition of the `SIGXFSZ` signal. See Table 10.2 and page 221 for more information on file size limits.

EMFILE	Returned if no more files can be opened by the calling process.
EMLINK	Returned by link() if the file being linked to already has the maximum number of links for the file system it is on (32,000 is currently the maximum on the standard Linux file system).
ENAMETOOLONG	A pathname was too long, either for the entire system or for the file system you were trying to access.
ENFILE	Returned if no more files can be opened by any process on the system.
ENODEV	Returned by mount() if the requested file system type is not available. Returned by open() if you attempt to open a special file for a device that does not have an associated device driver in the kernel.
ENOENT	No such file or directory. Returned when you try to access a file or directory that does not exist.
ENOEXEC	Executable format error. This might happen if you attempt to run an (obsolete) a.out binary on a system without support for a.out binaries. It will also happen if you attempt to run an ELF binary built for another CPU architecture.
ENOMEM	Out of memory. Returned by the brk() and mmap() functions if they fail to allocate memory.
ENOSPC	Returned by write() if you attempt to write a file longer than the file system has space for.
ENOSYS	System call is not implemented. Usually caused by running a recent binary on an old kernel that does not implement the system call.
ENOTBLK	The mount() system call returns this error if you attempt to mount as a file system a file that is not a block device special file.

ENOTDIR
:   An intermediate pathname component (that is, a directory name specified as part of a path) exists, but it is not a directory. Returned by any system call that takes a file name.

ENOTEMPTY
:   Returned by `rmdir()` if the directory you are trying to remove is not empty.

ENOTTY
:   Generally occurs when an application that is attempting to do terminal control is run with its input or output set to a pipe, but it can happen whenever you try to perform an operation on the wrong type of device. The standard error message for this, "not a typewriter," is rather misleading.

ENXIO
:   No such device or address. Usually generated by attempting to open a device special file that is associated with a piece of hardware that is not installed or configured.

EPERM
:   The process has insufficient permissions to complete the operation. This error most commonly happens with file operations. See Chapter 11.

EPIPE
:   Returned by `write()` if the reading end of the pipe or socket is closed and `SIGPIPE` is caught or ignored. See Chapter 12.

ERANGE
:   Not a system call error, `ERANGE` is set by math functions if the result is not representable by its return type, and by some functions if they are passed too short a buffer for a string return value. (This is `EINVAL` for the range.)

EROFS
:   Returned by `write()` if you attempt to write to a read-only file system.

ESPIPE
:   Returned by `lseek()` if you attempt to seek on a nonseekable file descriptor (including file descriptors for pipes, named pipes, and sockets). See Chapter 11 and Chapter 17.

ESRCH
:   No such process. See Chapter 10.

ETXTBSY   Returned by open() if you attempt to open, with write
                 mode enabled, an executable file or shared library that
                 is currently being run, or any other file which has been
                 mapped into memory with the MAP_DENYWRITE flag set
                 (see page 270). To work around this, rename the file,
                 then make a new copy with the same name as the old
                 one and work with the new copy. See Chapter 11 and its
                 discussion of inodes for why this happens.

EXDEV   Returned by link() if the source and destination files are
                 not on the same file system.

A few other relatively common error return codes happen only in regard
to networking; see page 469 for more information.

9.3 Finding Header and Library Files

Header files that come with your Linux system are in the /usr/include
directory hierarchy. The compiler will search for include files only in
/usr/include by default. (Header files may be stored outside /usr/include,
but they generally have links to them inside /usr/include; for example,
at the time of writing, the X include files are in /usr/X11R6/include/X11,
but a symbolic link is provided so that the compiler will find them through
the /usr/include/X11 path instead.)

Libraries are much the same way, with a twist. Libraries that are considered
critical to booting the system (and repairing it, if necessary) are in /lib.
Other system libraries are in /usr/lib, except for X11R6 libraries, which are
in /usr/X11R6/lib. The compiler will search for standard system libraries
by default.

Some libraries are intended to support development on the same system
against more than one major version of the library. In many of these cases,
special configuration utilities are available to provide the correct version
of the header files to include and the proper version of the libraries to link
against. A unified tool called pkg-config provides this information for
each version of every library that is built to support pkg-config.

Part 3

System Programming

CHAPTER 10

The Process Model

One of Unix's hallmarks is its process model. It is the key to understanding access rights, the relationships among open files, signals, job control, and most other low-level topics in this book. Linux adopted most of Unix's process model and added new ideas of its own to allow a truly lightweight threads implementation.

10.1 Defining a Process

What exactly is a process? In the original Unix implementations, a process was any executing program. For each program, the kernel kept track of

- The current location of execution (such as waiting for a system call to return from the kernel), often called the program's **context**

- Which files the program had access to

- The program's **credentials** (which user and group owned the process, for example)

- The program's current directory

- Which memory space the program had access to and how it was laid out

A process was also the basic scheduling unit for the operating system. Only processes were allowed to run on the CPU.

10.1.1 Complicating Things with Threads

Although the definition of a process may seem obvious, the concept of threads makes all of this less clear-cut. A thread allows a single program to run in multiple places at the same time. All the threads created (or spun off) by a single program share most of the characteristics that differentiate processes from each other. For example, multiple threads that originate from the same program share information on open files, credentials, current directory, and memory image. As soon as one of the threads modifies a global variable, all the threads see the new value rather than the old one.

Many Unix implementations (including AT&T's canonical System V release) were redesigned to make threads the fundamental scheduling unit for the kernel, and a process became a collection of threads that shared resources. As so many resources were shared among threads, the kernel could switch between threads in the same process more quickly than it could perform a full context switch between processes. This resulted in most Unix kernels having a two-tiered process model that differentiates between threads and processes.

10.1.2 The Linux Approach

Linux took another route, however. Linux context switches had always been extremely fast (on the same order of magnitude as the new "thread switches" introduced in the two-tiered approach), suggesting to the kernel developers that rather than change the scheduling approach Linux uses, they should allow processes to share resources more liberally.

Under Linux, a process is defined solely as a scheduling entity and the only thing unique to a process is its current execution context. It does not imply anything about shared resources, because a process creating a new child process has full control over which resources the two processes share (see the `clone()` system call described on page 153 for details on this). This model allows the traditional Unix process management approach to be retained while allowing a traditional thread interface to be built outside the kernel.

Luckily, the differences between the Linux process model and the two-tiered approach surface only rarely. In this book, we use the term **process** to refer to a set of (normally one) scheduling entities which share fundamental resources, and a **thread** is each of those individual scheduling entities. When a process consists of a single thread, we often use the terms interchangeably. To keep things simple, most of this chapter ignores threads completely. Toward the end, we discuss the `clone()` system call, which is used to create threads (and can also create normal processes).

10.2 Process Attributes

10.2.1 The pid and Parentage

Two of the most basic attributes are its **process ID**, or **pid**, and the pid of its parent process. A pid is a positive integer that uniquely identifies a running process and is stored in a variable of type `pid_t`. When a new process is created, the original process is known as the **parent** of the new process and is notified when the new child process ends.

When a process dies, its exit code is stored until the parent process requests it. The exit status is kept in the kernel's process table, which forces the kernel to keep the process's entry active until it can safely discard its exit status. Processes that have exited and are kept around only to preserve their exit status are known as **zombies**. Once the zombie's exit status has been collected, the zombie is removed from the system's process table.

If a process's parent exits (making the child process an **orphan process**), that process becomes a child of the **init process**. The init process is the first process started when a machine is booted and is assigned a pid of 1. One of the primary jobs of the init process is to collect the exit statuses of processes whose parents have died, allowing the kernel to remove the child processes from the process table. Processes can find their pid and their parent's pid through the `getpid()` and `getppid()` functions.

`pid_t getpid(void)`
> Returns the pid of the current process.

`pid_t getppid(void)`
> Returns the parent process's pid.

10.2.2 Credentials

Linux uses the traditional Unix security mechanisms of users and groups. User IDs (**uids**) and group IDs (**gids**) are integers[1] that are mapped to symbolic user names and group names through /etc/passwd and /etc/group, respectively (see Chapter 28 for more information on the user and group databases). However, the kernel knows nothing about the names—it is concerned only with the integer representation. The 0 uid is reserved for the system administrator, normally called **root**. All normal security checks are disabled for processes running as root (that is, with a uid of 0), giving the administrator complete control over the system.

In most cases, a process may be considered to have a single uid and gid associated with it. Those are the IDs that are used for most system security purposes (such as assigning ownerships to newly created files). The system calls that modify a process ownership are discussed later in this chapter.

As Unix developed, restricting processes to a single group turned out to create new difficulties. Users involved in multiple projects had to explicitly switch their gid when they wanted to access files whose access was restricted to members of different groups.

Supplemental groups were introduced in BSD 4.3 to eliminate this problem. Although every process still has its primary gid (which it uses as the gid for newly created files, for example), it also belongs to a set of **supplemental groups**. Security checks that used to ensure that a process belonged to a particular group (and only that group) now allow access as long as the group is one of the supplemental groups to which the process belongs. The `sysconf()` macro `_SC_NGROUPS_MAX` specifies how many supplemental groups a process may belong to. (See Chapter 6, page 54, for details on `sysconf()`.) Under Linux 2.4 and earlier, `_SC_NGROUPS_MAX` is 32; under Linux 2.6 and later, `_SC_NGROUPS_MAX` is 65536. Do not use a static array to store supplemental groups; instead, dynamically allocate memory, taking into account the return value of `sysconf(_SC_NGROUPS_MAX)`. Older code may use the `NGROUPS_MAX` macro to determine how many supplemental

---

1. uids and gids are normally positive integers, but negative ones work. Using -1 as an ID is problematic, however, as many of the uid- and gid-related system calls use -1 as an indication not to modify a value (see `setregid()` on page 114 for an example of this).

groups are supported by a system; using this macro does not function correctly when the code is compiled in one environment and used in another.

Setting the list of groups for a process is done through the setgroups() system call and may be done only by processes running with root permissions.

```
int setgroups(size_t num, const gid_t * list);
```

The list parameter points to an array of num gids. The process's supplemental group list is set to the gids listed in the list array.

The getgroups() function lets a process get a list of the supplemental groups to which it belongs.

```
int getgroups(size_t num, gid_t * list);
```

The list must point to an array of gid_t, which is filled in with the process's supplemental group list, and num specifies how many gid_ts list can hold. The getgroups() system call returns -1 on error (normally, if list is not large enough to hold the supplemental group list) or the number of supplemental groups. As a special case, if num is 0, getgroups() returns the number of supplemental groups for the process.

Here is an example of how to use getgroups():

```
gid_t *groupList;
int numGroups;

numGroups = getgroups(0, groupList);
if (numGroups) {
    groupList = alloca(numGroups * sizeof(gid_t));
    getgroups(numGroups, groupList);
}
```

A more complete example of getgroups() appears in Chapter 28.

Thus, a process has a uid, a primary gid, and a set of supplemental groups associated with it. Luckily, this is as much as most programmers ever have to worry about. There are two classes of programs that need very flexible management of uids and gids, however: setuid/setgid programs and system daemons.

System daemons are programs that are always running on a system and perform some action at the request of an external stimulus. For example, most World Wide Web (http) daemons are always running, waiting for a client to connect to it so that they can process the client's requests. Other daemons, such as the cron daemon (which runs requests periodically), sleep until a time when they need to perform actions. Most daemons need to run with root permissions but perform actions at the request of a user who may be trying to compromise system security through the daemon.

The ftp daemon is a good example of a daemon that needs flexible uid handling. It initially runs as root and then switches its uid to the uid of the user who logs into it (most systems start a new process to handle each ftp request, so this approach works quite well). This leaves the job of validating file accesses to the kernel where it belongs. Under some circumstances, however, the ftp daemon must open a network connection in a way that only root is allowed to do (see Chapter 17 for details on this). The ftp daemon cannot simply switch back to root, because user processes cannot give themselves superuser access (with good reason!), but keeping the root uid rather than switching to the user's uid would require the ftp daemon to check all file-system accesses itself. The solution to this dilemma has been applied symmetrically to both uids and primary gids, so we just talk about uids here.

A process actually has three uids: its **real uid**, **saved uid**, and **effective uid**.[2] The effective uid is used for all security checks and is the only uid of the process that normally has any effect.

The saved and real uids are checked only when a process attempts to change its effective uid. Any process may change its effective uid to the same value as either its saved or real uid. Only processes with an effective uid of 0 (processes running as root) may change their effective uid to an arbitrary value.

Normally, a process's effective, real, and saved uid's are all the same. However, this mechanism solves the ftp daemon's dilemma. When it starts, all its IDs are set to 0, giving it root permissions. When a user logs in, the daemon sets its effective uid to the uid of the user, leaving both the saved and real uids as 0. When the ftp daemon needs to perform an action

---

2. Linux processes also have a fourth uid and gid used for file system accesses. This is discussed on page 113.

restricted to root, it sets its effective uid to 0, performs the action, and then resets the effective uid to the uid of the user who is logged in.

Although the ftp daemon does not need the saved uid at all, the other class of programs that takes advantage of this mechanism, setuid and setgid binaries, does use it.

The passwd program is a simple example of why setuid and setgid functionality was introduced. The passwd program allows users to change their passwords. User passwords are usually stored in /etc/passwd. Only the root user may write to this file, preventing other users from changing user information. Users should be able to change their own passwords, however, so some way is needed to give the passwd program permission to modify /etc/passwd.

To allow this flexibility, the owner of a program may set special bits in the program's permission bits (see pages 158–162 for more information), which tells the kernel that whenever the program is executed, it should run with the same effective uid (or gid) as the user who owns the program file, regardless of what user runs the program. These programs are called **setuid** (or **setgid**) executables.

Making the passwd program owned by the root user and setting the setuid bit in the program's permission bits lets all users change their passwords. When a user runs passwd, the passwd program is run with an effective user ID of 0, allowing it to modify /etc/passwd and change the user's password. Of course, the passwd program has to be carefully written to prevent unintended side effects. Setuid programs are a popular target for system intruders, as poorly written setuid programs provide a simple way for users to gain unauthorized permissions.

There are many cases in which setuid programs need their special permissions only for short periods of time and would like to switch back to the uid of the actual user for the remainder of the time (like the ftp daemon). As setuid programs have only their effective uid set to the uid of the program's owner, they know the uid of the user who actually ran them (the saved uid), making switching back simple. In addition, they may set their real uid to the setuid value (without affecting the saved uid) and regain those special permissions as needed. In this situation, the effective, saved, and real uid's work together to make system security as simple as possible.

Unfortunately, using this mechanism can be confusing because POSIX and BSD take slightly different approaches, and Linux supports both. The BSD solution is more full-featured than the POSIX method. It is accessed with the setreuid() function.

```
int setreuid(uid_t ruid, uid_t euid);
```

The real uid of the process is set to ruid and the effective uid of the process is set to euid. If either of the parameters is -1, that ID is not affected by this call.

If the effective uid of the process is 0, this call always succeeds. Otherwise, the IDs may be set to either the saved uid or the real uid of the process. Note that this call never changes the saved uid of the current process; to do that, use POSIX's setuid() function, which can modify the saved uid.

```
int setuid(uid_t euid);
```

As in setreuid(), the effective uid of the process is set to euid as long as euid is the same as either the saved or real uid of the process, or as long as the process's effective uid at the time of the call is 0.

When setuid() is used by a process whose effective uid is 0, all the process's uids are changed to euid. Unfortunately, this makes it impossible for setuid() to be used in a setuid root program that needs to temporarily assume the permissions of another uid, because after calling setuid(), the process cannot recover its root privileges.

Although the ability to switch uids does make it easier to write code that cannot be tricked into compromising system security, it is not a panacea. There are many popular methods for tricking programs into executing arbitrary code [Lehey, 1995]. As long as either the saved or real uid of a process is 0, such attacks can easily set the effective uid of a process to 0. This makes switching uids insufficient to prevent serious vulnerabilities in system programs. However, if a process can give up any access to root privileges by setting its effective, real, and saved IDs to non-0 values, doing so limits the effectiveness of any attack against it.

10.2.3 The filesystem uid

In highly specialized circumstances, a program may want to keep its root permissions for everything but file-system access, for which it would rather use a user's uid. The user-space NFS server originally used by Linux illustrates the problem that can occur when a process assumes a user's uid. Although the NFS server in the past used `setreuid()` to switch uids while accessing the file system, doing so allowed the user whose uid the NFS server was assuming to kill the NFS server. After all, for a moment that user owned the NFS server process. To prevent this type of problem, Linux uses the **filesystem uid** (fsuid) for file-system access checks.

Whenever a process's effective uid is changed, the process's fsuid is set to the process's new effective user ID, making the fsuid transparent to most applications. Those applications that need the extra features provided by the separate fsuid must use the `setfsuid()` call to explicitly set the fsuid.

```
int setfsuid(uid_t uid);
```

The fsuid may be set to any of the current effective, saved, or real uids of the process. In addition, `setfsuid()` succeeds if the current fsuid is being retained or if the process's effective uid is 0.

10.2.4 User and Group ID Summary

Here is a summary of all the system calls that modify the access permissions of a running process. Most of the functions listed here that pertain to user IDs have been discussed in detail earlier in this chapter, but those related to group IDs have not. As those functions mirror similar functions that modify user IDs, their behavior should be clear.

All of these functions return -1 on error and 0 on success, unless otherwise noted. Most of these prototypes are in `<unistd.h>`. Those that are located elsewhere are noted below.

```
int setreuid(uid_t ruid, uid_t euid)
```
> Sets the real uid of the current process to `ruid` and the effective uid of the process to `euid`. If either of the parameters is -1, that uid remains unchanged.

`int setregid(gid_t rgid, gid_t egid)`

Sets the real gid of the current process to `rgid` and the effective gid of the process to `egid`. If either of the parameters is -1, that gid remains unchanged.

`int setuid(uid_t uid)`

If used by a normal user, sets the effective uid of the current process to `uid`. If used by a process with an effective uid of 0, it sets the real, effective, and saved uids to `uid`.

`int setgid(gid_t gid)`

If used by a normal user, sets the effective gid of the current process to `gid`. If used by a process with an effective gid of 0, sets the real, effective, and saved gids to `gid`.

`int seteuid(uid_t uid)`

Equivalent to `setreuid(-1, uid)`.

`int setegid(gid_t gid)`

Equivalent to `setregid(-1, gid)`.

`int setfsuid(uid_t fsuid)`

Sets the fsuid of the current process to `fsuid`. It is prototyped in `<sys/fsuid.h>`. It returns the previous fsuid.

`int setfsgid(gid_t fsgid)`

Sets the fsgid of the current process to `fsgid`. It is prototyped in `<sys/fsuid.h>`. It returns the previous fsgid.

`int setgroups(size_t num, const gid_t * list)`

Sets the supplemental groups for the current process to the groups specified in the array `list`, which must contain `num` items. The `sysconf()` macro `_SC_NGROUPS_MAX` tells how many groups may be in the list (likely 32 or 65536, depending on the Linux versions you are currently running). The `setgroups()` function is prototyped in `<grp.h>`.

`uid_t getuid()`

Returns the real uid of the process.

```
uid_t geteuid()
```
> Returns the effective uid of the process.

```
gid_t getgid()
```
> Returns the real gid of the process.

```
gid_t getegid()
```
> Returns the effective gid of the process.

```
size_t getgroups(size_t size, gid_t list[])
```
> Returns the current set of supplemental groups for the current process in the array `list`. `size` tells how many `gid_t`s the list can hold. If the list is not big enough to hold all of the groups, -1 is returned and `errno` is set to `EINVAL`. Otherwise, the number of groups in the list is returned. If `size` is 0, the number of groups in the list is returned, but `list` is not affected. The `getgroups()` function is prototyped in `<grp.h>`.

10.3 Process Information

The kernel makes available quite a bit of information about each process, and some information is passed to new programs when they are loaded. All of this information forms the execution environment for a process.

10.3.1 Program Arguments

There are two types of values passed to new programs when they are run: **command-line arguments** and **environment variables**. Various conventions have been set for their usage, but the system itself does not enforce any of these conventions. It is a good idea to stay within the conventions, however, to help your program fit into the Unix world.

Command-line arguments are a set of strings passed to the program. Usually, these are the text typed after the command name in a shell (hence the name), with optional arguments beginning with a dash (-) character.

Environment variables are a set of name/value pairs. Each pair is represented as a single string of the form *NAME=VALUE*, and the set of these strings makes up the program's **environment**. For example, the current user's home directory is normally contained in the `HOME` environment variable, so programs Joe runs often have `HOME=/home/joe` in their environment.

Both the command-line arguments and environment are made available to a program at startup. The command-line arguments are passed as parameters to the program's `main()` function, whereas a pointer to the environment is stored in the `environ` global variable, which is defined in `<unistd.h>`.[3]

Here is the complete prototype of `main()` in the Linux, Unix, and ANSI/ISO C world:

```
int main(int argc, char * argv[]);
```

You may be surprised to see that `main()` returns a value (other than `void`). The value `main()` returns is given to the process's parent after the process has exited. By convention, 0 indicates that the process completed successfully, and non-0 values indicate failure. Only the lower eight bits of a process's exit code are considered significant. The negative values between -1 and -128 are reserved for processes that are terminated abnormally by another process or by the kernel. An exit code of 0 indicates successful completion, and exit codes between 1 and 127 indicate the program exited because of an error.

The first parameter, `argc`, contains the number of command-line arguments passed to the program, whereas `argv` is an array of pointers to the argument strings. The first item in the array is `argv[0]`, which contains the name of the program being invoked (although not necessarily the complete path to the program). The next-to-last item in the array `argv[argc - 1]` points to the final command-line argument, and `argv[argc]` contains `NULL`.

To access the environment directly, use the following global variable:

```
extern char * environ[];
```

This provides `environ` as an array of pointers to each element in the program's environment (remember, each element is a `NAME=VALUE` pair), and

---

3. Most systems pass the environment as a parameter to `main()`, as well, but this method is not standardized by POSIX. The `environ` variable is the POSIX-approved method.

the final item in the array is `NULL`. This declaration appears in `<unistd.h>`, so you do not need to declare it yourself. The most common way of checking for elements in the environment is through `getenv`, which eliminates the need for directly accessing `environ`.

```
const char * getenv(const char * name);
```

The sole parameter to `getenv()` is the name of the environment variable whose value you are interested in. If the variable exists, `getenv()` returns a pointer to its value. If the variable does not exist in the current environment (the environment pointed to by `environ`), it returns `NULL`.

Linux provides two ways of adding strings to the program's environment, `setenv()` and `putenv()`. POSIX defines only `putenv()`, making it the more portable of the two.

```
int putenv(const char * string);
```

The `string` passed must be of the form *NAME=VALUE*. `putenv()` adds a variable named *NAME* to the current environment and gives it the value of *VALUE*. If the environment already contains a variable named *NAME*, its value is replaced with *VALUE*.

BSD defines `setenv()`, which Linux also provides, a more flexible and easier-to-use method for adding items to the environment.

```
int setenv(const char * name, const char * value, int overwrite);
```

Here, the name and the new value of the environment variable to manipulate are passed separately, which is usually easier for a program to do. If `overwrite` is 0, the environment is not modified if it already contains a variable called `name`. Otherwise, the variable's value is modified, as in `putenv()`.

Here is a short example of both of these functions. Both calls accomplish exactly the same thing, changing the current `PATH` environment variable for the running program.

```
putenv("PATH=/bin:/usr/bin");
setenv("PATH", "/bin:/usr/bin", 1);
```

Table 10.1 Process Resources Tracked by Linux

Type	Member	Description
struct timeval	ru_utime	Total time spent executing user mode code. This includes all the time spent running instructions in the application, but not the time the kernel spends fulfilling application requests.
struct timeval	ru_stime	Total time the kernel spent executing requests from the process. This does not include time spent while the process was blocked inside a system call.
long	ru_minflt	The number of **minor faults** that this process caused. Minor faults are memory accesses that force the processor into kernel mode but do not result in a disk access. These occur when a process tries to write past the end of its stack, forcing the kernel to allocate more stack space before continuing the process, for example.
long	ru_majflt	The number of **major faults** that this process caused. Major faults are memory accesses that force the kernel to access the disk before the program can continue to run. One common cause of major faults is a process accessing a part of its executable memory that has not yet been loaded into RAM from the disk or has been swapped out at some point.
long	ru_nswap	The number of memory pages that have been paged in from disk due to memory accesses from the process.

10.3.2 Resource Usage

The Linux kernel tracks how many resources each process is using. Although only a few resources are tracked, their measurement can be useful for developers, administrators, and users. Table 10.1 lists the process resources usage currently tracked by the Linux kernel, as of version 2.6.7.

A process may examine the resource usage of itself, the accumulated usages of all its children, or the sum of the two. The getrusage() system call returns a struct rusage (which is defined in <sys/resource.h>) that contains the current resources used.

```
int getrusage(int who, struct rusage * usage);
```

The first parameter, who, tells which of the three available resource counts should be returned. RUSAGE_SELF returns the usage for the current process, RUSAGE_CHILDREN returns the total usage for all of the current process's children, and RUSAGE_BOTH yields the total resources used by this process and all its children. The second parameter to getrusage() is a pointer to a struct rusage, which gets filled in with the appropriate resource utilizations. Although struct rusage contains quite a few members (the list is derived from BSD), most of those members are not yet used by Linux. Here is the complete definition of struct rusage. Table 10.1 describes the members currently used by Linux.

```
#include <sys/resource.h>
struct rusage
{
  struct timeval ru_utime;
  struct timeval ru_stime;
  long int ru_maxrss;
  long int ru_ixrss;
  long int ru_idrss;
  long int ru_isrss;
  long int ru_minflt;
  long int ru_majflt;
  long int ru_nswap;
  long int ru_inblock;
  long int ru_oublock;
  long int ru_msgsnd;
  long int ru_msgrcv;
  long int ru_nsignals;
  long int ru_nvcsw;
  long int ru_nivcsw;
};
```

10.3.3 Establishing Usage Limits

To help prevent runaway processes from destroying a system's performance, Unix keeps track of many of the resources a process can use and allows the system administrator and the users themselves to place limits on the resources a process may consume.

There are two classes of limits available: hard limits and soft limits. Hard limits may be lowered by any process but may be raised only by the super user. Hard limits are usually set to RLIM_INFINITY on system startup, which means no limit is enforced. The only exception to this is RLIMIT_CORE (the maximum size of a core dump), which Linux initializes to 0 to prevent unexpected core dumps. Many distributions reset this limit on startup, however, as most technical users expect core dumps under some conditions (see page 130 for information on what a core dump is). Soft limits are the limits that the kernel actually enforces. Any process may set the soft limit for a resource to any value less than or equal to that process's hard limit for the resource.

The various limits that may be set are listed in Table 10.2 and are defined in <sys/resource.h>. The getrlimit() and setrlimit() system calls get and set the limit for a single resource.

```
int getrlimit(int resource, struct rlimit *rlim);
int setrlimit(int resource, const struct rlimit *rlim);
```

Both of these functions use struct rlimit, which is defined as follows:

```
#include <sys/resource.h>

struct rlimit {
  long int rlim_cur;                 /* the soft limit */
  long int rlim_max;                 /* the hard limit */
};
```

The second member, rlim_max, indicates the hard limit for the limit indicated by the resource parameter, and rlim_cur contains the soft limit. These are the same sets of limits manipulated by the ulimit and limit commands, one or the other of which is built into most shells.

Table 10.2 Resource Limits

Value	Limit
RLIMIT_AS	Maximum amount of memory available to the process. This includes memory used for the stack, global variables, and dynamically allocated memory.
RLIMIT_CORE	Maximum size of a core file generated by the kernel (if the core file would be too large, none is created).
RLIMIT_CPU	Total CPU time used (in seconds). For more information on this limit, see the description of SIGXCPU on page 221
RLIMIT_DATA	Maximum size of data memory (in bytes). This doesn't include memory dynamically allocated by the program.
RLIMIT_FSIZE	Maximum size for an open file (checked on writes). For more information on this limit, see the description of SIGXFSZ on page 221.
RLIMIT_MEMLOCK	Maximum amount of memory that may be locked with mlock() (mlock() is decsribed on page 275).
RLIMIT_NOFILE	Maximum number of open files.
RLIMIT_NPROC	Maximum number of child processes the process may spawn. This limits only how many children the process may have at one time. It does not limit how many descendants it may have— each child may have up to RLIMIT_NPROC children of its own.
RLIMIT_RSS	Maximum amount of RAM used at any time (any memory usage exceeding this causes paging). This is known as a process's **resident set size**.
RLIMIT_STACK	Maximum size of stack memory (in bytes), including all local variables.

10.4 Process Primitives

Despite the relatively long discussion needed to describe a process, creating and destroying processes in Linux is straightforward.

10.4.1 Having Children

Linux has two system calls that create new processes: fork() and clone(). As mentioned earlier, clone() is used for creating threads and is discussed briefly later in this chapter. For now, we focus on fork(), which is the most popular method of process creation.

```
#include <unistd.h>

pid_t fork(void);
```

This system call has the unusual property of not returning once per invocation, but twice: once in the parent and once in the child. Note that we did not say "first in the parent"—writing code that makes any assumptions about the two processes executing in a deterministic order is a very bad idea.

Each return from the fork() system call returns a different value. In the parent process, the system call returns the pid of the newly created child process; in the child process, the call returns 0.

The difference in return value is the only difference apparent to the processes. Both have the same memory image, credentials, open files,[4] and signal handlers. Here is a simple example of a program that creates a child:

```
#include <sys/types.h>
#include <stdio.h>
#include <unistd.h>

int main(void) {
    pid_t child;

    if (!(child = fork())) {
        printf("in child\n");
        exit(0);
    }
    printf("in parent -- child is %d\n", child);
    return 0;
}
```

---

4. For details on how the parent's and child's open files relate to each other, see page 197.

10.4.2 Watching Your Children Die

Collecting the exit status of a child is called **waiting** on the process. There
are four ways this can be done, although only one of the calls is provided
by the kernel. The other three methods are implemented in the standard C
library. As the kernel system call takes four arguments, it is called wait4().

```
pid_t wait4(pid_t pid, int *status, int options, struct rusage *rusage);
```

The first argument, pid, is the process whose exit code should be returned.
It can take on a number of special values.

< -1   Waits for any child whose pgid is the same as the absolute
            value of pid.

= -1   Waits for any child to terminate.

= 0   Waits for a child in the same process group current process.[5]

> 0   Waits for process pid to exit.

The second parameter is a pointer to an integer that gets set to the exit
status of the process that caused the wait4() to return (which we hereafter
call the *examined* process). The format of the returned status is convoluted,
and a set of macros is provided to make sense of it.

Three events cause wait4() to return the status of the examined process:
The process could have exited, it could have been terminated by a kill()
(sent a fatal signal), or it could have been stopped for some reason.[6] You
can find out which of these occurred through the following macros, each
of which takes the returned status from wait4() as the sole parameter:

WIFEXITED(status)
        Returns true if the process exited normally. A process exits normally
        when its main() function returns or the program calls exit(). If
        WIFEXITED() is true, WEXITSTATUS(status) returns the process's
        exit code.

---

5. Process groups are described on pages 136–138.
6. See Chapter 15 for reasons why this might happen.

WIFSIGNALED(status)

> Returns true if the process was terminated due to a signal (this is what happens for processes terminated with kill()). If this is the case, WTERMSIG(status) returns the signal number that terminated the process.

WIFSTOPPED(status)

> If the process has been stopped by a signal, WIFSTOPPED() returns true and WSTOPSIG(status) returns the signal that stopped the process. wait4() returns information on stopped processes only if WUNTRACED was specified as an option.

The options argument controls how the call behaves. WNOHANG causes the call to return immediately. If no processes are ready to report their status, the call returns 0 rather than a valid pid. WUNTRACED causes wait4() to return if an appropriate child has been stopped. See Chapter 15 for more information on stopped processes. Both of these behaviors may be specified by bitwise OR'ing the two values together.

The final parameter to wait4(), a pointer to a struct rusage, gets filled in with the resource usage of the examined process and all the examined process's children. See the discussion of getrusage() and RUSAGE_BOTH on pages 118–119 for more information on what this entails. If this parameter is NULL, no status information is returned.

There are three other interfaces to wait4(), all of which provide subsets of its functionality. Here is a summary of the alternative interfaces.

pid_t wait(int *status)

> The only parameter to wait() is a pointer to the location to store the terminated process's return code. This function always blocks until a child has terminated.

pid_t waitpid(pid_t pid, int *status, int options)

> The waitpid() function is similar to wait4(); the only difference is that it does not return resource usage information on the terminated process.

pid_t wait3(int *status, int options, struct rusage *rusage)

> This function is also similar to wait4(), but it does not allow the caller to specify which child should be checked.

10.4.3 Running New Programs

Although there are six ways to run one program from another, they all do about the same thing—replace the currently running program with another. Note the word *replace*—all traces of the currently running program disappear. If you want to have the original program stick around, you must create a new process with fork() and then execute the new program in the child process.

The six functions feature only slight differences in the interface. Only one of these functions, execve(), is actually a system call under Linux. The rest of the functions are implemented in user-space libraries and utilize execve() to execute the new program. Here are the prototypes of the exec() family of functions:

```
int execl(const char * path, const char * arg0, ...);
int execlp(const char * file, const char * arg0, ...);
int execle(const char * path, const char * arg0, ...);
int execv(const char * path, const char ** argv);
int execvp(const char * file, const char ** argv);
int execve(const char * file, const char ** argv, const char ** envp);
```

As mentioned, all of these programs try to replace the current program with a new program. If they succeed, they never return (as the program that called them is no longer running). If they fail, they return -1 and the error code is stored in errno, as with any other system call. When a new program is run (or exec()ed) it gets passed an array of arguments (argv) and an array of environment variables (envp). Each element in envp is of the form *VARIABLE=value.*[7]

The primary difference between the various exec() functions is how the command line arguments are passed to the new program. The execl family passes each element in argv (the command-line arguments) as a separate argument to the function, and NULL terminates the entire list. Traditionally, the first element in argv is the command used to invoke the new program. For example, the shell command /bin/cat /etc/passwd /etc/group normally results in the following exec call:

---

7. This is the same format the command env uses to print the current environment variables settings, and the envp argument is of the same type as the environ global variable.

```
execl("/bin/cat", "/bin/cat", "/etc/passwd", "/etc/group", NULL);
```

The first argument is the full path to the program being executed and the rest of the arguments get passed to the program as `argv`. The final parameter to `execl()` must be `NULL`—it indicates the end of the parameter list. If you omit the `NULL`, the function call is likely to result in either a segmentation fault or return `EINVAL`. The environment passed to the new program is whatever is pointed to by the `environ` global variable, as mentioned on page 116.

The `execv` functions pass the command-line argument as a C array of strings,[8] which is the same format used to pass `argv` to the new program. The final entry in the `argv` array must be `NULL` to indicate the end of the array, and the first element (`argv[0]`) should contain the name of the program that was invoked. Our `./cat /etc/passwd /etc/group` example would be coded using `execv` like this:

```
char * argv[] = { "./cat", "/etc/passwd", "/etc/group", NULL };
execv("/bin/cat", argv);
```

If you need to pass a specific environment to the new program, `execle()` and `execve()` are available. They are exactly like `execl()` and `execv()` but they take a pointer to the environment as their final argument. The environment is set up just like `argv`.

For example, here is one way to execute `/usr/bin/env` (which prints out the environment it was passed) with a small environment:

```
char * newenv[] = { "PATH=/bin:/usr/bin",
                    "HOME=/home/sweethome", NULL };
execle("/usr/bin/env", "/usr/bin/env", NULL, newenv);
```

Here is the same idea implemented with `execve()`:

```
char * argv[] = { "/usr/bin/env", NULL };
char * newenv[] = { "PATH=/bin:/usr/bin",
                    "HOME=/home/sweethome", NULL };
execve("/usr/bin/env", argv, newenv);
```

---

8. Technically, a pointer to a `NULL`-terminated array of pointers to `'\0'` terminated arrays of characters. If this does not make sense, see [Kernighan, 1988].

The final two functions, `execlp()` and `execvp()`, differ from the first two by searching the current path (set by the `PATH` environment variable) for the program to execute. The arguments to the program are not modified, however, so `argv[0]` does not contain the full path to the program being run. Here are modified versions of our first example that search for `cat` in the current `PATH`:

```
execlp("cat", "cat", "/etc/passwd", "/etc/group", NULL);

char * argv[] = { "cat", "/etc/passwd", "/etc/group", NULL };
execvp("cat", argv);
```

If `execl()` or `execv()` were used instead, those code fragments would fail unless `cat` was located in the current directory.

If you are trying to run a program with a specific environment while still searching the path, you need to search the path manually and use `execle()` or `execve()`, because none of the available `exec()` functions does quite what you want.

Signal handlers are preserved across the `exec()` functions in a slightly nonobvious way; the mechanism is described on page 205.

10.4.4 Faster Process Creation with `vfork()`

Normally processes that `fork()` immediately `exec()` another program (this is what shells do every time you type a command), making the full semantics of `fork()` more computationally expensive than is necessary. To help optimize this common case, `vfork()` is provided.

```
#include <unistd.h>

pid_t vfork(void);
```

Rather than creating an entirely new execution environment for the new process, `vfork()` creates a new process that shares the memory of the original process. The new process is expected to either `_exit()` or `exec()` another process very quickly, and the behavior is undefined if it modifies any memory, returns from the function the `vfork()` is contained in, or calls any new functions. In addition, the original process is suspended until the new one either terminates or calls an exec() function.[9] Not all systems provide the memory-sharing and parent-suspending semantics of vfork(), however, and applications should never rely upon that behavior.

10.4.5 Killing Yourself

Processes terminate themselves by calling either exit() or _exit(). When a process's main() function returns, the standard C library calls exit() with the value returned from main() as the parameter.

```
void exit(int exitCode)
void _exit(int exitCode)
```

The two forms, exit() and _exit(), differ in that exit() is a function in the C library, while _exit() is a system call. The _exit() system call terminates the program immediately, and the exitCode is stored as the exit code of the process. When exit() is used, functions registered by atexit() are called before the library calls _exit(exitCode). Among other things, this allows the ANSI/ISO standard I/O library to flush all its buffers.

Registering functions to be run when exit() is used is done through the atexit() function.

```
int alexit(void (*function)(void));
```

The only parameter passed to atexit() is a pointer to a function. When exit() is invoked, all the functions registered with atexit() are called in the opposite order from which they were registered. Note that if _exit() is used or the process is terminated due to a signal (see Chapter 12 for details on signals), functions registered via atexit() are not called.

---

9. vfork() was motivated by older systems that needed to copy all of the memory used by the original process as part of the fork(). Modern operating systems use **copy-on-write**, which copies memory regions only as necessary, as discussed in most operating system texts [Vahalia, 1997] [Bach, 1986]. This facility makes fork() almost as fast as vfork(), and much easier to use.

10.4.6 Killing Others

Destroying other processes is almost as easy as creating a new one—just kill it:

```
int kill(pid_t pid, int signum);
```

pid should be the pid of the process to kill, and signum describes how to kill it. There are two choices[10] for how to kill a child. You can use SIGTERM to terminate the process gently. This means that the process can ask the kernel to tell it when someone is trying to kill it so that it can terminate gracefully (saving files, for example). The process may also ignore this type of request for it to terminate and, instead, continue running. Using SIGKILL for the signum parameter kills the process immediately, no questions asked. If signum is zero, then kill() checks to see if the process calling kill() has the proper permissions, and returns zero if so and nonzero if its permissions are insufficient. This provides a way for a process to check the validity of a pid.

The pid parameter can take on four types of values under Linux.

pid > 0   The signal is sent to the process whose pid is pid. If no process exists with that pid, ESRCH is returned.

pid < -1   The signal is sent to all the processes in the process group whose pgid is -pid. For example, kill(-5316, SIGKILL) immediately terminates all the processes in process group 5316. This ability is used by job control shells, as discussed in Chapter 15.

pid = 0   The signal is sent to all the processes in the current process's process group.

pid = -1   The signal is sent to all the processes on the system except the init process. This is used during system shutdown.

---

10. This is a gross oversimplification. kill() actually sends a signal, and signals are a complicated topic in their own right. See Chapter 12 for a complete description of what signals are and how to use them.

Processes can normally kill() only processes that share the same effective user ID as themselves. There are two exceptions to this rule. First, processes with an effective uid of 0 may kill() any process on the system. Second, any process can send a SIGCONT signal to any other process in the same session.[11]

10.4.7 Dumping Core

Although we just mentioned that passing SIGTERM and SIGKILL to kill() causes a process to terminate, you can use quite a few different values (Chapter 12 discusses all of them). Some of these, such as SIGABRT, cause the program to dump **core** before dying. A program's core dump contains a complete history of the state of the program when it died.[12] Most debuggers, including gdb, can analyze a core file and tell you what the program was doing when it died, as well as let you inspect the defunct process's memory image. Core dumps end up in the process's current working directory in a file called (simply enough) core.

When a process has violated some of the system's requirements (such as trying to access memory that it is not allowed to access), the kernel terminates the process by calling an internal version of kill() with a parameter that causes a core dump. The kernel may kill a process for several reasons, including arithmetic violations, such as division by zero; the programs running illegal instructions; and the programs trying to access inaccessible regions of memory. This last case causes a **segmentation fault**, which results in the message segmentation fault (core dumped). If you do any reasonable amount of Linux programming, you are sure to tire of this message!

If a process's resource limit for core files is 0 (see page 120 for details on the core resource limit), no core file is generated.

---

11. This is to allow job control shells to restart processes that have changed their effective user ID. See chapter Chapter 15 for more information on job control.
12. A once-popular form of computer memory consists of small iron rings arranged in a matrix, with each ring held in place by two wires that are used to sense and set the magnetic polarity of the ring. Each of the rings is called a core, and the whole thing is core memory. So a core dump is a copy of the state of the system's memory (or core) at a given time.

10.5 Simple Children

Although fork(), exec(), and wait() allow programs to make full use of the Linux process model, many applications do not need that much control over their children. There are two library functions that make it easier to use child processes: system() and popen().

10.5.1 Running and Waiting with system()

Programs regularly want to run another program and wait for it to finish before continuing. The system() function allows a program to do this easily.

```
int system(const char * cmd);
```

system() forks a child process that exec()s /bin/sh, which then runs cmd. The original process waits for the child shell to exit and returns the same status code that wait() does.[13] If you do not need the shell to hang around (which is rarely necessary), cmd should contain a preceding "exec", which causes the shell to exec() cmd rather than run cmd as a subprocess.

As cmd is run through the /bin/sh shell, normal shell rules for command expansion apply. Here is an example of system() that displays all the C source files in the current directory.

---

13. In the process, system() blocks SIGCHLD, which will cause a SIGCHLD signal to be delivered to the program immediately before system() returns (but after system() has called wait() on the process it spawned), so programs that use signal handlers need to be careful to handle this possibly spurious signal. The system() function also ignores SIGINT and SIGQUIT, which means that a tight loop calling system() repeatedly could be uninterruptible by everything except SIGSTOP and SIGKILL.

```
#include <stdlib.h>
#include <sys/wait.h>

int main() {
    int result;

    result = system("exec ls *.c");

    if (!WIFEXITED(result))
        printf("(abnormal exit)\n");

    exit(0);
}
```

The system() command should be used very carefully in programs that run with special permissions. As the system shell provides many powerful features and is strongly influenced by environment variables, system() provides many potential security weaknesses for intruders to exploit. As long as the application is not a system daemon or a setuid/setgid program, however, system() is perfectly safe.

10.5.2 Reading or Writing from a Process

Although system() displays the command's output on standard output and allows the child to read from standard input, this is not always ideal. Often, a process wants to read the output from a process or send it text on standard input. popen() makes it easy for a process to do this.[14]

```
FILE * popen(const char * cmd, const char * mode);
```

The cmd is run through the shell, just as with system(). The mode should be "r" if the parent wants to read the command's output and "w" to write to the child's standard input. Note that you cannot do both with popen();

---

14. While popen() makes this easy, it has some hidden behaviors that are not immediately obvious. It creates a child process that might terminate before pclose() is called, which would cause the wait() functions to return status on the process. When that process ends, it also causes a SIGCHLD to be generated, which could confuse a naively written signal handler.

two processes reading from and writing to each other is complex[15] and beyond popen()'s abilities.[16]

popen() returns a FILE * (as defined by the ANSI/ISO standard I/O library), which can be read from and written to just like any other stdio stream,[17] or NULL if the operation fails. When the parent process is finished, it should use pclose() to close the stream and terminate the child process if it is still running. Like system(), pclose() returns the child's status from wait4().

```
int pclose(FILE * stream);
```

Here is a simple calculator program that uses the **bc** program to do all of the real work. It is important to flush the popen()ed stream after writing to it to prevent stdio buffering from delaying output (see [Kernighan, 1988] for details on buffering in the ANSI/ISO C stdio library functions).

```
 1: /* calc.c */
 2:
 3: /* This is a very simple calculator which uses the external bc
 4:    command to do everything. It opens a pipe to bc, reads a command
 5:    in, passes it to bc, and exits. */
 6: #include <stdio.h>
 7: #include <sys/wait.h>
 8: #include <unistd.h>
 9:
10: int main(void) {
11:     char buf[1024];
12:     FILE * bc;
13:     int result;
14:
15:     /* open a pipe to bc, and exit if we fail */
16:     bc = popen("bc", "w");
17:     if (!bc) {
```

---

15. This type of processing often results in **deadlocks**, in which process A is waiting for process B to do something, while process B is waiting for process A, resulting in nothing at all getting done.
16. If you find yourself needing to do this, start the child with fork() and exec() and use poll() to read to and write from the child process. A program called **expect** is designed to do this.
17. For information on reading and writing from stdio streams, consult [Kernighan, 1988].

```
18:          perror("popen");
19:          return 1;
20:      }
21:
22:      /* prompt for an expression, and read it in */
23:      printf("expr: "); fflush(stdout);
24:      fgets(buf, sizeof(buf), stdin);
25:
26:      /* send the expression to bc for evaluation */
27:      fprintf(bc, "%s\n", buf);
28:      fflush(bc);
29:
30:      /* close the pipe to bc, and wait for it to exit */
31:      result = pclose(bc);
32:
33:      if (!WIFEXITED(result))
34:          printf("(abnormal exit)\n");
35:
36:      return 0;
37: }
```

Like system(), popen() runs commands through the system shell and should be used very cautiously by programs that run with root credentials.

10.6   Sessions and Process Groups

In Linux, as in other Unix systems, users normally interact with groups of related processes. Although they initially log in to a single terminal and use a single process (their **shell**, which provides a command-line interface), users end up running many processes as a result of actions such as

- Running noninteractive tasks in the background

- Switching among interactive tasks via **job control**, which is discussed more fully in Chapter 15

- Starting multiple processes that work together through pipes

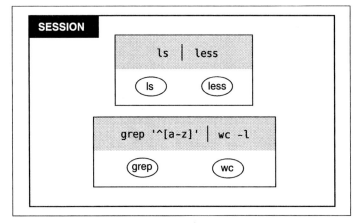

Figure 10.1   Sessions, Process Groups, and Processes

- Running a windowing system, such as the X Window System, which allows multiple terminal windows to be opened

In order to manage all of these processes, the kernel needs to group the processes in ways more complicated than the simple parent-child relationship we have already discussed. These groupings are called **sessions** and **process groups**. Figure 10.1 shows the relationship among sessions, process groups, and processes.

10.6.1 Sessions

When a user logs out of a system, the kernel needs to terminate all the processes the user had running (otherwise, users would leave a slew of old processes sitting around waiting for input that can never arrive). To simplify this task, processes are organized into sets of **sessions**. The session's ID is the same as the pid of the process that created the session through the setsid() system call. That process is known as the **session leader** for that session group. All of that process's descendants are then members of that session unless they specifically remove themselves from it. The setsid() function does not take any arguments and returns the new session ID.

```
#include <unistd.h>

pid_t setsid(void);
```

10.6.2 Controlling Terminal

Every session is tied to a terminal from which processes in the session get their input and to which they send their output. That terminal may be the machine's local console, a terminal connected over a serial line, or a pseudo terminal that maps to an X window or across a network (see Chapter 16 for information on pseudo terminal devices). The terminal to which a session is related is called the **controlling terminal** (or **controlling tty**) of the session. A terminal can be the controlling terminal for only one session at a time.

Although the controlling terminal for a session can be changed, this is usually done only by processes that manage a user's initial logging in to a system. Information on how to change a session's controlling tty appears in Chapter 16, on pages 338–339.

10.6.3 Process Groups

One of the original design goals of Unix was to construct a set of simple tools that could be used together in complex ways (through mechanisms like pipes). Most Linux users have done something like the following, which is a practical example of this philosophy:

```
ls | grep "^[aA].*\.gz" | more
```

Another popular feature added to Unix fairly early was job control. Job control allows users to suspend the current task (known as the **foreground** task) while they go and do something else on their terminals. When the suspended task is a sequence of processes working together, the system needs to keep track of which processes should be suspended when the user wants to suspend "the" foreground task. Process groups allow the system to keep track of which processes are working together and hence should be managed together via job control.

Processes are added to a process group through setpgid().

```
int setpgid(pid_t pid, pid_t pgid);
```

pid is the process that is being placed in a new process group (0 may be used to indicate the current process). pgid is the process group ID the process pid should belong to, or 0 if the process should be in a new process group whose pgid is the same as that process's pid. Like sessions, a **process group leader** is the process whose pid is the same as its process group ID (or **pgid**).

The rules for how setpgid() may be used are a bit complicated.

1. A process may set the process group of itself or one of its children. It may not change the process group for any other process on the system, even if the process calling setpgid() has root privileges.

2. A session leader may not change its process group.

3. A process may not be moved into a process group whose leader is in a different session from itself. In other words, all the processes in a process group must belong to the same session.

setpgid() call places the calling process into its own process group and its own session. This is necessary to ensure that two sessions do not contain processes in the same process group.

A full example of process groups is given when we discuss job control in Chapter 15.

When the connection to a terminal is lost, the kernel sends a signal (SIGHUP; see Chapter 12 for more information on signals) to the leader of the session containing the terminal's foreground process group, which is usually a shell. This allows the shell to terminate the user's processes unconditionally, notify the processes that the user has logged out (usually, through a SIGHUP), or take some other action (or inaction). Although this setup may seem complicated, it lets the session group leader decide how closed terminals should be handled rather than putting that decision in the kernel. This allows system administrators flexibile control over account policies.

Determining the process group is easily done through the getpgid() and getpgrp() functions.

pid_t getpgid(pid_t pid)
> Returns the pgid of process pid. If pid is 0, the pgid of the current process is returned. No special permissions are needed to use this

call; any process may determine the process group to which any other process belongs.

```
pid_t getpgrp(void)
```
Returns the pgid of the current process (equivalent to getpgid(0)).

10.6.4 Orphaned Process Groups

The mechanism for how processes are terminated (or allowed to continue) when their session disappears is quite complicated. Imagine a session with multiple process groups in it (Figure 10.1 may help you visualize this). The session is being run on a terminal, and a normal system shell is the session leader.

When the session leader (the shell) exits, the process groups are left in a difficult situation. If they are actively running, they can no longer use stdin or stdout as the terminal has been closed. If they have been suspended, they will probably never run again as the user of that terminal cannot easily restart them, but never running means they will not terminate either.

In this situation, each process group is called an **orphaned process group**. POSIX defines this as a process group whose parent is also a member of that process group, or is not a member of that group's session. This is another way of saying that a process group is not orphaned as long as a process in that group has a parent in the same session but a different group.

While both definitions are complicated, the concept is pretty simple. If a process group is suspended and there is not a process around that can tell it to continue, the process group is orphaned.[18]

When the shell exits, any of its child programs become children of init, but stay in their original session. Assuming that every program in the session is a descendant of the shell, all of the process groups in that session become orphaned.[19] When a process group is orphaned, every process in that

---

18. Chapter 15 makes all of this much clearer, and it may be worth rereading this section after reading that chapter.
19. But maybe not right away. There may be process groups that contain processes who have parents in other process groups in that session. As the parent-child relationship between processes is a tree, there will eventually be a process group that contained only processes whose parents were the shell, and when that process group exits another one becomes orphaned.

process group is sent a SIGHUP, which normally terminates the program. Programs that have chosen not to terminate on SIGHUP are sent a SIGCONT, which resumes any suspended processes. This sequence terminates most processes and makes sure that any processes that are left are able to run (are not suspended).[20]

Once a process has been orphaned, it is forcibly disassociated from its controlling terminal (to allow a new user to make use of that terminal). If programs that continue running try to access that terminal, those attempts result in errors, with errno set to EIO. The processes remain in the same session, and the session ID is not used for a new process ID until every program in that session has exited.

10.7 **Introduction to** ladsh

To help illustrate many ideas discussed in this book, we develop a subset of a Unix command shell as the book progresses. At the end of the book, the shell will support

- Simple built-in commands

- Command execution

- I/O redirection (>, |, and so on)

- Job control

The full source code of the final version of this shell, called ladsh4.c, appears in Appendix B. As new features are added to ladsh, the changes to the source code are described in the text. To reduce the number of changes made between the versions, some early versions of the shell are a bit more complicated than they need to be. These extra complications make it easier to develop the shell later in the book, however, so please be patient. Just take those pieces on faith for now; we explain them all to you later in the book.

---

20. This discussion will make much more sense after you read the chapters on signals (Chapter 12) and job control (Chapter 15).

10.7.1 Running External Programs with ladsh

Here is the first (and simplest) version of ladsh, called ladsh1:

```
 1: /* ladsh1.c */
 2:
 3: #include <ctype.h>
 4: #include <errno.h>
 5: #include <fcntl.h>
 6: #include <signal.h>
 7: #include <stdio.h>
 8: #include <stdlib.h>
 9: #include <string.h>
10: #include <sys/ioctl.h>
11: #include <sys/wait.h>
12: #include <unistd.h>
13:
14: #define MAX_COMMAND_LEN 250     /* max length of a single command
15:                                          string */
16: #define JOB_STATUS_FORMAT "[%d] %-22s %.40s\n"
17:
18: struct jobSet {
19:     struct job * head;      /* head of list of running jobs */
20:     struct job * fg;        /* current foreground job */
21: };
22:
23: struct childProgram {
24:     pid_t pid;              /* 0 if exited */
25:     char ** argv;           /* program name and arguments */
26: };
27:
28: struct job {
29:     int jobId;              /* job number */
30:     int numProgs;           /* total number of programs in job */
31:     int runningProgs;       /* number of programs running */
32:     char * text;            /* name of job */
33:     char * cmdBuf;          /* buffer various argv's point into */
34:     pid_t pgrp;             /* process group ID for the job */
35:     struct childProgram * progs; /* array of programs in job */
36:     struct job * next;      /* to track background commands */
37: };
38:
```

```
39: void freeJob(struct job * cmd) {
40:     int i;
41:
42:     for (i = 0; i < cmd->numProgs; i++) {
43:         free(cmd->progs[i].argv);
44:     }
45:     free(cmd->progs);
46:     if (cmd->text) free(cmd->text);
47:     free(cmd->cmdBuf);
48: }
49:
50: int getCommand(FILE * source, char * command) {
51:     if (source == stdin) {
52:         printf("# ");
53:         fflush(stdout);
54:     }
55:
56:     if (!fgets(command, MAX_COMMAND_LEN, source)) {
57:         if (source == stdin) printf("\n");
58:         return 1;
59:     }
60:
61:     /* remove trailing newline */
62:     command[strlen(command) - 1] = '\0';
63:
64:     return 0;
65: }
66:
67: /* Return cmd->numProgs as 0 if no command is present (e.g. an empty
68:    line). If a valid command is found, commandPtr is set to point to
69:    the beginning of the next command (if the original command had
70:    more than one job associated with it) or NULL if no more
71:    commands are present. */
72: int parseCommand(char ** commandPtr, struct job * job, int * isBg) {
73:     char * command;
74:     char * returnCommand = NULL;
75:     char * src, * buf;
76:     int argc = 0;
77:     int done = 0;
78:     int argvAlloced;
79:     char quote = '\0';
```

```
 80:    int count;
 81:    struct childProgram * prog;
 82:
 83:    /* skip leading white space */
 84:    while (**commandPtr && isspace(**commandPtr)) (*commandPtr)++;
 85:
 86:    /* this handles empty lines and leading '#' characters */
 87:        if (!**commandPtr || (**commandPtr=='#')) {
 88:        job->numProgs = 0;
 89:        *commandPtr = NULL;
 90:        return 0;
 91:    }
 92:
 93:    *isBg = 0;
 94:    job->numProgs = 1;
 95:    job->progs = malloc(sizeof(*job->progs));
 96:
 97:    /* We set the argv elements to point inside of this string. The
 98:        memory is freed by freeJob().
 99:
100:        Getting clean memory relieves us of the task of NULL
101:        terminating things and makes the rest of this look a bit
102:        cleaner (though it is, admittedly, a tad less efficient) */
103:    job->cmdBuf = command = calloc(1, strlen(*commandPtr) + 1);
104:    job->text = NULL;
105:
106:    prog = job->progs;
107:
108:    argvAlloced = 5;
109:    prog->argv = malloc(sizeof(*prog->argv) * argvAlloced);
110:    prog->argv[0] = job->cmdBuf;
111:
112:    buf = command;
113:    src = *commandPtr;
114:    while (*src && !done) {
115:        if (quote == *src) {
116:            quote = '\0';
117:        } else if (quote) {
118:            if (*src == '\\') {
119:                src++;
120:                if (!*src) {
```

```
121:                          fprintf(stderr,
122:                              "character expected after \\\n");
123:                          freeJob(job);
124:                          return 1;
125:                      }
126:
127:                      /* in shell, "\'" should yield \' */
128:                      if (*src != quote) *buf++ = '\\';
129:                  }
130:                  *buf++ = *src;
131:              } else if (isspace(*src)) {
132:                  if (*prog->argv[argc]) {
133:                      buf++, argc++;
134:                      /* +1 here leaves room for the NULL which
135:                          ends argv */
136:                      if ((argc + 1) == argvAlloced) {
137:                          argvAlloced += 5;
138:                          prog->argv = realloc(prog->argv,
139:                                  sizeof(*prog->argv) * argvAlloced);
140:                      }
141:                      prog->argv[argc] = buf;
142:                  }
143:              } else switch (*src) {
144:              case '"':
145:              case '\'':
146:                  quote = *src;
147:                  break;
148:
149:              case '#':                               /* comment */
150:                  done = 1;
151:                  break;
152:
153:              case '&':                               /* background */
154:                  *isBg = 1;
155:              case ';':                               /* multiple commands */
156:                  done = 1;
157:                  returnCommand = *commandPtr + (src - *commandPtr) + 1;
158:                  break;
159:
160:              case '\\':
161:                  src++;
```

```
162:                    if (!*src) {
163:                        freeJob(job);
164:                        fprintf(stderr, "character expected after \\\n");
165:                        return 1;
166:                    }
167:                    /* fallthrough */
168:                default:
169:                    *buf++ = *src;
170:                }
171:
172:                src++;
173:        }
174:
175:        if (*prog->argv[argc]) {
176:            argc++;
177:        }
178:        if (!argc) {
179:            freeJob(job);
180:            return 0;
181:        }
182:        prog->argv[argc] = NULL;
183:
184:        if (!returnCommand) {
185:            job->text = malloc(strlen(*commandPtr) + 1);
186:            strcpy(job->text, *commandPtr);
187:        } else {
188:            /* This leaves any trailing spaces, which is a bil sloppy */
189:
190:            count = returnCommand - *commandPtr;
191:            job->text = malloc(count + 1);
192:            strncpy(job->text, *commandPtr, count);
193:            job->text[count] = '\0';
194:        }
195:
196:        *commandPtr = returnCommand;
197:
198:        return 0;
199: }
200:
201: int runCommand(struct job newJob, struct jobSet * jobList,
202:                int inBg) {
```

```
203:        struct job * job;
204:
205:        /* handle built-ins here -- we don't fork() so we
206:           can't background these very easily */
207:        if (!strcmp(newJob.progs[0].argv[0], "exit")) {
208:            /* this should return a real exit code */
209:            exit(0);
210:        } else if (!strcmp(newJob.progs[0].argv[0], "jobs")) {
211:            for (job = jobList->head; job; job = job->next)
212:                printf(JOB_STATUS_FORMAT, job->jobId, "Running",
213:                        job->text);
214:            return 0;
215:        }
216:
217:        /* we only have one program per child job right now, so this is
218:           easy */
219:        if (!(newJob.progs[0].pid = fork())) {
220:            execvp(newJob.progs[0].argv[0], newJob.progs[0].argv);
221:            fprintf(stderr, "exec() of %s failed: %s\n",
222:                    newJob.progs[0].argv[0],
223:                    strerror(errno));
224:            exit(1);
225:        }
226:
227:        /* put our child in its own process group */
228:        setpgid(newJob.progs[0].pid, newJob.progs[0].pid);
229:
230:        newJob.pgrp = newJob.progs[0].pid;
231:
232:        /* find the ID for the job to use */
233:        newJob.jobId = 1;
234:        for (job = jobList->head; job; job = job->next)
235:            if (job->jobId >= newJob.jobId)
236:                newJob.jobId = job->jobId + 1;
237:
238:        /* add the job to the list of running jobs */
239:        if (!jobList->head) {
240:            job = jobList->head = malloc(sizeof(*job));
241:        } else {
242:            for (job = jobList->head; job->next; job = job->next);
243:            job->next = malloc(sizeof(*job));
```

```
244:            job = job->next;
245:        }
246:
247:        *job = newJob;
248:        job->next = NULL;
249:        job->runningProgs = job->numProgs;
250:
251:        if (inBg) {
252:            /* we don't wait for background jobs to return -- append it
253:                to the list of backgrounded jobs and leave it alone */
254:
255:            printf("[%d] %d\n", job->jobId,
256:                    newJob.progs[newJob.numProgs - 1].pid);
257:        } else {
258:            jobList->fg = job;
259:
260:            /* move the new process group into the foreground */
261:
262:            if (tcsetpgrp(0, newJob.pgrp))
263:                perror("tcsetpgrp");
264:        }
265:
266:        return 0;
267: }
268:
269: void removeJob(struct jobSet * jobList, struct job * job) {
270:        struct job * prevJob;
271:
272:        freeJob(job);
273:        if (job == jobList->head) {
274:            jobList->head = job->next;
275:        } else {
276:            prevJob = jobList->head;
277:            while (prevJob->next != job) prevJob = prevJob->next;
278:            prevJob->next = job->next;
279:        }
280:
281:        free(job);
282: }
283:
284: /* Checks to see if any background processes have exited -- if they
```

```
285:     have, figure out why and see if a job has completed */
286: void checkJobs(struct jobSet * jobList) {
287:     struct job * job;
288:     pid_t childpid;
289:     int status;
290:     int progNum;
291:
292:     while ((childpid = waitpid(-1, &status, WNOHANG)) > 0) {
293:         for (job = jobList->head; job; job = job->next) {
294:             progNum = 0;
295:             while (progNum < job->numProgs &&
296:                         job->progs[progNum].pid != childpid)
297:                 progNum++;
298:             if (progNum < job->numProgs) break;
299:         }
300:
301:         job->runningProgs--;
302:         job->progs[progNum].pid = 0;
303:
304:         if (!job->runningProgs) {
305:             printf(JOB_STATUS_FORMAT, job->jobId, "Done",
306:                     job->text);
307:             removeJob(jobList, job);
308:         }
309:     }
310:
311:     if (childpid == -1 && errno != ECHILD)
312:         perror("waitpid");
313: }
314:
315: int main(int argc, const char ** argv) {
316:     char command[MAX_COMMAND_LEN + 1];
317:     char * nextCommand = NULL;
318:     struct jobSet jobList = { NULL, NULL };
319:     struct job newJob;
320:     FILE * input = stdin;
321:     int i;
322:     int status;
323:     int inBg;
324:
325:     if (argc > 2) {
```

```
326:            fprintf(stderr, "unexpected arguments; usage: ladsh1 "
327:                            "<commands>\n");
328:            exit(1);
329:        } else if (argc == 2) {
330:            input = fopen(argv[1], "r");
331:            if (!input) {
332:                perror("fopen");
333:                exit(1);
334:            }
335:        }
336:
337:    /* don't pay any attention to this signal; it just confuses
338:       things and isn't really meant for shells anyway */
339:    signal(SIGTTOU, SIG_IGN);
340:
341:    while (1) {
342:        if (!jobList.fg) {
343:            /* no job is in the foreground */
344:
345:            /* see if any background processes have exited */
346:            checkJobs(&jobList);
347:
348:            if (!nextCommand) {
349:                if (getCommand(input, command)) break;
350:                nextCommand = command;
351:            }
352:
353:            if (!parseCommand(&nextCommand, &newJob, &inBg) &&
354:                            newJob.numProgs) {
355:                runCommand(newJob, &jobList, inBg);
356:            }
357:        } else {
358:            /* a job is running in the foreground; wait for it */
359:            i = 0;
360:            while (!jobList.fg->progs[i].pid) i++;
361:
362:            waitpid(jobList.fg->progs[i].pid, &status, 0);
363:
364:            jobList.fg->runningProgs--;
365:            jobList.fg->progs[i].pid = 0;
366:
```

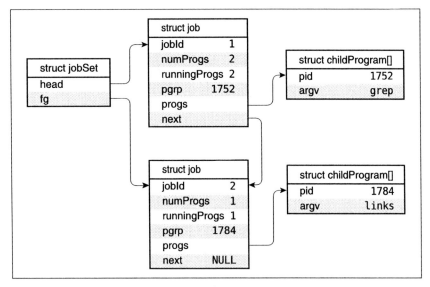

Figure 10.2   Job Data Structures for ladsh1.c

```
367:               if (!jobList.fg->runningProgs) {
368:                   /* child exited */
369:
370:                   removeJob(&jobList, jobList.fg);
371:                   jobList.fg = NULL;
372:
373:                   /* move the shell to the foreground */
374:                   if (tcsetpgrp(0, getpid()))
375:                       perror("tcsetpgrp");
376:               }
377:           }
378:       }
379:
380:    return 0;
381: }
```

This version does nothing more than run external programs with arguments, support # comments (everything after a # is ignored), and allow programs to be run in the background. It works as a shell script interpreter for simple scripts written using the #! notation, but it does not do much else. It is designed to mimic the usual shell interpreter used on Linux systems, although it is necessarily simplified.

First of all, let's look at the data structures it uses. Figure 10.2 illustrates the data structures `ladsh1.c` uses to keep track of child processes it runs, using a shell running `grep` in the background and `links` in the foreground as an example. `struct jobSet` describes a set of jobs that are running. It contains a linked list of jobs and a pointer to the job that is currently running in the foreground. If there is no foreground job, the pointer is `NULL`. ladsh1.c uses `struct jobSet` to keep track of all the jobs that are currently running as background tasks.

`struct childProgram` describes a single program being executed. This is not quite the same as a job; eventually, we will allow each job to be multiple programs tied together with pipes. For each child program, `ladsh` keeps track of the child's pid, the program that was run, and the command-line arguments. The first element of `argv`, `argv[0]`, holds the name of the program that was run, which is also passed as the first argument to the child.

Multiple commands are tied into a single job by `struct job`. Each job has a job ID unique within the shell, an arbitrary number of programs that constitute the job (stored through `progs`, a pointer to an array of `struct childProgram`), and a pointer to another (next) job, which allows the jobs to be tied together in a linked list (which `struct jobSet` relies on). The job also keeps track of how many individual programs originally comprised the job and how many of those programs are still running (as all of a job's component processes may not quit at the same time). The remaining two members, `text` and `cmdBuf`, are used as buffers that contain various strings used in the `struct childProgram` structures contained by the job.

Much of `struct jobSet` is made up of dynamically allocated memory that should be freed when the job is complete. The first function in ladsh1.c, `freeJob()`, frees the memory used by a job.

The next function, `getCommand()`, reads a command from the user and returns the string. If the commands are being read from a file, no prompting is done (which is why the code compares the input file stream against `stdin`).

`parseCommand()` breaks a command string into a `struct job` for `ladsh` to use. The first argument is a pointer to a pointer to the command. If there are multiple commands in the string, this pointer is advanced to the beginning of the second command. It is set to `NULL` once the final command from the string has been parsed. This allows parseCommand() to parse only a single command on each invocation and allows the caller to easily parse the entire string through multiple calls. Note that multiple programs piped together do not count as separate commands—only programs separated by ; or & are independent of each other. As parseCommand() is simply an exercise in string parsing, we shall not go over it in any detail.

The runCommand() function is responsible for running a single job. It takes a struct job describing the job to run, the list of jobs that are currently running, and a flag telling it whether the job should be run in the foreground or the background.

For now, ladsh does not support pipes, so each job may consist of only a single program (although much of the infrastructure for supporting pipes is already present in ladsh1.c). If the user runs exit, we exit the program immediately. This is an example of a **built-in** command that must be run by the shell itself to get the proper behavior. Another built-in, jobs, is also implemented here.

If the command is not a built-in, we need to execute a child command. As each job can consist only of a single program (until we implement pipes), this is pretty straightforward.

```
219:        if (!(newJob.progs[0].pid = fork())) {
220:            execvp(newJob.progs[0].argv[0], newJob.progs[0].argv);
221:            fprintf(stderr, "exec() of %s failed: %s\n",
222:                    newJob.progs[0].argv[0],
223:                    strerror(errno));
224:            exit(1);
225:        }
```

First of all, we fork() off the child process. The parent stores the child's pid in newJob.progs[0].pid, whereas the child process places a 0 there (remember, the parent and child have different memory images, although they are initially filled with the same values). This results in the child going into the body of the if statement while the parent skips the body. The child immediately runs the new program via execvp(). If the execvp() call fails, the child prints an error message and then exits. That is all that is necessary for spawning a simple child process.

After forking the child, the parent places the child into its own process group and records the job in the list of running jobs. If the process is meant to run in the foreground, the parent makes the new process group the foreground process group for the shell's controlling terminal.

The next function, `checkJobs()`, looks for background jobs that have exited and cleans up the list of running jobs as appropriate. For each process that has exited (remember `waitpid()` returns only information on exited processes unless `WUNTRACED` is specified), the shell

1. Finds the job the process was a part of

2. Marks the program as completed (by setting the stored pid for the program to 0) and reduces the number of running programs for the job by one

If the job containing the deceased process has no more running processes, which is always the case in this version of `ladsh`, the shell prints a message telling the user the process completed and removes the job from the list of background processes.

The `main()` routine for ladsh1.c controls the shell's execution flow. If an argument was passed to the shell when it was invoked, it treats that as a file name and reads subsequent commands from that file. Otherwise, `stdin` is used as the source of commands. The program then ignores the `SIGTTOU` signal. This is a bit of job-control magic that keeps things going smoothly, and it will make sense once you get to Chapter 15. Job control is not fully implemented, however, and when you are experimenting with ladsh1.c do not try job-control activities (especially those activities that involve suspending programs ladsh1.c has run); they simply will not work. A complete job-control implementation is added in Chapter 15; the setup here is only skeletal.

The remainder of `main()` is the main loop of the program. There is no exit condition for this loop; the program ends by calling `exit()` inside the `runCommand()` function.

The `nextCommand` variable points to the original (unparsed) string representation of the next command that should be run, or is `NULL` if the next command should be read from the input file, which is usually `stdin`. When no job is running in the foreground, ladsh calls checkJobs() to check for background jobs that have exited, reads the next command from the input file if nextCommand is NULL, and then parses and executes the next command.

When a foreground job is executing, ladsh1.c instead waits for one of the processes in the foreground job to terminate. Once all the processes in the foreground job have exited, the job is removed from the list of running jobs and ladsh1.c reads the next command as described previously.

10.8 Creating Clones

Although fork() is the traditional way of creating new processes in Unix, Linux also provides the clone() system call, which lets the process being duplicated specify what resources the parent process should share with its children.

```
int clone(int flags);
```

This is not much more than a fork(); the only difference is the flags parameter. It should be set to the signal that should be sent to the parent process when the child exits (usually, SIGCHLD), bitwise OR'ed with any number of the following flags, which are defined in <sched.h>:

CLONE_VM	The two processes share their virtual memory space (including the stack).
CLONE_FS	File-system information (such as the current directory) is shared.
CLONE_FILES	Open files are shared.
CLONE_SIGHAND	The signal handlers are shared for the two processes.

When two resources are shared, both processes see those resources identically. If the CLONE_SIGHAND is specified, when one of the processes changes the signal handler for a particular signal, both processes use the new handler (see Chapter 12 for details on signal handlers). When CLONE_FILES is used, not only is the set of open files shared, but the current location in each file is also shared. The return values for clone() are the same as for fork().

If a signal other than SIGCHLD is specified to be delivered to the parent on the death of a child process, the wait() family of functions will not, by default, return information on those processes. If you would like to get information on such processes, as well as on processes that use the normal SIGCHLD mechanism, the __WCLONE flag must be OR'ed with the flags parameter of the wait call. Although this behavior may seem odd, it allows greater flexibility. If wait() returned information on cloned processes, it would be more difficult to build standard thread libraries around clone(), because wait() would return information on other threads, as well as child processes.

Although it is not recommended that applications use clone() directly, numerous user-space libraries are available that use clone() and provide a fully POSIX-compatible thread implementation. The glibc library includes libpthread, which provides the most popular thread implementation. Several good books on POSIX thread programming are available [Butenhof, 1997] [Nichols, 1996].

CHAPTER 11

Simple File Handling

Files are the most ubiquitous resource abstraction used in the Unix world. Resources such as memory, disk space, devices, and interprocess communication (IPC) channels are represented as files. By providing a uniform abstraction of these resources, Unix reduces the number of software interfaces programmers must master. The resources accessed through file operations are as follows:

regular files   The kind of files most computer users think of. They serve as data repositories that can grow arbitrarily large and allow random access. Unix files are byte-oriented—any other logical boundaries are purely application conventions; the kernel knows nothing about them.

pipes   Unix's simplest IPC mechanism. Usually, one process writes information into the pipe while another reads from it. Pipes are what shells use to provide I/O redirection (for example, `ls -lR | grep notes` or `ls | more`), and many programs use pipes to feed input to programs that run as their subprocesses. There are two types of pipes: unnamed and named. **Unnamed pipes** are created as they are needed and disappear once both the read and the write ends of the pipe are closed. Unnamed pipes are so called because they do not exist in the file system and, therefore, have no file name.[1] **Named pipes** do have file names, and the file name is used to allow two independent

---

1. Under Linux, the /proc file system includes information on every file currently open on the system. Although this means that unnamed pipes can be found in a file system, they still do not have permanent file names, because they disappear when the processes using the pipe end.

processes to communicate through the pipe (similar to the way Unix domain sockets work[2]). Pipes are also known as FIFOs because the data is ordered in a first-in/first-out manner.

directories   Special files that consist of a list of files they contain. Old Unix implementations allowed programs to read and write them in exactly the same manner as regular files. To allow better abstraction, a special set of system calls was added to provide directory manipulation, although the directories are still opened and closed like regular files. Those functions are presented in Chapter 14.

device files   Most physical devices are represented as files. There are two types of device files: block devices and character devices. **Block device** files represent hardware devices[3] that cannot be read from a byte at a time; they must be read from in multiples of some block size. Under Linux, block devices receive special handling from the kernel[4] and can contain file systems.[5] Disk drives, including CD-ROM drives and RAM disks, are the most common block devices. **Character devices** can be read from a single character at a time, and the kernel provides no caching or ordering facilities for them. Modems, terminals, printers, sound cards, and mice are all character devices. Traditionally, special directory entries kept in the /dev directory allow user-space processes to access device resources as files.

symbolic links   A special kind of file that contains the path to another file. When a symbolic link (symlink) is opened, the system recognizes it as a symlink, reads its value, and opens the file it references instead of the symlink itself. When the

---

2. See Chapter 17 for more information on Unix domain sockets.
3. Not all block devices represent actual hardware. A better description of a block device is an entity on which a file system can reside; Linux's loopback block device maps a regular file to a logical block device that allows that file to contain a complete file system.
4. Most notably, they are cached and access to them is ordered.
5. This is different from some systems that are capable of mounting file systems on character devices, as well as block devices.

value stored in the symbolic link is used, the system is said to be *following the symlink*. Unless otherwise noted, system calls are assumed to follow symlinks that are passed to them.

sockets   Like pipes, sockets provide an IPC channel. They are more flexible than pipes, and can create IPC channels between processes running on different machines. Sockets are discussed in Chapter 17.

In many operating systems, there is a one-to-one correspondence between files and file names. Every file has a file name in a file system, and every file name maps to a single file. Unix divorces the two concepts, allowing for more flexibility.

The only unique identity a file has is its **inode** (an abbreviation of *information node*). A file's inode contains all the information about a file, including the access permissions associated with it, its current size, and how many file names it has (which could be zero, one, twenty, or more). There are two types of inodes. The **in-core inode** is the only type we normally care about; every open file on the system has one. The kernel keeps in-core inodes in memory, and they are the same for all file-system types. The other type of inodes are **on-disk inodes**. Every file on a file system has an on-disk inode, and their exact structure depends on the type of file system the file is stored on. When a process opens a file on a file system, the on-disk inode is loaded into memory and converted into an in-core inode. When the in-core inode has been modified, it is transformed back into an on-disk inode and stored in the file system.[6]

On-disk and in-core inodes do not contain exactly the same information. Only the in-core inode, for example, keeps track of how many processes on the system are currently using the file associated with the inode.

As on-disk and in-core inodes are synchronized by the kernel, most system calls end up updating both inodes. When this is the case, we just refer to updating the inode; it is implied that both the in-core and on-disk are

---

6. Linux has always used the term *inode* for both types, while other Unix variants have reserved inode for on-disk inodes and call in-core inodes *vnodes*. While using the vnode terminology is less confusing, we choose to use inode for both types to keep consistent with Linux standards.

affected. Some files (such as unnamed pipes) do not have any on-disk inode. In these cases, only the in-core inode is updated.

A file name exists only in a directory that relates that file name to the on-disk inode. You can think of the file name as a pointer to the on-disk inode for the file associated with it. The on-disk inode contains the number of file names that refer to that inode, called the **link count**. When a file is removed, the link count is decremented and if the link count is 0 and no processes already have the file open, the space is freed. If other processes have the file open, the disk space is freed when the final process has closed the file.

All of this means that it is possible to

- Have multiple processes access a file that has never existed in a file system (such as a pipe)

- Create a file on the disk, remove its directory entry, and continue to read and write from the file

- Change /tmp/foo and see the changes immediately in /tmp/bar, if both file names refer to the same inode

Unix has always worked this way, but these operations can be disconcerting to new users and programmers. As long as you keep in mind that a file name is merely a pointer to a file's on-disk inode, and that the inode is the real resource, you should be fine.

11.1 The File Mode

Every file on a system has a file type (such as unnamed pipe or character device), as well as a set of access permissions that define what processes may access that file. A file's type and access permissions are combined in a 16-bit value (a C short) called the **file mode**.

The bottom 12 bits of a file's mode represent the access permissions that govern access to the file, as well as file permission modifiers. The file permission modifiers serve a variety of functions. The most important functions are allowing the effective user and group IDs to change when the file is executed.

The file mode is usually written in up to six octal (base 8) digits. When represented in octal, the low-order three digits are the access bits, the next digit contains the file permission modifiers, and the high-order two digits indicate the file type. For example, a file whose mode is 0041777 has a file type of 04, a file permission modifier of 1, and access bits 0777.[7] Similarly, a file of mode 0100755 is of type 010, has no file permission modifiers set, and has access permissions of 0755.

11.1.1 File Access Permissions

Each of the three access digits represents the permissions for a different class of users. The first digit represents the permissions for the file's owner, the second digit represents permissions for users in the file's group, and the final digit represents the permissions for all other users. Each octal digit is made up of three bits, which represent read permission, write permission, and execute permission, from most significant to least significant bit. The term *world permissions* is commonly used to refer to the permission given to all three classes of users.

Let's try to make the previous paragraph a little more concrete through some examples. Linux's `chmod` command allows the user to specify an access mode in octal and then applies that mode to one or more files. If we have a file, `somefile`, which we would like to allow only the owner to write to but any user (including the owner) to read from, we would use mode 0644 (remember, this is in octal). The leading 6 is 110 in binary, which indicates that the type of user to which it refers (in this case, the owner) is given both read and write permission; the 4s are 010 binary, giving the other types of users (group and other) only read permissions.

```
$ chmod 0644 somefile
$ ls -l somefile
-rw-r--r--   1 ewt        devel        31 Feb 15 15:12 somefile
```

If we wanted to allow any member of group `devel` to write to the file, we would use mode 0664 instead.

---

7. This is the mode usually used for the /tmp directory.

```
$ chmod 0664 somefile
$ ls -l somefile
-rw-rw-r--   1 ewt       devel        31 Feb 15 15:12 somefile
```

If somefile is a **shell script** (programs that use #! at their beginning to specify a command interpreter) we want to execute, we must tell the system that the file is executable by turning on the execute bit—in this case, we are allowing the owner to read, write, and execute the file and members of group devel to read and execute the file. Other users may not manipulate the file in any way.

```
$ chmod 0750 somefile
$ ls -l somefile
-rwxr-x---   1 ewt       devel        31 Feb 15 15:12 somefile
```

Directories use the same set of access bits as normal files, but with slightly different semantics. Read permissions allow a process to access the directory itself, which lets a user list the contents of a directory. Write permissions allow a process to create new files in the directory and delete existing ones. The execute bit does not translate as well, however (what does it mean to execute a directory?). It allows a process to **search** a directory, which means it can access a file in that directory, as long as it knows the name of that file.

Most system directories on Linux machines have 0755 permissions and are owned by the root user. This lets all users on the system list the files in a directory and access those files by name, but restricts writing in that directory to the root user. Anonymous ftp sites that allow any person to submit files but do not want to let people download them until an administrator has looked at the contents of the files, normally set their incoming file directories to 0772. That allows all users to create new files in the directory without being allowed either to see the contents of the directory or access files in it.

More information on file access permissions may be found in any introductory Linux or Unix book [Sobell, 2002] [Welsh, 1996].

11.1.2 File Permission Modifiers

The file permission modifier digit is also a bitmask, whose values represent setuid, setgid, and the sticky bit. If the setuid bit is set for an executable file, the process's effective user ID is set to the owner of the file when the program is executed (see page 111 for information on why this is useful). The setgid bit behaves the same way, but sets the effective group ID to the file's group. The setuid bit has no meaning for files that are not executable, but if the setgid bit is set for a nonexecutable file, any locking done on the file is mandatory rather than advisory.[8] Under Linux, the setuid and setgid bits are ignored for shell scripts because setuid scripts tend to be insecure.

Neither setuid nor setgid bits have any obvious meaning for directories. The setuid bit actually has no semantics when it is set on a directory. If a directory's setgid bit is set, all new files created in that directory are owned by the same group that owns the directory itself. This makes it easier to use directories for collaborative work among users.

The sticky bit, the least significant bit in the file permission modifier digit, has an interesting history behind its name. Older Unix implementations had to load an entire program into memory before they could begin executing it. This meant big programs had long startup times, which could get quite annoying. If a program had the sticky bit set, the operating system would attempt to leave the program "stuck" in memory for as long as possible, even when the program was not running, reducing the startup time for those programs. Although this was a bit of a kludge, it worked reasonably well for commonly used programs, such as the C compiler. Modern Unix implementations, including Linux, use demand loading to run programs that load the program piece by piece, making the sticky bit unnecessary, and so Linux ignores the sticky bit for regular files.

The sticky bit is still used for directories. Usually, any user with write permissions to a directory can erase any file in that directory. If a directory's sticky bit is set, however, files may be removed only by the user who owns the file and the root user. This behavior is handy for directories that are repositories for files created by a wide variety of users, such as /tmp.

The final section of a file's mode specifies the file's type. It is contained in the high-order octal digits of the mode and is not a bitmask. Instead, the

---

8. See Chapter 13 for more information on file locking.

Table 11.1 File Permission Constants

Name	Value	Description
S_ISUID	0004000	The program is setuid.
S_ISGID	0002000	The program is setgid.
S_ISVTX	0001000	The sticky bit.
S_IRWXU	00700	The file's owner has read, write, and execute permissions.
S_IRUSR	00400	The file's owner has read permission.
S_IWUSR	00200	The file's owner has write permission.
S_IXUSR	00100	The file's owner has execute permission.
S_IRWXG	00070	The file's group has read, write, and execute permissions.
S_IRGRP	00040	The file's group has read permission.
S_IWGRP	00020	The file's group has write permission.
S_IXGRP	00010	The file's group has execute permission.
S_IRWXO	00007	Other users have read, write, and execute permissions.
S_IROTH	00004	Other users have read permission.
S_IWOTH	00002	Other users have write permission.
S_IXOTH	00001	Other users have execute permission.

value of those digits equates to a specific file type (04 indicates a directory; 06 indicates a block device). A file's type is set when the file is created. It can never be changed except by removing the file.

The include file <sys/stat.h> provides symbolic constants for all of the access bits, which can make code more readable. Both Linux and Unix users usually become comfortable with the octal representation of file modes, however, so it is common for programs to use the octal values directly. Table 11.1 lists the symbolic names used for both file access permissions and file permission modifiers.

11.1.3 File Types

The upper four bits of a file mode specify the file's type. Table 11.2 lists the constants that relate to the file's type. Bitwise AND'ing any of these constants with a file's mode yields non-0 if the bit is set.

The following macros take a file mode as an argument and return true or false:

Table 11.2 File Type Constants

Name	Value (Octal)	Description
S_IFMT	00170000	This value, bitwise ANDed with the mode, gives the file type (which equals one of the other S_IF values).
S_IFSOCK	0140000	The file is a socket.
S_IFLNK	0120000	The file is a symbolic link.
S_IFREG	0100000	The file is a regular file.
S_IFBLK	0060000	The file represents a block device.
S_IFDIR	0040000	The file is a directory.
S_IFCHR	0020000	The file represents a character device.
S_IFIFO	0010000	The file represents a first-in/first-out communications pipe.

S_ISLNK(m)	True if the file is a symbolic link
S_ISREG(m)	True if the file is a regular file
S_ISDIR(m)	True if the file is a directory
S_ISCHR(m)	True if the file represents a character device
S_ISBLK(m)	True if the file represents a block device
S_ISFIFO(m)	True if the file is a first-in/first-out pipe
S_ISSOCK(m)	True if the file is a socket

11.1.4 The Process's umask

The permissions given to newly created files depend on both a system's setup and an individual user's preferences. To relieve individual programs of the need to guess the permissions to use for a file, the system allows users to turn off particular permissions for newly created files (and directories, which are just special files). Every process has a **umask,** which specifies the permission bits to turn off when files are created. This allows a process to specify fairly liberal permissions (usually, world read and write permissions) and end up with the permissions the user would like. If the file is particularly sensitive, the creating process can specify more restrictive permissions than normal, because the umask never results in less restrictive permissions, only in more restrictive permissions.

The process's current umask is set by the `umask()` system call.

```
#include <sys/stat.h>

int umask(int newmask);
```

The old umask is returned, and the process's umask is set to the new value. Only read, write, and execute permissions may be specified for the file—you cannot use the umask to prevent the setuid, setgid, or sticky bits from being set. The `umask` command present in most shells allows the user to set the umask for the shell itself and its subsequent child processes.

As an example, the `touch` command creates new files with 0666 (world read and write) permissions. Because the user rarely wants this, he could force the `touch` command to turn off world and group write permissions for a file with a umask of 022, as shown by this example:

```
$ umask 022
$ touch foo
$ ls -l foo
-rw-r--r--   1 ewt        ewt             0 Feb 24 21:24 foo
```

If he prefers group write permissions, he can use a umask of 002 instead.

```
$ umask 002
$ touch foo2
$ ls -l foo2
-rw-rw-r--   1 ewt        ewt             0 Feb 24 21:24 foo2
```

If he wants all his files to be accessible only by himself, a 077 umask will accomplish the task.

```
$ umask 077
$ touch foo3
$ ls -l foo3
-rw-------   1 ewt        ewt             0 Feb 24 21:26 foo3
```

The process's umask affects the `open()`, `creat()`, `mknod()`, and `mkdir()` system calls.

11.2 Basic File Operations

As a large proportion of Linux's system calls manipulate files, we begin by showing you the functions that are most widely used. We discuss the more specialized functions later in this chapter. The functions used to read through directories are presented in Chapter 14 to help keep this chapter a bit more concise.

11.2.1 File Descriptors

When a process gains access to a file (usually called *opening* the file), the kernel returns a **file descriptor** that the process uses to perform subsequent operations on the file. File descriptors are small, positive integers, which serve as indices into an array of open files the kernel maintains for each process.

The first three file descriptors for a process (0, 1, and 2) have standard usages. The first, 0, is known as standard input (*stdin*) and is where programs should take their interactive input from. File descriptor 1 is called standard output (*stdout*), and most output from the program should be directed there. Errors should be sent to standard error (*stderr*), which is file descriptor 2. The standard C library follows these rules, so `gets()` and `printf()` use stdin and stdout, respectively, and these conventions allow shells to properly redirect a process's input and output.

The `<unistd.h>` header file provides the `STDIN_FILENO`, `STDOUT_FILENO`, and `STDERR_FILENO` macros, which evaluate to the stdin, stdout, and stderr file descriptors, respectively. Using these symbolic names can make code slightly more readable.

Many of the file operations that manipulate a file's inode are available in two forms. The first form takes a file name as an argument. The kernel uses that argument to look up the file's inode and performs the appropriate operation on the inode (this usually includes following symlinks). The second form takes a file descriptor as an argument and performs the operation on the inode it refers to. The two sets of system calls use similar names, with the system calls that expect a file descriptor argument prefixed with the letter *f*. For example, the `chmod()` system call changes the access permissions for the file referred to by the passed file name; `fchmod()` sets the access permissions for the file referred to by the specified file descriptor.

To make the rest of this discussion a bit less verbose, we present both versions of the system calls when they exist but discuss only the first version (which uses a file name).

11.2.2 Closing Files

One of the few operations that is the same for all types of files is closing the file. Here is how to close a file:

```
#include <unistd.h>

int close(int fd);
```

This is obviously a pretty basic operation. However, there is one important thing to remember about closing files—it could fail. Some systems (most notably, networked file systems such as NFS) do not try to store the final piece of written data in the file system until the file is closed. If that storage operation fails (the remote host may have crashed), then the `close()` returns an error. If your application is writing data but does not use synchronous writes (see the discussion of `O_SYNC` in the next section), you should always check the results of file closures. If `close()` fails, the updated file is corrupted in some unpredictable fashion! Luckily, this happens extremely rarely.

11.2.3 Opening Files in the File System

Although Linux provides many types of files, regular files are by far the most commonly used. Programs, configuration files, and data files all fall under that heading, and most applications do not (explicitly) use any other file type. There are two ways of opening files that have associated file names:

```
#include <fcntl.h>
#include <unistd.h>

int open(char * pathname, int flags, mode_t mode);
int creat(char * pathname, mode_t mode);
```

The open() function returns a file descriptor that references the file pathname. If the return value is less than 0, an error has occurred (as always, errno contains the error code). The flags argument describes the type of access the calling process wants, and also controls various attributes of how the file is opened and manipulated. An access mode must always be provided and is one of O_RDONLY, O_RDWR, and O_WRONLY, which request read-only, read-write, and write-only access, respectively. One or more of the following values may be bitwise OR'ed with the access mode to control other file semantics.

O_CREAT   If the file does not already exist, create it as a regular file.

O_EXCL   This flag should be used only with O_CREAT. When it is specified, open() fails if the file already exists. This flag allows a simple locking implementation, but it is unreliable across networked file systems like NFS.[9]

O_NOCTTY   The file being opened does not become the process's controlling terminal (see page 136 for more information on controlling terminals). This flag matters only when a process without any controlling terminal is opening a tty device. If it is specified any other time, it is ignored.

O_TRUNC   If the file already exists, the contents are discarded and the file size is set to 0.

O_APPEND   All writes to the file occur at the end of the file, although random access reads are still permitted.

O_NONBLOCK[10]   The file is opened in nonblocking mode. Operations on normal files always block because they are stored on local hard disks with predictable response times, but operations on certain file types have unpredictable completion times. For example, reading from a pipe that does not have any data in it blocks the reading process until data becomes available. If O_NONBLOCK is specified, the read returns zero bytes rather than block. Files that may take

---

9. For more information on file locking, see Chapter 13.
10. O_NDELAY is the original name for O_NONBLOCK, but it is now obsolete.

an indeterminate amount of time to perform an operation are called **slow files**.

O_SYNC   Normally, the kernel caches writes and records them to the hardware when it is convenient to do so. Although this implementation greatly increases performance, it is more likely to allow data loss than is immediately writing the data to disk. If O_SYNC is specified when a file is opened, all changes to the file are stored on the disk before the kernel returns control to the writing process. This is very important for some applications, such as database systems, in which write ordering is used to prevent data corruption in case of a system failure.

The mode parameter specifies the access permissions for the file if it is being created, and it is modified by the process's current umask. If O_CREAT is not specified, the mode is ignored.

The creat() function is exactly equivalent to

```
open(pathname, O_CREAT | O_WRONLY | O_TRUNC, mode)
```

We do not use creat() in this book because we find open() easier to read and to understand.[11]

11.2.4 Reading, Writing, and Moving Around

Although there are a few ways to read from and write to files, only the simplest is discussed here.[12] Reading and writing are nearly identical, so we discuss them simultaneously.

```
#include <unistd.h>

size_t read(int fd, void * buf, size_t length);
size_t write(int fd, const void * buf, size_t length);
```

---

11. creat() is misspelled, anyway.
12. readv(), writev(), and mmap() are discussed in Chapter 13; sendmsg() and recvmsg() are mentioned in Chapter 17.

Both functions take a file descriptor `fd`, a pointer to a buffer `buf`, and the `length` of that buffer. `read()` reads from the file descriptor and places the data read into the passed buffer; `write()` writes `length` bytes from the buffer to the file. Both functions return the number of bytes transferred, or -1 on an error (which implies no bytes were read or stored).

Now that we have covered these system calls, here is a simple example that creates the file `hw` in the current directory and writes `Hello World!` into it:

```
 1: /* hwwrite.c */
 2:
 3: #include <errno.h>
 4: #include <fcntl.h>
 5: #include <stdio.h>
 6: #include <stdlib.h>
 7: #include <unistd.h>
 8:
 9: int main(void) {
10:     int fd;
11:
12:     /* open the file, creating it if it's not there, and removing
13:        its contents if it is there */
14:     if ((fd = open("hw", O_TRUNC | O_CREAT | O_WRONLY, 0644)) < 0) {
15:         perror("open"),
16:         exit(1);
17:     }
18:
19:     /* the magic number of 13 is the number of characters which will
20:        be written */
21:     if (write(fd, "Hello World!\n", 13) != 13) {
22:         perror("write");
23:         exit(1);
24:     }
25:
26:     close(fd);
27:
28:     return 0;
29: }
```

Here is what happens when we run `hwwrite`:

```
$ cat hw
cat: hw: No such file or directory
$ ./hwwrite
$ cat hw
Hello World!
$
```

Changing this function to read from a file is a simple matter of changing the open() to

```
open("hw", O_RDONLY);
```

and changing the write() of a static string to a read() into a buffer.

Unix files can be divided into two catgories: seekable and nonseekable.[13] Nonseekable files are first-in/first-out channels that do not support random reads or writes, and data cannot be reread or overwritten. Seekable files allow the reads and the writes to occur anywhere in the file. Pipes and sockets are nonseekable files; block devices and regular files are seekable.

As FIFOs are nonseekable files, it is obvious where read() reads from (the beginning of the file) and write() writes to (the end of the file). Seekable files, on the other hand, have no obvious place for the operations to occur. Instead, both happen at the "current" location in the file and advance the current location after the operation. When a seekable file is initially opened, the current location is at the beginning of the file, or offset 0. If 10 bytes are read, the current position is then at offset 10, and a write of 5 more bytes overwrites the data, starting with the eleventh byte in the file (which is at offset 10, where the current position was). After such a write, the current position becomes offset 15, immediately after the overwritten data.

If the current position is the end of the file and the process tries to read from the file, read() returns 0 rather than an error. If more data is written at the end of the file, the file grows just enough to accommodate the extra data and the current position becomes the new end of the file. Each file descriptor keeps track of an independent current position[14] (it is not kept in the file's

---

13. Although this division is almost clean, TCP sockets support out-of-band data, which makes it a bit dirtier. Out-of-band data is outside the scope of this book; [Stevens, 2004] provides a complete description.
14. Almost independent; see the discussion of dup() on page 196 for the exceptions to this.

inode), so if a file is opened multiple times by multiple processes (or by the same process, for that matter), reads and writes through one of the file descriptors do not affect the location of reads and writes made through the other file descriptor. Of course, the multiple writes could corrupt the file in other ways, so some sort of locking may be needed in these situations.

Files opened with O_APPEND have a slightly different behavior. For such files, the current position is moved to the end of the file before the kernel writes any data. After the write, the current position is moved to the end of the newly written data, as normal. For append-only files, this guarantees that the file's current position is always at the end of the file immediately following a write().

Applications that want to read and write data from random locations in the file need to set the current position before reading and writing data, using lseek():

```
#include <unistd.h>

int lseek(int fd, off_t offset, int whence);
```

The current position for file fd is moved to offset bytes relative to whence, where whence is one of the following:

SEEK_SET[15]   The beginning of the file

SEEK_CUR   The current position in the file

SEEK_END   The end of the file

For both SEEK_CUR and SEEK_END the offset may be negative. In this case, the current position is moved toward the beginning of the file (from whence) rather than toward the end of the file. For example, the following code moves the current position to five bytes from the end of the file:

```
lseek(fd, -5, SEEK_END);
```

---

15. As most systems define SEEK_SET as 0, it is common to see lseek(fd, offset, 0) used instead of lseek(fd, offset, SEEK_SET). This is not as portable (or readable) as SEEK_SET, but it is fairly common in old code.

The lseek() system call returns the new current position in the file relative to the beginning of the file, or -1 if an error occurred. Thus, lseek(fd, 0, SEEK_END) is a simple way of finding out how large a file is, but make sure you reset the current position before trying to read from fd.

Although the current position is not disturbed by other processes that access the file at the same time,[16] that does not mean multiple processes can safely write to a file simultaneously. Imagine the following sequence:

Process A	Process B
lseek(fd, 0, SEEK_END);	
	lseek(fd, 0, SEEK_END);
	write(fd, buf, 10);
write(fd, buf, 5);	

In this case process A would have overwritten the first five bytes of process B's data, which is probably not what was intended. If multiple processes need to write to append to a file simultaneously, the O_APPEND flag should be used, which makes the operation atomic.

Under most POSIX systems, processes are allowed to move the current position past the end of the file. The file is grown to the appropriate size, and the current position becomes the new end of the file. The only catch is that most systems do not actually allocate any disk space for the portion of the file that was never written to; they change only the logical size of the file.

Portions of files that are "created" in this manner are known as **holes**. Reading from a hole in a file returns a buffer full of zeros, and writing to them could fail with an out-of-disk-space error. All of this means that lseek() should not be used to reserve disk space for later use because that space may not be allocated. If your application needs to allocate some disk space for later use, you must use write(). Files with holes in them are often used for files that have data sparsely spaced throughout them, such as files that represent hash tables.

---

16. Well, not usually, anyway. If processes share file descriptors (meaning file descriptors that arose from a single open() call), those processes share the same file structure and the same current position. The most common way for this to happen is for files after a fork(), as discussed on page 197. The other way this can happen is if a file descriptor is passed to another process through a Unix domain socket, which is described on pages 424–425.

For a simple, shell-based demonstration of file holes, look at the following example (note that /dev/zero is a character device that returns as many zeros as a process tries to read from it).

```
$ dd if=/dev/zero of=foo bs=1k count=10
10+0 records in
10+0 records out
$ ls -l foo
-rw-rw-r--  1 ewt      ewt         10240 Feb  6 21:50 foo
$ du foo
10      foo
$ dd if=/dev/zero of=bar bs=1k count=1 seek=9
1+0 records in
1+0 records out
$ ls -l bar
-rw-rw-r--  1 ewt      ewt         10240 Feb  6 21:50 bar
$ du bar
1       bar
$
```

Although both foo and bar are 10K in size, bar uses only 1K of disk space because the other 9K were seek() ed over when the file was created instead of written.

11.2.5 Partial Reads and Writes

Although both read() and write() take a parameter that specifies how many bytes to read or write, neither one is guaranteed to process the requested number of bytes, even if no error has occurred. The simplest example of this is trying to read from a regular file that is already positioned at the end of the file. The system cannot actually read any bytes, but it is not exactly an error condition either. Instead, the read() call returns 0 bytes. In the same vein, if the current position was 10 bytes from the end of the file and an attempt was made to read more than 10 bytes from the file, 10 bytes would be read and the read() call would return the value 10. Again, this is not considered an error condition.

The behavior of read() also depends on whether the file was opened with O_NONBLOCK. On many file types, O_NONBLOCK does not make any difference at all. Files for which the system can guarantee an operation's completion in a reasonable amount of time always block on reads and writes; they are sometimes referred to as **fast files**. This set of files includes local block devices and regular files. For other file types, such as pipes and such character devices as terminals, the process could be waiting for another process (or a human being) to either provide something for the process to read or free resources for the system to use when processing the write() request. In either case, the system has no way of knowing whether it will ever be able to complete the system call. When these files are opened with O_NONBLOCK, for each operation on the file, the system simply does as much as it is able to do immediately, and then returns to the calling process.

Nonblocking I/O is an important topic, and more examples of it are presented in Chapter 13. With the standardization of the poll() system call, however, the need for it (especially for reading) has diminished. If you find yourself using nonblocking I/O extensively, try to rethink your program in terms of poll() to see if you can make it more efficient.

To show a concrete example of reading and writing files, here is a simple reimplementation of **cat**. It copies stdin to stdout until there is no more input to copy.

```
 1: /* cat.c */
 2:
 3: #include <stdio.h>
 4: #include <unistd.h>
 5:
 6: /* While there is data on standard in (fd 0), copy it to standard
 7:    out (fd 1). Exit once no more data is available. */
 8:
 9: int main(void) {
10:     char buf[1024];
11:     int len;
12:
13:     /* len will be >= 0 while data is available, and read() is
14:        successful */
15:     while ((len = read(STDIN_FILENO, buf, sizeof(buf))) > 0) {
16:         if (write(1, buf, len) != len) {
17:             perror("write");
18:             return 1;
19:         }
20:     }
```

```
21:
22:     /* len was <= 0; If len = 0, no more data is available.
23:        Otherwise, an error occurred. */
24:     if (len < 0) {
25:         perror("read");
26:         return 1;
27:     }
28:
29:     return 0;
30: }
```

11.2.6 Shortening Files

Although regular files automatically grow when data is written to the end of them, there is no way for the system to automatically shrink files when the data at their end is no longer needed. After all, how would the system know when data becomes extraneous? It is a process's responsibility to notify the system when a file may be truncated at a certain point.

```
#include <unistd.h>

int truncate(const char * pathname, size_t length);
int ftruncate(int fd, size_t length);
```

The file's size is set to length, and any data in the file past the new end of the file is lost. If length is larger than the current size of the file, the file is actually grown to the indicated length (using holes if possible), although this behavior is not guaranteed by POSIX and should not be relied on in portable programs.

11.2.7 Synchronizing Files

When a program writes data to the file, the data is normally stored in a kernel cache until it gets written to the physical medium (such as a hard drive), but the kernel returns control to that program as soon as the data is copied into the cache. This provides major performance improvements as it allows the kernel to order writes on the disk and to group multiple writes into a single block operation. In the event of a system failure, however, it has a few drawbacks that could be important. For example, an application that assumes data is stored in a database before the index entry for that data is stored might not handle a failure that results in just the index's getting updated.

There are a few mechanisms applications can use to wait for data to get written to the physical medium. The O_SYNC flag, discussed on page 168, causes all writes to the file to block the calling process until the medium has been updated. While this certainly works, it is not a very neat approach. Normally, applications do not need to have every operation synchronized, more often they need to make sure a set of operations has completed before beginning another set. The fsync() and fdatasync() system calls provide this semantic:

```
#include <unistd.h>

int fsync(int fd);
int fdatasync(int fd);
```

Both system calls suspend the application until all of the data for the file fd has been written. The fsync() also waits for the file's inode information, such as the access time, to get updated.[17] Neither of these system calls can ensure that the data gets written to nonvolatile storage, however. Modern disk drives have large caches, and a power failure could cause some data stored in those caches to get lost.

11.2.8 Other Operations

Linux's file model does a good job of standardizing most file operations through generic functions such as read() and write() (for example, writing to a pipe is the same as writing to a file on disk). However, some devices have operations that are poorly modeled by this abstraction. For example, terminal devices, represented as character devices, need to provide a method to change the speed of the terminal, and a CD-ROM drive, represented by a block device, needs to know when it should play an audio track to help increase a programmer's productivity.

---

17. The inode information for files is listed in Table 11.3.

All of these miscellaneous operations are accessed through a single system call, `ioctl()` (short for I/O control), which is prototyped like this:

```
#include <sys/ioctl.h>

int ioctl(int fd, int request, ...);
```

although it is almost always used like this:

```
int ioctl(int fd, int request, void * arg);
```

Whenever `ioctl()` is used, its first argument is the file being manipulated and the second argument specifies what operation is being requested. The final argument is usually a pointer to *something*, but what that something is, as well as the exact semantics of the return code, depends on what type of file `fd` refers to and what type of operation was requested. For some operations, `arg` is a `long` value instead of a pointer; in these instances, a typecast is normally used. There are many examples of `ioctl()` in this book, and you do not need to worry about using `ioctl()` until you come across them.

11.3 Querying and Changing Inode Information

11.3.1 Finding Inode Information

The beginning of this chapter introduced an inode as the data structure that tracks information about a file rather than just a single process's view of it. For example, a file's size is a constant at any given time—it does not change for different processes that have access to the file (compare this with the current position in the file, which is unique for the result of each `open()` rather than a property of the file itself). Linux provides three ways of reading a file's inode information:

```
#include <sys/stat.h>

int stat(const char * pathname, struct stat * statbuf);
int lstat(const char *pathname, struct stat * statbuf);
int fstat(int fd, struct stat * statbuf);
```

The first version, stat(), returns the inode information for the file referenced by pathname, following any symlinks that are present. If you do not want to follow symlinks (to check if a file name is a symlink, for example), use lstat() instead, which does not follow them. The final version, fstat(), returns the inode referred to by an open file descriptor. All three system calls fill in the struct stat referenced by statbuf with information from the file's inode. Table 11.3 describes the information available from struct stat.

11.3.2 A Simple Example of stat()

Here is a simple program that displays information from lstat() for each file name passed as an argument. It illustrates how to use the values returned by the stat() family of functions.

```
 1: /* statsamp.c */
 2:
 3: /* For each file name passed on the command line, we display all of
 4:     the information lstat() returns on the file. */
 5:
 6: #include <errno.h>
 7: #include <stdio.h>
 8: #include <string.h>
 9: #include <sys/stat.h>
10: #include <sys/sysmacros.h>
11: #include <sys/types.h>
12: #include <time.h>
13: #include <unistd.h>
14:
15: #define TIME_STRING_BUF 50
16:
17: /* Make the user pass buf (of minimum length TIME_STRING_BUF) rather
18:     than using a static buf local to the function to avoid the use of
19:     static local variables and dynamic memory.  No error should ever
20:     occur so we don't do any error checking. */
21: char * timeString(time_t t, char * buf) {
22:     struct tm * local;
23:
24:     local = localtime(&t);
25:     strftime(buf, TIME_STRING_BUF, "%c", local);
```

Table 11.3 Members of `struct stat`

Type	Field	Description
`dev_t`	`st_dev`	The device number the file resides on.
`ino_t`	`st_ino`	The file's on-disk inode number. Each file has an on-disk inode number unique for the device it is on. Thus the (`st_dev`, `st_ino`) pair provides a unique identification of the file.
`mode_t`	`st_mode`	The mode of the file. This includes information on both the file permissions and the type of file.
`nlink_t`	`st_nlink`	The number of pathnames that reference this inode. This does not include symlinks, because symlinks reference other file names, not inodes.
`uid_t`	`st_uid`	The user ID that owns the file.
`gid_t`	`st_gid`	The group ID that owns the file.
`dev_t`	`st_rdev`	If the file is a character or block device, this gives the major and minor numbers of the file. See the discussion on `mknod()` on page 189 for more information on this member and the macros that manipulate its value.
`off_t`	`st_size`	The size of the file in bytes. This is defined only for regular files.
`unsigned long`	`st_blksize`	The block size for the file system storing the file.
`unsigned long`	`st_blocks`	The number of blocks allocated to the file. Normally, `st_blksize * st_blocks` is a little more than the `st_size` because some of the space in the final block is unused. However, for files with holes, `st_blksize * st_blocks` can be substantially smaller than `st_size`.
`time_t`	`st_atime`	The most recent access time of the file. This is updated whenever the file is opened or its inode is modified.
`time_t`	`st_mtime`	The most recent modification time of the file. It is updated whenever the file's data has changed
`time_t`	`st_ctime`	The most recent change time of the file or the inode, including owner, group, link count, and so on.

```
26:
27:      return buf;
28: }
29:
30: /* Display all of the information we get from lstat() on the file
31:    named as our sole parameter. */
32: int statFile(const char * file) {
33:     struct stat statbuf;
34:     char timeBuf[TIME_STRING_BUF];
35:
36:     if (lstat(file, &statbuf)) {
37:         fprintf(stderr, "could not lstat %s: %s\n", file,
38:                 strerror(errno));
39:         return 1;
40:     }
41:
42:     printf("Filename : %s\n", file);
43:     printf("On device: major %d/minor %d    Inode number: %ld\n",
44:             major(statbuf.st_dev), minor(statbuf.st_dev),
45:             statbuf.st_ino);
46:     printf("Size     : %-10ld          Type: %07o        "
47:             "Permissions: %05o\n", statbuf.st_size,
48:             statbuf.st_mode & S_IFMT, statbuf.st_mode & ~(S_IFMT));
49:     printf("Owner    : %d                Group: %d"
50:             "            Number of links: %d\n",
51:             statbuf.st_uid, statbuf.st_gid, statbuf.st_nlink);
52:     printf("Creation time: %s\n",
53:             timeString(statbuf.st_ctime, timeBuf));
54:     printf("Modified time: %s\n",
55:             timeString(statbuf.st_mtime, timeBuf));
56:     printf("Access time  : %s\n",
57:             timeString(statbuf.st_atime, timeBuf));
58:
59:     return 0;
60: }
61:
62: int main(int argc, const char ** argv) {
63:     int i;
64:     int rc = 0;
65:
66:     /* Call statFile() for each file name passed on the
```

```
67:        command line. */
68:    for (i = 1; i < argc; i++) {
69:        /* If statFile() ever fails, rc will end up non-zero. */
70:        rc |= statFile(argv[i]);
71:
72:        /* this prints a blank line between entries, but not after
73:            the last entry */
74:        if ((argc - i) > 1) printf("\n");
75:    }
76:
77:    return rc;
78: }
```

11.3.3 Easily Determining Access Rights

Although the mode of a file provides all the information a program needs to determine whether it is allowed to access a file, testing the set of permissions is tricky and error prone. As the kernel already includes the code to validate access permissions, a simple system call is provided that lets programs determine whether they may access a file in a certain way:

```
#include <unistd.h>

int access(const char * pathname, int mode);
```

The mode is a mask that contains one or more of the following values:

F_OK   The file exists. This requires execute permissions on all the directories in the path being checked, so it could fail for a file that does exist.

R_OK   The process may read from the file.

W_OK   The process may write to the file.

X_OK   The process may execute the file (or search the directory).

access() returns 0 if the specified access modes are allowed, and an EACCES error otherwise.

11.3.4 Changing a File's Access Permissions

A file's access permissions and access permission modifiers are changed by the chmod() system call.

```
#include <sys/stat.h>

int chmod(const char * pathname, mode_t mode);
int fchmod(int fd, mode_t mode);
```

Although chmod() allows you to specify a path, remember that file permissions are based on the inode, not on the file name. If a file has multiple hard links to it, changing the permissions of one of the file's names changes the file's permissions everywhere it appears in the file system. The mode parameter may be any combination of the access and access modifier bits just discussed, bitwise OR'ed together. As there are normally quite a few of these values specified at a time, it is common for programs to specify the new permission value directly in octal. Only the root user and the owner of a file are allowed to change the access permissions for a file—all others who attempt to do so get EPERM.

11.3.5 Changing a File's Owner and Group

Just like a file's permissions, a file's owner and group are stored in the file's inode, so all hard links to a file have the same owner and group. The same system call is used to change both the owner and the group of a file.

```
#include <unistd.h>

int chown(const char * pathname, uid_t owner, gid_t group);
int fchown(int fd, uid_t owner, gid_t group);
```

The owner and group parameters specify the new owner and group for the file. If either is -1, that value is not changed. Only the root user may change the owner of a file. When a file's owner is changed or the file is written to, the setuid bit for that file is always cleared for security reasons. Both the owner of a file and the root user may change the group that owns a file, but the owner must be a member of the group to which he is changing the file. If the file has its group execute bit set, the setgid bit is cleared for security reasons. If the setgid bit is set but the group execute bit is not, the file has mandatory locking enabled and the mode is preserved.

11.3.6 Changing a File's Timestamps

A file's owner may change the mtime and atime of a file to any arbitrary value. This makes these timestamps useless as audit trails, but it allows archiving tools like tar and cpio to reset a file's timestamps to the same values they had when the file was archived. The ctime is changed when the mtime and atime are updated, so tar and cpio are unable to restore it.

There are two ways of changing these stamps: utime() and utimes(). utime() originated in System V and was adopted by POSIX, whereas utimes() is from BSD. Both functions are equivalent; they differ only in the way the new timestamps are specified.

```
#include <utime.h>
int utime(const char * pathname, struct utimbuf * buf);

#include <sys/time.h>
int utimes(const char * pathname, struct timeval * tvp);
```

The POSIX version, utime(), takes a struct utimbuf, which is defined in <utime.h> as

```
struct utimbuf {
    time_t actime;
    time_t modtime;
}
```

BSD's utimes() instead passes the new atime and mtime through a struct timeval, which is defined in <sys/time.h>.

```
struct timeval {
    long tv_sec;
    long tv_usec;
}
```

The tv_sec element holds the new atime; tv_usec contains the new mtime for utimes().

Table 11.4 Extended File Attributes

Attribute	Definition
EXT3_APPEND_FL	If the file is opened for writing, O_APPEND must be specified.
EXT3_IMMUTABLE_FL	The file may not be modified or removed by any user, including root.
EXT3_NODUMP	The file should be ignored by the dump command.
EXT3_SYNC_FL	The file must be updated synchronously, as if O_SYNC had been specified on opening.

If NULL is passed as the second argument to either function, both timestamps are set to the current time. The new atime and mtime are specified in elapsed seconds since the epoch (just like the value time() returns), as defined in Chapter 18.

11.3.7 Ext3 Extended Attributes

The primary file system used on Linux systems is the Third Extended File System,[18] commonly abbreviated as ext3. Although the ext3 file system supports all the traditional features of Unix file systems, such as the meanings of the various bits in each file's mode, it allows for other attributes for each file. Table 11.4 describes the extra attributes currently supported, along with the symbolic name for each attribute. These flags may be set and inspected through the chattr and lsattr programs.

As the ext3 extended attributes are outside the standard file system interface, they cannot be modified through chmod() like the file attributes. Instead, ioctl() is used. Recall that ioctl() is defined as

```
#include <sys/ioctl.h>
#include <linux/ext3_fs.h>

int ioctl(int fd, int request, void * arg);
```

---

18. So named because it is a journaling version of the Second Extended File System, the successor to the Linux Extended File System, which was designed as a more complete file system than the Minix file system, the only one Linux originally supported.

The file whose attributes are being changed must be open, just as for fchmod(). The request is EXT3_IOC_GETFLAGS to check the current flags for the file and EXT3_IOC_SETFLAGS to set them. In either case, arg must point to an int. If EXT3_IOC_GETFLAGS is used, the long is set to the current value of the program's flags. If EXT3_IOC_SETFLAGS is used, the new value of the file's flags is taken from the int pointed to by arg.

The append and immutable flags may be changed only by the root user, as they restrict the operations the root user is able to perform. The other flags may be modified by either the root user or the owner of the file whose flags are being modified.

Here is a small program that displays the flags for any files specified on the command line. It works only for files on an ext3 file system,[19] however. The ioctl() fails for files on any other type of file system.

```
 1: /* checkflags.c */
 2:
 3: /* For each file name passed on the command line, display
 4:    information on that file's ext3 attributes. */
 5:
 6: #include <errno.h>
 7: #include <fcntl.h>
 8: #include <linux/ext3_fs.h>
 9: #include <stdio.h>
10: #include <string.h>
11: #include <sys/ioctl.h>
12: #include <unistd.h>
13:
14: int main(int argc, const char ** argv) {
15:     const char ** filename = argv + 1;
16:     int fd;
17:     int flags;
18:
19:     /* Iterate over each file name on the command line. The last
20:        pointer in argv[] is NULL, so this while() loop is legal. */
21:     while (*filename) {
```

---

19. It actually works just fine on an ext2 file system as well. The two file systems are very similar (an ext3 file system can even be mounted as an ext2 one), and the programs presented here work on both. In fact, if all of the places 3 appears in the source are changed to 2 the programs still compile and function identically.

```
22:           /* Unlike normal attributes, ext3 attributes can only
23:              be queried if we have a file descriptor (a file name
24:              isn't sufficient). We don't need write access to query
25:              the ext3 attributes, so O_RDONLY is fine. */
26:           fd = open(*filename, O_RDONLY);
27:           if (fd < 0) {
28:               fprintf(stderr, "cannot open %s: %s\n", *filename,
29:                       strerror(errno));
30:               return 1;
31:           }
32:
33:           /* This gets the attributes, and puts them into flags */
34:           if (ioctl(fd, EXT3_IOC_GETFLAGS, &flags)) {
35:               fprintf(stderr, "ioctl failed on %s: %s\n", *filename,
36:                       strerror(errno));
37:               return 1;
38:           }
39:
40:           printf("%s:", *filename++);
41:
42:           /* Check for each attribute, and display a message for each
43:              one which is turned on. */
44:           if (flags & EXT3_APPEND_FL) printf(" Append");
45:           if (flags & EXT3_IMMUTABLE_FL) printf(" Immutable");
46:           if (flags & EXT3_SYNC_FL) printf(" Sync");
47:           if (flags & EXT3_NODUMP_FL) printf(" Nodump");
48:
49:           printf("\n");
50:           close(fd);
51:       }
52:
53:       return 0;
54: };
```

The following is a similar program that sets the ext3 extended attributes for a given list of files. The first parameter must be a list of which flags should be set. Each flag is represented in the list by a single letter: A for append-only, I for immutable, S for sync, and N for the nodump flag. This program does not modify the current flags for the file; only the flags specified on the command line are set.

```
 1: /* setflags.c */
 2:
 3: /* The first parameter to this program is a string consisting of
 4:    0 (an empty string is okay) or more of the letters I, A, S, and
 5:    N. This string specifies which ext3 attributes should be turned
 6:    on for the files which are specified on the rest of the command
 7:    line -- the rest of the attributes are turned off. The letters
 8:    stand for immutable, append-only, sync, and nodump, respectively.
 9:
10:    For example, the command "setflags IN file1 file2" turns on the
11:    immutable and nodump flags for files file1 and file2, but turns
12:    off the sync and append-only flags for those files. */
13:
14: #include <errno.h>
15: #include <fcntl.h>
16: #include <linux/ext3_fs.h>
17: #include <stdio.h>
18: #include <string.h>
19: #include <sys/ioctl.h>
20: #include <unistd.h>
21:
22: int main(int argc, const char ** argv) {
23:     const char ** filename = argv + 1;
24:     int fd;
25:     int flags = 0;
26:
27:     /* Make sure the flags to set were specified, along with
28:        some file names. Allow a "0" to be set to indicate that all
29:        of the flags should be reset. */
30:     if (argc < 3) {
31:         fprintf(stderr, "setflags usage: [0][I][A][S][N] "
32:                         "<filenames>\n");
33:         return 1;
34:     }
35:
36:     /* each letter represents a flag; set the flags which are
37:        specified */
38:     if (strchr(argv[1], 'I')) flags |= EXT3_IMMUTABLE_FL;
39:     if (strchr(argv[1], 'A')) flags |= EXT3_APPEND_FL;
40:     if (strchr(argv[1], 'S')) flags |= EXT3_SYNC_FL;
41:     if (strchr(argv[1], 'N')) flags |= EXT3_NODUMP_FL;
```

```
42:
43:     /* iterate over all of the file names in argv[] */
44:     while (*(++filename)) {
45:         /* Unlike normal attributes, ext3 attributes can only
46:             be set if we have a file descriptor (a file name
47:             isn't sufficient). We don't need write access to set
48:             the ext3 attributes, so O_RDONLY is fine. */
49:         fd = open(*filename, O_RDONLY);
50:         if (fd < 0) {
51:             fprintf(stderr, "cannot open %s: %s\n", *filename,
52:                     strerror(errno));
53:             return 1;
54:         }
55:
56:         /* Sets the attributes as specified by the contents of
57:             flags. */
58:         if (ioctl(fd, EXT3_IOC_SETFLAGS, &flags)) {
59:             fprintf(stderr, "ioctl failed on %s: %s\n", *filename,
60:                     strerror(errno));
61:             return 1;
62:         }
63:         close(fd);
64:     }
65:
66:     return 0;
67: };
```

11.4   Manipulating Directory Entries

Remember that directory entries (file names) are nothing more than pointers to on-disk inodes; almost all the important information concerning a
file is stored in the inode. open() lets a process create directory entries
that are regular files, but other functions are needed to create other types
of files and to manipulate the entries themselves. The functions that allow
you to create, remove, and search directories are covered in Chapter 14;
socket files are introduced in Chapter 17. This section covers symbolic
links, device files, and FIFOs.

11.4.1 Creating Device and Named Pipe Entries

Processes create device file entries and named pipes in the file system through mknod().

```
#include <fcntl.h>
#include <unistd.h>

int mknod(const char * pathname, mode_t mode, dev_t dev);
```

The pathname is the file name to create, mode is both the access mode of the new file (which gets modified by the current umask) and the new file type (S_IFIFO, S_IFBLK, or S_IFCHR). The final parameter, dev, contains the major and minor numbers of the device to create. The type of device (character or block) and the major number of the device tell the kernel which device driver is responsible for operations on that device file. The minor number is used internally by the device driver to differentiate among multiple devices it provides. Only the root user is allowed to create device files; all users may create named pipes.

The <sys/sysmacros.h> header file provides three macros for manipulating dev_t values. The makedev() macro takes a major number as its first argument and a minor number as its second, and it returns a dev_t suitable for mknod(). The major() and minor() macros take a dev_t value as their sole argument and return the device's major and minor numbers, respectively.

The mknod program available under Linux provides a user-level interface to the mknod() system call (see man 1 mknod for details). Here is a simple reimplementation of mknod to illustrate the mknod() system call. Notice that the program creates the file with mode 0666 (giving read and write access to all users), and it depends on the process's umask setting to get the permissions right.

```
 1: /* mknod.c */
 2:
 3: /* Create the device or named pipe specified on the command line.
 4:    See the mknod(1) man page for details on the command line
 5:    parameters. */
 6:
 7: #include <errno.h>
```

```
 8: #include <stdio.h>
 9: #include <stdlib.h>
10: #include <string.h>
11: #include <sys/stat.h>
12: #include <sys/sysmacros.h>
13: #include <unistd.h>
14:
15: void usage(void) {
16:     fprintf(stderr, "usage: mknod <path> [b|c|u|p] "
17:                         "<major> <minor>\n");
18:      exit(1);
19: }
20:
21: int main(int argc, const char ** argv) {
22:     int major = 0, minor = 0;
23:     const char * path;
24:     int mode = 0666;
25:     char *end;
26:     int args;
27:
28:     /* We always need at least the type of inode to create, and
29:         the path for it. */
30:     if (argc < 3) usage();
31:
32:     path = argv[1];
33:
34:     /* the second argument tells us the type of node to create */
35:     if (!strcmp(argv[2], "b")) {
36:         mode |= S_IFBLK;
37:         args = 5;
38:     } else if (!strcmp(argv[2], "c") || !strcmp(argv[2], "u")) {
39:         mode |= S_IFCHR;
40:         args = 5;
41:     } else if (!strcmp(argv[2], "p")) {
42:         mode |= S_IFIFO;
43:         args = 3;
44:     } else {
45:         fprintf(stderr, "unknown node type %s\n", argv[2]);
46:         return 1;
47:     }
48:
```

```
49:        /* args tells us how many parameters to expect, as we need more
50:            information to create device files than named pipes */
51:        if (argc != args) usage();
52:
53:        if (args == 5) {
54:            /* get the major and minor numbers for the device file to
55:                create */
56:            major = strtol(argv[3], &end, 0);
57:            if (*end) {
58:                fprintf(stderr, "bad major number %s\n", argv[3]);
59:                return 1;
60:            }
61:
62:            minor = strtol(argv[4], &end, 0);
63:            if (*end) {
64:                fprintf(stderr, "bad minor number %s\n", argv[4]);
65:                return 1;
66:            }
67:        }
68:
69:        /* if we're creating a named pipe, the final parameter is
70:            ignored */
71:        if (mknod(path, mode, makedev(major, minor))) {
72:            fprintf(stderr, "mknod failed: %s\n", strerror(errno));
73:            return 1;
74:        }
75:
76:        return 0;
77: }
```

11.4.2 Creating Hard Links

When multiple file names in the file system refer to a single inode, the files
are called **hard links** to one other. All the file names must reside in the
same physical file system (normally, this means they must all be on the
same device). When a file has multiple hard links, each of those file names
is an exact peer—there is no way to tell which file name was originally
used. One benefit of this model is that removing one hard link does not
remove the file from the device—it stays until all the links to it are removed.
The link() system call links a new file name to an existing inode.

```
#include <unistd.h>

int link(const char * origpath, const char * newpath);
```

The origpath refers to a pathname that already exists; newpath is the path for the new hard link. Any user may create a link to a file he has read access to, as long as he has write access for the directory in which he is creating the link and execute permissions on the directory origpath is in. Only the root user has ever been allowed to create hard links to directories, but doing so was generally a bad idea, because most file systems and several utilities do not handle it very well; it is now entirely disallowed.

11.4.3 Using Symbolic Links

Symbolic links are a more flexible type of link than hard links, but they do not share the peer relationship that hard links enjoy. Whereas hard links share an inode, symbolic links point to other file names. If the destination file name is removed, the symbolic link then points to a file that does not exist, resulting in a **dangling link**. Using symbolic links between subdirectories is common, and symbolic links may also cross physical file system boundaries, which hard links cannot.

Almost all system calls that access files by their pathname automatically follow symbolic links to find the proper inode. The following calls do not follow symbolic links under Linux:

- chown()
- lstat()
- readlink()
- rename()
- unlink()

Creating symbolic links is just like creating hard links, but the symlink() system call is used instead.

```
#include <unistd.h>

int symlink(const char * origpath, const char * newpath);
```

If the call is successful, the file newpath gets created as a symbolic link pointing to origpath (often newpath is said to *contain* oldpath as its value).

Finding the value of the symbolic link is a bit more complicated.

```
#include <unistd.h>

int readlink(const char * pathname, char * buf,
             size_t bufsiz);
```

The buffer that buf points to is filled in by the contents of the pathname symlink as long as buf is long enough to hold the contents. bufsize should contain the length of buf in bytes. Usually, the PATH_MAX constant is used for the size of the buffer, as that should be big enough to hold the contents of any symlink.[20] One oddity of readlink() is that it does not end the string it writes to buf with a '\0' character, so buf is not a valid C string even if readlink() succeeds. It instead returns the number of bytes written to buf on success, and -1 on error. Thanks to this quirk, code that uses readlink() often looks like this:

```
char buf[PATH_MAX + 1];
int bytes;

if ((bytes = readlink(pathname, buf, sizeof(buf) - 1)) < 0) {
    perror("error in readlink");
} else {
    buf[bytes] = '\0';
}
```

---

20. Although PATH_MAX is not guaranteed to be large enough, it is, for all practical purposes. If you are dealing with pathological cases, you should call readlink() iteratively, making the buffer bigger until readlink() returns a value smaller than bufsiz.

11.4.4 Removing Files

Removing a file removes the pointer to its inode and removes the file's data if there are no other hard links to the file. If any processes have the file open, the file's inode is preserved until the final process closes the file, and then the inode and the file's data are both discarded. As there is no way of forcing a file to be removed immediately, this operation is called **unlinking** the file, since it removes a file name/inode link.

```
#include <unistd.h>

int unlink(char * pathname);
```

11.4.5 Renaming Files

A file name may be changed to any other file name as long as both names are on the same physical partition (this is the same limit that applies to creating hard links). If the new file name already references a file, that name is unlinked before the move takes place. The rename() system call is guaranteed to be atomic. Other processes on the system always see the file in existence under one name or the other; there is no point at which the file does not exist under either name, nor under both names. As open files are not related to file names (only to inodes), renaming a file that other processes have open does not affect those other processes in any way. Here is what the system call looks like:

```
#include <unistd.h>

int rename(const char * oldpath, const char * newpath);
```

After the call, the file referenced by oldpath may be referenced by newpath, but not by oldpath.

11.5 Manipulating File Descriptors

Nearly all the file-related system calls we have talked about, with the exception of `lseek()`, manipulate a file's inode, which causes their results to be shared among processes that have the file open. There are a few system calls that instead act on the file descriptor itself. The `fcntl()` system call can be used for numerous file descriptor manipulations. `fcntl()` looks like this:

```
#include <fcntl.h>

int fcntl(int fd, int command, long arg);
```

For many commands, `arg` is not used. We discuss most of `fcntl()`'s uses here. It is also used for file locking, file leases, and nonblocking I/O, which are discussed in Chapter 13, as well as directory change notification, which is presented in Chapter 14.

11.5.1 Changing the Access Mode for an Open File

The append mode (as indicated by the `O_APPEND` flag when the file is opened) and nonblocking mode (the `O_NONBLOCK` flag), can be turned on and off after a file has already been opened through the `fcntl()`'s `F_SETFL` command. The `arg` parameter should be the flags that should be set—if one of the flags is not specified, it is turned off for `fd`.

`F_GETFL` may be used to query the current flags for the file. It returns all the flags, including the read/write mode the file was opened in. `F_SETFL` allows only setting the flags mentioned above; any other flags that are present in the `arg` parameter are ignored.

```
fcntl(fd, F_SETFL, fcntl(fd, F_GETFL, 0) | O_RDONLY);
```

is perfectly legal, but it does not accomplish anything. Turning on append mode for a file descriptor looks like this:

```
fcntl(fd, F_SETFL, fcntl(fd, F_GETFL, 0) | O_APPEND);
```

Note that care was taken to preserve the `O_NONBLOCK` setting. Turning append mode off looks similar:

```
fcntl(fd, F_SETFL, fcntl(fd, F_GETFL, 0) & ~O_APPEND);
```

11.5.2 Modifiying the close-on-exec Flag

During an `exec()` system call, file descriptors are normally left open for the new program to use. In certain cases, you may wish to have files closed when you call `exec()`. Rather than closing them by hand, you can ask the system to close a certain file descriptor when `exec()` is called through `fcntl()`'s `F_GETFD` and `F_SETFD` commands. If the close-on-exec flag is set when `F_GETFD` is used, `fcntl()` returns non-0; otherwise, it returns 0. The close-on-exec flag is set through `F_SETFD`; it is disabled if `arg` is 0 and enabled otherwise.

Here is how you would force `fd` to be closed when the process `exec()`s:

```
fcntl(fd, F_SETFD, 1);
```

11.5.3 Duplicating File Descriptors

Occasionally, a process needs to create a new file descriptor that references a file that is already open. Shells use this functionality to redirect standard input, output, and error at the user's request. If the process does not care what file descriptor is used for the new reference, it should use `dup()`.

```
#include <unistd.h>

int dup(int oldfd);
```

`dup()` returns a file descriptor that references the same inode as `oldfd`, or -1 on an error. The `oldfd` is still a valid file descriptor and still references the original file. The new file descriptor is always the smallest file descriptor currently available. If the process needs the new file descriptor to have a particular value (such as 0 to change its standard input), it should use `dup2()` instead.

```
#include <unistd.h>

int dup2(int oldfd, int newfd);
```

If newfd references an already open file descriptor, that file descriptor is closed. If the call succeeds, it returns the new file descriptor and newfd references the same file as oldfd. The fcntl() system call provides almost the same functionality through the F_DUPFD command. The first argument, fd, is the already open file descriptor. The new file descriptor is the first available file descriptor that is the same or larger than the last argument to fcntl(). (This is different than how dup2() works.) You could implement dup2() through fcntl() like this:

```
int dup2(int oldfd, int newfd) {
    close(newfd);                        /* ensure newfd is available */
    return fcntl(oldfd, F_DUPFD, newfd);
}
```

Creating two duped file descriptors that reference the same file is not the same as opening a file twice. Nearly all duped file descriptors' attributes are shared; they share a common current position, access mode, and locks. (These items are stored in a **file structure**,[21] one of which is created each time the file is opened. A file descriptor refers to a file structure, and dup()ed file descriptors refer to a single file structure.) The only attribute that can be independently controlled for the two file descriptors is their close-on-exec status. After the process has fork()ed, the parent's open files are inherited by the child, and those pairs of file descriptors (one in the parent and one in the new child) behave exactly like a file descriptor that has been duped with the current position and most other attributes being shared.[22]

---

21. File structures are also known as file table entries or open file objects, depending on the operating system.
22. The file descriptor in each process refers to the same file structure.

11.6   Creating Unnamed Pipes

Unnamed pipes are similar to named pipes, but they do not exist in the file system. They have no pathnames associated with them, and they and all their remnants disappear after the final file descriptor that references them is closed. They are almost exclusively used for interprocess communication between a child and parent processes or between sibling processes.

Shells use unnamed pipes to execute commands such as `ls | head`. The `ls` process writes to the same pipe that `head` reads its input from, yielding the results the user intended.

Creating an unnamed pipe results in two file descriptors, one of which is read-only and the other one of which is write-only.

```
#include <unistd.h>

int pipe(int fds[2]);
```

The sole parameter is filled in with the two returned file descriptors, `fds[0]` for reading and `fds[1]` for writing.

11.7   Adding Redirection to `ladsh`

Now that we have covered the basics of file manipulation, we can teach `ladsh` to redirect input and output through files and pipes. ladsh2.c, which we present here, handles pipes (denoted by a | in `ladsh` commands, just as in most shells) and input and output redirection for arbitrary file descriptors. We show only the modified pieces of code here—full source to ladsh2.c is available from http://ladweb.net/lad/src/. The changes to `parseCommand()` are a simple exercise in string parsing, so we do not bother discussing them here.

11.7.1 The Data Structures

Although ladsh1.c included the concept of a job as multiple processes (presumably tied together by pipes), it did not provide a way of specifying which files to use for a child's input and output. To allow for this, new data structures are introduced and existing ones modified.

```
24:                          REDIRECT_APPEND };
25:
26: struct redirectionSpecifier {
27:     enum redirectionType type;  /* type of redirection */
28:     int fd;                     /* file descriptor being redirected */
29:     char * filename;            /* file to redirect fd to */
30: };
31:
32: struct childProgram {
33:     pid_t pid;                  /* 0 if exited */
34:     char ** argv;               /* program name and arguments */
35:     int numRedirections;        /* elements in redirection array */
36:     struct redirectionSpecifier * redirections;  /* I/O redirs */
37: };
```

`struct redirectionSpecifier` tells ladsh2.c how to set up a single file descriptor. It contains an `enum redirectionType` that tells us whether this redirection is an input redirection, an output redirection that should be appended to an already existing file, or an output redirection that replaces any existing file. It also includes the file descriptor that is being redirected, as well as the name of the file involved. Each child program (`struct childProgram`) now specifies an arbitrary number of redirections for itself.

These new data structures are not involved in setting up pipes between processes. As a job is defined as multiple child processes with pipes tying them together, there is no need for more explicit information describing the pipes. Figure 11.1 shows how these new data structures would look for the command `tail < input-file | sort > output-file`.

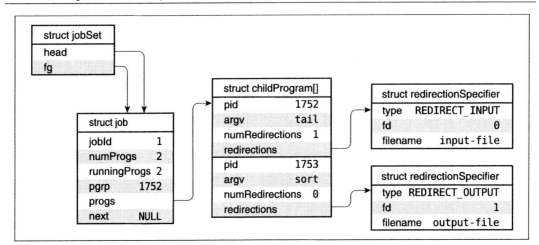

Figure 11.1 Job Data Structures for `ladsh2.c`

11.7.2 Changing the Code

Once `parseCommand()` has set up the data structures properly, running the commands in the proper sequence is easy enough, as long as you watch the details. First of all, we added a loop to `runCommand()` to start the child processes, because there could now be multiple children. Before entering the loop, we set up `nextin` and `nextout`, which are the file descriptors to use for the standard input and the standard output of the next process we start. To begin with, we use the same stdin and stdout as the shell.

Now we take a look at what happens inside the loop. The basic idea is as follows:

1. If this is the final process in the job, make sure `nextout` points at stdout. Otherwise, we need to connect the output of this job to the input side of an unnamed pipe.

2. Fork the new process. Inside the child, redirect stdin and stdout as specified by `nextout`, `nextin`, and any file redirections that were specified.

3. Back in the parent, we close the `nextin` and `nextout` used by the just-started child (unless they are the shell's own stdin or stdout).

4. Now set up the next process in the job to receive its input from output of the process we just created (through `nextin`).

Here is how these ideas translate into C:

```
365:    nextin = 0, nextout = 1;
366:    for (i = 0; i < newJob.numProgs; i++) {
367:        if ((i + 1) < newJob.numProgs) {
368:            pipe(pipefds);
369:            nextout = pipefds[1];
370:        } else {
371:            nextout = 1;
372:        }
373:
374:        if (!(newJob.progs[i].pid = fork())) {
375:            if (nextin != 0) {
376:                dup2(nextin, 0);
377:                close(nextin);
378:            }
379:
380:            if (nextout != 1) {
381:                dup2(nextout, 1);
382:                close(nextout);
383:            }
384:
385:            /* explicit redirections override pipes */
386:            setupRedirections(newJob.progs + i);
387:
388:            execvp(newJob.progs[i].argv[0], newJob.progs[i].argv);
389:            fprintf(stderr, "exec() of %s failed: %s\n",
390:                    newJob.progs[i].argv[0],
391:                    strerror(errno));
392:            exit(1);
393:        }
394:
395:        /* put our child in the process group whose leader is the
396:           first process in this pipe */
397:        setpgid(newJob.progs[i].pid, newJob.progs[0].pid);
398:
399:        if (nextin != 0) close(nextin);
400:        if (nextout != 1) close(nextout);
```

```
401:
402:          /* If there isn't another process, nextin is garbage
403:             but it doesn't matter */
404:          nextin = pipefds[0];
```

The only other code added to ladsh2.c to allow redirection was setupRedi-
rections(), the source of which appears unchanged in all subsequent versions of ladsh. Its job is to process the struct redirectionSpecifier
specifiers for a child job and modify the child's file descriptors as appropriate. We recommend reading over the function as it appears in Appendix B
to ensure you understand its implementation.

CHAPTER 12

Signal Processing

Signals are the simplest form of interprocess communication in the POSIX world. They allow a process to be asynchronously interrupted by another process (or by the kernel) to handle some event. Once the signal has been handled, the interrupted process resumes from the point of interruption. Signals are used for tasks such as terminating processes and telling daemons to reread their configuration file.

Signals have always been an integral part of Unix. The kernel uses them to inform a process of a variety of events, including:

- The death of one of the process's children.

- An alarm set by the process has expired.

- The size of the terminal window has changed.

All of these messages share an important property: They are all asynchronous. The process has no control over when one of its children exits—it could happen at any point during the parent's execution. Each of these events causes a signal to be sent to the process. When a process is signaled, the process can do one of three things:

1. Ignore the signal.

2. Have the kernel run a special part of the process before allowing the process to continue (called **catching** a signal).

3. Let the kernel invoke its default action, which depends on the particular signal being sent.

Conceptually, this is fairly straightforward. However, the age of the signal feature shows when you compare the different signal interfaces that are supported by the various flavors of Unix. BSD, System V, and System 3 supported different and incompatible signal APIs. POSIX defined a standard that is now supported by nearly all versions of Unix (including Linux), which was then extended to support new signal semantics (such as signal queuing) as part of the POSIX Real Time Signal definition. This chapter discusses the original implementation of Unix signals before explaining the base POSIX API and its Real Time Signal extensions, as many of the features in the POSIX API were motivated by weaknesses in earlier signal implementations.

12.1   Signal Concepts

12.1.1 Life Cycle of a Signal

Signals have a well-defined life; they are created, they are stored until the kernel can take an action based on the signal, and then they cause an action to occur. Creating a signal is variously called **raising**, **generating**, or **sending** a signal. Normally, a process *sends* a signal to another process while the kernel *generates* a signal to send to a process. When a process sends itself a signal, it is often called *raising* the signal. These terms are not used with complete consistency, however.

During the time between a signal being sent and the signal causing an action to occur, the signal is called **pending**. This means that the kernel knows the signal needs to be handled, but it has not yet had the chance to do so. Once the signal is given to the target process, the signal has been **delivered**. If delivering the signal causes a special piece of code (a **signal handler**) to be run, the signal has been **caught**. There are ways for a process to prevent asynchronous delivery of a signal but still handle the signal (through the `sigwait()` system call, for example). When this happens, the signal has been **accepted**.

To help keep things clear, we use this set of terminology throughout the book.[1]

---

1. This terminology is also used in much of the standards literature, including the Single Unix Specification.

12.1.2 Simple Signals

Originally, handling signals was simple. The `signal()` system call was used to tell the kernel how to deliver a particular signal to the process:

```
#include <signal.h>

void * signal(int signum, void * handler);
```

`signum` is the signal to handle, and `handler` defines the action to perform when the signal is delivered. Normally, the handler is a pointer to a function that takes no parameters and returns no value. When the signal is delivered to the process, the kernel executes the handler function as soon as possible. Once the function returns, the kernel resumes process execution wherever it was interrupted. System-level engineers will recognize this type of signal mechanism as analogous to hardware interrupt delivery; interrupts and signals are very similar and present many of the same problems.

There are many signal numbers available. Table 12.1 on page 217 lists all the non-real-time signals Linux currently supports. They have symbolic names that begin with `SIG`, and we use `SIGFOO` when we talk about a generic signal.

The `handler` can take on two special values, `SIG_IGN` and `SIG_DFL` (both of which are defined through `<signal.h>`). If `SIG_IGN` is specified, the signal is ignored; `SIG_DFL` tells the kernel to perform the default action for the signal, usually killing the process or ignoring the signal. Two signals, `SIGKILL` and `SIGSTOP`, cannot be caught. The kernel always performs the default action for these two signals, killing the process and stopping the process, respectively.

The `signal()` function returns the previous signal handler (which could have been `SIG_IGN` or `SIG_DFL`). Signal handlers are preserved when new processes are created by `fork()`, and any signals that are set to `SIG_IGN` remain ignored after an `exec()`.[2] All signals not being ignored are set to `SIG_DFL` after an `exec()`.

All this seems simple enough until you ask yourself: What will happen if `SIGFOO` is sent to a process that is already running a signal handler for

---

2. This is the mechanism used by the `nohup` utility.

SIGFOO? The obvious thing for the kernel to do is interrupt the process and run the signal handler again. This creates two problems. First, the signal handler must function properly if it is invoked while it is already running. Although this may be easy, signal handlers that manipulate program-wide resources, such as global data structures or files, need to be written very carefully. Functions that behave properly when they are called in this manner are called **reentrant functions**.[3]

The simple locking techniques that are sufficient to coordinate data access between concurrent processes do not allow reentrancy. For example, the file-locking techniques presented in Chapter 13 cannot be used to allow a signal handler that manipulates a data file to be reentrant. When the signal handler is called the first time, it can lock the data file just fine and begin writing to it. If the signal handler is then interrupted by another signal while it holds the lock, the second invocation of the signal handler cannot lock the file, because the first invocation holds the lock. Unfortunately, the invocation that holds the lock is suspended until the invocation that wants the lock finishes running.

The difficulty of writing reentrant signal handlers is a major reason for the kernel not to deliver signals that a process is already handling. Such a model also makes it difficult for processes to handle a large number of signals that are being sent to the process very rapidly. As each signal results in a new invocation of the signal handler, the process's stack grows without bound, despite the program itself being well-behaved.

The first solution to this problem was ill-conceived. Before the signal handler was invoked, the handler for that signal was reset to SIG_DFL and the signal handler was expected to set a more appropriate signal disposition as soon as it could. Although this did simplify writing signal handlers, it made it impossible for a developer to handle signals in a reliable fashion. If two occurrences of the same signal occurred quickly, the kernel handled the second signal in the default fashion. That meant that the second signal was ignored (and lost forever) or the process was terminated. This signal implementation is known as **unreliable signals** because it makes it impossible to write well behaved signal handlers.

---

3. The need for reentrant functions is not limited to signal handlers. Multithreaded applications must take great care to ensure proper reentrancy and locking.

Unfortunately, this is exactly the signal model used in the ANSI/ISO C standard.[4] Although **reliable signal** APIs that fix these shortcomings are widespread, ANSI/ISO's unreliable standardization of the `signal()` function will probably be around forever.

12.1.3 Reliable Signals

The implementers of BSD realized that a solution to the multiple signals problem would be to simply wait until the process finishes handling the first signal to deliver the second signal. This ensures that both signals are received and removes the risk of stack overflows. Recall that when the kernel is holding a signal for later delivery, the signal is said to be *pending*.

However, if a process is sent `SIGFOO` while a `SIGFOO` signal is already pending, only one of those `SIGFOO` signals is delivered to the process. There is no way for a process to know how many times a signal was sent to it, as multiple signals may have been coalesced into one. This is not normally much of a problem, however. As signals do not carry any information other than the signal number with them, sending a signal twice in a very short period of time is usually the same as sending it a single time, so if the program receives the signal only once, it does not matter much. This is different from performing the default action on the second signal (which occurs with unreliable signals).[5]

The idea of a signal's being automatically **blocked** has been extended to allow a process to explicitly block signals. This makes it easy to protect critical pieces of code, while still handling all the signals that are sent. Such protection lets the signal handlers manipulate data structures that are maintained by other pieces of the code by providing simple synchronization.

---

4. Well, not *exactly*. The ANSI/ISO C signal handling model is not as well specified as the one we just presented. It does, however, mandate that signal handlers be reset to `SIG_DFL` before a signal is delivered, forcing all ANSI/ISO C `signal()` functions to be unreliable.
5. The POSIX Real Time Signal specification allows some signals to be queued and for signals to carry a limited amount of data, changing this model significantly. Real-time signals are discussed on pages 227–230.

Although BSD provided the basic signal model POSIX adopted, the POSIX standard committee made it simpler for system calls to modify the disposition of groups of signals by introducing new system calls that operate on sets of signals. A set of signals is represented by the data type `sigset_t`, and a set of macros is provided to manipulate it.[6]

12.1.4 Signals and System Calls

A signal is often delivered to a process that is waiting for an external event to occur. For instance, a text editor is often waiting for `read()` to return input from the terminal. When the system administrator sends the process a `SIGTERM` signal (the normal signal sent by the `kill` command, allowing a process to terminate cleanly), the process could handle it in a few ways:

1. It could make no attempt to catch the signal and be terminated by the kernel (the default handling of `SIGTERM`). This would leave the user's terminal in a nonstandard configuration, making it difficult for them to continue.

2. It could catch the signal, have the signal handler clean up the terminal, and then exit. Although this is appealing, in complex programs it is difficult to write a signal handler that knows enough about what the program was doing when it was interrupted to clean it up properly.

3. It could catch the signal, set a flag indicating that the signal occurred, and somehow cause the blocked system call (in this case, `read()`) to exit with an error indicating something unusual happened. The normal execution pathway could then check for the flag and handle it appropriately.

As the final choice seems much cleaner and easier than the others, the original signal implementation caused **slow system calls** to return `EINTR` when they were interrupted by a signal, whereas **fast system calls** were completed before the signal was delivered.

---

6. This is similar to the `fd_set` type used by the `select()` system call discussed in Chapter 13.

Slow system calls take an indeterminate amount of time to complete. System calls that wait for unpredictable resources, such as other processes, network data, or a *Homo sapiens* to perform some action are considered slow. The wait() family of system calls, for example, does not normally return until a child process exits. As there is no way to know how long that may take, wait() is a slow system call. File access system calls are considered slow if they access slow files, and fast if they access fast files.[7]

It was the process's job to handle EINTR and restart system calls as necessary. Although this provided all the functionality people needed, it made it more difficult to write code that handled signals. Every time read() was called on a slow file descriptor, the code had to be modified to check for EINTR and restart the call, or the code might not perform as expected.

To "simplify" things, 4.2BSD automatically restarted certain system calls (notably read() and write()). For the most common operations, programs no longer needed to worry about EINTR because the system call would continue after the process handled the signal. Later versions of Unix changed which system calls would be automatically restarted, and 4.3BSD allows you to choose whether to restart system calls. The POSIX signal standard does not specify which behavior should be used, but all popular systems agree on how to handle this case. By default, system calls are not restarted, but for each signal, the process can set a flag that indicates that it would like the system to automatically restart system calls interrupted by that signal.

12.2 The Linux (and POSIX) Signal API

12.2.1 Sending Signals

Sending signals from one process to another is normally done through the kill() system call. This system call is discussed in detail on page 129. A variant of kill() is tkill(), which is not intended to be used directly by programs.

```
int tkill(pid_t pid, int signum);
```

---

7. The difference between fast files and slow files is the same as the difference between fast and slow system calls and is discussed in more detail on page 167.

There are two differences between kill() and tkill().[8] First, the pid must be a positive number; tkill() cannot be used to send signals to groups of processes like kill() can. The other difference allows signal handlers to detect whether kill() or tkill() was used to generate the signal; see page 232 for details.

The raise() function, which is how ANSI/ISO C specifies signal generation, uses the tkill() system call to generate the signal on Linux systems.

```
int raise(int signum);
```

The raise() function sends the signal specified by signum to the current process.[9]

12.2.2 Using sigset_t

Most POSIX signal functions take a set of signals as one of the parameters (or as part of one of the parameters). The sigset_t data type is used to represent a signal set, and it is defined in <signal.h>. POSIX defines five functions for manipulating signal sets:

```
#include <signal.h>

int sigemptyset(sigset_t *set);
int sigfillset(sigset_t *set);
int sigaddset(sigset_t *set, int signum);
int sigdelset(sigset_t *set, int signum);
int sigismember(const sigset_t *set, int signum);


int sigemptyset(sigset_t *set);
```
    Makes the signal set pointed to by set empty (no signals are present in the set).

```
int sigfillset(sigset_t *set);
```
    Includes all available signals in set.

---

8. There are some other differences between the two relating to multithreaded programs, which we do not cover in this book.
9. It actually sends the signal to the current thread of the current process.

```
int sigaddset(sigset_t *set, int signum);
```
     Adds signal signum to set.

```
int sigdelset(sigset_t *set, int signum);
```
     Removes signal signum from set.

```
int sigismember(const sigset_t *set, int signum);
```
     Returns non-0 if signal signum is in set, 0 otherwise.

The only way any of these functions can return an error is if their signum parameter is an invalid signal. In that case, they return EINVAL. Needless to say, this should never happen.

12.2.3 Catching Signals

Rather than use the signal() function (whose semantics were already irregular because of its evolution), POSIX programs register signal handlers through sigaction().

```
#include <signal.h>

int sigaction(int signum, struct sigaction * act,
              struct sigaction * oact);
```

This system call sets the handler for signal signum as defined by act. If oact is not NULL, it is set to describe the disposition of the signal before sigaction() was called. If act is NULL, the current signal disposition is left unchanged, allowing a program to discover the current disposition for a signal without modifying it. sigaction() returns 0 on success, non-0 on error. Errors occur only if one or more of the parameters passed to sigaction() are invalid.

The kernel's handling of a signal is fully described by struct sigaction.

```
#include <signal.h>

struct sigaction {
        __sighandler_t sa_handler;
        sigset_t sa_mask;
        int sa_flags;
};
```

`sa_handler` is a pointer to a function with the following prototype:

```
void handler(int signum);
```

where `signum` is set to the signal number that caused the function to be invoked. `sa_handlers` can point to a function of this type, or contain `SIG_IGN` or `SIG_DFL`.

A program also specifies a set of signals that should be blocked while the signal handler is being run. If a signal handler is designed to handle several different signals (which the `signum` parameter makes easy to do), this feature is essential to prevent race conditions. The `sa_mask` is a signal set that includes all the signals that should be blocked when the handler for the signal is invoked. However, the signal that is being delivered is blocked no matter what `sa_mask` contains—if you do not want it blocked, specify this through the `sa_flags` member of `struct sigaction`.

The `sa_flags` member lets the process modify various signal behaviors. It consists of one or more flags bitwise OR'ed together.[10]

`SA_NOCLDSTOP`	Normally, `SIGCHLD` is generated when one of a process's children has terminated or stopped (that is, whenever `wait4()` would return status information on the process). If `SA_NOCLDSTOP` has been specified for the `SIGCHLD` signal, the signal is generated only when a child process has terminated; children stopped do not cause any signal. `SA_NOCLDSTOP` has no effect on any other signal.
`SA_NODEFER`	When the process's signal handler is invoked, the signal is not automatically blocked. Using this flag results in unreliable signals and should be used only to emulate unreliable signals for applications that depend on this behavior. It is identical to System V's `SA_NOMASK` flag.
`SA_RESETHAND`	When this signal is sent, the signal handler is reset to `SIG_DFL`. This flag allows the ANSI/ISO C `signal()`

---

10. The flags given are those defined by the Single Unix Specification. Many of these have other names that are described in the text.

function to be emulated in a user-space library. This is identical to System V's `SIG_ONESHOT` flag.

SA_RESTART When the signal is sent to the process while it is executing a slow system call, the system call is restarted after the signal handler returns. If this flag is not specified, the system call instead returns an error and sets `errno` to `EINTR`.

12.2.4 Manipulating a Process's Signal Mask

It is common for a signal handler to manipulate data structures that are used in other parts of the program. Unfortunately, the asynchronous nature of signals makes this dangerous unless it is done carefully. Manipulating all but the most simple of data structures subjects a program to race conditions.

An example should make this problem a bit more clear. Here is a simple `SIGHUP` handler that changes the value of a string pointed to by the global variable `someString`:

```
void handleHup(int signum) {
    free(someString);
    someString = strdup("a different string");
}
```

In real-world programs, the new value for `someString` would probably be read from an external source (such as a FIFO), but the same concepts apply. Now assume the main part of a program is copying a string (this code is similar to the code in a `strcpy()` implementation, although not very optimized) when a `SIGHUP` signal arrives:

```
src = someString;
while (*src)
    *dest++ = *src++;
```

When the main part of the program resumes execution, src will be pointing to memory that was freed by the signal handler. Needless to say, this is a very bad idea.[11]

To solve this type of problem, the POSIX signal API allows a process to block an arbitrary set of signals from being delivered to the process. The signals are not thrown away—their delivery is delayed until the process indicates it is willing to handle those signals by unblocking them. To make the string copy shown earlier legal, the program would have to block SIGHUP before the string copy and unblock it afterward. After discussing the interface for manipulating the signal mask, we present a proper version of the code.

The set of signals that a process is currently blocking is often called the process's **signal mask**. The signal mask for a process is a sigset_t that contains the signals currently being blocked. The sigprocmask() function allows a process to control its current signal mask.

```
#include <signal.h>

int sigprocmask(int what, const sigset_t * set, sigset_t * oldset);
```

The first parameter, what, describes how the signal mask is to be manipulated. If set is NULL, what is ignored.

SIG_BLOCK   The signals in set are added to the current signal mask.

SIG_UNBLOCK   The signals in set are removed from the current signal mask.

SIG_SETMASK   Precisely the signals in set are blocked—the rest are unblocked.

In all three cases, the sigset_t pointed to by oldset is set to the original signal mask unless oldset is NULL, in which case oldset is ignored. The following finds the current signal mask for the running process:

---

11. Although referencing memory that has been freed may work on some systems, it is not portable. Some malloc() implementations return memory to the operating system, which causes referencing the returned memory to cause a segmentation fault; others overwrite portions of the freed memory with bookkeeping information.

```
sigprocmask(SIG_BLOCK, NULL, &currentSet);
```

The `sigprocmask()` system call allows us to fix the code presented earlier, which was afflicted by a race condition. All we need to do is block `SIGHUP` before we copy the string and unblock it afterward. The following change renders the code safe:

```
sigset_t hup;

sigemptyset(&hup);
sigaddset(&hup, SIGHUP);

sigprocmask(SIG_BLOCK, &hup, NULL);
src = someString;
while (*src)
    *dest++ = *src++;
sigprocmask(SIG_UNBLOCK, &hup, NULL);
```

The complexity of making signal handlers safe from race conditions should encourage you to keep your signal handlers as simple as possible.

12.2.5 Finding the Set of Pending Signals

It is easy to find out which signals are currently pending (signals that need to be delivered, but are currently blocked).

```
#include <signal.h>

int sigpending(sigset_t * set);
```

On return, the `sigset_t` pointed to by `set` contains the signals currently pending.

12.2.6 Waiting for Signals

When a program is built primarily around signals, it is often designed to wait for a signal to occur before continuing. The `pause()` system call provides a simple way of doing this.

```
#include <unistd.h>

int pause(void);
```

`pause()` does not return until after a signal has been delivered to the process. If a signal handler is present for that signal, the signal handler is run before `pause()` returns. `pause()` always returns -1 and sets `errno` to EINTR.

The `sigsuspend()` system call provides an alternate method of waiting for a signal call.

```
#include <signal.h>

int sigsuspend(const sigset_t * mask);
```

Like `pause()`, `sigsuspend()` suspends the process until a signal has been received (and processed by a signal handler, if one is available), returning -1 and setting `errno` to EINTR.

Unlike `pause()`, `sigsuspend()` temporarily sets the process's signal mask to the value pointed to by the `mask` parameter before waiting for a signal to occur. Once the signal occurs, the signal mask is restored to the value it had before `sigsuspend()` was called. This allows a process to wait for a particular signal to occur by blocking all other signals.[12]

---

12. Using `sigprocmask()` and `pause()` to get this behavior presents a race condition if the signal that is being waited for occurs between the two system calls.

Table 12.1 Signals

Signal	Description	Default Action
SIGABRT	Delivered by abort()	Terminate, core
SIGALRM	An alarm() has expired	Terminate
SIGBUS	Hardware-dependent error	Terminate, core
SIGCHLD	Child process terminated	Ignored
SIGCONT	Process has been continued after being stopped	Ignored
SIGFPE	Arithmetic point exception	Terminate, core
SIGHUP	The process's controlling tty was closed	Terminate
SIGILL	An illegal instruction was encountered	Terminate, core
SIGINT	User sent the interrupt character (^C)	Terminate
SIGIO	Asynchronous I/O has been received	Terminate
SIGKILL	Uncatchable process termination	Terminate
SIGPIPE	Process wrote to a pipe w/o any readers	Terminate
SIGPROF	Profiling segment ended	Terminate
SIGPWR	Power failure detected	Terminate
SIGQUIT	User sent the quit character (^\)	Terminate, core
SIGSEGV	Memory violation	Terminate, core
SIGSTOP	Stops the process without terminating it	Process stopped
SIGSYS	An invalid system call was made	Terminate, core
SIGTERM	Catchable termination request	Terminate
SIGTRAP	Breakpoint instruction encountered	Terminate, core
SIGTSTP	User sent suspend character (^Z)	Process stopped
SIGTTIN	Background process read from controlling tty	Process stopped
SIGTTOU	Background process wrote to controlling tty	Process stopped
SIGURG	Urgent I/O condition	Ignored
SIGUSR1	Process-defined signal	Terminate
SIGUSR2	Process-defined signal	Terminate
SIGVTALRM	setitimer() timer has expired	Terminate
SIGWINCH	Size of the controlling tty has changed	Ignored
SIGXCPU	CPU resource limit exceeded	Terminate, core
SIGXFSZ	File-size resource limit exceeded	Terminate, core

12.3 Available Signals

Linux has quite a few signals available for processes to use, all of which are summarized in Table 12.1. There are four default actions the kernel can take for a signal: ignore it, stop the process (it is still alive and can be restarted later), terminate the process, or terminate the process and generate a core dump.[13] The following are more detailed descriptions of each signal listed

---

13. See page 130 for more information on core dumps.

in Table 12.1:

SIGABRT   The abort() function sends this signal to the process that
           called it, terminating the process with a core file. Under
           Linux, the C library calls abort() whenever an assertion
           fails.[14]

SIGALRM   Sent when an alarm set by the alarm() system call has ex-
           pired. Alarms are the basis of the sleep() function dis-
           cussed in Chapter 18.

SIGBUS   When a process violates hardware constraints other than
           those related to memory protections, this signal is sent. This
           usually occurs on traditional Unix platforms when an un-
           aligned access occurs, but the Linux kernel fixes unaligned
           access and continues the process. Memory alignment is dis-
           cussed further on page 76.

SIGCHLD   This signal is sent to a process when one of that process's
           children has exited or stopped. This allows the process to
           avoid zombies by calling one of the wait() functions from
           the signal handler. If the parent always waits for its children
           to exit before continuing, this signal can be safely ignored.
           This signal is different from the SIGCLD signal provided by
           early releases of System V. SIGCLD is obsolete and should
           not be used anymore.

SIGCONT   This signal restarts a process that has been stopped. It may
           also be caught by a process, allowing it to take an action after
           being restarted. Most editors catch this signal and refresh
           the terminal when they are restarted. See Chapter 15 for
           more information on stopping and starting processes.

SIGFPE   This signal is sent when a process causes an arithmetic ex-
           ception. All floating-point exceptions, such as overflows and
           underflows, cause this signal, as does integer division by 0.

SIGHUP   When a terminal is disconnected, the session leader for the
           session associated with the terminal is sent a SIGHUP signal

---

14. Assertions are discussed in most introductory C books [Kernighan, 1988].

unless that terminal's `CLOCAL` flag has been set. If a session leader exits, `SIGHUP` is sent to the process group leader for each process group in the session. Most processes terminate when `SIGHUP` is received because it indicates the user is no longer present.

Many daemon processes interpret `SIGHUP` as a request to close and reopen log files and reread configuration files.

`SIGILL` The process attempted to run an illegal hardware instruction.

`SIGINT` This signal is sent to all processes in the foreground process group when the user presses the interrupt character (normally, ^C).

`SIGIO` An asynchronous I/O event has occurred. Asynchronous I/O is rarely used and is not documented in this book. We suggest consulting other books for information on using asynchronous I/O [Stevens, 1992].

`SIGKILL` This signal is generated only by `kill()` and allows a user to terminate a process unconditionally .

`SIGPIPE` The process has written to a pipe that has no readers.

`SIGPROF` The profile timer has expired. This signal is usually used by profilers, which are programs that examine another process's run-time characteristics. Profilers are normally used to optimize a program's execution speed by helping programmers to find execution bottlenecks.[15]

`SIGPWR` The system detected an impending loss of power. It is usually sent to init by a daemon that is monitoring the machine's power source, allowing the machine to be cleanly shut down before power failure.

`SIGQUIT` This signal is sent to all processes in the foreground process group when the user presses the quit character (usually, ^\).

---

15. The gprof utility, included with all Linux distributions, is a simple profiler.

SIGSEGV   This signal is sent when a process attempts to access memory it is not allowed to access. It is generated when a process tries to read from unmapped memory, execute a page of memory that has not been mapped with execute permissions, or write to memory it does not have write access to.

SIGSTOP   This signal is generated only by kill() and allows a user to unconditionally stop a process. See Chapter 15 for more information on stopping processes.

SIGSYS   When a program attempts a nonexistent system call, the kernel terminates the program with SIGSYS. This should never happen to programs that make system calls through the system's C library.

SIGTERM   This signal is generated only by kill() and allows a user to gracefully terminate a process. A process should exit as soon as possible after receiving this signal.

SIGTRAP   When a process has crossed a breakpoint, this signal is sent to the process. It is usually intercepted by a debugger process that set the breakpoint.

SIGTSTP   This signal is sent to all processes in the foreground process group when the user presses the suspend character (usually, ^Z). See Chapter 15 for more information on job control.

SIGTTIN   This signal is sent to a background process that has tried to read from its controlling terminal. See Chapter 15 for more information on job control.

SIGTTOU   This signal is sent to a background process that has tried to write to its controlling terminal. See Chapter 15 for more information on job control.

SIGURG   This signal is sent when out-of-band data has been received on a socket. Out-of-band data is an advanced networking topic outside the scope of this book; [Stevens, 2004] covers it thoroughly, however.

SIGUSR1   There is no defined use for this signal; processes may use it for whatever purposes they like.

SIGUSR2   There is no defined use for this signal; processes may use it for whatever purposes they like.

SIGVTALRM   Sent when a timer set by setitimer() has expired. For information on using timers, see Chapter 18.

SIGWINCH   When a terminal window has changed size, such as when an xterm is resized, all processes in the foreground process group for that process are sent SIGWINCH. See page 376 for information on finding the current size of the controlling terminal.

SIGXCPU   The process has exceeded its soft CPU limit. This signal is sent once per second until the process exceeds its hard CPU limit; once that happens the process is terminated with SIGKILL. For information on process resource limits, see pages 118–119.

SIGXFSZ   When a program exceeds its file size limit, SIGXFSZ is sent to it, which normally kills the process. If the signal is caught, the system call that would have exceeded the file size limit instead returns the error EFBIG. For information on process resource limits, see pages 118–119.

12.3.1 Describing Signals

Occasionally, an application needs a description of a signal to display to the user or put in a log. There are three ways to do this;[16] unfortunately, none of them is standardized.

The oldest method is through sys_siglist, which is an array of strings describing each signal, indexed by the signal number itself. It includes descriptions for all signals except the real-time signals. Using sys_siglist is more portable than the other methods described here. BSD systems

---

16. These methods parallel the ways of getting descriptions for system errors described in Chapter 9.

provide psignal(), which provides a shortcut for displaying messages. Here is a version of psignal():

```
#include <signal.h>
#include <stdio.h>

void psignal(int signum, const char * msg) {
    printf("%s: %s\n", msg, sys_siglist[signum]);
}
```

Note that it uses the same list of signals as sys_siglist, so real-time signals are excluded.

The GNU C library used by Linux provides one more method, strsignal(). This function is not provided by any standard, so to access the prototype C files need to define _GNU_SOURCE.

```
#define _GNU_SOURCE
#include <signal.h>

char * strsignal(int signum);
```

Like sys_siglist, strsignal() provides a description for signal number signum. It uses sys_siglist for most signals and constructs a description for the real-time signals. For example, SIGRTMIN + 5 would be described as "Real-time signal 5." For an example of strsignal() being used, look at lines 639–648 and 717 of ladsh4.c, which appears in Appendix B.

12.4 Writing Signal Handlers

Although a signal handler looks like a normal C function, it is not called like one. Rather than being run as part of a program's normal call sequence, signal handlers are called by the kernel. The key difference between the two cases is that a signal handler can be called at almost any time, even in the middle of a single C statement! There are only a few restrictions on when the system will call a signal handler on which you can rely:

1. The semantics of some signals restrict when they will be sent. SIGCHLD, for example, is not normally sent to a program that has no children.[17] Most signals are like SIGHUP, however, and are sent at unpredictable times.

2. If the process is in the middle of handling a particular signal, the signal handler is not reinvoked to handle the same signal unless the SA_NODEFER option was specified. The process can also block additional signals when a signal processor is running through the sa_mask member of struct sigaction.

3. The process can block signals while running a part of code through use of sigprocmask(). Page 215 has an example of using this facility to allow atomic updates to data structures.

Because signal handlers can be run at almost any time, it is important to write them so that they do not make unwarranted assumptions about what the rest of the program is doing at the time and so that they do not rearrange things in a way that could confuse the rest of the program when it starts running again.

One of the most important things to watch is modifying global data. Unless this is done carefully, race conditions result. The easiest way to keep updates of global data safe is simply to avoid them. The next best method is blocking all signal handlers that modify a particular data structure whenever the rest of the code is modifying it, ensuring that only one code segment is manipulating the data at a time.

Although it is safe for the signal handler to read a data structure when it has interrupted another reader of that structure, all other combinations are unsafe. It is no more safe for the signal handler to modify a data structure that the rest of the program is reading than it is for the signal handler to read a data structure the rest of the program is writing. Some specialized data structures have been designed to allow concurrent access, but those data structures are well beyond the scope of this book.

If you must access global data from a signal handler (which most signal handlers end up doing), keep the data structure simple. Although it is pretty

---

17. Although users can send SIGCHLD to any processes they own, programs are not expected to respond reasonably to unexpected signals.

easy to safely modify a single data element, such as an `int`, more complicated structures usually require blocking signals. Any global variables that a signal handler may modify should be declared with the `volatile` keyword. This tells the compiler that the variable may be changed outside the normal flow of the program and it should not try to optimize accesses to the variable.

The other thing to be careful of in signal handlers is calling other functions, as they may modify global data as well! The C stdio library tends to do this quite a bit and should never be used from a signal handler. Table 12.2 lists functions that are guaranteed to be safe to call from a signal handler;[18] all other system functions should be avoided.

12.5 Reopening Log Files

Most system daemons keep log files indicating what they have been busy doing. As many Unix systems stay up for months without interruption, these log files can grow quite large. Simply removing (or renaming) the log files occasionally is not a good solution because the daemons would simply keep writing to the files despite their inaccessibility, and having to stop and start each daemon while the log files are cleaned up would result in system downtime (albeit not much). A common way for daemons to manage this situation is to catch `SIGHUP` and reopen their log files. This allows **log rotation** (periodically starting new log files while keeping the old ones) to happen with a simple shell script like

```
cd /var/log
mv messages messages.old
killall -HUP syslogd
```

Logrotate[19] is one program that takes advantage of this feature to perform safe log rotation.

Including this ability in most daemons is straightforward. One of the easiest approaches is to include a global variable that indicates whether

---

18. The table lists functions that may not be present on some, or even any, Linux systems. We have included all of the functions that POSIX specifies as safe to call from signal handlers for completeness.

19. ftp://ftp.redhat.com/pub/redhat/code/logrotate/

Table 12.2 Reentrant Functions

abort()	accept()	access()
aio_error()	aio_return()	aio_suspend()
alarm()	bind()	cfgetispeed()
cfgetospeed()	cfsetispeed()	cfsetospeed()
chdir()	chmod()	chown()
close()	connect()	creat()
dup()	dup2()	execle()
execve()	_exit()	fchmod()
fchown()	fcntl()	fdatasync()
fork()	fpathconf()	fstat()
fsync()	getegid()	geteuid()
getgid()	getgroups()	getpeername()
getpgrp()	getpid()	getppid()
getuid()	kill()	link()
listen()	lseek()	lstat()
mkdir()	mkfifo()	open()
pathconf()	pause()	pipe()
poll()	posix_trace_event()	pselect()
raise()	read()	readlink()
recv()	recvfrom()	recvmsg()
rename()	rmdir()	select()
sem_post()	send()	sendmsg()
sendto()	setgid()	setpgid()
setsid()	setsockopt()	setuid()
shutdown()	sigaction()	sigaddset()
sigdelset()	sigemptyset()	sigfillset()
sigismember()	signal()	sigpause()
sigpending()	sigprocmask()	sigqueue()
sigset()	sigsuspend()	sleep()
socket()	socketpair()	stat()
symlink()	sysconf()	tcdrain()
tcflow()	tcflush()	tcgetattr()
tcgetpgrp()	tcsendbreak()	tcsetattr()
tcsetpgrp()	time()	timer_getoverrun()
timer_gettime()	timer_settime()	times()
umask()	uname()	unlink()
utime()	wait()	wait3()
wait4()	waitpid()	write()

the logs need to be reopened. Then a SIGHUP signal handler sets this
variable whenever it is invoked, and the main part of the program checks
the variable as often as possible. The following is an example program that
does this:

```
 1: /* sighup.c */
 2:
 3: #include <errno.h>
 4: #include <signal.h>
 5: #include <stdio.h>
 6: #include <string.h>
 7: #include <unistd.h>
 8:
 9: volatile int reopenLog = 0;      /* volatile as it is modified
10:                                     by a signal handler */
11:
12: /* write a line to the log */
13: void logstring(int logfd, char * str) {
14:     write(logfd, str, strlen(str));
15: }
16:
17: /* When SIGHUP occurs, make a note of it and continue. */
18: void hupHandler(int signum) {
19:     reopenLog = 1;
20: }
21:
22: int main() {
23:     int done = 0;
24:     struct sigaction sa;
25:     int rc;
26:     int logfd;
27:
28:     logfd = STDOUT_FILENO;
29:
30:     /* Set up a signal handler for SIGHUP. Use memset() to
31:        initialize the struct sigaction to be sure we clear all
32:        of it. */
33:     memset(&sa, 0, sizeof(sa));
34:     sa.sa_handler = hupHandler;
35:
36:     if (sigaction(SIGHUP, &sa, NULL)) perror("sigaction");
37:
38:     /* Log a message every two seconds, and reopen the log file
39:        as requested by SIGHUP. */
40:     while (!done) {
41:         /* sleep() returns nonzero if it didn't sleep long enough */
```

```
42:          rc = sleep(2);
43:          if (rc) {
44:              if (reopenLog) {
45:                  logstring(logfd,
46:                      "* reopening log files at SIGHUP's request\n");
47:                  reopenLog = 0;
48:              } else {
49:                  logstring(logfd,
50:                      "* sleep interrupted by unknown signal "
51:                          "-- dying\n");
52:                  done = 1;
53:              }
54:          } else {
55:              logstring(logfd, "Periodic message\n");
56:          }
57:      }
58:
59:      return 0;
60: }
```

To test this program, run it in one xterm and send it SIGHUP from another. For each SIGHUP the program receives, it prints out a message where it would ordinarily rotate its logs. Remember that if a signal arrives while another instance of the signal is already pending, only one instance of the signal is delivered, so do not send the signals too quickly.

12.6 Real-Time Signals

To address some of the limitations of the POSIX signal model, notably the lack of any data attached to the signal and the possibility of multiple signals being collapsed into a single delivery, the POSIX Real Time Signals extension was developed.[20] Systems that support real-time signals, including Linux, also support the traditional POSIX signals mechanism we described earlier. For the highest levels of portability between systems, we suggest using the standard POSIX interfaces unless there is a need for some of the extra features provided by the real-time extension.

---

20. *Real time* is a misnomer here, as the extension makes no attempt to provide guarantees on the latency of signal delivery. The features it does add are useful in building soft real-time implementations, however.

12.6.1 Signal Queueing and Ordering

Two of the limitations of the standard POSIX signal model are that when a signal is pending sending that signal again does not result in multiple signal deliveries and the lack of ordering guarantees for the delivery of multiple different signals (if you send a SIGTERM followed by a SIGKILL there is no way of knowing which one will be delivered first). The POSIX Real Time Signal extensions have added a new set of signals that are not subject to these constraints.

There are a number of real-time signals available, and they are not used by the kernel for any predefined purpose. All of the signals between SIGRTMIN and SIGRTMAX are real-time signals, although the exact number of these is not specified by POSIX (Linux provides 32 at the time of writing, but that could be increased in the future).

Real-time signals are always queued; every real-time signal sent to an application is delivered to that application (unless the application terminates before some of the signals have been delivered). The ordering of real-time signals is also well defined. Real-time signals with smaller signal numbers are always delivered before signals with larger signal numbers, and when multiple signals with the same signal number have been queued, they are delivered in the order they were sent. The ordering between non-real-time signals is not defined, nor is the ordering between non-real-time signals and real-time signals.

Here is some sample code to illustrate signal queuing and ordering:

```
 1: /* queued.c */
 2:
 3: /* get the definition of strsignal() from string.h */
 4: #define _GNU_SOURCE 1
 5:
 6: #include <sys/signal.h>
 7: #include <stdlib.h>
 8: #include <stdio.h>
 9: #include <string.h>
10: #include <unistd.h>
11:
12: /* Globals for building a list of caught signals */
13: int nextSig = 0;
```

```
14: int sigOrder[10];
15:
16: /* Catch a signal and record that it was handled. */
17: void handler(int signo) {
18:     sigOrder[nextSig++] = signo;
19: }
20:
21: int main() {
22:     sigset_t mask;
23:     sigset_t oldMask;
24:     struct sigaction act;
25:     int i;
26:
27:     /* Signals we're handling in this program */
28:     sigemptyset(&mask);
29:     sigaddset(&mask, SIGRTMIN);
30:     sigaddset(&mask, SIGRTMIN + 1);
31:     sigaddset(&mask, SIGUSR1);
32:
33:     /* Send signals to handler() and keep all signals blocked
34:         that handler() has been configured to catch to avoid
35:         races in manipulating the global variables. */
36:     act.sa_handler = handler;
37:     act.sa_mask = mask;
38:     act.sa_flags = 0;
39:
40:     sigaction(SIGRTMIN, &act, NULL);
41:     sigaction(SIGRTMIN + 1, &act, NULL);
42:     sigaction(SIGUSR1, &act, NULL);
43:
44:     /* Block the signals we're working with so we can see the
45:         queuing and ordering behavior. */
46:     sigprocmask(SIG_BLOCK, &mask, &oldMask);
47:
48:     /* Generate signals */
49:     raise(SIGRTMIN + 1);
50:     raise(SIGRTMIN);
51:     raise(SIGRTMIN);
52:     raise(SIGRTMIN + 1);
53:     raise(SIGRTMIN);
54:     raise(SIGUSR1);
```

```
55:        raise(SIGUSR1);
56:
57:        /* Enable delivery of the signals. They'll all be delivered
58:            right before this call returns (on Linux; this is NOT
59:            portable behavior). */
60:        sigprocmask(SIG_SETMASK, &oldMask, NULL);
61:
62:        /* Display the ordered list of signals we caught */
63:        printf("signals received:\n");
64:        for (i = 0; i < nextSig; i++)
65:            if (sigOrder[i] < SIGRTMIN)
66:                printf("\t%s\n", strsignal(sigOrder[i]));
67:            else
68:                printf("\tSIGRTMIN + %d\n", sigOrder[i] - SIGRTMIN);
69:
70:        return 0;
71: }
```

This program sends itself a number of signals and records the order the signals arrive in for display. While the signals are being sent, it blocks those signals to prevent them from being delivered immediately. It also blocks the signals whenever the signal handler is being run by setting the sa_mask member of struct sigaction when installing the signal handler for each signal. This prevents possible races accessing the global variables nextSig and sigOrder from inside the signal handler.

Running this program gives the following results:

```
signals received:
        User defined signal 1
        SIGRTMIN + 0
        SIGRTMIN + 0
        SIGRTMIN + 0
        SIGRTMIN + 1
        SIGRTMIN + 1
```

This shows that all of the real-time signals were delivered, while only a single instance of SIGUSR1 was delivered. You can also see the reordering of real-time signals, with all of the SIGRTMIN signals delivered before SIGRTMIN + 1.

12.7 Learning About a Signal

The signals we have discussed so far carry no data with them; the arrival of the signal is the only information the application gets. In some cases it would be nice to know what caused the signal to be sent (such as the illegal memory address that caused a `SIGSEGV`) or to be able to include data with application-generated signals. The Real Time Signal extensions address both of these needs.

12.7.1 Getting a Signal's Context

The information about how and why a signal was generated is called the signal's **context**.[21] Applications that wish to view a signal's context use a different signal handler than the normal one. It includes two more parameters, a pointer to a `siginfo_t`, which provides the signal's context and a pointer to `void *`, which can be used by some low-level system libraries.[22] Here is what the full handler prototype looks like:

```
void handler(int signum, siginfo_t * siginfo, void * context);
```

Applications need to tell the kernel to pass full context information by setting the `SA_SIGINFO` flag in the `sa_mask` member of the `struct sigaction` used to register the signal handler. The `sa_handler` member is also not used, as it is a pointer to a function with a different prototype. Instead, a new member, `sa_sigaction`, is set to point to the signal handler with the proper prototype.

To help reduce memory usage, `sa_handler` and `sa_sigaction` are allowed to use the same region of memory, so only one should be used at a time. To make this transparent, the C library defines `struct sigaction` like this:

---

21. Before the POSIX standards, applications could access a `struct sigcontext` for the same type of information now provided by `siginfo_t`, and the term context has stuck from this older implementation.
22. This third parameter is actually a pointer to a `struct ucontext`, which allows processes to do full context switching in user space. Doing this is beyond the scope of this book, but it is well documented in the Single Unix Specification.

```
#include <signal.h>

struct sigaction {
        union {
                __sighandler_t sa_handler;
                __sigaction_t sa_sigaction;
        } __sigaction_handler;
        sigset_t sa_mask;
        unsigned long sa_flags;
};


#define sa_handler    __sigaction_handler.sa_handler
#define sa_sigaction  __sigaction_handler.sa_sigaction
```

Using this combination of a union and macros allows the two members to overlap in memory without the data structure getting overly complicated from the application's view.

The `siginfo_t` structure contains information about where and why a signal was generated. Two members are available for all signals: `si_signo` and `si_code`. Which other members are available depends on the signal being delivered, and those members overlap in memory in a way similar to `sa_handler` and `sa_sigaction` in `struct sigaction`. The `si_signo` member contains the signal number that is being delivered and is the same as the first parameter passed to the signal handler, while `si_code` specifies why the signal was generated and changes depending on the signal number. For most signals, it is one of the following:

SI_USER   A user-space application used `kill()` to send the signal.[23]

SI_QUEUE A user-space application used `sigqueue()` to send the signal, which is discussed on page 237.

SI_TKILL The signal was sent by a user-space application using the `tkill()` system call. While the Linux kernel uses `SI_TKILL`, its value is not specified in current versions of the C library.

---

23. The `sigsend()` function, which Linux includes for compatibility with some other Unix systems, also causes `SI_USER`.

If you need to check for SI_TKILL, use the following code segment to define its value:

```
#ifndef SI_TKILL
#define SI_TKILL -6
#endif
```

SI_TKILL is not specified by any standard (but it is allowed by them), so it needs to be used with care in portable programs.

SI_KERNEL   The signal was generated by the kernel.[24]

When SIGILL, SIGFPE, SIGSEGV, SIGBUS, and SIGCHLD are sent by the kernel, si_code takes on the values shown in Table 12.3 instead of SI_KERNEL.[25]

To help clarify the various values si_code can take, here is an example that generates SIGCHLD in four different ways: kill(), sigqueue(), raise() (which uses the tkill() system call), and by creating a child that immediately terminates.

```
 1: /* sicode.c */
 2:
 3: #include <sys/signal.h>
 4: #include <stdlib.h>
 5: #include <stdio.h>
 6: #include <unistd.h>
 7:
 8: #ifndef SI_TKILL
 9: #define SI_TKILL -6
10: #endif
11:
12: void handler(int signo, siginfo_t * info, void * f) {
13:     static int count = 0;
14:
```

---

24. There are more values for si_code than we talk about here, related to features like asynchronous I/O, message queues, and real-time timers, which are outside the scope of this book.
25. It also takes on special values for SIGTRAP, which is used by debuggers, and SIGPOLL, which is used by an unreliable asynchronous I/O mechanism. Neither of these topics is covered in this book, so the details on these signals have been omitted from Table 12.3.

Table 12.3 Values of `si_code` for Special Signals

Signal	`si_code`	Description
SIGILL	ILL_ILLOPC	Illegal opcode
	ILL_ILLOPC	Illegal operand
	ILL_ILLOPC	Illegal addressing mode
	ILL_ILLOPC	Illegal trap
	ILL_ILLOPC	Privileged opcode
	ILL_ILLOPC	Privileged register
	ILL_ILLOPC	Internal stack error
	ILL_ILLOPC	Coprocessor error
SIGFPE	FPE_INTDIV	Integer divide by zero
	FPE_INTOVF	Integer overflow
	FPE_FLTDIV	Floating point divide by zero
	FPE_FLTOVF	Floating point overflow
	FPE_FLTUND	Floating point underflow
	FPE_FLTRES	Floating point inexact result
	FPE_FLTINV	Floating point invalid operation
	FPE_FLTSUB	Floating point subscript out of range
SIGSEGV	SEGV_MAPERR	Address not mapped in an object
	SEGV_ACCERR	Invalid permissions for address
SIGBUS	BUS_ADRALN	Invalid address alignment
	BUS_ADRERR	Nonexistent physical address
	BUS_OBJERR	Object specific hardware error
SIGCHLD	CLD_EXITED	Child has exited
	CLD_KILLED	Child was killed without a core file
	CLD_DUMPED	Child was killed and a core file was created
	CLD_TRAPPED	Child has hit a breakpoint
	CLD_STOPPED	Child has stopped

```
15:        printf("caught signal sent by ");
16:        switch (info->si_code) {
17:        case SI_USER:
18:            printf("kill()\n"); break;
19:        case SI_QUEUE:
20:            printf("sigqueue()\n"); break;
21:        case SI_TKILL:
22:            printf("tkill() or raise()\n"); break;
23:        case CLD_EXITED:
24:            printf("kernel telling us child exited\n"); exit(0);
25:        }
26:
27:        if (++count == 4) exit(1);
```

```
28: }
29:
30: int main() {
31:     struct sigaction act;
32:     union sigval val;
33:     pid_t pid = getpid();
34:
35:     val.sival_int = 1234;
36:
37:     act.sa_sigaction = handler;
38:     sigemptyset(&act.sa_mask);
39:     act.sa_flags = SA_SIGINFO;
40:     sigaction(SIGCHLD, &act, NULL);
41:
42:     kill(pid, SIGCHLD);
43:     sigqueue(pid, SIGCHLD, val);
44:     raise(SIGCHLD);
45:
46:     /* To get a SIGCHLD from the kernel we create a child and
47:        have it exit immediately. The signal handler exits after
48:        receiving the signal from the kernel, so we just sleep for
49:        a while and let the program terminate that way. */
50:
51:     if (!fork()) exit(0);
52:     sleep(60);
53:
54:     return 0;
55: }
```

If si_code is SI_USER, SI_QUEUE, or SI_TKILL, two additional members of siginfo_t are available, si_pid and si_uid, which provide the process ID that sent the signal and the real user ID of that process.

When a SIGCHLD is sent by the kernel, the si_pid, si_status, si_utime, and si_stime members are available. The first, si_pid, gives the pid of the process whose status has changed.[26] Information on the new status is available in both si_code (as specified by Table 12.3) and si_status, which is identical to the status integer returned by the wait() family of functions. The final two members, si_utime and si_stime, specify the

---

26. Recall that SIGCHLD is sent not only when a child has exited, but also when a child has stopped or resumed.

amount of the time the child application has spent in user space and kernel space, respectively (this is similar to measures wait3() and wait4() return in struct rusage). They are measured in clock ticks, which is an integer. The number of clock ticks per second is defined by the _SC_CLK_TCK macro, defined in <sysconf.h>.

SIGSEGV, SIGBUS, SIGILL, and SIGFPE all provide si_addr, which specifies the address that caused the fault described by si_code.

Here is a simple example of examining a signal's context. It installs a signal handler for SIGSEGV that prints out the context for that signal and then terminates the process. A segmentation violation is generated by trying to dereference NULL.

```
 1: /* catch-segv.c */
 2:
 3: #include <sys/signal.h>
 4: #include <stdlib.h>
 5: #include <stdio.h>
 6:
 7: void handler(int signo, siginfo_t * info, void * f) {
 8:     printf("caught ");
 9:     if (info->si_signo == SIGSEGV)
10:         printf("segv accessing %p", info->si_addr);
11:     if (info->si_code == SEGV_MAPERR)
12:         printf(" SEGV_MAPERR");
13:     printf("\n");
14:
15:     exit(1);
16: }
17:
18: int main() {
19:     struct sigaction act;
20:
21:     act.sa_sigaction = handler;
22:     sigemptyset(&act.sa_mask);
23:     act.sa_flags = SA_SIGINFO;
24:     sigaction(SIGSEGV, &act, NULL);
25:
26:     *((int *) NULL) = 1;
27:
```

```
28:        return 0;
29: }
```

12.7.2 Sending Data with a Signal

The `siginfo_t` mechanism also allows signals sent from programs to attach a single data element to the signal (this element may be a pointer, allowing an arbitrary amount of data to be passed indirectly). To send data, a `union sigval` is used.

```
#include <signal.h>

union sigval {
        int sival_int;
        void * sival_ptr;
};
```

Either `sival_int` or `sival_ptr` may be set to an arbitrary value that is included in the `siginfo_t` delivered with the signal. To generate a signal with a `union sigval`, `sigqueue()` must be used.

```
#include <signal.h>

void * sigqueue(pid_t pid, int signum, const union sigval value);
```

Unlike `kill()`, `pid` must be a valid process ID number (no negative values are allowed). The `signum` specifies the signal number to send. Like `kill()`, `sigqueue()` allows `signum` to be zero to check whether the calling process is allowed to send the target `pid` a signal without actually sending one. The final parameter, `value`, provides the datum that is delivered along with the signal.

To receive the `union sigval`, the process catching the signal must use `SA_SIGINFO` when registering its signal handler with `sigaction()`. When the `si_code` member of `siginfo_t` is `SI_QUEUE`, `siginfo_t` provides a `si_value` member that is the same as the `value` passed to `sigqueue`.

Here is an example of sending data elements with a signal. It queues three `SIGRTMIN` signals with different data elements. It demonstrates that the signals were delivered in the same order they were sent, which is what we would expect for queued real-time signals.[27] A more involved example uses signals to monitor changes in directories and is presented on page 319.

```
 1: /* sigval.c */
 2:
 3: #include <sys/signal.h>
 4: #include <stdlib.h>
 5: #include <stdio.h>
 6: #include <string.h>
 7: #include <unistd.h>
 8:
 9: /* Catch a signal and record that it was handled. */
10: void handler(int signo, siginfo_t * si, void * context) {
11:     printf("%d\n", si->si_value.sival_int);
12: }
13:
14: int main() {
15:     sigset_t mask;
16:     sigset_t oldMask;
17:     struct sigaction act;
18:     int me = getpid();
19:     union sigval val;
20:
21:     /* Send signals to handler() and keep all signals blocked
22:         that handler() has been configured to catch to avoid
23:         races in manipulating the global variables. */
24:     act.sa_sigaction = handler;
25:     act.sa_mask = mask;
26:     act.sa_flags = SA_SIGINFO;
27:
28:     sigaction(SIGRTMIN, &act, NULL);
29:
30:     /* Block SIGRTMIN so we can see the queueing and ordering */
31:     sigemptyset(&mask);
32:     sigaddset(&mask, SIGRTMIN);
33:
34:     sigprocmask(SIG_BLOCK, &mask, &oldMask);
35:
36:     /* Generate signals */
```

---

27. For more examples of signal handling, look at the sample programs for file leases (page 287), tty handling (page 355), and interval timers (page 493).

```
37:     val.sival_int = 1;
38:     sigqueue(me, SIGRTMIN, val);
39:     val.sival_int++;
40:     sigqueue(me, SIGRTMIN, val);
41:     val.sival_int++;
42:     sigqueue(me, SIGRTMIN, val);
43:
44:     /* Enable delivery of the signals. */
45:     sigprocmask(SIG_SETMASK, &oldMask, NULL);
46:
47:     return 0;
48: }
```

CHAPTER 13

Advanced File Handling

Files are used for a large number of tasks in the Linux world, such as persistent data storage in regular files, networking through sockets, and device access through device files. The variety of applications for files has led to the development of many specialized ways of manipulating files. Chapter 11 introduced the most common operations on files, and this chapter discusses some more specialized file operations. In this chapter, we cover using multiple files simultaneously, mapping files into system memory, file locking, and scatter/gather reads and writes.

13.1 Input and Output Multiplexing

Many client/server applications need to read input from or write output to multiple file descriptors at a time. For example, modern Web browsers open many simultaneous network connections to reduce the loading time for a Web page. This allows them to download the multiple images that appear on most Web pages more quickly than consecutive connections would allow. Along with the interprocess communication (IPC) channel that graphical browsers use to contact the X server on which they are displayed, browsers have many file descriptors to keep track of.

The easiest way to handle all these files is for the browser to read from each file in turn and process whatever data that file delivers (a read() system call on a network connection, as on a pipe, returns whatever data is currently available and blocks only if no bytes are ready). This approach works fine, as long as all the connections are delivering data fairly regularly.

If one of the network connections gets behind, problems start. When the browser next reads from that file, the browser stops running while the read() blocks, waiting for data to arrive. Needless to say, this is not the behavior the browser's user would prefer.

To help illustrate these problems, here is a short program that reads from two files: p1 and p2. To try it, open three X terminal sessions (or use three virtual consoles). Make named pipes named p1 and p2 (with the mknod command), then run cat > p1 and cat > p2 in two of the terminals while running mpx-blocks in the third. Once everything is running, type some text in each of the cat windows and watch how it appears. Remember that the two cat commands will not write any data into the pipes until the end of a line.

```
 1: /* mpx-blocks.c */
 2:
 3: #include <fcntl.h>
 4: #include <stdio.h>
 5: #include <unistd.h>
 6:
 7: int main(void) {
 8:     int fds[2];
 9:     char buf[4096];
10:     int i;
11:     int fd;
12:
13:     if ((fds[0] = open("p1", O_RDONLY)) < 0) {
14:         perror("open p1");
15:         return 1;
16:     }
17:
18:     if ((fds[1] = open("p2", O_RDONLY)) < 0) {
19:         perror("open p2");
20:         return 1;
21:     }
22:
23:     fd = 0;
24:     while (1) {
25:         /* if data is available read it and display it */
26:         i = read(fds[fd], buf, sizeof(buf) - 1);
27:         if (i < 0) {
```

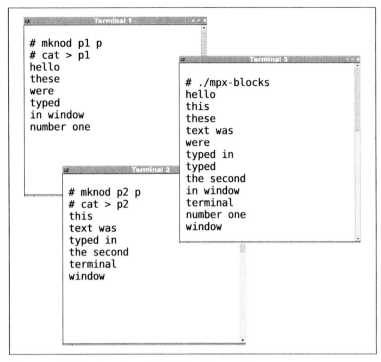

Figure 13.1   Running Multiplex Examples

```
28:                perror("read");
29:                return 1;
30:            } else if (!i) {
31:                printf("pipe closed\n");
32:                return 0;
33:            }
34:
35:            buf[i] = '\0';
36:            printf("read: %s", buf);
37:
38:            /* read from the other file descriptor */
39:            fd = (fd + 1) % 2;
40:        }
41: }
```

Although mpx-blocks does read from both pipes, it does not do a very nice
job of it. It reads from only one pipe at a time. When it starts, it reads from
the first file until data becomes available on it; the second file is ignored

until the read() from the first file returns. Once that read does return, the first file is ignored until data is read from the second file. This method does not perform anything like smooth data multiplexing. Figure 13.1 shows what mpx-blocks looks like when it is run.

13.1.1 Nonblocking I/O

Recall from Chapter 11 that we may specify a file is nonblocking through the fcntl() system call. When a slow file is nonblocking, read() always returns immediately. If no data is available, it simply returns 0. Nonblocking I/O provides a simple solution to multiplexing by preventing operations on files from ever blocking.

Here is a modified version of mpx-blocks that takes advantage of nonblocking I/O to alternate between p1 and p2 more smoothly:

```
 1: /* mpx-nonblock.c */
 2:
 3: #include <errno.h>
 4: #include <fcntl.h>
 5: #include <stdio.h>
 6: #include <unistd.h>
 7:
 8: int main(void) {
 9:     int fds[2];
10:     char buf[4096];
11:     int i;
12:     int fd;
13:
14:     /* open both pipes in nonblocking mode */
15:     if ((fds[0] = open("p1", O_RDONLY | O_NONBLOCK)) < 0) {
16:         perror("open p1");
17:         return 1;
18:     }
19:
20:     if ((fds[1] = open("p2", O_RDONLY | O_NONBLOCK)) < 0) {
21:         perror("open p2");
22:         return 1;
23:     }
24:
```

```
25:        fd = 0;
26:        while (1) {
27:            /* if data is available read it and display it */
28:            i = read(fds[fd], buf, sizeof(buf) - 1);
29:            if ((i < 0) && (errno != EAGAIN)) {
30:                perror("read");
31:                return 1;
32:            } else if (i > 0) {
33:                buf[i] = '\0';
34:                printf("read: %s", buf);
35:            }
36:
37:            /* read from the other file descriptor */
38:            fd = (fd + 1) % 2;
39:        }
40: }
```

One important difference between mpx-nonblock and mpx-blocks is that
mpx-nonblock does not exit when one of the pipes it is reading from is
closed. A nonblocking read() from a pipe with no writers returns 0 bytes;
from a pipe with writers but no data read() returns EAGAIN.

Although nonblocking I/O allows us to switch easily between file descriptors, it has a high price. The program is always polling the two file descriptors for input—it *never* blocks. As the program is constantly running, it
inflicts a heavy performance penalty on the system as the operating system
can never put the process to sleep (try running 10 copies of mpx-nonblock
on your system and see how it affects system performance).

13.1.2 Multiplexing with poll()

To allow efficient multiplexing, Linux provides the poll() system call,
which allows a process to block on multiple file descriptors simultaneously.
Rather than constantly check each file descriptor it is interested in, a process
makes a single system call that specifies which file descriptors the process
would like to read from or write to. When one or more of those files have
data available for reading or can accept data written to them, the poll()
returns and the application can read and write from those file descriptors
without worrying about blocking. Once those files have been handled, the

process makes another poll() call, which blocks until a file is ready for more attention. Here is the definition of poll():

```
#include <sys/poll.h>

int poll(struct pollfd * fds, int numfds, int timeout);
```

The last two parameters are straightforward; numfds specifies the number of items in the array pointed to by the first parameter and timeout specifies how long poll() should wait for an event to occur. If 0 is used as the timeout, poll() never times out.

The first parameter, fds, describes which file descriptors should be monitored and what types of I/O they should be monitored for. It is a pointer to an array of struct pollfd structures.

```
struct pollfd {
    int fd;        /* file descriptor */
    short events;   /* I/O events to wait for */
    short revents;  /* I/O events that occurred */
};
```

The first element, fd, is a file descriptor being monitored, and the events element describes what types of events are of interest. It is one or more of the following flags logically OR'ed together:

POLLIN   Normal data is available for reading from the file descriptor.

POLLPRI   Priority (out-of-band[1]) data is available for reading.

POLLOUT   The file descriptor is able to accept some data being written to it.

The revents element of struct pollfd is filled in by the poll() system call, and reflects the status of file descriptor fd. It is similar to the events member, but instead of specifying what types of I/O events are of interest to the application, it specifies what types of I/O events are available. For

---

1. This is almost the only place in this book we ever mention out-of-band data. For more information, consult [Stevens, 2004].

example, if the application is monitoring a pipe both for reading and writing (events is set to POLLIN | POLLOUT), then after the poll() succeeds revents has the POLLIN bit set if the pipe has data ready to be read, and the POLLOUT bit set if there is room in the pipe for more data to be written. If both are true, both bits are set.

There are a few bits that the kernel can set in revents that do not make sense for events;

POLLERR	There is an error pending on the file descriptor; performing a system call on the file descriptor will cause errno to be set to the appropriate code.
POLLHUP	The file has been disconnected; no more writing to it is possible (although there may be data left to be read). This occurs if a terminal has been disconnected or the remote end of a pipe or socket has been closed.
POLLNVAL	The file descriptor is invalid (it does not refer to an open file).

The return value of poll() is zero if the call times out, -1 if an error occurs (such as fds being an invalid pointer; errors on the files themselves cause POLLERR to get set), or a positive number describing the number of files with nonzero revents members.

Rather than the inefficient method we used earlier to multiplex input and output from pipes, poll() lets us solve the same problem quite elegantly. By using poll() on the file descriptors for both pipes simultaneously, we know when poll() returns, one of the pipes has data ready to be read or has been closed. We check the revents member for both file descriptors to see what actions need to be taken and go back to the poll() call once we are done. Most of the time is now spent blocking on the poll() call rather than continuously checking the file descriptors using nonblocking I/O, significantly reducing load on the system. Here is mpx-poll:

```
 1: /* mpx-poll.c */
 2:
 3: #include <fcntl.h>
 4: #include <stdio.h>
 5: #include <sys/poll.h>
```

```
 6: #include <unistd.h>
 7:
 8: int main(void) {
 9:     struct pollfd fds[2];
10:     char buf[4096];
11:     int i, rc;
12:
13:     /* open both pipes */
14:     if ((fds[0].fd = open("p1", O_RDONLY | O_NONBLOCK)) < 0) {
15:         perror("open p1");
16:         return 1;
17:     }
18:
19:     if ((fds[1].fd = open("p2", O_RDONLY | O_NONBLOCK)) < 0) {
20:         perror("open p2");
21:         return 1;
22:     }
23:
24:     /* start off reading from both file descriptors */
25:     fds[0].events = POLLIN;
26:     fds[1].events = POLLIN;
27:
28:     /* while we're watching one of fds[0] or fds[1] */
29:     while (fds[0].events || fds[1].events) {
30:         if (poll(fds, 2, 0) < 0) {
31:             perror("poll");
32:             return 1;
33:         }
34:
35:         /* check to see which file descriptors are ready to be
36:            read from */
37:         for (i = 0; i < 2; i++) {
38:             if (fds[i].revents) {
39:                 /* fds[i] is ready for reading, go ahead... */
40:                 rc = read(fds[i].fd, buf, sizeof(buf) - 1);
41:                 if (rc < 0) {
42:                     perror("read");
43:                     return 1;
44:                 } else if (!rc) {
45:                     /* this pipe has been closed, don't try
46:                        to read from it again */
```

```
47:                          fds[i].events = 0;
48:                      } else {
49:                          buf[rc] = '\0';
50:                          printf("read: %s", buf);
51:                      }
52:                  }
53:              }
54:          }
55:
56:      return 0;
57: }
```

13.1.3 Multiplexing with select()

The poll() system call was originally introduced as part of the System V Unix tree. The BSD development efforts solved the same basic problem in a similar way by introducing the select() system call.

```
#include <sys/select.h>

int select(int numfds, fd_set * readfds, fd_set * writefds,
           fd_set * exceptfds, struct timeval * timeout);
```

The middle three parameters, readfds, writefds, and exceptfds, specify which file descriptors should be watched. Each parameter is a pointer to an fd_set, a data structure that allows a process to specify an arbitrary number of file descriptors.[2] It is manipulated through the following macros:

FD_ZERO(fd_set * fds);
> Clears fds—no file descriptors are contained in the set. This macro is used to initialize fd_set structures.

FD_SET(int fd, fd_set * fds);
> Adds fd to the fd_set.

FD_CLR(int fd, fd_set * fds);
> Removes fd from the fd_set.

---

2. This is similar to sigset_t used for signal masks.

```
FD_ISSET(int fd, fd_set * fds);
```
       Returns true if `fd` is contained in set `fds`.

The first of `select()`'s file descriptor sets, `readfds`, contains the set of file descriptors that will cause the `select()` call to return when they are ready to be read from[3] or (for pipes and sockets) when the process on the other end of the file has closed the file. When any of the file descriptors in `writefds` are ready to be written, `select()` returns. `exceptfds` contains the file descriptors to watch for exceptional conditions. Under Linux (as well as Unix), this occurs only when out-of-band data has been received on a network connection. Any of these may be `NULL` if you are not interested in that type of event.

The final parameter, `timeout`, specifies how long, in milliseconds, the `select()` call should wait for something to happen. It is a pointer to a `struct timeval`, which looks like this:

```
#include <sys/time.h>

struct timeval {
    int tv_sec;      /* seconds */
    int tv_usec;     /* microseconds */
};
```

The first element, `tv_sec`, is the number of seconds to wait, and `tv_usec` is the number of microseconds to wait. If the `timeout` value is `NULL`, `select()` blocks until something happens. If it points to a `struct timeval` that contains zero in both its elements, `select()` does not block. It updates the file descriptor sets to indicate which file descriptors are currently ready for reading or writing, then returns immediately.

The first parameter, `numfds`, causes the most difficulty. It specifies how many of the file descriptors (starting from file descriptor 0) may be specified by the `fd_sets`. Another (and perhaps easier) way of thinking of `numfds` is as one greater than the maximum file descriptor `select()` is meant to consider.[4] As Linux normally allows each process to have up to 1,024 file

---

3. When a network socket being `listen()`ed to is ready to be `accept()`ed, it is considered ready to be read from for `select()`'s purposes; information on sockets is in Chapter 17.
4. If you compare this to the `numfds` parameter for `poll()` you'll see where the confusion comes from.

descriptors, numfds prevents the kernel from having to look through all 1,024 file descriptors each fd_set could contain, providing a performance increase.

On return, the three fd_set structures contain the file descriptors that have input pending, may be written to, or are in an exceptional condition. Linux's select() call returns the total number of items set in the three fd_set structures, 0 if the call timed out, or -1 if an error occurred. However, many Unix systems count a particular file descriptor in the return value only once, even if it occurs in both readfds and writefds, so for portability, it is a good idea to check only whether the return value is greater than 0. If the return value is -1, do not assume the fd_set structures remain pristine. Linux updates them only if select() returns a value greater than 0, but some Unix systems behave differently.

Another portability concern is the timeout parameter. Linux kernels[5] update it to reflect the amount of time left before the select() call would have timed out, but most other Unix systems do not update it.[6] However, other systems do not update the timeout, to conform to the more common implementation. For portability, do not depend on either behavior and explicitly set the timeout structure before calling select().

Now let's look at a couple of examples of using select(). First of all, we use select for something unrelated to files, constructing a subsecond sleep() call.

```
#include <sys/select.h>
#include <sys/stdlib.h>

int usecsleep(int usecs) {
    struct timeval tv;

    tv.tv_sec = 0;
    tv.tv_usec = usecs;

    return select(0, NULL, NULL, NULL, &tv);
}
```

---

5. Except for some experimental kernels in the 2.1 series.
6. When Linus Torvalds first implemented select(), the BSD man page for select() listed the BSD kernel's failure to update the timeout as a bug. Rather than write buggy code, Linus decided to "fix" this bug. Unfortunately, the standards committees decided they liked BSD's behavior.

This code allows highly portable pauses of less than one second (which BSD's usleep() library function allows, as well, but select() is much more portable). For example, usecsleep(500000) causes a minimum of a half-second pause.

The select() call can also be used to solve the pipe multiplexing example we have been working with. The solution is very similar to the one using poll().

```
 1: /* mpx-select.c */
 2:
 3: #include <fcntl.h>
 4: #include <stdio.h>
 5: #include <sys/select.h>
 6: #include <unistd.h>
 7:
 8: int main(void) {
 9:     int fds[2];
10:     char buf[4096];
11:     int i, rc, maxfd;
12:     fd_set watchset;        /* fds to read from */
13:     fd_set inset;           /* updated by select() */
14:
15:     /* open both pipes */
16:     if ((fds[0] = open("p1", O_RDONLY | O_NONBLOCK)) < 0) {
17:         perror("open p1");
18:         return 1;
19:     }
20:
21:     if ((fds[1] = open("p2", O_RDONLY | O_NONBLOCK)) < 0) {
22:         perror("open p2");
23:         return 1;
24:     }
25:
26:     /* start off reading from both file descriptors */
27:     FD_ZERO(&watchset);
28:     FD_SET(fds[0], &watchset);
29:     FD_SET(fds[1], &watchset);
30:
31:     /* find the maximum file descriptor */
32:     maxfd = fds[0] > fds[1] ? fds[0] : fds[1];
33:
```

```
34:     /* while we're watching one of fds[0] or fds[1] */
35:     while (FD_ISSET(fds[0], &watchset) ||
36:            FD_ISSET(fds[1], &watchset)) {
37:         /* we copy watchset here because select() updates it */
38:         inset = watchset;
39:         if (select(maxfd + 1, &inset, NULL, NULL, NULL) < 0) {
40:             perror("select");
41:             return 1;
42:         }
43:
44:         /* check to see which file descriptors are ready to be
45:            read from */
46:         for (i = 0; i < 2; i++) {
47:             if (FD_ISSET(fds[i], &inset)) {
48:                 /* fds[i] is ready for reading, go ahead... */
49:                 rc = read(fds[i], buf, sizeof(buf) - 1);
50:                 if (rc < 0) {
51:                     perror("read");
52:                     return 1;
53:                 } else if (!rc) {
54:                     /* this pipe has been closed, don't try
55:                        to read from it again */
56:                     close(fds[i]);
57:                     FD_CLR(fds[i], &watchset);
58:                 } else {
59:                     buf[rc] = '\0';
60:                     printf("read: %s", buf);
61:                 }
62:             }
63:         }
64:     }
65:
66:     return 0;
67: }
```

13.1.4 Comparing `poll()` and `select()`

Although `poll()` and `select()` perform the same basic function, there are real differences between the two. The most obvious is probably the timeout, which has millisecond precision for `poll()` and microsecond precision for select(). In reality, this difference is almost meaningless as neither are going to be accurate down to the microsecond.

The more important difference is performance. The poll() interface differs from select() in a few ways that make it much more efficient.

1. When select() is used, the kernel must check all of the file descriptors between 0 and numfds - 1 to see if the application is interested in I/O events for that file descriptor. For applications with large numbers of open files, this can cause substantial waste as the kernel checks which file descriptors are of interest.

2. The set of file descriptors is passed to the kernel as a bitmap for select() and as a list for poll(). The somewhat complicated bit operations required to check and set the fd_set data structures are less efficient than the simple checks needed for struct pollfd.

3. As the kernel overwrites the data structures passed to select(), the application is forced to reset those structures every time it needs to call select(). With poll() the kernel's results are limited to the revents member, removing the need for data structures to be rebuilt before every call.

4. Using a set-based structure like fd_set does not scale as the number of file descriptors available to a process increases. Since it is a static size (rather than dynamically allocated; note the lack of a corresponding macro like FD_FREE), it cannot grow or shrink with the needs of the application (or the abilities of the kernel). Under Linux, the maximum file descriptor that can be set in an fd_set is 1023. If a larger file descriptor may be needed, select() will not work.

The only advantage select() offers over poll() is better portability to old systems. As very few of those implementations are still in use, you should consider select() of interest primarily for understanding and maintaining existing code bases.

To illustrate how much less efficient select() is than poll(), here is a short program that measures the number of system calls that can be performed in a second:

```
 1: /* select-vs-poll.c */
 2:
 3: #include <fcntl.h>
 4: #include <stdio.h>
 5: #include <sys/poll.h>
 6: #include <sys/select.h>
 7: #include <sys/signal.h>
 8: #include <unistd.h>
 9:
10: int gotAlarm;
11:
12: void catch(int sig) {
13:     gotAlarm = 1;
14: }
15:
16: #define HIGH_FD 1000
17:
18: int main(int argc, const char ** argv) {
19:     int devZero;
20:     int count;
21:     fd_set selectFds;
22:     struct pollfd pollFds;
23:
24:     devZero = open("/dev/zero", O_RDONLY);
25:     dup2(devZero, HIGH_FD);
26:
27:     /* use a signal to know when time's up */
28:     signal(SIGALRM, catch);
29:
30:     gotAlarm = 0;
31:     count = 0;
32:     alarm(1);
33:     while (!gotAlarm) {
34:         FD_ZERO(&selectFds);
35:         FD_SET(HIGH_FD, &selectFds);
36:
37:         select(HIGH_FD + 1, &selectFds, NULL, NULL, NULL);
38:         count++;
39:     }
40:
41:     printf("select() calls per second: %d\n", count);
```

```
42:
43:        pollFds.fd = HIGH_FD;
44:        pollFds.events = POLLIN;
45:        count = 0;
46:        gotAlarm = 0;
47:        alarm(1);
48:        while (!gotAlarm) {
49:            poll(&pollFds, 0, 0);
50:            count++;
51:        }
52:
53:        printf("poll() calls per second: %d\n", count);
54:
55:        return 0;
56: }
```

It uses /dev/zero, which provides an infinite number of zeros so that the system calls return immediately. The HIGH_FD value can be changed to see how select() degrades as the file descriptor values increase.

On one particular system and a HIGH_FD value of 2 (which is not very high), this program showed that the kernel could handle four times as many poll() calls per second as select() calls. When HIGH_FD was increased to 1,000, poll() became forty times more efficient than select().

13.1.5 Multiplexing with epoll

The 2.6 version of the Linux kernel introduced a third method for multiplexed I/O, called epoll. While epoll is more complicated than either poll() or select(), it removes a performance bottleneck common to both of those methods.

Both the poll() and select() system calls pass a full list of file descriptors to monitor each time they are called. Every one of those file descriptors must be processed by the system call, even if only one of them is ready for reading or writing. When tens, or hundreds, or thousands of file descriptors are being monitored, those system calls become bottlenecks; the kernel spends a large amount of time checking to see which file descriptors need to be checked by the application.

When epoll is used, applications provide the kernel with a list of file descriptors to monitor through one system call, and then monitor those file descriptors using a different system call. Once the list has been created, the kernel continually monitors those file descriptors for the events the application is interested in,[7] and when an event occurs, it makes a note that something interesting just happened. As soon as the application asks the kernel which file descriptors are ready for further processing, the kernel provides the list it has been maintaining without having to check every file descriptor.

The performance advantages of epoll require a system call interface that is more complicated than those of poll() and select(). While poll() uses an array of struct pollfd to represent a set of file descriptors and select() uses three different fd_set structures for the same purpose, epoll moves these file descriptor sets into the kernel rather than keeping them in the program's address space. Each of these sets is referenced through an epoll descriptor, which is a file descriptor that can be used only for epoll system calls. New epoll descriptors are allocated by the epoll_create() system call.

```
#include <sys/epoll.h>

int epoll_create(int numDescriptors);
```

The sole parameter numDescriptors is the program's best guess at how many file descriptors the newly created epoll descriptor will reference. This is not a hard limit, it is just a hint to the kernel to help it initialize its internal structures more accurately. epoll_create() returns an epoll descriptor, and when the program has finished with that descriptor it should be passed to close() to allow the kernel to free any memory used by that descriptor.

Although the epoll descriptor is a file descriptor, there are only two system calls it should be used with.

---

7. The kernel actually sets a callback on each file, and when those events occur the callback is invoked. This mechanism eliminates the scaling problems with very large numbers of file descriptors as polling is not used at any point.

```
#include <sys/epoll.h>

int epoll_ctl(int epfd, int op, int fd, struct epoll_event * event);
int epoll_wait(int epfd, struct epoll_event * events, int maxevents,
               int timeout);
```

Both of these use parameters of the type `struct epoll_event`, which is defined as follows:

```
#include <sys/epoll.h>

struct epoll_event {
    int events;
    union {
        void * ptr;
        int fd;
        unsigned int u32;
        unsigned long long u64;
    } data;
};
```

This structure serves three purposes: It specifies what types of events should be monitored, specifies what types of events occurred, and allows a single data element to be associated with the file descriptor. The `events` field is for the first two functions, and is one or more of the following values logically OR'ed together:[8]

EPOLLIN   Indicates that a `read()` operation will not block; either data is ready or there is no more data to be read.

EPOLLOUT   The associated file is ready to be written to.

EPOLLPRI   The file has out-of-band data ready for reading.

The second member of `struct epoll_event`, `data`, is a union that contains an integer (for holding a file descriptor), a pointer, and 32-bit and 64-bit

---

8. `EPOLLET` is one more value `events` can have, which switches `epoll` from being level-triggered to edge-triggered. This topic is beyond the scope of this book, and edge-triggered `epoll` should be used only under very special circumstances.

integers.[9] This data element is kept by epoll and returned to the program whenever an event of the appropriate type occurs. The data element is the only way the program has to know which file descriptor needs to be serviced; the epoll interface does not pass the file descriptor to the program, unlike poll() and select() (unless data contains the file descriptor). This method gives extra flexibility to applications that track files as something more complicated than simple file descriptors.

The epoll_ctl() system call adds and removes file descriptors from the set the epfd epoll descriptor refers to.

The second parameter, op, describes how the file descriptor set should be modified, and is one of the following:

EPOLL_CTL_ADD

>The file descriptor fd is added to the file descriptor set with the event set events. If the file descriptor is already present, it returns EEXIST. (It is possible that multiple threads will be able to add the same file descriptor to an epoll set more than once, and doing so does not change anything.)

EPOLL_CTL_DEL

>The file descriptor fd is removed from the set of file descriptors that is being monitored. The events parameter must point to a struct epoll_event, but the contents of that structure are ignored. (This is another way of saying events needs to be a valid pointer; it cannot be NULL.)

EPOLL_CTL_MOD

>The struct epoll_event for fd is updated from the information pointed to by events. This allows the set of events being monitored and the data element associated with the file descriptor to be updated without introducing any race conditions.

The final system call used by epoll is epoll_wait(), which blocks until one or more of the file descriptors being monitored has data to read or

---

9. The structure shown in the text gives the right member sizes on most platforms, but it is not correct for machines that define an int as 64 bits.

is ready to be written to. The first argument is the epoll descriptor, and the last provides a timeout in seconds. If no file descriptors are ready for processing before the timeout expires, epoll_wait() returns 0.

The middle two parameters specify a buffer for the kernel to copy a set struct epoll_event structures into. The events parameter points to the buffer, maxevents specifies how many struct epoll_event structures fit in that buffer, and the return value tells the program how many structures were placed in that buffer (unless the call times out or an error occurs).

Each struct epoll_event tells the program the full status of a file descriptor that is being monitored. The events member can have any of the EPOLLIN, EPOLLOUT, or EPOLLPRI flags set, as well as two new flags.

EPOLLERR   An error condition is pending on the file; this can occur if an error occurs on a socket when the application is not reading from or writing to it.

EPOLLHUP   A hangup occurred on the file descriptor; see page 138 for information on when this can occur.

While all of this seems complicated, it is actually very similar to how poll() works. Calling epoll_create() is the same as allocating the struct pollfd array, and epoll_ctl() is the same step as initializing the members of that array. The main loop that is processing file descriptors uses epoll_wait() instead of the poll() system call, and close() is analogous to freeing the struct pollfd array. These parallels make switching programs that were originally written around poll() or select() to epoll quite straightforward.

The epoll interface allows one more trick that cannot really be compared to poll() or select(). Since the epoll descriptor is really a file descriptor (which is why it can be passed to close()), you can monitor that epoll descriptor as part of another epoll descriptor, or via poll() or select(). The epoll descriptor will appear as ready to be read from whenever calling epoll_wait() would return events.

Our final solution to the pipe multiplexing problem we have used throughout this section uses epoll. It is very similar to the other examples, but some of the initialization code has been moved into a new `addEvent()` function to keep the program from getting longer than necessary.

```c
 1: /* mpx-epoll.c */
 2:
 3: #include <fcntl.h>
 4: #include <stdio.h>
 5: #include <stdlib.h>
 6: #include <sys/epoll.h>
 7: #include <unistd.h>
 8:
 9: #include <sys/poll.h>
10:
11: void addEvent(int epfd, char * filename) {
12:     int fd;
13:     struct epoll_event event;
14:
15:     if ((fd = open(filename, O_RDONLY | O_NONBLOCK)) < 0) {
16:         perror("open");
17:         exit(1);
18:     }
19:
20:     event.events = EPOLLIN;
21:     event.data.fd = fd;
22:
23:     if (epoll_ctl(epfd, EPOLL_CTL_ADD, fd, &event)) {
24:         perror("epoll_ctl(ADD)");
25:         exit(1);
26:     }
27: }
28:
29: int main(void) {
30:     char buf[4096];
31:     int i, rc;
32:     int epfd;
33:     struct epoll_event events[2];
34:     int num;
35:     int numFds;
36:
37:     epfd = epoll_create(2);
38:     if (epfd < 0) {
39:         perror("epoll_create");
```

```
40:            return 1;
41:        }
42:
43:    /* open both pipes and add them to the epoll set */
44:    addEvent(epfd, "p1");
45:    addEvent(epfd, "p2");
46:
47:    /* continue while we have one or more file descriptors to
48:       watch */
49:    numFds = 2;
50:    while (numFds) {
51:        if ((num = epoll_wait(epfd, events,
52:                           sizeof(events) / sizeof(*events),
53:                              -1)) <= 0) {
54:            perror("epoll_wait");
55:            return 1;
56:        }
57:
58:        for (i = 0; i < num; i++) {
59:            /* events[i].data.fd is ready for reading */
60:
61:            rc = read(events[i].data.fd, buf, sizeof(buf) - 1);
62:            if (rc < 0) {
63:                perror("read");
64:                return 1;
65:            } else if (!rc) {
66:                /* this pipe has been closed, don't try
67:                   to read from it again */
68:                if (epoll_ctl(epfd, EPOLL_CTL_DEL,
69:                             events[i].data.fd, &events[i])) {
70:                    perror("epoll_ctl(DEL)");
71:                    return 1;
72:                }
73:
74:                close(events[i].data.fd);
75:
76:                numFds--;
77:            } else {
78:                buf[rc] = '\0';
79:                printf("read: %s", buf);
80:            }
```

```
81:          }
82:      }
83:
84:      close(epfd);
85:
86:      return 0;
87: }
```

13.1.6 Comparing `poll()` and `epoll`

The differences between `poll()` and `epoll` are straightforward; `poll()` is well standardized but does not scale well, while `epoll` exists only on Linux but scales very well. Applications that watch a small number of file descriptors and value portability should use `poll()`, but any application that needs to monitor a large number of descriptors is better off with `epoll` even if it also needs to support `poll()` for other platforms.

The performance differences between the two methods can be quite dramatic. To illustrate how much better `epoll` scales, poll-vs-epoll.c measures how many `poll()` and `epoll_wait()` system calls can be made in one second for file descriptor sets of various sizes (the number of file descriptors to put in the set is specified on the command line). Each file descriptor refers to the read portion of a pipe, and they are created through `dup2()`.

Table 13.1 summarizes the results of running poll-vs-epoll.c for set sizes ranging from a single file descriptor to 100,000 file descriptors.[10] While the number of system calls per second drops off rapidly for `poll()`, it stays nearly constant for `epoll`.[11] As this table makes clear, `epoll` places far less load on the system than `poll()` does, and scales far better as a result.

```
1: /* poll-vs-epoll.c */
2:
3: #include <errno.h>
4: #include <fcntl.h>
5: #include <stdio.h>
6: #include <sys/epoll.h>
```

10. The program needs to be run as root for sets larger than about 1,000 descriptors.
11. This testing was not done particularly scientifically. Only a single test run was done, so the results show a little bit of jitter that would disappear over a large number of repetitions.

Table 13.1 Comparing `poll()` and `epoll`

File Descriptors	poll()	epoll
1	310,063	714,848
10	140,842	726,108
100	25,866	726,659
1,000	3,343	729,072
5,000	612	718,424
10,000	300	730,483
25,000	108	717,097
50,000	38	729,746
100,000	18	712,301

```
 7: #include <sys/poll.h>
 8: #include <sys/signal.h>
 9: #include <unistd.h>
10: #include <sys/resource.h>
11: #include <string.h>
12: #include <stdlib.h>
13:
14: #include <sys/select.h>
15:
16: int gotAlarm;
17:
18: void catch(int sig) {
19:     gotAlarm = 1;
20: }
21:
22: #define OFFSET 10
23:
24: int main(int argc, const char ** argv) {
25:     int pipeFds[2];
26:     int count;
27:     int numFds;
28:     struct pollfd * pollFds;
29:     struct epoll_event event;
30:     int epfd;
31:     int i;
32:     struct rlimit lim;
33:     char * end;
34:
35:     if (!argv[1]) {
```

```
36:            fprintf(stderr, "number expected\n");
37:            return 1;
38:        }
39:
40:        numFds = strtol(argv[1], &end, 0);
41:        if (*end) {
42:            fprintf(stderr, "number expected\n");
43:            return 1;
44:        }
45:
46:        printf("Running test on %d file descriptors.\n", numFds);
47:
48:        lim.rlim_cur = numFds + OFFSET;
49:        lim.rlim_max = numFds + OFFSET;
50:        if (setrlimit(RLIMIT_NOFILE, &lim)) {
51:            perror("setrlimit");
52:            exit(1);
53:        }
54:
55:        pipe(pipeFds);
56:
57:        pollFds = malloc(sizeof(*pollFds) * numFds);
58:
59:        epfd = epoll_create(numFds);
60:        event.events = EPOLLIN;
61:
62:        for (i = OFFSET; i < OFFSET + numFds; i++) {
63:            if (dup2(pipeFds[0], i) != i) {
64:                printf("failed at %d: %s\n", i, strerror(errno));
65:                exit(1);
66:            }
67:
68:            pollFds[i - OFFSET].fd = i;
69:            pollFds[i - OFFSET].events = POLLIN;
70:
71:            event.data.fd = i;
72:            epoll_ctl(epfd, EPOLL_CTL_ADD, i, &event);
73:        }
74:
75:        /* use a signal to know when time's up */
76:        signal(SIGALRM, catch);
```

```
 77:
 78:        count = 0;
 79:        gotAlarm = 0;
 80:        alarm(1);
 81:        while (!gotAlarm) {
 82:            poll(pollFds, numFds, 0);
 83:            count++;
 84:        }
 85:
 86:        printf("poll() calls per second: %d\n", count);
 87:
 88:        alarm(1);
 89:
 90:        count = 0;
 91:        gotAlarm = 0;
 92:        alarm(1);
 93:        while (!gotAlarm) {
 94:            epoll_wait(epfd, &event, 1, 0);
 95:            count++;
 96:        }
 97:
 98:        printf("epoll() calls per second: %d\n", count);
 99:
100:        return 0;
101: }
```

13.2 Memory Mapping

Linux allows a process to map files into its address space. Such a mapping creates a one-to-one correspondence between data in the file and data in the mapped memory region. Memory mapping has a number of applications.

1. High-speed file access. Normal I/O mechanisms, such as read() and write(), force the kernel to copy the data through a kernel buffer

rather than directly between the file that holds the device and the user-space process. Memory maps eliminate this middle buffer, saving a memory copy.[12]

2. Executable files can be mapped into a program's memory, allowing a program to dynamically load new executable sections. This is how dynamic loading, described in Chapter 27, is implemented.

3. New memory can be allocated by mapping portions of /dev/zero, a special device that is full of zeros,[13] or through an anonymous mapping. Electric Fence, described in Chapter 7, uses this mechanism to allocate memory.

4. New memory allocated through memory maps can be made executable, allowing it to be filled with machine instructions, which are then executed. This feature is used by just-in-time compilers.

5. Files can be treated just like memory and read using pointers instead of system calls. This can greatly simplify programs by eliminating the need for `read()`, `write()`, and `lseek()` calls.

6. Memory mapping allows processes to share memory regions that persist across process creation and destruction. The memory contents are stored in the mapped file, making it independent of any process.

13.2.1 Page Alignment

System memory is divided into chunks called **pages**. The size of a page varies with architecture, and on some processors the page size can be changed by the kernel. The `getpagesize()` function returns the size, in bytes, of each page on the system.

```
#include <unistd.h>

size_t getpagesize(void);
```

---

12. Although saving a memory copy may not seem that important, thanks to Linux's efficient caching mechanism, these copy latencies are the slowest part of writing to data files that do not have `O_SYNC` set.
13. Although most character devices cannot be mapped, /dev/zero can be mapped for exactly this type of application.

For each page on the system, the kernel tells the hardware how each process may access the page (such as write, execute, or not at all). When a process attempts to access a page in a manner that violates the kernel's restrictions, a segmentation fault (`SIGSEGV`) results, which normally terminates the process.

A memory address is said to be **page aligned** if it is the address of the beginning of a page. In other words, the address must be an integral multiple of the architecture's page size. On a system with 4K pages, 0, 4,096, 16,384, and 32,768 are all page-aligned addresses (of course, there are many more) because the first, second, fifth, and ninth pages in the system begin at those addresses.

13.2.2 Establishing Memory Mappings

New memory maps are created by the `mmap()` system call.

```
#include <sys/mman.h>

caddr_t mmap(caddr_t address, size_t length, int protection, int flags,
             int fd, off_t offset);
```

The `address` specifies where in memory the data should be mapped. Normally, `address` is `NULL`, which means the process does not care where the new mapping is, allowing the kernel to pick any address. If an address is specified, it must be page aligned and not already in use. If the requested mapping would conflict with another mapping or would not be page aligned, `mmap()` may fail.

The second parameter, `length`, tells the kernel how much of the file to map into memory. You can successfully map more memory than the file has data, but attempting to access it may result in a `SIGSEGV`.[14]

The process controls which types of access are allowed to the new memory region. It should be one or more of the values from Table 13.2 bitwise OR'ed together, or `PROT_NONE` if no access to the mapped region should be allowed. A file can be mapped only for access types that were also

---

14. A segmentation fault will result when you try to access an unallocated page.

Table 13.2 mmap() Protections

Flag	Description
PROT_READ PROT_WRITE PROT_EXEC	The mapped region may be read. The mapped region may be written. The mapped region may be executed.

Table 13.3 mmap() Flags

Flag	POSIX?	Description
MAP_ANONYMOUS	Yes	Ignore fd, create an anonymous mapping.
MAP_FIXED	Yes	Fail if address is invalid.
MAP_PRIVATE	Yes	Writes are private to process.
MAP_SHARED	Yes	Writes are copied to the file.
MAP_DENYWRITE	No	Do not allow normal writes to the file.
MAP_GROWSDOWN	No	Grow the memory region downward.
MAP_LOCKED	No	Lock the pages into memory.

requested when the file was originally opened. For example, a file that was opened O_RDONLY cannot be mapped for writing with PROT_WRITE.

The enforcement of the specified protection is limited by the hardware platform on which the program is running. Many architectures cannot allow code to execute in a memory region while disallowing reading from that memory region. On such hardware, mapping a region with PROT_EXEC is equivalent to mapping it with PROT_EXEC | PROT_READ. The memory protections passed to mmap() should be relied on only as minimal protections for this reason.

The flags specify other attributes of the mapped region. Table 13.3 summarizes all the flags. Many of the flags that Linux supports are not standard but may be useful in special circumstances. Table 13.3 differentiates between the standard mmap() flags and Linux's extra flags. All calls to mmap() must specify one of MAP_PRIVATE or MAP_SHARED; the remainder of the flags are optional.

MAP_ANONYMOUS

Rather than mapping a file, an **anonymous mapping** is returned. It behaves like a normal mapping, but no physical file is involved. Although this memory region cannot be shared with other processes, nor is it automatically saved to a file, anonymous mappings allow processes to allocate new memory for private use. Such mapping is often used by implementations of malloc(), as well as by more specialized applications. The fd parameter is ignored if this flag is used.

MAP_FIXED   If the mapping cannot be placed at the requested address, mmap() fails. If this flag is not specified, the kernel will try to place the map at address but will map it at an alternate address if it cannot. If the address has already been used by mmap(), the item mapped into that region will be replaced by a new memory map. This means that it is a very good idea to pass only addresses which were returned by previous calls to mmap(); if arbitrary addresses are used, the memory region used by system libraries may be overwritten.

MAP_PRIVATE

Modifications to the memory region should be private to the process, neither shared with other processes that map the same file (other than related processes that are forked after the memory map is created) nor reflected in the file itself. Either MAP_SHARED or MAP_PRIVATE must be used. If the memory region is not writeable, it does not matter which is used.

MAP_SHARED

Changes that are made to the memory region are copied back to the file that was mapped and shared with other processes that are mapping the same file. (To write changes to the memory region, PROT_WRITE must have been specified; otherwise, the memory region is immutable.) Either MAP_SHARED or MAP_PRIVATE must be specified.

MAP_DENYWRITE

Usually, system calls for normal file access (like write()) may modify a mapped file. If the region is being executed, this may not be a good idea, however. MAP_DENYWRITE causes writes to the file, other than those writes done through memory maps, to return ETXTBSY.

MAP_GROWSDOWN

Trying to access the memory immediately before a mapped region normally causes a SIGSEGV. This flag tells the kernel to extend the region to lower memory addresses, one page at a time, if a process tries to access the memory in the lower adjacent page, and continue the process as normal. This is used to allow the kernel to automatically grow processes' stacks on platforms that have stacks that grow down (the most common case). This is a platform-specific flag that is normally used only for system code.

The only limit on MAP_GROWSDOWN is the stack-size resource limit, discussed on pages 120–120. If no limit is set, the kernel will grow the mapped segment whenever doing so would be beneficial. It will not grow the segment past other mapped regions, however.

MAP_GROWSUP

This flag works just like MAP_GROWSDOWN, but it is for those (rare) platforms that have stacks that grow up, which means that the region is extended only with higher rather than lower addresses. (As of kernel 2.6.7, only the parisc architecture has stacks that grow up.) Like MAP_GROWSDOWN, this flag is normally reserved for system code, and the stack-size resource limit is applied.

MAP_LOCKED

The region is *locked* into memory, meaning it will never be swapped. This is important for real-time applications (mlock(), discussed on page 275, provides another method for memory locking). This normally may be specified only by the root user; normal users cannot lock pages into memory. Some Linux systems allow limited allocation of locked memory by users other than root, and it is possible that this capability will be added to the standard Linux kernel in the future.

After the flags comes the file descriptor, fd, for the file that is to be mapped into memory. If MAP_ANONYMOUS was used, this value is ignored. The final parameter specifies where in the file the mapping should begin, and it must be an integral multiple of the page size. Most applications begin the mapping from the start of the file by specifying an offset of zero.

mmap() returns an address that should be stored in a pointer. If an error occurred, it returns the address that is equivalent to -1. To test for this, the -1 constant should be typecast to a caddr_t rather than typecasting the returned address to an int. This ensures that you get the right result no matter what the sizes of pointers and integers.

Here is a program that acts like cat and expects a single name as a command-line argument. It opens that file, maps it into memory, and writes the entire file to standard output through a single write() call. It may be instructional to compare this example with the simple cat implementation on page 174. This example also illustrates that memory mappings stay in place after the mapped file is closed.

```
 1: /* map-cat.c */
 2:
 3: #include <errno.h>
 4: #include <fcntl.h>
 5: #include <sys/mman.h>
 6: #include <sys/stat.h>
 7: #include <sys/types.h>
 8: #include <stdio.h>
 9: #include <unistd.h>
10:
11: int main(int argc, const char ** argv) {
12:     int fd;
13:     struct stat sb;
14:     void * region;
15:
16:     if ((fd = open(argv[1], O_RDONLY)) < 0) {
17:         perror("open");
18:         return 1;
19:     }
20:
21:     /* stat the file so we know how much of it to map into memory */
22:     if (fstat(fd, &sb)) {
23:         perror("fstat");
24:         return 1;
25:     }
```

```
26:
27:     /* we could just as well map it MAP_PRIVATE as we aren't writing
28:        to it anyway */
29:     region = mmap(NULL, sb.st_size, PROT_READ, MAP_SHARED, fd, 0);
30:     if (region == ((caddr_t) -1)) {
31:         perror("mmap");
32:         return 1;
33:     }
34:
35:     close(fd);
36:
37:     if (write(1, region, sb.st_size) != sb.st_size) {
38:         perror("write");
39:         return 1;
40:     }
41:
42:     return 0;
43: }
```

13.2.3 Unmapping Regions

After a process is finished with a memory mapping, it can unmap the memory region through munmap(). This causes future accesses to that address to generate a SIGSEGV (unless the memory is subsequently remapped) and saves some system resources. All memory regions are unmapped when a process terminates or begins a new program through an exec() system call.

```
#include <sys/mman.h>

int munmap(caddr_t addr, int length);
```

The addr is the address of the beginning of the memory region to unmap, and length specifies how much of the memory region should be unmapped. Normally, each mapped region is unmapped by a single munmap() call. Linux can fragment maps if only a portion of a mapped region is unmapped, but this is not a portable technique.

13.2.4 Syncing Memory Regions to Disk

If a memory map is being used to write to a file, the modified memory pages and the file will be different for a period of time. If a process wishes to immediately write the pages to disk, it may use msync().

```
#include <sys/mman.h>

int msync(caddr_t addr, size_t length, int flags);
```

The first two parameters, addr and length, specify the region to sync to disk. The flags parameter specifies how the memory and disk should be synchronized. It consists of one or more of the following flags bitwise OR'ed together:

MS_ASYNC	The modified portions of the memory region are scheduled to be synchronized "soon." Only one of MS_ASYNC and MS_SYNC may be used.
MS_SYNC	The modified pages in the memory region are written to disk before the msync() system call returns. Only one of MS_ASYNC and MS_SYNC may be used.
MS_INVALIDATE	This option lets the kernel decide whether the changes are ever written to disk. Although this does not ensure that they will not be written, it tells the kernel that it does not have to save the changes. This flag is used only under special circumstances.
0	Passing 0 to msync() works on Linux kernels, though it is not well documented. It is similiar to MS_ASYNC, but means that pages should be written out to disk whenever it is appropriate to do so. This normally means they will be flushed when the bdflush kernel thread next runs (it normally runs every 30 seconds), whereas MS_ASYNC writes the pages out more aggressively.

13.2.5 Locking Memory Regions

Under Linux and most other modern operating systems, memory regions may be paged to disk (or discarded if they can be replaced in some other manner) when memory becomes scarce. Applications that are sensitive to external timing constraints may be adversely affected by the delay that results from the kernel paging memory back into RAM when the process needs it. To make these applications more robust, Linux allows a process to **lock** memory in RAM to make these timings more predictable. For security reasons, only processes running with root permission may lock memory.[15] If any process could lock regions of memory, a rogue process could lock all the system's RAM, making the system unusable. The total amount of memory locked by a process cannot exceed its RLIMIT_MEMLOCK usage limit.[16]

The following calls are used to lock and unlock memory regions:

```
#include <sys/mman.h>

int mlock(caddr_t addr, size_t length);
int mlockall(int flags);
int munlock(caddr_t addr, size_t length);
int munlockall(void);
```

The first of these, mlock(), locks length bytes starting at address addr. An entire page of memory must be locked at a time, so mlock() actually locks all the pages between the page containing the first address and the page containing the final address to lock, inclusively. When mlock() returns, all the affected pages will be in RAM.

If a process wants to lock its entire address space, mlockall() should be used. The flags argument is one or both of the following flags bitwise OR'ed together:

MCL_CURRENT   All the pages currently in the process's address space are locked into RAM. They will all be in RAM when mlock-all() returns.

---

15. This may change in the future as finer-grained system permissions are implemented in the kernel.
16. See pages 118–119 for information on resource limits.

MCL_FUTURE   All pages added to the process's address space will be locked into RAM.

Unlocking memory is nearly the same as locking it. If a process no longer needs any of its memory locked, munlockall() unlocks all the process's pages. munlock() takes the same arguments as mlock() and unlocks the pages containing the indicated region.

Locking a page multiple times is equivalent to locking it once. In either case, a single call to munlock() unlocks the affected pages.

13.3   File Locking

Although it is common for multiple processes to access a single file, doing so must be done carefully. Many files include complex data structures, and updating those data structures creates the same race conditions involved in signal handlers and shared memory regions.

There are two types of file locking. The most common, **advisory locking**, is not enforced by the kernel. It is purely a convention that all processes that access the file must follow. The other type, **mandatory locking**, is enforced by the kernel. When a process locks a file for writing, other processes that attempt to read or write to the file are suspended until the lock is released. Although this may seem like the more obvious method, mandatory locks force the kernel to check for locks on every read() and write(), substantially decreasing the performance of those system calls.

Linux provides two methods of locking files: lock files and record locking.

13.3.1 Lock Files

Lock files are the simplest method of file locking. Each data file that needs locking is associated with a lock file. When that lock file exists, the data file is considered locked and other processes do not access it. When the lock file does not exist, a process creates the lock file and then accesses the file. As long as the procedure for creating the lock file is atomic, ensuring that only one process at a time can "own" the lock file, this method guarantees that only one process accesses the file at a time.

This idea is pretty simple. When a process wants to access a file, it locks the file as follows:

```
fd = open("somefile.lck", O_RDONLY, 0644);
if (fd >= 0) {
    close(fd);
    printf("the file is already locked");
    return 1;
} else {
    /* the lock file does not exist, we can lock it and access it */
    fd = open("somefile.lck", O_CREAT | O_WRONLY, 0644");
    if (fd < 0) {
        perror("error creating lock file");
        return 1;
    }
    /* we could write our pid to the file */
    close(fd);
}
```

When the process is done with the file, it calls `unlink("somefile.lck");` to release the lock.

Although the above code segment may look correct, it would allow multiple processes to lock the same file under some circumstances, which is exactly what locking is supposed to avoid. If a process checks for the lock file's existence, sees that the lock does not exist, and is then interrupted by the kernel to let other processes run, another process could lock the file before the original process creates the lock file! The `O_EXCL` flag to `open()` is available to make lock file creation atomic, and hence immune to race conditions. When `O_EXCL` is specified, `open()` fails if the file already exists. This simplifies the creation of lock files, which is properly implemented as follows.

```
fd = open("somefile.lck", O_WRONLY | O_CREAT | O_EXCL, 0644);
if (fd < 0 && errno == EEXIST) {
    printf("the file is already locked");
    return 1;
} else if (fd < 0) {
    perror("unexpected error checking lock");
    return 1;
}

/* we could write our pid to the file */
close(fd);
```

Lock files are used to lock a wide variety of standard Linux files, including serial ports and the /etc/passwd file. Although they work well for many applications, they do suffer from a number of serious drawbacks.

- Only one process may have the lock at a time, preventing multiple processes from reading a file simultaneously. If the file is updated atomically,[17] processes that read the file can ignore the locking issue, but atomic updates are difficult to guarantee for complex file structures.

- The O_EXCL flag is reliable only on local file systems. None of the network file systems supported by Linux preserve O_EXCL semantics between multiple machines that are locking a common file.[18]

- The locking is only advisory; processes can update the file despite the existence of a lock.

- If the process that holds the lock terminates abnormally, the lock file remains. If the pid of the locking process is stored in the lock file, other processes can check for the existence of the locking process and remove the lock if it has terminated. This is, however, a complex procedure that is no help if the pid is being reused by another process when the check is made.

---

17. /etc/passwd is updated only by processes that create a new copy of the file with the modifications and then replace the original through a rename() system call. As this sequence provides an atomic update, processes may read from /etc/passwd at any time.
18. The Andrew Filesystem (AFS), which is available for Linux but not included in the standard kernel, does support O_EXCL across a network.

13.3.2 Record Locking

To overcome the problems inherent with lock files, **record locking** was added to both System V and BSD 4.3 through the `lockf()` and `flock()` system calls, respectively. POSIX defined a third mechanism for record locking that uses the `fcntl()` system call. Although Linux supports all three interfaces, we discuss only the POSIX interface, as it is now supported by nearly all Unix platforms. The `lockf()` function is implemented as an interface to `fcntl()`, however, so the rest of this discussion applies to both techniques.

There are two important distinctions between record locks and lock files. First of all, record locks lock an arbitrary portion of the file. For example, process A may lock bytes 50–200 of a file while another process locks bytes 2,500–3,000, without having the two locks conflict. Fine-grained locking is useful when multiple processes need to update a single file. The other advantage of record locking is that the locks are held by the kernel rather than the file system. When a process is terminated, all the locks it holds are released.

Like lock files, POSIX locks are also advisory. Linux, like System V, provides a mandatory variant of record locking that may be used but is not as portable. File locking may or may not work across networked file systems. Under recent versions of Linux, file locking works across NFS as long as all of the machines participating in the locks are running the NFS locking daemon `lockd`.

Record locking provides two types of locks: **read locks** and **write locks**. Read locks are also known as **shared locks**, because multiple processes may simultaneously hold read locks over a single region. It is always safe for multiple processes to read a data structure that is not being updated. When a process needs to write to a file, it must get a write lock (or **exclusive lock**). Only one process may hold a write lock for a record, and no read locks may exist for the record while the write lock is in place. This ensures that a process does not interfere with readers while it is writing to a region.

Multiple locks from a single process never conflict.[19] If a process has a read lock on bytes 200–250 and tries to get a write lock on the region 200–225,

---

19. This situation is more complicated for threads. Many Linux kernels and libraries treat threads as different processes, which raises the potential of file lock conflicts between threads (which is incompatible with the standard POSIX threads model).

it will succeed. The original lock is moved and becomes a read lock on bytes 226–250, and the new write lock from 200–225 is granted.[20] This rule prevents a process from forcing itself into a deadlock (although multiple processes can still deadlock).

POSIX record locking is done through the fcntl() system call. Recall from Chapter 11 that fcntl() looks like this:

```
#include <fcntl.h>

int fcntl(int fd, int command, long arg);
```

For all of the locking operations, the third parameter (arg) is a pointer to a struct flock.

```
#include <fcntl.h>

struct flock {
    short l_type;
    short l_whence;
    off_t l_start;
    off_t l_len;
    pid_t l_pid;
};
```

The first element, l_type, tells what type of lock is being set. It is one of the following:

F_RDLCK   A read (shared) lock is being set.

F_WRLCK   A write (exclusive) lock is being set.

F_UNLCK   An existing lock is being removed.

Linux is moving toward a more conventional thread model which shares file locks between all of the threads of a single process, but threaded programs should use the POSIX thread locking mechanisms instead of relying on either behavior for file locks.

20. This lock manipulation happens atomically—there is no point at which any part of the region is unlocked.

The next two elements, l_whence and l_start, specify where the region begins in the same manner file offsets are passed to lseek(). l_whence tells how l_start is to be interpreted and is one of SEEK_SET, SEEK_CUR, and SEEK_END; see page 171 for details on these values. The next entry, l_len, tells how long, in bytes, the lock is. If l_len is 0, the lock is considered to extend to the end of the file. The final entry, l_pid, is used only when locks are being queried. It is set to the pid of the process that owns the queried lock.

There are three fcntl() commands that pertain to locking the file. The operation is passed as the second argument to fcntl(). fcntl() returns -1 on error and 0 otherwise. The command argument should be set to one of the following:

F_SETLK   Sets the lock described by arg. If the lock cannot be granted because of a conflict with another process's locks, EAGAIN is returned. If the l_type is set to F_UNLCK, an existing lock is removed.

F_SETLKW   Similar to F_SETLK, but blocks until the lock is granted. If a signal occurs while the process is blocked, the fcntl() call returns EAGAIN.

F_GETLK   Checks to see if the described lock would be granted. If the lock would be granted, the struct flock is unchanged except for l_type, which is set to F_UNLCK. If the lock would not be granted, l_pid is set to the pid of the process that holds the conflicting lock. Success (0) is returned whether or not the lock would be granted.

Although F_GETLK allows a process to check whether a lock would be granted, the following code sequence could still fail to get a lock:

```
fcntl(fd, F_GETLK, &lockinfo);
if (lockinfo.l_type != F_UNLCK) {
    fprintf(stderr, "lock conflict\n");
    return 1;
}
lockinfo.l_type = F_RDLCK;
fcntl(fd, F_SETLK, &lockinfo);
```

Another process could lock the region between the two fcntl() calls, causing the second fcntl() to fail to set the lock.

As a simple example of record locking, here is a program that opens a file, obtains a read lock on the file, frees the read lock, gets a write lock, and then exits. Between each step, the program waits for the user to press return. If it fails to get a lock, it prints the pid of a process that holds a conflicting lock and waits for the user to tell it to try again. Running this sample program in two terminals makes it easy to experiment with POSIX locking rules.

```
 1: /* lock.c */
 2:
 3: #include <errno.h>
 4: #include <fcntl.h>
 5: #include <stdio.h>
 6: #include <unistd.h>
 7:
 8: /* displays the message, and waits for the user to press
 9:     return */
10: void waitforuser(char * message) {
11:     char buf[10];
12:
13:     printf("%s", message);
14:     fflush(stdout);
15:
16:     fgcts(buf, 9, stdin);
17: }
18:
19: /* Gets a lock of the indicated type on the fd which is passed.
20:     The type should be either F_UNLCK, F_RDLCK, or F_WRLCK */
21: void getlock(int fd, int type) {
22:     struct flock lockinfo;
23:     char message[80];
24:
25:     /* we'll lock the entire file */
26:     lockinfo.l_whence = SEEK_SET;
27:     lockinfo.l_start = 0;
28:     lockinfo.l_len = 0;
29:
30:     /* keep trying until we succeed */
31:     while (1) {
```

```
32:          lockinfo.l_type = type;
33:          /* if we get the lock, return immediately */
34:          if (!fcntl(fd, F_SETLK, &lockinfo)) return;
35:
36:          /* find out who holds the conflicting lock */
37:          fcntl(fd, F_GETLK, &lockinfo);
38:
39:          /* there's a chance the lock was freed between the F_SETLK
40:             and F_GETLK; make sure there's still a conflict before
41:             complaining about it */
42:          if (lockinfo.l_type != F_UNLCK) {
43:             sprintf(message, "conflict with process %d... press "
44:                     "<return> to retry:", lockinfo.l_pid);
45:             waitforuser(message);
46:          }
47:      }
48: }
49:
50: int main(void) {
51:     int fd;
52:
53:     /* set up a file to lock */
54:     fd = open("testlockfile", O_RDWR | O_CREAT, 0666);
55:     if (fd < 0) {
56:         perror("open");
57:         return 1;
58:     }
59:
60:     printf("getting read lock\n");
61:     getlock(fd, F_RDLCK);
62:     printf("got read lock\n");
63:
64:     waitforuser("\npress <return> to continue:");
65:
66:     printf("releasing lock\n");
67:     getlock(fd, F_UNLCK);
68:
69:     printf("getting write lock\n");
70:     getlock(fd, F_WRLCK);
71:     printf("got write lock\n");
72:
```

```
73:      waitforuser("\npress <return> to exit:");
74:
75:      /* locks are released when the file is closed */
76:
77:      return 0;
78: }
```

Locks are treated differently from other file attributes. Locks are associated with a *(pid, inode)* tuple, unlike most attributes of open files, which are associated with a file descriptor or file structure. This means that if a process

1. Opens a single file twice, resulting in two different file descriptors

2. Gets read locks on a single region in both file descriptors

3. Closes one of the file descriptors

then the file is no longer locked by the process. Only a single read lock was granted because only one *(pid, inode)* pair was involved (the second lock attempt succeeded because a process's locks can never conflict), and after one of the file descriptors is closed, the process does not have any locks on the file!

After a fork(), the parent process retains its file locks, but the child process does not. If child processes were to inherit locks, two processes would end up with a write lock on the same region of a file, which file locks are supposed to prevent.

File locks are inherited across an exec(), however. While POSIX does not define what happens to locks after an exec(), all variants of Unix preserve them.[21]

---

21. The effect of fork() and exec() calls on file locks is the biggest difference between POSIX file locking (and hence lockf() file locking) and BSD's flock() file locking.

13.3.3 Mandatory Locks

Both Linux and System V provide mandatory locking, as well as normal locking. Mandatory locks are established and released through the same `fcntl()` mechanism that is used for advisory record locking. The locks are mandatory if the locked file's setgid bit is set but its group execute bit is not set. If this is not the case, advisory locking is used.

When mandatory locking is enabled, the `read()` and `write()` system calls block when they conflict with locks that have been set. If a process tries to `write()` to a portion of a file that a different process has a read or write lock on, the process without the lock blocks until the lock is released. Similarly, `read()` calls block on regions that are included in mandatory write locks.

Mandatory record locking causes a larger performance loss than advisory locking, because every `read()` and `write()` call must be checked for conflicts with locks. It is also not as portable as POSIX advisory locks, so we do not recommend using mandatory locking in most applications.

13.3.4 Leasing a File

Both advisory and mandatory locking are designed to prevent a process from accessing a file, or part of a file, that another process is using. When a lock is in place, the process that needs access to the file has to wait for the process owning the lock to finish. This structure is fine for most applications, but occasionally a program would like to use a file until someone else needs it, and is willing to give up exclusive access to the file if necessary. To allow this, Linux provides **file leases** (other systems call these opportunistic locks, or **oplocks**).[22]

Putting a lease on a file allows a process to be notified (via a signal) when that file is accessed by another process. There are two types of leases available: read leases and write leases. A read lease causes a signal to be sent when the file is opened for writing, opened with `O_TRUNC`, or `truncate()` is called for that file. A write lease also sends a signal when the file is opened

---

22. By far the most common user of file leases is the samba file server, which uses file leases to allow clients to cache their writes to increase performance.

for reading.[23] File leases work only for modifications made to the file by the same system running the application that owns the lease. If the file is a local file (not a file being accessed across the network), any appropriate file access triggers a signal. If the file is being accessed across the network, only processes on the same machine as the leaseholder cause the signal to be sent; accesses from any other machine proceed as if the lease were not in place.

The fcntl() system call is used to create, release, and inquire about file leases. Leases can be placed only on normal files (they cannot be placed on files such as pipes or directories), and write leases are granted only to the owner of a file. The first argument to fcntl() is the file descriptor we are interested in monitoring, and the second argument, command, specifies what operation to perform.

F_SETLEASE   A lease is created or released, depending on the value of the final argument to fcntl(); F_RDLCK creates a read lease, F_WRLCK creates a write lock, and F_UNLCK releases any lease that may be in place. If a new lease is requested, the new lease replaces any lease already in place. If an error occurs, a negative value is returned; zero or a positive value indicates success.[24]

F_GETLEASE   The type of lease currently in place for the file is returned (one of F_RDLCK, F_WRLCK, or F_UNLCK).

When one of the monitored events occurs on a leased file, the kernel sends the process holding the lease a signal. By default, SIGIO is sent, but the process can choose which signal is sent for that file by calling fcntl() with the second argument set to F_SETSIG and the final argument set to the signal that should be used instead.

---

23. If it seems a little strange that a write lease notifies the process of opening the file for reading, think of it from the point of view of the process taking out the lease. It would need to know if another process wanted to read from the file only if it was itself writing to that file.
24. Older kernels could return either zero or one on success, while newer ones always return zero on success. In either case, checking for negative or nonnegative works fine.

Using F_SETSIG has one other important effect. By default, no siginfo_t is passed to the handler when SIGIO is delivered. If F_SETSIG has been used, even if the signal the kernel is told to deliver is SIGIO, and SA_SIGINFO was specified when the signal handler was registered, the file descriptor whose lease triggered the event is passed to the signal handler as the si_fd member of the siginfo_t passed to the signal handler. This allows a single signal to be used for leases on multiple files, with si_fd letting the signal handler know which file needs attention.[25]

The only two system calls that can cause a signal to be sent for a leased file are open() and truncate(). When they are called by a process on a file that has a lease in place, those system calls block[26] and the process holding the lease is sent a signal. The open() or truncate() completes after the lease has been removed from the file (or the file is closed by the process holding the lease, which causes the lease to be released). If the process holding the lease does not remove the release within the amount of time specified in the file /proc/sys/fs/lease-break-time, the kernel breaks the lease and lets the triggering system call complete.

Here is an example of using file leases to be notified when another process needs to access a file. It takes a list of files from the command line and places write leases on each of them. When another process wants to access the file (even for reading, since a write lock was used) the program releases its lock on the file, allowing that other process to continue. It also prints a message saying which file was released.

```
 1: /* leases.c */
 2:
 3: #define _GNU_SOURCE
 4:
 5: #include <fcntl.h>
 6: #include <signal.h>
 7: #include <stdio.h>
 8: #include <string.h>
 9: #include <unistd.h>
10:
```

---

25. If one signal is used for leases on multiple files, make sure the signal is a real-time signal so that multiple lease events are queued. If a regular signal is used, signals may get lost if the lease events occur close together.
26. Unless O_NONBLOCK was specified as a flag to open(), in which case EWOULDBLOCK would be returned.

```
11: const char ** fileNames;
12: int numFiles;
13:
14: void handler(int sig, siginfo_t * siginfo, void * context) {
15:     /* When a lease is up, print a message and close the file.
16:         We assume that the first file we open will get file
17:         descriptor 3, the next 4, and so on. */
18:
19:     write(1, "releasing ", 10);
20:     write(1, fileNames[siginfo->si_fd - 3],
21:             strlen(fileNames[siginfo->si_fd - 3]));
22:     write(1, "\n", 1);
23:     fcntl(siginfo->si_fd, F_SETLEASE, F_UNLCK);
24:     close(siginfo->si_fd);
25:     numFiles--;
26: }
27:
28: int main(int argc, const char ** argv) {
29:     int fd;
30:     const char ** file;
31:     struct sigaction act;
32:
33:     if (argc < 2) {
34:         fprintf(stderr, "usage: %s <filename>+\n", argv[0]);
35:         return 1;
36:     }
37:
38:     /* Register the signal handler. Specifying SA_SIGINFO lets
39:         the handler learn which file descriptor had the lease
40:         expire. */
41:     act.sa_sigaction = handler;
42:     act.sa_flags = SA_SIGINFO;
43:     sigemptyset(&act.sa_mask);
44:     sigaction(SIGRTMIN, &act, NULL);
45:
46:     /* Store the list of filenames in a global variable so that
47:         the signal handler can access it. */
48:     fileNames = argv + 1;
49:     numFiles = argc - 1;
50:
51:     /* Open the files, set the signal to use, and create the
```

```
52:          lease */
53:      for (file = fileNames; *file; file++) {
54:          if ((fd = open(*file, O_RDONLY)) < 0) {
55:              perror("open");
56:              return 1;
57:          }
58:
59:          /* We have to use F_SETSIG for the siginfo structure to
60:              get filled in properly */
61:          if (fcntl(fd, F_SETSIG, SIGRTMIN) < 0) {
62:              perror("F_SETSIG");
63:              return 1;
64:          }
65:
66:          if (fcntl(fd, F_SETLEASE, F_WRLCK) < 0) {
67:              perror("F_SETLEASE");
68:              return 1;
69:          }
70:      }
71:
72:      /* As long as files remain open, wait for signals. */
73:      while (numFiles)
74:          pause();
75:
76:      return 0;
77: }
```

13.4 Alternatives to read() and write()

While the read() and write() system calls are all applications need to
retrieve and store data in a file, they are not always the fastest method.
They allow a single piece of data to be manipulated; if multiple pieces of
data need to be written, multiple system calls are required. Similarly, if the
application needs to access data in different locations in the file, it must
call lseek() between every read() or write(), doubling the number of
system calls needed. To improve efficiency, there are other system calls
that improve things.

13.4.1 Scatter/Gather Reads and Writes

Applications often want to read and write various types of data to consecutive areas of a file. Although this can be done fairly easily through multiple read() and write() calls, this solution is not particularly efficient. Applications could instead move all the data into a consecutive memory region, allowing a single system call, but doing so results in many unnecessary memory operations.

Linux provides readv() and writev(), which implement scatter/gather reads and writes.[27] Instead of being passed a single pointer and buffer size, as their standard siblings are, these system calls are passed an array of records, each record describing a buffer. The buffers get read from or written to in the order they are listed in the array. Each buffer is described by a struct iovec.

```
#include <sys/uio.h>

struct iovec {
    void * iov_base;    /* buffer address */
    size_t iov_len;     /* buffer length */
};
```

The first element, iov_base, points to the buffer space. The iov_len item is the number of characters in the buffer. These items are the same as the second and third parameters passed to read() and write().

Here are the prototypes for readv() and writev():

```
#include <sys/uio.h>

int readv(int fd, const struct iovec * vector, size_t count);
int writev(int fd, const struct iovec * vector, size_t count);
```

The first argument is the file descriptor to be read from or written to. The second, vector, points to an array of count struct iovec items. Both functions return the total number of bytes read or written.

---

27. They are so named because the reads scatter data across memory, and the writes gather data from different memory regions. They are also known as vector reads and writes, which is the origin of the v at the end of readv() and writev().

Here is a simple example program that uses writev() to display a simple message on standard output:

```
 1: /* gather.c */
 2:
 3: #include <sys/uio.h>
 4:
 5: int main(void) {
 6:     struct iovec buffers[3];
 7:
 8:     buffers[0].iov_base = "hello";
 9:     buffers[0].iov_len = 5;
10:
11:     buffers[1].iov_base = " ";
12:     buffers[1].iov_len = 1;
13:
14:     buffers[2].iov_base = "world\n";
15:     buffers[2].iov_len = 6;
16:
17:     writev(1, buffers, 3);
18:
19:     return 0;
20: }
```

13.4.2 Ignoring the File Pointer

Programs that use binary files often look something like this:

```
lseek(fd, SEEK_SET, offset1);
read(fd, buffer, bufferSize);
offset2 = someOperation(buffer);
lseek(fd, SEEK_SET, offset2);
read(fd, buffer2, bufferSize2);
offset3 = someOperation(buffer2);
lseek(fd, SEEK_SET, offset3);
read(fd, buffer3, bufferSize3);
```

The need to lseek() to a new location before every read() doubles the number of system calls, as the file pointer is never positioned correctly after a read() because the data is not stored in the file consecutively. There are alternatives to read() and write() that require the file offset as a parameter, and neither alternative uses the file pointer to know what part of the file to access or to update it. Both functions work only on seekable files, as nonseekable files can be read from and written to only at the current location.

```
#define _XOPEN_SOURCE 500
#include <unistd.h>

size_t pread(int fd, void *buf, size_t count, off_t offset);
size_t pwrite(int fd, void *buf, size_t count, off_t offset);
#endif
```

These look just like the prototypes for read() and write() with a fourth parameter, offset. The offset specifies which point in the file the data should be read from or written to. Like their namesakes, these functions return the number of bytes that were transferred. Here is a version of pread() implemented using read() and lseek() that should make its function easy to understand:[28]

```
int pread(int fd, void * data, int size, int offset) {
    int oldOffset;
    int rc;
    int oldErrno;

    /* move the file pointer to the new location */
    oldOffset = lseek(fd, SEEK_SET, offset);
    if (oldOffset < 0) return -1;

    rc = read(fd, data, size);

    /* restore the file pointer, being careful to save errno */
    oldErrno = errno;
    lseek(fd, SEEK_SET, oldOffset);
    errno = oldErrno;

    return rc;
}
```

---

28. This emulated version gets most of the behavior right, but it acts differently than the actual system call if signals are received while it is being executed.

CHAPTER 14

Directory Operations

Linux, like many other operating systems, uses directories to organize files. Directories (which are just special types of files that contain lists of file names) contain files, as well as other directories, allowing a file hierarchy to be built. All Linux systems have a root directory, known as /, through which (directly or indirectly) you access all the files on the system.

14.1 The Current Working Directory

14.1.1 Finding the Current Working Directory

The getcwd() function allows a process to find the name of its current directory relative to the system's root directory.

```
#include <unistd.h>
char * getcwd(char * buf, size_t size);
```

The first parameter, buf, points to a buffer that is filled in with the path to the current working directory. If the current path is larger than size - 1 bytes long (the -1 allows the path to be '\0' terminated), the function returns an error of ERANGE. If the call succeeds, buf is returned; NULL is returned if an error occurs. Although most modern shells maintain a PWD environment variable that contains the path to the current directory, it does not necessarily have the same value a call to getcwd() would return. PWD often includes path elements that are symbolic links to other directories, but getcwd() always returns a path free from symbolic links.

If the current path is unknown (such as at program startup), the buffer that holds the current directory must be dynamically allocated because the current path may be arbitrarily large. Code that properly reads the current path looks like this:

```
char * buf;
int len = 50;

buf = malloc(len);
while (!getcwd(buf, len) && errno == ERANGE) {
    len += 50;
    buf = realloc(buf, len);
}
```

Linux, along with many other Unix systems, provides a useful extension to the POSIX getcwd() specification. If buf is NULL, the function allocates a buffer large enough to contain the current path through the normal malloc() mechanism. Although the caller must take care to properly free() the result, using this extension can make code look much cleaner than using a loop, as was shown in the earlier example.

BSD's getwd() function is a commonly used alternative to getcwd(), but it suffers from certain defects that led to the development of getcwd().

```
#include <unistd.h>
char * getwd(char * buf);
```

Like getcwd(), getwd() fills in buf with the current path, although the function has no idea how large buf is. getwd() never writes more than PATH_MAX (defined through <limits.h>) to the buffer, which allows programs to avoid buffer overruns, but does not give the program any mechanism for finding the correct path if it is longer than PATH_MAX bytes![1] This function is supported by Linux only for legacy applications and should not be used by new applications. Instead, use the correct and more portable getcwd() function.

If the current directory path is displayed to users, it is normally a good idea to check the PWD environment variable. If it is set, it contains the path the user thinks he is using (which may contain symbolic links for some of the elements in the path), which is generally what the user would like an

---

1. That is right; PATH_MAX is not an actual limit. POSIX considers it *indeterminate*, which is morally equivalent to "do not use this."

application to display. To make this easier, Linux's C library provides the get_current_dir_name() function, which is implemented like this:

```
char * get_current_dir_name() {
    char * env = getenv("PWD");

    if (env)
        return strdup(env);
    else
        return getcwd(NULL, 0);
}
```

14.1.2 The . and .. Special Files

Every directory, including the root directory, includes two special files, called . and .., which are useful in some circumstances. The first, ., is the same as the current directory. This means that the file names somefile and ./somefile are equivalent.

The other special file name, .., is the current directory's parent directory. For the root directory, .. refers to the root directory itself (because the root directory has no parent).

Both . and .. can be used wherever a directory name can be used. It is common to see symbolic links refer to paths such as ../include/mylib, and file names like /./foo/.././bar/./fubar/../../usr/bin/less are perfectly legal (although admittedly convoluted).[2]

14.1.3 Changing the Current Directory

There are two system calls that change a process's current directory: chdir() and fchdir().

```
#include <unistd.h>
int chdir(const char * pathname);
int fchdir(int fd);
```

---

2. For the curious, that pathname is equivalent to the much simpler /usr/bin/less.

The first of these takes the name of a directory as its sole argument; the second takes a file descriptor that is an open directory. In either case, the specified directory is made the current working directory. These functions can fail if their arguments specify a file that is not a directory or if the process does not have proper permissions.

14.2   Changing the Root Directory

Although the system has a single root directory, the meaning of / may be changed for each process on the system. This is usually done to prevent suspect processes (such as ftp daemons handling requests from untrusted users) from accessing the complete file system. For example, if /home/ftp is specified as the process's root directory, running chdir("/") will make the process's current directory /home/ftp, and getcwd() will return / to keep things consistent for the process in question. To ensure security, if the process tries to chdir("/.."), it is left in its / directory (the system-wide /home/ftp directory), just as normal processes that chdir("/..") are left in the system-wide root directory. A process may easily change its current root directory through the chroot() system call. The process's new root directory path is interpreted with the current root directory in place, so chroot("/") does not modify the process's current root directory.

```
#include <unistd.h>
int chroot(const char * path);
```

Here, the path specifies the new root directory for the process. This system call does *not* change the current working directory of the process, however. The process can still access files in the current directory, as well as relative to it (that is, ../../directory/file). Most processes that chroot() themselves immediately change their current working directory to be inside the new root hierarchy with chdir("/"), or something similar, and not doing so would be a security problem in some applications.

14.3   Creating and Removing Directories

14.3.1 Creating New Directories

Creating new directories is straightforward.

```
#include <fcntl.h>
#include <unistd.h>
int mkdir(const char * dirname, mode_t mode);
```

The path specified by dirname is created as a new directory with permissions mode (which is modified by the process's umask). If dirname specifies an existing file or if any of the elements of dirname are not a directory or a symbolic link to a directory, the system call fails.

14.3.2 Removing Directories

Removing a directory is almost exactly the same as removing a file; only the name of the system call is different.

```
#include <unistd.h>
int rmdir(char * pathname);
```

For rmdir() to succeed, the directory must be empty (other than the omnipresent . and .. entries); otherwise, ENOTEMPTY is returned.

14.4   Reading a Directory's Contents

It is common for a program to need a list of the files contained in a directory. Linux provides a set of functions that allow a directory to be handled as an abstract entity to avoid forcing programs to depend on the exact format of directories employed by a file system. Opening and closing directories is straightforward.

```
#include <dirent.h>
DIR * opendir(const char * pathname);
int closedir(DIR * dir);
```

opendir() returns a pointer to a DIR data type, which is abstract (just like stdio's FILE structure) and should not be manipulated outside the C library. As directories may be opened only for reading, it is not necessary to specify what mode the directory is opened with. opendir() succeeds only if the directory exists—it cannot be used to create new directories (use mkdir() for that). Closing a directory can fail only if the dir parameter is invalid.

Once the directory has been opened, directory entries are read sequentially until the end of the directory is reached.

readdir() returns the name of the next file in the directory. Directories are not ordered in any way, so do not assume that the contents of the directory are sorted. If you need a sorted list of files, you must sort the file names yourself. The readdir() function is defined like this:

```
#include <dirent.h>
struct dirent * readdir(DIR * dir);
```

A pointer to a struct dirent is returned to the caller. Although struct dirent contains multiple members, the only one that is portable is d_name, which holds the file name of the directory entry. The rest of struct dirent's members are system specific. The only interesting one of these is d_ino, which contains the inode number of the file.

The only tricky part of this is determining when an error has occurred. Unfortunately, readdir() returns NULL if an error occurs or if there are no more entries in the directory. To differentiate between the two cases, you must check errno. This task is made more difficult by readdir() not changing errno unless an error occurs, which means errno must be set to a known value (normally, 0) before calling readdir() to allow proper error checking. Here is a simple program that writes the names of the files in the current directory to stdout:

```
1: /* dircontents.c */
2:
3: #include <errno.h>
4: #include <dirent.h>
5: #include <stdio.h>
6:
7: int main(void) {
8:     DIR * dir;
```

```
 9:      struct dirent * ent;
10:
11:      /* "." is the current directory */
12:      if (!(dir = opendir("."))) {
13:          perror("opendir");
14:          return 1;
15:      }
16:
17:      /* set errno to 0, so we can tell when readdir() fails */
18:      errno = 0;
19:      while ((ent = readdir(dir))) {
20:          puts(ent->d_name);
21:          /* reset errno, as puts() could modify it */
22:          errno = 0;
23:      }
24:
25:      if (errno) {
26:          perror("readdir");
27:          return 1;
28:      }
29:
30:      closedir(dir);
31:
32:      return 0;
33: }
```

14.4.1 Starting Over

If you need to reread the contents of a directory that has already been opened with opendir(), rewinddir() resets the DIR structure so that the next call to readdir() returns the first file in the directory.

```
#include <dirent.h>
int rewinddir(DIR * dir);
```

14.5 File Name Globbing

Most Linux users take it for granted that running ls *.c does not tell them all about the file in the current directory called *.c. Instead, they expect to see a list of all the file names in the current directory whose names end with .c. This file-name expansion from *.c to ladsh.c dircontents.c (for example) is normally handled by the shell, which **globs** all the parameters to programs it runs. Programs that help users manipulate files often need to glob file names, as well. There are two common ways to glob file names from inside a program.

14.5.1 Use a Subprocess

The oldest method is simply to run a shell as a child process and let it glob the file names for you. The standard popen()[3] function makes this simple—just run the command ls *.c through popen() and read the results. Although this may seem simplistic, it is a simple solution to the globbing problem and is highly portable (which is why applications like Perl use this approach).

Here is a program that globs all its arguments and displays all of the matches:

```
 1: /* popenglob.c */
 2:
 3: #include <stdio.h>
 4: #include <string.h>
 5: #include <sys/wait.h>
 6: #include <unistd.h>
 7:
 8: int main(int argc, const char ** argv) {
 9:     char buf[1024];
10:     FILE * ls;
11:     int result;
12:     int i;
13:
14:     strcpy(buf, "ls ");
```

---

3. See page 132 for information on popen().

```
15:
16:        for (i = 1; i < argc; i++) {
17:            strcat(buf, argv[i]);
18:            strcat(buf, " ");
19:        }
20:
21:        ls = popen(buf, "r");
22:        if (!ls) {
23:            perror("popen");
24:            return 1;
25:        }
26:
27:        while (fgets(buf, sizeof(buf), ls))
28:            printf("%s", buf);
29:
30:        result = pclose(ls);
31:
32:        if (!WIFEXITED(result)) return 1;
33:
34:        return 0;
35: }
```

14.5.2 Internal Globbing

If you need to glob many file names, running many subshells through
popen() may be too inefficient. The glob() function allows you to glob
file names without running any subprocesses, at the price of increased complexity and reduced portability. Although glob() is specified by POSIX.2,
many Unix variants do not yet support it.

```
#include <glob.h>
int glob(const char *pattern, int flags,
        int errfunc(const char * epath, int eerrno), glob_t * pglob);
```

The first parameter, pattern, specifies the pattern that file names must
match. This function understands the *, ?, and [] globbing operators,
and optionally also the {, }, and ~ globbing operators, and treats them
identically to the standard shells. The final parameter is a pointer to a
structure that gets filled in with the results of the glob. The structure is
defined like this:

```
#include <glob.h>

typedef struct {
    int gl_pathc;      /* number of paths in gl_pathv */
    char **gl_pathv;   /* list of gl_pathc matched pathnames */
    int gl_offs;       /* slots to reserve in gl_pathv for GLOB_DOOFS */
} glob_t;
```

The flags are of one or more of the following values bitwise OR'ed together:

GLOB_ERR	Returned if an error occurs (if the function cannot read the contents of a directory due to permissions problems, for example).
GLOB_MARK	If the pattern matches a directory name, that directory name will have a / appended to it on return.
GLOB_NOSORT	Normally, the returned pathnames are sorted alphabetically. If this flag is specified, they are not sorted.
GLOB_DOOFS	If set, the first pglob->gl_offs strings in the returned list of pathnames are left empty. This allows glob() to be used while building a set of arguments that will be passed directly to execv().
GLOB_NOCHECK	If no file names match the pattern, the pattern itself is returned as the sole match (usually, no matches are returned). In either case, if the pattern does not contain any globbing operators, the pattern is returned.
GLOB_APPEND	pglob is assumed to be a valid result from a previous call to glob(), and any results from this invocation are appended to the results from the previous call. This makes it easy to glob multiple patterns.
GLOB_NOESCAPE	Usually, if a backslash (\) precedes a globbing operator, the operator is taken as a normal character instead of being assigned its special meaning. For example, the pattern a* usually matches only a file named a*. If

GLOB_NOESCAPE is specified, \ loses this special meaning, and a* matches any file name that begins with the characters a\. In this case, a\ and a\bcd would be matched, but arachnid would not because it does not contain a \.

GLOB_PERIOD

Most shells do not allow glob operators to match files whose names begin with a . (try ls * in your home directory and compare it with ls -a .). The glob() function generally behaves this way, but GLOB_PERIOD allows the globbing operators to match a leading . character. GLOB_PERIOD is not defined by POSIX.

GLOB_BRACE

Many shells (following the lead of csh) expand sequences with braces as alternatives; for example, the pattern "{a,b}" is expanded to "a b", and the pattern "a{,b,c}" to "a ab ac". The GLOB_BRACE enables this behavior. GLOB_BRACE is not defined by POSIX.

GLOB_NOMAGIC

Acts just like GLOB_NOCHECK except that it appends the pattern to the list of results only if it contains no special characters. GLOB_NOMAGIC is not defined by POSIX.

GLOB_TILDE

Turns on tilde expansion, in which ~ or the substring ~/ is expanded to the path to the current user's home directory, and ~user is expanded to the path to *user's* home directory. GLOB_TILDE is not defined by POSIX.

GLOB_ONLYDIR

Matches only directories, not any other type of file. GLOB_ONLYDIR is not defined by POSIX.

Often, glob() encounters directories to which the process does not have access, which causes an error. Although the error may need to be handled in some manner, if the glob() returns the error (thanks to GLOB_ERR), there is no way to restart the globbing operation where the previous globbing operation encountered the error. As this makes it difficult both to handle errors that occur during a glob() and to complete the glob, glob() allows the errors to be reported to a function of the caller's choice, which is specified in the third parameter to glob(). It should be prototyped as follows:

```
int globerr(const char * pathname, int globerrno);
```

The function is passed the pathname that caused the error and the errno value that resulted from one of opendir(), readdir(), or stat(). If the error function returns nonzero, glob() returns with an error. Otherwise, the globbing operation is continued.

The results of the glob are stored in the glob_t structure referenced by pglob. It includes the following members, which allow the caller to find the matched file names:

gl_pathc   The number of pathnames that matched the pattern

gl_pathv   Array of pathnames that matched the pattern

After the returned glob_t has been used, the memory it uses should be freed by passing it to globfree().

```
void globfree(glob_t * pglob);
```

glob() returns GLOB_NOSPACE if it ran out of memory, GLOB_ABEND if a read error caused the function to fail, GLOB_NOMATCH if no matches were found, or 0 if the function succeeded and found matches.

To help illustrate glob(), here is a program called globit, which accepts multiple patterns as arguments, globs them all, and displays the result. If an error occurs, a message describing the error is displayed, but the glob operation is continued.

```
 1: /* globit.c */
 2:
 3: #include <errno.h>
 4: #include <glob.h>
 5: #include <stdio.h>
 6: #include <string.h>
 7: #include <unistd.h>
 8:
 9: /* This is the error function we pass to glob(). It just displays
10:    an error and returns success, which allows the glob() to
11:    continue. */
```

```
12: int errfn(const char * pathname, int theerr) {
13:     fprintf(stderr, "error accessing %s: %s\n", pathname,
14:             strerror(theerr));
15:
16:     /* We want the glob operation to continue, so return 0 */
17:     return 0;
18: }
19:
20: int main(int argc, const char ** argv) {
21:     glob_t result;
22:     int i, rc, flags;
23:
24:     if (argc < 2) {
25:         printf("at least one argument must be given\n");
26:         return 1;
27:     }
28:
29:     /* set flags to 0; it gets changed to GLOB_APPEND later */
30:     flags = 0;
31:
32:     /* iterate over all of the command-line arguments */
33:     for (i = 1; i < argc; i++) {
34:         rc = glob(argv[i], flags, errfn, &result);
35:
36:         /* GLOB_ABEND can't happen thanks to errfn */
37:         if (rc == GLOB_NOSPACE) {
38:             fprintf(stderr, "out of space during glob operation\n");
39:             return 1;
40:         }
41:
42:         flags |= GLOB_APPEND;
43:     }
44:
45:     if (!result.gl_pathc) {
46:         fprintf(stderr, "no matches\n");
47:         rc = 1;
48:     } else {
49:         for (i = 0; i < result.gl_pathc; i++)
50:             puts(result.gl_pathv[i]);
51:         rc = 0;
52:     }
```

```
53:
54:     /* the glob structure uses memory from the malloc() pool, which
55:         needs to be freed */
56:     globfree(&result);
57:
58:     return rc;
59: }
```

14.6 Adding Directories and Globbing to ladsh

The evolution of ladsh continues here by adding four new features to
ladsh3.c.

1. The cd built-in, to change directories.

2. The pwd built-in, to display the current directory.

3. File name globbing.

4. Some new messages are displayed to take advantage of strsignal().
    These changes are discussed on page 222 of Chapter 12.

14.6.1 Adding cd and pwd

Adding the built-in commands is a straightforward application of chdir()
and getcwd(). The code fits into runProgram() right where all the other
built-in commands are handled. Here is how the built-in command-
handling section looks in ladsh3.c:

```
422:     if (!strcmp(newJob.progs[0].argv[0], "exit")) {
423:         /* this should return a real exit code */
424:         exit(0);
425:     } else if (!strcmp(newJob.progs[0].argv[0], "pwd")) {
426:         len = 50;
427:         buf = malloc(len);
428:         while (!getcwd(buf, len) && errno == ERANGE) {
429:             len += 50;
```

```
430:                buf = realloc(buf, len);
431:            }
432:            printf("%s\n", buf);
433:            free(buf);
434:            return 0;
435:        } else if (!strcmp(newJob.progs[0].argv[0], "cd")) {
436:            if (!newJob.progs[0].argv[1] == 1)
437:                newdir = getenv("HOME");
438:            else
439:                newdir = newJob.progs[0].argv[1];
440:            if (chdir(newdir))
441:                printf("failed to change current directory: %s\n",
442:                        strerror(errno));
443:            return 0;
444:        } else if (!strcmp(newJob.progs[0].argv[0], "jobs")) {
445:            for (job = jobList->head; job; job = job->next)
446:                printf(JOB_STATUS_FORMAT, job->jobId, "Running",
447:                        job->text);
448:            return 0;
449:        }
```

14.6.2 Adding File Name Globbing

File name globbing, in which the shell expands the *, [], and ? characters
into matching file names, is a bit tricky to implement because of the various
quoting methods. The first modification is to build up each argument as a
string suitable for passing to glob(). If a globbing character is quoted by a
shell quoting sequence (enclosed in double quotes, for example), then the
globbing character is prefixed by a \ to prevent glob() from expanding it.
Although this sounds tricky, it is easy to do.

Two parts of parseCommand()'s command parsing need to be slightly modified. The " and ' sequences are handled near the top of the loop, which
splits a command string into arguments. If we are in the middle of a quoted
string and we encounter a globbing character, we quote the globbing character with a \ while parsing it, which looks like this:

```
189:        } else if (quote) {
190:            if (*src == '\\') {
191:                src++;
```

```
192:                    if (!*src) {
193:                        fprintf(stderr,
194:                                "character expected after \\\n");
195:                        freeJob(job);
196:                        return 1;
197:                    }
198:
199:                    /* in shell, "\'" should yield \' */
200:                    if (*src != quote) *buf++ = '\\';
201:                } else if (*src == '*' || *src == '?' || *src == '[' ||
202:                        *src == ']')
203:                    *buf++ = '\\';
204:                *buf++ = *src;
205:            } else if (isspace(*src)) {
```

Only the middle else if and the assignment statement in its body were
added to the code. Similar code needs to be added to the handling of \
characters that occur outside quoted strings. This case is handled at the
end of parseCommand()'s main loop. Here is the modified code:

```
329:        case '\\':
330:            src++;
331:            if (!*src) {
332:                freeJob(job);
333:                fprintf(stderr, "character expected after \\\n");
334:                return 1;
335:            }
336:            if (*src == '*' || *src == '[' || *src == ']'
337:                        || *src == '?')
338:                *buf++ = '\\';
339:            /* fallthrough */
340:        default:
341:            *buf++ = *src;
```

The same code was added here to quote the globbing characters.

Those two sequences of code ensure that each argument may be passed
to glob() without finding unintended matches. Now we add a function,
globLastArgument(), which globs the most recently found argument for
a child program and replaces it with whatever matches it finds.

To help ease the memory management, a glob_t called globResult, which is used to hold the results of all glob operations, has been added to struct childProgram. We also added an integer, freeGlob, which is nonzero if freeJob() should free the globResult contained in the structure. Here is the complete definition for struct childProgram in ladsh3.c:

```
35: struct childProgram {
36:     pid_t pid;                       /* 0 if exited */
37:     char ** argv;                    /* program name and arguments */
38:     int numRedirections;             /* elements in redirection array */
39:     struct redirectionSpecifier * redirections;  /* I/O redirs */
40:     glob_t globResult;               /* result of parameter globbing */
41:     int freeGlob;                    /* should we free globResult? */
42: };
```

The first time globLastArgument() is run for a command string (when argc for the current child is 1), it initializes globResult. For the rest of the arguments, it takes advantage of GLOB_APPEND to add new matches to the end of the existing matches. This prevents us from having to allocate our own memory for globbing because our single glob_t is automatically expanded as necessary.

If globLastArgument() does not find any matches, the quoting \ characters are removed from the argument. Otherwise, all the new matches are copied into the list of arguments being constructed for the child program.

Here is the complete implementation of globLastArgument(). All the tricky parts are related to memory management; the actual globbing is similar to the globit.c sample program presented earlier in this chapter.

```
87: void globLastArgument(struct childProgram * prog, int * argcPtr,
88:                        int * argcAllocedPtr) {
89:     int argc = *argcPtr;
90:     int argcAlloced = *argcAllocedPtr;
91:     int rc;
92:     int flags;
93:     int i;
94:     char * src, * dst;
95:
96:     if (argc > 1) {           /* cmd->globResult already initialized */
97:         flags = GLOB_APPEND;
```

```
 98:            i = prog->globResult.gl_pathc;
 99:        } else {
100:            prog->freeGlob = 1;
101:            flags = 0;
102:            i = 0;
103:        }
104:
105:        rc = glob(prog->argv[argc - 1], flags, NULL, &prog->globResult);
106:        if (rc == GLOB_NOSPACE) {
107:            fprintf(stderr, "out of space during glob operation\n");
108:            return;
109:        } else if (rc == GLOB_NOMATCH ||
110:                    (!rc && (prog->globResult.gl_pathc - i) == 1 &&
111:                        !strcmp(prog->argv[argc - 1],
112:                            prog->globResult.gl_pathv[i]))) {
113:            /* we need to remove whatever \ quoting is still present */
114:            src = dst = prog->argv[argc - 1];
115:            while (*src) {
116:                if (*src != '\\') *dst++ = *src;
117:                src++;
118:            }
119:            *dst = '\0';
120:        } else if (!rc) {
121:            argcAlloced += (prog->globResult.gl_pathc - i);
122:            prog->argv = realloc(prog->argv,
123:                                argcAlloced * sizeof(*prog->argv));
124:            memcpy(prog->argv + (argc - 1),
125:                    prog->globResult.gl_pathv + i,
126:                    sizeof(*(prog->argv)) *
127:                        (prog->globResult.gl_pathc - i));
128:            argc += (prog->globResult.gl_pathc - i - 1);
129:        }
130:
131:        *argcAllocedPtr = argcAlloced;
132:        *argcPtr = argc;
133: }
```

The final changes are the calls to globLastArgument() that need to be
made once a new argument has been parsed. The calls are added in two
places: when white space is found outside a quoted string and when the
entire command string has been parsed. Both of the calls look like this:

```
globLastArgument(prog, &argc, &argvAlloced);
```

The complete source code for ladsh3.c is available on the LAD Web site at
http://ladweb.net/lad/src/.

14.7 Walking File System Trees

There are two functions available that make it easy for applications to look
at all of the files in a directory, including files in subdirectories. Recursing
through all entries in a tree (such as a file system) is often called **walking**
the structure, and is the reason these two functions are called ftw() and
nftw(), which stand for *file tree walk* and *new file tree walk*. As the names
suggest, nftw() is an enhanced version of ftw.

14.7.1 Using ftw()

```
#include <ftw.h>

int ftw(const char *dir, ftwFunctionPointer callback, int depth);
```

The ftw() function starts in the directory dir and calls the function pointed
to by callback for every file it finds in that directory and any subdirectories. The function is called for all file types, including symbolic links and
directories. The implementation of ftw() opens every directory it finds
(using up a file descriptor), and, to improve performance, it does not close
them until it is finished reading all of the entries in that directory. This
means that it uses as many file descriptors as there are levels of subdirectories. To prevent the application from running out of file descriptors, the
depth parameter limits how many file descriptors ftw() will leave open at
one time. If this limit is hit, performance slows down, because directories
need to be opened and closed repeatedly.

The callback points to a function defined as follows:

```
int ftwCallbackFunction(const char *file, const struct stat * sb,
                        int flag);
```

This function is called once for every file in the directory tree, and the first parameter, `file`, gives the name of the file beginning with the `dir` passed to `ftw()`. For example, if the `dir` was `"."`, one file name might be `"././.bashrc"`. If `"/etc"` was used instead, a file name would be `/etc/hosts`.

The second argument to the callback, `sb`, points to a `struct stat` that resulted from a `stat()` on the file.[4] The `flag` argument provides information on the file, and takes one of the following values:

FTW_F   The file is not a symbolic link or a directory.

FTW_D   The file is a directory or a symbolic link pointing to a directory.

FTW_DNR   The file is a directory that the application does not have permission to read (so it cannot be traversed).

FTW_SL   The file is a symbolic link.

FTW_NS   The file is an object on which `stat()` failed. An example of this would be a file in a directory that the application has read permission for (allowing the application to get a list of the files in that directory) but not execute permission for (preventing the `stat()` call from succeeding on the files in that directory).

When a file is a symbolic link, `ftw()` attempts to follow that link and return information on the file it points to (`ftw()` traverses the same directory multiple times if there are multiple symbolic links to that directory, although it is smart enough to avoid loops). If it is a broken link, however, it is not defined whether `FTW_SL` or `FTW_NS` is returned. This is a good reason to use `nftw()` instead.

If the callback function returns zero, the directory traversal continues. If a nonzero value is returned, the file tree walk ends and that value is returned by `ftw()`. If the traversal completes normally, `ftw()` returns zero, and it returns -1 if an error occurs as part of `ftw()`.

---

4. `ftw()` has to stat every file it finds to determine whether or not it is a directory, and passing this information to the callback prevents the callback from having to stat the files again in many cases.

14.7.2 File Tree Walks with nftw()

The new version of ftw(), nftw() addresses the symbolic link ambiguities inherent in ftw() and includes some additional features. To have nftw() properly defined by the header files, the application needs to define _XOPEN_SOURCE to be 500 or greater. Here is the prototype for nftw():

```
#define _XOPEN_SOURCE 600
#include <ftw.h>

int nftw(const char *dir, ftwFunctionPointer callback, int depth, int
flags);

int nftwCallbackFunction(const char *file, const struct stat * sb,
                         int flag, struct FTW * ftwInfo);
```

Comparing nftw() to ftw() shows a single new parameter, flags. It can be one or more of the following flags logically OR'ed together:

FTW_CHDIR   nftw() does not normally change the current directory of the program. When FTW_CHDIR is specified, nftw() changes the current directory to whatever directory is being currently read. In other words, when the callback is invoked, the file name it is passed is always in the current directory.

FTW_DEPTH   By default, nftw() reports a directory name before the files in the directory. This flag causes that order to be reversed, with the contents of a directory being reported before the directory itself.[5]

FTW_MOUNT   This flag prevents nftw() from crossing a file system boundary during the traversal. If you are not sure what a file system is, refer to [Sobell, 2002].

FTW_PHYS   Rather than follow symbolic links, nftw() will report the links but not follow them. A side effect of this is that the callback gets the result of an lstat() call rather than a stat() call.

---

5. This flag causes nftw() to provide a depth first search. There is no similar flag for a breadth first search.

The flag argument to the callback can take on two new values for nftw(), in addition to the values we have already mentioned for ftw().

FTW_DP   The item is a directory whose contents have already been reported (this can occur only if FTW_DEPTH was specified).

FTW_SLN   The item is a symbolic link that points to a nonexistent file (it is a broken link). This can occur only if FTW_PHYS was not specified; if it was, FTW_SL would be passed.

These extra flag values make the behavior nftw() for symbolic links well specified. If FTW_PHYS is used, all symbolic links return FTW_SL. Without nftw(), broken links yield FTW_NS and other symbolic links give the same result as the target of the link.

The callback for nftw() takes one more argument, ftwInfo. It is a pointer to a struct FTW, which is defined as:

```
#define _XOPEN_SOURCE 600
#include <ftw.h>

struct FTW {
    int base;
    int level;
};
```

The base is the offset of the file name within the full path passed to the callback. For example, if the full path passed was /usr/bin/ls, the base would be 9, and file + ftwInfo->base would give the file name ls. The level is the number of directories below the original directory this file is. If ls was found in an nftw() that began in /usr, the level would be 1. If the search began in /usr/bin, the level would instead be 0.

14.7.3 **Implementing** find

The find command searches one or more directory trees for files that match
certain characteristics. Here is a simple implementation of find that is built
around nftw(). It uses fnmatch()[6] to implement the -name switch, and
illustrates many of the flags nftw() understands.

```
 1: /* find.c */
 2:
 3: #define _XOPEN_SOURCE 600
 4:
 5: #include <fnmatch.h>
 6: #include <ftw.h>
 7: #include <limits.h>
 8: #include <stdio.h>
 9: #include <stdlib.h>
10: #include <string.h>
11:
12: const char * name = NULL;
13: int minDepth = 0, maxDepth = INT_MAX;
14:
15: int find(const char * file, const struct stat * sb, int flags,
16:         struct FTW * f) {
17:     if (f->level < minDepth) return 0;
18:     if (f->level > maxDepth) return 0;
19:     if (name && fnmatch(name, file + f->base, FNM_PERIOD)) return 0;
20:
21:     if (flags == FTW_DNR) {
22:         fprintf(stderr, "find: %s: permission denied\n", file);
23:     } else {
24:         printf("%s\n", file);
25:     }
26:
27:     return 0;
28: }
29:
30: int main(int argc, const char ** argv) {
31:     int flags = FTW_PHYS;
32:     int i;
33:     int problem = 0;
```

---

6. The fnmatch() function is described on pages 555–556.

```
34:        int tmp;
35:        int rc;
36:        char * chptr;
37:
38:        /* look for first command line parameter (which must occur after
39:           the list of paths */
40:        i = 1;
41:        while (i < argc && *argv[i] != '-') i++;
42:
43:        /* handle the command line options */
44:        while (i < argc && !problem) {
45:            if (!strcmp(argv[i], "-name")) {
46:                i++;
47:                if (i == argc)
48:                    problem = 1;
49:                else
50:                    name = argv[i++];
51:            } else if (!strcmp(argv[i], "-depth")) {
52:                i++;
53:                flags |= FTW_DEPTH;
54:            } else if (!strcmp(argv[i], "-mount") ||
55:                       !strcmp(argv[i], "-xdev")) {
56:                i++;
57:                flags |= FTW_MOUNT;
58:            } else if (!strcmp(argv[i], "-mindepth") ||
59:                       !strcmp(argv[i], "-maxdepth")) {
60:                i++;
61:                if (i == argc)
62:                    problem = 1;
63:                else {
64:                    tmp = strtoul(argv[i++], &chptr, 10);
65:                    if (*chptr)
66:                        problem = 1;
67:                    else if (!strcmp(argv[i - 2], "-mindepth"))
68:                        minDepth = tmp;
69:                    else
70:                        maxDepth = tmp;
71:                }
72:            }
73:        }
74:
```

```
75:        if (problem) {
76:            fprintf(stderr, "usage: find <paths> [-name <str>] "
77:                    "[-mindepth <int>] [-maxdepth <int>]\n");
78:            fprintf(stderr, "        [-xdev] [-depth]\n");
79:            return 1;
80:        }
81:
82:        if (argc == 1 || *argv[1] == '-') {
83:            argv[1] = ".";
84:            argc = 2;
85:        }
86:
87:        rc = 0;
88:        i = 1;
89:        flags =0;
90:        while (i < argc && *argv[i] != '-')
91:            rc |= nftw(argv[i++], find, 100, flags);
92:
93:        return rc;
94: }
```

14.8 Directory Change Notification

Applications may wish to know when the contents of a directory change. File managers, for example, may list the contents of a directory in a window and would like to keep that window up-to-date when other programs modify that directory. While the application could recheck the directory at regular intervals, Linux can send a program a signal when a directory is modified, allowing timely updates without the overhead (and delays) of polling.

The fcntl() system call is used to register for notifications of updates to a directory. Recall from Chapter 11 that this system call takes three arguments, the first is the file descriptor we are interested in, the second is the command we want fcntl() to perform, and the final one is an integer value specific to that command. For directory notifications, the first argument is a file descriptor referring to the directory of interest. This is the only case in which a directory should be opened through the normal open() system call instead of opendir(). The command to register for notifications is F_NOTIFY, and the last argument specifies what types of events cause a signal to be sent. It should be one or more of the following flags logically OR'ed together:

DN_ACCESS   A file in the directory has been read from.

DN_ATTRIB   The ownership or permissions of a file in the directory were changed.

DN_CREATE   A new file was created in the directory (this includes new hard links being made to existing files).

DN_DELETE   A file was removed from the directory.

DN_MODIFY   A file in the directory was modified (truncation is a type of modification).

DN_RENAME   A file in the directory was renamed.

To cancel event notification, call fcntl() with a command of F_NOTIFY and a final argument of zero.

Normally, directory notification is automatically canceled after a single signal has been sent. To keep directory notification in effect, the final argument to fcntl() should be OR'ed with DN_MULTISHOT, which causes signals to be sent for all appropriate events until the notification is canceled.

By default, SIGIO is sent for directory notification. If the application wants to use a different signal for this (it may want to use different signals for different directories, for example), the F_SETSIG command of fcntl() can be used, with the final argument to fcntl() specifying the signal to send for that directory. If F_SETSIG is used (even if the signal specified is SIGIO, the kernel also places the file descriptor for the directory in the si_fd member of the siginfo_t argument of the signal handler,[7] letting the application know which of the directories being monitored was updated.[8] If multiple directories are being monitored and a single signal is used for all of them, it is critical to use a real-time signal to make sure no events are lost.

---

7. This is exactly the same as the method used for file leases, discussed in Chapter 13.
8. The signal handler still must be registered with the SA_SIGINFO flag for the file descriptor to reach the signal handler properly.

Here is an example program that uses directory change notification to display messages when files are removed or added to any of the directories it is monitoring (any number of which may be specified on the command line). It registers to receive SIGRTMIN whenever a directory changes, and uses si_fd to discover which directory has been modified. To prevent any race conditions, the program uses queued signals and signal blocking. The only time a signal can be delivered is when sigsuspend() is called on line 203. This ensures that any changes to a directory that occur while that directory is being scanned force a rescan of that directory; otherwise those changes might not be noticed. Using queued signals lets any number of directory changes occur while the program is working; those signals are delivered as soon as sigsuspend() is called again, making sure nothing is forgotten.

```
 1: /* dirchange.c */
 2:
 3: #define _GNU_SOURCE
 4: #include <dirent.h>
 5: #include <errno.h>
 6: #include <fcntl.h>
 7: #include <signal.h>
 8: #include <stdio.h>
 9: #include <stdlib.h>
10: #include <string.h>
11: #include <unistd.h>
12:
13: /* We use a linked list to store the names of all of the files in
14:     each directory. The exists field is used for housekeeping work
15:     when we check for changes. */
16: struct fileInfo {
17:     char * name;
18:     struct fileInfo * next;
19:     int exists;
20: };
21:
22: /* This is a global array. It matches file descriptors to directory
23:     paths, stores a list of files in the directory, and gives a place
24:     for the signal handler to indicate that the directory needs to be
25:     rescanned. The last entry has a NULL path to mark the end of the
26:     array. */
27:
```

```
28: struct directoryInfo {
29:     char * path;
30:     int fd;
31:     int changed;
32:     struct fileInfo * contents;
33: } * directoryList;
34:
35: /* This will never return an empty list; all directories contain at
36:    least "." and ".." */
37: int buildDirectoryList(char * path, struct fileInfo ** listPtr) {
38:     DIR * dir;
39:     struct dirent * ent;
40:     struct fileInfo * list = NULL;
41:
42:     if (!(dir = opendir(path))) {
43:         perror("opendir");
44:         return 1;
45:     }
46:
47:     while ((ent = readdir(dir))) {
48:         if (!list) {
49:             list = malloc(sizeof(*list));
50:             list->next = NULL;
51:             *listPtr = list;
52:         } else {
53:             list->next = malloc(sizeof(*list));
54:             list = list->next;
55:         }
56:
57:         list->name = strdup(ent->d_name);
58:     }
59:
60:     if (errno) {
61:         perror("readdir");
62:         closedir(dir);
63:         return 1;
64:     }
65:
66:     closedir(dir);
67:
68:     return 0;
```

```
 69: }
 70:
 71: /* Scans the directory path looking for changes from the previous
 72:    contents, as specified by the *listPtr. The linked list is
 73:    updated to reflect the new contents, and messages are printed
 74:    specifying what changes have occured. */
 75: int updateDirectoryList(char * path, struct fileInfo ** listPtr) {
 76:     DIR * dir;
 77:     struct dirent * ent;
 78:     struct fileInfo * list = *listPtr;
 79:     struct fileInfo * file, * prev;
 80:
 81:     if (!(dir = opendir(path))) {
 82:         perror("opendir");
 83:         return 1;
 84:     }
 85:
 86:     for (file = list; file; file = file->next)
 87:         file->exists = 0;
 88:
 89:     while ((ent = readdir(dir))) {
 90:         file = list;
 91:         while (file && strcmp(file->name, ent->d_name))
 92:             file = file->next;
 93:
 94:         if (!file) {
 95:             /* new file, add it to the list */
 96:             printf("%s created in %s\n", ent->d_name, path);
 97:             file = malloc(sizeof(*file));
 98:             file->name = strdup(ent->d_name);
 99:             file->next = list;
100:             file->exists = 1;
101:             list = file;
102:         } else {
103:             file->exists = 1;
104:         }
105:     }
106:
107:     closedir(dir);
108:
109:     file = list;
```

```
110:        prev = NULL;
111:        while (file) {
112:            if (!file->exists) {
113:                printf("%s removed from %s\n", file->name, path);
114:                free(file->name);
115:
116:                if (!prev) {
117:                    /* removing the head node */
118:                    list = file->next;
119:                    free(file);
120:                    file = list;
121:                } else {
122:                    prev->next = file->next;
123:                    free(file);
124:                    file = prev->next;
125:                }
126:            } else {
127:                prev = file;
128:                file = file->next;
129:            }
130:        }
131:
132:        *listPtr = list;
133:
134:        return 0;
135: }
136:
137: void handler(int sig, siginfo_t * siginfo, void * context) {
138:        int i;
139:
140:        for (i = 0; directoryList[i].path; i++) {
141:            if (directoryList[i].fd == siginfo->si_fd) {
142:                directoryList[i].changed = 1;
143:                return;
144:            }
145:        }
146: }
147:
148: int main(int argc, char ** argv) {
149:        struct sigaction act;
150:        sigset_t mask, sigio;
```

```
151:        int i;
152:
153:        /* Block SIGRTMIN. We don't want to receive this anywhere but
154:            inside of the sigsuspend() system call. */
155:        sigemptyset(&sigio);
156:        sigaddset(&sigio, SIGRTMIN);
157:        sigprocmask(SIG_BLOCK, &sigio, &mask);
158:
159:        act.sa_sigaction = handler;
160:        act.sa_flags = SA_SIGINFO;
161:        sigemptyset(&act.sa_mask);
162:        sigaction(SIGRTMIN, &act, NULL);
163:
164:        if (!argv[1]) {
165:            /* no arguments given, fix up argc/argv to look like "." was
166:                given as the only argument */
167:            argv[1] = ".";
168:            argc++;
169:        }
170:
171:        /* each argument is a directory to watch */
172:        directoryList = malloc(sizeof(*directoryList) * argc);
173:        directoryList[argc - 1].path = NULL;
174:
175:        for (i = 0; i < (argc - 1); i++) {
176:            directoryList[i].path = argv[i + 1];
177:            if ((directoryList[i].fd =
178:                    open(directoryList[i].path, O_RDONLY)) < 0) {
179:                fprintf(stderr, "failed to open %s: %s\n",
180:                        directoryList[i].path, strerror(errno));
181:                return 1;
182:            }
183:
184:            /* monitor the directory before scanning it the first time,
185:                ensuring we catch files created by someone else while
186:                we're scanning it. If someone does happen to change it,
187:                a signal will be generated (and blocked until we're
188:                ready for it) */
189:            if (fcntl(directoryList[i].fd, F_NOTIFY, DN_DELETE |
190:                        DN_CREATE | DN_RENAME | DN_MULTISHOT)) {
191:                perror("fcntl F_NOTIFY");
```

```
192:              return 1;
193:          }
194:
195:          fcntl(directoryList[i].fd, F_SETSIG, SIGRTMIN);
196:
197:          if (buildDirectoryList(directoryList[i].path,
198:                              &directoryList[i].contents))
199:              return 1;
200:      }
201:
202:      while (1) {
203:          sigsuspend(&mask);
204:
205:          for (i = 0; directoryList[i].path; i++)
206:              if (directoryList[i].changed)
207:                  if (updateDirectoryList(directoryList[i].path,
208:                                  &directoryList[i].contents))
209:                      return 1;
210:      }
211:
212:      return 0;
213: }
```

Job Control

Job control, a feature standardized by POSIX.1 and mandated by many standards, allows a single terminal to run multiple jobs. Each job is a group of one or more processes, usually connected by pipes. Mechanisms are provided to move jobs between the foreground and the background and to prevent background jobs from accessing the terminal.

15.1 Job Control Basics

Recall from Chapter 10 that each active terminal runs a single group of processes, called a session. Each session is made up of process groups, and each process group contains one or more individual processes.

One of the process groups in a session is the foreground process group. The rest are background process groups. The foreground process group may be changed to any process group belonging to the session, allowing the user to switch among foreground process groups. Processes that are members of the foreground process group are often called foreground processes; processes that are not are called background processes.

15.1.1 Restarting Processes

Every process is in one of three states: running, stopped, or zombied. Running processes are terminated by calling the `exit()` system call or by being sent a fatal signal. Processes are moved between the running and stopped states exclusively through signals generated by another process, the kernel, or themselves.[1]

When a process receives SIGCONT, the kernel moves it from the stopped state to the running state; if the process is already running, the signal does not affect its state. The process may catch the signal, with the kernel moving the process to the running state before delivering the signal.

15.1.2 Stopping Processes

Four signals move a running process to the stopped state. SIGSTOP is never generated by the kernel. It is provided to allow users to stop arbitrary processes. It cannot be caught or ignored; it always stops the target process. The other three signals that stop processes, SIGTSTP, SIGTTIN, and SIGTTOU, may be generated by the terminal on which the process is running or by another process. Although these signals behave similarly, they are generated under different circumstances.

SIGTSTP   This signal is sent to every process in a terminal's foreground process group when a user presses the terminal's suspend key.[2]

SIGTTIN   When a background process attempts to read from the terminal, it is sent SIGTTIN.

SIGTTOU   This process is normally generated by a background process attempting to write to its terminal. The signal is generated only if the terminal's TOSTOP attribute is set, as discussed on page 387.

This signal is also generated by a background process calling either tcflush(), tcflow(), tcsetattr(), tcsetpgrp(), tcdrain(), or tcsendbreak().

The default action of each of these three signals is to stop the process. They all may be caught or ignored. In both cases, the process is not stopped.

---

1. Stopped processes cannot generate signals, however, so they cannot restart themselves either.
2. Normally, the suspend key is Ctrl-Z. The stty program allows users to change the suspend key for a terminal, and Chapter 16 details how a program can change it.

15.1.3 Handling Job Control Signals

Although many applications can be stopped and restarted with no ill effects, other processes need to handle process stops and starts. Most editors, for example, need to modify many of the terminal parameters while they are running. When users suspend the process, they expect their terminal to be restored to its default state.

When a process needs to perform actions before being suspended, it needs to provide a signal handler for SIGTSTP. This lets the kernel notify the process that it needs to suspend itself.

Upon receiving SIGTSTP, the process should immediately perform whatever actions it needs to take in order to allow suspension (such as restoring the terminal to its original state) and suspend itself. The simplest way for the process to suspend itself is by sending itself SIGSTOP. Most shells display messages that indicate which signal caused the process to stop, however, and if the process sent itself SIGSTOP, it would look different from most suspended processes. To avoid this nuisance, most applications reset their SIGTSTP handler to SIG_DFL and send themselves a SIGTSTP.

Processes that require special code for clean suspensions normally need to perform special actions when they are restarted. This is easily done by providing a signal handler for SIGCONT, which performs such actions. If the process suspends itself with SIGTSTP, such special actions probably include setting a signal handler for SIGTSTP.

The following code provides a simple signal handler for both SIGCONT and SIGTSTP. When the user suspends or restarts the process, the process displays a message before stopping or continuing.

```
 1: /* monitor.c */
 2:
 3: #include <signal.h>
 4: #include <stdio.h>
 5: #include <string.h>
 6: #include <unistd.h>
 7:
 8: void catchSignal(int sigNum, int useDefault);
 9:
10: void handler(int signum) {
```

```
11:      if (signum == SIGTSTP) {
12:          write(STDOUT_FILENO, "got SIGTSTP\n", 12);
13:          catchSignal(SIGTSTP, 1);
14:          kill(getpid(), SIGTSTP);
15:      } else {
16:          write(STDOUT_FILENO, "got SIGCONT\n", 12);
17:          catchSignal(SIGTSTP, 0);
18:      }
19: }
20:
21: void catchSignal(int sigNum, int useDefault) {
22:      struct sigaction sa;
23:
24:      memset(&sa, 0, sizeof(sa));
25:
26:      if (useDefault)
27:          sa.sa_handler = SIG_DFL;
28:      else
29:          sa.sa_handler = handler;
30:
31:      if (sigaction(sigNum, &sa, NULL)) perror("sigaction");
32: }
33:
34: int main() {
35:      catchSignal(SIGTSTP, 0);
36:      catchSignal(SIGCONT, 0);
37:
38:      while (1) ;
39:
40:      return 0;
41: }
```

15.2 **Job Control in** ladsh

Adding job control to ladsh is the last addition to the simple shell, the final source code to which appears in Appendix B. The first step is to add a member to each of struct childProgram, struct job, and struct jobSet. As ladsh has not been discussed for a while, it may help to refer back to page 149, where these data structures were first introduced. Here is the final definition of `struct childProgram`:

```
35: struct childProgram {
36:     pid_t pid;                  /* 0 if exited */
37:     char ** argv;              /* program name and arguments */
38:     int numRedirections;       /* elements in redirection array */
39:     struct redirectionSpecifier * redirections;  /* I/O redirs */
40:     glob_t globResult;         /* result of parameter globbing */
41:     int freeGlob;              /* should we free globResult? */
42:     int isStopped;             /* is the program currently running? */
43: };
```

We already differentiate between running children and terminated children through the `pid` member of `struct childProgram`—it is zero if the child has terminated and it contains a valid pid otherwise. The new member, `isStopped`, is nonzero if the process has been stopped and zero otherwise. Note that its value is meaningless if the `pid` member is zero.

An analogous change needs to be made to `struct job`. It previously kept track of the number of programs in a job and how many of those processes were still running. Its new member, `stoppedProgs`, records how many of the job's processes are currently stopped. It could be calculated from the `isStopped` members of the children that comprise the job, but it is convenient to track it separately. This change gives the final form for `struct job`:

```
45: struct job {
46:     int jobId;                 /* job number */
47:     int numProgs;              /* number of programs in job */
48:     int runningProgs;          /* number of programs running */
49:     char * text;               /* name of job */
50:     char * cmdBuf;             /* buffer various argv's point to */
51:     pid_t pgrp;                /* process group ID for the job */
52:     struct childProgram * progs; /* array of programs in job */
53:     struct job * next;         /* to track background commands */
54:     int stoppedProgs;          /* num of programs alive, but stopped */
55: };
```

Like previous versions of `ladsh`, ladsh4.c ignores `SIGTTOU`. It does this to allow `tcsetpgrp()` to be used even when the shell is not a foreground process. As the shell will have proper job control now, however, we do not want our children to ignore the signal. As soon as a new process is fork() ed by runCommand(), it sets the handler for SIGTTOU to SIG_DFL. This allows the terminal driver to suspend background processes that attempt to write to (or otherwise manipulate) the terminal. Here is the code that begins creating the child process, where SIGTTOU is reset and some additional synchronization work is performed:

```
514:            pipe(controlfds);
515:
516:            if (!(newJob.progs[i].pid = fork())) {
517:                signal(SIGTTOU, SIG_DFL);
518:
519:                close(controlfds[1]);
520:                /* this read will return 0 when the write side closes */
521:                read(controlfds[0], &len, 1);
522:                close(controlfds[0]);
```

The controlfds pipe is used to suspend the child process until after the shell has moved the child into the proper process group. By closing the write side of the pipe and reading from the read side, the child process stops until the parent closes the write side of the pipe, which happens after the setpgid() call on line 546. This type of mechanism is necessary to ensure that the child gets moved into the process group before the exec() occurs. If we waited until after the exec(), we are not assured that the process would be in the right process group before it starts accessing the terminal (which may not be allowed).

ladsh checks for terminated children in two places. The primary place is when it wait() s for processes in the foreground process group. When the foreground process has terminated or been stopped, ladsh checks for changes in the states of its background processes through the checkJobs() function. Both of these code paths need to be modified to handle stopped children, as well as terminated ones.

Adding the WUNTRACED flag to the waitpid() call, which waits on foreground processes, allows it to notice stopped processes, as well. When a process has been stopped rather than terminated, the child's isStopped flag is set and the job's stoppedProgs count is incremented. If all the programs in the job have been stopped, ladsh moves itself back to the foreground and waits for a user's command. Here is how the portion of ladsh's main loop that waits on the foreground process now looks:

```
708:                /* a job is running in the foreground; wait for it */
709:                i = 0;
710:                while (!jobList.fg->progs[i].pid ||
711:                        jobList.fg->progs[i].isStopped) i++;
712:
713:                waitpid(jobList.fg->progs[i].pid, &status, WUNTRACED);
714:
715:                if (WIFSIGNALED(status) &&
716:                        (WTERMSIG(status) != SIGINT)) {
717:                    printf("%s\n", strsignal(status));
718:                }
719:
720:                if (WIFEXITED(status) || WIFSIGNALED(status)) {
721:                    /* the child exited */
722:                    jobList.fg->runningProgs--;
723:                    jobList.fg->progs[i].pid = 0;
724:
725:                    if (!jobList.fg->runningProgs) {
726:                        /* child exited */
727:
728:                        removeJob(&jobList, jobList.fg);
729:                        jobList.fg = NULL;
730:
731:                        /* move the shell to the foreground */
732:                        if (tcsetpgrp(0, getpid()))
733:                            perror("tcsetpgrp");
734:                    }
735:                } else {
736:                    /* the child was stopped */
737:                    jobList.fg->stoppedProgs++;
738:                    jobList.fg->progs[i].isStopped = 1;
739:
740:                    if (jobList.fg->stoppedProgs ==
741:                                    jobList.fg->runningProgs) {
742:                        printf("\n" JOB_STATUS_FORMAT,
743:                            jobList.fg->jobId,
744:                            "Stopped", jobList.fg->text);
745:                        jobList.fg = NULL;
746:                    }
747:                }
748:
```

```
749:                    if (!jobList.fg) {
750:                        /* move the shell to the foreground */
751:                        if (tcsetpgrp(0, getpid()))
752:                            perror("tcsetpgrp");
753:                    }
754:                }
```

Similarly, background tasks may be stopped by signals. We again add
WUNTRACED to the waitpid(), which checks the states of background processes. When a background process has been stopped, the isStopped flag
and stoppedProgs counter are updated, and if the entire job has been
stopped, a message is printed.

The final ability that ladsh requires is to be able to move jobs between
running in the foreground, running in the background, and being stopped.
Two built-in commands allow this: fg and bg. They are limited versions
of the normal shell commands that go by the same name. Both take a
single parameter, which is a job number preceded by a % (for compatibility
with standard shells). The fg command moves the specified job to the
foreground; bg sets it running in the background.

Both chores are done by sending SIGCONT to every process in the process
group being activated. Although it could send the signal to each process
through separate kill() calls, it is slightly simpler to send it to the entire
process group using a single kill(). Here is the implementation of the fg
and bg built-in commands:

```
461:        } else if (!strcmp(newJob.progs[0].argv[0], "fg") ||
462:                   !strcmp(newJob.progs[0].argv[0], "bg")) {
463:            if (!newJob.progs[0].argv[1] || newJob.progs[0].argv[2]) {
464:                fprintf(stderr,
465:                        "%s: exactly one argument is expected\n",
466:                        newJob.progs[0].argv[0]);
467:                return 1;
468:            }
469:
470:            if (sscanf(newJob.progs[0].argv[1], "%%%d", &jobNum) != 1) {
471:                fprintf(stderr, "%s: bad argument '%s'\n",
472:                        newJob.progs[0].argv[0],
473:                        newJob.progs[0].argv[1]);
474:                return 1;
```

```
475:            }
476:
477:            for (job = jobList->head; job; job = job->next)
478:                if (job->jobId == jobNum) break;
479:
480:            if (!job) {
481:                fprintf(stderr, "%s: unknown job %d\n",
482:                        newJob.progs[0].argv[0], jobNum);
483:                return 1;
484:            }
485:
486:            if (*newJob.progs[0].argv[0] == 'f') {
487:                /* Make this job the foreground job */
488:
489:                if (tcsetpgrp(0, job->pgrp))
490:                    perror("tcsetpgrp");
491:                jobList->fg = job;
492:            }
493:
494:            /* Restart the processes in the job */
495:            for (i = 0; i < job->numProgs; i++)
496:                job->progs[i].isStopped = 0;
497:
498:            kill(-job->pgrp, SIGCONT);
499:
500:            job->stoppedProgs = 0;
501:
502:            return 0;
503:        }
```

Job control was the final ability that ladsh required in order to be usable. It is still missing many features present in regular shells, such as shell and environment variables, but it illustrates all the low-level tasks that shells perform. The complete source code to the final version of ladsh appears in Appendix B.

CHAPTER 16

Terminals and Pseudo Terminals

Devices designed for interactive use[1] all have a similar interface derived from the one created decades ago for serial TeleType paper-display terminals and thus dubbed the **tty** interface. The tty interface is used for accessing serial terminals, consoles, xterms, network logins, and more.

This tty interface is simple in conception but complex in implementation. It is flexible and powerful, which makes it possible to write applications that do not know much about how they get their input and output and can run over the network, on a local screen, or through a modem. Applications can even run under the control of another program without being aware of it.

Unfortunately, it took the Unix implementors several tries to get the interface right. They have left us with three distinct interfaces for connecting to tty devices. The BSD **sgtty** and System V **termio** interfaces have now been superseded by the POSIX **termios** interface, which is a superset of the termio interface. Because all current systems support the termios interface, and because it is the most powerful of the interfaces, we document only termios, not the earlier interfaces. (For the sake of supporting legacy source code, Linux supports termio, as well as termios. It also used to support the sgtty interface in a limited way, but that support has been removed because it was never perfect, and because there was no longer significant demand for it.)

Not only does the termios interface have to support interactive program use, but it must also support other kinds of data traffic. The same serial

---

1. That is, devices used both for input and for output.

line over which you log in using a modem you might also use for dialing out via a modem, to talk to a serial printer, or to talk to some specialized piece of hardware.

A tty device has two ends. The simplistic view is that one end is attached to the program and the other end is attached to the hardware device. This is true for a serial port; in this case, the serial device driver attaches the serial port (and thereby the terminal or modem) to a shell, editor, or other program. It is also true for the console; the console driver connects the keyboard and screen to the same types of programs. But in some cases, there is a program on each end; in these cases, one of the ends takes the place of hardware. For instance, with a network connection, one end of the tty device is connected to a program that provides the network connection, and the other end is connected to the shell, editor, or other potentially interactive program. When there is a program at each end, you need to keep a clear idea of which end is emulating hardware; in the case of network connections, the side that connects to the network is the hardware side.

tty devices that have software at both ends are called **pseudo ttys,** or, simply, **ptys.** For the first part of this chapter, you can pretend that they do not exist, because the "software" end of a pty is handled just like any tty device. Later on, we talk about programming the "hardware" end of a pty.

16.1   tty Operations

tty devices provide a large number of processing options; they are among the most complicated devices in the kernel. You can set input processing, output processing, and data flow processing options. You can also control a limited amount of data manipulation that occurs at the device driver level.

ttys operate in two basic modes: raw and cooked. **Raw mode** passes data to the application as it is received, with no changes made. **Cooked mode**, also known as **canonical mode**, provides a limited line editor inside the device driver and sends edited input to the application one line at a time. This mode is primarily derived from mainframe systems, in which dedicated input processing units provided cooked mode without interrupting the CPU at all.

Cooked mode processes certain control characters; for example, by default, ^U **kills** (erases) the current line, ^W erases the current word, backspace (^H) or delete erases the previous character, and ^R erases and then retypes the current line. Each of these control actions can be reassigned to a different character. For instance, on many terminals, DEL (character 127) is assigned the backspace action.

16.1.1 Terminal Utility Functions

Sometimes you do not know whether a file descriptor corresponds to a tty. This is most commonly the case for the standard output file descriptor. Programs that output text to standard output often format differently when they are writing to a pipe than when they are displaying information for human consumption. For example, when you use ls to list files, it will print multiple columns when you simply run it (most convenient for a human to read), but when you pipe it to another program, it will print one file per line (most convenient for a program to read). Run ls and ls | cat and see the difference.

You can determine whether a file descriptor corresponds to a tty by using the isatty() function, which takes a file descriptor as its argument and returns 1 if the descriptor corresponds to a tty, and 0 otherwise.

```
#include <unistd.h>

int isatty(int fd);
```

The ttyname() function provides a canonical name for the terminal (if any) associated with a file descriptor. It takes as its argument any file descriptor, and returns a pointer to a character string.

```
#include <unistd.h>

char *ttyname(int fd);
```

Because that character string is (the standard says "may be", but we all know better) in static space, you need to make a copy of the returned string before calling ttyname() again; it is not re-entrant. ttyname() returns NULL on any error, including if it is passed a file descriptor that is not associated with a tty.

16.1.2 Controlling Terminals

Every session (see Chapter 10) is tied to a terminal from which processes in the session get their input and to which they send their output. That terminal may be the machine's local console, a terminal connected over a serial line, or a pseudo terminal that maps to an X window or across a network (see page 389 later in this chapter for more on pseudo terminals). The terminal to which a session is related is called the **controlling terminal** (or **controlling tty**) of the session. A terminal can be the controlling terminal for only one session at a time.

Normal processes cannot change their controlling terminal; only a session leader can do that. Under Linux, a change in the session leader's controlling terminal is not propagated to other processes in that session. Session leaders almost always set a controlling terminal when they initially start running, before they create any child processes, in order to ensure that all the processes in the session share a common controlling terminal.

There are two interfaces for changing a session group leader's controlling tty. The first is through the normal `open()` and `close()` system calls:

1. Close all file descriptors that reference the current controlling terminal.

2. Open a new terminal without specifying the `O_NOCTTY` flag.

The other method involves `ioctl()`s on separate file descriptors that reference the old and the new terminal devices:

1. `TIOCNOTTY` on a file descriptor tied to the original controlling tty (usually, `ioctl(0, TIOCNOTTY, NULL)` works fine). This breaks the bond between the session and the tty.

2. `TIOCSCTTY` on the file descriptor tied to the new controlling tty. This sets a new controlling tty.

A terminal that is being used by a session keeps track of which process group is considered the **foreground process group**. Processes in that process group are allowed to read from and write to the terminal, whereas processes in other process groups are not (see Chapter 15 for details on what happens when background processes try to read and write from the controlling terminal). The `tcsetpgrp()` function allows a process running on a terminal to change the foreground process group for that terminal.[2]

```
int tcsetpgrp(int ttyfd, pid_t pgrp);
```

The first parameter specifies the tty whose controlling process group is being changed, and `pgrp` is the process group that should be moved to the foreground. Processes may change the foreground process group only for their controlling terminal. If the process making the change is not in the foreground process group on that terminal, a `SIGTTOU` is generated, unless that signal is being ignored or is blocked.[3]

16.1.3 Terminal Ownership

There are two system databases used to keep track of logged-in users; **utmp** is used specifically for currently logged-in users, and **wtmp** is a record of all previous logins since the file was created. The **who** command uses the utmp database to print out its list of logged-in users, and the **last** command uses the wtmp database to print out its list of users who have logged into the system since the wtmp database was regenerated. On Linux systems, the utmp database is stored in the file /var/run/utmp, and the wtmp database is stored in the file /var/log/wtmp.

Programs that use ttys for user login sessions (whether or not they are associated with a graphical login) should update the two system databases, unless the user explicitly requests otherwise; for example, some users do not want every shell session they are running in a terminal emulator under the X Window System to be listed as a login process. Only add interactive sessions, because utmp and wtmp are not meant for logging automated programs. Any tty that is not a controlling terminal should normally not be added to the utmp and wtmp databases.

---

2. Older implementations of Unix provided this functionality through the `TIOCSPGRP` `ioctl()`, which is still supported in Linux. For comparison, `tcsetpgrp()` could be implemented as `ioctl(ttyfd, TIOCSPGRP, &pgrp)`.
3. For more information on signals and their interaction with job control, see Chapter 12.

16.1.4 Recording with utempter

Applications that use ptys and that are written with security in mind rarely have sufficient permissions to modify the database files. These applications should provide the option to use a simple helper program that is available on most Linux systems and some other systems, but is not standardized: the utempter utility. The utempter utility is setgid (or setuid if necessary) with sufficient permissions to modify the utmp and wtmp databases, and it is accessed through a simple library. The utempter utility checks to make sure that the process owns the tty that it is trying to log into the utmp database before allowing the operation. utempter is meant to be used only for ptys; other ttys are generally opened by daemons with sufficient permissions to modify the system database files.

```
#include <utempter.h>

void addToUtmp(const char *pty, const char *hostname, int ptyfd);
void removeLineFromUtmp(const char *pty, int ptyfd);
void removeFromUtmp(void);
```

The addToUtmp() function takes three arguments. The first, pty, is the full path to the pty being added. The second, hostname, may be NULL; if not, it is the network name of the system from which a network connection using this pty originated (this sets ut_host, as documented on page 343). The third, ptyfd, must be an open file descriptor referencing the pty device named in the pty argument.

The removeLineFromUtmp() function takes two arguments; they are defined exactly like the arguments of the same name passed to the addToUtmp() function.

Some existing applications are written with a structure that makes it difficult to keep the name and file descriptor around to clean up the utmp entry. Because of this, the utempter library keeps a cache of the more recent device name and file descriptor passed to addToUtmp() and a convenience function removeFromUtmp() that takes no arguments and acts like removeLineFromUtmp() on the information it has cached. This works only for applications that add only one utmp entry; more complex applications that use more than one pty must use removeLineFromUtmp() instead.

16.1.5 Recording by Hand

The area of utmp and wtmp handling is one of those inconsistent areas where mechanisms have differed between systems and changed over the years; even the definition of what information is available in utmp and wtmp still differs between systems. Originally, utmp and wtmp were essentially just arrays of structures written to disk; over time, APIs were created to handle the records reliably.

At least two such interfaces have been officially standardized; the original utmp interface (specified in XSI, XPG2, and SVID2) and the extended **utmpx** interface (specified in XPG4.2 and in recent editions of POSIX). Conveniently, both interfaces (utmp and utmpx) are available on Linux. The utmp interface, which varies widely between machines, has a set of defines to make it possible to write portable code that take advantage of the extensions that glibc provides. The utmpx interface, which is more strictly standardized, does not (currently) provide those defines but still provides the extensions.

The Linux utmp interface was originally constructed as a superset of other existing utmp interfaces, and utmpx was standardized as a superset of other existing utmp interfaces; happily, the two supersets are essentially the same, so on Linux, the difference between the utmp and utmpx data structures is the letter x.

If you do not wish to use any extensions, we recommend that you use the utmpx interface, because as long as you are using no extensions, it is the most portable; it is strictly standardized.

If you do wish to use extensions, however, we recommend that you use the utmp interface, because glibc provides defines that let you write portable code that takes advantage of the extensions.

There is also a hybrid approach—include both header files and use the defines that glibc provides for the utmp interface to decide whether to use extensions in the utmpx interface. We recommend against this because there is no guarantee that the utmp.h and utmpx.h header files will not conflict on non-Linux systems. If you want both maximum portability and maximum functionality, this is one of those areas where you may have to write some code twice—one version using utmpx for easy portability to new systems, and then one version with #ifdefs for maximum functionality on each new system you port to.

We document here only the most commonly used extensions; the glibc documentation covers all the extensions that it supports. The utmp functions operate in terms of struct utmp; we ignore some of the extensions. The utmpx structure and functions operate exactly the same as the utmp structure and functions, and so we do not document them separately. Note that the same structure is used for both utmp and wtmp, because the two databases are so similar.

```
struct utmp {
    short int ut_type;          /* type of login */
    pid_t ut_pid;               /* process id of login process */
    char ut_line[UT_LINESIZE];  /* 32 characters */
    char ut_id[4];              /* inittab id */
    char ut_user[UT_NAMESIZE];  /* 32 characters */
    char ut_host[UT_HOSTSIZE];  /* 256 characters */
    struct timeval ut_tv;
    struct exit_status ut_exit; /* status of dead processes */
    long ut_session;
    int32_t ut_addr_v6[4];
};
```

Many of the same members are part of struct utmpx by the same name. The members that are not required to be members of struct utmpx are annotated as "not standardized by POSIX" (none of them are standardized as part of struct utmp since struct utmp is itself not standardized).

The character array members are not necessarily NULL-terminated strings. Use sizeof() or other size limitations judiciously.

ut_type   One of the following values: EMPTY, INIT_PROCESS, LOGIN_PROCESS, USER_PROCESS, DEAD_PROCESS, BOOT_TIME, NEW_TIME, OLD_TIME, RUN_LVL, or ACCOUNTING, each of which is described below.

ut_tv   The time associated with the event. This is the only member beside ut_type that POSIX specifies as always valid for nonempty entries. Some systems have instead a ut_time member instead that is measured only in seconds.

ut_pid
The process id of the associated process, for all types ending in _PROCESS.

ut_id
The inittab id of the associated process, for all types ending in _PROCESS. This is the first field in noncomment lines in the file /etc/inittab, where fields are separated by : characters. Network logins, which are not associated with inittab, may use this in other ways; for example, they may include parts of the device information here.

ut_line
The line (basename of the device or local display number for X) associated with the process. The POSIX specification is unclear about the status of ut_line; it does not list ut_line as meaningful for LOGIN_PROCESS, but in another place it implies that it is meaningful for LOGIN_PROCESS, and this makes sense in practice. POSIX says that ut_line is meaningful for USER_PROCESS. In practice, it is often also meaningful for DEAD_PROCESS, depending on the origin of the dead process.

ut_user
Normally, the name of the logged-in user; it can also be the name of the login process (normally, LOGIN) depending on the value of ut_type.

ut_host
The name of the remote host that has logged in (or is otherwise associated) with this process. The ut_host member applies only to USER_PROCESS. This member is not standardized by POSIX.

ut_exit
ut_exit.e_exit gives the exit code as provided by the WEXITSTATUS() macro, and ut_exit.e_termination gives the signal that caused the process to terminate (if it was terminated by a signal), as provided by the WTERMSIG() macro. This member is not standardized by POSIX.

ut_session
The session ID in the X Window System. This member is not standardized by POSIX.

ut_addr_v6
The IP address of the remote host, in the case of a USER_PROCESS initiated by a connection from a remote host.

Use the `inet_ntop()` function to generate printable content. If only the first quad is nonzero, then it is an IPV4 address (`inet_ntop()` takes the `AF_INET` argument); otherwise it is an IPV6 address (`inet_ntop()` takes the `AF_INET6` argument). This member is not standardized by POSIX.

The `ut_type` member defines how all the rest of the members are defined. Some `ut_type` values are reserved for recording system information; these are useful only for specialized system programs. We do not document these fully.

EMPTY
: There is no valid information in this utmp record (such records may be reused later), so ignore the contents of this record. None of the other structure members have meaning.

INIT_PROCESS
: The listed process was spawned directly from init. This value may be set by system programs (normally only the init process itself); applications should read and recognize this value but never set it. The `ut_pid`, `ut_id`, and `ut_tv` members are meaningful.

LOGIN_PROCESS
: Instances of the login program waiting for a user to log in. The `ut_id`, `ut_pid`, and `ut_tv` members are useful; the `ut_user` member is nominally useful (on Linux, it will say `LOGIN` but this name of the login process is implementation-defined according to POSIX.

USER_PROCESS
: This entry denotes a session leader for a logged-in user. This may be the login program after a user has logged in, the display manager or session manager for an X Window System login, a terminal emulator program configured to mark login sessions, or any other interactive user login. The `ut_id`, `ut_user`, `ut_line`, `ut_pid`, and `ut_tv` members are meaningful.

DEAD_PROCESS
: The listed process was a session leader for a logged-in user, but has exited. The `ut_id`, `ut_pid`, and `ut_tv` members are meaningful according to POSIX. The `ut_exit`

member (not specified by POSIX) is meaningful only in this context.

BOOT_TIME   The time the system booted. In utmp this will be the most recent boot; in wtmp there will be an entry for every system boot since wtmp was cleared. Only ut_tv is meaningful.

OLD_TIME and NEW_TIME

These are used only for recording times that the clock time jumped, and are recorded in pairs. Do not depend on these entries being recorded on the system even if the clock time is changed for any reason.

RUN_LVL and ACCOUNTING

These are internal system values; do not use in applications.

The interfaces defined by XPG2, SVID 2, and FSSTND 1.2 are:

```
#include <utmp.h>

int utmpname(char *file);
struct utmp *getutent(void);
struct utmp *getutid(const struct utmp *id);
struct utmp *getutline(const struct utmp *line);
struct utmp *pututline(const struct utmp *ut);
void setutent(void);
void endutent(void);
void updwtmp(const char *file, const struct utmp *ut);
void logwtmp(const char *line, const char *name, const char *host);
```

Each record in a utmp or wtmp database is called a *line*. All the functions that return a pointer to a struct utmp return a pointer to static data on success, and a NULL pointer on failure. Note that the static data is overwritten by every new call to any function that returns a struct utmp. Also, the POSIX standard (for utmpx) requires that the static data be cleared by the application before some searches.

The utmpx versions of these functions take struct utmpx instead of struct utmp, require including utmpx.h, and are named getutxent, getutxid, getutxline, pututxline, setutxent, and endutxent, but are otherwise identical to the utmp versions of these functions on Linux. There is no utmpxname() function defined by POSIX, although some platforms may choose to define it anyway (as does glibc).

The utmpname() function is used to determine which database you are looking at. The default database is the utmp database, but you can use this function to point to wtmp instead. Two predefined names are _PATH_UTMP for the utmp file and _PATH_WTMP for the wtmp file; for testing you might choose instead to point to a local copy. The utmpname() function returns zero on success, nonzero on failure, but success may simply mean that it was able to copy a filename into the library; it does not mean that a database actually exists at the path you have provided to it!

The getutent() function simply returns the next line from the database. If the database has not been opened yet, it returns the contents of the first line. If no more lines are available, it returns NULL.

The getutid() function takes a struct utmp and looks only at one or two members. If the ut_type is BOOT_TIME, OLD_TIME, or NEW_TIME, then it returns the next line of that type. If the ut_type is any of INIT_PROCESS, LOGIN_PROCESS, USER_PROCESS, or DEAD_PROCESS, then getutid() returns the next line matching *any* of those types that also has a ut_id value matching the ut_id value in the struct utmp passed to getutid(). You must clear the data in the struct utmp returned by getutid() before calling it again; otherwise, it is allowed by POSIX to return the same line as the previous invocation. If no matching lines are available, it returns NULL.

The getutline() function returns the next line with ut_id set to LOGIN_PROCESS or USER_PROCESS that also has a ut_line value matching the ut_line value in the struct utmp passed to getutline(). Like getutid(), you must clear the data in the struct utmp returned by getutline() before calling it again; otherwise, it is allowed by POSIX to return the same line as the previous invocation. If no matching lines are available, it returns NULL.

The pututline() function modifies (or adds, if necessary) the database record matching the ut_line member of its struct utmp argument. It does this only if the process has sufficient permissions to modify the database. If it succeeds in modifying the database, it returns a struct utmp that matches the data it wrote to the database. Otherwise, it returns NULL. The `pututline()` function is not portably applicable to the wtmp database. To modify the wtmp database, use `updwtmp()` or `logwtmp()` instead.

The `setutent()` function rewinds the database to the beginning.

The `endutent()` function closes the database. This closes the file descriptor and frees any associated data. Call `endutent()` before using `utmpname()` to access a different utmp file, as well as after you are done accessing utmp data.

BSD defined two functions that are also available as part of glibc, which are the most robust way to modify the wtmp database.

The `updwtmp()` function takes the filename of the wtmp database (normally `_PATH_WTMP`) and a filled-in `struct utmp`, and attempts to append the entry to the wtmp file. Failure is not reported.

The `logwtmp()` function is a convenience function that fills in a `struct utmp` and calls `updwtmp()` with it. The `line` argument is copied to `ut_line`, `name` is copied to `ut_user`, `host` is copied to `ut_host`, `ut_tv` is filled in from the current time, and `ut_pid` is filled in from the current process id. Like `updwtmp()`, it does not report failure.

The utmp program demonstrates several methods of reading utmp and wtmp databases:

```
 1: /* utmp.c */
 2:
 3: #include <stdio.h>
 4: #include <unistd.h>
 5: #include <string.h>
 6: #include <time.h>
 7: #include <sys/time.h>
 8: #include <sys/types.h>
 9: #include <sys/socket.h>
10: #include <netinet/in.h>
11: #include <arpa/inet.h>
12: #include <utmp.h>
13: #include <popt.h>
14:
15: void print_utmp_entry(struct utmp *u) {
```

```
16:     struct tm *tp;
17:     char *type;
18:     char addrtext[INET6_ADDRSTRLEN];
19:
20:     switch (u->ut_type) {
21:         case EMPTY: type = "EMPTY"; break;
22:         case RUN_LVL: type = "RUN_LVL"; break;
23:         case BOOT_TIME: type = "BOOT_TIME"; break;
24:         case NEW_TIME: type = "NEW_TIME"; break;
25:         case OLD_TIME: type = "OLD_TIME"; break;
26:         case INIT_PROCESS: type = "INIT_PROCESS"; break;
27:         case LOGIN_PROCESS: type = "LOGIN_PROCESS"; break;
28:         case USER_PROCESS: type = "USER_PROCESS"; break;
29:         case DEAD_PROCESS: type = "DEAD_PROCESS"; break;
30:         case ACCOUNTING: type = "ACCOUNTING"; break;
31:     }
32:     printf("%-13s:", type);
33:     switch (u->ut_type) {
34:         case LOGIN_PROCESS:
35:         case USER_PROCESS:
36:         case DEAD_PROCESS:
37:             printf(" line: %s", u->ut_line);
38:             /* fall through */
39:         case INIT_PROCESS:
40:             printf("\n  pid: %6d id: %4.4s", u->ut_pid, u->ut_id);
41:     }
42:     printf("\n");
43:     tp = gmtime(&u->ut_tv.tv_sec);
44:     printf("  time: %24.24s.%lu\n", asctime(tp), u->ut_tv.tv_usec);
45:     switch (u->ut_type) {
46:         case USER_PROCESS:
47:         case LOGIN_PROCESS:
48:         case RUN_LVL:
49:         case BOOT_TIME:
50:             printf("  user: %s\n", u->ut_user);
51:     }
52:     if (u->ut_type == USER_PROCESS) {
53:         if (u->ut_session)
54:             printf("  sess: %lu\n", u->ut_session);
55:         if (u->ut_host)
56:             printf("  host: %s\n", u->ut_host);
```

```
57:            if (u->ut_addr_v6[0]) {
58:                if (!(u->ut_addr_v6[1] |
59:                        u->ut_addr_v6[2] |
60:                        u->ut_addr_v6[3])) {
61:                    /* only first quad filled in implies IPV4 address */
62:                    inet_ntop(AF_INET, u->ut_addr_v6,
63:                            addrtext, sizeof(addrtext));
64:                    printf("  IPV4: %s\n", addrtext);
65:                } else {
66:                    inet_ntop(AF_INET6, u->ut_addr_v6,
67:                            addrtext, sizeof(addrtext));
68:                    printf("  IPV6: %s\n", addrtext);
69:                }
70:            }
71:        }
72:        if (u->ut_type == DEAD_PROCESS) {
73:            printf("  exit: %u:%u\n",
74:                    u->ut_exit.e_termination,
75:                    u->ut_exit.e_exit);
76:        }
77:        printf("\n");
78: }
79:
80: struct utmp * get_next_line(char *id, char *line) {
81:        struct utmp request;
82:
83:        if (!id && !line)
84:            return getutent();
85:
86:        memset(&request, 0, sizeof(request));
87:
88:        if (line) {
89:            strncpy(&request.ut_line[0], line, UT_LINESIZE);
90:            return getutline(&request);
91:        }
92:
93:        request.ut_type = INIT_PROCESS;
94:        strncpy(&request.ut_id[0], id, 4);
95:        return getutid(&request);
96: }
97:
```

```
 98: void print_file(char * name, char *id, char *line) {
 99:     struct utmp *u;
100:
101:     if (utmpname(name)) {
102:         fprintf(stderr, "utmp database %s open failed\n", name);
103:         return;
104:     }
105:     setutent();
106:     printf("%s:\n=====================\n", name);
107:     while ((u=get_next_line(id, line))) {
108:         print_utmp_entry(u);
109:         /* POSIX requires us to clear the static data before
110:          * calling getutline or getutid again
111:          */
112:         memset(u, 0, sizeof(struct utmp));
113:     }
114:     endutent();
115: }
116:
117: int main(int argc, const char **argv) {
118:     char *id = NULL, *line = NULL;
119:     int show_utmp = 1, show_wtmp = 0;
120:     int c;
121:     poptContext optCon;
122:     struct poptOption optionsTable[] = {
123:         { "utmp", 'u', POPT_ARG_NONE|POPT_ARGFLAG_XOR,
124:             &show_utmp, 0,
125:             "toggle showing contents of utmp file", NULL },
126:         { "wtmp", 'w', POPT_ARG_NONE|POPT_ARGFLAG_XOR,
127:             &show_wtmp, 0,
128:             "toggle showing contents of wtmp file", NULL },
129:         { "id", 'i', POPT_ARG_STRING, &id, 0,
130:             "show process entries for specified inittab id",
131:             "<inittab id>" },
132:         { "line", 'l', POPT_ARG_STRING, &line, 0,
133:             "show process entries for specified device line",
134:             "<line>" },
135:         POPT_AUTOHELP
136:         POPT_TABLEEND
137:     };
138:
```

```
139:        optCon = poptGetContext("utmp", argc, argv, optionsTable, 0);
140:        if ((c = poptGetNextOpt(optCon)) < -1) {
141:            fprintf(stderr, "%s: %s\n",
142:                poptBadOption(optCon, POPT_BADOPTION_NOALIAS),
143:                poptStrerror(c));
144:            return 1;
145:        }
146:        poptFreeContext(optCon);
147:
148:        if (id && line)
149:            fprintf(stderr, "Cannot choose both by id and line, "
150:                            "choosing by line\n");
151:
152:        if (show_utmp)
153:            print_file(_PATH_UTMP, id, line);
154:        if (show_utmp && show_wtmp)
155:            printf("\n\n\n");
156:        if (show_wtmp)
157:            print_file(_PATH_WTMP, id, line);
158:
159:        return 0;
160: }
```

16.2 termios Overview

All tty manipulation is done through one structure, struct termios, and through several functions, all defined in the <termios.h> header file. Of those functions, only six are commonly used, and when you do not have to set line speeds, you are likely to use only two of them. The two most important functions are the tcgetattr() and tcsetattr() functions:

```
#include <termios.h>

struct termios {
    tcflag_t c_iflag;    /* input mode flags */
    tcflag_t c_oflag;    /* output mode flags */
    tcflag_t c_cflag;    /* control mode flags */
    tcflag_t c_lflag;    /* local mode flags */
    cc_t c_line;         /* line discipline */
```

```
    cc_t c_cc[NCCS];    /* control characters */
};

int tcgetattr (int fd, struct termios *tp);
int tcsetattr (int fd, int oact, struct termios *tp);
```

In almost every situation, programs should use tcgetattr() to get a device's current settings, modify those settings, and then use tcsetattr() to make the modified settings active. Many programs also save a copy of the original settings and restore them before terminating. In general, modify only the settings that you know you care about; changing other settings may make it difficult for users to work around unusual system configurations (or bugs in your code).

tcsetattr() may not honor all the settings you choose; it is allowed to ignore arbitrary settings. In particular, if the hardware simply does not support a setting, tcsetattr() ignores it rather than return an error. If you care that a setting really takes effect, you must use tcgetattr() after tcsetattr() and test to make sure that your change took effect.

To get a tty device's settings, you have to open the device and use the file descriptor in the tcgetattr() call. This poses a problem with some tty devices; some normally may be opened only once, to prevent device contention. Fortunately, giving the O_NONBLOCK flag to open() causes it to be opened immediately and not block on any operations. However, you may still prefer to block on read(); if so, use fcntl() to turn off O_NONBLOCK mode before you read or write to it:

```
    fcntl(fd, F_SETFL, fcntl(fd, F_GETFL, 0) & ~O_NONBLOCK);
```

The four termios flags control four distinct parts of managing input and output. The input flag, c_iflag, determines how received characters are interpreted and processed. The output flag, c_oflag, determines how characters your process writes to the tty are interpreted and processed. The control flag, c_cflag, determines serial protocol characteristics of the device and is useful only for physical devices. The local flag, c_lflag, determines how characters are collected and processed before they are sent to output processing. Figure 16.1 shows a simplified view of how each of these flags fits into the grand scheme of character processing.

We first demonstrate ways to use termios, and then present a short reference to it.

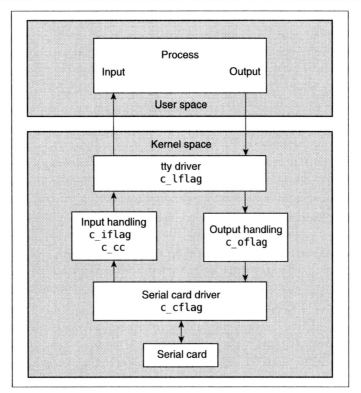

Figure 16.1 Simplified View of tty Processing

16.3 termios Examples

16.3.1 Passwords

One common reason to modify termios settings is to read a password without echoing characters. To do this, you want to turn off local echo while reading the password. Your code should look like this:

```
struct termios ts, ots;
```

One structure keeps the original termios settings so that you can restore them, and the other one is a copy to modify.

```
tcgetattr(STDIN_FILENO, &ts);
```

Generally, you read passwords from standard input.

```
ots = ts;
```

Keep a copy of the original termios settings to restore later.

```
ts.c_lflag &= ~ECHO;
ts.c_lflag |= ECHONL;
tcsetattr(STDIN_FILENO, TCSAFLUSH, &ts);
```

Turn off echoing characters except newlines, after all currently pending output is completed. (The first l in c_lflag stands for local processing.)

```
read_password();
```

Here, you read the password. This may be as simple as a single fgets() or read() call, or it may include more complex processing, depending on whether the tty is in raw mode or cooked mode, and depending on the requirements of your program.

```
tcsetattr(STDIN_FILENO, TCSANOW, &ots);
```

This restores the original termios settings and does so immediately. (We explain other options later, in the reference section on page 371.)

A full example program, readpass, looks like this:

```
 1: /* readpass.c */
 2:
 3: #include <stdio.h>
 4: #include <stdlib.h>
 5: #include <termios.h>
 6: #include <unistd.h>
 7:
 8: int main(void) {
 9:     struct termios ts, ots;
10:     char passbuf[1024];
11:
12:     /* get and save current termios settings */
13:     tcgetattr(STDIN_FILENO, &ts);
14:     ots = ts;
15:
16:     /* change and set new termios settings */
```

```
17:        ts.c_lflag &= ~ECHO;
18:        ts.c_lflag |= ECHONL;
19:        tcsetattr(STDIN_FILENO, TCSAFLUSH, &ts);
20:
21:        /* paranoia: check that the settings took effect */
22:        tcgetattr(STDIN_FILENO, &ts);
23:        if (ts.c_lflag & ECHO) {
24:            fprintf(stderr, "Failed to turn off echo\n");
25:            tcsetattr(STDIN_FILENO, TCSANOW, &ots);
26:            exit(1);
27:        }
28:
29:        /* get and print the password */
30:        printf("enter password: ");
31:        fflush(stdout);
32:        fgets(passbuf, 1024, stdin);
33:        printf("read password: %s", passbuf);
34:        /* there was a terminating \n in passbuf */
35:
36:        /* restore old termios settings */
37:        tcsetattr(STDIN_FILENO, TCSANOW, &ots);
38:
39:        exit(0);
40: }
```

16.3.2 Serial Communications

As an example of programming both ends of a tty, here is a program that connects the current terminal to a serial port. On one tty, the program, called robin, is talking to you as you type. On another tty, it is communicating with the serial port. In order to multiplex input to and output from the local tty and the serial port, the program uses the poll() system call described on page 245.

Here is robin.c in its entirety, followed by an explanation:

```
1: /* robin.c */
2:
3: #include <sys/poll.h>
4: #include <errno.h>
```

```
 5: #include <fcntl.h>
 6: #include <popt.h>
 7: #include <stdio.h>
 8: #include <stdlib.h>
 9: #include <signal.h>
10: #include <string.h>              /* for strerror() */
11: #include <termios.h>
12: #include <unistd.h>
13:
14: void die(int exitcode, const char *error, const char *addl) {
15:     if (error) fprintf(stderr, "%s: %s\n", error, addl);
16:     exit(exitcode);
17: }
18:
19: speed_t symbolic_speed(int speednum) {
20:     if (speednum >= 460800) return B460800;
21:     if (speednum >= 230400) return B230400;
22:     if (speednum >= 115200) return B115200;
23:     if (speednum >= 57600) return B57600;
24:     if (speednum >= 38400) return B38400;
25:     if (speednum >= 19200) return B19200;
26:     if (speednum >= 9600) return B9600;
27:     if (speednum >= 4800) return B4800;
28:     if (speednum >= 2400) return B2400;
29:     if (speednum >= 1800) return B1800;
30:     if (speednum >= 1200) return B1200;
31:     if (speednum >= 600) return B600;
32:     if (speednum >= 300) return B300;
33:     if (speednum >= 200) return B200;
34:     if (speednum >= 150) return B150;
35:     if (speednum >= 134) return B134;
36:     if (speednum >= 110) return B110;
37:     if (speednum >= 75) return B75;
38:     return B50;
39: }
40:
41: /* These need to have file scope so that we can use them in
42:  * signal handlers */
43: /* old port termios settings to restore */
44: static struct termios pots;
45: /* old stdout/in termios settings to restore */
```

```
46: static struct termios sots;
47: /* port file descriptor */
48: int    pf;
49:
50: /* restore original terminal settings on exit */
51: void cleanup_termios(int signal) {
52:     tcsetattr(pf, TCSANOW, &pots);
53:     tcsetattr(STDIN_FILENO, TCSANOW, &sots);
54:     exit(0);
55: }
56:
57: /* handle a single escape character */
58: void send_escape(int fd, char c) {
59:     switch (c) {
60:     case 'q':
61:         /* restore termios settings and exit */
62:         cleanup_termios(0);
63:         break;
64:     case 'b':
65:         /* send a break */
66:         tcsendbreak(fd, 0);
67:         break;
68:     default:
69:         /* pass the character through */
70:         /* "C-\ C-\" sends "C-\" */
71:         write(fd, &c, 1);
72:         break;
73:     }
74:     return;
75: }
76:
77: /* handle escape characters, writing to output */
78: void cook_buf(int fd, char *buf, int num) {
79:     int current = 0;
80:     static int in_escape = 0;
81:
82:     if (in_escape) {
83:         /* cook_buf last called with an incomplete escape
84:            sequence */
85:         send_escape(fd, buf[0]);
86:         num--;
```

```
87:             buf++;
88:             in_escape = 0;
89:         }
90:     while (current < num) {
91: #       define CTRLCHAR(c) ((c)-0x40)
92:         while ((current < num) && (buf[current] != CTRLCHAR('\\')))
93:             current++;
94:         if (current) write (fd, buf, current);
95:         if (current < num) {
96:             /* found an escape character */
97:             current++;
98:             if (current >= num) {
99:                 /* interpret first character of next sequence */
100:                 in_escape = 1;
101:                 return;
102:             }
103:             send_escape(fd, buf[current]);
104:         }
105:         num -= current;
106:         buf += current;
107:         current = 0;
108:     }
109:     return;
110: }
111:
112: int main(int argc, const char *argv[]) {
113:     char    c;              /* used for argument parsing */
114:     struct  termios pts;    /* termios settings on port */
115:     struct  termios sts;    /* termios settings on stdout/in */
116:     const char  *portname;
117:     int     speed = 0;      /* used in argument parsing for speed */
118:     struct  sigaction sact;/* used to initialize signal handler */
119:     struct  pollfd ufds[2]; /* communicate with poll() */
120:     int     raw = 0;        /* raw mode? */
121:     int     flow = 0;       /* type of flow control, if any */
122:     int     crnl = 0;       /* send carriage return with newline? */
123:     int     i = 0;          /* used in the multiplex loop */
124:     int     done = 0;
125: #   define BUFSIZE 1024
126:     char    buf[BUFSIZE];
127:     poptContext optCon;     /* context for command-line options */
```

```
128:        struct poptOption optionsTable[] = {
129:                { "bps", 'b', POPT_ARG_INT, &speed, 0,
130:                  "signaling rate for current maching in bps",
131:                  "<BPS>" },
132:                { "crnl", 'c', POPT_ARG_VAL, &crnl, 'c',
133:                  "send carriage return with each newline", NULL },
134:                { "hwflow", 'h', POPT_ARG_VAL, &flow, 'h',
135:                  "use hardware flow control", NULL },
136:                { "swflow", 's', POPT_ARG_VAL, &flow, 's',
137:                  "use software flow control", NULL },
138:                { "noflow", 'n', POPT_ARG_VAL, &flow, 'n',
139:                  "disable flow control", NULL },
140:                { "raw", 'r', POPT_ARG_VAL, &raw, 1,
141:                  "enable raw mode", NULL },
142:                POPT_AUTOHELP
143:                { NULL, '\0', 0, NULL, '\0', NULL, NULL }
144:        };
145:
146: #ifdef DSLEEP
147:     /* wait 10 minutes so we can attach a debugger */
148:     sleep(600);
149: #endif
150:
151:     optCon = poptGetContext("robin", argc, argv, optionsTable, 0);
152:     poptSetOtherOptionHelp(optCon, "<port>");
153:
154:     if (argc < 2) {
155:         poptPrintUsage(optCon, stderr, 0);
156:         die(1, "Not enough arguments", "");
157:     }
158:
159:     if ((c = poptGetNextOpt(optCon)) < -1) {
160:         /* an error occurred during option processing */
161:         fprintf(stderr, "%s: %s\n",
162:                 poptBadOption(optCon, POPT_BADOPTION_NOALIAS),
163:                 poptStrerror(c));
164:         return 1;
165:     }
166:     portname = poptGetArg(optCon);
167:     if (!portname) {
168:         poptPrintUsage(optCon, stderr, 0);
```

```
169:            die(1, "No port name specified", "");
170:        }
171:
172:        pf = open(portname, O_RDWR);
173:        if (pf < 0) {
174:            poptPrintUsage(optCon, stderr, 0);
175:            die(1, strerror(errno), portname);
176:        }
177:        poptFreeContext(optCon);
178:
179:        /* modify the port configuration */
180:        tcgetattr(pf, &pts);
181:        pots = pts;
182:        /* some things we want to set arbitrarily */
183:        pts.c_lflag &= ~ICANON;
184:        pts.c_lflag &= ~(ECHO | ECHOCTL | ECHONL);
185:        pts.c_cflag |= HUPCL;
186:        pts.c_cc[VMIN] = 1;
187:        pts.c_cc[VTIME] = 0;
188:
189:        /* Standard CR/LF handling: this is a dumb terminal.
190:         * Do no translation:
191:         *   no NL -> CR/NL mapping on output, and
192:         *   no CR -> NL mapping on input.
193:         */
194:        pts.c_oflag &= ~ONLCR;
195:        pts.c_iflag &= ~ICRNL;
196:
197:        /* Now deal with the local terminal side */
198:        tcgetattr(STDIN_FILENO, &sts);
199:        sots = sts;
200:        /* again, some arbitrary things */
201:        sts.c_iflag &= ~(BRKINT | ICRNL);
202:        sts.c_iflag |= IGNBRK;
203:        sts.c_lflag &= ~ISIG;
204:        sts.c_cc[VMIN] = 1;
205:        sts.c_cc[VTIME] = 0;
206:        sts.c_lflag &= ~ICANON;
207:        /* no local echo: allow the other end to do the echoing */
208:        sts.c_lflag &= ~(ECHO | ECHOCTL | ECHONL);
209:
```

```
210:     /* option handling will now modify pts and sts */
211:     switch (flow) {
212:     case 'h':
213:         /* hardware flow control */
214:         pts.c_cflag |= CRTSCTS;
215:         pts.c_iflag &= ~(IXON | IXOFF | IXANY);
216:         break;
217:     case 's':
218:         /* software flow control */
219:         pts.c_cflag &= ~CRTSCTS;
220:         pts.c_iflag |= IXON | IXOFF | IXANY;
221:         break;
222:     case 'n':
223:         /* no flow control */
224:         pts.c_cflag &= ~CRTSCTS;
225:         pts.c_iflag &= ~(IXON | IXOFF | IXANY);
226:         break;
227:     }
228:     if (crnl) {
229:         /* send CR with NL */
230:         pts.c_oflag |= ONLCR;
231:     }
232:
233:     /* speed is not modified unless -b is specified */
234:     if (speed) {
235:         cfsetospeed(&pts, symbolic_speed(speed));
236:         cfsetispeed(&pts, symbolic_speed(speed));
237:     }
238:
239:     /* set the signal handler to restore the old
240:      * termios handler */
241:     sact.sa_handler = cleanup_termios;
242:     sigaction(SIGHUP, &sact, NULL);
243:     sigaction(SIGINT, &sact, NULL);
244:     sigaction(SIGPIPE, &sact, NULL);
245:     sigaction(SIGTERM, &sact, NULL);
246:
247:     /* Now set the modified termios settings */
248:     tcsetattr(pf, TCSANOW, &pts);
249:     tcsetattr(STDIN_FILENO, TCSANOW, &sts);
250:
```

```
251:        ufds[0].fd = STDIN_FILENO;
252:        ufds[0].events = POLLIN;
253:        ufds[1].fd = pf;
254:        ufds[1].events = POLLIN;
255:
256:        do {
257:            int r;
258:
259:            r = poll(ufds, 2, -1);
260:            if ((r < 0) && (errno != EINTR))
261:                die(1, "poll failed unexpectedly", "");
262:
263:            /* First check for an opportunity to exit */
264:            if ((ufds[0].revents | ufds[1].revents) &
265:                (POLLERR | POLLHUP | POLLNVAL)) {
266:                done = 1;
267:                break;
268:            }
269:
270:            if (ufds[1].revents & POLLIN) {
271:                /* pf has characters for us */
272:                i = read(pf, buf, BUFSIZE);
273:                if (i >= 1) {
274:                    write(STDOUT_FILENO, buf, i);
275:                } else {
276:                    done = 1;
277:                }
278:            }
279:            if (ufds[0].revents & POLLIN) {
280:                /* standard input has characters for us */
281:                i = read(STDIN_FILENO, buf, BUFSIZE);
282:                if (i >= 1) {
283:                    if (raw) {
284:                        write(pf, buf, i);
285:                    } else {
286:                        cook_buf(pf, buf, i);
287:                    }
288:                } else {
289:                    done = 1;
290:                }
291:            }
```

```
292:        } while (!done);
293:
294:        /* restore original terminal settings and exit */
295:        tcsetattr(pf, TCSANOW, &pots);
296:        tcsetattr(STDIN_FILENO, TCSANOW, &sots);
297:        exit(0);
298: }
```

robin.c starts out by including a few header files (read the man page for each system call and library function to see which include files you need to include, as usual), then defines a few useful functions.

The symbolic_speed() function at line 19 converts an integer speed into a symbolic speed that termios can handle. Unfortunately, termios is not designed to handle arbitrary speeds, so each speed you wish to use must be part of the user–kernel interface.[4]

Note that it includes some rather high speeds. Not all serial ports support speeds as high as 230,400 or 460,800 bps; the POSIX standard defines speeds only up to 38,400 bps. To make this program portable, each line above the one that sets the speed to 38,400 bps would have to be expanded to three lines, like this:

```
#   ifdef B460800
    if (speednum >= 460800) return B460800;
#   endif
```

That still allows users to specify speeds beyond what the serial ports may be able to handle, but the source code will now compile on any system with POSIX termios. (As discussed on page 352 and page 371, any serial port has the option of refusing to honor any termios setting it is incapable of handling, and that includes speed settings. So just because B460800 is defined does not mean you can set the port speed to 460,800 bits per second.)

Next, on lines 44 through 55, we see a few global variables for communicating some variables to a signal handler, and the signal handler itself. The signal handler is designed to restore termios settings on both tty interfaces when a signal is delivered, so it needs to be able to access the structures

---

4. See man setserial for a Linux-specific way to get around this limitation on a limited basis.

containing the old termios settings. It also needs to know the file descriptor of the serial port (the file descriptor for standard input does not change, so it is compiled into the binary). The code is identical to that in the normal exit path, which is described later. The signal handler is later attached to signals that would terminate the process if they were ignored.

The `send_escape()` and `cook_buf()` functions are discussed later. They are used as part of the input processing in the I/O loop at the end of the `main()` function.

The conditionally compiled `sleep(600)` at the beginning of the `main()` function is there for debugging. In order to debug programs that modify termios settings for standard input or standard output, it is best to *attach* to the process from a different window or terminal session. However, that means that you cannot just set a breakpoint on the main function and step into the process one instruction at a time. You have to start the program running, find its pid, and attach to it from within the debugger. This process is described in more detail on page 370.

Therefore, if we are debugging and need to debug code that runs before the program waits for input, we need the program to sleep for a while to give us time to attach. Once we attach, we interrupt the sleep, so there is no harm in using a long sleep time. Compile robin.c with `-DDSLEEP` in order to activate this feature.

Ignoring debugging, we first parse the options using the popt library described in Chapter 26, and then open the serial port to which we will talk.

Next, we use the `tcgetattr()` function to get the existing termios configuration of the serial port, then we save a copy in `pots` so that we can restore it when we are through.

Starting with line 183, we modify settings for the serial port:

```
183:    pts.c_lflag &= ~ICANON;
```

This line turns off canonicalization in the serial port driver—that is, puts it in raw mode. In this mode, no characters are special—not newlines, not control characters:

```
184:    pts.c_lflag &= ~(ECHO | ECHOCTL | ECHONL);
```

This turns off all local echoing on the serial port:

```
185:      pts.c_cflag |= HUPCL;
```

If there is a modem connected, HUPCL arranges for it to be told to hang up when the final program closes the device:

```
186:      pts.c_cc[VMIN] = 1;
187:      pts.c_cc[VTIME] = 0;
```

When a tty is in raw mode, these two settings determine the read() system call's behavior. This particular setting says that when we call read(), we want read() to wait to return until one or more bytes have been read. We never call read() unless we know that there is at least one byte to read, so this is functionally equivalent to a nonblocking read(). The definition of VMIN and VTIME is complex, as we demonstrate on page 387.

The default termios settings include some end-of-line character translation. That is okay for dial-in lines and for terminal sessions, but when we are connecting two ttys, we do not want the translation to happen twice. We do not want to map newline characters to a carriage return/newline pair on output, and we do not want to map a received carriage return to a newline on input, because we are already receiving carriage return/newline pairs from the remote system:

```
194:      pts.c_oflag &= ~ONLCR;
195:      pts.c_iflag &= ~ICRNL;
```

Without these two lines, using robin to connect to another Linux or Unix computer would result in the remote system seeing you press Return twice each time you press it once, and each time it tries to display a new line on your screen, you will see two lines. So each time you press Return (assuming you manage to log in with these terminal settings), you will see two prompts echoed back to you, and if you run vi, you will see ~ characters on every other line rather than on every line.

At this point, we have made all the changes to the serial port's termios settings that we know we need to make before we process the command-line arguments. We now turn to modifying the settings for the tty that gives us standard input and output. Since it is one tty, we need to deal with only one file descriptor of the pair. We have chosen standard input, following the convention set by the **stty** program. We start out, again, by getting and saving attributes.

Then we modify some flags:

```
201:        sts.c_iflag &= ~(BRKINT | ICRNL);
202:        sts.c_iflag |= IGNBRK;
203:        sts.c_lflag &= ~ISIG;
```

Turning off BRKINT makes a difference only if robin is being called from a login session attached to another serial port on which a break can be received. Turning it off means that the tty driver does not send a SIGINT to robin when a break condition occurs on robin's standard input, since robin does not have anything useful to do when it receives a break. Turning off ICRNL prevents any received carriage-return ('\r') characters from being reported to robin as newline ('\n') characters. Like turning off BRKINT, this applies only when the login session is attached to another serial port. In addition, it applies only if carriage-return characters are not being ignored (that is, if the IGNCR flag is not set).

The IGNBRK function tells the tty driver to ignore breaks. Turning on IGNBRK is actually redundant here. If IGNBRK is set, then BRKINT is ignored. But it does not hurt to set both.

Those are input processing flags. We also modify a local processing flag: We turn off ISIG. This keeps the tty driver from sending SIGINT, SIGQUIT, and SIGTSTP when the respective character (INTR, QUIT, or SUSP) is received. We do this because we want those characters to be sent to the remote system (or whatever is connected to the serial port) for processing there.

Next comes option handling. In some cases, the default modifications we made to the termios settings might not be sufficient, or they might be too much. In these cases, we provide some command-line options to modify the termios options.

By default, we leave the serial port in whatever flow-control state we find it in. However, at line 212, there are options to do hardware flow control (which uses the CTS and RTS flow-control wires), software flow control (reserving ^S and ^Q for STOP and START, respectively), and explicitly disable flow control entirely:

```
212:        case 'h':
213:            /* hardware flow control */
214:            pts.c_cflag |= CRTSCTS;
215:            pts.c_iflag &= ~(IXON | IXOFF | IXANY);
216:            break;
217:        case 's':
218:            /* software flow control */
219:            pts.c_cflag &= ~CRTSCTS;
220:            pts.c_iflag |= IXON | IXOFF | IXANY;
221:            break;
222:        case 'n':
223:            /* no flow control */
224:            pts.c_cflag &= ~CRTSCTS;
225:            pts.c_iflag &= ~(IXON | IXOFF | IXANY);
226:            break;
```

Note that software flow control involves three flags:

IXON   Stop sending output if a STOP character (usually, ^S) is received, and start again when a START character (usually, ^Q) is received.

IXOFF   Send a STOP character when there is too much data in the incoming buffer, and send a START character when enough of the data has been read.

IXANY   Allow any received character, not just START, to restart *output*. (This flag is commonly implemented on Unix systems, but it is not specified by POSIX.)

When robin is being used as a helper program by another program, doing any special character processing (robin usually interprets a control-\ character specially) may get in the way, so we provide raw mode to sidestep all such processing. On line 120, we provide a variable that determines whether raw mode is enabled; the default is not to enable raw mode. On line 140, we tell popt how to inform us that the -r or --raw option was given on the command line, enabling raw mode.

Some systems require that you send them a carriage-return character to represent a newline. The word *systems* should be taken broadly here; as an example, this is true of many smart peripherals, such as UPSs, that have serial ports, because they were designed to function in the DOS world, where a carriage return/newline pair is always used to denote a new line. Line 228 allows us to specify this DOS-oriented behavior:

```
228:    if (crnl) {
229:        /* send CR with NL */
230:        pts.c_oflag |= ONLCR;
231:    }
```

The final bit of option handling controls the *bits per second*[5] rate. Rather than include a large nested switch statement here, we call symbolic_speed(), already described, to get a speed_t that termios understands, as shown on line 233.

```
233:    /* speed is not modified unless -b is specified */
234:    if (speed) {
235:        cfsetospeed(&pts, symbolic_speed(speed));
236:        cfsetispeed(&pts, symbolic_speed(speed));
237:    }
```

Having determined the actual speed and gotten the symbolic value that represents it, we need to put that speed into the termios structure for the serial port. Since the termios structure supports asynchronous devices that can have different input and output speeds, we need to set both speeds to the same value here.

Before committing the changes we have made in our copies of the termios structures to the devices, on line 241 we register signal handlers for important signals that might otherwise kill us, causing us to leave the ttys in their raw state. For more information on signal handlers, see Chapter 12.

```
241:    sact.sa_handler = cleanup_termios;
242:    sigaction(SIGHUP, &sact, NULL);
243:    sigaction(SIGINT, &sact, NULL);
244:    sigaction(SIGPIPE, &sact, NULL);
245:    sigaction(SIGTERM, &sact, NULL);
```

---

5. Note: "bits per second" or "bps," not "baud." *Bits per second* indicates the rate at which information is sent. *Baud* is an engineering term that describes phase changes per second. Baud is irrelevant to termios, but the word *baud* unfortunately has made its way into some termios flags that are not covered in this book.

Once the signal handler is in place to restore the old termios settings if robin is killed, we can safely put the new termios settings in place:

```
248:        tcsetattr(pf, TCSANOW, &pts);
249:        tcsetattr(STDIN_FILENO, TCSANOW, &sts);
```

Note that we use the TCSANOW option when setting these options, indicating that we want them to take effect immediately. Sometimes, it is appropriate to use other options; they are covered later in the reference section.

At this point, robin is ready to read and write characters. robin has two file descriptors to read from: data coming from the serial port and data coming from the keyboard. We use poll() to multiplex I/O between the four file descriptors, as described on page 245.

The poll() loop makes the simplifying assumption that it can always write as much as it was able to read. This is almost always true and does not cause problems in practice, because blocking for short periods is not noticeable in normal circumstances. The loop never reads from a file descriptor unless poll() has already said that that file descriptor has data waiting to be read, so we know that we do not block while reading.

For data coming from the keyboard, we may need to process escape sequences before writing, if the user did not select raw mode when running robin. Rather than include that code in the middle of this loop, we call cook_buf() (line 78), which calls send_escape() (line 58) when necessary. Both of these functions are simple. The only tricks are that cook_buf() may be called once with the escape character, then a second time with the character to interpret, and that it is optimized to call the write() function as little as is reasonably possible.

cook_buf() calls the send_escape() function once for every character that is preceded by an unescaped control-\ character. A q character restores the original termios settings and quits by calling the signal handler (with a bogus signal number of 0), which restores the termios settings appropriately before exiting. A b character generates a break condition, which is a long string of continuous 0 bits. Any other character, including a second control-\ character, is passed through to the serial port verbatim.

If either input file descriptor returns an end-of-file condition, robin exits the poll() loop and falls through to the exit processing, which is the same as the signal handler: It restores the old termios settings on both input file descriptors and exits. In raw mode, the only ways to get robin to quit are to close one of the file descriptors or to send it a signal.

16.4 termios Debugging

Debugging tty code is not always easy. The options overlap in meaning and affect each other in various ways, often in ways that you do not intend. But you cannot easily see what is happening with only a debugger, because the processing that you are trying to manage is happening in the kernel.

One effective way to debug code that communicates over a serial port is to use the script program. While developing robin, we connected two computers with a serial cable and verified that the connection worked by running the already-working kermit program. While still running kermit on the local computer, we ran the script program on the remote computer, which started keeping a log of all the characters in the file typescript. Then we quit kermit and ran script on the local computer, which put a typescript file in the current directory on the local computer. We then tried to run robin under script and compared the two typescript files at each end after each run to see the differences in characters. We thereby deciphered the effects of the processing options we had chosen.

Another debugging method takes advantage of the stty program. If, while you are testing a program, you think you recognize a mistake in the termios settings, you can use the stty program to make the change immediately rather than recompile your program first. If you are working on /dev/ttyS0, and you want to set the ECHOCTL flag, simply run the command

```
stty echoctl < /dev/ttyS0
```

while your program is running.

Similarly, you can view the current status of the port you are using with

```
stty -a < /dev/ttyS0
```

As we explained before, it is hard to use the same tty for running the debugger and for running the tty-mangling program you are debugging.

Instead, you want to attach to the process. This is not difficult to do. In one X-terminal session (do this under X so that you can see both ttys at once), run the program you want to debug. If you need to, put a long `sleep()` in it at the point at which you wish to attach to it:

```
$ ./robin -b 38400 /dev/ttyS1
```

Now, from another X-terminal session, find the pid of the program you are trying to debug, in one of two ways:

```
$ ps | grep robin
30483  ?  S    0:00 ./robin -b 38400 /dev/ttyS1
30485  ?  S    0:00 grep robin
$ pidof robin
30483
```

pidof is more convenient, but may not be available on every system. Keep the number you found (here, 30483) in mind and start a debugging session the same way you normally would.

```
$ gdb robin 30483
GDB is free software...
...
Attaching to program '.../robin', process 30483
Reading symbols from ...
0x40075d88 in sigsuspend ()
```

From this point, you can set breakpoints and watchpoints, step through the program, or whatever you like.

16.5 termios Reference

The termios interface is composed of a structure, a set of functions that operate on it, and a multitude of flags that you can set individually:

```
#include <termios.h>

struct termios {
    tcflag_t c_iflag;    /* input mode flags */
    tcflag_t c_oflag;    /* output mode flags */
    tcflag_t c_cflag;    /* control mode flags */
    tcflag_t c_lflag;    /* local mode flags */
    cc_t c_line;         /* line discipline */
    cc_t c_cc[NCCS];     /* control characters */
};
```

The c_line member is used only in very system-specific applications[6] that are beyond the scope of this book. The other five members, however, are relevant in almost all situations that require you to manipulate terminal settings.

16.5.1 Functions

The termios interface defines several functions, all of which are declared in <termios.h>. Four of them are convenience functions for manipulating a struct termios in a portable way; the rest are system calls. Those that start with cf are convenience functions; those functions that start with tc are *terminal control* system calls. All of the terminal control system calls generate SIGTTOU if the process is currently running in the background and tries to manipulate its controlling terminal (see Chapter 15).

Except as noted, these functions return 0 to indicate success and -1 to indicate failure. The function calls you may use for terminal control are:

int tcgetattr(int fd, struct termios *t);
    Retrieves the current settings for the file descriptor fd and places them in the structure to which t points.

int tcsetattr(int fd, int options, struct termios *t);
    Sets the current terminal settings for the file descriptor fd to the settings specified in t. Always use tcgetattr() to fill in t, then modify it. Never fill in t by hand: Some systems require that flags

---

6. Such as setting up networking protocols that communicate through tty devices.

beyond the flags specified by POSIX be set or cleared, so filling in t by hand is nonportable.

The options argument determines when the change takes effect.

TCSANOW   The change takes effect immediately.

TCSADRAIN   The change takes effect after all the output that already has been written to fd has been transmitted; it drains the queue before taking effect. You should generally use this when you change output parameters.

TCSAFLUSH   The change takes effect after the output queue has been drained; the input queue is discarded (flushed) before the change takes effect.

If the system cannot handle some settings, such as data rate, it is allowed to *ignore* those settings silently without returning any error. The only way to see whether the settings were accepted is to use tcgetattr() and compare the contents of the structure it returns to the one you passed to tcsetattr().

Thus, most portable applications use code something like this:

```
#include <termios.h>

struct termios save;
struct termios set;
struct termios new;
int fd;
...
tcgetattr(fd, &save);
set = save;
cfsetospeed(&set, B2400);
cfsetispeed(&set, B2400);
tcsetattr(fd, &set);
tcgetattr(fd, &new);
if ((cfgetospeed(&set) != B2400) ||
    (cfgetispeed(&set) != B2400)) {
  /* complain */
}
```

Note that if you do not care if a termios setting sticks, it is fine to ignore the condition, as we do in robin.

```
speed_t cfgetospeed(struct termios *t);
speed_t cfgetispeed(struct termios *t);
```
Retrieve the output or input speed, respectively, from t. These functions return a symbolic speed, the same as is given to cfsetospeed() and cfsetispeed().

```
int cfsetospeed(struct termios *t, speed_t speed);
int cfsetispeed(struct termios *t, speed_t speed);
```
Set the output or input speed, respectively, in t to speed. Note that this function does not change the speed of the connection on any file descriptor; it merely sets the speed in the termios structure. The speed, like other characteristics, is applied to a file descriptor by tcsetattr().

These functions take a symbolic speed—that is, a number that matches the definition of one of the following macros whose names indicate the bits-per-second rate: B0 (0 bits per second indicates a disconnected state), B50, B75, B110, B134,[7] B150, B200, B300, B600, B1200, B1800, B2400, B4800, B9600, B19200, B38400, B57600, B115200, B230400, B460800, B500000, B576000, B921600, B1000000, B1152000, B1500000, B2000000, B2500000, B3000000, B3500000, or B4000000. B57600 and higher are not specified by POSIX; portable source code uses them only if they are protected by #ifdef statements.

More symbolic speeds will be added to the header file as Linux drivers are written for hardware that supports other data rates.

Currently, input speed is ignored. The termios interface specifies separate input and output speeds for some asynchronous hardware that allows split speeds, but little such hardware exists. Just call cfsetospeed() and cfsetispeed() in pairs so that your code will continue to work on systems that support split speeds.

Not all ttys support all rates. In particular, the serial ports on standard PCs do not support over 115,200 bps. As noted above, if you

---

7. B134 is really 134.5 bps, a rate used by an obsolete IBM terminal.

care whether this setting takes effect, you need to use `tcgetattr()` to check after you attempt to set it with `tcsetattr()`. Also, note that the rate you set is advisory. Some ttys, like local consoles, cheerfully accept and ignore any rate you give them.

`int tcsendbreak(int fd, int duration)`
> Sends a stream of zero-valued bits on `fd` for a specified `duration`, which is known as a **break**. If `duration` is `0`, the break is at least 250 milliseconds and no more than 500 milliseconds long. Unfortunately, POSIX did not bother to specify the unit in which the duration is measured, so the only portable value for `duration` is `0`. Under Linux, duration multiplies the break; `0` or `1` specify between a quarter second and a half second; `2` specifies between a half second and a second, and so on.

`int tcdrain(int fd)`
> Waits until all currently pending output on the file descriptor `fd` has been sent.

`int tcflush(int fd, int queue_selector)`
> Discards some data on file descriptor `fd`, depending on the value of `queue_selector`:

`TCIFLUSH`	Flush all data that the interface has received but that has not yet been read.
`TCOFLUSH`	Flush all data that has been written to the interface that has not yet been sent.
`TCIOFLUSH`	Flush all pending data, input and output.

`int tcflow(int fd, int action)`
> Suspend or resume output or input on the file descriptor `fd`. Exactly what to do is determined by `action`:

`TCOOFF`	Suspend output.
`TCOON`	Resume output.

TCIOFF   Send a STOP character, requesting that the other end of the connection stop sending characters.

TCION   Send a START character, requesting that the other end of the connection resume sending characters.

Note that TCIOFF and TCION are only advisory, and that even if the other end of the connection does honor them, there may be a delay before it does so.

16.5.2 Window Sizes

There are two ioctl() requests that, unfortunately, were not codified as part of the termios interface, although they should have been. The size of the tty, measured in rows and columns, ought to be managed with tcgetwinsize() and tcsetwinsize(), but as they do not exist, you must use ioctl() instead. For both requesting the current size and setting a new size, use a struct winsize:

```
#include <termios.h>

struct winsize {
    unsigned short ws_row;      /* number of rows */
    unsigned short ws_col;      /* number of columns */
    unsigned short ws_xpixel;   /* unused */
    unsigned short ws_ypixel;   /* unused */
};
```

To request the current size, use

```
    struct winsize ws;

    ioctl(fd, TIOCGWINSZ, &ws);
```

To set a new size, fill in a struct winsize and call

```
    ioctl(fd, TIOCSWINSZ, &ws);
```

See page 389 for an example of the conditions in which you would want to set a new window size.

When the window size changes, the signal SIGWINCH is sent to the foreground process group leader on that tty. Your code can catch this signal; use TIOCGWINSZ to query the new size and make any appropriate changes within your program.

16.5.3 Flags

The four flag variables, c_iflag, c_oflag, c_cflag, and c_lflag, hold flags that control various characteristics. The <termios.h> header file provides symbolic constant bitmasks that represent those flags. Set them with |= and unset them with &= ~, like this:

```
t.c_iflag |= BRKINT;
t.c_iflag &= ~IGNBRK;
```

A few of these symbolic defines are actually bitmasks that cover several related constants. They are used to extract parts of the structure for comparison:

```
if ((t.c_cflag & CSIZE) == CS7)
    character_size = 7;
```

The set of flags differs from system to system. The most important flags are specified by POSIX, but Linux follows System V in including several useful flags that POSIX does not define. This documentation is not complete; Linux supports some flags that you will probably never need. We cover the flags that you might possibly have a reason to use and refrain from confusing you with the rest.

In order to enable you to write portable software, we have labelled every flag that is not specified by the POSIX standard. For those flags, you should write code like this:

```
#ifdef IUCLC
    t.c_iflag |= IUCLC;
#endif
```

Also, some areas that present particular portability problems are mentioned, and we even break our rule of not confusing you with details from other implementations by presenting a few details about what other systems do.

16.5.4 Input Flags

The input mode flags affect input processing even though they sometimes have an effect on output. The flags that operate on c_iflag are as follows:

BRKINT and IGNBRK

> If IGNBRK is set, break conditions (see tcsendbreak(), mentioned earlier) are ignored.
>
> If IGNBRK is not set and BRKINT is set, break conditions cause the tty to flush all queued input and output data and send a SIGINT to processes in the foreground process group for the tty.
>
> If IGNBRK is not set and BRKINT is not set, break conditions are read as a zero-valued character ('\0'), except if PARMRK is set, in which case a framing error is detected and the three bytes '\377' '\0' '\0' are delivered to the application instead.

PARMRK and IGNPAR

> If IGNPAR is set, received bytes containing parity or framing errors are ignored (except as specified for break conditions earlier).
>
> If IGNPAR is not set and PARMRK is set, a received byte with a parity or framing error is reported to the application as the three-byte sequence '\377' '\0' '\n', where n is the byte as it was received. In this case, if ISTRIP is not set, a valid '\377' character is reported to the application as the two-character sequence '\377' '\377'; if ISTRIP is set, a '\377' character has its high bit stripped and is reported as '\177'.
>
> If neither PARMRK nor IGNPAR is set, a received byte with a parity or framing error other than a break condition is reported to the application as a single '\0' character.

INPCK   If INPCK is set, parity checking is enabled. If it is not enabled, PARMRK and IGNPAR have no effect on received parity errors.

ISTRIP   If ISTRIP is set, the high-order bit is stripped from all received bytes, limiting them to seven bits.

INLCR   If INLCR is set, received newline ('\n') characters are translated to carriage-return ('\r') characters.

IGNCR   If IGNCR is set, received carriage returns ('\r') are ignored (not reported to the application).

ICRNL   If ICRNL is set and IGNCR is not set, received carriage-return ('\r') characters are reported to the application as newline ('\n') characters.

IUCLC   If IUCLC and IEXTEN are set, received uppercase characters are reported to the application as lowercase characters. This flag is not specified by POSIX.

IXOFF   If IXOFF is set, the tty may send Control-S and Control-Q characters to the terminal to request that it stop and resume output (that is, sending data to the computer), respectively, to avoid overflowing the tty's input buffers. This is relevant only to serial terminals, as network and local terminals have more direct forms of flow control. Even serial terminals often have hardware flow control, which is controlled by the control flag (c_cflag) and which makes software flow control (Control-S and Control-Q) irrelevant.

IXON   If IXON is set, a received Control-S character stops output to this tty and a received Control-Q character restarts output to this tty. This is relevant to any form of terminal I/O, as some users type literal Control-S and Control-Q characters to suspend and resume output.

IXANY   If IXANY is set, any received character (not just Control-Q) restarts output. This flag is not specified by POSIX.

IMAXBEL   If IMAXBEL is set, the alert ('\a') character is sent whenever a character is received and the input buffer is already full. This flag is not specified by POSIX.

16.5.5 Output Flags

The output mode flags modify output processing *only if* OPOST *is set.* None of these flags are portable, because POSIX defines only OPOST and calls it "implementation defined." However, you will find that real terminal-handling applications often do need output processing, and the output flags available under Linux are generally available on most Unix systems, including SVR4.

The terminal code keeps track of the **current column**, which allows it to suppress extra carriage-return characters ('\r') and to convert tabs to spaces when appropriate. This current column is zero-based; the first column is column zero. The current column is set to zero whenever a carriage return ('\r') is sent or implied, as it may be by a newline character ('\n') when ONLRET or ONLCR is set, or when the current column is set to one and a backspace character ('\b') is sent.

The flags that operate on c_oflag are as follows:

OPOST   This is the only output flag specified by POSIX, which says that it turns on "implementation-defined" output processing. If OPOST is not set, none of the other output mode flags are consulted and no output processing is done.

OLCUC   If OLCUC is set, lowercase characters are sent to the terminal as uppercase characters. This flag is not specified by POSIX.

ONLCR   If ONLCR is set, when a newline character ('\n') is sent, a carriage return ('\r') is sent before the newline. The current column is set to zero. This flag is not specified by POSIX.

ONOCR   If ONOCR is set, carriage-return characters ('\r') are neither processed nor sent if the current column is zero. This flag is not specified by POSIX.

OCRNL   If OCRNL is set, carriage-return characters ('\r') are translated into newline characters ('\n'). If, in addition, ONLRET is set, the current column is set to zero. This flag is not specified by POSIX.

ONLRET   If ONLRET is set, when a newline character ('\n') or carriage-return character ('\r') is sent, the current column is set to zero. This flag is not specified by POSIX.

OXTABS   If OXTABS is set, tabs are expanded to spaces. Tab stops are assumed to be every eight characters, and the number of space characters that are sent is determined by the current column. This flag is not specified by POSIX.

In addition, there are delay flags that you never need to set; they are designed to compensate for old, badly designed, and, by now, mercifully rare hardware. The termcap and terminfo libraries are responsible for managing delay flags, which means that you should never have to modify them. *termcap & terminfo* [Strang, 1991B], which documents them, describes them as obsolete. The Linux kernel does not currently implement them, and as there has been no demand for this feature, they likely will never be implemented.

16.5.6 Control Flags

The control mode flags affect protocol parameters, such as parity and flow control.[8] The flags that operate on c_cflag are as follows:

CLOCAL   If CLOCAL is set, modem control lines are ignored. If it is not set, then open() will block until the modem announces an off-hook condition by asserting the carrier-detect line.

CREAD   Characters can be received only if CREAD is set. It cannot necessarily be unset.[9]

CSIZE   CSIZE is a mask for the codes that set the size of a transmitted character in bits. The character size should be set to:
CS5   for five bits per character
CS6   for six bits per character
CS7   for seven bits per character
CS8   for eight bits per character

---

8. Linux also uses c_cflag to hold the speed, but relying on that is completely non-portable. Use cfsetospeed() and cfsetispeed() instead.
9. Try running stty -cread!

CSTOPB If CSTOPB is set, two stop bits are generated at the end of each transmitted character frame. If CSTOPB is not set, only one stop bit is generated. Obsolete equipment that requires two stop bits is rare.

HUPCL If HUPCL is set, then when the final open file descriptor on the device is closed, the DTR and RTS lines on the serial port (if they exist) will be lowered to signal the modem to hang up. This means, for example, that when a user who logged in through a modem then logs out, the modem will be hung up. If a communications program has the device open for outbound calls and the process then closes the device (or exits), the modem will be hung up.

PARENB and PARODD

If PARENB is set, a parity bit is generated. If PARODD is not set, even parity is generated. If PARODD is set, odd parity is generated.

If PARENB is not set, PARODD is ignored.

CRTSCTS Use hardware flow control (RTS and CTS lines). At high speeds (19,200 bps and higher) software flow control via the XON and XOFF characters becomes ineffective and hardware flow control must be used instead.

This flag is not specified by POSIX and is not available by this name on most other Unix systems. This is a particularly non-portable area of terminal control, despite the common need for hardware flow control on modern systems. SVR4 is particularly egregious in that it provides no way to enable hardware flow control through termios, only through a different interface called termiox.

16.5.7 Control Characters

Control characters are characters that have special meanings that may differ depending on whether the terminal is in canonical input mode or raw input mode and on the settings of various control flags. Each offset (except for VMIN and VTIME) in the c_cc array designates an action and holds the character code that is assigned that action. For example, set the interrupt character to Control-C with code like this:

```
ts.c_cc[VINTR] = CTRLCHAR('C');
```

CTRLCHAR() is a macro defined as

```
#define CTRLCHAR(ch) ((ch)&0x1F)
```

Some systems have a CTRL() macro defined in <termios.h>, but it is not defined on all systems, so defining our own version is more portable.

We use the ^C notation to designate Control-C.

The character positions that are not specified by POSIX are active only if the IEXTEN local control (c_lflag) flag is set.

The control characters that you can use as subscripts to the c_cc array are:

VINTR   Offset VINTR is usually set to ^C. It normally flushes the input and output queues and sends SIGINT to the members of the foreground process group associated with the tty. Processes that do not explicitly handle SIGINT will exit immediately.

VQUIT   Offset VQUIT is usually set to ^\. It normally flushes the input and output queues and sends SIGQUIT to the members of the foreground process group associated with the tty. Processes that do not explicitly handle SIGQUIT will abort, dumping core if possible (see page 120).

VERASE   Offset VERASE is usually set to ^H or ^?. In canonical mode, it normally erases the previous character on the line. In raw mode, it is meaningless.

VKILL   Offset VKILL is usually set to ^U. In canonical mode, it normally erases the entire line. In raw mode, it is meaningless.

VEOF

Offset VEOF is usually set to ^D. In canonical mode, it causes read() on that file descriptor to return 0, signaling an end-of-file condition. On some systems, it may share space with the VMIN character, which is active only in raw mode. (This is not an issue if you save a struct termios with canonical mode settings to restore once you are done with raw mode, which is proper termios programming practice, anyway.)

VSTOP

Offset VSTOP is usually set to ^S. It causes the tty to pause output until the VSTART character is received, or, if IXANY is set, until any character is received.

VSTART

Offset VSTART is usually set to ^Q. It restarts paused tty output.

VSUSP

Offset VSUSP is usually set to ^Z. It causes the current foreground process group to be sent SIGTSTP; see Chapter 15 for details.

VEOL and VEOL2

In canonical mode, these characters, in addition to the newline character ('\n'), signal an end-of-line condition. This causes the collected buffer to be transmitted and a new buffer started. On some systems, VEOL may share space with the VTIME character, which is active only in raw mode, just as VEOF may share space with VMIN. The VEOL2 character is not specified by POSIX.

VREPRINT

Offset VREPRINT is usually set to ^R. In canonical mode, if the ECHO local flag is set, it causes the VREPRINT character to be echoed locally, a newline (and a carriage return, if appropriate) to be echoed locally, and the whole current buffer to be reprinted. This character is not specified by POSIX.

VWERASE

Offset VWERASE is usually set to ^W. In canonical mode, it erases any white space at the end of the buffer, then all adjacent non-white-space characters, which has the effect of erasing the previous word on the line. This character is not specified by POSIX.

VLNEXT

Offset VLNEXT is usually set to ^V. It is not itself entered into the buffer, but it causes the next character input to be put into the buffer literally, even if it is one of the control characters. Of course, to enter a single literal VLNEXT character, type it twice. This character is not specified by POSIX.

To disable any control character position, set its value to _POSIX_VDISABLE. This only works if _POSIX_VDISABLE is defined, and is defined as something other than -1. _POSIX_VDISABLE works on Linux, but a portable program will, unfortunately, not be able to depend on disabling control character positions on all systems.

16.5.8 Local Flags

The local mode flags affect local processing, which (roughly) refers to how characters are collected before they are output. When the device is in canonical (cooked) mode, characters are echoed locally without being sent to the remote system until a newline character is encountered. At that point, the whole line is sent, and the remote end processes it without echoing it again. In raw mode, each character is sent to the remote system as it is received. Sometimes the character is echoed only by the remote system; sometimes only by the local system; and sometimes, such as when reading a password, it is not echoed at all.

Some flags may act differently, depending on whether the terminal is in canonical mode or raw mode. Those that act differently in canonical and raw mode are marked.

The flags that operate on c_lflag are as follows:

ICANON   If ICANON is set, canonical mode is enabled. If ICANON is not set, raw mode is enabled.

ECHO   If ECHO is set, local echo is enabled. If ECHO is not set, all the other flags whose names start with ECHO are effectively disabled and function as if they are not set, except for ECHONL.

ECHOCTL If ECHOCTL is set, control characters are printed as ^C, where C is the character formed by adding octal 0100 to the control character, mod octal 0200. So Control-C is displayed as ^C, and Control-? (octal 0177) is represented as ^? (? is octal 77). This flag is not specified by POSIX.

ECHOE   In canonical mode, if ECHOE is set, then when the ERASE character
         is received, the previous character on the display is erased if
         possible.

ECHOK and ECHOKE
         In canonical mode, when the KILL character is received, the
         entire current line is erased from the buffer.

         If neither ECHOK, ECHOKE, nor ECHOE is set, the ECHOCTL represen-
         tation of the KILL character (^U by default) is printed to indicate
         that the line has been erased.

         If ECHOE and ECHOK are set but ECHOKE is not set, the ECHOCTL
         representation of the KILL character is printed, followed by a
         newline, which is then processed appropriately by OPOST han-
         dling if OPOST is set.

         If ECHOE, ECHOK, and ECHOKE are all set, the line is erased.

         See the description of ECHOPRT for another variation on this
         theme.

         The ECHOKE flag is not specified by POSIX. On systems without
         the ECHOKE flag, setting the ECHOK flag may be equivalent to
         setting both the ECHOK and ECHOKE flags under Linux.

ECHONL   In canonical mode, if ECHONL is set, newline ('\n') characters
         are echoed even if ECHO is not set.

ECHOPRT In canonical mode, if ECHOPRT is set, characters are printed as
         they are erased when the ERASE or WERASE (or KILL, if ECHOK
         and ECHOKE are set) characters are received. When the first erase
         character in a sequence is received, a \ is printed, and when the
         final erased character is printed (the end of the line is reached or
         a nonerasing character is typed), a / is printed. Every normal
         character you type is merely echoed. So typing asdf, followed
         by two ERASE characters, followed by df, followed by a KILL
         character, would look like asdf\fd/df\fdsa/

         This is useful for debugging and for using hardcopy terminals,
         such as the original teletype, where the characters are printed

on paper, and is otherwise useless. This flag is not specified by POSIX.

ISIG   If ISIG is set, the INTR, QUIT, and SUSP control characters cause the corresponding signal (SIGINT, SIGQUIT, or SIGTSTP, respectively; see Chapter 12) to be sent to all the processes in the current foreground process group on that tty.

NOFLSH   Usually, when the INTR and QUIT characters are received, the input and output queues are flushed. When the SUSP character is received, only the input queue is flushed. If NOFLSH is set, neither queue is flushed.

TOSTOP   If TOSTOP is set, then when a process that is not in the current foreground process group attempts to write to its controlling terminal, SIGTTOU is sent to the entire process group of which the process is a member. By default, this signal stops a process, as if the SUSP character had been pressed.

IEXTEN   This flag is specified as implementation-dependent by POSIX. It enables implementation-defined processing of input characters. Although portable programs do not set this bit, the IUCLC and certain character-erasing facilities in Linux depend on it being set. Fortunately, it is generally enabled by default on Linux systems, because the kernel initially enables it when setting up ttys, so you should not normally need to set it for any reason.

16.5.9 Controlling read()

Two elements in the c_cc array are not control characters and are relevant only in raw mode: VTIME and VMIN. In raw mode only, these determine when read() returns. In canonical mode, read() returns only when lines have been assembled or end-of-file is reached, unless the O_NONBLOCK option is set.

In raw mode, it would not be efficient to read one byte at a time, and it is also inefficient to poll the port by reading in nonblocking mode. This leaves two complementary methods of reading efficiently.

The first is to use poll(), as documented in Chapter 13 and demonstrated in robin.c. If poll() says that a file descriptor is ready to read, you know that you can read() some number of bytes immediately. However, combining poll() with the second method can make your code even more efficient by making it possible to read more bytes at a time.

The VTIME and VMIN "control characters" have a complex relationship. VTIME specifies an amount of time to wait in tenths of seconds (which cannot be larger than a cc_t, usually an 8-bit unsigned char), which may be zero. VMIN specifies the minimum number of bytes to wait for (not to read—read()'s third argument specifies the maximum number of bytes to read), which may also be zero.

- If VTIME is zero, VMIN specifies the number of bytes to wait for. A read() call does not return until at least VMIN bytes have been read or a signal has been received.

- If VMIN is zero, VTIME specifies the number of tenths of seconds for read() to wait before returning, even if no data is available. In this case, read() returning zero does not necessarily indicate an end-of-file condition, as it usually does.

- If neither VTIME nor VMIN is zero, VTIME specifies the number of tenths of seconds for read() to wait after at least one byte is available. If data is available when read() is called, a timer starts immediately. If data is not available when read() is called, a timer is started when the first byte arrives. The read() call returns either when at least VMIN bytes have arrived or when the timer expires, whichever comes first. It always returns at least one byte because the timer does not start until at least one byte is available.

- If VTIME and VMIN are both zero, read() always returns immediately, even if no data is available. Again, zero does not necessarily indicate an end-of-file condition.

16.6   Pseudo ttys

A pseudo tty, or pty, is a mechanism that allows a user-level program to take the place (logically speaking) of a tty driver for a piece of hardware. The pty has two distinct ends: The end that emulates hardware is called the **pty master**, and the end that provides programs with a normal tty interface is called the **pty slave**. The slave looks like a normal tty; the master is like a standard character device and is not a tty.

A serial port driver is generally implemented as an interrupt-driven piece of code in the kernel, to which programs talk through a specific device file. That does not have to be the case, however. For example, at least one SCSI-based terminal server exists that uses a generic interface to the SCSI protocol to have a user-level program that talks to the terminal server and provides access to the serial ports via ptys.

Network terminal sessions are done in the same manner; the rlogind and telnetd programs connect a network socket to a pty master and run a shell on a pty slave to make network connections act like ttys, allowing you to run interactive programs over a non-tty network connection. The screen program multiplexes several pty connections onto one tty, which may or may not itself be a pty, connected to the user. The expect program allows programs that insist on being run in interactive mode on a tty to be run on a pty slave under the control of another program connected to a pty master.

16.6.1 Opening Pseudo ttys

There are broad categories of ways to open pseudo ttys: The way everyone actually does it (in Linux, at least), the more or less standard-compliant way based on SysV, and the mostly abandoned way based on old BSD practice. The most common method among Linux system programmers is a set of BSD extensions that also have been implemented as part of glibc. The less common method is documented as part of the 1998 Unix98 standard, and documented differently in the 2000 revision of the Unix98 standard.

Historically, there have been two different methods of opening pseudo ttys on Unix and Unix-like systems. Linux originally followed the BSD model, even though it is more complex to use, because the SysV model is explicitly written in terms of STREAMS, and Linux does not implement STREAMS. The BSD model, however, requires that each application search for an unused pty master by knowing about many specific device names. Between 64 and 256 pty devices are normally available, and to find the first open device, programs search through the devices in order by minor number. They do this by searching in the peculiar lexicographic manner demonstrated in the ptypair program included in this section.

The BSD model presents several problems:

- Each application must know the entire space of available names. When the set of possible pseudo ttys is expanded, each application that uses pseudo ttys must be modified with explicit knowledge of all possible device names. This is inconvenient and error-prone.

- The time taken to search becomes measurable when you are searching through thousands of device nodes in a well-populated /dev directory, wasting system time and slowing down access to the system, so this scales very poorly to large systems.

- Permission handing can be problematic. For example, if a program terminates abnormally, it can leave pseudo tty device files with inappropriate permissions.

Because the SysV model is explicitly written in terms of STREAMS, and requires using STREAMS ioctl() calls to set up the slave devices, the SysV model was not really an option for Linux. However, the Unix98 interface does not specify the STREAMS-specific functionality, and in 1998 Linux added support for Unix98-style pseudo ttys.

The Linux kernel can be compiled without support for the Unix98 interface, and you may encounter older systems without Unix98-style pseudo ttys, so we present code that attempts to open Unix98-style pseudo ttys, but is also able to fall back to the BSD interface. (We do not document the STREAMS-specific parts of the SysV model; see [Stevens, 1992] for details on the STREAMS interface specifics. You should not normally need the STREAMS-specific code; the Unix98 specification does not require it.)

16.6.2 Opening Pseudo ttys the Easy Ways

In the libutil library, glibc provides `openpty()` and `forkpty()`, two functions which do nearly all the work of pseudo tty handling for you.

```
#include <pty.h>

int openpty(int *masterfd, int *slavefd, char *name,
            struct termios *term, struct winsize *winp);
int forkpty(int *masterfd, char *name,
            struct termios *term, struct winsize *winp);
```

`openpty()` opens a set of master and slave pseudo ttys, and optionally uses `struct termios` and `struct winsize` structures passed in as options to set up the slave pseudo tty, returning 0 to indicate success and -1 to indicate failure. The master and slave file descriptors are passed back in the `masterfd` and `slavefd` arguments, respectively. The `term` and `winp` arguments may be `NULL`, in which case they are ignored and no setup is done.

`forkpty()` works the same way as `openpty()`, but instead of returning the slave file descriptor, it forks and sets up the slave pseudo tty as the controlling terminal on stdin, stdout, and stderr for the child process, and then, like `fork()`, returns the pid of the child in the parent and 0 in the child, or -1 to indicate failure.

Even these convenient interfaces have a major problem: the `name` argument was originally intended to pass the name of the pseudo tty device back to the calling code, but it cannot be used in a safe fashion, because `openpty()` and `forkpty()` have no way of knowing how large the buffer is. Always pass `NULL` as the `name` argument. Use the `ttyname()` function, described on page 337, to get the pathname of the pseudo tty device file.

The normally preferred way of working with `struct termios` is to use a read-modify-write cycle, but that does not apply here, for two reasons: You can pass `NULL` and take the default values, which should be sufficient for most cases; and when you do want to provide termios settings, you often are borrowing settings from another tty, or know exactly what the settings should be for some other reason (for example, the SCSI serial port concentrator described earlier in this chapter). Ignoring errors for clarity:

```
tcgetattr(STDIN_FILENO, &term);
ioctl(STDIN_FILENO, TIOCGWINSZ, &ws);
pid = forkpty(&masterfd, NULL, &term, &ws);
```

16.6.3 Opening Pseudo ttys the Hard Ways

The Unix98 interface for allocating a pseudo tty pair is a set of functions:

```
#define _XOPEN_SOURCE 600
#include <stdlib.h>
#include <fcntl.h>

int posix_openpt(int oflag);
int grantpt(int fildes);
int unlockpt(int fildes);
char *ptsname(int fildes);
```

The `posix_openpt()` function is the same as opening the `/dev/ptmx` device but is theoretically more portable (once it is accepted everywhere). We recommend using `open("/dev/ptmx", oflag)` at this time for maximum practical portability. You want one or two `open()` or `posix_openpt()` flags: Use `O_RDWR` normally; if you are not opening the controlling tty for the process, instead use `O_RDWR|O_NOCTTY`. `open()` or `posix_openpt()` returns an open file descriptor for the master pseudo tty. You then call `grantpt()` with the master pseudo tty file descriptor returned from `posix_openpt()` to change the mode and ownership of the slave pseudo tty, and then `unlockpt()` to make the slave pseudo tty available to be opened. The Unix98 interface for opening the slave pseudo tty is simply to open the name returned by `ptsname()`. These functions all return -1 on error, except for `ptsname()`, which returns `NULL` on error.

The functions in ptypair.c allocate a matched pair of pty devices. The example `get_master_pty()` function on line 22 of ptypair.c opens a master pty and returns the file descriptor to the parent, and also provides the name of the corresponding slave pty to open. It first tries the Unix98 interface for allocating a master pty, and if that does not work (for example, if the kernel has been compiled without Unix98 pty support, a possibility for embedded systems), it falls back to the old BSD-style interface. The corresponding

get_slave_pty() function on line 87 can be used after a fork() to open
the corresponding slave pty device:

```
 1: /* ptypair.c */
 2:
 3: #define _XOPEN_SOURCE 600
 4: #include <errno.h>
 5: #include <fcntl.h>
 6: #include <grp.h>
 7: #include <stdlib.h>
 8: #include <string.h>
 9: #include <sys/types.h>
10: #include <sys/stat.h>
11: #include <unistd.h>
12:
13:
14: /* get_master_pty() takes a double-indirect character pointer in
15:  * which to put a slave name, and returns an integer file
16:  * descriptor. If it returns < 0, an error has occurred. Otherwise,
17:  * it has returned the master pty file descriptor, and fills in
18:  * *name with the name of the corresponding slave pty. Once the
19:  * slave pty has been opened, you are responsible to free *name.
20:  */
21:
22: int get_master_pty(char **name) {
23:     int i, j;
24:     /* default to returning error */
25:     int master = -1;
26:     char *slavename;
27:
28:     master = open("/dev/ptmx", O_RDWR);
29:     /* This is equivalent to, though more widely implemented but
30:      * theoretically less portable than:
31:      * master = posix_openpt(O_RDWR);
32:      */
33:
34:     if (master >= 0 && grantpt (master) >= 0 &&
35:                         unlockpt (master) >= 0) {
36:         slavename = ptsname(master);
37:         if (!slavename) {
38:             close(master);
39:             master = -1;
```

```
40:                   /* fall through to fallback */
41:             } else {
42:                 *name = strdup(slavename);
43:                 return master;
44:             }
45:         }
46:
47:         /* The rest of this function is a fallback for older systems */
48:
49:         /* create a dummy name to fill in */
50:         *name = strdup("/dev/ptyXX");
51:
52:         /* search for an unused pty */
53:         for (i=0; i<16 && master <= 0; i++) {
54:             for (j=0; j<16 && master <= 0; j++) {
55:                 (*name)[8] = "pqrstuvwxyzPQRST"[i];
56:                 (*name)[9] = "0123456789abcdef"[j];
57:                 /* open the master pty */
58:                 if ((master = open(*name, O_RDWR)) < 0) {
59:                     if (errno == ENOENT) {
60:                         /* we are out of pty devices */
61:                         free (*name);
62:                         return (master);
63:                     }
64:                 }
65:             }
66:         }
67:
68:         if ((master < 0) && (i == 16) && (j == 16)) {
69:             /* must have tried every pty unsuccessfully */
70:             free (*name);
71:             return (master);
72:         }
73:
74:         /* By substituting a letter, we change the master pty
75:          * name into the slave pty name.
76:          */
77:         (*name)[5] = 't';
78:
79:         return (master);
80: }
```

```
81:
82: /* get_slave_pty() returns an integer file descriptor.
83:  * If it returns < 0, an error has occurred.
84:  * Otherwise, it has returned the slave file descriptor.
85:  */
86:
87: int get_slave_pty(char *name) {
88:     struct group *gptr;
89:     gid_t gid;
90:     int slave = -1;
91:
92:     if (strcmp(name, "/dev/pts/")) {
93:         /* The Unix98 interface has not been used, special
94:          * permission or ownership handling is necessary.
95:          *
96:          * chown/chmod the corresponding pty, if possible.
97:          * This will work only if the process has root permissions.
98:          * Alternatively, write and exec a small setuid program
99:          * that does just this.
100:         *
101:         * Alternatively, just ignore this and use only the Unix98
102:         * interface.
103:         */
104:         if ((gptr = getgrnam("tty")) != 0) {
105:             gid = gptr->gr_gid;
106:         } else {
107:             /* if the tty group does not exist, don't change the
108:              * group on the slave pty, only the owner
109:              */
110:             gid = -1;
111:         }
112:
113:         /* Note that we do not check for errors here.  If this is
114:          * code where these actions are critical, check for errors!
115:          */
116:         chown(name, getuid(), gid);
117:
118:         /* This code makes the slave read/writeable only for the
119:          * user. If this is for an interactive shell that will
120:          * want to receive "write" and "wall" messages, OR S_IWGRP
121:          * into the second argument below.  In that case, you will
```

```
122:              * want to move this line outside the if() clause so that
123:              * it is run for * both BSD-style and Unix98-style
124:              * interfaces.
125:              */
126:             chmod(name, S_IRUSR|S_IWUSR);
127:         }
128:
129:     /* open the corresponding slave pty */
130:     slave = open(name, O_RDWR);
131:
132:     return (slave);
133: }
```

The get_slave_pty() function does nothing new. Every function in it is described elsewhere in this book, so we do not explain it here.

16.6.4 Pseudo tty Examples

Perhaps one of the simplest programs that can be written to use ptys is a program that opens a pty pair and runs a shell on the slave pty, connecting it to the master pty. Having written that program, you can expand it in any way that you wish. forkptytest.c is an example using the forkpty() function; ptytest.c is an example that uses the functions defined in ptypair.c, and it is by necessity more complicated.

```
 1: /* forkptytest.c */
 2:
 3: #include <errno.h>
 4: #include <signal.h>
 5: #include <stdio.h>
 6: #include <stdlib.h>
 7: #include <sys/ioctl.h>
 8: #include <sys/poll.h>
 9: #include <termios.h>
10: #include <unistd.h>
11: #include <pty.h>
12:
13:
14: volatile int propagate_sigwinch = 0;
15:
```

```
16: /* sigwinch_handler
17:  * propagate window size changes from input file descriptor to
18:  * master side of pty.
19:  */
20: void sigwinch_handler(int signal) {
21:     propagate_sigwinch = 1;
22: }
23:
24:
25: /* forkptytest tries to open a pty pair with a shell running
26:  * underneath the slave pty.
27:  */
28: int main (void) {
29:     int master;
30:     int pid;
31:     struct pollfd ufds[2];
32:     int i;
33: #define BUFSIZE 1024
34:     char buf[1024];
35:     struct termios ot, t;
36:     struct winsize ws;
37:     int done = 0;
38:     struct sigaction act;
39:
40:     if (ioctl(STDIN_FILENO, TIOCGWINSZ, &ws) < 0) {
41:         perror("ptypair: could not get window size");
42:         exit(1);
43:     }
44:
45:     if ((pid = forkpty(&master, NULL, NULL, &ws)) < 0) {
46:         perror("ptypair");
47:         exit(1);
48:     }
49:
50:     if (pid == 0) {
51:         /* start the shell */
52:         execl("/bin/sh", "/bin/sh", 0);
53:
54:         /* should never be reached */
55:         exit(1);
56:     }
```

```
57:
58:     /* parent */
59:     /* set up SIGWINCH handler */
60:     act.sa_handler = sigwinch_handler;
61:     sigemptyset(&(act.sa_mask));
62:     act.sa_flags = 0;
63:     if (sigaction(SIGWINCH, &act, NULL) < 0) {
64:         perror("ptypair: could not handle SIGWINCH ");
65:         exit(1);
66:     }
67:
68:     /* Note that we only set termios settings for standard input;
69:      * the master side of a pty is NOT a tty.
70:      */
71:     tcgetattr(STDIN_FILENO, &ot);
72:     t = ot;
73:     t.c_lflag &= ~(ICANON | ISIG | ECHO | ECHOCTL | ECHOE | \
74:                     ECHOK | ECHOKE | ECHONL | ECHOPRT );
75:     t.c_iflag |= IGNBRK;
76:     t.c_cc[VMIN] = 1;
77:     t.c_cc[VTIME] = 0;
78:     tcsetattr(STDIN_FILENO, TCSANOW, &t);
79:
80:     /* This code comes nearly verbatim from robin.c
81:      * If the child exits, reading master will return -1
82:      * and we exit.
83:      */
84:     ufds[0].fd = STDIN_FILENO;
85:     ufds[0].events = POLLIN;
86:     ufds[1].fd = master;
87:     ufds[1].events = POLLIN;
88:
89:     do {
90:         int r;
91:
92:         r = poll(ufds, 2, -1);
93:         if ((r < 0) && (errno != EINTR)) {
94:             done = 1;
95:             break;
96:         }
97:
```

```
 98:            /* First check for an opportunity to exit */
 99:            if ((ufds[0].revents | ufds[1].revents) &
100:                (POLLERR | POLLHUP | POLLNVAL)) {
101:                done = 1;
102:                break;
103:            }
104:
105:            if (propagate_sigwinch) {
106:                /* signal handler has asked for SIGWINCH propagation */
107:                if (ioctl(STDIN_FILENO, TIOCGWINSZ, &ws) < 0) {
108:                    perror("ptypair: could not get window size");
109:                }
110:                if (ioctl(master, TIOCSWINSZ, &ws) < 0) {
111:                    perror("could not restore window size");
112:                }
113:
114:                /* now do not do this again until next SIGWINCH */
115:                propagate_sigwinch = 0;
116:
117:                /* poll may have been interrupted by SIGWINCH,
118:                 * so try again.
119:                 */
120:                continue;
121:            }
122:
123:            if (ufds[1].revents & POLLIN) {
124:                i = read(master, buf, BUFSIZE);
125:                if (i >= 1) {
126:                    write(STDOUT_FILENO, buf, i);
127:                } else {
128:                    done = 1;
129:                }
130:            }
131:
132:            if (ufds[0].revents & POLLIN) {
133:                i = read(STDIN_FILENO, buf, BUFSIZE);
134:                if (i >= 1) {
135:                    write(master, buf, i);
136:                } else {
137:                    done = 1;
138:                }
```

```
139:            }
140:
141:     } while (!done);
142:
143:     tcsetattr(STDIN_FILENO, TCSANOW, &ot);
144:     exit(0);
145: }
```

forkptytest.c does very little that we have not seen before. Signal handling is described in Chapter 12, and the poll() loop is almost exactly straight from robin.c on page 355 (minus the escape-character processing), as is the code modifying termios settings.

This leaves propagating window-size changes to be explained here.

On line 105, after poll() exits, we check to see if the reason that poll() exited was the SIGWINCH signal being delivered to the sigwinch_handler function on line 20. If it was, we need to get the new current window size from standard input and propagate it to the slave's pty. By setting the window size, SIGWINCH is sent *automatically* to the process running on the pty; we should not explicitly send a SIGWINCH to that process.

Now, by contrast, see how much more complicated this code is when you have to use the functions we have defined in ptypair.c:

```
 1: /* ptytest.c */
 2:
 3: #include <errno.h>
 4: #include <fcntl.h>
 5: #include <signal.h>
 6: #include <stdio.h>
 7: #include <stdlib.h>
 8: #include <string.h>
 9: #include <sys/ioctl.h>
10: #include <sys/poll.h>
11: #include <sys/stat.h>
12: #include <termios.h>
13: #include <unistd.h>
14: #include "ptypair.h"
15:
16:
```

```
17: volatile int propagate_sigwinch = 0;
18:
19: /* sigwinch_handler
20:  * propagate window size changes from input file descriptor to
21:  * master side of pty.
22:  */
23: void sigwinch_handler(int signal) {
24:     propagate_sigwinch = 1;
25: }
26:
27:
28: /* ptytest tries to open a pty pair with a shell running
29:  * underneath the slave pty.
30:  */
31: int main (void) {
32:     int master;
33:     int pid;
34:     char *name;
35:     struct pollfd ufds[2];
36:     int i;
37: #define BUFSIZE 1024
38:     char buf[1024];
39:     struct termios ot, t;
40:     struct winsize ws;
41:     int done = 0;
42:     struct sigaction act;
43:
44:     if ((master = get_master_pty(&name)) < 0) {
45:         perror("ptypair: could not open master pty");
46:         exit(1);
47:     }
48:
49:     /* set up SIGWINCH handler */
50:     act.sa_handler = sigwinch_handler;
51:     sigemptyset(&(act.sa_mask));
52:     act.sa_flags = 0;
53:     if (sigaction(SIGWINCH, &act, NULL) < 0) {
54:         perror("ptypair: could not handle SIGWINCH ");
55:         exit(1);
56:     }
57:
```

```
58:        if (ioctl(STDIN_FILENO, TIOCGWINSZ, &ws) < 0) {
59:            perror("ptypair: could not get window size");
60:            exit(1);
61:        }
62:
63:        if ((pid = fork()) < 0) {
64:            perror("ptypair");
65:            exit(1);
66:        }
67:
68:        if (pid == 0) {
69:            int slave;  /* file descriptor for slave pty */
70:
71:            /* We are in the child process */
72:            close(master);
73:
74:            if ((slave = get_slave_pty(name)) < 0) {
75:                perror("ptypair: could not open slave pty");
76:                exit(1);
77:            }
78:            free(name);
79:
80:            /* We need to make this process a session group leader,
81:             * because it is on a new PTY, and things like job control
82:             * simply will not work correctly unless there is a session
83:             * group leader and process group leader (which a session
84:             * group leader automatically is). This also disassociates
85:             * us from our old controlling tty.
86:             */
87:            if (setsid() < 0) {
88:                perror("could not set session leader");
89:            }
90:
91:            /* Tie us to our new controlling tty. */
92:            if (ioctl(slave, TIOCSCTTY, NULL)) {
93:                perror("could not set new controlling tty");
94:            }
95:
96:            /* make slave pty be standard in, out, and error */
97:            dup2(slave, STDIN_FILENO);
98:            dup2(slave, STDOUT_FILENO);
```

```
 99:            dup2(slave, STDERR_FILENO);
100:
101:            /* at this point the slave pty should be standard input */
102:            if (slave > 2) {
103:                close(slave);
104:            }
105:
106:            /* Try to restore window size; failure isn't critical */
107:            if (ioctl(STDOUT_FILENO, TIOCSWINSZ, &ws) < 0) {
108:                perror("could not restore window size");
109:            }
110:
111:            /* now start the shell */
112:            execl("/bin/sh", "/bin/sh", 0);
113:
114:            /* should never be reached */
115:            exit(1);
116:        }
117:
118:        /* parent */
119:        free(name);
120:
121:        /* Note that we only set termios settings for standard input;
122:         * the master side of a pty is NOT a tty.
123:         */
124:        tcgetattr(STDIN_FILENO, &ot);
125:        t = ot;
126:        t.c_lflag &= ~(ICANON | ISIG | ECHO | ECHOCTL | ECHOE | \
127:                       ECHOK | ECHOKE | ECHONL | ECHOPRT );
128:        t.c_iflag |= IGNBRK;
129:        t.c_cc[VMIN] = 1;
130:        t.c_cc[VTIME] = 0;
131:        tcsetattr(STDIN_FILENO, TCSANOW, &t);
132:
133:        /* This code comes nearly verbatim from robin.c
134:         * If the child exits, reading master will return -1 and
135:         * we exit.
136:         */
137:        ufds[0].fd = STDIN_FILENO;
138:        ufds[0].events = POLLIN;
139:        ufds[1].fd = master;
```

```
140:        ufds[1].events = POLLIN;
141:
142:    do {
143:        int r;
144:
145:        r = poll(ufds, 2, -1);
146:        if ((r < 0) && (errno != EINTR)) {
147:            done = 1;
148:            break;
149:        }
150:
151:        /* First check for an opportunity to exit */
152:        if ((ufds[0].revents | ufds[1].revents) &
153:            (POLLERR | POLLHUP | POLLNVAL)) {
154:            done = 1;
155:            break;
156:        }
157:
158:        if (propagate_sigwinch) {
159:            /* signal handler has asked for SIGWINCH propagation */
160:            if (ioctl(STDIN_FILENO, TIOCGWINSZ, &ws) < 0) {
161:                perror("ptypair: could not get window size");
162:            }
163:            if (ioctl(master, TIOCSWINSZ, &ws) < 0) {
164:                perror("could not restore window size");
165:            }
166:
167:            /* now do not do this again until next SIGWINCH */
168:            propagate_sigwinch = 0;
169:
170:            /* poll may have been interrupted by SIGWINCH,
171:             * so try again. */
172:            continue;
173:        }
174:
175:        if (ufds[1].revents & POLLIN) {
176:            i = read(master, buf, BUFSIZE);
177:            if (i >= 1) {
178:                write(STDOUT_FILENO, buf, i);
179:            } else {
180:                done = 1;
```

```
181:                    }
182:                }
183:
184:            if (ufds[0].revents & POLLIN) {
185:                    i = read(STDIN_FILENO, buf, BUFSIZE);
186:                    if (i >= 1) {
187:                        write(master, buf, i);
188:                    } else {
189:                        done = 1;
190:                    }
191:                }
192:        } while (!done);
193:
194:        tcsetattr(STDIN_FILENO, TCSANOW, &ot);
195:        exit(0);
196: }
```

All the added complexity of ptytest.c beyond forkptytest.c is to handle the complexity of the old interface. This has been described in this chapter, except for starting a child process, which is introduced in Chapter 10.

CHAPTER 17

Networking with Sockets

As the computer world becomes more networked, network-aware applications are increasingly important. Linux provides the Berkeley socket API, which has become the standard networking API. We discuss the basics of using Berkeley sockets for both TCP/IP networking and simple **interprocess communication** (IPC) through Unix-domain sockets.

This chapter is not intended to be a complete guide to network programming. Network programming is a complicated topic, and we recommend dedicated network programming books for programmers who intend to do serious work with sockets [Stevens, 2004]. This chapter should be sufficient to allow you to write simple networked applications, however.

17.1 Protocol Support

The Berkeley socket API was designed as a gateway to multiple protocols. Although this does necessitate extra complexity in the interface, it is much easier than inventing (or learning) a new interface for every new protocol you encounter. Linux uses the socket API for many protocols, including TCP/IP (both version 4 and version 6), AppleTalk, and IPX.

We discuss using sockets for two of the protocols available through Linux's socket implementation. The most important protocol that Linux supports is TCP/IP,[1] which is the protocol that drives the Internet. We also cover

---

1. The 2.6.x kernels covered by this book support both version 4 and version 6 (commonly referred to as IPv6 of the TCP/IP suite).

Unix domain sockets, an IPC mechanism restricted to a single machine. Although they do not work across networks, Unix domain sockets are widely used for applications that run on a single computer.

Protocols normally come in groups, or protocol families. The popular TCP/IP protocol family includes the TCP and UDP protocols (among others). Making sense of the various protocols requires you to know a few networking terms.

17.1.1 Nice Networking

Most users consider networking protocols to provide the equivalent of Unix pipes between machines. If a byte (or sequence of bytes) goes in one end of the connection, it is guaranteed to come out the other end. Not only is it guaranteed to come out the other end, but it also comes out right after the byte that was sent before it and immediately before the byte that was sent after it. Of course, all of these bytes should be received exactly as they were sent; no bytes should change. Also, no other process should be able to interject extra bytes into the conversation; it should be restricted to the original two parties.

A good visualization of this idea is the telephone. When you speak to your friends, you expect them to hear the same words you speak, and in the order you speak them.[2] Not only that, you do not expect your mother to pick up her phone (assuming she is not in the same house as you) and start chatting away happily to you and your friend.

17.1.2 Real Networking

Although this may seem pretty basic, it is not at all how underlying computer networks work. Networks tend to be chaotic and random. Imagine a first-grade class at recess, except they are not allowed to speak to each other and they have to stay at least five feet apart. Now, chances are those kids are going to find some way to communicate—perhaps even with paper airplanes!

---

2. Well, this depends on the character of the friends and how late they were out the night before the conversation.

Imagine that whenever students want to send letters to one another they simply write the letters on pieces of paper, fold them into airplanes, write the name of the intended recipient on the outside, and hurl them toward someone who is closer to the final recipient than the sender is. This intermediate looks at the airplane, sees who the intended target is, and sends it toward the next closest person. Eventually, the intended recipient will (well, *may*) get the airplane and unfold it to read the message.

Believe it or not, this is almost exactly how computer networks operate.[3] The intermediaries are called **routers** and the airplanes are called **packets**, but the rest is the same. Just as in the first-grade class, some of those airplanes (or packets) are going to get lost. If a message is too long to fit in a single packet, it must be split across multiple ones (each of which may be lost). All the students in between can read the packets if they like[4] and may simply throw the message away rather than try to deliver it. Also, anyone can interrupt your conversation by sending new packets into the middle of it.

17.1.3 Making Reality Play Nice

Confronted with the reality of millions of paper airplanes, protocol designers endeavor to present a view of the network more on par with the telephone than the first-grade class. Various terms have evolved to describe networking protocols.

- **Connection-oriented** protocols have two endpoints, like a telephone conversation. The connection must be established before any communication takes place, just as you answer the phone by saying "hello" rather than just talking immediately. Other users cannot (or should not be able to) intrude into the connection. Protocols that do not have these characteristics are known as **connectionless**.

- Protocols provide **sequencing** if they ensure the data arrives in the same order it was sent.

---

3. This is how **packet-switched** networks work, anyway. An alternative design, **circuit-switched** networks, acts more like telephone connections. They are not widely used in computer networking, however.
4. This is why cryptography has gained so much importance since the advent of the Internet.

- Protocols provide **error control** if they automatically discard messages that have been corrupted and arrange to retransmit the data.

- **Streaming** protocols recognize only byte boundaries. Sequences of bytes may be split up and are delivered to the recipient as the data arrives.

- **Packet-based** protocols handle packets of data, preserving the packet boundaries and delivering complete packets to the receiver. Packet-based protocols normally enforce a maximum packet size.

Although each of these attributes is independent of the others, two major types of protocols are commonly used by applications. **Datagram** protocols are packet-oriented transports that provide neither sequencing nor error control; UDP, part of the TCP/IP protocol family, is a widely used datagram protocol. **Stream** protocols, such as the TCP portion of TCP/IP, are streaming protocols that provide both sequencing and error control.

Although datagram protocols, such as UDP, can be useful,[5] we focus on using stream protocols because they are easier to use for most applications. More information on protocol design and the differences between various protocols is available from many books [Stevens, 2004] [Stevens, 1994].

17.1.4 Addresses

As every protocol has its own definition of a network address, the sockets API must abstract addresses. It uses a `struct sockaddr` as the basic form of an address; its contents are defined differently for each protocol family. Whenever a `struct sockaddr` is passed to a system call, the process also passes the size of the address that is being passed. The type `socklen_t` is defined as a numeric type large enough to hold the size of any socket address used by the system.

All `struct sockaddr` types conform to the following definition:

---

5. Many higher-level protocols, such as BOOTP and NFS, are built on top of UDP.

```
#include <sys/socket.h>

struct sockaddr {
    unsigned short sa_family;
    char sa_data[MAXSOCKADDRDATA];
}
```

The first two bytes (the size of a short) specifies the **address family** this address belongs to. A list of the common address families that Linux applications use is in Table 17.1, on page 413.

17.2 Utility Functions

All of the examples in this section use two functions, copyData() and die(). copyData() reads data from a file descriptor and writes it to another as long as data is left to be read. die() calls perror() and exits the program. We put both of these functions in the file sockutil.c to keep the example programs a bit cleaner. For reference, here is the implementation of these two functions:

```
 1: /* sockutil.c */
 2:
 3: #include <stdio.h>
 4: #include <stdlib.h>
 5: #include <unistd.h>
 6:
 7: #include "sockutil.h"
 8:
 9: /* issue an error message via perror() and terminate the program */
10: void die(char * message) {
11:     perror(message);
12:     exit(1);
13: }
14:
15: /* Copies data from file descriptor 'from' to file descriptor
16:    'to' until nothing is left to be copied. Exits if an error
17:    occurs. This assumes both from and to are set for blocking
18:    reads and writes. */
```

```
19: void copyData(int from, int to) {
20:     char buf[1024];
21:     int amount;
22:
23:     while ((amount = read(from, buf, sizeof(buf))) > 0) {
24:         if (write(to, buf, amount) != amount) {
25:             die("write");
26:             return;
27:         }
28:     }
29:     if (amount < 0)
30:         die("read");
31: }
```

17.3 Basic Socket Operations

Like most other Linux resources, sockets are implemented through the file abstraction. They are created through the socket() system call, which returns a file descriptor. Once the socket has been properly initialized, that file descriptor may be used for read() and write() requests, like any other file descriptor. When a process is finished with a socket, it should be close()ed to free the resources associated with it.

This section presents the basic system calls for creating and initializing sockets for any protocol. It is a bit abstract due to this protocol independence, and does not contain any examples for the same reason. The next two sections of this chapter describe how to use sockets with two different protocols, Unix Domain and TCP/IP, and those sections include full examples of how to use most of the system calls introduced here.

17.3.1 Creating a Socket

New sockets are created by the socket() system call, which returns a file descriptor for the *uninitialized* socket. The socket is tied to a particular protocol when it is created, but it is not connected to anything. As it is not connected, it cannot yet be read from or written to.

Table 17.1 Protocol and Address Families

Address	Protocol	Protocol Description
AF_UNIX	PF_UNIX	Unix domain
AF_INET	PF_INET	TCP/IP (version 4)
AF_INET6	PF_INET6	TCP/IP (version 6)
AF_AX25	PF_AX25	AX.25, used by amateur radio
AF_IPX	PF_IPX	Novell IPX
AF_APPLETALK	PF_APPLETALK	AppleTalk DDS
AF_NETROM	PF_NETROM	NetROM, used by amateur radio

Table 17.2 IP Protocols

Protocol	Description
IPPROTO_ICMP	Internet Control Message Protocol for IPv4
IPPROTO_ICMPV6	Internet Control Message Protocol for IPv6
IPPROTO_IPIP	IPIP tunnels
IPPROTO_IPV6	IPv6 headers
IPPROTO_RAW	Raw IP packets
IPPROTO_TCP	Transmission Control Protocol (TCP)
IPPROTO_UDP	User Datagram Protocol (UDP)

```
#include <sys/socket.h>

int socket(int domain, int type, int protocol);
```

Like open(), socket() returns a value less than 0 on error and a file descriptor, which is greater than or equal to 0, on success. The three parameters specify the protocol to use.

The first parameter specifies the protocol family that should be used and is usually one of the values specified in Table 17.1.

The next parameter, type, is SOCK_STREAM, SOCK_DGRAM, or SOCK_RAW.[6] SOCK_STREAM specifies a protocol from the specified family that provides a stream connection, whereas SOCK_DGRAM specifies a datagram protocol from the same family. SOCK_RAW provides the ability to send packets directly to a network device driver, which enables user space applications to provide networking protocols that are not understood by the kernel.

---

6. A couple of other values are available, but they are not usually used by application code.

The final parameter specifies which protocol is to be used, subject to the constraints specified by the first two parameters. Usually this parameter is 0, letting the kernel use the default protocol of the specified type and family. For the PF_INET protocol family, Table 17.2 lists some of protocols allowed, with IPPROTO_TCP being the default stream protocol and IPPROTO_UDP the default datagram protocol.

17.3.2 Establishing Connections

After you create a stream socket, it needs to be connected to something before it is of much use. Establishing socket connections is an inherently asymmetric task; each side of the connection does it differently. One side gets its socket ready to be connected to something and then waits for someone to connect to it. This is usually done by server applications that are started and continuously run, waiting for other processes to connect to them.

Client processes instead create a socket, tell the system which address they want to connect it to, and then try to establish the connection. Once the server (which has been waiting for a client) accepts the connection attempt, the connection is established between the two sockets. After this happens, the socket may be used for bidirectional communication.

17.3.3 Binding an Address to a Socket

Both server and client processes need to tell the system which address to use for the socket. Attaching an address to the local side of a socket is called **binding** the socket and is done through the bind() system call.

```
#include <sys/socket.h>

int bind(int sock, struct sockaddr * my_addr, socklen_t addrlen);
```

The first parameter is the socket being bound, and the other parameters specify the address to use for the local endpoint.

17.3.4 Waiting for Connections

After creating a socket, server processes `bind()` the socket to the address they are listening to. After the socket is bound to an address, the process tells the system it is willing to let other processes establish connections to that socket (at the specified address) by calling `listen()`. Once a socket is bound to an address, the kernel is able to handle processes' attempts to connect to that address. However, the connection is not immediately established. The `listen()`ing process must first accept the connection attempt through the `accept()` system call. New connection attempts that have been made to addresses that have been `listen()`ed to are called **pending connections** until the connections has been `accept()`ed.

Normally, `accept()` blocks until a client process tries to connect to it. If the socket has been marked as nonblocking through `fcntl()`, `accept()` instead returns `EAGAIN` if no client process is available.[7] The `select()`, `poll()`, and `epoll` system calls may also be used to determine whether a connection to a socket is pending (those calls mark the socket as ready to be read from).[8]

Here are the prototypes of `listen()` and `accept()`.

```
#include <sys/socket.h>

int listen(int sock, int backlog);
int accept(int sock, struct sockaddr * addr, socklen_t * addrlen);
```

Both of these functions expect the socket's file descriptor as the first parameter. `listen()`'s other parameter, `backlog`, specifies how many connections may be pending on the socket before further connection attempts are refused. Network connections are not established until the server has `accept()`ed the connection; until the `accept()`, the incoming connection is considered pending. By providing a small queue of pending connections,

---

7. The `connect()` system call can also be nonblocking, which allows clients to open multiple TCP connections much more quickly (it lets the program continue to run while TCP's three-way handshake is performed). Details on how to do this can be found in [Stevens, 2004].
8. The various forms of `select()` mark a socket as ready for reading when an `accept()` would not block even if the socket is not marked as nonblocking. For maximum portability, `select()` should be used only for accepting connections with nonblocking sockets, although under Linux it is not actually necessary. [Stevens, 2004] talks about the reasons for this in detail.

the kernel relaxes the need for server processes to be constantly prepared to accept() connections. Applications have historically set the maximum backlog to five, although a larger value may sometimes be necessary. listen() returns zero on success and nonzero on failure.

The accept() call changes a pending connection to an established connection. The established connection is given a new file descriptor, which accept() returns. The new file descriptor inherits its attributes from the socket that was listen()ed to. One unusual feature of accept() is that it returns networking errors that are pending as errors from accept().[9] Servers should not abort when accept() returns an error if errno is one of ECONNABORTED, ENETDOWN, EPROTO, ENOPROTOOPT, EHOSTDOWN, ENONET, EHOSTUNREACH, EOPNOTSUPP, or ENETUNREACH. All of these should be ignored, with the server just calling accept() once more.

The addr and addrlen parameters point to data that the kernel fills in with the address of the remote (client) end of the connection. Initially, addrlen should point to an integer containing the size of the buffer addr points to. accept() returns a file descriptor, or less than zero if an error occurs, just like open().

17.3.5 Connecting to a Server

Like servers, clients may bind() the local address to the socket immediately after creating it. Usually, the client does not care what the local address is and skips this step, allowing the kernel to assign it any convenient local address.

After the bind() step (which may be omitted), the client connect()s to a server.

```
#include <sys/socket.h>

int connect(int sock, struct sockaddr * servaddr, socklen_t addrlen);
```

The process passes to connect() the socket that is being connected, followed by the address to which the socket should be connected.

Figure 17.1 shows the system calls usually used to establish socket connections, and the order in which they occur.

---

9. BSD variants do not have this behavior; on those systems the errors go unreported.

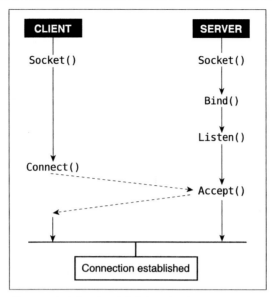

Figure 17.1 Establishing Socket Connections

17.3.6 Finding Connection Addresses

After a connection has been established, applications can find the addresses for both the local and remote end of a socket by using getpeername() and getsockname().

```
#include <sys/socket.h>

int getpeername(int s, struct sockaddr * addr, socklen_t * addrlen);
int getsockname(int s, struct sockaddr * addr, socklen_t * addrlen);
```

Both functions fill in the structures pointed to by their addr parameters with addresses for the connection used by socket s. The address for the remote side is returned by getpeername(), while getsockname() returns the address for the local part of the connection. For both functions, the integer pointed to by addrlen should be initialized to the amount of space pointed to by addr, and that integer is changed to the number of bytes in the address returned.

17.4 Unix Domain Sockets

Unix domain sockets are the simplest protocol family available through the sockets API. They do not actually represent a network protocol; they can connect only to sockets on the same machine. Although this restricts their usefulness, they are used by many applications because they provide a flexible IPC mechanism. Their addresses are pathnames that are created in the file system when a socket is bound to the pathname. Socket files, which represent Unix domain addresses, can be `stat()`ed but cannot be opened through `open()`; the socket API must be used instead.

The Unix domain provides both datagram and stream interfaces. The datagram interface is rarely used and is not discussed here. The stream interface, which is discussed here, is similar to named pipes. Unix domain sockets are not identical to named pipes, however.

When multiple processes open a named pipe, any of the processes may read a message sent through the pipe by another process. Each named pipe is like a bulletin board. When a process posts a message to the board, any other process (with sufficient permission) may take the message from the board.

Unix domain sockets are connection-oriented; each connection to the socket results in a new communication channel. The server, which may be handling many simultaneous connections, has a different file descriptor for each. This property makes Unix domain sockets much better suited to many IPC tasks than are named pipes. This is the primary reason they are used by many standard Linux services, including the X Window System and the system logger.

17.4.1 Unix Domain Addresses

Addresses for Unix domain sockets are pathnames in the file system. If the file does not already exist, it is created as a socket-type file when a socket is bound to the pathname through `bind()`. If a file (even a socket) exists with the pathname being bound, `bind()` fails and returns `EADDRINUSE`. `bind()` sets the permissions of newly created socket files to 0666, as modified by the current umask.

To `connect()` to an existing socket, the process must have read and write permissions for the socket file.[10]

Unix domain socket addresses are passed through a `struct sockaddr_un` structure.

```
#include <sys/socket.h>
#include <sys/un.h>

struct sockaddr_un {
    unsigned short sun_family;      /* AF_UNIX */
    char sun_path[UNIX_PATH_MAX];   /* pathname */
};
```

In the Linux 2.6.7 kernel, `UNIX_PATH_MAX` is 108, but that may change in future versions of the Linux kernel.

The first member, `sun_family`, must contain `AF_UNIX` to indicate that the structure contains a Unix domain address. The `sun_path` holds the pathname to use for the connection. When the size of the address is passed to and from the socket-related system calls, the passed length should be the number of characters in the pathname plus the size of the `sun_family` member. The `sun_path` does not need to be `'\0'` terminated, although it usually is.

17.4.2 Waiting for a Connection

Listening for a connection to be established on a Unix domain socket follows the procedure we described earlier: Create the socket, `bind()` an address to the socket, tell the system to `listen()` for connection attempts, and then `accept()` the connection.

Here is a simple server that repeatedly accepts connections on a Unix domain socket (the file `sample-socket` in the current directory) and reads all the data available from the socket, displaying it on standard output:

```
1: /* userver.c */
```

---

10. For both `bind()` and `connect()`, the process must have execute permission for the directories traversed during the pathname lookup, just as with opening normal files.

```
 2:
 3: /* Waits for a connection on the ./sample-socket Unix domain
 4:    socket. Once a connection has been established, copy data
 5:    from the socket to stdout until the other end closes the
 6:    connection, and then wait for another connection to the
 7:    socket. */
 8:
 9: #include <stdio.h>
10: #include <sys/socket.h>
11: #include <sys/un.h>
12: #include <unistd.h>
13:
14: #include "sockutil.h"          /* some utility functions */
15:
16: int main(void) {
17:     struct sockaddr_un address;
18:     int sock, conn;
19:     size_t addrLength;
20:
21:     if ((sock = socket(PF_UNIX, SOCK_STREAM, 0)) < 0)
22:         die("socket");
23:
24:     /* Remove any preexisting socket (or other file) */
25:     unlink("./sample-socket");
26:
27:     address.sun_family = AF_UNIX;        /* Unix domain socket */
28:     strcpy(address.sun_path, "./sample-socket");
29:
30:     /* The total length of the address includes the sun_family
31:        element */
32:     addrLength = sizeof(address.sun_family) +
33:                   strlen(address.sun_path);
34:
35:     if (bind(sock, (struct sockaddr *) &address, addrLength))
36:         die("bind");
37:
38:     if (listen(sock, 5))
39:         die("listen");
40:
41:     while ((conn = accept(sock, (struct sockaddr *) &address,
42:                           &addrLength)) >= 0) {
```

```
43:              printf("---- getting data\n");
44:              copyData(conn, 1);
45:              printf("---- done\n");
46:              close(conn);
47:          }
48:
49:      if (conn < 0)
50:          die("accept");
51:
52:      close(sock);
53:      return 0;
54: }
```

Although this program is small, it illustrates how to write a simple server process. This server is an **iterative server** because it handles one client at a time. Servers may also be written as **concurrent servers,** which handle multiple clients simultaneously.[11]

Notice the unlink() call before the socket is bound. Because bind() fails if the socket file already exists, this allows the program to be run more than once without requiring that the socket file be manually removed.

The server code typecasts the struct sockaddr_un pointer passed to both bind() and accept() to a (struct sockaddr *). All the various socket-related system calls are prototyped as taking a pointer to struct sockaddr; the typecast keeps the compiler from complaining about pointer type mismatches.

---

11. While it may seem like most real-world server programs would need to be concurrent, many of them are actually written as iterative servers. Many Web servers, for example, handle only a single connection at a time per process. To allow more clients to connect, the server is run as many individual processes. This makes the Web server much simpler to write, and if a bug causes one of those processes to terminate it affects only a single client connection.

17.4.3 Connecting to a Server

Connecting to a server through a Unix domain socket consists of creating a socket and connect()ing to the desired address. Once the socket is connected, it may be treated like any other file descriptor.

The following program connects to the same socket that the example server uses and copies its standard input to the server:

```
 1: /* uclient.c */
 2:
 3: /* Connect to the ./sample-socket Unix domain socket, copy stdin
 4:    into the socket, and then exit. */
 5:
 6: #include <sys/socket.h>
 7: #include <sys/un.h>
 8: #include <unistd.h>
 9:
10: #include "sockutil.h"          /* some utility functions */
11:
12: int main(void) {
13:     struct sockaddr_un address;
14:     int sock;
15:     size_t addrLength;
16:
17:     if ((sock = socket(PF_UNIX, SOCK_STREAM, 0)) < 0)
18:         die("socket");
19:
20:     address.sun_family = AF_UNIX;    /* Unix domain socket */
21:     strcpy(address.sun_path, "./sample-socket");
22:
23:     /* The total length of the address includes the sun_family
24:        element */
25:     addrLength = sizeof(address.sun_family) +
26:                  strlen(address.sun_path);
27:
28:     if (connect(sock, (struct sockaddr *) &address, addrLength))
29:         die("connect");
30:
31:     copyData(0, sock);
32:
33:     close(sock);
```

```
34:
35:      return 0;
36: }
```

The client is not much different than the server. The only changes were replacing the bind(), listen(), accept() sequence with a single connect() call and copying a slightly different set of data.

17.4.4 Running the Unix Domain Examples

The previous two example programs, one a server and the other a client, are designed to work together. Run the server from one terminal, then run the client from another terminal (but in the same directory). As you type lines into the client, they are sent through the socket to the server. When you exit the client, the server waits for another connection. You can transmit files through the socket by redirecting the input to the client program.

17.4.5 Unnamed Unix Domain Sockets

Because Unix domain sockets have some advantages over pipes (such as being full duplex), they are often used as an IPC mechanism. To facilitate this, the socketpair() system call was introduced.

```
#include <sys/socket.h>

int socketpair(int domain, int type, int protocol, int sockfds[2]);
```

The first three parameters are the same as those passed to socket(). The final parameter, sockfds(), is filled in by socketpair() with two file descriptors, one for each end of the socket. A sample application of socketpair() is shown on page 425.

17.4.6 Passing File Descriptors

Unix domain sockets have a unique ability: File descriptors can be passed through them. No other IPC mechanism supports this facility. It allows a process to open a file and pass the file descriptor to another—possibly unrelated—process. All the access checks are done when the file is opened, so the receiving process gains the same access rights to the file as the original process.

File descriptors are passed as part of a more complicated message that is sent using the sendmsg() system call and received using recvmsg().

```
#include <sys/socket.h>

int sendmsg(int fd, const struct msghdr * msg, unsigned int flags);
int recvmsg(int fd, struct msghdr * msg, unsigned int flags);
```

The fd parameter is the file descriptor through which the message is transmitted; the second parameter is a pointer to a structure describing the message. The flags are not usually used and should be set to zero for most applications. More advanced network programming books discuss the available flags [Stevens, 2004].

A message is described by the following structure:

```
#include <sys/socket.h>
#include <sys/un.h>

struct msghdr {
    void * msg_name;              /* optional address */
    unsigned int msg_namelen;     /* size of msg_name */
    struct iovec * msg_iov;       /* scatter/gather array */
    unsigned int msg_iovlen;      /* number of elements in msg_iov */
    void * msg_control;           /* ancillary data */
    unsigned int msg_controllen;  /* ancillary data buffer len */
    int msg_flags;                /* flags on received message */
};
```

The first two members, msg_name and msg_namelen, are not used with stream protocols. Applications that send messages across stream sockets should set msg_name to NULL and msg_namelen to zero.

msg_iov and msg_iovlen describe a set of buffers that are sent or received. Scatter/gather reads and writes, as well as struct iovec, are discussed on pages 290–291. The final member of the structure, msg_flags, is not currently used and should be set to zero.

The two members we skipped over, msg_control and msg_controllen, provide the file descriptor passing ability. The msg_control member points to an array of control message headers; msg_controllen specifies how many bytes the array contains. Each control message consists of a struct cmsghdr followed by extra data.

```
#include <sys/socket.h>

struct cmsghdr {
    unsigned int cmsg_len;      /* length of control message */
    int cmsg_level;             /* SOL_SOCKET */
    int cmsg_type;              /* SCM_RIGHTS */
    int cmsg_data[0];           /* file descriptor goes here */
};
```

The size of the control message, including the header, is stored in cmsg_len. The only type of control message currently defined is SCM_RIGHTS, which passes file descriptors.[12] For this message type, cmsg_level and cmsg_type must be set to SOL_SOCKET and SCM_RIGHTS, respectively. The final member, cmsg_data, is an array of size zero. This is a gcc extension that allows an application to copy data to the end of the structure (see the following program for an example of this).

Receiving a file descriptor is similar. Enough buffer space must be left for the control message, and a new file descriptor follows each struct cmsghdr that arrives.

To illustrate the use of these nested structures, we wrote an example program that is a fancy cat. It takes a file name as its sole argument, opens the specified file in a child process, and passes the resulting file descriptor to the parent through a Unix domain socket. The parent then copies the file to standard output. The file name is sent along with the file descriptor for illustrative purposes.

---

12. This is sometimes called passing access rights.

```
 1: /* passfd.c */
 2:
 3: /* We behave like a simple /bin/cat, which only handles one
 4:    argument (a file name). We create Unix domain sockets through
 5:    socketpair(), and then fork(). The child opens the file whose
 6:    name is passed on the command line, passes the file descriptor
 7:    and file name back to the parent, and then exits. The parent
 8:    waits for the file descriptor from the child, then copies data
 9:    from that file descriptor to stdout until no data is left. The
10:    parent then exits. */
11:
12: #include <alloca.h>
13: #include <fcntl.h>
14: #include <stdio.h>
15: #include <string.h>
16: #include <sys/socket.h>
17: #include <sys/uio.h>
18: #include <sys/un.h>
19: #include <sys/wait.h>
20: #include <unistd.h>
21:
22: #include "sockutil.h"            /* simple utility functions */
23:
24: /* The child process. This sends the file descriptor. */
25: int childProcess(char * filename, int sock) {
26:     int fd;
27:     struct iovec vector;        /* some data to pass w/ the fd */
28:     struct msghdr msg;          /* the complete message */
29:     struct cmsghdr * cmsg;      /* the control message, which */
30:                                 /* wil linclude the fd */
31:
32:     /* Open the file whose descriptor will be passed. */
33:     if ((fd = open(filename, O_RDONLY)) < 0) {
34:         perror("open");
35:         return 1;
36:     }
37:
38:     /* Send the file name down the socket, including the trailing
39:        '\0' */
40:     vector.iov_base = filename;
41:     vector.iov_len = strlen(filename) + 1;
```

```
42:
43:        /* Put together the first part of the message. Include the
44:           file name iovec */
45:        msg.msg_name = NULL;
46:        msg.msg_namelen = 0;
47:        msg.msg_iov = &vector;
48:        msg.msg_iovlen = 1;
49:
50:        /* Now for the control message. We have to allocate room for
51:           the file descriptor. */
52:        cmsg = alloca(sizeof(struct cmsghdr) + sizeof(fd));
53:        cmsg->cmsg_len = sizeof(struct cmsghdr) + sizeof(fd);
54:        cmsg->cmsg_level = SOL_SOCKET;
55:        cmsg->cmsg_type = SCM_RIGHTS;
56:
57:        /* copy the file descriptor onto the end of the control
58:           message */
59:        memcpy(CMSG_DATA(cmsg), &fd, sizeof(fd));
60:
61:        msg.msg_control = cmsg;
62:        msg.msg_controllen = cmsg->cmsg_len;
63:
64:        if (sendmsg(sock, &msg, 0) != vector.iov_len)
65:            die("sendmsg");
66:
67:        return 0;
68: }
69:
70: /* The parent process. This receives the file descriptor. */
71: int parentProcess(int sock) {
72:        char buf[80];                /* space to read file name into */
73:        struct iovec vector;         /* file name from the child */
74:        struct msghdr msg;           /* full message */
75:        struct cmsghdr * cmsg;       /* control message with the fd */
76:        int fd;
77:
78:        /* set up the iovec for the file name */
79:        vector.iov_base = buf;
80:        vector.iov_len = 80;
81:
82:        /* the message we're expecting to receive */
```

```
 83:
 84:        msg.msg_name = NULL;
 85:        msg.msg_namelen = 0;
 86:        msg.msg_iov = &vector;
 87:        msg.msg_iovlen = 1;
 88:
 89:        /* dynamically allocate so we can leave room for the file
 90:           descriptor */
 91:        cmsg = alloca(sizeof(struct cmsghdr) + sizeof(fd));
 92:        cmsg->cmsg_len = sizeof(struct cmsghdr) + sizeof(fd);
 93:        msg.msg_control = cmsg;
 94:        msg.msg_controllen = cmsg->cmsg_len;
 95:
 96:        if (!recvmsg(sock, &msg, 0))
 97:            return 1;
 98:
 99:        printf("got file descriptor for '%s'\n",
100:                (char *) vector.iov_base);
101:
102:        /* grab the file descriptor from the control structure */
103:        memcpy(&fd, CMSG_DATA(cmsg), sizeof(fd));
104:
105:        copyData(fd, 1);
106:
107:        return 0;
108: }
109:
110: int main(int argc, char ** argv) {
111:        int socks[2];
112:        int status;
113:
114:        if (argc != 2) {
115:            fprintf(stderr, "only a single argument is supported\n");
116:            return 1;
117:        }
118:
119:        /* Create the sockets. The first is for the parent and the
120:           second is for the child (though we could reverse that
121:           if we liked. */
122:        if (socketpair(PF_UNIX, SOCK_STREAM, 0, socks))
123:            die("socketpair");
```

```
124:
125:    if (!fork()) {
126:        /* child */
127:        close(socks[0]);
128:        return childProcess(argv[1], socks[1]);
129:    }
130:
131:    /* parent */
132:    close(socks[1]);
133:    parentProcess(socks[0]);
134:
135:    /* reap the child */
136:    wait(&status);
137:
138:    if (WEXITSTATUS(status))
139:        fprintf(stderr, "child failed\n");
140:
141:    return 0;
142: }
```

17.5   Networking Machines with TCP/IP

The primary use for sockets is to allow applications running on different machines to talk to one another. The TCP/IP protocol family [Stevens, 1994] is the protocol used on the Internet, the largest set of networked computers in the world. Linux provides a complete, robust TCP/IP implementation that allows it to act as both a TCP/IP server and client.

The most widely deployed version of TCP/IP is version 4 (IPv4). Version 6 of TCP/IP (IPv6) has become available for most operating systems and network infrastructure products, although IPv4 is still dominant. We concentrate here on writing applications for IPv4, but we touch on the differences for IPv6 applications, as well as for programs that need to support both.

17.5.1 Byte Ordering

TCP/IP networks are usually heterogenous; they include a wide variety of machines and architectures. One of the most common differences between architectures is how they store numbers.

Computer numbers are made up of a sequence of bytes. C integers are commonly 4 bytes (32 bits), for example. There are quite a few ways of storing those four bytes in memory. **Big-endian** architectures store the most significant byte at the lowest hardware address, and the other bytes follow in order from most significant to least significant. **Little-endian** machines store multibyte values in exactly the opposite order: The least significant byte is stored at the smallest memory address. Other machines store bytes in different orders yet.

Because multiple byte quantities are needed as part of the TCP/IP protocol, the protocol designers adopted a single standard for how multibyte values are sent across the network.[13] TCP/IP mandates that **big-endian** byte order be used for transmitting protocol information and suggests that it be used for application data, as well (although no attempt is made to enforce the format of an application's data stream).[14] The ordering used for multibyte values sent across the network is known as the **network byte order**.

Four functions are available for converting between host byte order and network byte order:

```
#include <netinet/in.h>

unsigned int htonl(unsigned int hostlong);
unsigned short htons(unsigned short hostshort);
unsigned int ntohl(unsigned int netlong);
unsigned short ntohs(unsigned short netshort);
```

Although each of these functions is prototyped for unsigned quantities, they all work fine for signed quantities, as well.

---

13. Although it may seem like this is an obvious thing to do, some protocols allow the sender to use any byte order and depend on the recipient to convert the information to the proper (native) order. This gives a performance boost when like machines communicate, at the expense of algorithmic complexity.
14. All Intel and Intel-compatible processors store data as **little-endian**, so getting the conversions right is important for programs to ever work properly.

The first two functions, `htonl()` and `htons()`, convert longs and shorts, respectively, from host order to network order. The final two, `ntohl()` and `ntohs()`, convert longs and shorts from network order to the host byte ordering.

Although we use the term *long* in the descriptions, that is a misnomer. `htonl()` and `ntohl()` both expect 32-bit quantities, not values that are C `long`s. We prototype both functions as manipulating `int` values, as all Linux platforms currently use 32-bit integers.

17.5.2 IPv4 Addressing

IPv4 connections are a 4-tuple of (*local host, local port, remote host, remote port*). Each part of the connection must be determined before a connection can be established. *Local host* and *remote host* are each IPv4 addresses. IPv4 addresses are 32-bit (4-byte) numbers unique across the entire connected network. Usually they are written as *aaa.bbb.ccc.ddd*, with each element in the address being the decimal representation of one of the bytes in the machine's address. The left-most number in the address corresponds to the most significant byte in the address. This format for IPv4 addresses is known as **dotted-decimal notation**.

As most machines need to run multiple concurrent TCP/IP applications, an IP number does not provide a unique identification for a connection on a single machine. **Port numbers** are 16-bit numbers that uniquely identify one endpoint of a connection on a single host. The combination of an IPv4 address and a port number identifies a connection endpoint anywhere on a single TCP/IP network (the Internet is a single TCP/IP network). Two connection endpoints form a TCP connection, so two IP number/port number pairs uniquely identify a TCP/IP connection on a network.

Determining which port numbers to use for various protocols is done by a part of the Internet standards known as **well-known port numbers**, maintained by the **Internet Assigned Numbers Authority** (IANA).[15] Common Internet protocols, such as ftp, telnet, and http, are each assigned a port number. Most servers provide those services at the assigned numbers, making them easy to find. Some servers are run at alternate port numbers,

---

15. See http://www.iana.org for information on the IANA.

usually to allow multiple services to be provided by a single machine.[16] As well-known port numbers do not change, Linux uses a simple mapping between protocol names (commonly called **services**) and port numbers through the /etc/services file.

Although the port numbers range from 0 to 65,535, Linux divides them into two classes. The **reserved ports**, numbering from 0 to 1,024, may be used only by processes running as root. This allows client programs to trust that a program running on a server is not a Trojan horse started by a user.[17]

IPv4 addresses are stored in struct sockaddr_in, which is defined as follows:

```
#include <sys/socket.h>
#include <netinet/in.h>

struct sockaddr_in {
    short int           sin_family; /* AF_INET */
    unsigned short int  sin_port;   /* port number */
    struct in_addr      sin_addr;   /* IP address */
}
```

The first member must be AF_INET, indicating that this is an IP address. The next member is the port number in network byte order. The final member is the IP number of the machine for this TCP address. The IP number, stored in sin_addr, should be treated as an opaque type and not accessed directly.

If either sin_port or sin_addr is filled with \0 bytes (normally, by memset()), that indicates a "do not care" condition. Server processes usually do not care what IP address is used for the local connection, for example, as they are willing to accept connections to any address the machine has. If an application wishes to listen for connections only on a single interface, however, it would specify the address. This address is sometimes called **unspecified** as it is not a complete specification of the connection's address, which also needs an IP address.[18]

---

16. Or, increasingly, to hide them from broadband ISPs who do not want their low-dollar customers running servers at home.
17. It may still be a Trojan horse started by the superuser, however.
18. The value for IPv4 unspecified addresses is contained in the constant INADDR_ANY, which is a 32-bit numeric value.

17.5.3 IPv6 Addressing

IPv6 uses the same (*local host*, *local port*, *remote host*, *remote port*) tuple as IPv4, and the port numbers are the same between both versions (16-bit values).

The local and remote host IPv6 addresses are 128-bit (16 bytes) numbers instead of the 32-bit numbers used for IPv4. Using such large addresses gives the protocol plenty of addresses for the future (it could easily give a unique address to every atom in the Milky Way). While this probably seems like overkill, network architectures tend to waste large numbers of addresses, and the designers of IPv6 felt that it was better to change to 128-bit addresses now than to worry about the need for a possible address change in the future.

IPv6's equivalent of IPv4's dotted-decimal notation is colon-separated notation. As the name suggests, colons are used to separate each pair of bytes in the address (instead of a period separating each individual byte). As the addresses are so long, IPv6 addresses are written in hexadecimal (instead of decimal) form to help keep the length of the addresses down. Here are some examples of what an IPv6 address looks like in colon-separated notation:[19]:

```
1080:0:0:0:8:800:200C:417A
FF01:0:0:0:0:0:0:43
0:0:0:0:0:0:0:1
```

As these addresses are quite unwieldy and tend to contain quite a few zeros, a shorthand is available. Any zeros may be left out of the written address, and groups of more than two sequential colons may be written as exactly two colons. Applying these rules to the addresses above leaves us with

```
1080::8:800:200C:417A
FF01::43
::1
```

Taken to the extreme, the address 0:0:0:0:0:0:0:0 becomes just ::.[20]

---

19. These examples were borrowed from RFC 1884, which defines the IPv6 addressing architecture
20. This is the unspecified address for IPv6.

A final method for writing IPv6 addresses is to write the last 32 bits in dotted-decimal notation, and the first 96 bits in colon-separated form. This lets us write the IPv6 loopback address, `::1`, as either `::0.0.0.1` or `0:0:0:0:0:0:0.0.0.1`.

IPv6 defines any address with 96 leading zeros (except for the loopback address and unspecified address) as a compatible IPv4 address, which allows network routers to easily route (tunnel) packets intended for IPv4 hosts through IPv6 networks. The colon shorthand makes it easy to write an IPv4 address as an IPv6 address by prepending the normal dotted-decimal address with `::`; this type of address is called an "IPv4-compatible IPv6 address." This addressing is used only by routers; normal programs cannot take advantage of it.

Programs running on IPv6 machines that need to address IPv4 machines can use mapped IPv4 addresses. They prepend the IPV4 address with 80 leading zeros and the 16-bit value `0xffff`, which is written as `::ffff:` followed by the machine's dotted-decimal IPv4 address. This addressing lets most programs on an IPv6-only system communicate transparently with an IPv4-only node.

IPv6 addresses are stored in variables of type `struct sockaddr_in6`.

```
#include <sys/socket.h>
#include <netinet/in.h>

struct sockaddr_in6 {
    short int           sin6_family;    /* AF_INET6 */
    unsigned short int  sin6_port;      /* port number */
    unsigned int        sin6_flowinfo;  /* IPv6 traffic flow info */
    struct in6_addr     sin6_addr;      /* IP address */
    unsigned int        sin6_scope_id;  /* set of scope interfaces */
}
```

This structure is quite similar to `struct sockaddr_in`, with the first member holding the address family (`AF_INET6` in this case) and the next holding a 16-bit port number in network byte order. The fourth member holds the binary representation of an IPv6 address, performing the same function as the final member of `struct sockaddr_in`. The other two members of the structure, `sin6_flowinfo` and `sin6_scope_id`, are for advanced uses, and should be set to zero for most applications.

The standards restrict `struct sockaddr_in` to exactly three members, while `struct sockaddr_in6` may have extra members. For that reason programs that manually fill in a `struct sockaddr_in6` should zero out the data structure using `memset()`.

17.5.4 Manipulating IP Addresses

Applications often need to convert IP addresses between a human readable notation (either dotted-decimal or colon-separated) and `struct in_addr`'s binary representation. `inet_ntop()` takes a binary IP address and returns a pointer to a string containing the dotted-decimal or colon-separated form.

```
#include <arpa/inet.h>

const char * inet_ntop(int family, const void * address, char * dest,
                       int size);
```

The `family` is the address family of the address being passed as the second parameter; only `AF_INET` and `AF_INET6` are supported. The next parameter points to a `struct in_addr` or a `struct in6_addr6` as specified by the first parameter. The `dest` is a character array in which the human-readable address is stored, and is an array of `size` elements. If the address was successfully formatted, `inet_ntop()` returns `dest`; otherwise, it returns `NULL`. There are only two reasons `inet_ntop()` can fail: If the destination buffer is not large enough to hold the formatted address `errno` is set to `ENOSPC`, or if the `family` is invalid, `errno` contains `EAFNOSUPPORT`.

`INET_ADDRSTRLEN` is a constant that defines the largest size `dest` needs to be to hold any IPv4 address while `INET6_ADDRSTRLEN` defines the maximum array size for an IPv6 address.

The netlookup.c sample program gives an example of using `inet_ntop()`; the full program starts on page 445.

```
120:            if (addr->ai_family == PF_INET) {
121:                struct sockaddr_in * inetaddr = (void *) addr->ai_addr;
122:                char nameBuf[INET_ADDRSTRLEN];
123:
124:                if (serviceName)
125:                    printf("\tport %d", ntohs(inetaddr->sin_port));
```

```
126:
127:              if (hostName)
128:                  printf("\thost %s",
129:                       inet_ntop(AF_INET, &inetaddr->sin_addr,
130:                                 nameBuf, sizeof(nameBuf)));
131:          } else if (addr->ai_family == PF_INET6) {
132:              struct sockaddr_in6 * inetaddr =
133:                                    (void *) addr->ai_addr;
134:              char nameBuf[INET6_ADDRSTRLEN];
135:
136:              if (serviceName)
137:                  printf("\tport %d", ntohs(inetaddr->sin6_port));
138:
139:              if (hostName)
140:                  printf("\thost %s",
141:                       inet_ntop(AF_INET6, &inetaddr->sin6_addr,
142:                                 nameBuf, sizeof(nameBuf)));
143:          }
```

To perform the inverse, converting a string containing a dotted-decimal or colon-separated address into a binary IP address, use inet_pton().

```
#include <arpa/inet.h>

int inet_pton(int family, const char * address, void * dest);
```

The family specifies the type of address being converted, either AF_INET or AF_INET6, and address points to a string containing the character representation of the address. If AF_INET is used, the dotted-decimal string is converted to a binary address stored in the struct in_addr dest points to. For AF_INET6, the colon-separated string is converted and stored in the struct in6_addr dest points to. Unlike most library functions, inet_pton() returns 1 if the conversion was successful, 0 if dest did not contain a valid address, and -1 if the family was not AF_INET or AF_INET6.

The example program reverselookup, which starts on page 451, uses inet_pton() to convert IPv4 and IPv6 addresses given by the user into struct sockaddr structures. Here is the code region that performs the conversions of the IP address pointed to by hostAddress. At the end of this code, the struct sockaddr * addr points to a structure containing the converted address.

```
 79:        if (!hostAddress) {
 80:            addr4.sin_family = AF_INET;
 81:            addr4.sin_port = portNum;
 82:        } else if (!strchr(hostAddress, ':')) {
 83:            /* If a colon appears in the hostAddress, assume IPv6.
 84:               Otherwise, it must be IPv4 */
 85:
 86:            if (inet_pton(AF_INET, hostAddress,
 87:                            &addr4.sin_addr) <= 0) {
 88:                fprintf(stderr, "error converting IPv4 address %s\n",
 89:                        hostAddress);
 90:                return 1;
 91:            }
 92:
 93:            addr4.sin_family = AF_INET;
 94:            addr4.sin_port = portNum;
 95:        } else {
 96:
 97:            memset(&addr6, 0, sizeof(addr6));
 98:
 99:            if (inet_pton(AF_INET6, hostAddress,
100:                            &addr6.sin6_addr) <= 0) {
101:                fprintf(stderr, "error converting IPv6 address %s\n",
102:                        hostAddress);
103:                return 1;
104:            }
105:
106:            addr6.sin6_family = AF_INET6;
107:            addr6.sin6_port = portNum;
108:            addr = (struct sockaddr *) &addr6;
109:            addrLen = sizeof(addr6);
110:        }
```

17.5.5 Turning Names into Addresses

Although long strings of numbers are a perfectly reasonable identification method for computers to use for recognizing each other, people tend to get dismayed at the idea of dealing with large numbers of digits. To allow humans to use alphabetic names for computers instead of numeric ones, the TCP/IP protocol suite includes a distributed database for converting between hostnames and IP addresses. This database is called the **Domain Name System** (DNS) and is covered in depth by many books [Stevens, 1994] [Albitz, 1996].

DNS provides many features, but the only one we are interested in here is its ability to convert between IP addresses and hostnames. Although it may seem like this should be a one-to-one mapping, it is actually a many-to-many mapping: Every IP address corresponds to zero or more hostnames and every hostname corresponds to zero or more IP addresses.

Although using a many-to-many mapping between hostnames and IP addresses may seem strange, many Internet sites use a single machine for their ftp site and their Web site. They would like `www.some.org` and `ftp.some.org` to refer to a single machine, and they have no need for two IP addresses for the machine, so both hostnames resolve to a single IP address. Every IP address has one primary, or **canonical hostname**, which is used when an IP address needs to be converted to a single hostname during a **reverse name lookup**.

The most popular reason for mapping a single hostname to multiple IP addresses is load balancing. Name servers (programs that provide the service of converting hostnames to IP addresses) are often configured to return different addresses at different times for the same name, allowing multiple physical machines to provide a single service.

The arrival of IPv6 provides another reason for a single hostname to have multiple addresses; many machines now have both IPv4 and IPv6 addresses.

The `getaddrinfo()`[21] library function provides programs easy access to DNS's hostname resolution.

---

21. If you have done much socket programming in the past (or are comparing this book to its first edition) you'll notice that the functions used for hostname resolution have changed dramatically. These changes allow programs to be written completely independently of the protocol they use. The changes were made to make it easy to write programs that work on both IPv4 and IPv6 machines, but they should extend to other protocols as well, although `getaddrinfo()` works only on IPv4 and IPv6 at this time.

```
#include <sys/types.h>
#include <socket.h>
#include <netdb.h>

int getaddrinfo(const char * hostname, const char * servicename,
                const struct addrinfo * hints, struct addrinfo ** res);
```

This function is conceptually quite simple, but it is very powerful, so the details are a bit tricky. The idea is for it to take a hostname, a service name, or both, turn it into a list of IP addresses, and use the hints to filter out some of those addresses that the application is not interested in. The final list is returned as a linked list in res.

The hostname that is being looked up is in the first parameter, and may be NULL if only a service lookup is being done. The hostname may be a name (such as www.ladweb.net) or an IP address in either dotted-decimal or colon-separated form, which getaddrinfo() converts to a binary address.

The second parameter, servicename, specifies the name of the service whose well-known port is needed. If it is NULL, no service lookup is done.

struct addrinfo is used for both the hints that are used to filter the full list of addresses and for returning the final list of addresses to the application.

```
#include <netdb.h>

struct addrinfo {
    int ai_flags;
    int ai_family;
    int ai_socktype;
    int ai_protocol;
    socklen_t ai_addrlen;
    struct sockaddr_t * ai_addr;
    char * ai_canonname;
    struct addrinfo * next;
}
```

When struct addrinfo is used for the hints parameter, only the first four members are used; the rest should be set to zero or NULL. If ai_family is set, getaddrinfo() returns addresses only for the protocol family (such as

PF_INET) it specifies. Similarly, if ai_socktype is set, only addresses for that type of socket are returned.

The ai_protocol member allows the results to be limited to a particular protocol. It should never be used unless ai_family is set as well, as the numeric value of a protocol (such as IPPROTO_TCP) is not unique across all protocols; it is well defined only for PF_INET and PF_INET6.

The final member that is used for the hints is ai_flags, which is one or more of the following values logically OR'ed together:

AI_ADDRCONFIG   By default, getaddrinfo() returns all of the addresses that match the query. This flag tells it to return only addresses for protocols that have addresses configured on the local system. In other words, it returns only IPv4 addresses on systems with IPv4 interfaces configured, and returns only IPv6 addresses on systems with IPv6 interfaces configured.

AI_CANONNAME   On return, the ai_canonname field will contain the canonical hostname for the address specified by that struct addrinfo. Finding this takes an extra search in the DNS, and is not normally necessary.

AI_NUMERICHOST   The hostname parameter must be an address in colon-separated or dotted-decimal form; no hostname conversions are done. This prevents getaddrinfo() from performing any hostname lookups, which can be a lengthy process.

AI_PASSIVE   When hostname is NULL and this flag is present, the address returned is unspecified, which allows a server to wait for connections on all interfaces. If this flag is not specified when hostname is NULL, the loopback address is returned.[22]

The final parameter to getaddrinfo(), res, should be the address of a pointer to a struct addrinfo. On successful completion, the variable

---

22. The loopback address is a special address that lets programs talk through TCP/IP to applications on the same machine only.

pointed to by res is set to point to the first entry in a singly linked list of addresses that match the query. The ai_next member of the struct addrinfo points to the next member in the linked list, and the last node in the list has ai_next set to NULL. When the application is finished with the linked list that is returned, freeaddrinfo() frees the memory used by the list.

```
#include <sys/types.h>
#include <socket.h>
#include <netdb.h>

void freeaddrinfo(struct addrinfo * res);
```

The sole parameter to freeaddrinfo is a pointer to the first node in the list.

Each node in the returned list is of type struct addrinfo, and specifies a single address that matches the query. Each address includes not only the IPv4 or IPv6 address, but also specifies the type of connection (datagram, for example) and the protocol (such as udp). If the query matches multiple types of connections for a single IP address, that address is included in multiple nodes.

Each node contains the following information:

- ai_family is the protocol family (PF_INET or PF_INET6) the address belongs to.

- ai_socktype is the type of connection for the address and is normally SOCK_STREAM, SOCK_DGRAM, or SOCK_RAW.

- ai_protocol is the protocol for the address (normally IPPROTO_TCP or IPPROTO_UDP).

- If AI_CANONNAME was specified in the hints parameter, ai_canonname contains the canonical name for the address.

- ai_addr points to a struct sockaddr for the appropriate protocol. If ai_family is PF_INET, then ai_addr points to a struct sockaddr_in, for example. The ai_addrlen member contains the length of the structure ai_addr points to.

- If a servicename was provided, the port number in each address is set to the well-known port for that service; otherwise, the port number for each address is zero.

- If no hostname was provided, the port numbers are set for each address but the IP address is set to either the loopback address or the unspecified address, as specified above in the description of the AI_PASSIVE flag.

While all of this seems very complicated, there are only two different ways getaddrinfo() is normally used. Most client programs want to turn a hostname supplied by the user and a service name known by the program into a fully specified address to which the client can connect. Accomplishing this is pretty straightforward; here is a program that takes a hostname as its first argument and a service name as its second and performs the lookups:

```
 1: /* clientlookup.c */
 2:
 3: #include <netdb.h>
 4: #include <stdio.h>
 5: #include <string.h>
 6:
 7: int main(int argc, const char ** argv) {
 8:     struct addrinfo hints, * addr;
 9:     const char * host = argv[1], * service = argv[2];
10:     int rc;
11:
12:     if (argc != 3) {
13:         fprintf(stderr, "exactly two arguments are needed\n");
14:         return 1;
15:     }
16:
17:     memset(&hints, 0, sizeof(hints));
18:
19:     hints.ai_socktype = SOCK_STREAM;
20:     hints.ai_flags = AI_ADDRCONFIG;
21:     if ((rc = getaddrinfo(host, service, &hints, &addr)))
22:         fprintf(stderr, "lookup failed\n");
23:     else
24:         freeaddrinfo(addr);
```

```
25:
26:        return 0;
27: }
```

The interesting part of this program is lines 17–24. After clearing the hints structure, the application asks for SOCK_STREAM addresses that use a protocol configured on the local system (by setting the AI_ADDRCONFIG flag). It then calls getaddrinfo() with the hostname, service name, and hints, and displays a message if the lookup failed. On success, the first node in the linked list pointed to by addr is an appropriate address for the program to use to contact the specified service and host; whether that connection is best made using IPv4 or IPv6 is transparent to the program.

Server applications are a little bit simpler; they normally want to accept connection on a particular port, but on all addresses. Setting the AI_PASSIVE flags tells getaddrinfo() to return the address that tells the kernel to allow connections to any address it knows about when NULL is passed as the first parameter. As in the client example, AI_ADDRCONFIG is used to ensure that the returned address is for a protocol the machine supports.

```
 1: /* serverlookup.c */
 2:
 3: #include <netdb.h>
 4: #include <stdio.h>
 5: #include <string.h>
 6:
 7: int main(int argc, const char ** argv) {
 8:     struct addrinfo hints, * addr;
 9:     const char * service = argv[1];
10:     int rc;
11:
12:     if (argc != 3) {
13:         fprintf(stderr, "exactly one argument is needed\n");
14:         return 1;
15:     }
16:
17:     memset(&hints, 0, sizeof(hints));
18:
19:     hints.ai_socktype = SOCK_STREAM;
20:     hints.ai_flags = AI_ADDRCONFIG | AI_PASSIVE;
21:     if ((rc = getaddrinfo(NULL, service, &hints, &addr)))
```

```
22:              fprintf(stderr, "lookup failed\n");
23:      else
24:          freeaddrinfo(addr);
25:
26:      return 0;
27: }
```

After `getaddrinfo()` returns successfully, the first node in the linked list can be used by the server for setting up its socket.

The next example is a much more useful program. It provides a command line interface to most of the capabilities of `getaddrinfo()`. It allows the user to specify the hostname or service name to look up (or both), the type of socket (stream or datagram), the address family, and the protocol (TCP or UDP). The user can also ask that it display the canonical name, and that it display only addresses for protocols for which the machine is configured (via the `AI_ADDRCONFIG` flag). Here is how the program can be used to find the addresses to use for a telnet connection to the local machine (this machine has been configured for both IPv4 and IPv6):

```
$ ./netlookup --host localhost --service telnet
IPv6    stream  tcp     port 23 host ::1
IPv6    dgram   udp     port 23 host ::1
IPv4    stream  tcp     port 23 host 127.0.0.1
IPv4    dgram   udp     port 23 host 127.0.0.1
```

As there is no protocol for telnet over a datagram connection defined (although a well-known port for such a service has been reserved), it is probably a good idea to restrict the search to stream protocols.

```
[ewt@patton code]$ ./netlookup --host localhost --service telnet --stream
IPv6    stream  tcp     port 23 host ::1
IPv4    stream  tcp     port 23 host 127.0.0.1
```

After unconfiguring the local machine for IPv6, the same command looks like this:

```
[ewt@patton code]$ ./netlookup --host localhost --service telnet --stream
IPv4    stream  tcp     port 23 host 127.0.0.1
```

Here is what a lookup looks like for an Internet host that has both IPv4 and IPv6 configurations:

```
$ ./netlookup --host www.6bone.net --stream
IPv6    stream  tcp     host 3ffe:b00:c18:1::10
IPv4    stream  tcp     host 206.123.31.124
```

For a complete list of the command-line options netlookup.c supports, run it without any parameters.

```
 1: /* netlookup.c */
 2:
 3: #include <netdb.h>
 4: #include <arpa/inet.h>
 5: #include <netinet/in.h>
 6: #include <stdio.h>
 7: #include <string.h>
 8: #include <stdlib.h>
 9:
10: /* Called when errors occur during command line processing;
11:     this displays a brief usage message and exits */
12: void usage(void) {
13:     fprintf(stderr, "usage: netlookup [--stream] [--dgram] "
14:             "[--ipv4] [--ipv6] [--name] [--udp]\n");
15:     fprintf(stderr, "                      [--tcp] [--cfg] "
16:             "[--service <service>] [--host <hostname>]\n");
17:     exit(1);
18: }
19:
20: int main(int argc, const char ** argv) {
21:     struct addrinfo * addr, * result;
22:     const char ** ptr;
23:     int rc;
24:     struct addrinfo hints;
25:     const char * serviceName = NULL;
26:     const char * hostName = NULL;
27:
28:     /* clear the hints structure */
29:     memset(&hints, 0, sizeof(hints));
30:
31:     /* parse the command line arguments, skipping over argv[0]
32:
33:         The hints structure, serviceName, and hostName will be
34:         filled in based on which arguments are present. */
```

```
35:        ptr = argv + 1;
36:        while (*ptr && *ptr[0] == '-') {
37:            if (!strcmp(*ptr, "--ipv4"))
38:                hints.ai_family = PF_INET;
39:            else if (!strcmp(*ptr, "--ipv6"))
40:                hints.ai_family = PF_INET6;
41:            else if (!strcmp(*ptr, "--stream"))
42:                hints.ai_socktype = SOCK_STREAM;
43:            else if (!strcmp(*ptr, "--dgram"))
44:                hints.ai_socktype = SOCK_DGRAM;
45:            else if (!strcmp(*ptr, "--name"))
46:                hints.ai_flags |= AI_CANONNAME;
47:            else if (!strcmp(*ptr, "--cfg"))
48:                hints.ai_flags |= AI_ADDRCONFIG;
49:            else if (!strcmp(*ptr, "--tcp")) {
50:                hints.ai_protocol = IPPROTO_TCP;
51:            } else if (!strcmp(*ptr, "--udp")) {
52:                hints.ai_protocol = IPPROTO_UDP;
53:            } else if (!strcmp(*ptr, "--host")) {
54:                ptr++;
55:                if (!*ptr) usage();
56:                hostName = *ptr;
57:            } else if (!strcmp(*ptr, "--service")) {
58:                ptr++;
59:                if (!*ptr) usage();
60:                serviceName = *ptr;
61:            } else
62:                usage();
63:
64:            ptr++;
65:        }
66:
67:        /* we need a hostName, serviceName, or both */
68:        if (!hostName && !serviceName)
69:            usage();
70:
71:        if ((rc = getaddrinfo(hostName, serviceName, &hints,
72:                              &result))) {
73:            fprintf(stderr, "service lookup failed: %s\n",
74:                    gai_strerror(rc));
75:            return 1;
```

```
76:      }
77:
78:      /* walk through the linked list, displaying all results */
79:      addr = result;
80:      while (addr) {
81:          switch (addr->ai_family) {
82:              case PF_INET:      printf("IPv4");
83:                                 break;
84:              case PF_INET6:     printf("IPv6");
85:                                 break;
86:              default:           printf("(%d)", addr->ai_family);
87:                                 break;
88:          }
89:
90:          switch (addr->ai_socktype) {
91:              case SOCK_STREAM:  printf("\tstream");
92:                                 break;
93:              case SOCK_DGRAM:   printf("\tdgram");
94:                                 break;
95:              case SOCK_RAW:     printf("\traw  ");
96:                                 break;
97:              default:           printf("\t(%d)",
98:                                         addr->ai_socktype);
99:                                 break;
100:         }
101:
102:         if (addr->ai_family == PF_INET ||
103:                 addr->ai_family == PF_INET6)
104:             switch (addr->ai_protocol) {
105:                 case IPPROTO_TCP:  printf("\ttcp");
106:                                    break;
107:                 case IPPROTO_UDP:  printf("\tudp");
108:                                    break;
109:                 case IPPROTO_RAW:  printf("\traw");
110:                                    break;
111:                 default:           printf("\t(%d)",
112:                                            addr->ai_protocol);
113:                                    break;
114:             }
115:         else
116:             printf("\t");
```

```
117:
118:            /* display information for both IPv4 and IPv6 addresses */
119:
120:            if (addr->ai_family == PF_INET) {
121:                struct sockaddr_in * inetaddr = (void *) addr->ai_addr;
122:                char nameBuf[INET_ADDRSTRLEN];
123:
124:                if (serviceName)
125:                    printf("\tport %d", ntohs(inetaddr->sin_port));
126:
127:                if (hostName)
128:                    printf("\thost %s",
129:                            inet_ntop(AF_INET, &inetaddr->sin_addr,
130:                                    nameBuf, sizeof(nameBuf)));
131:            } else if (addr->ai_family == PF_INET6) {
132:                struct sockaddr_in6 * inetaddr =
133:                                        (void *) addr->ai_addr;
134:                char nameBuf[INET6_ADDRSTRLEN];
135:
136:                if (serviceName)
137:                    printf("\tport %d", ntohs(inetaddr->sin6_port));
138:
139:                if (hostName)
140:                    printf("\thost %s",
141:                            inet_ntop(AF_INET6, &inetaddr->sin6_addr,
142:                                    nameBuf, sizeof(nameBuf)));
143:            }
144:
145:            if (addr->ai_canonname)
146:                printf("\tname %s", addr->ai_canonname);
147:
148:            printf("\n");
149:
150:            addr = addr->ai_next;
151:        }
152:
153:        /* free the results of getaddrinfo() */
154:        freeaddrinfo(result);
155:
156:        return 0;
157: }
```

Table 17.3 Address and Name Lookup Errors

Error	Description
EAI_EAGAIN	The name could not be found, but trying again later might succeed.
EAI_BADFLAGS	The flags passed to the function were invalid.
EAI_FAIL	The lookup process had a permanent error occur.
EAI_FAMILY	The address family was not recognized.
EAI_MEMORY	A memory allocation request failed.
EAI_NONAME	The name or address cannot be converted.
EAI_OVERFLOW	An buffer passed was too small.
EAI_SERVICE	The service does not exist for the socket type.
EAI_SOCKTYPR	An invalid socket type was given.
EAI_SYSTEM	A system error occured, and the error is in errno.

Unlike most library functions, getaddrinfo() returns an integer that is zero on success, and describes the error on failure; errno is not normally used by these functions. Table 17.3 summarizes the various error codes that these functions can return.

These error codes can be converted to a string describing the failure through gai_strerror().

```
#include <netdb.h>

const char * gai_strerror(int error);
```

The error should be the nonzero return value from getaddrinfo(). If the error is EAI_SYSTEM, the program should instead use strerror(errno) to get a good description.

17.5.6 Turning Addresses into Names

Fortunately, turning IP addresses and port numbers into host and service names is simpler than going the other way.

```
#include <sys/socket.h>
#include <netdb.h>

int getnameinfo(struct sockaddr * addr, socklen_t addrlen,
                char * hostname, size_t hostlen,
                char * servicename, size_t servicelen,
                int flags);
```

The addr parameter points to either a struct sockaddr_in or struct sockaddr_in6 structure, and addrlen contains the size of the structure addr points to. The IP address and port number specified by addr are converted to a hostname, which is stored at the location pointed to by hostname and a service name, which is stored in servicename. Either one may be NULL, causing getnameinfo() to not perform any name lookup for that parameter.

The hostlen and servicelen parameters specify how many bytes are available in the buffers pointed to by hostname and servicename respectively. If the either name does not fit in the space available, the buffers are filled up and an error (EAI_OVERFLOW) is returned.

The final argument, flags, changes how getnameinfo() performs name lookups. It should be zero or more of the following values logically OR'ed together:

NI_DGRAM   The UDP service name for the specified port is looked up
                    instead of the TCP service name.[23]

NI_NAMEREQD   If the IP address to hostname lookup fails and this flag
                    is specified, getnameinfo() returns an error. Otherwise,
                    it returns the IP address formatted in dotted-decimal or
                    colon-separated form.

NI_NOFQDN   Hostnames are normally returned as full qualified do-
                    main names; this means that the complete hostname is
                    returned rather than a local abbreviation. If this flag is set,

---

23. The two are almost always identical, but there are a few ports that are defined only for UDP ports (the SNMP trap protocol is one) and a few cases where the same port number is used for different TCP and UDP services (port 512 is used for the TCP exec service and the UDP biff service, for example).

your host is `digit.iana.org`, and you lookup the IP address corresponding to `www.iana.org`, for example, then the returned hostname will be `www`. Hostname lookups for other machines are not affected; in the previous example, looking up the address for `www.ietf.org` will return the full hostname, `www.ietf.org`.

NI_NUMERICHOST

Rather than performing a hostname lookup, `getnameinfo()` converts the IP address to an IP address like `inet_ntop()` does.

NI_NUMERICSERV

The port number is placed in `servicename` as a formatted numeric string rather than converted to a service name.

The return codes for `getnameinfo()` are the same as for `gethostinfo()`; zero is returned on success and an error code is returned on failure. A full list of the possible errors is in Table 17.3, and `gai_strerror()` can be used to convert those errors into descriptive strings.

Here is an example of how to use `getnameinfo()` to perform some reverse name lookups for both IPv4 and IPv6 addresses:

```
$ ./reverselookup --host ::1
hostname: localhost
$ ./reverselookup --host 127.0.0.1
hostname: localhost
$ ./reverselookup --host 3ffe:b00:c18:1::10
hostname: www.6bone.net
$ ./reverselookup --host 206.123.31.124 --service 80
hostname: www.6bone.net
service name: http

  1: /* reverselookup.c */
  2:
  3: #include <netdb.h>
  4: #include <arpa/inet.h>
  5: #include <netinet/in.h>
  6: #include <stdio.h>
  7: #include <string.h>
```

```
 8: #include <stdlib.h>
 9:
10: /* Called when errors occur during command line processing; this
11:    displays a brief usage message and exits */
12: void usage(void) {
13:     fprintf(stderr, "usage: reverselookup [--numerichost] "
14:             "[--numericserv] [--namereqd] [--udp]\n");
15:     fprintf(stderr, "                     [--nofqdn] "
16:             "[--service <service>] [--host <hostname>]\n");
17:     exit(1);
18: }
19:
20: int main(int argc, const char ** argv) {
21:     int flags;
22:     const char * hostAddress = NULL;
23:     const char * serviceAddress = NULL;
24:     struct sockaddr_in addr4;
25:     struct sockaddr_in6 addr6;
26:     struct sockaddr * addr = (struct sockaddr *) &addr4;
27:     int addrLen = sizeof(addr4);
28:     int rc;
29:     int portNum = 0;
30:     const char ** ptr;
31:     char hostName[1024];
32:     char serviceName[256];
33:
34:     /* clear the flags */
35:     flags = 0;
36:
37:     /* parse the command line arguments, skipping over argv[0] */
38:     ptr = argv + 1;
39:     while (*ptr && *ptr[0] == '-') {
40:         if (!strcmp(*ptr, "--numerichost")) {
41:             flags |= NI_NUMERICHOST;
42:         } else if (!strcmp(*ptr, "--numericserv")) {
43:             flags |= NI_NUMERICSERV;
44:         } else if (!strcmp(*ptr, "--namereqd")) {
45:             flags |= NI_NAMEREQD;
46:         } else if (!strcmp(*ptr, "--nofqdn")) {
47:             flags |= NI_NOFQDN;
48:         } else if (!strcmp(*ptr, "--udp")) {
```

```
49:                    flags |= NI_DGRAM;
50:            } else if (!strcmp(*ptr, "--host")) {
51:                ptr++;
52:                if (!*ptr) usage();
53:                hostAddress = *ptr;
54:            } else if (!strcmp(*ptr, "--service")) {
55:                ptr++;
56:                if (!*ptr) usage();
57:                serviceAddress = *ptr;
58:            } else
59:                usage();
60:
61:            ptr++;
62:    }
63:
64:    /* we need a hostAddress, serviceAddress, or both */
65:    if (!hostAddress && !serviceAddress)
66:        usage();
67:
68:    if (serviceAddress) {
69:        char * end;
70:
71:        portNum = htons(strtol(serviceAddress, &end, 0));
72:        if (*end) {
73:            fprintf(stderr, "failed to convert %s to a number\n",
74:                    serviceAddress);
75:            return 1;
76:        }
77:    }
78:
79:    if (!hostAddress) {
80:        addr4.sin_family = AF_INET;
81:        addr4.sin_port = portNum;
82:    } else if (!strchr(hostAddress, ':')) {
83:        /* If a colon appears in the hostAddress, assume IPv6.
84:           Otherwise, it must be IPv4 */
85:
86:        if (inet_pton(AF_INET, hostAddress,
87:                    &addr4.sin_addr) <= 0) {
88:            fprintf(stderr, "error converting IPv4 address %s\n",
89:                    hostAddress);
```

```
 90:            return 1;
 91:        }
 92:
 93:        addr4.sin_family = AF_INET;
 94:        addr4.sin_port = portNum;
 95:    } else {
 96:
 97:        memset(&addr6, 0, sizeof(addr6));
 98:
 99:        if (inet_pton(AF_INET6, hostAddress,
100:                    &addr6.sin6_addr) <= 0) {
101:            fprintf(stderr, "error converting IPv6 address %s\n",
102:                    hostAddress);
103:            return 1;
104:        }
105:
106:        addr6.sin6_family = AF_INET6;
107:        addr6.sin6_port = portNum;
108:        addr = (struct sockaddr *) &addr6;
109:        addrLen = sizeof(addr6);
110:    }
111:
112:    if (!serviceAddress) {
113:        rc = getnameinfo(addr, addrLen, hostName, sizeof(hostName),
114:                        NULL, 0,  flags);
115:    } else if (!hostAddress) {
116:        rc = getnameinfo(addr, addrLen, NULL, 0,
117:                        serviceName, sizeof(serviceName), flags);
118:    } else {
119:        rc = getnameinfo(addr, addrLen, hostName, sizeof(hostName),
120:                        serviceName, sizeof(serviceName), flags);
121:    }
122:
123:    if (rc) {
124:        fprintf(stderr, "reverse lookup failed: %s\n",
125:                gai_strerror(rc));
126:        return 1;
127:    }
128:
129:    if (hostAddress)
130:        printf("hostname: %s\n", hostName);
```

```
131:        if (serviceAddress)
132:            printf("service name: %s\n", serviceName);
133:
134:        return 0;
135: }
```

17.5.7 Listening for TCP Connections

Listening for TCP connections is nearly identical to listening for Unix domain connections. The only differences are the protocol and address families. Here is a version of the example Unix domain server that works over TCP sockets instead:

```
 1: /* tserver.c */
 2:
 3: /* Waits for a connection on port 4321. Once a connection has been
 4:    established, copy data from the socket to stdout until the other
 5:    end closes the connection, and then wait for another connection
 6:    to the socket. */
 7:
 8: #include <arpa/inet.h>
 9: #include <netdb.h>
10: #include <netinet/in.h>
11: #include <stdio.h>
12: #include <string.h>
13: #include <sys/socket.h>
14: #include <unistd.h>
15:
16: #include "sockutil.h"              /* some utility functions */
17:
18: int main(void) {
19:     int sock, conn, i, rc;
20:     struct sockaddr address;
21:     size_t addrLength = sizeof(address);
22:     struct addrinfo hints, * addr;
23:
24:     memset(&hints, 0, sizeof(hints));
25:
26:     hints.ai_socktype = SOCK_STREAM;
27:     hints.ai_flags = AI_PASSIVE | AI_ADDRCONFIG;
```

```
28:        if ((rc = getaddrinfo(NULL, "4321", &hints, &addr))) {
29:            fprintf(stderr, "hostname lookup failed: %s\n",
30:                    gai_strerror(rc));
31:            return 1;
32:        }
33:
34:        if ((sock = socket(addr->ai_family, addr->ai_socktype,
35:                            addr->ai_protocol)) < 0)
36:            die("socket");
37:
38:        /* Let the kernel reuse the socket address. This lets us run
39:           twice in a row, without waiting for the (ip, port) tuple
40:           to time out. */
41:        i = 1;
42:        setsockopt(sock, SOL_SOCKET, SO_REUSEADDR, &i, sizeof(i));
43:
44:        if (bind(sock, addr->ai_addr, addr->ai_addrlen))
45:            die("bind");
46:
47:        freeaddrinfo(addr);
48:
49:        if (listen(sock, 5))
50:            die("listen");
51:
52:        while ((conn = accept(sock, (struct sockaddr *) &address,
53:                            &addrLength)) >= 0) {
54:            printf("---- getting data\n");
55:            copyData(conn, 1);
56:            printf("---- done\n");
57:            close(conn);
58:        }
59:
60:        if (conn < 0)
61:            die("accept");
62:
63:        close(sock);
64:        return 0;
65: }
```

Notice that the IP address bound to the socket specifies a port number,
4321, but not an IP address. This leaves the kernel free to use whatever
local IP address it likes.

The other thing that needs some explaining is this code sequence on lines
41–42:

```
41:     i = 1;
42:     setsockopt(sock, SOL_SOCKET, SO_REUSEADDR, &i, sizeof(i));
```

Linux's TCP implementation, like that of most Unix systems, restricts how
soon a (*local host*, *local port*) can be reused.[24] This code sets an option on the
socket that bypasses this restriction and allows the server to be run twice in
a short period of time. This is similar to the reason the Unix domain socket
example server removed any preexisting socket file before calling bind().

The setsockopt() allows you to set many socket- and protocol-specific
options:

```
#include <sys/socket.h>

int setsockopt(int sock, int level, int option,
               const void * valptr, int vallength);
```

The first argument is the socket whose option is being set. The second
argument, level, specifies what type of option is being set. In our server,
we used SOL_SOCKET, which specifies that a generic socket option is being
set. The option parameter specifies the option to be changed. A pointer to
the new value of the option is passed through valptr and the size of the
value pointed to by valptr is passed as vallength. For our server, we use
a pointer to a non-zero integer, which turns on the SO_REUSEADDR option.

17.5.8 TCP Client Applications

TCP clients are similar to Unix domain clients. Usually, a socket is created and immediately connect()ed to the server. The only differences
are in how the address passed to connect() is set. Rather than use a
file name, most TCP clients look up the hostname to connect to through
getaddrinfo(), which provides the information for connect().

Here is a simple TCP client that talks to the server presented in the previous
section. It takes a single argument, which is the name or IP number (in

---

24. For TCP ports, the combination may not be used within a two-minute period.

dotted-decimal notation) of the host the server is running on. It otherwise behaves like the sample Unix domain socket client presented on page 422.

```
 1: /* tclient.c */
 2:
 3: /* Connect to the server whose hostname or IP is given as an
 4:    argument, at port 4321. Once connected, copy everything on
 5:    stdin to the socket, then exit. */
 6:
 7: #include <arpa/inet.h>
 8: #include <netdb.h>
 9: #include <netinet/in.h>
10: #include <stdio.h>
11: #include <stdlib.h>
12: #include <string.h>
13: #include <sys/socket.h>
14: #include <unistd.h>
15:
16: #include "sockutil.h"            /* some utility functions */
17:
18: int main(int argc, const char ** argv) {
19:     struct addrinfo hints, * addr;
20:     struct sockaddr_in * addrInfo;
21:     int rc;
22:     int sock;
23:
24:     if (argc != 2) {
25:         fprintf(stderr, "only a single argument is supported\n");
26:         return 1;
27:     }
28:
29:     memset(&hints, 0, sizeof(hints));
30:
31:     hints.ai_socktype = SOCK_STREAM;
32:     hints.ai_flags = AI_ADDRCONFIG;
33:     if ((rc = getaddrinfo(argv[1], NULL, &hints, &addr))) {
34:         fprintf(stderr, "hostname lookup failed: %s\n",
35:                 gai_strerror(rc));
36:         return 1;
37:     }
38:
39:     /* this lets us access the sin_family and sin_port (which are
```

```
40:          in the same place as sin6_family and sin6_port */
41:       addrInfo = (struct sockaddr_in *) addr->ai_addr;
42:
43:       if ((sock = socket(addrInfo->sin_family, addr->ai_socktype,
44:                          addr->ai_protocol)) < 0)
45:          die("socket");
46:
47:       addrInfo->sin_port = htons(4321);
48:
49:       if (connect(sock, (struct sockaddr *) addrInfo,
50:                   addr->ai_addrlen))
51:          die("connect");
52:
53:       freeaddrinfo(addr);
54:
55:       copyData(0, sock);
56:
57:       close(sock);
58:
59:       return 0;
60: }
```

17.6 Using UDP Datagrams

While most network applications benefit from the streaming TCP protocol, some prefer to use UDP. Here are some reasons that the connectionless datagram model provided by UDP might be useful:

- Connectionless protocols handle machine restarts more gracefully as there are no connections that need to be reestablished. This can be very attractive for network file systems (like NFS, which is UDP based), since it allows the file server to be restarted without the clients having to be aware of it.

- Protocols that are very simple may run much faster over a datagram protocol. The Domain Name System (DNS) uses UDP for just this reason (although it optionally supports TCP as well). When a TCP connection is being established, the client machine needs to send a message to the server to establish the connection, get an acknowledgment back from the server saying the connection is available, and then tell the server when the client side has been established.[25] Once this occurs, the client can send its hostname query to the server, which responds. All of this took five messages, ignoring the error checking and sequencing for the actual query and response. By using UDP, hostname queries are sent as the first packet to the server, which then responds with one more UDP packet, reducing the total packet count to five. If the client does not get a response, it simply resends the query.

- When computers are first initialized, they often need to establish an IP address and then download the first part of the operating system over the network.[26] Using UDP for these operations makes the protocol stack that is embedded on such machines much simpler than it would be if a full TCP implementation were required.

17.6.1 Creating a UDP Socket

Like any other socket, UDP sockets are created through `socket()`, but the second argument should be `SOCK_DGRAM`, and the final argument is either `IPPROTO_UDP` or just zero (as UDP is the default IP datagram protocol).

Once the socket is created, it needs to have a local port number assigned to it. This occurs when a program does one of three things:

- A port number is explicitly set by calling `bind()`. Servers that need to receive datagrams on a well-known port number need to do this, and the system call is exactly the same as for TCP servers.

- A datagram is sent through the socket. The kernel assigns a UDP port number to that socket the first time data is sent through it. Most client programs use this technique, as they do not care what port number is used.

---

25. This is known as TCP's three-way handshake, which is actually more complicated than described here.
26. This process is called network booting.

- A remote address is set for the socket by connect() (which is optional for UDP sockets).

There are also two different ways of assigning the remote port number. Recall that TCP sockets have the remote address assigned by connect(), which can also be used for UDP sockets.[27] While TCP's connect() causes packets to be exchanged to initialize the connection (making connect() a slow system call), calling connect() for UDP sockets simply assigns a remote IP address and port number for outgoing datagrams, and is a fast system call. Another difference is applications can connect() a TCP socket only once; UDP sockets can have their destination address changed by calling connect() again.[28]

One advantage of using connected UDP sockets is that only the machine and port that are specified as the remote address for the socket can send datagrams to that socket. Any IP address and port can send datagrams to an unconnected UDP socket, which is required in some cases (this is how new clients initially contact servers), but forces programs to keep track of where datagrams are being sent from.

17.6.2 Sending and Receiving Datagrams

Four system calls are normally used for sending and receiving UDP packets,[29] send(), sendto(), recv(), and recvfrom().[30]

---

27. UDP sockets that have permanant destinations assigned by connect() are sometimes called connected UDP sockets.
28. It is also possible to use connect() to make a connected socket an unconnected one, but doing so is not well standardized. See [Stevens, 2004] for information on how to do this if it is needed.
29. These functions can be used to send data across any socket, and occasionally there are reasons to use them for TCP connections.
30. The sendmsg() and recvmsg() system calls can also be used, but there is rarely a reason to do so.

```
#include <sys/types.h>
#include <sys/sockets.h>

int send(int s, const void * data, size_t len, int flags);
int sendto(int s, const void * data, size_t len, int flags,
           const struct sockaddr * to, socklen_t toLen);
int recv(int s, void * data, size_t maxlen, int flags);
int recvfrom(int s, void * data, size_t maxlen, int flags,
             struct sockaddr * from, socklen_t * fromLen);
```

For our purposes, the `flags` for all of these are always zero. There are many values it can take, and [Stevens, 2004] discusses them in detail.

The first of the system calls, `send()`, can be used only for sockets whose destination IP address and port have been specified by calling `connect()`. It sends the first `len` bytes pointed to by `data` to the other end of the socket `s`. The data is sent as a single datagram. If `len` is too long to the data to be passed in a single datagram, `EMSGSIZE` is returned in `errno`.

The next system call, `sendto()` works like `send()` but allows the destination IP address and port number to be specified for sockets that have not been connected. The last two parameters are a pointer to the socket address and the length of the socket address. Using this function does not set a destination address for the socket; it remains unconnected and future `sendto()` calls can send datagrams to different destinations. If the `to` argument is `NULL`, `sendto()` behaves exactly like `send()`.

The `recv()` and `recvfrom()` system calls are analogous to `send()` and `sendto()`, but they receive datagrams instead of sending them. Both write a single datagram to `data`, up to `*maxlen` bytes, and discard any part of the datagram that does not fit in the buffer. The remote address that sent the datagram is stored in the `from` parameter of `recvmsg()` as long as it is no more than `fromLen` bytes long.

17.6.3 A Simple tftp Server

This simple tftp server illustrates how to send and receive UDP datagrams for both connected and unconnected sockets. The tftp protocol is a very simple file transfer protocol that is built on UDP.[31] It is often used by a computer's firmware to download an initial boot image during a network boot. The server we implement has a number of limitations that make it ill-suited for any real work:

- Only a single client can talk to the server at a time (although this is easy to fix).

- Files can only be sent by the server; it cannot receive them.

- There are no provisions for restricting what files the server sends to an anonymous remote user.

- Very little error checking is done, making it quite likely that there are exploitable security problems in the code.

A tftp client starts a tftp session by sending a "read request packet," which contains a file name it would like to receive and a mode. The two primary modes are netascii, which performs some simple translations of the file, and octet, which sends the file exactly as it appears on the disk. This server supports only octet mode, as it is simpler.

Upon receiving the read request, the tftp server sends the file 512 bytes at a time. Each datagram contains the block number (starting from 1), and the client knows that the file has been properly received when it receives a data block containing less than 512 bytes. After each datagram, the client sends a datagram containing the block number, which acknowledges that the block has been received. Once the server sees this acknowledgment, it sends the next block of data.

The basic format of a datagram is defined by lines 17–46. Some constants are defined that specify the type of datagram being sent, along with an error code that is sent if the requested file does not exist (all other errors are handled quite unceremoniously by the server, which simply exits). The

---

31. Full descriptions of tftp can be found in both [Stevens, 2004] and [Stevens, 1994].

struct tftpPacket outlines what a datagram looks like, with an opcode followed by data that depends on the datagram type. The union nested inside of the structure then defines the rest of the datagram format for error, data, and acknowledgment packets.

The first part of main(), in lines 156–169, creates the UDP socket and sets up the local port number (which is either the well-known service for tftp or the port specified as the program's sole command-line argument) by calling bind(). Unlike our TCP server example, there is no need to call either listen() or accept() as UDP is connectionless.

Once the socket has been created, the server waits for a datagram to be sent to by calling recvfrom(). The handleRequest() function is invoked on line 181, which transmits the file requested and then returns. After this call, the server once more calls recvfrom() to wait for another client to make a request. The comment right above the call to handleRequest() notes that it is quite easy to switch this server from an iterative server to a concurrent one by letting each call to handleRequest() run as its own process.

While the main part of the program used an unconnected UDP socket (which allowed any client to connect to it), handleSocket() uses a connected UDP socket to transfer the file.[32] After parsing out the file name that needs to be sent and making sure the transfer mode is correct, line 93 creates a socket of the same family, type, and protocol that the server was contacted on. It then uses connect() to set the remote end of the socket to the address that requested the file, and begins sending the file. After sending each block, the server waits for an acknowledgment packet before continuing. After the last one is received, it closes the socket and goes back to the main loop.

This server should normally be run with a port number as its only argument. To test it, the normal tftp client program can be used, with the first argument being the hostname to connect to (localhost is probably a good choice) and the second being the port number the server is running on. Once the client is running, the bin command should be issued to it so that it requests files in octet mode rather than the default netascii. Once this

---

32. The tftp protocol specification requires servers to send data to a client on a port number other than the port the server is waiting for new requests on. It also makes it easier to write a concurrent server as each server socket is intended for exactly one client.

has been done, a get command will be able to transfer any file from the server to the client.

```
 1: /* tftpserver.c */
 2:
 3: /* This is a partial implementation of tftp. It doesn't ever time
 4:    out or resend packets, and it doesn't handle unexpected events
 5:    very well. */
 6:
 7: #include <netdb.h>
 8: #include <stdio.h>
 9: #include <stdlib.h>
10: #include <string.h>
11: #include <sys/socket.h>
12: #include <unistd.h>
13: #include <fcntl.h>
14:
15: #include "sockutil.h"          /* some utility functions */
16:
17: #define RRQ     1              /* read request */
18: #define DATA    3              /* data block */
19: #define ACK     4              /* acknowledgement */
20: #define ERROR   5              /* error occured */
21:
22: /* tftp error codes */
23: #define FILE_NOT_FOUND  1
24:
25: struct tftpPacket {
26:     short opcode;
27:
28:     union {
29:        char bytes[514];        /* largest packet we can handle has 2
30:                                   bytes for block number and 512
31:                                   for data */
32:        struct {
33:            short code;
34:            char message[200];
35:        } error;
36:
37:        struct {
38:            short block;
39:            char bytes[512];
```

```
40:          } data;
41:
42:          struct {
43:              short block;
44:          } ack;
45:      } u;
46: };
47:
48: void sendError(int s, int errorCode) {
49:      struct tftpPacket err;
50:      int size;
51:
52:      err.opcode = htons(ERROR);
53:
54:      err.u.error.code = htons(errorCode);   /* file not found */
55:      switch (errorCode) {
56:      case FILE_NOT_FOUND:
57:          strcpy(err.u.error.message, "file not found");
58:          break;
59:      }
60:
61:      /* 2 byte opcode, 2 byte error code, the message and a '\0' */
62:      size = 2 + 2 + strlen(err.u.error.message) + 1;
63:      if (send(s, &err, size, 0) != size)
64:          die("error send");
65: }
66:
67: void handleRequest(struct addrinfo tftpAddr,
68:                    struct sockaddr remote, int remoteLen,
69:                    struct tftpPacket request) {
70:      char * fileName;
71:      char * mode;
72:      int fd;
73:      int s;
74:      int size;
75:      int sizeRead;
76:      struct tftpPacket data, response;
77:      int blockNum = 0;
78:
79:      request.opcode = ntohs(request.opcode);
80:      if (request.opcode != RRQ) die("bad opcode");
```

```
81:
82:        fileName = request.u.bytes;
83:        mode = fileName + strlen(fileName) + 1;
84:
85:        /* we only support bin mode */
86:        if (strcmp(mode, "octet"))  {
87:            fprintf(stderr, "bad mode %s\n", mode);
88:            exit(1);
89:        }
90:
91:        /* we want to send using a socket of the same family and type
92:           we started with, */
93:        if ((s = socket(tftpAddr.ai_family, tftpAddr.ai_socktype,
94:                        tftpAddr.ai_protocol)) < 0)
95:            die("send socket");
96:
97:        /* set the remote end of the socket to the address which
98:           initiated this connection */
99:        if (connect(s, &remote, remoteLen))
100:            die("connect");
101:
102:        if ((fd = open(fileName, O_RDONLY)) < 0) {
103:            sendError(s, FILE_NOT_FOUND);
104:            close(s);
105:            return ;
106:        }
107:
108:        data.opcode = htons(DATA);
109:        while ((size = read(fd, data.u.data.bytes, 512)) > 0) {
110:            data.u.data.block = htons(++blockNum);
111:
112:            /* size is 2 byte opcode, 2 byte block number, data */
113:            size += 4;
114:            if (send(s, &data, size, 0) != size)
115:                die("data send");
116:
117:            sizeRead = recv(s, &response, sizeof(response), 0);
118:            if (sizeRead < 0) die("recv ack");
119:
120:            response.opcode = ntohs(response.opcode);
121:            if (response.opcode != ACK) {
```

```
122:                fprintf(stderr, "unexpected opcode in response\n");
123:                exit(1);
124:            }
125:
126:            response.u.ack.block = ntohs(response.u.ack.block);
127:            if (response.u.ack.block != blockNum) {
128:                fprintf(stderr, "received ack of wrong block\n");
129:                exit(1);
130:            }
131:
132:            /* if the block we just sent had less than 512 data
133:                bytes, we're done */
134:            if (size < 516) break;
135:        }
136:
137:        close(s);
138: }
139:
140: int main(int argc, char ** argv) {
141:        struct addrinfo hints, * addr;
142:        char * portAddress = "tftp";
143:        int s;
144:        int rc;
145:        int bytes, fromLen;
146:        struct sockaddr from;
147:        struct tftpPacket packet;
148:
149:        if (argc > 2) {
150:            fprintf(stderr, "usage: tftpserver [port]\n");
151:            exit(1);
152:        }
153:
154:        if (argv[1]) portAddress = argv[1];
155:
156:        memset(&hints, 0, sizeof(hints));
157:
158:        hints.ai_socktype = SOCK_DGRAM;
159:        hints.ai_flags = AI_ADDRCONFIG | AI_PASSIVE;
160:        if ((rc = getaddrinfo(NULL, portAddress, &hints, &addr)))
161:            fprintf(stderr, "lookup of port %s failed\n",
162:                    portAddress);
```

```
163:
164:        if ((s = socket(addr->ai_family, addr->ai_socktype,
165:                        addr->ai_protocol)) < 0)
166:          die("socket");
167:
168:        if (bind(s, addr->ai_addr, addr->ai_addrlen))
169:          die("bind");
170:
171:        /* The main loop waits for a tftp request, handles the
172:           request, and then waits for another one. */
173:        while (1) {
174:            bytes = recvfrom(s, &packet, sizeof(packet), 0, &from,
175:                             &fromLen);
176:            if (bytes < 0) die("recvfrom");
177:
178:            /* if we forked before calling handleRequest() and had
179:               the child exit after the function returned, this server
180:               would work perfectly well as a concurrent tftp server */
181:            handleRequest(*addr, from, fromLen, packet);
182:        }
183: }
```

17.7 Socket Errors

A number of `errno` values occur only with sockets. Here is a list of socket-specific errors and a short description of each:

`EADDRINUSE`
> A requested address is already in use and cannot be reassigned.

`EADDRNOTAVAIL`
> An unavailable address was requested.

`EAFNOSUPPORT`
> An unsupported address family was specified.

`ECONNABORTED`
> The connection was aborted by software.

ECONNREFUSED

> The remote machine refused the connection attempt.

ECONNRESET

> The connection was reset by the remote end. This usually indicates that the remote machine was restarted.

EDESTADDRREQ

> An attempt was made to send data over a socket without providing the destination address. This can occur only for datagram sockets.

EHOSTDOWN

> The remote host is not on the network.

EHOSTUNREAD

> The remote host cannot be reached.

EISCONN

> A connection is already established for the socket.

EMSGSIZE

> The data being sent through a socket is too large to be sent as a single, atomic message.

ENETDOWN

> The network connection is down.

ENETRESET

> The network was reset, causing the connection to be dropped.

ENETUNREACH

> The specified network cannot be reached.

ENOBUFS

> Not enough buffer space is available to handle the request.

ENOPROTOOPT

> An attempt to set an invalid option was made.

ENOTCONN

> A connection must be established before the operation can succeed.

ENOTSOCK

A socket-specific operation was attempted on a file descriptor that references a file other than a socket.

EPFNOSUPPORT

An unsupported protocol family was specified.

EPROTONOSUPPORT

A request was made for an unsupported protocol.

EPROTOTYPE

An inappropriate protocol type was specified for the socket.

ESOCKTNOSUPPORT

An attempt was made to create an unsupported socket type.

ETIMEDOUT

The connection timed out.

17.8 Legacy Networking Functions

There are a number of library functions related to TCP/IP networking that should not be used in new applications. They are widely used in existing IPv4-only programs, however, so they are covered here to aid in understanding and updating this older code.

17.8.1 IPv4 Address Manipulation

The inet_ntop() and inet_pton() functions are relatively new and were introduced to allow a single set of functions to handle both IPv4 and IPv6 addresses. Before they were around, programs used inet_addr(), inet_aton(), and inet_ntoa(), all of which are IPv4 specific.

Recall that struct sockaddr_in is defined as

```
struct sockaddr_in {
    short int           sin_family; /* AF_INET */
    unsigned short int  sin_port;   /* port number */
    struct in_addr      sin_addr;   /* IP address */
}
```

The `sin_addr` member is a `struct in_addr`, which these legacy functions use as a parameter.[33] This structure is meant to be opaque; application programs should never manipulate a `struct in_addr` except through library functions. The old function for converting an IPv4 address to its dotted-decimal form is `inet_ntoa()`.

```
#include <netinet/in.h>
#include <arpa/inet.h>
char * inet_ntoa(struct in_addr address);
```

The address passed is converted to a string in dotted-decimal form, and a pointer to that string is returned. The string is stored in a static buffer in the C library and will be destroyed on the next call to `inet_ntoa()`.[34]

There are two functions that provide the inverse, converting a dotted-decimal string to a binary IP address. The older of the two, `inet_addr()` function has two problems, both caused by its returning a `long`. Not returning a `struct in_addr`, which is what the rest of the standard functions expect, forced programmers into ugly casts. In addition, if a `long` was 32 bits, programs could not differentiate between a return of -1 (indicating an error, such as a malformed address) and the binary representation of 255.255.255.255.

```
#include <netinet/in.h>
#include <arpa/inet.h>

unsigned long int inet_addr(const char * ddaddress);
```

The function takes the passed string, which should contain a dotted-decimal IP address, and converts it to a binary IP address.

---

33. Using this structure directly made it impossible to extend these functions for IPv6 without changing their interface.
34. Functions using static memory to store results make it difficult to build threaded applications, as locks need to be added by the application code to protect those static buffers.

To remedy the shortcomings of `inet_addr()`, `inet_aton()` was introduced.

```
#include <netinet/in.h>
#include <arpa/inet.h>


int inet_aton(const char * ddaddress, struct in_addr * address);
```

This function expects a string containing a dotted-decimal IP address and fills in the `struct in_addr` pointed to by `address` with the binary representation of the address. Unlike most library functions, `inet_aton()` returns zero if an error occurred and non-zero if the conversion was successful.

17.8.2 Hostname Resolution

The `getaddrinfo()` `getnameinfo()` functions, which make it easy to write a program that supports both IPv4 and IPv6, were added to do just that. The original hostname functions could not be easily extended for IPv6, and their interfaces require applications to know quite a bit about the version-specific structures that store IP addresses; the new interfaces are abstract and so support IPv4 and IPv6 equally.

Rather than returning a linked list like `getaddrinfo()` does, the older hostname functions use `struct hostent`, which can contain all the hostnames and addresses for a single host.

```
#include <netdb.h>


struct hostent {
    char * h_name;        /* canonical hostname              */
    char ** h_aliases;    /* aliases (NULL terminated)       */
    int h_addrtype;       /* host address type               */
    int h_length;         /* length of address               */
    char ** h_addr_list;  /* list of addresses (NULL term)   */
};
```

The `h_name` is the canonical name for the host. The `h_aliases` array contains any aliases for the host. The final entry in `h_aliases` is a `NULL` pointer, signaling the end of the array.

h_addrtype tells the type of address the host has. For the purposes of this chapter, it is always AF_INET. Applications that were written to support IPv6 will see other address types.[35] The next member, h_length, specifies the length of the binary addresses for this host. For AF_INET addresses, it is equal to sizeof(struct in_addr). The final member, h_addr_list, is an array of pointers to the addresses for this host, with the final pointer being NULL to signify the end of the list. When h_addrtype is AF_INET, each pointer in this list points to a struct in_addr.

Two library functions convert between IP numbers and hostnames. The first, gethostbyname(), returns a struct hostent for a hostname; the other, gethostbyaddr(), returns information on a machine with a particular IP address.

```
#include <netdb.h>

struct hostent * gethostbyname(const char * name);
struct hostent * gethostbyaddr(const char * addr, int len, int type);
```

Both functions return a pointer to a struct hostent. The structure may be overwritten by the next call to either function, so the program should save any values it will need later. gethostbyname() takes a single parameter, a string containing a hostname. gethostbyaddr() takes three parameters, which together specify an address. The first, addr, should point to a struct in_addr. The next, len, specifies how long the information pointed to by addr is. The final parameter, type, specifies the type of address that should be converted to a hostname—AF_INET for IPv4 addresses.

When errors occur during hostname lookup, an error code is set in h_errno. The herror() function call prints a description of the error, behaving almost identically to the standard perror() function.

The only error code that most programs test for is NETDB_INTERNAL, which indicates a failed system call. When this error is returned, errno contains the error that led to the failure.

---

35. There probably are not any IPv6 programs that use struct hostaddr, but it is possible for them to do so. The functions we discuss here return only IPv4 information by default and we do not talk about using these functions with IPv6.

17.8.3 Legacy Host Information Lookup Example

Here is a sample program that makes use of inet_aton(), inet_ntoa(), gethostbyname(), and gethostbyaddr(). It takes a single argument that may be either a hostname or an IP address in dotted-decimal notation. It looks up the host and prints all the hostnames and IP addresses associated with it.

Any argument that is a valid dotted-decimal address is assumed to be an IP number, not a hostname.

```
 1: /* lookup.c */
 2:
 3: /* Given either a hostname or IP address on the command line, print
 4:    the canonical hostname for that host and all of the IP numbers
 5:    and hostnames associated with it. */
 6:
 7: #include <netdb.h>               /* for gethostby* */
 8: #include <sys/socket.h>
 9: #include <netinet/in.h>          /* for address structures */
10: #include <arpa/inet.h>           /* for inet_ntoa() */
11: #include <stdio.h>
12:
13: int main(int argc, const char ** argv) {
14:     struct hostent * answer;
15:     struct in_addr address, ** addrptr;
16:     char ** next;
17:
18:     if (argc != 2) {
19:         fprintf(stderr, "only a single argument is supported\n");
20:         return 1;
21:     }
22:
23:     /* If the argument looks like an IP, assume it was one and
24:        perform a reverse name lookup */
25:     if (inet_aton(argv[1], &address))
26:         answer = gethostbyaddr((char *) &address, sizeof(address),
27:                                 AF_INET);
28:     else
29:         answer = gethostbyname(argv[1]);
30:
31:     /* the hostname lookup failed :-( */
```

```
32:        if (!answer) {
33:            herror("error looking up host");
34:            return 1;
35:        }
36:
37:        printf("Canonical hostname: %s\n", answer->h_name);
38:
39:        /* if there are any aliases, print them all out */
40:        if (answer->h_aliases[0]) {
41:            printf("Aliases:");
42:            for (next = answer->h_aliases; *next; next++)
43:                printf(" %s", *next);
44:            printf("\n");
45:        }
46:
47:        /* display all of the IP addresses for this machine */
48:        printf("Addresses:");
49:        for (addrptr = (struct in_addr **) answer->h_addr_list;
50:                    *addrptr; addrptr++)
51:            printf(" %s", inet_ntoa(**addrptr));
52:        printf("\n");
53:
54:        return 0;
55: }
```

Here is what this program looks like when it is run:

```
$ ./lookup ftp.netscape.com
Canonical hostname: ftp25.netscape.com
Aliases: ftp.netscape.com anonftp10.netscape.com
Addresses: 207.200.74.21
```

17.8.4 Looking Up Port Numbers

While getaddrinfo() and getnameinfo() make it easy for application to
convert service names to port numbers at the same time hostname resolution is performed, the older functions for service name lookups are
completely independent of hostname lookups. Service names are accessed
through the getservbyname() function.

```
#include <netdb.h>

struct servent * getservbyname(const char * name,
                               const char * protocol);
```

The first parameter, `name`, is the service name about which the application needs information. The `protocol` parameter specifies the protocol to use. The services database contains information on other protocols (especially UDP); specifying the protocol allows the function to ignore information on other protocols. The `protocol` is usually the string `"tcp"`, although other protocol names, such as `"udp"`, may be used.

`getservbyname()` returns a pointer to a structure that contains information on the queried service. The information may be overwritten by the next call to `getservbyname()`, so any important information should be saved by the application. Here is the information returned by `getservbyname()`:

```
#include <netdb.h>

struct servent {
    char * s_name;       /* service name */
    char ** s_aliases;   /* service aliases */
    int s_port;          /* port number */
    char * s_proto;      /* protocol to use */
}
```

Each service may have multiple names associated with it but only one port number. `s_name` lists the canonical name of the service, `s_port` contains the well-known port number for the service (in network byte order), and `s_proto` is the protocol for the service (such as `"tcp"`). The `s_aliases` member is an array of pointers to aliases for the service, with a `NULL` pointer marking the end of the list.

If the function fails, it returns `NULL` and sets `h_errno`.

Here is an example program that looks up a TCP service specified on the command line and displays the service's canonical name, port number, and all of its aliases:

```
 1: /* services.c */
 2:
```

```
 3: #include <netdb.h>
 4: #include <netinet/in.h>
 5: #include <stdio.h>
 6:
 7: /* display the TCP port number and any aliases for the service
 8:    which is named on the command line */
 9:
10: /* services.c - finds the port number for a service */
11: int main(int argc, const char ** argv) {
12:     struct servent * service;
13:     char ** ptr;
14:
15:     if (argc != 2) {
16:         fprintf(stderr, "only a single argument is supported\n");
17:         return 1;
18:     }
19:
20:     /* look up the service in /etc/services, give an error if
21:        we fail */
22:     service = getservbyname(argv[1], "tcp");
23:     if (!service) {
24:         herror("getservbyname failed");
25:         return 1;
26:     }
27:
28:     printf("service: %s\n", service->s_name);
29:     printf("tcp port: %d\n", ntohs(service->s_port));
30:
31:     /* display any aliases this service has */
32:     if (*service->s_aliases) {
33:         printf("aliases:");
34:         for (ptr = service->s_aliases; *ptr; ptr++)
35:             printf(" %s", *ptr);
36:         printf("\n");
37:     }
38:
39:     return 0;
40: }
```

Here is an example of running the program; notice it can look up services by either their canonical name or an alias:

```
$ ./services http
service: http
tcp port: 80
$ ./services source
service: chargen
tcp port: 19
aliases: ttytst source
```

CHAPTER 18

Time

18.1 Telling Time and Dates

18.1.1 Representing Time

Unix and Linux keep track of time in seconds before or after the **epoch**, which is defined as midnight, January 1, 1970 UTC.[1] Positive time values are after the epoch; negative time values are before the epoch. In order to provide processes with the current time, Linux, like all versions of Unix, provides a system call called `time()`:

```
#include <time.h>
time_t time(time_t *t);
```

`time()` returns the number of seconds since the epoch, and if `t` is non-null, it also fills in `t` with the number of seconds since the epoch.

Some problems require higher resolution. Linux provides another system call, `gettimeofday()`, which provides more information:

```
#include <sys/time.h>
#include <unistd.h>

int gettimeofday(struct timeval *tv, struct timezone *tz);

struct timeval {
    int tv_sec;             /* seconds */
```

---

1. UTC: Universal Coordinated Time, also sometimes improperly referred to as UCT; roughly equivalent to Greenwich Mean Time (GMT) and Zulu. Time zone designations involve technical detail far beyond the scope of this book.

```
    int tv_usec;        /* microseconds */
};

struct timezone {
    int tz_minuteswest; /* minutes west of Greenwich */
    int tz_dsttime;     /* type of dst correction */
};
```

On most platforms, including the i386 platform, Linux is able to provide very accurate time measurements. Industry-standard PCs have a hardware clock that provides microsecond-accurate time information. Alpha and SPARC hardware also provides a high-resolution timer. On some other platforms, however, Linux can keep track of time only within the resolution of the system timer, which is generally set to 100Hz, so the tv_usec member of the timeval structure may be less accurate on those systems.

Five macros are provided in sys/time.h for operating on timeval structures:

timerclear(struct timeval *)
       This clears a timeval structure.

timerisset(struct timeval *)
       This checks to see if a timeval structure has been filled in (that is, if either element is nonzero).

timercmp(struct timeval *t0, struct timeval *t1, operator)
       This allows you to compare two timeval structures in the time domain. It evaluates the logical equivalent of t0 operator t1, if t0 and t1 were arithmetic types. Note that timercmp() does not work for the <= and >= operators. Use !timercmp(t1, t2, >) and !timercmp(t1, t2, <) instead.

timeradd(struct timeval *t0, struct timeval *t1, struct timeval *result)
       Adds t0 to t1 and places the sum in result.

timersub(struct timeval *t0, struct timeval *t1, struct timeval *result)
       Subtracts t1 from t0 and places the difference in result.

A third representation of time, `struct tm`, puts the time in terms that are more human-oriented:

```
struct tm {
{
    int tm_sec;
    int tm_min;
    int tm_hour;
    int tm_mday;
    int tm_mon;
    int tm_year;
    int tm_wday;
    int tm_yday;
    int tm_isdst;
    long int tm_gmtoff;
    const char *tm_zone;
};
```

The first nine elements are standard; the final two are nonstandard but useful when they exist, as they do on Linux systems.

tm_sec	The number of elapsed seconds in the minute. Will be between 0 and 61 (two extra seconds are allocated to deal with leap seconds).
tm_min	The number of elapsed minutes in the hour. Will be between 0 and 59.
tm_hour	The number of elapsed hours in the day. Will be between 0 and 23.
tm_mday	The number of the day of the month. Will be between 1 and 31. This is the only member that will never be 0.
tm_mon	The number of elapsed months in the year. Will be between 0 and 11.
tm_year	The number of elapsed years since 1900.
tm_wday	The number of elapsed days in the week (since Sunday). Will be between 0 and 6.

tm_yday   The number of elapsed days in the year. Will be between 0 and 365.

tm_isdst   Whether some sort of daylight savings time is in effect in the expressed time value in the current time zone, if applicable. tm_isdst will be positive if daylight savings time is in effect, 0 if it is not in effect, and -1 if the system does not know.

tm_gmtoff   This is not portable as it does not exist on all systems. If it exists, it may also be named _ _tm_gmtoff. It specifies seconds east of UTC or negative seconds west of UTC for time zones east of the date line.

tm_zone   This is not portable as it does not exist on all systems. If it exists, it may also be named _ _tm_zone. It holds a name for the current time zone (some time zones may have several names).

Finally, the POSIX.1b real-time processing standard allows even higher resolution than the microsecond resolution available in struct timeval. struct timespec uses nanoseconds instead and provides larger places to put the numbers:

```
struct timespec {
    long int tv_sec;   /* seconds     */
    long int tv_nsec;  /* nanoseconds */
};
```

18.1.2 Converting, Formatting, and Parsing Times

Four functions are available for converting among times expressed in terms of time_t and times expressed in terms of struct tm. Three are standard and are available on all Linux and Unix systems. The fourth, although useful, is not universally available, although it is available on all current Linux systems. A fifth function, which is standard, calculates the difference in seconds between time_t times. (Notice that even the time_t arguments are passed as pointers, not just the struct tm arguments.)

`struct tm * gmtime(const time_t *t)`

> Short for Greenwich Mean Time, `gmtime()` converts a `time_t` value into a `struct tm` that expresses that time in UTC.

`struct tm * localtime(const time_t *t)`

> `localtime()` acts like `gmtime()` except that it creates the `struct tm` expressed in terms of local time. Local time is defined for the whole system by the settings of the zoneinfo files, and that can be overridden by a `TZ` environment variable by users who are working from a different time zone than the one the computer is in.

`time_t mktime(struct tm *tp);`

> `mktime()` converts a `struct tm` to a `time_t`, assuming that the `struct tm` is expressed in terms of local time.

`time_t timegm(struct tm *tp);`

> `timegm()` acts like `mktime()` except that it assumes that the `struct tm` is expressed in terms of UTC. It is not a standard function.

`double difftime(time_t time1, time_t time0);`

> `difftime()` returns a floating-point number representing the difference in time in seconds between two `time_t` values. Although `time_t` is guaranteed to be an arithmetic type, the unit is not specified by ANSI/ISO C; `difftime()` returns the difference in seconds, regardless of the units of `time_t`.

Four more functions are available to convert time between computer-friendly numbers and human-friendly textual representations. Again, the final one is not standard, despite its obvious general usefulness.

`char *asctime(struct tm *tp);`
`char *ctime(time_t *t);`

> `asctime()` and `ctime()` both convert a time value into a standard Unix date string that looks something like this:
>
> `Tue Jun 17 23:17:29 1997`
>
> In both cases, the string is 26 characters long and includes a final newline character and the terminating `'\0'`.

The length of the string may not be guaranteed to be 26 characters in all locales, as it is in the default C locale.

`ctime()` expresses this date in local time. `asctime()` expresses this date in whatever time zone the `struct tm` specifies; if it was created with `gmtime()`, it is in UTC, but if it was created with `localtime()`, it is in local time.

`size_t strftime(char *s, size_t max, char *fmt, struct tm *tp);`
`strftime()` is like `sprintf()` for time. It formats a `struct tm` according to the format `fmt` and places the result in no more than `max` bytes (including the terminating `'\0'`) of the string `s`.

Like `sprintf()`, `strftime()` uses the `%` character to introduce escape sequences into which data is substituted. All of the substituted strings are expressed in terms of the current locale. However, the escape sequences are completely different. In several cases, lowercase letters are used for abbreviations and uppercase letters are used for full names. Unlike `sprintf()`, you do not have the option of using numbers in the middle of an escape sequence to limit the length of the substituted string; `%.6A` is invalid. Like `sprintf()`, `strftime()` returns the number of characters printed into the `s` buffer. If it is equal to `max`, the buffer is not large enough for the current locale; allocate a larger buffer and try again.

`strftime()` uses the same substitutions used by the date program. These definitions of the substitutions are for the default locale and are here to help you identify the type of information they provide; they may be somewhat different in other locales.

`%a` The three-character abbreviation for the name of the weekday.

`%A` The full name of the weekday.

`%b` The three-character abbreviation for the name of the month.

`%B` The full name of the month.

`%c` The preferred local expression of the date and time, as returned by `ctime()` and `asctime()`.

%d	The numeric day of the month, counting from zero.
%H	The hour of the day, in 24-hour time, counting from zero.
%I	The hour of the day, in 12-hour time, counting from zero.
%j	The day of the year, counting from one.
%m	The month of the year, counting from one.
%M	The minute of the hour, counting from zero.
%p	The correct string for the local equivalent of AM or PM.
%S	The second of the minute, counting from zero.
%U	The numeric week of the year, where week one starts on the first Sunday of the year.
%W	The numeric week of the year, where week one starts on the first Monday of the year.
%w	The numeric day of the week, counting from zero.
%x	The preferred local expression of the date only, without the time.
%X	The preferred local expression of the time only, without the date.
%y	The two-digit representation of the year, without the century. (Do not use this—it is a potent source of year-2000 problems.)
%Y	The full four-digit numeric representation of the year.
%Z	The name or standard abbreviation of the time zone.
%%	The literal character %.

```
char *strptime(char *s, char *fmt, struct tm *tp);
```
Like scanf(), strptime() converts a string to a parsed format.
It tries to be liberal in interpreting the s input string according

to the `fmt` format string. It takes the same escape sequences that `strftime()` takes, but for each type of input, it accepts both abbreviations and full names. It does not distinguish between upper and lower case, and it does not recognize `%U` and `%W`.

`strptime()` also provides a few extra escape sequences and interprets a few sequences slightly differently than does `strftime()`. Only the significantly different escape sequences (that is, beyond the changes already mentioned) are documented in this list. Numbers may have leading zeros, but they are not required.

`%h`   Equivalent to `%b` and `%B`.

`%c`   Reads the date and time as printed by `strftime()` with the format string `%x %X`.

`%C`   Reads the date and time as printed by `strftime()` with the format string `%c`.

`%e`   Equivalent to `%d`.

`%D`   Reads the date as printed by `strftime()` with the format string `%m/%d/%y`.

`%k`   Equivalent to `%H`.

`%l`   Equivalent to `%I`.

`%r`   Reads the time as printed by `strftime()` with the format string `%I:%M:%S %p`.

`%R`   Reads the time as printed by `strftime()` with the format string `%H:%M`.

`%T`   Reads the time as printed by `strftime()` with the format string `%H:%M:%S`.

`%y`   Reads the year within the twentieth century. 1900 is added to the value, and only values of 0–99 are allowed.

%Y   Reads the full year. Use this instead of %y if you possibly can, to avoid year-2000 problems.

strptime() returns a pointer to the character in s one character beyond the final character that it reads while parsing.

The strptime() function is, unfortunately, specified neither by ANSI/ISO nor POSIX, which limits its portability.

18.1.3 The Limits of Time

On 32-bit Linux systems, like most Unix systems, time_t is a signed integer 32 bits long. This means that it will overflow Monday, January 18, 2038, at 10:14:07 PM. So Monday, January 18, 2038, 10:14:08 PM will be represented as Friday, December 13th, 3:45:52 PM, 1901. As you can see, Linux did not exhibit a year-2000 problem (as far as the native time libraries are concerned), but it does have a year-2038 problem.

On 64-bit platforms, time_t is instead a 64-bit signed long. This is effectively forever; signed 64-bit time is truly astronomical, as it will not overflow until well after the sun is predicted to envelop the Earth as it becomes a red giant.

To find the beginning of time, the current time, and the end of time for the system you are using, you can build and run this program, daytime.c:

```
 1: /* daytime.c */
 2:
 3: #include <stdio.h>
 4: #include <sys/time.h>
 5: #include <unistd.h>
 6:
 7: int main() {
 8:     struct timeval tv;
 9:     struct timezone tz;
10:     time_t now;
11:     /* beginning_of_time is smallest time_t-sized value */
12:     time_t beginning_of_time = 1L<<(sizeof(time_t)*8 - 1);
13:     /* end_of_time is largest time_t-sized value */
14:     time_t end_of_time = ~beginning_of_time;
```

```
15:
16:     printf("time_t is %d bits long\n\n", sizeof(time_t)*8);
17:
18:     gettimeofday(&tv, &tz);
19:     now = tv.tv_sec;
20:     printf("Current time of day represented as a struct timeval:\n"
21:             "tv.tv_sec = 0x%08x, tv.tv_usec = 0x%08x\n"
22:             "tz.tz_minuteswest = 0x%08x, tz.tz_dsttime = 0x%08x\n\n",
23:             tv.tv_sec, tv.tv_usec, tz.tz_minuteswest, tz.tz_dsttime);
24:
25:     printf("Demonstrating ctime()%s:\n",
26:             sizeof(time_t)*8 <= 32 ? "" :
27:             " (may hang after printing first line; press "
28:             "control-C)");
29:     printf("time is now %s", ctime(&now));
30:     printf("time begins %s", ctime(&beginning_of_time));
31:     printf("time ends %s", ctime(&end_of_time));
32:
33:     exit (0);
34: }
```

Unfortunately, the ctime() function is iterative by nature, which means that it (for all practical purposes) never terminates on 64-bit systems for astronomical dates like the 64-bit beginning and end of time. Use Control-C to terminate the program when you become tired of waiting for it to complete.

18.2 Using Timers

A timer is simply a way of scheduling an event to happen at some point in the future. Instead of looping around, looking at the current time, and wasting CPU cycles, a program can ask the kernel to notify it when at least a certain amount of time has passed.

There are two ways to use timers: synchronously and asynchronously. The only way to use a timer synchronously is to wait for the timer to expire—sleeping. Using a timer asynchronously, like every other asynchronous facility, involves signals. What may be surprising is that using a timer synchronously may also involve signals.

18.2.1 Sleeping

A process requesting that it not be scheduled for at least a certain amount of time is called *sleeping*. Four functions are available for sleeping; each measures time in different units. They also have slightly different behavior and interact with other parts of the system differently.

`unsigned int sleep(unsigned int seconds);`
> `sleep()` causes the current process to sleep at least `seconds` seconds *or* until a signal that the process does not ignore is received by the process. On most platforms, `sleep()` is implemented in terms of the `SIGALRM` signal, and therefore it does not mix well with using the `alarm()` system call, creating a `SIGALRM` handler, ignoring the `SIGALRM` signal, or using `ITIMER_REAL` interval timers (described later), which share the same timer and signal.
>
> If `sleep()` does not sleep for the full time allotted, it returns the number of seconds left to sleep. If it has slept at least as long as requested, it returns zero.

`void usleep(unsigned long usec);`
> `usleep()` causes the current process to sleep at least `usec` microseconds. No signals are used. On most platforms, `usleep()` is implemented via `select()`.

`int select(0, NULL, NULL, NULL, struct timeval tv);`
> `select()`, documented in Chapter 13, provides a portable way to sleep for a precise amount of time. Simply fill in the `struct timeval` with the minimum amount of time you wish to wait, and do not wait for any events to occur.

`int nanosleep(struct timespec *req, struct timespec *rem);`
> `nanosleep()` causes the current process to sleep at least the amount of time specified in `req` (see page 484 for `timespec`), unless a signal is received by the process. If `nanosleep()` terminates early due to a received signal, it returns -1 and sets `errno` to `EINTR` and, if `rem` is not `NULL`, sets `rem` to represent the amount of time remaining in the sleep period.
>
> `nanosleep()` is currently the least portable of these functions, because it was specified as part of the POSIX.1b (previously called

POSIX.4) real-time specification, which is not implemented on all versions of Unix. However, all new Unix implementations implement it, because the POSIX.1b functions are now a standard part of the Single Unix Specification.

Not all platforms that provide the `nanosleep()` function provide high accuracy, but Linux, like other real-time operating systems, attempts to honor short waits with extreme accuracy for real-time processes. See *Programming for the Real World* [Gallmeister, 1995] for more information on real-time programming.

18.2.2 Interval Timers

Interval timers, once enabled, continually deliver signals to a process on a regular basis. Exactly what *regular* means depends on which interval timer you use. Each process has three interval timers associated with it.

ITIMER_REAL

Tracks time in terms of the clock on the wall—real time, regardless of whether the process is executing—and delivers a `SIGALRM` signal. It conflicts with the `alarm()` system call, which is used by the `sleep()` function. Use neither `alarm()` nor `sleep()` if you have a real itimer active.

ITIMER_VIRTUAL

Counts time only when the process is executing—excluding any system calls the process makes—and delivers a `SIGVTALRM` signal.

ITIMER_PROF

Counts time when the process is executing—including the time the kernel spends executing system calls on the behalf of the process, but not including any time spent processing interrupts on behalf of the process—and delivers a `SIGPROF` signal. Accounting for time spent processing interrupts would be so expensive that it would change the timings.

The combination of `ITIMER_VIRTUAL` and `ITIMER_PROF` is often used for profiling code.

Each of these timers generates its associated signal within one system clock tick (normally 1–10 milliseconds) of the timer expiring. If the process is currently running when the signal is generated, it is delivered immediately; otherwise, it is delivered soon afterward, depending on system load. Since ITIMER_VIRTUAL is tracked only when the process is running, it is always delivered immediately.

Use a struct itimerval to query and set itimers:

```
struct itimerval {
    struct timeval it_interval;
    struct timeval it_value;
};
```

The it_value member is the amount of time left until the next signal is sent. The it_interval member is the amount of time between signals; it_value is set to this value each time the timer goes off.

There are two system calls for dealing with interval timers. Both take a which argument that specifies which timer to manipulate.

```
int getitimer(int which, struct itimerval *val);
```
Fills in val with the current state of the which timer.

```
  int setitimer(int which, struct itimerval *new,
                            struct itimerval *old);
```
Sets the which timer to new and fills in old with the previous setting if it is non-NULL.

Setting a timer's it_value to zero immediately disables it; the timer will no longer be called. Setting a timer's it_interval to zero disables it after the next time the timer triggers.

In the following example, a parent process starts a child process, runs a one-second ITIMER_REAL timer, sleeps for 10 seconds, and then kills the child process:

```
1: /* itimer.c */
2:
3: #include <stdio.h>
4: #include <stdlib.h>
```

```
 5: #include <sys/wait.h>
 6: #include <unistd.h>
 7: #include <string.h>
 8: #include <signal.h>
 9: #include <sys/time.h>
10:
11:
12: void catch_signal (int ignored) {
13:     static int iteration=0;
14:
15:     printf("caught interval timer signal, iteration %d\n",
16:             iteration++);
17: }
18:
19: pid_t start_timer (int interval) {
20:     pid_t child;
21:     struct itimerval it;
22:     struct sigaction sa;
23:
24:     if (!(child = fork())) {
25:         memset(&sa, 0, sizeof(sa));
26:         sa.sa_handler = catch_signal;
27:         sigemptyset(&sa.sa_mask);
28:         sa.sa_flags = SA_RESTART;
29:
30:         sigaction(SIGALRM, &sa, NULL);
31:
32:         memset(&it, 0, sizeof(it));
33:         it.it_interval.tv_sec = interval;
34:         it.it_value.tv_sec = interval;
35:         setitimer(ITIMER_REAL, &it, NULL);
36:
37:         while (1) pause();
38:     }
39:
40:     return child;
41: }
42:
43: void stop_timer (pid_t child) {
44:     kill (child, SIGTERM);
45: }
```

```
46:
47: int main (int argc, const char **argv) {
48:     pid_t timer = 0;
49:
50:     printf("Demonstrating itimers for 10 seconds, "
51:             "please wait...\n");
52:     timer = start_timer(1);
53:     sleep(10);
54:     stop_timer(timer);
55:     printf("Done.\n");
56:
57:     return 0;
58: }
```

CHAPTER 19

Random Numbers

The word *random* means different things to different programmers at different times. For most applications, the pseudo-random numbers provided by the C library are quite sufficient. Because they allow you to reproduce conditions if necessary (perhaps for debugging purposes), they are preferable to truly random numbers.

But certain applications, including cryptography, require truly random numbers for best results. The Linux kernel samples events from the unpredictable outside world to provide cryptographically strong random numbers.

Computers are predictable. Most of the tasks that we want computers to do are tasks in which predictability is the most important thing. Even when bugs appear in your program, you want them to appear predictably so that you can find them and squash them.

19.1   Pseudo-Random Numbers

Sometimes you want to provide the appearance of unpredictability, however. The C library contains functions for generating a well-respected series of pseudo-random numbers. These functions are easy to use and are the same on every Unix platform. Here is an example of how these functions are typically used:

```
#include <stdlib.h>
#include <time.h>...
    srand(time(NULL) + getpid());
    for (...; ...; ...) {
        do_something(rand());
    }
```

It is common to *seed* the pseudo-random number generator with the current date, as returned by the time() function. time() returns the number of seconds since January 1, 1970, so the seed changes once per second and is therefore unique over a long time span (approximately 49,710 days on a 32-bit computer). If you want to keep a program from acting the same for two people who start it in the same second, add the current process ID to the time.

The numbers subsequently returned by the rand() function satisfy the mathematical property of random distribution but not of high entropy: For large enough samples, they are relatively well distributed within the space of possible 32-bit numbers, but it is possible to infer other numbers given one number. This means that these kinds of pseudo-random numbers are useful for almost every application that requests a random distribution of numbers. This includes games, Monte Carlo methods (here it is important to save the seed so that you or others can verify your results), and protocols that handle collision by inserting random delays.

Note that for debugging purposes, you may want to save the seed you used when you called srand() so that if a bug occurs that relies on data produced by the rand() function, you can use the same seed to produce the same stream of random numbers to reproduce the bug.

19.2 Cryptography and Random Numbers

The authors of this book are not cryptography experts. Writing cryptographic software is a particularly subtle pursuit, and anyone who attempts it without proper research will fail to write robust and secure cryptographic applications. This chapter has two, and only two, purposes:

- To convince people who are not experts in cryptography that this is an area best left to experts.

- To let experts in cryptography know that a particularly useful tool is available for their use.

If you are not an expert in cryptography but need to use it, we suggest *Applied Cryptography* [Schneier, 1996] as an excellent overview and introduction to the topic.

Cryptography is generally no different from other software in its predictability requirements; when you give a program the key to decrypt data, you want it to decrypt the data the same way every time. There is one exception: choosing a truly random key. No matter how sophisticated an encryption algorithm is, it is worthless if an attacker can guess what key was used to generate the data. For example, many encrypted messages include some sort of timestamp that tells approximately when they were created. If you then use the current time to seed a common pseudo-random number generator, it would not take long for the attacker to decrypt the data by simply using the time when the message was created to seed common pseudo-random number generators and try keys based on those numbers.

It does not work much better to ask a human to provide a key. In general, people pick keys that are hardly random. Their keys are generally related to natural language text, which is highly predictable in terms of information theory. Natural language is said to have *low entropy*; a truly random key has *high entropy*.

If every computer had a small radiation source, the unpredictable amount of time between the particles emitted by decaying atoms could be used to produce truly random numbers, numbers that could not be predicted based on any other information. No other known data would be sufficient to predict which numbers might have been created by the emission of radiation.

Since most computers are not equipped with such devices, Linux improvises. Ted Ts'o wrote code that examines timings of external events (mouse clicks, keyboard keypresses, and so on) and extracts information from them, storing it in an *entropy pool*. There are components of human (and other external) interaction with the computer that are essentially random. The code that fills the entropy pool attempts to distinguish the amount of entropy that is being added, which allows the programmer to determine the amount of entropy used to generate random information. Recently, many computers have started to provide hardware-based sources of cryptographically random data; on Linux, this random data is fed into the system entropy pool as needed so that all Linux programs can use the same interface regardless of the hardware they use.

Programmers who need random numbers based on unpredictable events can take random numbers from the entropy pool through one of two similar devices: /dev/random and /dev/urandom. The /dev/random device returns only as many bytes of random data as the device currently estimates are in the entropy pool. The /dev/urandom device does not try to offer any guarantees about the amount of entropy in the information it returns; it generates as much random data as you want, based on the entropy pool. Whenever either device is read, it subtracts the number of bytes read from the entropy count.

When you read data from either device, it does not simply return the data that is in the entropy pool. It returns data stirred by a one-way hash algorithm that does not reveal the state of the pool in its output.

- Use neither /dev/random nor /dev/urandom for data you want to replicate. They are particularly useless sources of data for Monte Carlo methods; even 1,2...*n-1,n* would be better; it is at least a repeatable series.

- If you need only a certain amount of entropy, but need more raw data than entropy, you can read a small amount of data from one of the random devices (depending on what quality you need guaranteed) and then extend it with a hash function such as MD5 or SHA.

The source code to the random driver, drivers/char/random.c, includes considerable documentation on the details. If you do intend to write cryptographic code that uses the data provided by one of the interfaces, we recommend that you read that documentation first.

CHAPTER 20

Programming Virtual Consoles

The Linux virtual console programming interface is modeled on the one provided with some versions of UNIX. It is not a complete reimplementation (although it is complete enough for source code compatibility with almost all programs), and it provides several valuable extensions.

Linux can multiplex multiple terminal sessions over one screen and one keyboard. Special key sequences allow the user to control which terminal session is currently being displayed. Each of these login sessions has its own keyboard settings (such as whether the Caps Lock key is engaged), terminal settings (such as what the terminal size is, whether the screen is in graphics mode, and what the fonts are), and device entries (such as /dev/tty1, /dev/vcs1, and /dev/vcsa1).

The keyboard and terminal settings together make up **virtual consoles** (VCs), so called because of their similarity to virtual memory, in which the system uses disk space to provide more usable memory than is physically present in the machine.

Unless you wish to manage or manipulate VCs, you can skip this chapter. A few programming libraries manage VCs for you, but you may still need to know what they are doing behind your back, so that you work with them rather than against them.

For instance, svgalib, a library for using graphics on several types of graphics controllers, has functions that do most of the basic VC manipulation for you. It still requires that you avoid writing random bits to the graphics controller while it is in text mode; doing so would scramble the screen. The current lack of documentation for svgalib makes it even more important that you know what is going on underneath.[1]

VCs provide users with many options, but the majority of users ignore the options and simply use the X Window System. Those users who do use VCs can

- Choose a separate font for each VC

- Choose a separate terminal size for each VC

- Choose key mappings (more on these later) for *all* VCs

- Choose a different keystroke encoding for *all* VCs

- Switch VCs on command with user-specifiable keystrokes

The Linux Documentation Project (LDP) has documents explaining how the user can use programs that already exist in order to take advantage of these capabilities. Your goal is different—you wish to program VCs, not just use them. Although font setting and keyboard settings are well encapsulated in utilities[2] that you can simply call from within your programs, there are cases in which those external programs are insufficient.

20.1 Getting Started

Here is a list of some of the things that you can do with VCs. Some are specific to an individual VC (usually, the currently active VC); some apply to all VCs in use:

---

1. We do not recommend using svgalib to do graphics programming. Many books document programming for the X Window System, and X provides a far saner, safer, and portable method of graphics programming. On the other hand, if you actually want to program the X Window server, you may need to program VCs. You have then come full circle and still need to read this chapter.
2. Read the man pages for the loadkeys, dumpkeys, keytables, setfont, and mapscrn utilities.

- Find the current VC

- Initiate a VC switch

- Refuse or allow a switch to or from a VC

- Disable VC switching completely

- Find an unused VC

- Allocate and deallocate VCs dynamically in the kernel

- Make simple sounds

In all cases, the same preparation is needed. You will use `ioctl()` commands on /dev/tty—so you need to start out by including the header files that define the `ioctl()` arguments:

```
#include <signal.h>
#include <sys/ioctl.h>
#include <sys/vt.h>
#include <sys/kd.h>
#include <sys/param.h>
```

Then open /dev/tty:

```
if ((fd = open("/dev/tty", O_RDWR)) < 0) {
    perror("myapp: could not open /dev/tty");
    exit (1);
}
```

If you find that you cannot open /dev/tty, you probably have a permission problem: /dev/tty should be readable and writable by everyone.

Note that in addition to ioctl.h, there are two main header files that define the `ioctl()` calls that manipulate VCs. vt.h defines calls that start with VT and control the virtual terminal, or screen, part of the virtual consoles. kd.h defines calls that start with KD and that control the keyboard and fonts. You can ignore most of the contents of kd.h because the functionality it covers is so nicely encapsulated in utility programs, but it is useful for making the console beep at controlled frequencies.

Those two main header files also define structures that are used with the ioctl()s.

You use the vt_mode structure to find and change the current VC:

```
struct vt_mode {
    char mode;
    char waitv;
    short relsig;
    short acqsig;
    short frsig;
};
```

- mode is either VT_AUTO, which tells the kernel to switch VCs automatically when keys are pressed or when a program sends a request to the kernel to change VCs, or VT_PROCESS, which tells the kernel to ask before switching.

- waitv is unused, but should be set to one for SVR4 compatibility.

- relsig names a signal that the kernel should raise to request that the process release the VC.

- acqsig names a signal that the kernel should raise to alert the process that it has acquired the VC.

- frsig is unused and should be set to zero for SVR4 compatibility.

```
struct vt_stat {
    unsigned short v_active;
    unsigned short v_signal;
    unsigned short v_state;
};
```

- v_active holds the number of the currently active VC.

- v_signal is not implemented.

- v_state holds a bitmask telling which of the *first 16* VCs are currently open (Linux supports up to 63). There is rarely any reason to consult this bitmask under Linux; you should probably ignore it because it is not sufficiently large to contain complete information, and because in most cases you need to know only the number of some open VC, which you can get with VT_OPENQRY (see page 507).

20.2 Beeping

Last things first: Causing the console to beep for a certain amount of time at a certain frequency is fairly simple. There are two ways to make the console beep. The first is to turn on or off a constant tone. KIOCSOUND turns off the sound if its argument is zero; if its argument is nonzero, it specifies the frequency in a rather bizarre way, as this code shows:

```
void turn_tone_on(int fd, int hertz) {
    ioctl(fd, KIOCSOUND, 1193180/hertz)
}
void turn_tone_off(int fd) {
    ioctl(fd, KIOCSOUND, 0)
}
```

The second way to cause the console to beep is to use the KDMKTONE ioctl to turn on a tone for a period specified in **jiffies**, which are ticks of the system clock. Unfortunately, the time per tick varies from architecture to architecture; the HZ macro defined by sys/param.h gives ticks per second. The tone() function below shows how to derive the number of ticks from hundredths of a second and the value of HZ:[3]

---

3. This interface is flawed; it should have been specified in some constant fraction of a second and converted. HZ is no longer constant even on a particular platform, but at least for the Intel i86 architecture, Linus Torvalds has decreed that all interfaces specified in regard to HZ shall present a synthetic 100Hz interface. It is possible that in the future, there will be no periodic system clock, in which case jiffies will become a completely synthetic concept.

```
#include <sys/param.h>
void tone(int fd, int hertz, int hundredths) {
    unsigned int ticks = hundredths * HZ / 100;

    /* ticks & 0xffff will not work if ticks == 0xf0000
     * need to round off to highest legal value instead */
    if (ticks > 0xffff) ticks = 0xffff;
    /* now the other rounding error */
    if (hundredths && ticks == 0) ticks = 1;
    ioctl(fd, KDMKTONE, (ticks<<16 | (1193180/hertz)));
}
```

20.3   Determining Whether the Terminal Is a VC

To find out whether the current terminal is a VC, you can open /dev/tty
and use VT_GETMODE to query the mode:

```
struct vt_mode vtmode;

fd = open("/dev/tty", O_RDWR);
retval = ioctl(fd, VT_GETMODE, &vtmode);
if (retval < 0) {
    /* This terminal is not a VC; take appropriate action */
}
```

20.4   Finding the Current VC

To find the number of the current VC, use the VT_GETSTATE ioctl, which
takes a pointer to a struct vt_stat and returns the number of the current
VC in the v_active element:

```
unsigned short get_current_vc(int fd) {
    struct vt_stat vs;

    ioctl(fd, VT_GETSTATE, &vs);
    return (vs.v_active);
}
```

To locate the correct device entry for the current VC, use

```
sprintf(ttyname, "/dev/tty%d", get_current_vc(fd));
```

20.5 Managing VC Switching

To find an unused VC (that is, a VC currently referenced by no processes'
open file descriptors) to activate, use the VT_OPENQRY ioctl:

```
retcode = ioctl(fd, VT_OPENQRY, &vtnum);
if ((retcode < 0) || (vtnum == -1)) {
    perror("myapp: no available virtual terminals");
    /* take appropriate action /*
}
```

If fewer than 63 VCs are in use and all the currently allocated VCs are in
use, a new VC is allocated dynamically by the kernel.[4]

To trigger a switch to another VC (perhaps the available one that you just
found), use the VT_ACTIVATE ioctl. Use the VT_WAITACTIVE ioctl if you wish
to wait for the VC to become active. Changing VCs can take some time—
possibly several seconds—because the console to which you are switching
may be in graphical mode and the contents of the screen may have to be
reconstructed from memory, fetched from swap, or rebuilt in some other
time-consuming manner.[5]

```
ioctl(fd, VT_ACTIVATE, vtnum);
ioctl(fd, VT_WAITACTIVE, vtnum);
```

---

4. Most other systems with virtual consoles or virtual terminals do not dynamically
   allocate them.
5. Certain systems (but not Linux) initiate a switch automatically if one is not in
   progress and VT_WAITACTIVE is called.

To exercise control over when VC switches take place, or simply to be notified of such switches, you must provide reliable signal handlers with sigaction, as discussed in Chapter 12. We use SIGUSR1 and SIGUSR2 here; if you prefer, you can reuse almost any other two signals that you do not intend to use otherwise, such as SIGPROF or SIGURG. Just make sure that the signals you choose meet the following criteria:

- They are not needed for other system functions, especially signals that cannot be trapped or ignored.

- They are not used elsewhere in your application for other purposes.

- They are not the same signal number with two different names, such as SIGPOLL and SIGIO (see the definitions in /usr/include/asm/signal.h, or restrict yourself to signals from Table 12.1 on page 217).

```
void relsig (int signo) {
    /* take appropriate action to release VC */
}
void acqsig (int signo) {
    /* take appropriate action to acquire VC */
}

void setup_signals(void) {
    struct sigaction sact;

    /* Do not mask any signals while these
     * handlers are being called. */
    sigemptyset(&sact.sa_mask);
    /* You may wish to add calls to sigaddset()
     * here if there are signals that you wish to mask
     * during VC switching. */
    sact.flags = 0;
    sact.sa_handler = relsig;
    sigaction(SIGUSR1, &sact, NULL);
    sact.sa_handler = acqsig;
    sigaction(SIGUSR2, &sact, NULL);
}
```

You then need to change the VC mode from VT_AUTO (the default) to VT_PROCESS, while telling the VC about your signal handlers by setting relsig and acqsig:

```
void control_vc_switching(int fd) {
    struct vt_mode vtmode;

    vtmode.mode = VT_PROCESS;
    vtmode.waitv = 1;
    vtmode.relsig = SIGUSR1;
    vtmode.acqsig = SIGUSR2;
    vtmode.frsig = 0;
    ioctl(fd, VT_SETMODE, &vtmode);
}
```

The signal handlers that are called when a VC is in VT_PROCESS mode do not have to agree to the switch. More precisely, the relsig handler may refuse to allow the VC switch to take place. The acqsig handler usually manages the process of taking over the console, but it could conceivably initiate a switch to yet another VC. Be careful in coding your signal handlers not to call any nonreentrant library functions that cannot be called from a signal handler. POSIX.1 specifies that the functions listed in Table 12.2 are reentrant; you should consider all others nonreentrant, especially if you wish to write a portable program. Note in particular that malloc() and printf() are nonreentrant.

Here are examples of relsig() and acqsig() functions that do useful work. Note that, for the relsig() function, calling VT_RELDISP is required, but for the acqsig() function, calling VT_RELDISP is recommended only for the sake of portability.

```
void relsig (int signo) {
    if (change_vc_ok()) {
        /* VC switch allowed */
        save_state();
        ioctl(fd, VT_RELDISP, 1);
    } else {
        /* VC switch disallowed */
        ioctl(fd, VT_RELDISP, 0);
    }
}
```

```
void acqsig (int signo) {
    restore_state();
    ioctl(fd, VT_RELDISP, VT_ACKACQ);
}
```

It is up to you to implement the change_vc_ok(), save_state(), and restore_state() code.

VCs are allocated dynamically when they are opened, but they are *not* reaped automatically when they are closed. To reap the kernel memory used to store the state of a VC, you need to call an ioctl:

```
ioctl(fd, VT_DISALLOCATE, vtnum);
```

You can disable and reenable VC switching completely with a few simple ioctls:

```
void disallow_vc_switch(int fd) {
    ioctl(fd, VT_LOCKSWITCH, 0);
}
void allow_vc_switch(int fd) {
    ioctl(fd, VT_UNLOCKSWITCH, 0);
}
```

20.6   Example: The open Command

Here is sample code to find an unused VC, to run a shell on it, to wait for the shell to exit, and to switch back and deallocate the VC when the program exits. The open program, which is distributed with Linux, does the same, but it has more options and error checking, and is thus more robust. Although this version works, it is hardly friendly, robust, or secure.

```
1: /* minopen.c */
2:
3: #include <stdio.h>
4: #include <unistd.h>
5: #include <stdlib.h>
6: #include <signal.h>
7: #include <fcntl.h>
```

```
 8: #include <sys/ioctl.h>
 9: #include <sys/vt.h>
10: #include <sys/stat.h>
11: #include <sys/types.h>
12: #include <sys/wait.h>
13:
14: int main (int argc, const char **argv) {
15:     int vtnum;
16:     int vtfd;
17:     struct vt_stat vtstat;
18:     char device[32];
19:     int child;
20:
21:     vtfd = open("/dev/tty", O_RDWR, 0);
22:     if (vtfd < 0) {
23:         perror("minopen: could not open /dev/tty");
24:         exit (1);
25:     }
26:     if (ioctl(vtfd, VT_GETSTATE, &vtstat) < 0) {
27:         perror("minopen: tty is not virtual console");
28:         exit (1);
29:     }
30:     if (ioctl(vtfd, VT_OPENQRY, &vtnum) < 0) {
31:         perror("minopen: no free virtual consoles");
32:         exit (1);
33:     }
34:     sprintf(device, "/dev/tty%d", vtnum);
35:     if (access(device, (W_OK|R_OK)) < 0) {
36:         perror("minopen: insufficient permission on tty");
37:         exit (1);
38:     }
39:     child = fork();
40:     if (child == 0) {
41:         ioctl(vtfd, VT_ACTIVATE, vtnum);
42:         ioctl(vtfd, VT_WAITACTIVE, vtnum);
43:         setsid();
44:         close (0); close (1); close (2);
45:         close (vtfd);
46:         vtfd = open(device, O_RDWR, 0); dup(vtfd); dup(vtfd);
47:         execlp("/bin/bash", "bash", NULL);
48:     }
```

```
49:     wait (&child);
50:     ioctl(vtfd, VT_ACTIVATE, vtstat.v_active);
51:     ioctl(vtfd, VT_WAITACTIVE, vtstat.v_active);
52:     ioctl(vtfd, VT_DISALLOCATE, vtnum);
53:     exit(0);
54: }
```

CHAPTER 21

The Linux Console

The Linux console normally imitates a serial terminal. By writing special character sequences to the console device, you control all aspects of the screen presentation. You will usually use S-Lang, curses, or some other screen-drawing library to draw to the screen; they use these escape sequences. The console can also be read and modified through an alternative full-screen interface, which is particularly useful for some specialized programs.

DOS programmers introduced for the first time to Linux programming often are dismayed to find that writing characters to the screen is not a simple matter of initializing a pointer to the address of the screen in memory and writing blindly through it. Some complain loudly about this "backwards" system that forces them to pretend that they are writing to a serial terminal, writing **escape sequences** in between the characters that are written to the screen to control cursor movement, color, screen clearing, and so on.

There are several good reasons to treat the console as a fancy serial terminal. Not the least is that when the program *is* being run on a serial terminal, it still works. More important—in these Internet-conscious times—the program runs correctly across networks and—in these GUI-conscious times—the program runs correctly in a terminal emulator window under X or any other GUI. Furthermore, programs that are run remotely, either via a network or a serial connection, display properly on your console.

Furthermore, you will find that the escape codes are a reasonable low-level interface to the screen, and they are a good base on which to build higher-level primitives, such as curses, documented in *Programming with curses* [Strang, 1991A]. This is no accident; serial terminals are a venerable technology, fine-tuned over the years in response to programmers' real needs. The Linux console is based on the most popular family of serial terminals, the descendants of the DEC VT100.

Most escape sequences use the ANSI escape character, which has no convenient printed representation. We follow the termcap and terminfo libraries in using `^[` to denote the ANSI escape character; be aware when reading them that they sometimes refer to the same character as `\E`. As elsewhere in this book, as well as in termcap and terminfo, `^C` indicates the Control-C character.

21.1 Capability Databases

The actions controlled by these escape sequences are often called **capabilities**. Some escape sequences are shared among many terminals, and many of those sequences are specified in the ANSI X3.64-1979 standard. Nearly all color-capable terminals use the same sequences to choose colors to display. However, many terminals have wildly different escape sequences. For instance, on a Wyse 30 terminal, pressing F1 sends the sequence `^A@\r`, whereas pressing F1 on your Linux console sends the sequence `^[[[A`. Similarly, to move the cursor up on a Wyse 30, you send it a `^K` character; to move the cursor up on the Linux console, send the `^[[A` sequence. To write a program that can work on either terminal, you clearly need a way to abstract these differences, which would allow you to program with the capabilities rather than the raw character sequences.

The most common programming library that provides this abstraction is called **curses**,[1] documented in *Programming with curses* [Strang, 1991A]. It has two important conceptual levels. The first level provides functions that (generally speaking) send one escape sequence to accomplish one action, such as move the cursor up, move it down, scroll the screen, and so on. The second level provides a concept of "windows": independent screen areas that can be manipulated separately, with curses quietly figuring out the shortest character sequences to send to effect the changes you request.

---

1. The curses library is defined by X/Open. The implementation included in Linux is currently base-level conformant with X/Open XSI Curses.

The curses library determines which sequences to send to the terminal by consulting a database that, for each terminal, maps capability names to the strings that need to be sent.

Linux, like all modern Unix systems, provides two databases that describe terminals in terms of the capabilities they possess and which escape sequences map to which capabilities. The older database is called **termcap** (short for *terminal capabilities*) and is kept in one large ASCII flat file called /etc/termcap. This file has become unwieldy; it has grown to approximately half a megabyte. The newer database is called **terminfo** (short for *terminal information*) and is kept in many binary files, one per terminal, normally in subdirectories of the /usr/lib/terminfo directory.

Within each database, the capability information for each terminal is indexed by one or more unique names. Both databases use the same name for the same terminal. For instance, the Linux console is called linux in both termcap and terminfo. You tell programs which terminal entry to use by setting the TERM environment variable. When writing programs that use termcap and terminfo, you rarely need to look at the TERM environment variable; usually, the low-level libraries for accessing the termcap or terminfo databases automatically take care of that.

However, if you wish to do Linux-specific optimizations, especially if you want to use some of Linux's unusual capabilities that are not described in the capability databases, you can check the TERM environment variable with code like this:

```
if (!strcmp("linux", getenv("TERM"))) {
    /* should be a Linux console */
} else {
    /* handle as a normal serial terminal */
}
```

Also, if you wish to write programs in programming languages without easy access to curses or some other terminal abstraction library, you may find it convenient to use this documentation.

Of course, that your terminal type is linux does not guarantee that your program is running on a local terminal. If the terminal type is linux, you know you have access to the escape sequences documented in this chapter, but you do not know if you have access to the vcs devices (documented later in this chapter) or ioctl()s. POSIX specifies a ttyname() function that you can use to find the name of the device file for the controlling terminal. On a Linux system, the virtual consoles are named /dev/tty*n* for *n* between 1 and 63 (/dev/tty0 is always the current console).

Complete documentation for the termcap and terminfo systems is available in *termcap & terminfo* [Strang, 1991B]. Eric Raymond currently maintains the termcap and terminfo databases, which he makes available via the Web at http://www.ccil.org/~esr/terminfo/ The source code to ncurses (new curses, the implementation of curses used on Linux) includes an introduction to curses programming in the misc/ncurses-intro.html file.

21.2   Glyphs, Characters, and Maps

When you write a character to any terminal, several steps of translation may happen. The value written to the terminal is the character number, or character code. That character code is not enough to determine what to display on the screen, however. The shape depends on what font is being used. The character code 97 may be printed as an a in a font designed for rendering Latin-based languages, but might be rendered as an   in a font designed for rendering Greek or mathematics. The shape that is displayed is called a **glyph**. The translation from character codes to glyphs is called a map.

21.3   Linux Console Capabilities

The Linux console,[2] like most terminals, is **modal**: Its response to data depends on what mode it is in. By default, it prints on the screen the characters you send to it unless it receives an escape or control character. A **control character** simply causes some control action to be taken, but the next character is read normally; there is no change in processing mode. An **escape character** signals the beginning of an escape sequence and changes the processing mode to escape mode.

---

2. This description owes a considerable amount of organization to an excellent usenet post to the comp.os.linux.announce newsgroup by Peter Jones on September 30, 1995.

For example, consider the following C string:

```
"this is a line\na \033[1mbold\033[0m word\n"
```

The console processes the string in the following sequence:

1. Starting from the current cursor position, the console prints the words "this is a line".

2. It encounters the linefeed (\n) control character, so (because Linux and Unix traditionally operate in a mode in which a linefeed signals a carriage return, as well) it moves the cursor to the beginning of the next line, scrolling the whole display up one line if the cursor was already on the bottom line.

3. It displays the string "a " at the beginning of that line.

4. It encounters the escape character, "\033", and moves into escape mode.

5. It reads the "[" character, and moves into **Command Sequence Introduction** (CSI) mode.

6. In CSI mode, it reads a series of ASCII-coded decimal numbers separated by "; ", which are called parameters, until a letter is encountered. The letter determines what action to take, modified by the data in the parameters. In this case, there is one parameter, "1", and the letter "m" means that the parameter is used to determine *character rendition*; the "1" sets the bold attribute on.

7. It prints the string "bold" in a bold rendition.

8. Another character rendition sequence follows, which resets all attributes to their default, so it prints " word" in a normal rendition.

9. Finally, it encounters and processes another newline.

So, assuming that the cursor was at the beginning of a line to start with, the output from the entire string will look something like this:

```
this is a line
a bold word
```

21.3.1 Control Characters

The console reads control characters immediately, acts on them, and then continues to read characters in normal mode.

In termcap and terminfo files and documentation, control characters are represented by ^c. We use that convention often in this book, because it will be more generally useful to you than octal C escape sequences. To find the numeric value of a control character, some systems provide a CTRL() macro in <termios.h>, but it is not standard on all systems. Instead, we provide our own version, CTRLCHAR():

```
#define CTRLCHAR(ch) ((ch)&0x1F)
```

It is used like this:

```
if (c == CTRLCHAR('C')) {
    /* control-C was pressed */
}
```

The control characters understood by the Linux console are described in Table 21.1. The ^? character is actually '?'+0100, not '?'-0100, so it is not really a control-question-mark, but ^? is the standard name for it anyway. Its value is 0177 (octal), 127 (decimal), 7F (hexadecimal). You will not be able to use the CTRL macro just described to test for it. Instead, use the numeric value 127.

Note that the effect of some of these codes depends on the tty settings. Although the console itself is precisely documented here, the tty settings may alter what characters are sent. For instance, sending a ^J (LF) usually causes the tty layer also to send a ^M (CR), and ^? (DEL) can be set to send ^H (BS) instead.

The ALT-^[character is not an ASCII character at all. It is an ESC character with the eighth bit set—ASCII specifies only 7-bit characters. You can use it as a shortcut for entering the CSI sequence, but we recommend that you avoid it because it requires an 8-bit-clean communications link, which might keep your program from running remotely on another Linux system connected, perhaps, by a serial link that transmits only seven bits out of every byte.

Table 21.1 Console Control Characters

Control Character	ASCII Name	Description
^G	BEL	Sounds a tone
^H	BS	Moves cursor to previous character without over-writing it if the cursor is not in the first column already
^I	HT	Horizontal tab; moves cursor to next tab stop
^J	LF	Line feed; moves cursor to next line, scrolls scrolling region if already at the bottom of the scrolling region
^K	VT	Vertical tab; treated like a line feed
^L	FF	Form feed; treated like a line feed
^M	CR	Carriage return; moves cursor to beginning of current line
^N	SO	Shift out; use alternate (G1) character set to display glyphs, display glyphs for control characters
^O	SI	Shift in; use normal (G0) character set to display glyphs, do not display glyphs for control characters
^X	CAN	Cancels any escape sequence in progress
^Z	SUB	Cancels any escape sequence in progress
^[	ESC	ESCape; begins an escape sequence
^?	DEL	Ignored
ALT-^[	n/a	Introduces a command sequence, described later

For more information on the ASCII characters, see the ascii(7) online manual page. Similarly, the iso_8859_1(7) manual page covers the 8-bit ISO Latin 1 character set (more properly, ISO 8859 Latin Alphabet number 1); this newer standard is becoming the de facto replacement for ASCII, which is now officially called ISO 646-IRV.

21.3.2 Escape Sequences

There are several distinct types of escape sequences. The simplest type of escape sequence consists of the escape character (^[) followed by a single command character. (Although the escape character is represented in C strings as \033, it is represented as ^[in termcap and terminfo files and documentation.) Five of those single command characters preface more complex escape sequences called *command sequences,* and the rest cause the

Table 21.2 Console Control Sequences

Escape Sequence	Description
^[M	Moves cursor up one line in current column, back-scrolling screen if necessary (reverse line feed)
^[D	Moves cursor down one line in current column, scrolling screen if necessary (line feed)
^[E	Carriage return and line feed
^[H	Sets tab stop in current column
^[7	Stores cursor position and attributes
^[8	Restores cursor position and attributes
^[>	Puts keypad in numeric mode (normal)
^[=	Puts keypad in application mode (act like DEC VT102 function keys)
^[c	Resets every terminal setting that can be set through control characters and escape sequences
^[Z	Requests terminal ID. Response is ^[[?6c, saying that the console faithfully emulates a DEC VT102 (it includes a large superset of the DEC VT102's capabilities)

console to take simple actions and immediately leave escape mode. The simple escape sequences are documented in Table 21.2

Storing and restoring the cursor position (^[7 and ^[8) are not done on a stack; if you do two stores in a row, the second stored position overwrites the first stored position. Conversely, after storing the cursor position once, you can restore it as many times as you wish. Each time, the cursor will revert to the same location. When you restore the cursor position, you also restore character rendition attributes, current character set, and character set definitions, all described later in this chapter.

Cursor position is given in terms of a *character cell address*, an *x,y* pair of numbers that names one position on the screen. Character cell addresses on most terminals, including the Linux console, do not follow standard computer-science practice of counting from zero. The upper-left character on the screen is the **origin** and is addressed as character cell 1,1.

Note that control characters may be included in the middle of an escape sequence. For example, ^[^G8 first beeps and then restores the cursor position and attributes. The sequence ^[^X8 simply prints an 8.

Table 21.3 Complex Console Escape Sequences

Escape Sequence	Description
^[[	Begins a CSI sequence (ALT-^[is a synonym for this)
^[]	Begins a palette-setting sequence
^[%	Begins a UTF (UTF-8 wide-character Unicode) sequence
^[(	Chooses font mapping for G0 character set
^[)	Chooses font mapping for G1 character set
^[#8	DEC private test sequence; fills screen with E characters

21.3.3 Testing Sequences

To test most sequences, you merely need to log into a virtual console and run cat. Type the sequences you wish to test, and watch the results. For ^[, press the Escape key.

Terminal responses to commands such as the ^[Z terminal identification command or the CSIn command documented later show up as escape sequences that disappear in terminal handling. In cases in which you wish to see such a response, you can simply run

```
cat > /tmp/somefile
```

Then type the commands, followed by a return and a ^D. Use less, vi, Emacs, or some other program that can handle arbitrary characters to read /tmp/somefile, where you will find the responses directly following the sequences you typed.

21.3.4 Complex Escape Sequences

Five two-character escape sequences are really prefixes to longer, more-complex escape sequences, as shown in Table 21.3. We describe each of these sequences, in turn.

CSI sequences have three or four parts.

1. ^[[starts a CSI sequence, putting the terminal in CSI mode.

Table 21.4 CSI Sequences

Char	Description	
h	Sets mode; see page 525	
l	Clears mode; see page 525	
n	*par1*=5	Status report: Terminal responds with ^[[0n, which means "OK"
	par1=6	Cursor position report: Terminal responds with ^[[x;yR, where *y* is relative to the origin rather than the region if origin mode is selected (see Table 21.9)
G or '	Sets cursor horizontal position to column *par1*	
A	Moves cursor vertical position up by *par1* rows	
B or e	Moves cursor vertical position down by *par1* rows	
C or a	Moves cursor horizontal position right by *par1* columns	
D	Moves cursor horizontal position left by *par1* columns	
E	Moves cursor to beginning of line and down *par1* rows (1 by default)	
F	Moves cursor to beginning of line and up *par1* rows (1 by default)	
d	Sets cursor vertical position to row *par1*	
H or f	Sets cursor vertical position to row *par1* and horizontal position to column *par2* (both default to zero, moving the cursor to the origin)	
J	*par1*=0	Clears from cursor to end of display
	par1=1	Clears from origin to cursor
	par1=2	Clears entire display
K	*par1*=0	Clears from cursor to end of line
	par1=1	Clears from start of line to cursor
	par1=2	Clears entire line
L	Inserts *par1* lines above the current line	
M	Deletes *par1* lines, starting with the current line	
P	Deletes *par1* characters at the current position, shifting the rest of the line left	
c	Responds with ^[[?6c (synonym for ^[Z)	
g	*par1*=0	Clears tab in current column (default)
	par1=3	Clears all tabs
m	Character rendition sequence; see Table 21.7	
q	Turns keyboard LED *par1* on and others off (0 turns all off)	
r	Sets scrolling region (applied only in DEC origin mode; see page 525):	
	par1	First line of region, must be between 1 (default) and *par2*-1
	par2	Last line of region, must be between *par1*+1 and bottom line (default)
s	Stores cursor position and attributes (synonym for ^[7)	
u	Restores cursor position and attributes (synonym for ^[8)	
X	Erases up to *par1* characters, up to the end of the current line	
@	Erases up to *par1* characters, up to the end of the current line	
]	setterm sequences; see Table 21.10	

Table 21.5 Color Codes

N	Color	N	Bright Color
0	Black	8	Dark gray
1	Red	9	Bright red
2	Green	10	Bright green
3	Brown	11	Yellow
4	Blue	12	Bright blue
5	Magenta	13	Bright magenta
6	Cyan	14	Bright cyan
7	Gray	15	White

2. For the h and l sequences only, you can include a ? character to allow you to set or clear DEC private modes (see page 525).

3. You may provide up to 16 parameters. Parameters are decimal numbers separated by ; characters. 1;23;45 is a list of three parameters: 1, 23, and 45. (If the ; parameter separator is found after 16 parameters have already been read, the CSI sequence is terminated immediately and the terminal goes into normal mode, printing the rest of the sequence.)

4. A *command character* terminates the sequence and determines how to interpret the parameters the terminal has already encountered.

The parameters are usually referred to as *par1* through *par16*. If you do not set a parameter explicitly, its value is automatically set to 0 or 1, depending on what makes the most sense. The CSI command characters are documented in Table 21.4.

Several sequences take arguments describing colors; they all use the same mapping from numbers to colors, documented in Table 21.5. Sequences that describe background colors accept only color numbers between 0 and 7; sequences that describe foreground colors accept numbers between 8 and 15 that describe bold or bright colors.

These colors are actually offsets into a table—the color names in the table describe the default colors stored at those offsets. However, you can change those colors with a palette-setting sequence; the ^[]P sequence sets an individual palette entry, and the ^[]R sequence resets the palette to the system default palette. Palette entries are defined by seven hexadecimal

Table 21.6 Color Palette Components

Digit Number	Defines
1	Palette entry to redefine
2*16+3	Value of red component of palette entry
4*16+5	Value of green component of palette entry
6*16+7	Value of blue component of palette entry

Table 21.7 Character Rendition Parameters

par	Description
0	Default rendition: normal intensity, no underline, not reverse video, no blinking, and the default color scheme (white on black unless set otherwise by the setterm store sequence ^[[]8)
1	Bold intensity
2	Dim intensity
4	Enables underline
5	Enables blink
7	Enables reverse video
10	Selects primary font (ISO latin 1), does not display control characters, unsets bit 8 on output
11	Selects alternate font (IBM Codepage 437), displays control characters as graphics, unsets bit 8 on output
12	Selects alternate font (IBM Codepage 437), displays control characters as graphics, leaves bit 8 set on output
21 22	Normal intensity
24	Disables underline
25	Disables blink
27	Disables reverse video
30 – 37	Sets foreground color to par || 30; see Table 21.5
38	Enables underline and uses default foreground color
39	Disables underline and uses default foreground color
40 – 47	Sets background color to par || 40; see Table 21.5
49	Uses default background color

digits that follow ^[]P, as documented in Table 21.6. So for each palette entry, you can provide a 24-bit color definition with eight bits for each color.

The character rendition sequences denoted by the CSI m command may have up to 16 parameters, documented in Table 21.7, in any order. They are applied to the terminal in the order in which they are given, so if 0 to

Table 21.8 ANSI Modes

par	Description
3	Displays control characters
4	Insert mode
20	CRLF mode (produces a carriage return when a linefeed is received)

Table 21.9 DEC Private Modes

par	Description
1	Cursor keys as *application keys*; in application mode, they are pre-fixed with ^[O instead of the usual ^[[
3	Unimplemented; may switch between 80- and 132-column mode in the future
5	Sets entire screen in inverse video
6	Sets DEC origin mode, in which scrolling regions are honored, and goes to the origin (of the current scrolling region, if any)
7	Sets autowrap mode (on by default), in which characters that would go beyond the screen cause an automatic CRLF. When autowrap mode is turned off, extra characters over-write the right-most character on the current line
8	Sets keyboard auto-repeat mode (on by default)
9	Mouse reporting mode 1 (support may be provided by an external program)
25	Makes cursor visible (on by default)
1000	Mouse reporting mode 2 (support may be provided by an external program)

set the default rendition is followed by 1 to set bold, the result is a bold—but not blinking, reverse video, or underlined—character, regardless of the previous rendition settings.

Related somewhat to the character rendition sequences are the mode sequences. There are two types of modes: ANSI modes and DEC private modes. The CSI h sequence sets ANSI modes, documented in Table 21.8, and the CSI l sequence clears them. More than one parameter can be included in a sequence. The CSI ?h sequence sets DEC private modes, documented in Table 21.9, and the CSI ?l sequence clears them. Again, more than one parameter can be included.

Table 21.10 Console setterm Sequences

par	Description
1	Sets color to use to represent **underline** attribute to *par2*
2	Sets color to use to represent **dim** attribute to *par2*
8	Stores current setterm attributes as the defaults, making them the default character rendition attributes
9	Sets screen-blank interval to *par2* minutes, but no more than 60 minutes. *par2* set to 0 disables screen-blank
10	Sets the console bell frequency to *par2* Hz or to the default pitch if *par2* is unspecified
11	Sets the console bell duration to *par2* milliseconds if *par2* is specified and is less than 2000. If *par2* is not specified, resets the duration to the default
12	If console *par2* is allocated, makes console *par2* active (see Chapter 20)
13	Unblanks the screen
14	Sets VESA power-down interval to *par2* minutes, but no more than 60 minutes. *par2* set to 0 disables VESA power down

The setterm sequences are a set of CSI sequences with the command character]. They are documented in Table 21.10.

There is more to conversing with the console than telling it what to display; you also must recognize key sequences and know which keys they are attached to—and although some of them are specified in the terminfo database, others are not. To make life even more interesting, the keyboard is modal. In *application mode,* the cursor keys produce different codes. As shown in Table 21.9, they are prefixed with ^[0 instead of ^[[. This is to support legacy applications that assume that they are talking to DEC terminals.

The key sequences are documented in Table 21.11. Note that the function-key numbering has gaps and that it is designed so that people without F11 and F12 keys are not handicapped.

21.4 Direct Screen Writing

There are some cases in which being able to write characters to the screen is simply insufficient, partially because it is impossible to determine the current state of the screen. Although standard Unix practice is to ignore

Table 21.11   Function-Key Encodings

Key Sequence	Key(s)
^[[A	F1
^[[B	F2
^[[C	F3
^[[D	F4
^[[E	F5
^[[17~	F6
^[[18~	F7
^[[19~	F8
^[[20~	F9
^[[21~	F10
^[[23~	F11, Shift-F1, Shift-F11
^[[24~	F12, Shift-F2, Shift-F11
^[[25~	Shift-F3
^[[26~	Shift-F4
^[[28~	Shift-F5
^[[29~	Shift-F6
^[[31~	Shift-F7
^[[32~	Shift-F8
^[[33~	Shift-F9
^[[34~	Shift-F10
^[[A	Up arrow
^[[D	Left arrow
^[[B	Down arrow
^[[C	Right arrow
^[[1~	Home
^[[2~	Insert
^[[3~	Delete
^[[4~	End
^[[5~	Page Up
^[[6~	Page Down

the state of the screen—to set it up as you need it, make changes to it as you have changes to make, and to redraw it completely any time the user requests it (usually by pressing ^L)—you may have other applications in mind.

In particular, screen capture and restore programs and functions need access to the current contents of the screen. Linux provides this through two interfaces. One provides only the text contents of the screen, and one contains attributes (color and so forth), as well.

The simple text device is called **vcs**, which presumably stands for **virtual console screen**.[3] The /dev/vcs0 device when read produces the contents of the current virtual console as it is being viewed at the time it is read. If the screen is currently scrolled back (the Control-PageUp and Control-PageDown keys are set up to control console scrolling by default), /dev/vcs0 contains the scrolled-back contents that are being viewed. The rest of the vcs devices, /dev/vcs*n*, each represent the current state of the virtual console *n*, normally accessed through /dev/tty*n*.

When you read /dev/vcs*, you are given no indication of new lines or of console size other than an EOF at the end of the screen. If you read 2,000 bytes and then receive an EOF, there is no indication whether the screen is 80 columns and 25 lines or 40 columns and 50 lines. No newline characters are produced to mark the ends of lines, and every empty character cell, whether or not it was ever written to, is denoted by a space character. There are several popular screen configurations, and there is no guarantee that each of them has a unique number of lines and columns. The vcs device provides an easy way for a savvy sysadmin or developer to see what is on any virtual console, but it is not very useful from a programmer's standpoint, at least alone.

One useful way to use vcs is from within X. XFree86, by default, starts the X server on the first free virtual console, not on the console that the program was started from. If you start XFree86 from virtual console 1, you do not need to change back to virtual console 1 to see the detection messages that XFree86 left on the screen; bring up a terminal window the same size as the console (normally 80 columns by 25 lines), become superuser (in order to gain access to the vcs device), and run `cat /dev/vcs1`. The contents of the first virtual console will fill your terminal window.

In order to write reliable programs, however, you need some basic knowledge about the state of the screen that a vcs device does not provide

- Colors

- Other attributes (such as blinking)

---

3. This section belongs logically to Chapter 20 because it is related to virtual consoles, but it belongs in this chapter in a practical sense—you would not know to look in Chapter 20 unless you did not need to read this book in the first place.

- Current cursor position

- Screen configuration (number of rows and columns)

The **vcsa** device (which presumably stands for **virtual console screen with attributes**) provides all this. The first four bytes of /dev/vcsa*n* (for the same *n* as vcs devices) contain a header that gives the current cursor position and screen configuration. The first byte contains the number of rows, the second the number of columns, the third the cursor's current column, and the fourth the cursor's current row. The rest of the file contains alternating bytes that represent the text and text attribute bytes of the console in question.

So, if you need to know only the size of the console and its textual contents, you can read the first two bytes of the appropriate vcsa device and from then on use only the vcs device. If you want to set the current cursor position, write to the third and fourth bytes of the vcsa device (the first two bytes are read-only, so the first two characters arc placeholders; we prefer to use spaces or some other similar character to make this more obvious). As an example, to move the cursor on the fourth virtual console to the eighth row and the twentieth column (counting from zero):

```
echo -n -e '..\023\007' > /dev/vcsa4
```

The -n keeps echo from adding a newline character to the end, and the -e makes it interpret escape codes, so that *nnn* is interpreted as octal character *nnn*.

The attributes and character contents are represented as alternating bytes, the first containing the character and the second containing the attributes to apply to the character. The attribute byte is normally defined like the attribute byte used on VGA hardware. Other kinds of hardware, including the TGA cards used on many Linux/Alpha machines and the SPARC console driver, emulate the VGA attribute handling. On video hardware without color support but with underline support, it can be read slightly differently; it is designed in such a way that you can pretend that it is all VGA hardware, and all other hardware will behave somewhat reasonably.

For each attribute byte, the bits are interpreted as documented in Table 21.12. That is the VGA representation; some color hardware replaces blink

Table 21.12 Attributes

Bit(s)	Effect
7	Blink
6-4	Background
3	Bold
2-0	Foreground

by a bright background. The monochrome representation uses bit 0 of the foreground color to indicate underline.

CHAPTER 22

Writing Secure Programs

The vast majority of computers running Linux are connected to the Internet, and many of them are used by multiple people. Keeping a computer and its software secure from anonymous threats that arrive over its network connection, as well as from local users who are trying to gain unauthorized levels of access, requires careful programming in both the core operating system and many of its applications.

This chapter gives an overview of some of the things to think about when you are writing C programs that need to be secure. We discuss what types of programs need to think carefully about their security and how to minimize the risks, and mention some of the most common security pitfalls. This is meant to be an introduction to writing secure programs; for more information look at David A. Wheeler's *Secure Programming for Linux and UNIX HOWTO* at http://www.dwheeler.com/secure-programs/. It includes an excellent bibliography as well.

22.1 When Security Matters

Computer programs are complicated things. Even the most simple "Hello World" program is surprisingly involved. Ignoring everything that happens in the kernel, the C library has to find the right shared libraries, load them into the system, and initialize the standard I/O routines. On the computer used to write this chapter, the full program took 25 system calls, only one of which was the `write()` call used to print the words "Hello World."

As programs get larger, complexity grows quite rapidly. Most real-world programs accept input from multiple locations (such as the command line, configuration files, and the terminal) and manipulate that input in complicated ways. Any mistakes in this process provide for unexpected behavior, and those surprises can often be manipulated by a savvy programmer with undesirable consequences. Add a few complicated libraries into this mix, and it is very difficult for any programmer (let alone a team of programmers) to fully understand just how a program will react to any particular set of inputs.

While most programs are carefully tested to make sure they give the proper results for correct input sequences, most are poorly tested for unexpected ones.[1] While the kernel has been carefully designed to prevent failures in user-space programs from compromising the system, mistakes in some types of programs can affect the system's integrity.

There are three main types of programs whose programmers need to constantly think about security.

- Programs that handle data that could come from an untrustworthy source are very prone to vulnerabilities. That data can have attacks hidden in it that exploit bugs in programs, causing those programs to behave unexpectedly; they can often be manipulated into allowing anonymous users full access to the machine. Any program that accesses data across a network (both clients and servers) is an obvious candidate for attacks, but programs as innocuous as word processors can also be attacked through corrupted data files.[2]

- Any program that switches user or group context when it is run (via the setuid or setgid bits on the executable) has the potential of being tricked into doing things as the other (privileged) user, things that the unpriviliged user is probably not allowed to do.

---

1. A popular way of testing early Linux kernels was to generate a sequence of completely random bytes and start executing them as a program. While this would never do anything particularly useful (let alone write *Hamlet*), it would quite often cause the kernel to completely lock up. While trying to execute completely random code sequences is not in the kernel's job description, user-space programs should never cause the kernel to stop running properly, so this technique found a large number of bugs that needed to be fixed.
2. Attacking application software is now the primary method viruses use to spread.

- Any program that runs as a system daemon can be a security problem. Those programs are running as a privileged user on the system (quite often they are run as root), and any interaction they have with normal users provides the opportunity for system compromises.

22.1.1 When Security Fails

Security bugs in programs lead to four broad categories of attacks: remote exploits, local exploits, remote denial-of-service attacks, and local denial-of-service attacks. Remote exploits let users who can access the machine's network services run arbitrary code on that machine. For a remote exploit to occur, there must be a failure in a program that accesses the network. Traditionally, these mistakes have been in network servers, allowing a remote attacker to trick that server into giving him access to the system. More recently, bugs in network clients have been exploited. For example, if a web browser had a flaw in how it parsed HTML data, a web page loaded by that browser could cause the browser to run an arbitrary code sequence.

Local exploits let users perform action they do not normally have permission to perform (and are commonly referred to as allowing *local privilege escalation*, such as masquerading as other users on the system. This type of exploit typically targets local daemons (such as the `cron` or `sendmail` server) and setuid programs (such as `mount` or `passwd`).

Denial-of-service attacks do not let the attacker gain control of a system, but they allow them to prevent legitimate uses of that system. These are the most insidious bugs, and many of these can be very difficult to eliminate. Many programs that use lock files are subject to these, for example, as an attacker can create the lock file by hand and no program will ever remove it. One of the simplest denial-of-service attacks is for users to fill their home directories with unnecessary files, preventing other users on that file system from creating new files.[3] As a general rule, there are many more opportunities for local denial-of-service attacks than remote denial-of-service attacks. We do not talk much about denial-of-service attacks here, as they are often the result of program architecture rather than any single flaw.

---

3. System quotas prevent this attack from working.

22.2 Minimizing the Opportunity for Attack

One of the best strategies for making a program secure against attempts to exploit their privileges is to make the parts of a program that can be attacked as simple as possible. While this strategy can be difficult to employ for network programs and system daemons, programs that must be run with special permissions (via the setuid or setgid bits, or run by the root user) can usually use a few common mechanisms to limit their areas of vulnerability.

22.2.1 Giving Up Permissions

Many programs that need special privileges use those privileges only at startup time. For example, many networking daemons need to be run by the root user so they can `listen()` on a reserved port, but they do not need any special permissions after that. Most web servers use this technique to limit their exposure to attack by switching to a different user (normally a user called `nobody` or `apache`) right after they open TCP/IP port 80. While the server may still be subject to remote exploits, at least those exploits will no longer give the attacker access to a process running as root. Network clients who need reserved ports, such as `rsh`, can employ a similar strategy. They are run as setuid to root, which allows them to open the proper port. Once the port is open, there is no longer any need for root privileges, so they can drop those special abilities.

One or more of `setuid()`, `setgid()`, and `setgroups()` need to be used to reset the processes permissions. This technique is effective only if the real, effective, file system, and saved uids (or gids) are all set to their proper values. If the program is running setuid (or setgid), the process probably wants to set those uids to its saved uid. System daemons that are changing to a different user after being run by root need to change their user and group ids, and should also clear their supplemental group list. For more information on how a process can change its credentials, see page 108.

22.2.2 Getting a Helping Hand

If a program needs special permissions during more than just its initial startup, helper programs may provide a good solution. Rather than making the entire application run with elevated privileges, the main program runs as the normal user who invoked it, and runs another, very small program that has the proper credentials to perform the task that requires them. By architecting the application in this way, the complexity of the code that can be attacked is dramatically reduced. This reduction makes the code much easier to get correct and to audit for any mistakes. If there are problems in the main application that allow the user to perform arbitrary actions, those actions can be performed only with the user's normal credentials, rendering any attack useful only against that user, not the user with elevated capabilities.

Using small helper programs in this way has become quite popular in the Linux community. The `utempter` library, discussed on page 340, uses a setgid helper program to update the utmp database. The helper is very careful to validate its command-line arguments and to ensure that the application calling it is allowed to update the utmp database. By providing this service through a helper application, programs that use `utempter` do not need to have any special permissions themselves; before this library was written, any program that used pseudo ttys needed to be setgid to the group that owned the utmp database.

Another example of a helper program is the `unix_chkpwd` program used by PAM (PAM, or Pluggable Authentication Modules, is discussed in detail starting on page 635). Passwords on most Linux systems are stored in a file that is readable only by the root user; this prevents dictionary attacks on the users' encrypted passwords.[4] Some programs want to make sure the person currently at the computer is the one who is logged in (`xscreensaver`, which can be used to lock a system's screen until the user returns, is a common program that does this), but do not normally run as root. Rather than make those programs setuid root so they can validate the user's password, PAM's normal Unix-style authentication calls `unix_chkpwd` to validate the password for it, so that only `unix_chkpwd` needs to be setuid root. Not only does this remove the need for `xscreensaver` to be written as a privileged

---

4. A dictionary attack is a brute force method of discovering passwords where an automated program runs through a large list of common passwords, such as words in a dictionary, until one works.

program, but it also means that any vulnerabilities in the X11 libraries it depends on do not allow local exploits.

Using helper programs in this way is a very good way of eliminating the possibility of security problems in applications. Writing these helpers is normally quite straightforward, and their correctness is relatively simple to determine. There are a couple of things to watch out for in their design, however.

Quite often, confidential data is passed between the main application and the helper program. For `unix_chkpwd`, the user's unencrypted password must be supplied for the helper program to validate. Some care needs to be taken in how that information is passed; while it is tempting to use a command-line argument, that would allow any user who runs `ps` at just the right time to see a user's unencrypted passwords. If a pipe is used to transmit the data instead (normally set as the helper program's stdin), then the data is transmitted without other programs being able to see it.

The helper program also needs to carefully ensure that the program calling it is allowed to perform the action it is requesting. The `unx_chkpwd` helper does not let a program validate the passwords of any user other than the one running it. It uses its own real uid to validate that the program that calls it is allowed to check the password of the user it has requested. The `utempter` helper does similar checks to make sure that programs cannot remove terminals from the utmp database unless it is appropriate to do so.

22.2.3 Restricting File System Access

One more way of keeping coding mistakes from providing the potential for an attack is to limit the set of files to which a program has access by using the `chroot()` system call. As discussed on page 296, `chroot()` followed by a `chdir()` call changes the root directory of the process, limiting the set of files that process is able to access. This does not prevent an exploit, but it can sometimes contain the damage. If a network server running as a user other than root is remotely exploited, it becomes much more difficult for that remote user to use that server as the base of a local exploit if it cannot access any setuid files (the most common programs local exploits can take advantage of).

Anonymous ftp servers are the most common programs that take advantage of the `chroot()` mechanism. In recent years it has become more popular in other programs, and many system administrators have used the `chroot` command to force system daemons into running in a restricted environment as a precaution against intruders.

22.3 Common Security Holes

Now that we have looked at ways of reducing the potential impact of insecure code, we go over some of the most common programming mistakes that lead to security problems. While the rest of this chapter highlights some of the things to look out for, it is by no means a definitive list. Anyone writing programs that need to be secure needs to look beyond just this chapter for guidance.

22.3.1 Buffer Overflows

By far the most common programming mistake that leads to local and remote exploits is a buffer overflow. Here is an example of a program with an exploitable buffer overflow:

```
 1: /* bufferoverflow.c */
 2:
 3: #include <limits.h>
 4: #include <stdio.h>
 5: #include <string.h>
 6:
 7: int main(int argc, char ** argv) {
 8:     char path[_POSIX_PATH_MAX];
 9:
10:     printf("copying string of length %d\n", strlen(argv[1]));
11:
12:     strcpy(path, argv[1]);
13:
14:     return 0;
15: }
16:
```

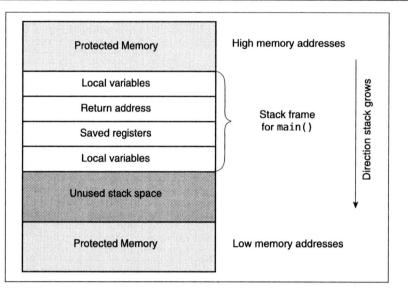

Figure 22.1   Memory Map of an Application's Stack

This looks pretty innocuous at first glance; after all, the program does not even really do anything. It does, however, copy a string provided by the user into a fixed space on the stack without making sure there is room on the stack for it. Try running this program with a single, long command-line argument (say, 300 characters). It causes a segmentation fault when the strcpy() writes beyond the space allocated for the path array.

To better understand how a program's stack space is allocated, take a look at Figure 22.1. On most systems, the processor stack grows down; that is, the earlier something is placed on the stack, the higher the logical memory address it gets. Above the first item on the stack is a protected region of memory; any attempt to access it is an error and causes a segmentation fault.

The next area on the stack contains local variables used by the code that starts the rest of the program. Here, we have called that function _main(), although it may actually get quite complex as it involves things like dynamic loading. When this startup code calls the main() routine for a program, it stores the address that the main() routine should return to after it is finished on the stack. When main() begins, it may need to store some of the microprocessor's registers on the stack so it can reuse those registers, and then it allocates space for its local variables.

Returning to our buffer overflow example, this means that the `path` variable gets allocated at the bottom of the stack. The byte `path[0]` is at the very bottom, the next byte is `path[1]`, and so on. When our sample program writes more than `_POSIX_PATH_MAX` bytes into `path`, it starts to overwrite other items on the stack. If it keeps going, it tries to write past the top of the stack and causes the segmentation fault we saw.

The real problem occurs if the program writes past the return address on the stack, but does not cause a segmentation fault. That lets it change the return address from the function that is running to any arbitrary address in memory; when the function returns, it will go to this arbitrary address and continue execution at that point.

Exploits that take advantage of buffer overflows typically include some code in the array that is written to the stack, and they set the return address to that code. This technique allows the attacker to execute any arbitrary code with the permissions of the program being attacked. If that program is a network daemon running as root, it allows any remote user root access on the local system!

String handling is not the only place where buffer overflows occur (although it is probably the most common). Reading files is another common location. File formats often store the size of a data element followed by the data item itself. If the store size is used to allocate a buffer, but the end of the data field is determined by some other means, then a buffer overflow could occur. This type of error has made it possible for Web sites to refer to files that have been corrupted in such a way that reading them causes a remote exploit.

Reading data over a network connection provides one more opportunity for buffer overflows. Many network protocols specify a maximum size for data fields. The BOOTP protocol,[5] for example, fixes all packet sizes at 300 bytes. However, there is nothing stopping another machine from sending a 350-byte BOOTP packet to the network. If some programs on the network are not written properly, they could try and copy that rogue 350-byte packet into space intended for a valid 300-byte BOOTP packet and cause a buffer overflow.

---

5. BOOTP is the predecessor to DHCP, which allows machines to learn their IP addresses automatically when they enable their network interfaces.

Localization and translation are two other instigators of buffer overflows. When a program is written for the English language, there is no doubt that a string of 10 characters is long enough to hold the name of a month loaded from a table. When that program gets translated into Spanish, "September" becomes "Septiembre" and a buffer overflow could result. Whenever a program supports different languages and locations, most of the formerly static strings become dynamic, and internal string buffers need to take this into account.

It should be obvious by now that buffer overflows are critical security problems. They are easy to overlook when you are programming (after all, who must worry about file names that are longer than _POSIX_PATH_MAX?) and easy to exploit.

There are a number of techniques to eliminate buffer overflows from code. Well-written programs use many of them to carefully allocate buffers of the right size.

The best way of allocating memory for objects is through malloc(), which avoids the problems incurred by overwriting the return address since malloc() does not allocate memory from the stack. Carefully using strlen() to calculate how large a buffer needs to be and dynamically allocating it on the program's heap provides good protection against overflows. Unfortunately, it also provides a good source of memory leaks as every malloc() needs a free(). Some good ways of tracking down memory leaks are discussed in Chapter 7, but even with these tools it can be difficult to know when to free the memory used by an object, especially if dynamic object allocation is being retrofitted into existing code. The alloca() function provides an alternative to malloc():

```
#include <alloca.h>

void * alloca(size_t size);
```

Like malloc(), alloca() allocates a region of memory size bytes long, and returns a pointer to the beginning of that region. Rather than using memory from the program's heap, it instead allocates memory from the bottom of the program's stack, the same place local variables are stored. Its primary advantage over local variables is that the number of bytes needed can be calculated programmatically rather than guessed; its advantage over malloc() is that the memory is automatically freed when the function returns. This makes `alloca()` an easy way to allocate memory that is needed only temporarily. As long as the size is calculated properly (do not forget the `'\0'` at the end of every C language string!), there will not be any buffer overflows.[6]

There are a couple of other functions that can make avoiding buffer overflows easier. The `strncpy()` and `strncat()` library routines can make it easier to avoid buffer overruns when copying strings around.

```
#include <string.h>

char * strncpy(char * dest, const char * src, size_t max);
char * strncat(char * dest, const char * src, size_t max);
```

Both functions behave like their similarly named cousins, `strcpy()` and `strcat()`, but the functions return once `max` bytes have been copied to the destination string. If that limit is hit, the resulting string will not be `'\0'` terminated, so normal string functions will no longer work. For this reason, it is normally a good idea to explicitly end the string after calling one of these functions like this:

```
strncpy(dest, src, sizeof(dest));
dest[sizeof(dest) - 1] = '\0';
```

It is a very common mistake when using `strncat()` to pass the total size of `dest` as the `max` parameter. This leads to a potential buffer overflow as `strncat()` *appends* up to `max` bytes onto `dest`; it does not stop copying bytes when the total length of `dest` reaches `max` bytes.

While using these functions may make the program perform incorrectly if long strings are present (by making those strings get truncated), this technique prevents buffer overflows in static-sized buffers. In many cases, this is an acceptable trade-off (and does not make the program perform any worse than it would if the buffer overflow were allowed to occur).

---

6. `alloca()` is not a standard feature of the C language, but the gcc compiler provides `alloca()` on most operating systems it supports. In older versions of the gcc compiler (before version 3.3), `alloca()` did not always interact properly with dynamically sized arrays (another GNU extension), so consider using only one of the two.

While strncpy() solves the problem of copying a string into a static buffer without overflowing the buffer, the strdup() functions automatically allocate a buffer large enough to hold a string before copying the original string into it.

```
#include <string.h>

char * strdup(const char * src);
char * strdupa(const char * src);
char * strndup(const char * src, int max);
char * strndupa(const char * src, int max);
```

The first of these, strdup(), copies the src string into a buffer allocated by malloc(), and returns the buffer to the caller while the second, strdupa() allocated the buffer with alloca(). Both functions allocate a buffer just long enough to hold the string and the trailing '\0'.

The other two functions, strndup() and strndupa() copy at most max bytes from str into the buffer (and allocated at most max + 1 bytes) along with a trailing '\0'. strndup() allocates the buffer with malloc() while strndupa() uses alloca().

Another function that often causes buffer overflows is sprintf(). Like strcat() and strcpy(), sprintf() has a variant that makes it easier to protect against overflows.

```
#include <stdio.h>

int snprintf(char * str, size_t max, char * format, ...);
```

Trying to determine the size of a buffer required by sprintf() can be tricky, as it depends on items such as the magnitude of any numbers that are formatted (which may or may not need number signs), the formatting arguments that are used, and the length of any strings that are being used by the format. To make it easier to avoid buffer overflows, snprintf() fills in no more than max characters in str, including the terminating '\0'. Unlike strcat() and strncat(), snprintf() also terminates the string properly, omitting a character from the formatted string if necessary. It returns the number of characters that would be used by the final string if enough space were available, whether or not the string had to be truncated to max (not including the final '\0').[7] If the return value is less than max, then the function completed successfully; if it is the same or greater, then the max limit was encountered.

The vsprintf() function has similar problems, and vsnprintf() provides a way to overcome them.

22.3.2 Parsing Filenames

It is quite common for privileged applications to provide access to files to untrusted users and let those users provide the filenames they would like to access. A web server is a good example of this; an HTTP URL contains a filename that the web server is requested to send to the remote (untrusted) user. The web server needs to make sure that the file it returns is one that it has been configured to send, and checking filenames for validity must be done carefully.

Imagine a web server that serves files from home/httpd/html, and it does this by simply adding the filename from the URL it is asked to provide to the end of /home/httpd/html. This will serve up the right file, but it also allows remote users to see any file on the system the web server has access to by requesting a file like ../../../etc/passwd. Those .. directories need to be checked for explicitly and disallowed. The chroot() system call is a good way to make filename handling in programs simpler.

If those filenames are passed to other programs, even more checking needs to be done. For example, if a leading - is used in the filename, it is quite likely that the other program will interpret that filename as a command-line option.

---

7. On some obsolete versions of the C library, it will instead return -1 if the string does not fit; the old version of the C library is no longer maintained and secure programs will not use it, but the snprintf() man page demonstrates code that can handle both variants.

22.3.3 Environment Variables

Programs run with setuid or setgid capabilities need to be extremely careful with their environment settings as those variables are set by the person running the program, allowing an avenue for attack. The most obvious attack is through the PATH environment variable, which changes what directories execlp() and execvp() look for programs. If a privileged program runs other programs, it needs to make sure it runs the right ones! A user who can override a program's search path can easily compromise that program.

There are other environment variables that could be very dangerous; the LD_PRELOAD environment variable lets the user specify a library to load before the standard C library. This can be useful, but is very dangerous in privileged applications (the environment variable is ignored if the real and effective uids are the same for exactly this reason).

If a program is localized, NLSPATH is also problematic. It lets a user switch the language catalog a program uses, which specifies how strings are translated. This means that, in translated programs, the user can specify the value for any translated string. The string can be made arbitrarily long, necessitating extreme vigilance in buffer allocation. Even more dangerously, if a format string for a function like printf() is translated, the format can change. This means that a string like Hello World, today is %s could become Hello World, today is %c%d%s. It is hard to tell what effect this type of change would have on a program's operation!

All of this means that the best solution for a setuid or setgid program's environment variables is to eliminate them. The clearenv()[8] function erases all values from the environment, leaving it empty. The program can then add back any environment variables it has to have with known values.

---

8. Unfortunately, clearenv() has not been well standardized. It is included in recent versions of POSIX but was left out of the Single Unix Standard, and is not available on all Unix-type systems. If you need to support an operating system that does not include it, environ = NULL; should work just as well.

22.3.4 Running the Shell

Running the system shell from any program where security is a concern is a bad idea. It makes a couple of the problems that already have been discussed more difficult to protect against.

Every string passed to a shell needs to be very carefully validated. A '\n' or ; embedded in a string could cause the shell to see two commands instead of one, for example. If the string contains back tick characters (') or the $() sequence, the shell runs another program to build the full command-line argument. Normal shell expansion also takes place, making environment variables and globbing available to attackers. The IFS environment variable lets characters other than space and tab separate fields when command lines are parsed by the string, opening up new avenues of attack. Other special characters, like <, >, and |, provide even more ways to build up command lines that do not behave as a program intended.

Checking all of these possibilities is very difficult to get right. The best way, by far, of avoiding all of the possible attacks against a shell is to avoid running one in the first place. Functions like pipe(), fork(), exec(), and glob() make it reasonably easy to perform most tasks the shell is normally used for without opening the Pandora's box of shell command-line expansion.

22.3.5 Creating Temporary Files

It is quite common for programs to use temporary files; Linux even provides special directories (/tmp and /var/tmp) for this purpose. Unfortunately, using temporary files in a secure manner can be very tricky. The best way to use temporary files is to create them in a directory that can be accessed only by the program's effective uid; the home directory of that user would be a good choice. This approach makes using temporary files safe and easy; most programmers do not like this approach as it clutters directories and those files will probably never get erased if the program fails unexpectedly.

Imagine a program that is run by the root user that creates a shell script in a temporary file and then runs that script. To let multiple copies of the program run at the same time, perhaps it includes the program's pid as part of the filename, and creates the file with code like this:

```
char fn[200];
    int fd;

    sprintf(fn, "/tmp/myprogram.%d", getpid());
    fd = open(fn, O_CREAT | O_RDWR | O_TRUNC, 0600);
```

The program creates a unique filename and truncates whatever file used to be there before writing to it. While it may look reasonable at first glance, it is actually trivial to exploit. If the file the program tries to create already exists as a symbolic link, the open call follows that symbolic link and opens whatever file it points to. One exploit is to create symbolic links in /tmp using many (or all) possible pids that point to a file like /etc/passwd, which would cause the system's password file to be overwritten when this program is run, resulting in a denial-of-service attack.

A more dangerous attack is for those symbolic links to be pointed at a file the attacker owns (or, equivalently, for the attacker to create regular files in /tmp with all of the possible names). When the file is opened, the targeted file will be truncated, but between the time the file is opened and the time the program gets executed, the attacker (who still owns the file) can write anything they like into it (adding a line like chmod u+s /bin/sh would certainly be advantageous in a shell script running as root!), creating an easy attack. While this may seem difficult to time properly, these types of race conditions are often exploited, leading to security compromises. If the program was setuid instead of run as root, the exploit actually becomes much easier as the user can send SIGSTOP to the program right after it opens the file, and then send SIGCONT after exploiting this race condition.

Adding O_EXCL to the open() call prevents open() from opening a file that is a symbolic link as well as a file that already exists. In this particular case, a simple denial-of-service attack also exists, as the code will fail if the first filename tried exists, but this is easily remedied by placing the open() in a loop that tries different filenames until one works.

A better way to create temporary files is by using POSIX's `mkstemp()` library function, which ensures that the file was created properly.[9]

```
int mkstemp(char * template);
```

The `template` is a filename whose last six characters must be `"XXXXXX"`. The last part is replaced with a number that allows the filename to be unique in the file system; this approach allows `mkstemp()` to try different filenames until one is found that works. The `template` is updated to contain the filename that was used (allowing the program to remove the file) and a file descriptor referring to the temporary file is returned. If the function fails, -1 is returned.

Older versions of Linux's C library created the file with mode 0666 (world read/write), and depended on the program's umask to get the proper permissions on the file. More recent versions allow only the user to read and write from the file, but as POSIX does not specify either behavior, it is a good idea to explicitly set the process's umask (077 would be a good choice!) before calling `mkstemp()`.

Linux, and a few other operating systems, provide `mkdtemp()` for creating temporary directories.

```
char * mkdtemp(char * template);
```

The `template` works the same as it does for `mkstemp()`, but the function returns a pointer to `template` on success and `NULL` if it fails.

Most operating systems that provide `mkdtemp()` also provide a `mktemp` program that allows shell scripts to create both temporary files and directories in a secure manner.

There are other problems with temporary files that have not been covered here. They include race conditions added by temporary directories residing on networked (especially NFS) file systems as well as by programs that regularly remove old files from those directories, and the extreme care that needs to be taken to reopen temporary files after they have been created.

---

9. There are a few other library functions that deal with temporary files, such as `tmpnam()`, `tempnam()`, `mktemp()`, and `tmpfile()`. Unfortunately, using any of them is little help as they leave exploitable race conditions in programs that are not carefully implemented.

For details on these and other problems with temporary files, take a look at David A. Wheeler's HOWTO mentioned on page 531. If you need to do any of these things, it is probably a better idea just to figure out how to create the files in the effective user's home directory instead.

22.3.6 Race Conditions and Signal Handlers

Any time an attacker can cause a program to behave in an incorrect manner there is the potential for an exploit. Mistakes that seem as innocuous as freeing the same portion of memory twice have been successfully exploited in the past, highlighting the need for privileged programs to be very carefully written.

Race conditions, and the signal handlers that can easily cause race conditions, are a rich source of program bugs. Common mistakes in writing signal handlers include:

- Performing dynamic memory allocation. Memory allocation functions are not reentrant, and should not be used from a signal handler.

- Using functions other than those appearing in Table 12.2 is always a mistake. Programs that call functions such as `printf()` from a signal handler have race conditions, as `printf()` has internal buffers and is not reentrant.

- Not properly blocking other signals. Most signal handlers are not meant to be reentrant, but it is quite common for a signal handler that handles multiple signals to not automatically block those other signals. Using `sigaction()` makes it easy to get this right as long as the programmer is diligent.

- Not blocking signals around areas of code that modify variables that a signal handler also accesses. (These code regions are often called *critical regions*.)

While signal-induced race conditions may not seem dangerous, networking code, setuid, and setgid programs can all have signals sent by untrusted users. Sending out-of-band data to a program can cause a `SIGURG` to be sent, while setuid and setgid programs can be sent signals by the user who runs them as the real uid of those processes does not change. Even if those programs change their real uids to prevent signals from being sent, when the user closes a terminal, all programs using that terminal are sent a SIGHUP.

22.3.7 Closing File Descriptors

On Linux and Unix systems, file descriptors are normally inherited across exec() system calls (and are always inherited across fork() and vfork()). In most cases, this behavior is not particularly desirable, as it is only stdin, stdout, and stderr that ought to be shared. To prevent programs that a privileged process runs from having access to files they should not have via an inherited file descriptor, it is important that programs carefully close all of the file descriptors to which the new program should not have access, which can be problematic if your program calls library functions which open files without closing them. One way of closing these file descriptors is to blindly close all of the file descriptors from descriptor number 3 (the one just after stderr) to an arbitrary, large value (say, 100 or 1024).[10] For most programs, this ensures that all of the proper file descriptors have been closed.[11]

A better approach is for programs to set the close-on-exec flag for every file it leaves open for an extended period of time (including sockets and device files), which prevents any new programs that are run from having access to those files. For details on the close-on-exec flag, see page 196.

---

10. Linux allows programs to open a very large number of files. Processes that are run as root can open millions of files simultaneously, but most distributions set a resource limit on the number of files a user process can open. This resource limit also limits the maximum file descriptor that can be used with dup2(), providing a usable upper limit for closing file descriptor.

11. Another way of closing all of the files a program has open is to walk through the process's /proc file system directory that lists all of the files it has open and close each of them. The directory /proc/PID/fd (where PID is the pid of the running process) contains a symbolic link for each file descriptor the process has open, and the name of each symbolic link is the file descriptor to which it corresponds. By reading the contents of the directory, the program can easily close all of the file descriptors it no longer needs.

22.4 Running as a Daemon

Programs that are designed to run as system daemons need to be a little careful how they become daemons to get all of the details right. Here is a list of things that should be done:

1. Most of the initialization work should be done before the program becomes an actual daemon. This allows any errors to be reported to the user starting the program and a meaningful exit code to be returned. This type of work includes parsing configuration files and opening sockets.

2. The current directory should be changed to whatever is appropriate. This is often the root directory, but it is never the directory from which the program was run. If the daemon does not do this, it may work properly, but it is preventing the directory from which it was started from being removed, as it is still a program's current directory. It is a good idea to `chroot()` to a directory if it is possible to do so for the reasons discussed earlier in this chapter.

3. Any unneeded file descriptors should be closed. This may seem obvious, but it can be easy to neglect to close file descriptors that have been inherited instead of opened by the program itself. See page 549 for information on how to do this.

4. The program should then call `fork()` and the parent process should call `exit()`, allowing the program that ran the daemon (often a shell) to continue.

5. The child process, which is continuing, should close stdin, stdout, and stderr, as it will no longer use the terminal. Rather than reuse file descriptors 0, 1, or 2, it is a good idea to open those files as `/dev/null`. This ensures that any library functions that report error conditions to stdout or stderr do not write those errors into other files the daemon has opened, and it allows the daemon to run external programs without worrying about their output.

6. To completely disassociate from the terminal from which the daemon was run, it should call `setsid()` to place it in its own process group.

This prevents it from getting signals when the terminal is closed, as well as job-control signals.

The C library provides a `daemon()` function that handles some of these tasks.

```
int daemon(int nochdir, int noclose);
```

This function forks immediately, and if the fork succeeds, the parent process calls `_exit()` with an exit code of 0. The child process then changes to the root directory unless `nochdir` is nonzero and redirects stdin, stdout, and stderr to `/dev/null` unless `noclose` is nonzero. It also calls `setsid()` before returning to the child. This could still leave open inherited file descriptors, so programs that use `daemon()` should check for that. If possible, the programs should also use `chroot()`.

Part 4

Development Libraries

String Matching

There is more to comparing strings than `strcmp()` or even `strncmp()`. Linux provides several general string-matching functions that make your programming tasks simpler. We start with the simple tasks and then cover the more complex ones.

23.1   Globbing Arbitrary Strings

Chapter 14 explains how to glob file names using the `glob()` function, but people used to globbing capabilities sometimes wish to apply them to other sorts of strings. The `fnmatch()` function allows you to apply globbing rules to arbitrary strings:

```
#include <fnmatch.h>

int fnmatch(const char *pattern, const char *string, int flags);
```

The pattern is a standard glob expression with four special characters, modified by the `flags` argument:

*   Matches any string, including an empty one.

?   Matches exactly one character, any character.

[Starts a list of characters to match, or, if the next character is ^, a list of characters not to match. The whole list matches, or does not match, a single character. The list is terminated by a] .

\   Causes the next character to be interpreted literally instead of as a special character.

The flags argument affects some details of the glob, and is mostly there to be useful for globbing against file names. If you are not globbing file names, you probably want to set flags to 0.

FNM_NOESCAPE

Treat \ as an ordinary character, not a special character.

FNM_PATHNAME

Do not match / characters in string with a *, ?, or even a [/] sequence in pattern; match it only with a literal, nonspecial /.

FNM_PERIOD

A leading . character in pattern matches a . character in string only if it is the first character in string or if FNM_PATHNAME is set and the . character in string directly follows a \.

fnmatch() returns zero if the pattern matches the string, FNM_NOMATCH if the pattern does not match the string, or some other unspecified value if an error occurs.

An example of using fnmatch() is provided in the example program on pages 315–317 in Chapter 14, where it is used as part of a simple reimplementation of the find command.

23.2 Regular Expressions

Regular expressions, as used in sed, awk, grep, vi, and countless other Unix programs through the years, have become a major part of the Unix programming environment. They are also available for use within C programs. This section explains how to use them and then presents a simple file parser using these functions.

23.2.1 Linux Regular Expressions

Regular expressions have two flavors: **basic regular expressions** (BREs) and **extended regular expressions** (EREs). They correspond (roughly) to the `grep` and `egrep` commands. Both forms of regular expressions are explained in the grep man page, in the POSIX.2 standard [IEEE, 1993], in *A Practical Guide to Red Hat Linux 8* [Sobell, 2002], and in other places, so we do not describe their syntax here, only the function interface that allows you to use regular expressions from within your programs.

23.2.2 Regular Expression Matching

POSIX specifies four functions to provide regular expression handling:

```
#include <regex.h>

int regcomp(regex_t *preg, const char *regex, int cflags);
int regexec(const regex_t *preg, const char *string, size_t nmatch,
            regmatch_t pmatch[], int eflags);
void regfree(regex_t *preg);
size_t regerror(int errcode, const regex_t *preg, char *errbuf,
                size_t errbuf_size);
```

Before you can compare a string to a regular expression, you need to **compile** it with the `regcomp()` function. The `regex_t *preg` holds all the state for the regular expression. You need one `regex_t` for each regular expression that you wish to have available concurrently. The `regex_t` structure has only one member on which you should rely: `re_nsub`, which specifies the number of parenthesized subexpressions in the regular expression. Consider the rest of the structure opaque.

The `cflags` argument determines many things about how the regular expression `regex` is interpreted. It may be zero, or it may be the bitwise OR of any of the following four items:

REG_EXTENDED
    If set, use ERE syntax instead of BRE syntax.

REG_ICASE
    If set, do not differentiate between upper- and lowercase.

REG_NOSUB

> If set, do not keep track of substrings. The regexec() function then ignores the nmatch and pmatch arguments.

REG_NEWLINE

> If REG_NEWLINE is not set, the newline character is treated essentially the same as any other character. The ^ and $ characters match only the beginning and end of the entire string, not adjacent newline characters. If REG_NEWLINE is set, you get the same behavior as you do with grep, sed, and other standard system tools; ^ anchors both to the beginning of a string and to the character after a newline (technically, it matches zero-length strings following a newline character); $ anchors to the end of the string and to newline characters (technically, it matches a zero-length string preceding the newline character); and . does not match a newline character.

A typical invocation looks like this:

```
if ((rerr = regcomp(&p, "(^(.*[^\\])#.*$)|(^[^#]+$)",
            REG_EXTENDED|REG_NEWLINE))) {
    if (rerr == REG_NOMATCH) {
        /* string simply did not match regular expression */
    } else {
        /* some other error, such as a badly formed expression */
    }
}
```

This ERE finds lines of a file that are not commented out, or that are, at most, partially commented out, by # characters not prefixed with \ characters. This kind of regular expression might be useful as part of a simple parser for an application's configuration file.

Even if you are compiling an expression that you know is good, you should still check for errors. regcomp() returns zero for a successful compilation and a nonzero error code for an error. Most errors involve invalid regular expressions of one sort or another, but another possible error is running out of memory. See page 562 for a description of the regerror() function.

```
#include <regex.h>

int regexec(const regex_t *preg, const chat *string, size_t nmatch,
            regmatch_t pmatch[], int eflags);
```

The regexec() function tests a string against a compiled regular expression. The eflags argument may be zero, or it may be the bitwise OR of any of the following symbols:

REG_NOTBOL

> If set, the first character of the string does not match a ^ character. Any character following a newline character still matches ^ as long as REG_NEWLINE was set in the call to regcomp().

REG_NOTEOL

> If set, the final character of the string does not match a $ character. Any character preceding a newline character still matches $ as long as REG_NEWLINE was set in the call to regcomp().

An array of regmatch_t structures is used to represent the location of subexpressions in the regular expression:

```
#include <regex.h>

typedef struct {
    regoff_t rm_so;   /* byte index within string of start of match */
    regoff_t rm_eo;   /* byte index within string of end of match */
} regmatch_t;
```

The first regmatch_t element describes the entire string that was matched; note that any newline, including a trailing newline, is included in this entire string, regardless of whether REG_NEWLINE is set or not.

Following array elements express parenthesized subexpressions in the order they are expressed in the regular expression, in order by the location of the opening parenthesis. (In C code, element i is equivalent to the replacement expression \i in sed or awk.) Subexpressions that do not match have a value of -1 in their regmatch_t.rm_so member.

This code matches a string against a regular expression with subexpressions, and prints out all the subexpressions that match:

```
 1: /* match.c */
 2:
 3: #include <alloca.h>
 4: #include <sys/types.h>
 5: #include <regex.h>
 6: #include <stdlib.h>
 7: #include <string.h>
 8: #include <stdio.h>
 9:
10: void do_regerror(int errcode, const regex_t *preg) {
11:     char *errbuf;
12:     size_t errbuf_size;
13:
14:     errbuf_size = regerror(errcode, preg, NULL, 0);
15:     errbuf = alloca(errbuf_size);
16:     if (!errbuf) {
17:         perror("alloca");
18:         return;
19:     }
20:
21:     regerror(errcode, preg, errbuf, errbuf_size);
22:     fprintf(stderr, "%s\n", errbuf);
23: }
24:
25: int main() {
26:
27:     regex_t p;
28:     regmatch_t *pmatch;
29:     int rerr;
30:     char *regex = "(^(.*[^\\])#.*$)|(^[^#]+$)";
31:     char string[BUFSIZ+1];
32:     int i;
33:
34:     if ((rerr = regcomp(&p, regex, REG_EXTENDED | REG_NEWLINE))) {
35:         do_regerror(rerr, &p);
36:     }
37:
38:     pmatch = alloca(sizeof(regmatch_t) * (p.re_nsub+1));
39:     if (!pmatch) {
```

```
40:            perror("alloca");
41:        }
42:
43:    printf("Enter a string: ");
44:    fgets(string, sizeof(string), stdin);
45:
46:    if ((rerr = regexec(&p, string, p.re_nsub+1, pmatch, 0))) {
47:        if (rerr == REG_NOMATCH) {
48:            /* regerror can handle this case, but in most cases
49:             * it is handled specially
50:             */
51:            printf("String did not match %s\n", regex);
52:        } else {
53:            do_regerror(rerr, &p);
54:        }
55:    } else {
56:        /* match succeeded */
57:        printf("String matched regular expressioon %s\n", regex);
58:        for(i = 0; i <= p.re_nsub; i++) {
59:            /* print the matching portion(s) of the string */
60:            if (pmatch[i].rm_so != -1) {
61:                char *submatch;
62:                size_t matchlen = pmatch[i].rm_eo - pmatch[i].rm_so;
63:                submatch = malloc(matchlen+1);
64:                strncpy(submatch, string+pmatch[i].rm_so,
65:                        matchlen);
66:                submatch[matchlen] = '\0';
67:                printf("matched subexpression %d: %s\n", i,
68:                        submatch);
69:                free(submatch);
70:            } else {
71:                printf("no match for subexpression %d\n", i);
72:            }
73:        }
74:    }
75:    exit(0);
76: }
```

In the sample regular expression given in match.c, there are three subexpressions: The first is an entire line containing text followed by a comment character, the second is the text in that line that precedes the comment character, and the third is an entire line containing no comment character. For a line with a comment character at the beginning, the second and third elements of `pmatch[]` have `rm_so` set to -1; for a line with a comment character at the beginning, the first and second are set to -1; and for a line with no comment characters, the second and third are set to -1.

Whenever you are done with a compiled regular expression, you need to free it to avoid a memory leak. You must use the `regfree()` function to free it, not the `free()` function:

```
#include <regex.h>

void regfree(regex_t *preg);
```

The POSIX standard does not explicitly specify whether you need to use `regfree()` each time you call `regcomp()` or only after the final time you call `regcomp()` on one `regex_t` structure. Therefore, `regfree()` your `regex_t` structures between uses to avoid memory leaks.

Whenever you get a nonzero return code from `regcomp()` or `regexec()`, the `regerror()` function can provide a detailed message explaining what went wrong. It writes as much as possible of an error message into a buffer and returns the size of the total message. Because you do not know beforehand how big the error message might be, you first ask for its size, then allocate the buffer, and then use the buffer, as demonstrated in our sample code below. Because that kind of error handling gets old fast, and because you need to include that error handling code at least twice (once after `regcomp()` and once after `regexec()`), we recommend that you write your own wrapper around `regerror()`, as shown on line 10 of match.c.

23.2.3 A Simple grep

Grep is a popular utility, specified by POSIX, which provides regular expression searching in text files. Here is a simple (not POSIX-compliant) version of grep implemented using the standard regular expression functions:

```
1: /* grep.c */
2:
3: #include <alloca.h>
```

```
 4: #include <ctype.h>
 5: #include <popt.h>
 6: #include <regex.h>
 7: #include <stdio.h>
 8: #include <string.h>
 9: #include <unistd.h>
10:
11: #define MODE_REGEXP        1
12: #define MODE_EXTENDED      2
13: #define MODE_FIXED         3
14:
15: void do_regerror(int errcode, const regex_t *preg) {
16:     char *errbuf;
17:     size_t errbuf_size;
18:
19:     errbuf_size = regerror(errcode, preg, NULL, 0);
20:     errbuf = alloca(errbuf_size);
21:     if (!errbuf) {
22:         perror("alloca");
23:         return;
24:     }
25:
26:     regerror(errcode, preg, errbuf, errbuf_size);
27:     fprintf(stderr, "%s\n", errbuf);
28: }
29:
30: int scanFile(FILE * f, int mode, const void * pattern,
31:              int ignoreCase, const char * fileName,
32:              int * maxCountPtr) {
33:     long lineLength;
34:     char * line;
35:     int match;
36:     int rc;
37:     char * chptr;
38:     char * prefix = "";
39:
40:     if (fileName) {
41:         prefix = alloca(strlen(fileName) + 4);
42:         sprintf(prefix, "%s: ", fileName);
43:     }
44:
```

```
45:        lineLength = sysconf(_SC_LINE_MAX);
46:        line = alloca(lineLength);
47:
48:        while (fgets(line, lineLength, f) && (*maxCountPtr)) {
49:            /* if we don't have a final '\n' we didn't get the
50:               whole line */
51:            if (line[strlen(line) - 1] != '\n') {
52:                fprintf(stderr, "%sline too long\n", prefix);
53:                return 1;
54:            }
55:
56:            if (mode == MODE_FIXED) {
57:                if (ignoreCase) {
58:                    for (chptr = line; *chptr; chptr++) {
59:                        if (isalpha(*chptr)) *chptr = tolower(*chptr);
60:                    }
61:                }
62:                match = (strstr(line, pattern) != NULL);
63:            } else {
64:                match = 0;
65:                rc = regexec(pattern, line, 0, NULL, 0);
66:                if (!rc)
67:                    match = 1;
68:                else if (rc != REG_NOMATCH)
69:                    do_regerror(match, pattern);
70:            }
71:
72:            if (match) {
73:                printf("%s%s", prefix, line);
74:                if (*maxCountPtr > 0)
75:                    (*maxCountPtr)--;
76:            }
77:        }
78:
79:        return 0;
80: }
81:
82: int main(int argc, const char ** argv) {
83:     const char * pattern = NULL;
84:     regex_t regPattern;
85:     const void * finalPattern;
```

```
 86:        int mode = MODE_REGEXP;
 87:        int ignoreCase = 0;
 88:        int maxCount = -1;
 89:        int rc;
 90:        int regFlags;
 91:        const char ** files;
 92:        poptContext optCon;
 93:        FILE * f;
 94:        char * chptr;
 95:        struct poptOption optionsTable[] = {
 96:                { "extended-regexp", 'E', POPT_ARG_VAL,
 97:                    &mode, MODE_EXTENDED,
 98:                    "pattern for match is an extended regular "
 99:                    "expression" },
100:                { "fixed-strings", 'F', POPT_ARG_VAL,
101:                    &mode, MODE_FIXED,
102:                    "pattern for match is a basic string (not a "
103:                    "regular expression)", NULL },
104:                { "basic-regexp", 'G', POPT_ARG_VAL,
105:                    &mode, MODE_REGEXP,
106:                    "pattern for match is a basic regular expression" },
107:                { "ignore-case", 'i', POPT_ARG_NONE, &ignoreCase, 0,
108:                    "perform case insensitive search", NULL },
109:                { "max-count", 'm', POPT_ARG_INT, &maxCount, 0,
110:                    "terminate after N matches", "N" },
111:                { "regexp", 'e', POPT_ARG_STRING, &pattern, 0,
112:                    "regular expression to search for", "pattern" },
113:                POPT_AUTOHELP
114:                { NULL, '\0', POPT_ARG_NONE, NULL, 0, NULL, NULL }
115:        };
116:
117:        optCon = poptGetContext("grep", argc, argv, optionsTable, 0);
118:        poptSetOtherOptionHelp(optCon, "<pattern> <file list>");
119:
120:        if ((rc = poptGetNextOpt(optCon)) < -1) {
121:            /* an error occurred during option processing */
122:            fprintf(stderr, "%s: %s\n",
123:                    poptBadOption(optCon, POPT_BADOPTION_NOALIAS),
124:                    poptStrerror(rc));
125:            return 1;
126:        }
```

```
127:
128:     files = poptGetArgs(optCon);
129:     /* if we weren't given a pattern it must be the first
130:        leftover */
131:     if (!files && !pattern) {
132:         poptPrintUsage(optCon, stdout, 0);
133:         return 1;
134:     }
135:
136:     if (!pattern) {
137:         pattern = files[0];
138:         files++;
139:     }
140:
141:     regFlags = REG_NEWLINE | REG_NOSUB;
142:     if (ignoreCase) {
143:         regFlags |= REG_ICASE;
144:         /* convert the pattern to lower case; this doesn't matter
145:            if we're ignoring the case in a regular expression, but
146:            it lets strstr() handle -i properly */
147:         chptr = alloca(strlen(pattern) + 1);
148:         strcpy(chptr, pattern);
149:         pattern = chptr;
150:
151:         while (*chptr) {
152:             if (isalpha(*chptr)) *chptr = tolower(*chptr);
153:             chptr++;
154:         }
155:     }
156:
157:
158:     switch (mode) {
159:     case MODE_EXTENDED:
160:         regFlags |= REG_EXTENDED;
161:     case MODE_REGEXP:
162:         if ((rc = regcomp(&regPattern, pattern, regFlags))) {
163:             do_regerror(rc, &regPattern);
164:             return 1;
165:         }
166:         finalPattern = &regPattern;
167:         break;
```

```
168:
169:        case MODE_FIXED:
170:            finalPattern = pattern;
171:            break;
172:        }
173:
174:        if (!*files) {
175:            rc = scanFile(stdin, mode, finalPattern, ignoreCase, NULL,
176:                            &maxCount);
177:        } else if (!files[1]) {
178:            /* this is handled separately because the file name should
179:                not be printed */
180:            if (!(f = fopen(*files, "r"))) {
181:                perror(*files);
182:                rc = 1;
183:            } else {
184:                rc = scanFile(f, mode, finalPattern, ignoreCase, NULL,
185:                                &maxCount);
186:                fclose(f);
187:            }
188:        } else {
189:            rc = 0;
190:
191:            while (*files) {
192:                if (!(f = fopen(*files, "r"))) {
193:                    perror(*files);
194:                    rc = 1;
195:                } else {
196:                    rc |= scanFile(f, mode, finalPattern, ignoreCase,
197:                                    *files, &maxCount);
198:                    fclose(f);
199:                }
200:                files++;
201:                if (!maxCount) break;
202:            }
203:        }
204:
205:        return rc;
206: }
```

CHAPTER 24

Terminal Handling with S-Lang

The S-Lang library, written by John E. Davis, provides midlevel access to terminals. It encapsulates all the low-level terminal handling through a set of routines that allow direct access to the video terminal and automatically handle scrolling and color. Although little direct support for windows is present and no widgets (or controls) are available in the S-Lang library, S-Lang provides a suitable base for such services.[1]

S-Lang is also available under DOS, which makes it attractive for applications that must be built for both Unix and DOS platforms. John E. Davis based his jed editor on S-Lang, allowing it to work on a wide variety of platforms, including DOS.

S-Lang's terminal handling abilities fall into two categories. First, it provides a set of functions for reading keystrokes from the terminal in a controlled manner. Second, it provides routines for full-screen output to the terminal. These routines hide many terminal capabilities from the programmer but still take advantage of each terminal's abilities.[2] This chapter discusses how to use S-Lang in each of these capacities and ends with an example program that uses both.

---

1. One of the authors of this book has written a higher-level windowing toolkit based on S-Lang called `newt`, which is included with most Linux distributions.
2. As described by the terminfo database.

24.1 Input Handling

Terminal input-handling is one of the least portable subsystems in the Unix world. BSD sgtty, System V termio, and POSIX termios have all been widely used. The S-Lang library hides this complexity through a few functions designed to make keyboard handling more straightforward and portable.

Writing a program to read one character at a time from the terminal and print each character onto its own line is fairly straightforward:

```
 1: /* slecho.c */
 2:
 3: #include <ctype.h>
 4: #include <slang/slang.h>
 5: #include <stdio.h>
 6:
 7: int main(void) {
 8:     char ch = '\0';
 9:
10:     /*
11:         Start SLANG tty handling, with:
12:          -1 default interrupt character (normally, Ctrl-C)
13:           0 no flow control, allowing all characters (except
14:              interrupt) to pass through to the program
15:           1 enable OPOST output processing of escape sequences
16:     */
17:     SLang_init_tty(-1, 0, 1);
18:
19:     while (ch != 'q') {
20:         ch = SLang_getkey();
21:         printf("read: %c 0x%x\n", isprint(ch) ? ch : ' ', ch);
22:     }
23:
24:     SLang_reset_tty();
25:
26:     return 0;
27: }
```

This program assumes that /usr/include/slang contains all the S-Lang header files. If this is not the case for your system, you need to change the code (and all other examples in this chapter) appropriately. When you compile and link this sample program, be sure to add -lslang to the link command so that the linker finds the S-Lang functions.

24.1.1 Initializing S-Lang Input Handling

Before any other input handling functions can work, the terminal must be placed in the state that S-Lang expects through the SLang_init_tty() function:

```
int SLang_init_tty(int abort_char, int flow_ctrl, int opost);
```

The first parameter to SLang_init_tty() is an abort character to use. If -1 is passed, the current tty interrupt character (usually, Ctrl-C) is retained; otherwise, the interrupt character is set to the value passed. Whenever the abort character is entered on the terminal, the kernel sends a SIGINT to the process, which normally terminates the application. Chapter 12 discusses how to handle signals such as SIGINT.

The next parameter turns flow control on and off. Terminal-level flow control allows the user to pause output to the terminal to prevent scrolling and then restart it. Normally, Ctrl-S is used to suspend terminal output and Ctrl-Q enables it. Although this feature is convenient for some line-oriented utilities, programs that take advantage of S-Lang are normally screen-oriented, so it may not be necessary. S-Lang allows applications to turn off this capability, which allows the program to use the Stop and Start keystrokes for other commands. To enable flow control, pass a nonzero value as the second parameter to SLang_init_tty().

The final parameter enables output post processing on the terminal. All the kernel's post processing mechanisms are enabled if the final parameter is nonzero. See page 380 for information on output processing.

24.1.2 Restoring the Terminal State

Once the terminal state has been modified by `SLang_init_tty()`, the program must explicitly restore the terminal to its original state before exiting. If you do not do this, the terminal will be extremely difficult to use after your program exits. `SLang_reset_tty()` does not take any arguments, nor does it return one.

If you are writing a program that should suspend properly (normally when the user presses Ctrl-Z), this function also needs to be called when `SIGTSTP` is received. For more information on handling `SIGTSTP` properly, see Chapter 15.

When you are developing programs with S-Lang, the program will likely crash more than once during your development, leaving your terminal in a nonstandard state. You can easily fix this by running the command `stty sane`.

24.1.3 Reading Characters from the Terminal

Once the terminal has been initialized properly, reading single keystrokes is straightforward. The function `SLang_getkey()` returns a single character from the terminal. However, that does not mean it returns a single keystroke—in Unix, many keystrokes return multiple characters. For example, on a VT100 terminal (as well as on many other terminals, including the Linux console) pressing F1 sends four characters to the screen—`ESC [ [ A` (try running slecho and pressing F1 to see what characters it received). Those multiple-character sequences can be mapped to keystrokes via the terminfo database [Strang, 1991B].

`SLang_getkey()` waits indefinitely for a character to be present before returning. If an error occurs, the function returns `0xFFFF` rather than a valid character.[3]

---

3. An error occurs if a signal is received while S-Lang is waiting for a keystroke.

24.1.4 Checking for Pending Input

In many cases, you want to check for available characters without blocking. This is handy whenever a program needs to do background processing while polling the user for input (this is especially popular in video games). `SLang_input_pending()` is defined as follows:

```
int SLang_input_pending(int timeout);
```

`SLang_input_pending()` returns true if characters become available within n tenths of seconds. It returns as soon as the characters are available; it returns false if no characters become available within the timeout period. If a timeout period of zero is given, `SLang_input_pending()` tells whether characters are currently available.

This behavior is easy to see. Just replace the test on the while loop in slecho.c with

```
while (ch != 'q' && SLang_input_pending(20))
```

The program now waits a maximum of two seconds for more input. Once two seconds pass without any input, it exits.

24.2 Output Handling

Internally, S-Lang's terminal output functions are divided into two sets: terminal-handling functions (the `SLtt` family) and higher-level screen management functions (the `SLsmg` family).

The `SLtt` function family works directly with the terminal; it includes functions that map closely with capabilities defined in the terminal database. It also includes routines for defining foreground and background color pairs and turning the cursor on and off. Only a few of these functions are normally used by application programmers; the rest are called internally by S-Lang.

The `SLsmg` family provides a higher-level abstraction of the display terminal. Although these functions use the `SLtt` functions for terminal handling, they provide a much more powerful interface for application developers.

These functions include string output, line drawing, and screen-querying functions. For performance reasons, these routines write to an internal buffer rather than directly to the terminal. When the application instructs S-Lang to update the physical terminal, S-Lang compares the new display to the original one and optimizes the output sequence appropriately.

24.2.1 Initializing Screen Management

Before using S-Lang's terminal output functions, a program must tell S-Lang to look up the current terminal (as determined by the TERM environment variable) in the terminal database. This is done by calling

```
void SLtt_get_terminfo(void);
```

One of the primary functions of SLtt_get_terminfo() is to set the physical size of the screen to the size listed in the terminal database. The number of rows and columns on the terminal are stored in SLtt_Screen_Rows and SLtt_Screen_Cols, respectively. Although the terminal database is often correct, resizeable terminals (such as xterms) are popular these days, and once they are resized from the defaults, the terminal database no longer contains the correct size for the terminal. To compensate for this, S-Lang allows programs to reset the values of SLtt_Screen_Rows and SLtt_Screen_Cols after the call to SLtt_get_terminfo(). Under Linux, the current terminal size is always available through the TIOCGWINSZ ioctl, which is discussed in detail on page 376.

Initializing the S-Lang's screen management layer is straightforward:

```
void SLsmg_init_smg(void);
SLsmg_init_smg()
```

24.2.2 Updating the Display

Before the results of a sequence of SLsmg routines gets reflected on the physical terminal, you must call the SLsmg_refresh() function. This function does not take any arguments or return a value, but it does update the physical terminal with the results of any screen drawing that has been done since the previous time it was called.

24.2.3 Moving the Cursor

As in most programs, the terminal cursor is used by S-Lang as both the default location for text output and a cue for the user. S-Lang programs can move the cursor with the following code:

```
extern void SLsmg_gotorc (int row, int column);
```

Note that the upper-left corner of the screen is (0, 0) and the bottom-right corner is (SLtt_Screen_Rows - 1, SLtt_Screen_Cols - 1).

24.2.4 Finishing Screen Management

When a program that uses SLsmg has finished, it needs to tell S-Lang it is done, allowing S-Lang to free buffers and restore the terminal state. Before doing this, it is a good idea to move the cursor to the bottom of the screen and refresh the display to make sure all output has been shown to the user.

24.2.5 Skeleton Screen Management

Here is a program that initializes S-Lang's screen management abilities and then closes them. Although it certainly does not do much, it does illustrate the basics of using S-Lang's SLsmg functionality.

```
 1: /* slinit.c */
 2:
 3: #include <slang/slang.h>
 4: #include <stdio.h>
 5: #include <sys/ioctl.h>
 6: #include <termios.h>
 7:
 8: int main(void) {
 9:     struct winsize ws;
10:
11:     /* get the size of the terminal connected to stdout */
12:     if (ioctl(1, TIOCGWINSZ, &ws)) {
13:         perror("failed to get window size");
14:         return 1;
15:     }
```

```
16:
17:        SLtt_get_terminfo();
18:
19:        SLtt_Screen_Rows = ws.ws_row;
20:        SLtt_Screen_Cols = ws.ws_col;
21:
22:        SLsmg_init_smg();
23:
24:        /* heart of the program goes here */
25:
26:        SLsmg_gotorc(SLtt_Screen_Rows - 1, 0);
27:        SLsmg_refresh();
28:        SLsmg_reset_smg();
29:        SLang_reset_tty();
30:
31:        return 0;
32: }
```

24.2.6 Switching Character Sets

Most modern terminals (including the VT100, which the Linux console closely emulates) support at least two character sets. The primary one is usually ISO-8859-1 or something similar; the second is used primarily for line-drawing characters. S-Lang allows you to choose which character set is used for drawing characters.

```
void SLsmg_set_char_set(int useAlternate)
```

When SLsmg_set_char_set() is called with a nonzero argument, new characters written to the display are mapped through the alternate character set. Calling SLsmg_set_char_set() with zero as its parameter disables this mapping, allowing characters to appear normally.

S-Lang defines a set of symbolic names for the commonly used line-drawing characters contained in the alternate character set. Table 24.1 shows the available line-drawing characters and S-Lang's name for each.

Table 24.1 Line Characters

Glyph	Symbolic Constant
—	SLSMG_HLINE_CHAR
│	SLSMG_VLINE_CHAR
┌	SLSMG_ULCORN_CHAR
┐	SLSMG_URCORN_CHAR
└	SLSMG_LLCORN_CHAR
┘	SLSMG_LRCORN_CHAR
┤	SLSMG_RTEE_CHAR
├	SLSMG_LTEE_CHAR
┬	SLSMG_UTEE_CHAR
┴	SLSMG_DTEE_CHAR
+	SLSMG_PLUS_CHAR

24.2.7 Writing to the Screen

Although there are a number of ways to write strings to the screen under S-Lang, they all look about the same. Here is the entire set of functions:

```
void SLsmg_write_char(char ch);
void SLsmg_write_string(char * str);
void SLsmg_write_nchars(char * chars, int length);
void SLsmg_write_nstring(char * str, int length);
void SLsmg_printf(char * format, ...);
void SLsmg_vprintf(char * format, va_list args);
void SLsmg_write_wrapped_string(char * str, int row, int column,
                                int height, int width, int fill);
```

All of these functions, except SLsmg_write_wrapped_string(), write the requested string into the screen buffer[4] at the current cursor location using the current color and character set. They all have different ways of deciding what string to write, however. After the information has been written, the cursor is advanced to the end of the area affected, just as on a normal terminal. Any strings that extend past the right side of the screen are truncated rather than wrapped. Although this is different from normal terminal output, it is reasonable for most full-screen applications, in which wrapped text has an adverse effect on the screen's layout.

---

4. Remember, the physical terminal is updated only by SLsmg_refresh().

SLsmg_write_char()

> Of all the screen output functions, this one is the simplest. It writes the character passed to the current cursor position and advances the cursor.

SLsmg_write_string()

> The string that is passed to the function is written to the screen.

SLsmg_write_nchars()

> The length characters pointed to by chars are written to the screen. NULL termination is ignored—a '\0' is written if one is found, and the routine continues past the end of the string.

SLsmg_write_nstring()

> At most length characters from str are written to the screen. If str is shorter than length characters, the remainder of the space is filled with blank characters.

SLsmg_printf()

> As the name implies, this routine acts like the standard printf() function, formatting the first argument, with the remainder of the arguments used as parameters for the formatting. The formatted string is then written to the screen.

SLsmg_vprintf()

> Like the C library's vfprintf() function, this routine expects a va_arg argument, which it uses to format the first parameter. The formatted string is then displayed.

SLsmg_write_wrapped_string()

> Although S-Lang truncates strings rather than wrap them, it does provide a simple function for writing strings wrapped to an arbitrary rectangle on the screen. SLsmg_write_wrapped_string() writes str to the rectangle that begins at row and column of size height and width.

> Although this routine does wrap on word boundaries, a \n in the string forces it to go to the next line. If final parameter fill is nonzero, every line is filled to the full width of the rectangle, with spaces used for padding where necessary.

24.2.8 Drawing Lines and Boxes

Although `SLsmg_set_char_set()` provides all the functionality needed to draw simple line graphics on a terminal, S-Lang provides some shortcut functions that are easier to use.

```
void SLsmg_draw_hline(int row);
void SLsmg_draw_vline(int column);
void SLsmg_draw_box(int row, int column, int height, int width);
```

The `SLsmg_draw_hline()` function draws a single horizontal line at row row; `SLsmg_draw_vline()` draws a single vertical line at column `col`.

`SLsmg_draw_box()` draws a box starting at `row` and `col` that extends for `height` rows and `width` columns. `SLsmg_draw_box()` is similar to a combination of `SLsmg_draw_hline()` and `SLsmg_draw_vline()`, but it gets the corners right, as well.

Here is an example program that draws a screen containing the normal character set and the alternate character set. It also demonstrates a simple use of `SLsmg_draw_box()`.

```
 1: /* slcharset.c */
 2:
 3: #include <slang/slang.h>
 4: #include <stdio.h>
 5: #include <sys/ioctl.h>
 6: #include <termios.h>
 7:
 8: /* displays a table containing 256 characters in a single character
 9:    set, starting a column col.  The 'label' is displayed over the
10:    table, and the alternate character set is displayed iff
11:    isAlternate is nonzero */
12: static void drawCharSet(int col, int isAlternate, char * label) {
13:     int i, j;
14:     int n = 0;
15:
16:     /* draw the box */
17:     SLsmg_draw_box(0, col, 20, 38);
18:
19:     /* center the label */
20:     SLsmg_gotorc(0, col + 2);
```

```
21:        SLsmg_write_string(label);
22:
23:
24:        /* draw the horizontal legend */
25:        SLsmg_gotorc(2, col + 4);
26:        SLsmg_write_string("0 1 2 3 4 5 6 7 8 9 A B C D E F");
27:
28:        /* set the character set to use */
29:        SLsmg_set_char_set(isAlternate);
30:
31:        /* this iterates over the 4 most significant bits */
32:        for (i = 0; i < 16; i++) {
33:            SLsmg_gotorc(3 + i, 2 + col);
34:            SLsmg_write_char(i < 10 ? i + '0' : (i - 10) + 'A');
35:
36:            /* this iterates over the 4 least significant bits */
37:            for (j = 0; j < 16; j++) {
38:                SLsmg_gotorc(3 + i, col + 4 + (j * 2));
39:                SLsmg_write_char(n++);
40:            }
41:        }
42:
43:        SLsmg_set_char_set(0);
44: }
45:
46: int main(void) {
47:     struct winsize ws;
48:
49:     /* get the size of the terminal connected to stdout */
50:     if (ioctl(1, TIOCGWINSZ, &ws)) {
51:         perror("failed to get window size");
52:         return 1;
53:     }
54:
55:     SLtt_get_terminfo();
56:
57:     SLtt_Screen_Rows = ws.ws_row;
58:     SLtt_Screen_Cols = ws.ws_col;
59:
60:     SLsmg_init_smg();
61:     SLang_init_tty(-1, 0, 1);
```

```
62:
63:        drawCharSet(0, 0, "Normal Character Set");
64:        drawCharSet(40, 1, "Alternate Character Set");
65:
66:        SLsmg_refresh();
67:        SLang_getkey();
68:
69:        SLsmg_gotorc(SLtt_Screen_Rows - 1, 0);
70:        SLsmg_refresh();
71:        SLsmg_reset_smg();
72:        SLang_reset_tty();
73:
74:        return 0;
75: }
```

24.2.9 Using Color

S-Lang makes it easy to add color to an application. It allows the user to use a palette of 256 entries[5], each defining a foreground and a background color. Most applications use a palette entry for one type of rendered object, such as window frame or listbox entry. A palette's colors are set through SLtt_set_color().

```
void SLtt_set_color(int entry, char * name, char * fg, char * bg);
```

The first parameter specifies the palette entry being modified. The name parameter is currently ignored and should be passed as NULL. The final two entries name the new foreground and background colors for that palette entry. Table 24.2 lists the colors S-Lang supports; the fg and bg should both be strings containing the name of the color to use. All the colors on the left side of the table may be used for the foreground or background color. However, the colors on the right side must be used only for foreground colors. Using them for background colors would give unpredictable results.[6]

Writes to the screen are done using the current palette entry, which is set by the SLsmg_set_color() function.

---

5. This number could be increased in the future, but it is doubtful such a change will ever be necessary.
6. Results might include blinking text on some systems.

Table 24.2   S-Lang Colors

Foreground or Background	Foreground
black	gray
red	brightred
green	brightgreen
brown	yellow
blue	brightblue
magenta	brightmagenta
cyan	brightcyan
lightgray	white

```
void SLsmg_set_color(int entry);
```

This sets the current palette entry to the specified entry. The colors specified by this entry are used for future screen writes.

Although an application may use the color-related functions on any terminal type, a number of factors control whether colors are displayed. The SLtt_Use_Ansi_Colors global variable controls whether colors are displayed. If it is set to zero, no colors are used. Any other value allows colors to be displayed.

SLtt_get_terminfo() tries to guess whether color should be enabled on the current terminal. Unfortunately, many termcap and terminfo databases are incomplete in this regard. If the COLORTERM environment variable is set, S-Lang sets SLtt_Use_Ansi_Colors no matter what the terminal database indicates.

Most applications that provide color support also provide a command-line option to allow users to selectively enable color support. When the option is used, the application explicitly sets SLtt_Use_Ansi_Colors.

CHAPTER 25

A Hashed Database Library

Applications commonly wish to store some form of binary data in a file. Storing such data for efficient retrieval is tricky and error-prone. There are a number of libraries that provide simple APIs for storing information in files. The **dbm** library was an early part of Unix systems (and was later reimplemented as **ndbm**), which led later to the the **Berkeley db library** and the **gdbm** library from the GNU Project. All of these libraries provide easy access to files that are set up as hash tables, with a binary key providing access to a binary data region.[1]

While gdbm and Berkeley db are both widely available on Linux systems, the licenses for each of them make them unsuitable for commercial development.[2] The **qdbm** library is quite similar to those other choices, but is licensed under the LGPL, making it more attractive to many developers. The basic API for each of these libraries is quite similar to the others, however, and porting code between the libraries is straightforward.

Full source code and documentation for qdbm are available from the http://qdbm.sourceforge.net Web site. This chapter describes all of the functions most applications need to use qdbm (all of which have close analogues in Berkeley db, gdbm, and ndbm). There are other API functions available, all of which are documented at the qdbm Web site.

---

1. The Berkeley db library has been greatly extended, and now includes a B-Tree implementation and full transaction capabilities.
2. Berkeley db is now developed by a for-profit organization, and they sell alternative licenses for their library that are attractive for certain applications.

25.1 Overview

Qdbm provides quite a few different APIs. The most basic of them, **Depot**, is the lowest-level API and the one we discuss here. The **Curia** interface allows the database to be split into multiple files (for better scalability or to work around file system limits) and the **Villa** functions provide both B-Trees and a transaction model. Inverted indexes[3] are available through the **Odeon** API. The final two APIs are **Relic** and **Hovel**, which provide reimplementations of the **ndbm** and **gdbm** APIs.

The Depot functions provide basic key/value operations, where a key is used to retrieve the value. Both the key and value are arbitrary binary streams that have their size passed separately from the data; the library does not need to know anything about their structure. However, Depot has a couple of features that make using strings as both keys and data items more convenient. First, whenever the size of a key or data item is passed into the library, -1 can be passed instead, which tells Depot to use `strlen()` to calculate the size to use. Second, most functions that read keys and data items automatically append a 0 byte to the returned value. This extra character is not included in the size returned, so it can be ignored if the value is not a string. If it is a string, the returned value can be treated as a string without the application having to `NULL`-terminate it.

Depot uses the global integer `dpecode` to store error codes; when Depot functions return failures, `dpecode` tells what went wrong (this is just like the `errno` variable used by system calls and the C library). Text error messages are provided by `dperrmsg()`.

```
#include <depot.h>

const char * dperrmsg(int ecode);
```

Like `strerror()`, `dperrmsg()` takes an error code (normally from `dpecode`) and returns a string describing what went wrong.

The functions in the Depot API use a pointer to a `DEPOT` structure. This structure is opaque (programs that use Depot cannot inspect the values in

---

3. Inverted indexes are a data structure designed for full text searches

the structure itself), but contains all of the information the library uses to maintain the on-disk file.

25.2 Basic Operations

25.2.1 Opening a qdbm File

The `dpopen()` library function is used to open db files.

```
#include <depot.h>

DB * dpopen(const char * filename, int omode, int bnum);
```

The first argument is the name of the file to use for the database.[4] The `omode` specifies how the file should be accessed, and should be `DP_OREADER` or `DP_OWRITER`, depending on whether the program wants read or write access to the database. By default, the database is locked to allow multiple programs read access or a single program write access. If the application does not want qdbm to perform any locking, `DP_ONOLCK` may be bitwise OR'ed with `omode`.

When applications are creating new databases, they should also bitwise OR `DP_CREAT` to tell qdbm to create a new file if it does not already exist. The `DP_OTRUNC` flag causes whatever contents `filename` originally contained to be erased and replaced with an empty database.

The final parameter for `dpopen()`, `bnum`, tells qdbm how many buckets to use in the hash array. The lower this number is, the smaller the database; the larger it is, the faster it is, due to reducing the number of hash collisions. The qdbm documentation recommends that this number be anywhere from half to four times the number of items that are expected to be in the database.[5] If you are not sure what number to use, zero gives a default value.[6]

---

4. Unlike some database libraries that use multiple files, commonly ending with `.pag` and `.dir`, the Depot library uses a single file.
5. For a good introduction to hash tables, see [Cormen, 1992].
6. This value can be changed only by optimizing the database with `dpoptimize()`, which is documented on the qdbm Web site.

dpopen() returns a pointer to a DEPOT structure, which is passed into the rest of the Depot functions. If an error occurs, dpopen() returns NULL and sets dpecode.

25.2.2 Closing a Database

Database files are closed through dpclose().

```
int dpclose(DEPOT * depot);
```

The dpclose() function returns zero on success, and nonzero if it fails, which can occur if the database's buffers cannot be flushed for any reason. Here is an example program that opens a database file in the current directory and immediately closes it:

```
 1: /* qdbmsimple.c */
 2:
 3: #include <depot.h>
 4: #include <errno.h>
 5: #include <fcntl.h>
 6: #include <stdio.h>
 7:
 8: int main(void) {
 9:     DEPOT * dp;
10:
11:     dp = dpopen("test.db", DP_OWRITER | DP_OCREAT, 0);
12:     if (!dp) {
13:         printf("error: %s\n", dperrmsg(dpecode));
14:         return 1;
15:     }
16:
17:     dpclose(dp);
18:
19:     return 0;
20: }
```

25.2.3 Obtaining the File Descriptor

While qdbm provides automatic locking, some programs may wish to substitute their own locking logic. To enable this, qdbm provides access to the file descriptor that refers to the database.

```
int dpfdesc(DEPOT * depot);
```

This function returns the file descriptor the database referred to by depot.[7]

25.2.4 Syncing the Database

Qdbm caches data in RAM to provide faster database access, and the Linux kernel caches disk writes for low-latency write() calls. An application can ensure that the on-disk database is consistent with the buffered structures by syncing the database. When a database is synced, qdbm flushes all its internal buffers and calls fsync() on the file descriptor.

```
int dpsync(DEPOT * depot);
```

25.3 Reading Records

There are two ways to read records from the database: looking up a record by its key, and reading sequential key/value pairs.

25.3.1 Reading a Particular Record

Both dpget() and dpgetwb() look up database entries by a key.

```
int dpget(DEPOT * depot, const char * key, int keySize, int start,
          int max, int * dataSize);
```

---

7. While qdbm makes the file descriptor available, be careful how you use it. All reading and writing to the file should be done through the qdbm library; operations that do not modify the data of the file, such as locking or setting the close-on-exec flag are acceptable.

The key is the item to look up in the database, and keySize is the length of the key (or -1, in which case Depot uses strlen(key) to determine the length). The next two parameters, start and max, allow partial records to be read in; start is the offset in the data where the read begins, and max is the maximum number of bytes to be read. If the data region were an array of 4 byte int values, for example, setting start to 12 and max to 8 would read in the fourth and fifth elements from the array. If less than start bytes are available, dpget() returns NULL. To read in all of the bytes from the data, set max to -1.

If the final parameter, dataSize, is not NULL, the integer it points to is filled in with the number of bytes read.

This function returns NULL on failure and a pointer to the data read in when it succeeds. If it fails, dpecode tells what caused the failure. In particular, if the item does not exist or has less than start bytes of data, it sets dpecode to DP_ENOITEM.

When dpget() returns data, a 0 byte is appended to the data, allowing it to be used as a string. The pointer is allocated using malloc(), and the application is responsible for freeing the memory when it is finished with it. If applications would like to read into a buffer rather than having Depot allocate one with malloc(), they should instead use the dpgetwb() function.

```
int dpgetwb(DEPOT * depot, const char * key, int keySize, int start,
            int max, const char * data);
```

The only parameters that are different between dpgetwb() and dpget() are max (which is interpreted differently) and data (which replaces the dataSize parameter from dpgetwb()). data should point to a buffer of max bytes for dpgetwb() to fill in with the data read from the database. The max parameter should not be -1 for dpgetwb() and the buffer does not have a 0 byte automatically appended to it by dpgetwb(). This function returns the number of bytes stored at data, and -1 if the record was not found, the data was smaller than start bytes, or an error occurred.

25.3.2 Reading Records Sequentially

Applications can iterate over all of the keys in the database by using dpi-
terinit() and dpiternext(). The keys are not returned in any particular
order[8] and the database should not be modified while the application is
iterating over it.

```
int dpiterinit(DEPOT * depot);
char * dpiternext(DEPOT * depot, int * keySize);
```

Calling dpiterinit() tells qdbm to return the first key in the database the
next time dpiternext() is called.

dpiternext() returns a pointer to either the first key in the database (if
dpiterinit() was just called) or the key in the database just after the key
it returned the previous time. If there are no more keys in the database, it
returns NULL. If keySize is not NULL, the integer it points to is set to the
size of the key returned.

The buffer dpiternext() returns a pointer to is allocated with malloc(),
and the pointer needs to be deallocated with free() when the application
is done with the key. The buffer is also NULL terminated, allowing it to be
used as a string, if appropriate.

25.4 Modifying the Database

There are two operations that modify qdbm databases: adding records and
removing records. Updating records is done using the same function as
adding records.

---

8. Well, they are returned in the order the items are referenced from the hash bucket.
   While this is an order, it is not a useful one.

25.4.1 Adding Records

New and updated records are recorded in the database through the dpput()
function.

```
int dpput(DEPOT * depot, const char * key, int keySize,
          const char * data, int dataSize, int dmode);
```

The key is the index value that can later be used to retrieve the information
referenced by data. Both keySize and dataSize may be -1, which tells
dpput() to use strlen() to get the size of that field. It looks at the dmode
parameter only if there is already a data item associated with key in the
database. dmode can have one of the following values:

DP_DCAT   The new data is appended to the end of the data already in
            the database.

DP_DKEEP   The database is not modified; dpput() returns failure and
            dpecode is set to DP_EKEEP.

DP_DOVER   The data in the database is overwritten with the new value.

dpput() returns zero if an error occurred (or if the key already existed and
DP_DKEEP was specified), and nonzero if the data for the key was updated
successfully.

25.4.2 Removing Records

Remove records from the database by passing the key whose data should
be removed to dpout().

```
int dpout(DEPOT * depot, const char * key, int keySize);
```

The specified key and the data associated with it are removed from the
database, and a nonzero value is returned. If there is no data for that key,
zero is returned. As for all of the other functions that take a key, if the
keySize is -1, dpout uses strlen() to find the length of the key.

25.5 Example

To help make all of this more concrete, here is a sample application that makes use of most of qdbm's features. It is intended as a simple phone database, although it can be used to store any simple name/value pairs. It stores its database in the user's home directory as .phonedb.

The -a flag adds an entry to the database. If -f is specified, any existing entry is overwritten with the new data. The next parameter is the key value to use, and the last parameter is the data (usually a phone number).

The -q flag queries the database for a particular key, which should be the only other parameter specified. Entries are removed from the database through the -d flag, which takes the key value to remove as the only other parameter.

If -l is specified, all the key/value pairs in the database are listed.

Here is an example of using phones:

```
$ ./phones -a Erik 374-5876
$ ./phones -a Michael 642-4235
$ ./phones -a Larry 527-7976
$ ./phones -a Barbara 227-2272
$ ./phones -q Larry
Larry 527-7976
$ ./phones -l
Larry 527-7976
Erik 374-5876
Michael 642-4235
Barbara 227-2272
$ ./phones -d Michael
$ ./phones -l
Larry 527-7976
Erik 374-5876
Barbara 227-2272
```

This program does something quite useful, has fewer than 200 lines of source code, and is well suited to managing large numbers of key/value pairs, clearly illustrating the value of the qdbm library.

```
 1: /* phones.c */
 2:
 3: /* This implements a very simple phone database. Full usage
 4:    information is given in the text. */
 5:
 6: #include <alloca.h>
 7: #include <depot.h>
 8: #include <errno.h>
 9: #include <fcntl.h>
10: #include <stdio.h>
11: #include <stdlib.h>
12: #include <string.h>
13: #include <unistd.h>
14:
15: void usage(void) {
16:     fprintf(stderr, "usage: phones -a [-f] <name> <phone>\n");
17:     fprintf(stderr, "              -d <name>\n");
18:     fprintf(stderr, "              -q <name>\n");
19:     fprintf(stderr, "              -l\n");
20:     exit(1);
21: }
22:
23: /* Opens the database $HOME/.phonedb. If writeable is nonzero,
24:    the database is opened for updating. If writeable is 0, the
25:    database is opened read-only. */
26: DEPOT * openDatabase(int writeable) {
27:     DEPOT * dp;
28:     char * filename;
29:     int flags;
30:
31:     /* Set the open mode */
32:     if (writeable) {
33:         flags = DP_OWRITER | DP_OCREAT;
34:     } else {
35:         flags = DP_OREADER;
36:     }
37:
38:     filename = alloca(strlen(getenv("HOME")) + 20);
39:     strcpy(filename, getenv("HOME"));
40:     strcat(filename, "/.phonedb");
41:
```

```
42:        dp = dpopen(filename, flags, 0);
43:        if (!dp) {
44:            fprintf(stderr, "failed to open %s: %s\n", filename,
45:                    dperrmsg(dpecode));
46:            return NULL;
47:        }
48:
49:        return dp;
50: }
51:
52: /* add a new record to the database; this parses the
53:    command-line arguments directly */
54: int addRecord(int argc, char ** argv) {
55:        DEPOT * dp;
56:        char * name, * phone;
57:        int rc = 0;
58:        int overwrite = 0;
59:        int flag;
60:
61:        /* check for our parameters; -f means overwrite an
62:           existing entry, and the name and phone number should
63:           be all that remains */
64:        if (!argc) usage();
65:        if (!strcmp(argv[0], "-f")) {
66:            overwrite = 1;
67:            argc--, argv++;
68:        }
69:
70:        if (argc != 2) usage();
71:
72:        name = argv[0];
73:        phone = argv[1];
74:
75:        /* open the database for writing */
76:        if (!(dp = openDatabase(1))) return 1;
77:
78:        /* if we shouldn't overwrite an existing entry, check
79:           to see if this name is already used */
80:        if (!overwrite) {
81:            flag = DP_DKEEP;
82:        } else {
```

```
83:            flag = DP_DOVER;
84:        }
85:
86:    if (!dpput(dp, name, -1, phone, -1, flag)) {
87:        if (dpecode == DP_EKEEP) {
88:            fprintf(stderr, "%s already has a listing\n", name);
89:        } else {
90:            fprintf(stderr, "put failed: %s\n", dperrmsg(dpecode));
91:        }
92:
93:        rc = 1;
94:    }
95:
96:    dpclose(dp);
97:
98:    return rc;
99: }
100:
101: /* looks up a name, and prints the phone number associated
102:    with it; parses the command line directly */
103: int queryRecord(int argc, char ** argv) {
104:    DEPOT * dp;
105:    int rc;
106:    char * phone;
107:
108:    /* only one argument is expected, a name to look up */
109:    if (argc != 1) usage();
110:
111:    /* open the database for reading */
112:    if (!(dp = openDatabase(0))) return 1;
113:
114:    phone = dpget(dp, argv[0], -1, 0, -1, NULL);
115:    if (!phone) {
116:        if (dpecode == DP_ENOITEM)
117:            fprintf(stderr, "%s is not listed\n", argv[0]);
118:        else
119:            fprintf(stderr, "error reading database: %s\n",
120:                    dperrmsg(dpecode));
121:
122:        rc = 1;
123:    } else {
```

```
124:            printf("%s %s\n", argv[0], (char *) phone);
125:            rc = 0;
126:        }
127:
128:        dpclose(dp);
129:
130:        return rc;
131: }
132:
133: /* delete the specified record; the name is passed as a
134:    command-line argument */
135: int delRecord(int argc, char ** argv) {
136:        DEPOT * dp;
137:        int rc;
138:
139:        /* only a single argument is expected */
140:        if (argc != 1) usage();
141:
142:        /* open the database for updating */
143:        if (!(dp = openDatabase(1))) return 1;
144:
145:        if (!(rc = dpout(dp, argv[0], -1))) {
146:            if (dpecode == DP_ENOITEM)
147:                fprintf(stderr, "%s is not listed\n", argv[0]);
148:            else
149:                fprintf(stderr, "error removing item: %s\n",
150:                        dperrmsg(dpecode));
151:
152:            rc = 1;
153:        }
154:
155:        dpclose(dp);
156:
157:        return rc;
158: }
159:
160: /* lists all of the records in the database */
161: int listRecords(void) {
162:        DEPOT * dp;
163:        char * key, * value;
164:
```

```
165:     /* open the database read-only */
166:     if (!(dp = openDatabase(0))) return 1;
167:
168:     dpiterinit(dp);
169:
170:     /* iterate over all of the records */
171:     while ((key = dpiternext(dp, NULL))) {
172:         value = dpget(dp, key, -1, 0, -1, NULL);
173:         printf("%s %s\n", key, value);
174:     }
175:
176:     dpclose(dp);
177:
178:     return 0;
179: }
180:
181: int main(int argc, char ** argv) {
182:     if (argc == 1) usage();
183:
184:     /* look for a mode flag, and call the appropriate function
185:        with the remainder of the arguments */
186:     if (!strcmp(argv[1], "-a"))
187:         return addRecord(argc - 2, argv + 2);
188:     else if (!strcmp(argv[1], "-q"))
189:         return queryRecord(argc - 2, argv + 2);
190:     else if (!strcmp(argv[1], "-d"))
191:         return delRecord(argc - 2, argv + 2);
192:     else if (!strcmp(argv[1], "-l")) {
193:         if (argc != 2) usage();
194:         return listRecords();
195:     }
196:
197:     usage();  /* did not recognize any options */
198:     return 0; /* doesn't get here due to usage() */
199: }
```

CHAPTER 26

Parsing Command-Line Options

Most Linux programs allow the user to specify command-line options. Such options perform a wide variety of functions but are fairly uniform in their syntax. **Short options** consist of a - character followed by a single alphanumeric character. **Long options**, common in GNU utilities, consist of two - characters followed by a string made up of letters, numbers, and hyphens. Either type of option may be followed by an argument. A space separates a short option from its arguments; either a space or an = separates a long option from an argument.

There are many ways of parsing command-line options. The most popular method is parsing the `argv` array by hand. The library functions `getopt()` and `getopt_long()` provide some assistance for option parsing. `getopt()` is provided by many Unix implementations, but it supports only short options. The `getopt_long()` function is available on Linux and allows automated parsing of both short and long options.[1]

A library called popt exists specifically for option parsing. It includes a number of advantages over the `getopt()` functions.

- It does not make use of global variables, which allows it to be used when multiple passes are needed to parse `argv`.

- It can parse an arbitrary array of `argv`-style elements. This allows popt to be used for parsing command-line-style strings from any source.

---

1. The `glibc` library also provides the `argp` library, which provides yet another alternative for option parsing.

- Many argument types can be parsed by the library without any extra code in the application.

- It provides a standard method of option aliasing. Programs that use popt can easily allow users to add new command-line options, which are defined as combinations of already-existing options. This allows the user to define new, complex behaviors or change the default behaviors of existing options.

- There is a straightforward mechanism for allowing libraries to parse some options while the main application parses other options.

- It can automatically generate a usage message summarizing the options a program understands, as well as a more detailed help message.

- Common error messages are provided by the library.

Like `getopt_long()`, the popt library supports short and long style options.

The popt library is highly portable and should work on any POSIX platform. The latest version is available from ftp://ftp.rpm.org/pub/rpm/. There are some features of popt that we do not discuss in this chapter, but the popt man page is quite good and contains documention on the features we have skipped.

It may be redistributed under either the GNU General Public License or the GNU Library General Public License, at the distributor's discretion.

26.1 The Option Table

26.1.1 Defining the Options

Applications provide popt with information on their command-line options through an array of `struct poptOption` structures.

Table 26.1   popt Argument Types

Value	Description	arg Type
POPT_ARG_NONE	No argument is expected	int
POPT_ARG_STRING	No type checking should be performed	char *
POPT_ARG_INT	An integer argument is expected	int
POPT_ARG_LONG	A long integer is expected	long
POPT_ARG_FLOAT	A float integer is expected	float
POPT_ARG_DOUBLE	A double integer is expected	double
POPT_ARG_VAL	No argument is expected (see text)	int

```
#include <popt.h>

struct poptOption {
    const char * longName;    /* may be NULL */
    char shortName;           /* may be '\0' */
    int argInfo;
    void * arg;               /* depends on argInfo */
    int val;                  /* 0 means do not return, just update flag */
    char * descrip;           /* optional description of the option */
    char * argDescrip;        /* optional argument description */
};
```

Each member of the table defines a single option that may be passed to the program. Long and short options are considered a single option that may occur in two different forms. The first two members, longName and shortName, define the names of the option; the first is a long name, and the latter is a single character.

The argInfo member tells popt what type of argument is expected after the argument. If no option is expected, POPT_ARG_NONE should be used. The rest of the valid values are summarized in Table 26.1.[2]

The next element, arg, allows popt to update program variables automatically when the option is used. If arg is NULL, it is ignored and popt takes no special action. Otherwise, it should point to a variable of the type indicated in the right-most column of Table 26.1.

---

2. getopt() connoisseurs will note that argInfo is the only required member of struct poptOption that is not directly analogous to a member in the getopt_long() argument table. The similarity between the two allows for easy transitions from getopt_long() to popt.

If the option takes no argument (`argInfo` is `POPT_ARG_NONE`), the variable pointed to by `arg` is set to one when the option is used. If the option does take an argument, the variable that `arg` points to is updated to reflect the value of the argument. Any string is acceptable for `POPT_ARG_STRING` arguments, but `POPT_ARG_INT`, `POPT_ARG_LONG`, `POPT_ARG_FLOAT`, and `POPT_ARG_DOUBLE` arguments are converted to the appropriate type, and an error is returned if the conversion fails.

If `POPT_ARG_VAL` is used, then no argument is expected. Instead, popt copies the integer value stored in the `val` member into the address pointed to by `arg`. This is useful when a program has a set of mutually exclusive arguments, and the last one specified wins. By specifying different `val` values for each option, having each option's `arg` member point to the same integer, and specifying `POPT_ARG_VAL` for each one, it is easy to know which of those options was the last one specified. If you need to give an error if more than one of the options was given, this does not work.

The `val` member specifies the value popt's parsing function should return when the option is encountered, unless `POPT_ARG_VAL` is used. If it is zero, the parsing function continues parsing with the next command-line argument rather than return.

The last two members are optional, and should be set to `NULL` if they are not needed.[3] The first of these, `descrip`, is a string describing the option. It is used by popt when it generates a help message describing all of the options available. The `descrip` member provides a sample argument for the option that is also used to display help. Help message generation is described on pages 606–608.

The final structure in the table should have all the pointer values set to `NULL` and all the arithmetic values set to 0, marking the end of the table.

Let's look at how an option table would be defined for a common application. Here is the options table for a simple version of `grep` utility:[4]

---

3. Note that the C language clears all remaining members of a structure that is given a partial default value when it is declared, making this happen automatically in most cases.

4. The full source code for this example is on pages 562–567 in Chapter 23.

```
const char * pattern = NULL;
int mode = MODE_REGEXP;
int ignoreCase = 0;
int maxCount = -1;

struct poptOption optionsTable[] = {
    { "extended-regexp", 'E', POPT_ARG_VAL, &mode, MODE_EXTENDED,
        "pattern for match is an extended regular expression", NULL },
    { "fixed-strings", 'F', POPT_ARG_VAL, &mode, MODE_FIXED,
        "pattern for match is a basic string (not a "
        "regular expression)", NULL },
    { "basic-regexp", 'G', POPT_ARG_VAL, &mode, MODE_REGEXP,
        "pattern for match is a basic regular expression" },
    { "ignore-case", 'i', POPT_ARG_NONE, &ignoreCase, 0,
        "perform case insensitive search", NULL },
    { "max-count", 'm', POPT_ARG_INT, &maxCount, 0,
        "terminate after N matches", "N" },
    { "regexp", 'e', POPT_ARG_STRING, &pattern, 0,
        "regular expression to search for", "pattern" },
    { NULL, '\0', POPT_ARG_NONE, NULL, 0, NULL, NULL }
};
```

The `retry` argument does not take an argument, so popt sets the `retry` variable to one if `--retry` is specified. The `bytes` and `lines` options both take integer arguments, which are stored in the identically named variables. The final option, `follow`, may be either the literal `name` or `descriptor`. The `followType` variable is set to point to whatever value is given on the command line, and needs to be checked for correctness. By setting it to point to `"descriptor"` initially, a useful default value is provided.

26.1.2 Nesting Option Tables

Some libraries provide implementation of some common command-line options. For example, one of the original X Windows toolkits handled the `-geometry` and `-display` options for applications, giving most X Windows programs a standard set of command-line options for controlling basic behaviors. Unfortunately, there is not an easy way of doing this. Passing `argc` and `argv` to an initialization function in the library lets the library handle the appropriate options, but the application has to know to ignore

those options when it parses argv. To prevent this problem, XtAppIni-
tialize() took argc and argv as parameters and returned new values for
each of them with the options handled by the library removed. This approach, while workable, becomes cumbersome as the number of libraries
increases.

To address this, popt allows the nesting of option tables. This lets libraries
define the options they want to handle (which could include further nesting), and the main program can provide those options by nesting the
libraries option table within its own.

An option table that is going to be nested is defined just like any other
one. To include it in another table, a new option is created with empty
longName and shortName options. The argInfo field must be set to
POPT_ARG_INCLUDE_TABLE and the arg member points to the table to be
nested. Here is an example of an option table that includes another:

```
struct poptOption nestedArgs[] = {
    { "option1", 'a', POPT_ARG_NONE, NULL, 'a' },
    { "option2", 'b', POPT_ARG_NONE, NULL, 'b' },
    { NULL, '\0', POPT_ARG_NONE, NULL, 0 }
};

struct poptOption mainArgs[] = {
    { "anoption", 'o', POPT_ARG_NONE, NULL, 'o' },
    { NULL, '\0', POPT_ARG_INCLUDE_TABLE, nestedArgs, 0 },
    { NULL, '\0', POPT_ARG_NONE, NULL, 0 }
};
```

In this example, the application ends up providing three options, --
option1, --option2, and --anoption. A more complete example of nested
option tables appears on pages 610–612.

26.2   Using the Option Table

26.2.1 Creating a Context

popt can interleave the parsing of multiple command-line sets. It does this
by keeping all the state information for a particular set of command-line

arguments in a `poptContext` data structure, an opaque type that should not be modified outside the popt library.

New popt contexts are created by `poptGetContext()`.

```
#include <popt.h>

poptContext poptGetContext(char * name, int argc, const char ** argv,
                           struct poptOption * options, int flags);
```

The first parameter, `name`, is used for alias handling and in help messages, and should be the name of the application whose options are being parsed. The next two arguments specify the command-line arguments to parse. These are generally passed to `poptGetContext()` exactly as they were passed to the program's `main()` function.[5] The `options` parameter points to the table of command-line options, which was described in the previous section. The final parameter, `flags`, modifies how options are parsed, and consists of the following flags (which may be logically OR'ed together):

`POPT_CONTEXT_KEEP_FIRST`
> Normally, popt ignores the value in `argv[0]` as it is typically the name of the program being run rather than a command-line argument. Specifying this flag causes popt to treat `argv[0]` as an option.

`POPT_CONTEXT_POSIXMEHARDER`
> Strict POSIX compliance requires that all options occur before extra command-line parameters. For example, according to POSIX, `rm -f file1 file2` would force the files `file1` and `file2` to be removed, while `rm file1 file -f` would cause normal removal of the three files `file1`, `file2`, and `-f`. Most Linux programs ignore this particular convention, so popt does not use this rule by default. This flag tells popt to parse options according to this convention.[6]

A `poptContext` keeps track of which options have already been parsed and which remain, among other things. If a program wishes to restart option

---

5. A common mistake is to define `argv` as `char **` rather than `const char **`, which is more correct. The prototype for `poptGetContext()` causes a compiler warning if `argv` is not defined in the correct manner.
6. The "posix me harder" terminology is popular among Linux applications when some (often unpleasant) strict POSIX compatibility mode is provided.

processing of a set of arguments, it can reset the poptContext by passing the context as the sole argument to poptResetContext().

When argument processing is complete, the process should free the popt-Context as it contains dynamically allocated components. The popt-FreeContext() function takes a poptContext as its sole argument and frees the resources the context is using.

Here are the prototypes of both poptResetContext() and poptFreeContext():

```
#include <popt.h>

void poptFreeContext(poptContext con);
void poptResetContext(poptContext con);
```

26.2.2 Parsing the Command Line

After an application has created a poptContext, it may begin parsing arguments. The poptGetNextOpt() performs the actual argument parsing.

```
#include <popt.h>

int poptGetNextOpt(poptContext con);
```

Taking the context as its sole argument, this function parses the next command-line argument found. After finding the next argument in the option table, the function fills in the object pointed to by the option table entry's arg pointer if it is not NULL. If the val entry for the option is nonzero, the function then returns that value. Otherwise, poptGetNextOpt() continues on to the next argument.

poptGetNextOpt() returns -1 when the final argument has been parsed, and other negative values when errors occur. This makes it a good idea to keep the val elements in the option table greater than zero.

If all of the command-line options are handled through arg pointers, command-line parsing is reduced to the following line of code:

```
rc = poptGetNextOpt(poptcon);
```

Many applications require more complex command-line parsing than this, however, and use the following structure:

```
while ((rc = poptGetNextOpt(poptcon)) > 0) {
    switch (rc) {
        /* specific arguments are handled here */
    }
}
```

When returned options are handled, the application needs to know the value of any arguments that were specified after the option. There are two ways to discover them. One is to ask popt to fill in a variable with the value of the option through the option table's arg elements. The other is to use poptGetOptArg().

```
#include <popt.h>

char * poptGetOptArg(poptContext con);
```

This function returns the argument given for the final option returned by poptGetNextOpt(), or it returns NULL if no argument was specified.

26.2.3 Leftover Arguments

Many applications take an arbitrary number of command-line arguments, such as a list of file names. When popt encounters an argument that does not begin with a -, it assumes it is such an argument and adds it to a list of leftover arguments. Three functions allow applications to access such arguments:

```
char * poptGetArg(poptContext con);
```
> This function returns the next leftover argument and marks it as processed.

```
char * poptPeekArg(poptContext con);
```
> The next leftover argument is returned but not marked as processed. This allows an application to look ahead into the argument list, without modifying the list.

```
char ** poptGetArgs(poptContext con);
```
All the leftover arguments are returned in a manner identical to argv. The final element in the returned array points to NULL, indicating the end of the arguments.

26.2.4 Automatic Help Messages

One of the benefits of using popt is its ability to generate help and usage messages automatically. Help messages list each command-line option along with a reasonably detailed description of that option, while usage messages provide a concise list of the available options without any descriptive text. popt provides a function to create each type of message.

```
#include <popt.h>

void poptPrintHelp(poptContext con, FILE * f, int flags);
void poptPrintUsage(poptContext con, FILE * f, int flags);
```

These two functions behave almost identically, writing the appropriate type of message to the file f. The flags argument is not currently used by either function, and should be set to zero for compatibility with future versions of popt.

Since the help message is normally provided by the --help option, and the usage message by the --usage option, popt provides an easy way of adding those two options to your program. The POPT_AUTOHELP macro can be used in the option table to add these options,[7] which displays the appropriate messages on STDOUT and exit with a return code of 0.[8] This example shows the option table in grep.c with the single line we need to add to the option table for grep to enable automatic help text:

```
95:     struct poptOption optionsTable[] = {
96:         { "extended-regexp", 'E', POPT_ARG_VAL,
97:             &mode, MODE_EXTENDED,
98:             "pattern for match is an extended regular "
99:             "expression" },
```

---

7. It also adds a -? option that is the same as --help.
8. The POPT_AUTOHELP macro expands to add a nested option table that defines the new options and a callback that implements the options.

```
100:                { "fixed-strings", 'F', POPT_ARG_VAL,
101:                    &mode, MODE_FIXED,
102:                    "pattern for match is a basic string (not a "
103:                    "regular expression)", NULL },
104:                { "basic-regexp", 'G', POPT_ARG_VAL,
105:                    &mode, MODE_REGEXP,
106:                    "pattern for match is a basic regular expression" },
107:                { "ignore-case", 'i', POPT_ARG_NONE, &ignoreCase, 0,
108:                    "perform case insensitive search", NULL },
109:                { "max-count", 'm', POPT_ARG_INT, &maxCount, 0,
110:                    "terminate after N matches", "N" },
111:                { "regexp", 'e', POPT_ARG_STRING, &pattern, 0,
112:                    "regular expression to search for", "pattern" },
113:                POPT_AUTOHELP
114:                { NULL, '\0', POPT_ARG_NONE, NULL, 0, NULL, NULL }
115:        };
```

Here is what the help message generated by this table looks like:

```
Usage: grep [OPTION...]
  -E, --extended-regexp       pattern for match is an extended regular
expression
  -F, --fixed-strings         pattern for match is a basic string (not a
regular
                              expression)
  -G, --basic-regexp       pattern for match is a basic regular expression
  -i, --ignore-case        perform case insensitive search
  -m, --max-count=N        terminate after N matches
  -e, --regexp=pattern     regular expression to search for

Help options:
  -?, --help               Show this help message
  --usage                  Display brief usage message
```

While this looks quite good, it is not quite right. The first line does not
mention that the command expects file names on the command line. The
[OPTION...] text that does appear there is popt's default, and this can be
changed to be more descriptive through the poptSetOtherOptionHelp()
function.

```
#include <popt.h>

poptSetOtherOptionHelp(poptContext con, const char * text);
```

The context is the first parameter and the second specifies the text that should appear after the program's name. Adding this call

```
poptSetOtherOptionHelp(optCon, "<pattern> <file list>");
```

changes the first line of our help message to

```
Usage: grep <pattern> <file list>
```

which is much nicer.

The final nicety of help message generation is how nested tables are handled. Look again at the help message for our `grep` program; the help options are in their own section of the help message. When a `POPT_ARG_INCLUDE_TABLE` option table entry provides a `descrip` member, that string is used as a description for all of the options in the nested table, and those options are displayed in their own section of the help message (like the help options for `tail`). If the `descrip` is `NULL`, the options for the nested table are displayed with the options from the main table rather than in their own section.

Occasionally, programs provide options that probably should not be used; they may be there for support with legacy applications or designed for testing only. Automatic help message generation for that option can be suppressed by logically OR'ing `POPT_ARGFLAG_DOC_HIDDEN` with the `arg` member of the the `struct poptOption` that defines that option.

26.3 Using Callbacks

We have shown two ways of handling options with popt: having an option returned by `poptGetNextOpt()` and having variables changed automatically when options are present. Unfortunately, neither of these are satisfactory for nested tables. Returning options defined by a nested table for the application to handle is obviously unworkable as nested tables are designed to prevent the application from having to know about options provided by a library. Setting variables does not work very well either as it is not clear what variables would get set. Using global variables is often a bad idea, and there are no local variables available for the library to use as the parsing happens from the main application, not from a library. To provide flexible option handling in nested applications, popt provides a callback facility.

Each table can define its own callback function, which overrides normal processing for the options defined in that table. Instead, the callback function gets called for each option that is found. Options defined in other option tables (including tables nested inside of a table defining a callback) get handled using the normal rules, unless those other tables define their own callbacks.

Callbacks can be defined only in the first entry in an option table. When that entry defines a callback, the `argInfo` member is `POPT_ARG_CALLBACK` and `arg` points to the callback function. The `descrip` member can be any pointer value, and it is passed to the callback each time it is invoked, allowing any arbitrary data to be accessed by the callback. All of the other members of `struct poptOption` should be zero or `NULL`.

Callbacks can be called at three points during option processing: before processing starts, when an option in the table for that callback is found, and when processing is complete. This gives libraries the opportunity to initialize any structures they need to (including the data defined by the `descrip` member) and to perform any housekeeping that may need to occur when processing is completed (perhaps cleaning up dynamic memory allocated for the `descrip` member). They are always called when options are found, but the option table needs to specify that they should be called in the other two places. To do this, `POPT_CBFLAG_PRE` or `POPT_CBFLAG_POST` (or both) should be logically OR'ed with the `POPT_ARG_CALLBACK` value set in the `arg` member of the structure specifying the callback.

Here is the prototype that should be used to define the callback function:

```
void callback(poptContext con, enum poptCallbackReason reason,
    const struct poptOption * opt, const char * arg,
    const void * data);
```

The first option is the context that is being parsed when the callback gets invoked. The next option is `POPT_CALLBACK_REASON_PRE` if option processing has not yet begun, `POPT_CALLBACK_REASON_POST` if option processing is finished, or `POPT_CALLBACK_REASON_OPTION` if an option in the table for this callback has been found. If it is the latter, the `opt` argument points to the option table entry for the option that was found, and the `arg` argument points to the string that defines the argument for the option. If a nonstring argument is expected, the callback is responsible for checking the type and converting the argument. The last parameter to the callback, data, is the value of the descrip field in the option table entry that sets up the callback.

Here is an example of a library that uses a nested popt table and callbacks to parse some command-line options. The data structure is initialized before the command-line parsing begins, and the final values are displayed afterward.

```
 1: /* popt-lib.c */
 2:
 3: #include <popt.h>
 4: #include <stdlib.h>
 5:
 6: struct params {
 7:     int height, width;
 8:     char * fg, * bg;
 9: };
10:
11: static void callback(poptContext con,
12:                      enum poptCallbackReason reason,
13:                      const struct poptOption * opt,
14:                      const char * arg,
15:                      const void * data);
16:
17: /* Store the parsed variables here. A global is not normally
18:    preferred, but it is simpler. */
19: struct params ourParam;
20:
21: struct poptOption libTable[] = {
22:     { NULL, '\0',
23:       POPT_ARG_CALLBACK | POPT_CBFLAG_PRE | POPT_CBFLAG_POST,
24:       callback, '\0', (void *) &ourParam, NULL },
25:     { "height", 'h', POPT_ARG_STRING, NULL, '\0', NULL, NULL },
26:     { "width", 'w', POPT_ARG_STRING, NULL, '\0', NULL, NULL },
27:     { "fg", 'f', POPT_ARG_STRING, NULL, '\0', NULL, NULL },
28:     { "bg", 'b', POPT_ARG_STRING, NULL, '\0', NULL, NULL },
29:     { NULL, '\0', POPT_ARG_NONE, NULL, '\0', NULL, NULL }
30: };
31:
32: static void callback(poptContext con,
```

```
33:                         enum poptCallbackReason reason,
34:                         const struct poptOption * opt,
35:                         const char * arg,
36:                         const void * data) {
37:     struct params * p = (void *) data;
38:     char * chptr = NULL;
39:
40:     if (reason == POPT_CALLBACK_REASON_PRE) {
41:         p->height = 640;
42:         p->width = 480;
43:         p->fg = "white";
44:         p->bg = "black";
45:     } else if (reason == POPT_CALLBACK_REASON_POST) {
46:         printf("using height %d width %d fg %s bg %s\n",
47:                 p->height, p->width, p->fg, p->bg);
48:
49:     } else {
50:         switch (opt->shortName) {
51:             case 'h': p->height = strtol(arg, &chptr, 10); break;
52:             case 'w': p->width = strtol(arg, &chptr, 10); break;
53:             case 'f': p->fg = (char *) arg; break;
54:             case 'b': p->bg = (char *) arg; break;
55:         }
56:
57:         if (chptr && *chptr) {
58:             fprintf(stderr, "numeric argument expected for %s\n",
59:                     opt->longName);
60:             exit(1);
61:         }
62:     }
63: }
64:
```

Programs that want to provide these command-line arguments need to include a single extra line in their popt table. Normally, this line would be a macro provided by a header file (like POPT_AUTOHELP is implemented), but for simplicity we just explicitly listed the line for this example.

```
1: /* popt-nest.c */
2:
3: #include <popt.h>
4:
```

```
 5: /* this would normally be declared in a header file */
 6: extern struct poptOption libTable[];
 7:
 8: int main(int argc, const char * argv[]) {
 9:     poptContext optCon;
10:     int rc;
11:     struct poptOption options[] = {
12:         { "app1", '\0', POPT_ARG_NONE, NULL, '\0' },
13:         { NULL, '\0', POPT_ARG_INCLUDE_TABLE, libTable,
14:           '\0', "Nested:", },
15:         POPT_AUTOHELP
16:         { NULL, '\0', POPT_ARG_NONE, NULL, '\0' }
17:     };
18:
19:     optCon = poptGetContext("popt-nest", argc, argv, options, 0);
20:
21:     if ((rc = poptGetNextOpt(optCon)) < -1) {
22:         fprintf(stderr, "%s: %s\n",
23:                 poptBadOption(optCon, POPT_BADOPTION_NOALIAS),
24:                 poptStrerror(rc));
25:         return 1;
26:     }
27:
28:     return 0;
29: }
```

26.4   Error Handling

All of the popt functions that can return errors return integers. When an error occurs, a negative error code is returned. Table 26.2 summarizes the error codes that occur. Here is a more detailed discussion of each error:

POPT_ERROR_NOARG

An option that requires an argument was specified on the command line, but no argument was given. This can be returned only by poptGetNextOpt().

Table 26.2 popt Errors

Error	Description
POPT_ERROR_NOARG	An argument is missing for an option.
POPT_ERROR_BADOPT	An option's argument could not be parsed.
POPT_ERROR_OPTSTOODEEP	Option aliasing is nested too deeply.
POPT_ERROR_BADQUOTE	Quotations do not match.
POPT_ERROR_BADNUMBER	An option could not be converted to a number.
POPT_ERROR_OVERFLOW	A given number was too big or too small.

POPT_ERROR_BADOPT

> An option was specified in argv but is not in the option table. This error can be returned only from poptGetNextOpt().

POPT_ERROR_OPTSTOODEEP

> A set of option aliases is nested too deeply. Currently, popt follows options only 10 levels deep to prevent infinite recursion. Only poptGetNextOpt() can return this error.

POPT_ERROR_BADQUOTE

> A parsed string has a quotation mismatch (such as a single quotation mark). poptParseArgvString(), poptReadConfigFile(), or poptReadDefaultConfig() can return this error.

POPT_ERROR_BADNUMBER

> A conversion from a string to a number (int or long) failed due to the string's containing nonnumeric characters. This occurs when poptGetNextOpt() processes an argument of type POPT_ARG_INT or POPT_ARG_LONG.

POPT_ERROR_OVERFLOW

> A string-to-number conversion failed because the number was too large or too small. Like POPT_ERROR_BADNUMBER, this error can occur only when poptGetNextOpt() processes an argument of type POPT_ARG_INT or POPT_ARG_LONG.

POPT_ERROR_ERRNO

> A system call returned with an error, and errno still contains the error from the system call. Both poptReadConfigFile() and poptReadDefaultConfig() can return this error.

Two functions are available to make it easy for applications to provide good error messages.

`const char * poptStrerror(const int error);`
> This function takes a popt error code and returns a string describing the error, just as with the standard `strerror()` function.

`char * poptBadOption(poptContext con, int flags);`
> If an error occurred during `poptGetNextOpt()`, this function returns the option that caused the error. If the `flags` argument is set to `POPT_BADOPTION_NOALIAS`, the outermost option is returned. Otherwise, `flags` should be zero, and the option that is returned may have been specified through an alias.

These two functions make popt error handling trivial for most applications. When an error is detected from most of the functions, an error message is printed along with the error string from `poptStrerror()`. When an error occurs during argument parsing, code similar to the following displays a useful error message:

```
fprintf(stderr, "%s: %s\n",
        poptBadOption(optCon, POPT_BADOPTION_NOALIAS),
        poptStrerror(rc));
```

26.5 Option Aliasing

One of the primary benefits of using popt over `getopt()` is the ability to use option aliasing. This lets the user specify options that popt expands into other options when they are specified. If the standard grep program made use of popt, users could add a `--text` option that expanded to `-i` `-n` `-E` `-2` to let them more easily find information in text files.

26.5.1 Specifying Aliases

Aliases are normally specified in two places: /etc/popt and the .popt file in the user's home directory (found through the `HOME` environment variable). Both files have the same format, an arbitrary number of lines formatted like this:

```
appname alias newoption expansion
```

The `appname` is the name of the application, which must be the same as the `name` parameter passed to `poptGetContext()`. This allows each file to specify aliases for multiple programs. The `alias` keyword specifies that an alias is being defined; currently, popt configuration files support only aliases, but other abilities may be added in the future. The next option is the option that should be aliased, and it may be either a short or a long option. The rest of the line specifies the expansion for the alias. It is parsed similarly to a shell command, which allows \, ", and ' to be used for quoting. If a backslash is the final character on a line, the next line in the file is assumed to be a logical continuation of the line containing the backslash, just as in shell.

The following entry would add a `--text` option to the `grep` command, as suggested at the beginning of this section:

```
grep alias --text -i -n -E -2
```

26.5.2 Enabling Aliases

An application must enable alias expansion for a `poptContext` before calling `poptGetNextOpt()` for the first time. There are three functions that define aliases for a context.

```
int poptReadDefaultConfig(poptContext con, int flags);
```
>   This function reads aliases from /etc/popt and the .popt file in the user's home directory. Currently, `flags` should be zero, as it is provided only for future expansion.

```
int poptReadConfigFile(poptContext con, char * fn);
```
> The file specified by fn is opened and parsed as a popt configuration file. This allows programs to use program-specific configuration files.

```
int poptAddAlias(poptContext con, struct poptAlias alias, int flags);
```
> Occasionally, programs want to specify aliases without having to read them from a configuration file. This function adds a new alias to a context. The flags argument should be zero, as it is currently reserved for future expansion. The new alias is specified as a struct poptAlias, which is defined as

```
struct poptAlias {
    char * longName;             /* may be NULL */
    char shortName;              /* may be '\0' */
    int argc;
    char ** argv;                /* must be free()able */
};
```

> The first two elements, longName and shortName, specify the option that is aliased. The final two, argc and argv, define the expansion to use when the aliases option is encountered.

26.6 Parsing Argument Strings

Although popt is usually used for parsing arguments already divided into an argv-style array, some programs need to parse strings that are formatted identically to command lines. To facilitate this, popt provides a function that parses a string into an array of string, using rules similar to normal shell parsing.

```
#include <popt.h>

int poptParseArgvString(char * s, int * argcPtr, char *** argvPtr);
```

The string s is parsed into an argv-style array. The integer pointed to by the second parameter, argcPtr, contains the number of elements parsed, and the pointer pointed to by the final parameter is set to point to the newly created array. The array is dynamically allocated and should be `free()`ed when the application is finished with it.

The `argvPtr` created by `poptParseArgvString()` is suitable to pass directly to `poptGetContext().`[9]

26.7 Handling Extra Arguments

Some applications implement the equivalent of option aliasing but need to do so through special logic. The `poptStuffArgs()` function allows an application to insert new arguments into the current `poptContext`.

```
#include <popt.h>

int poptStuffArgs(poptContext con, char ** argv);
```

The passed `argv` must have a `NULL` pointer as its final element. When `poptGetNextOpt()` is next called, the "stuffed" arguments are the first to be parsed. popt returns to the normal arguments once all the stuffed arguments have been exhausted.

26.8 Sample Application

Several of the examples in other chapters of this book use popt for option processing. A simple implementation of grep is on pages 562–567 and robin appears on pages 355–363. Both provide good examples of how popt is used in most applications.

RPM, a popular Linux package management program, makes heavy use of popt's features. Many of its command-line arguments are implemented through popt aliases, which makes RPM an excellent example of how to take advantage of the popt library.[10] For more information on RPM, see http://www.rpm.org.

---

9. This is often a good time to use `POPT_CONTEXT_KEEP_FIRST`.
10. popt was originally implemented for RPM, and many of RPM's query options are implemented as simple popt macros.

Logrotate is a program to help manage a system's log files. It provides a simpler example of using popt than RPM does, and is included with most Linux distributions.

CHAPTER 27

Dynamic Loading at Run Time

Loading shared objects at run time can be a useful way to structure your applications. Done right, it can make your applications extensible, and it also forces you to partition your code into logically separate modules, which is a useful coding discipline.

Many Unix applications, particularly large ones, are mostly implemented by separate blocks of code, often called *plugins* or *modules*. In some cases, they are implemented as completely different programs, which communicate with the application's core code via pipes or some other form of interprocess communication (IPC). In other cases, they are implemented as shared objects.

Shared objects are normally built like standard shared libraries (see Chapter 8), but they are used in a completely different way. The linker is never told about the shared objects, and they do not even need to exist when the application is linked. They do not need to be installed on the system in the same way most shared libraries do.

Just like normal shared libraries, a shared object should be linked explicitly against each library it calls. This ensures that the dynamic loader resolves all external references correctly when the shared object is loaded. If this is not done, then the external references are resolved only in the context of the application loading the shared object in that case. Theoretically, shared objects can be standard object files, but this is not recommended because it does not reliably resolve external shared library dependencies, just like a shared library that is not explicitly linked against all the libraries on which it depends.

The symbol names used in shared objects do not need to be unique among different shared objects loaded into the same program; in fact, they usually are not unique. Different shared objects written for the same interface usually use entry points with the same names. With normal shared libraries, this would be a disaster; with shared objects dynamically loaded at run time, it is the obvious thing to do.

Perhaps the most common use of shared objects loaded at run time is to create an interface to some generic type of capability that might have many different implementations. For instance, consider saving a graphics file. An application might have one internal format for managing its graphics, but there are a lot of file formats in which it might want to save graphics, and more are created on an irregular basis [Murray, 1996]. A generic interface for saving a graphics file that is exported to shared objects loaded at run time allows programmers to add new graphics file formats to the application without recompiling the application. If the interface is well documented, it is even possible for third parties who do not have the application's source code to add new graphics file formats.

A similar use is *framework* code that provides only an interface, not an implementation. For example, the PAM (Pluggable Authentication Modules) framework provides a general interface to challenge–response authentication methods, such as usernames and passwords. All the authentication is done by modules, and the choice of which authentication modules to use with which application is done at run time, not compile time, by consulting configuration files. The interface is well defined and stable, and new modules can be dropped into place and used at any time without recompiling either the framework or the application. The framework is loaded as a shared library, and code in that shared library loads and unloads the modules that provide the authentication methods.

27.1 The dl Interface

Dynamic loading consists of opening a library, looking up any number of symbols, handling any errors that occur, and closing the library. All the dynamic loading functions are declared in one header file, `<dlfcn.h>`, and are defined in libdl (link the application with `-ldl` to use the dynamic loading functionality).

The dlerror() function returns a string describing the most recent error that occurred in one of the other three dynamic loading functions:

```
const char * dlerror (void);
```

Each time it returns a value, it clears the error condition. Until another error condition is created, it continues to return NULL instead of a string. The reason for this unusual behavior is detailed in the description of the dlsym() function.

The dlopen() function opens a library. This involves finding the library file, opening the file, and doing some preliminary processing. Environment variables and the options passed to dlopen() determine the details:

```
void * dlopen (const char *filename, int flag);
```

If filename is an absolute path (that is, it begins with a / character), dlopen() does not need to search for the library. This is the usual way to use dlopen() from within application code. If filename is a simple file name, dlopen() searches for the filename library in these places:

- A colon-separated set of directories specified in the environment variable LD_ELF_LIBRARY_PATH, or, if LD_ELF_LIBRARY_PATH does not exist, in LD_LIBRARY_PATH.

- The libraries specified in the file /etc/ld.so.cache. That file is generated by the ldconfig program, which lists every library it finds in a directory listed in /etc/ld.so.conf at the time that it is run.

- /usr/lib

- /lib

If filename is NULL, dlopen() opens an instance of the current executable. This is useful only in rare cases. dlopen() returns NULL on failure.

Finding the files is the easy part of dlopen()'s job; resolving the symbols is more complex. There are two fundamentally different types of symbol resolution, immediate and lazy. Immediate resolution causes dlopen() to resolve all the unresolved symbols before it returns; lazy resolution means that symbol resolution occurs on demand.

If most of the symbols will end up being resolved in the end, it is more efficient to perform immediate resolution. However, for libraries with many unresolved symbols, the time spent resolving the symbols may be noticeable; if this significantly affects your user interface, you may prefer lazy resolution. The difference in overall efficiency is not significant.

While developing and debugging, you will almost always want to use immediate resolution. If your shared objects have unresolvable symbols, you want to know about it immediately, not when your program crashes in the middle of seemingly unrelated code. Lazy resolution will be a source of hard-to-reproduce bugs if you do not test your shared objects with immediate resolution first.

This is especially true if you have shared objects that depend on other shared objects to supply some of their symbols. If shared object A depends on a symbol b in shared object B, and B is loaded after A, lazy resolution of b will succeed if it happens after B is loaded, but it will fail before B is loaded. Developing your code with immediate resolution enabled will help you catch this type of bug before it causes problems.

This implies that you should always load modules in reverse order of their dependencies: If A depends on B for some of its symbols, you should load B before you load A, and you should unload A before you unload B. Fortunately, most applications of dynamically loaded shared objects have no such interdependencies.

By default, the symbols in a shared object are not exported and so will not be used to resolve symbols in other shared objects. They will be available only for you to look up and use, as will be described in the next section. However, you may choose to export all the symbols in a shared object to all other shared objects; they will be available to all subsequently loaded shared objects.

All of this is controlled by the `flags` argument. It must be set to `RTLD_LAZY` for lazy resolution or `RTLD_NOW` for immediate resolution. Either of these may be OR'ed with `RTLD_GLOBAL` in order to export its symbols to other modules.

If the shared object exports a routine named `_init`, that routine is run before `dlopen()` returns.

The dlopen() function returns a *handle* to the shared object it has opened. This is an opaque object handle that you should use only as an argument to subsequent dlsym() and dlclose() function calls. If a shared object is opened multiple times, dlopen() returns the same handle each time, and each call increments a reference count.

The dlsym() function looks up a symbol in a library:

```
void * dlsym (void *handle, char *symbol);
```

The handle must be a handle returned by dlopen(), and symbol is a NULL-terminated string naming the symbol you wish to look up. dlsym() returns the address of the symbol that you specified, or it returns NULL if a fatal error occurs. In cases in which you know that NULL is not the correct address of the symbol (such as looking up the address of a function), you can test for errors by checking to see if it returned NULL. However, in the more general case, some symbols may be zero-valued and be equal to NULL. In those cases, you need to see if dlerror() returns an error. Since dlerror() returns an error only once and then reverts to returning NULL, you should use code like this:

```
/* clear any error condition that has not been read yet */
dlerror();
p = dlsym(handle, "this_symbol");
if ((error = dlerror()) != NULL) {
    /* error handling */
}
```

Since dlsym() returns a void *, you need to use casts to make the C compiler stop complaining. When you store the pointer that dlsym() returns, store it in a variable of the type that you want to use, and make your cast when you call dlsym(). Do not store the result in a void * variable; you would have to cast it every time you use it.

The dlclose() function closes a library.

```
void * dlclose (void *handle);
```

dlclose() checks the reference count that was incremented on each duplicate dlopen() call, and if it is zero, it closes the library. This reference count allows libraries to use dlopen() and dlclose() on arbitrary objects without worrying that the code that called it has already opened any of those objects.

27.1.1 Example

In Chapter 8, we presented an example of using a normal shared library. The shared library that we built, libhello.so, can also be loaded at run time. The loadhello program loads libhello.so dynamically and calls the print_hello function it loads from the library.

Here is loadhello.c:

```
 1: /* loadhello.c */
 2:
 3: #include <dlfcn.h>
 4: #include <stdio.h>
 5: #include <stdlib.h>
 6:
 7: typedef void (*hello_function)(void);
 8:
 9: int main (void) {
10:    void *library;
11:    hello_function hello;
12:    const char *error;
13:
14:    library = dlopen("libhello.so", RTLD_LAZY);
15:    if (library == NULL) {
16:       fprintf(stderr, "Could not open libhello.so: %s\n",
17:               dlerror());
18:       exit(1);
19:    }
20:
21:    /* while in this case we know that the print_hello symbol
22:     * should never be null, that is not true for looking up
23:     * arbitrary symbols.  So we demonstrate checking dlerror()'s
24:     * return code instead of dlsym()'s.
25:     */
26:    dlerror();
27:    hello = dlsym(library, "print_hello");
28:    error = dlerror();
```

```
29:     if (error) {
30:         fprintf(stderr, "Could not find print_hello: %s\n", error);
31:         exit(1);
32:     }
33:
34:     (*hello)();
35:     dlclose(library);
36:     return 0;
37: }
```

CHAPTER 28

User Identification and Authentication

Linux's security model uses numbers to identify users and groups, but people prefer names. The names are stored, along with other important information, in two system databases.

28.1   ID-to-Name Translation

When you type `ls -l` to list the contents of the current directory, the third and fourth columns give the user ID and group ID that owns each file. It looks like this:

```
drwxrwxr-x    5 christid christid    1024 Aug 15 02:30 christid
drwxr-xr-x   73 johnsonm root        4096 Jan 18 12:48 johnsonm
drwxr-xr-x   25 kim      root        2048 Jan 12 21:13 kim
drwxrwsr-x    2 tytso    tytso       1024 Jan 30  1996 tytso
```

But the kernel does not store the string `christid` anywhere; the ls program is translating from kernel-supplied numbers to names. It gets numbers from the `stat()` system call and looks up the names in two system databases. These are normally kept in the /etc/passwd and /etc/group files, although on some systems the information is stored somewhere on the network or in other, less standard, file locations. As a programmer, you do not have to worry about where the information is stored; generic functions are provided in the C library that read configuration files to determine where the information is stored, fetch the information, and return it to you transparently.

To demonstrate what ls gets from the kernel, run `ls -ln`:

```
drwxrwxr-x   5 500      500         1024 Aug 15 02:30 christid
drwxr-xr-x  73 100        0         4096 Jan 18 12:48 johnsonm
drwxr-xr-x  25 101        0         2048 Jan 12 21:13 kim
drwxrwsr-x   2 1008     1008        1024 Jan 30  1996 tytso
```

The structure that represents entries in /etc/passwd (or equivalent databases for a system) is contained in <pwd.h>:

```
struct passwd {
  char *pw_name;           /* Username        */
  char *pw_passwd;         /* Password        */
  __uid_t pw_uid;          /* User ID         */
  __gid_t pw_gid;          /* Group ID        */
  char *pw_gecos;          /* Real name       */
  char *pw_dir;            /* Home directory  */
  char *pw_shell;          /* Shell program   */
};
```

- pw_name is the *unique* username.

- pw_passwd may be the encrypted password or something else related to authentication. This is system-dependent.

- pw_uid is the (usually unique) number that the kernel uses to identify the user.

- pw_gid is the primary group that the kernel associates with the user.

- pw_gecos is a system-dependent member that stores information about the user. This generally includes the user's real name; on many systems, it is a comma-separated list of members that includes home and office phone numbers.

- pw_dir is the home directory associated with the user. Normal login sessions start with this directory as the current directory.

- pw_shell is the shell that is started on normal logins for the user. This is usually something like /bin/bash, /bin/tcsh, /bin/zsh, and so on. However, entries used for other purposes may have other shells. /bin/false is used for passwd entries that should not be used for logins. Specialized shells are often used for purposes beyond the scope of this book.

The structure that represents entries in /etc/group (again, or equivalent databases) is contained in <grp.h>:

```
struct group {
  char *gr_name;          /*  Group name   */
  char *gr_passwd;        /*  Password     */
  __gid_t gr_gid;         /*  Group ID     */
  char **gr_mem;          /*  Member list  */
};
```

- gr_name is the unique name of the group.

- gr_passwd is the (usually unused) password. The same caveats apply to this member as to pw_passwd, only more so.

- gr_gid is the (usually unique) number the kernel uses to identify the group.

- gr_mem is a comma-separated list of group members. This is a list of usernames that are assigned to this group on a secondary basis (see Chapter 10).

There are two common reasons to access the system identification databases: if the kernel gives you a number and you want a name, or if someone or some program gives you a name and you need to give the kernel a number. There are two functions that look up numeric IDs, getpwuid() and getgrgid(), which take an integer ID and return a pointer to a structure containing information from the relevant system database. Similarly, there are two functions that look up names, getpwnam() and getgrnam(), and they return the same two structures. Here is a summary:

	User Database	Group Database
Number	getpwuid()	getgrgid()
Name	getpwnam()	getgrnam()

All of these functions return pointers to structures. The structures are static structures that are overwritten the next time the function is called, so if you need to keep a structure around for any reason, you need to make a copy of it.

The four functions above are essentially shortcuts providing the most commonly needed functions for accessing the system databases. Lower-level functions called `getpwent()` and `getgrent()` iterate over the lines in the databases rather than search for some record in particular. Each time you call one of these functions, it reads another entry from the relevant system database and returns it. When you are finished reading the entries in, call `endpwent()` or `endgrent()` to close the relevant file.

As an example, here is `getpwuid()` written in terms of `getpwent()`:

```
struct passwd *getpwuid(uid_t uid) {
    struct passwd *pw;

    while (pw = getpwent()) {
        if (!pw)
            /* error occurred;
             * fall through to error processing */
            break;
        if (pw->pw_uid == uid) {
            endpwent();
            return (pw);
        }
    }
    endpwent();
    return NULL;
}
```

28.1.1 Example: The `id` Command

The `id` command uses many of these functions and provides some excellent examples of how to work with them. It also uses some of the kernel features described in Chapter 10.

```
1: /* id.c */
2:
```

```
 3: #include <grp.h>
 4: #include <pwd.h>
 5: #include <sys/types.h>
 6: #include <stdlib.h>
 7: #include <stdio.h>
 8: #include <string.h>
 9: #include <unistd.h>
10:
11: void usage(int die, char *error) {
12:     fprintf(stderr, "Usage: id [<username>]\n");
13:     if (error) fprintf(stderr, "%s\n", error);
14:     if (die) exit(die);
15: }
16:
17: void die(char *error) {
18:     if (error) fprintf(stderr, "%s\n", error);
19:     exit(3);
20: }
21:
22: int main(int argc, const char *argv[]) {
23:     struct passwd *pw;
24:     struct group  *gp;
25:     int       current_user = 0;
26:     uid_t   id;
27:     int i;
28:
29:     if (argc > 2)
30:         usage(1, NULL);
31:
32:     if (argc == 1) {
33:         id = getuid();
34:         current_user = 1;
35:         if (!(pw = getpwuid(id)))
36:             usage(1, "Username does not exist");
37:     } else {
38:         if (!(pw = getpwnam(argv[1])))
39:             usage(1, "Username does not exist");
40:         id = pw->pw_uid;
41:     }
42:
43:     printf("uid=%d(%s)", id, pw->pw_name);
```

```
44:        if ((gp = getgrgid(pw->pw_gid)))
45:            printf(" gid=%d(%s)", pw->pw_gid, gp->gr_name);
46:
47:        if (current_user) {
48:            gid_t *gid_list;
49:            int      gid_size;
50:
51:            if (getuid() != geteuid()) {
52:                id = geteuid();
53:                if (!(pw = getpwuid(id)))
54:                    usage(1, "Username does not exist");
55:                printf(" euid=%d(%s)", id, pw->pw_name);
56:            }
57:
58:            if (getgid() != getegid()) {
59:                id = getegid();
60:                if (!(gp = getgrgid(id)))
61:                    usage(1, "Group does not exist");
62:                printf(" egid=%d(%s)", id, gp->gr_name);
63:            }
64:
65:            /* use getgroups interface to get current groups */
66:            gid_size = getgroups(0, NULL);
67:            if (gid_size) {
68:                gid_list = malloc(gid_size * sizeof(gid_t));
69:                getgroups(gid_size, gid_list);
70:
71:                for (i = 0; i < gid_size; i++) {
72:                    if (!(gp = getgrgid(gid_list[i])))
73:                        die("Group does not exist");
74:                    printf("%s%d(%s)", (i == 0) ? " groups=" : ",",
75:                                            gp->gr_gid, gp->gr_name);
76:                }
77:
78:                free(gid_list);
79:            }
80:        } else {
81:            /* get list of groups from group database */
82:            i = 0;
83:            while ((gp = getgrent())) {
84:                char *c = *(gp->gr_mem);
```

```
 85:
 86:                while (c && *c) {
 87:                    if (!strncmp(c, pw->pw_name, 16)) {
 88:                        printf("%s%d(%s)",
 89:                            (i++ == 0) ? " groups=" : ",",
 90:                            gp->gr_gid, gp->gr_name);
 91:                        c = NULL;
 92:                    } else {
 93:                        c++;
 94:                    }
 95:                }
 96:            }
 97:            endgrent();
 98:        }
 99:
100:        printf("\n");
101:        exit(0);
102: }
```

The argument-handling code that starts on line 29 calls a few important functions. When called with no command-line arguments, id looks up information based on what user ran it and reports on that. getuid() is documented in Chapter 10; it returns the user ID of the process that calls it. getpwuid() then looks up the password file entry for that user ID. If id is given a username as a command-line argument, it instead looks up the entry based on the name that it is given, regardless of the ID of the user that runs it.

The id program first prints the user's numeric ID and name. The password file includes the name of the user's primary group. If that group exists in the group file, id prints its number and name.

Chapter 10 documents all the different forms of IDs that the kernel uses. id needs to use geteuid() and getegid() to check the effective uid and gid and print them if they differ from the real uid and gid. Again, we look up password and group structures by numeric ID.

Finally, id needs to print out all the supplementary groups. This is a little tricky because there are two ways to determine the list of supplementary groups. If a user is running id with no arguments, then id uses the getgroups() function to determine what groups the user is a member of. Otherwise, it gets a list of groups out of the group database.

Using getgroups() is preferable because it lists the groups that the current process belongs to rather than the groups that the user would belong to if he logged in at that moment. That is, if the user has already logged in and has been assigned a set of supplementary groups, and then the group database is changed, getgroups() gets the set of groups that apply to that login process; examining the group database gets the set of groups that will be applied to the user's *next* login session.

As documented in Chapter 10, the getgroups() function has an unusual (but convenient) usage: Call it once with 0 size and an ignored pointer (which can, as here, be NULL) and it returns the number of data items it wants to return. So then id allocates the exact-right-size list and calls getgroups() again, this time with the correct size and a list capable of holding the information it wants.

Next, id iterates over the list, getting the entries it wants from the group database. Note that this is different from using the group database to get the list of groups to which a user belongs. In this case, id is using the group database only to map group numbers to group names. A more efficient interface would use getgrent() to iterate over the group database and look up entries in the list, rather than the other way around; that is left as an easy exercise. Remember to use endgrent() when you are done. Not doing so would leave a file handle open, which may cause later code to fail if that code assumes (reasonably enough) that getgrent() starts with the first entry.

Note that there is no guarantee that the entries in the list returned by getgroups() is sorted in the same order that they appear in the group database, although it is often the case that they are.

If the user provided a username as a command-line argument, id needs to iterate over the group file, looking for groups in which the provided username is specified. Remember to call endgrent() to clean up after yourself!

28.2 Pluggable Authentication Modules

The C library interface is fine for looking up user information, but does not allow the system administrator sufficient control over how authentication is performed.

Pluggable Authentication Modules, or PAM, is a specification and library specifically for configuring authentication on a system. The library provides a standard and relatively simple interface for authenticating users and for changing authentication information (such as a user's password). The Linux-PAM implementation[1] includes full documentation on how to program to the PAM interface, including documentation on how to write new PAM modules (*The Module Writers' Manual*) and how to write applications that make use of PAM (*The Application Developers' Manual*). Here, we merely show simple use of PAM for an application that wishes to check passwords appropriately.

PAM is a standard interface, specified by DCE, X/Open, and The Open Group. It is included as a part of several versions of Unix and practically all versions of Linux. It is a portable interface, so we recommend that you authenticate users using PAM. If you need to port code written to the PAM standard to an operating system that does not support PAM, the port will be trivial. However, because PAM is a somewhat rigid standard, it can be less easy to port applications that do not support PAM to a system that does use PAM.

Beyond authentication services (determining whether a user really is who he says he is, changing authentication information like passwords), PAM also does account management (determining whether this user is allowed to log in at this time and on this terminal), and credential management (typically, authentication tokens such as those used for X and Kerberos—but expressly not uids and gids).

The Linux-PAM implementation provides both the standard `libpam` library and a set of nonstandard helper functions in the `libpam_misc` library. The main header file for writing PAM-aware applications is `<security/pam_appl.h>`.

---

1. http://www.kernel.org/pub/linux/libs/pam/

We describe the core routines used to build an application that depends on PAM for its user authentication, and then provide a sample application, pamexample, that uses both the libpam library and the libpam_misc library.

28.2.1 PAM Conversations

PAM separates policy from mechanism; the PAM modules that implement the policy do not directly interact with the user, and the application does not set policy. All policy is established by the system administrator in a policy definition file, and is implemented by the modules invoked by the policy definition file. The *conversation structure*, struct pam_conv, tells modules how to ask the application to request information from the user.

```
#include <security/pam_appl.h>
struct pam_conv {
    int (*conv)(int num_msg, const struct pam_message **msg,
                struct pam_response **resp, void *appdata_ptr);
    void *appdata_ptr;
};
```

The conv() member is a pointer to a *conversation function* that accepts messages to give to the user in struct pam_message and returns the user-supplied information in struct pam_response. The libpam_misc library provides a conversation function called misc_conv that works fine for text-based console applications. To use it (which we recommend that you do if possible), you need to include <security/pam_misc.h> and fill in the conv member with misc_conv. The "pamexample" program presented on page 641 uses this simple mechanism.

Alternatively, you will have to implement your own conversation function. To do so, you need to understand two more data structures:

```
struct pam_message {
    int msg_style;
    const char *msg;
};
struct pam_response {
    char *resp;
    int resp_retcode;    /* currently unused, zero expected */
};
```

The conversation function is passed an array of pointers to `pam_message` structures and an array of pointers to `pam_response` structures, each of length `num_msg`. Provide the response, if any, to each `pam_message` structure in the `pam_response` structure with the same array index. The `msg_style` can be one of the following:

PAM_PROMPT_ECHO_OFF

> Print text specified in `msg` as informational text (for example, on the standard output file descriptor), ask user for a response without echoing the characters typed (as for a password), and return the text in a newly allocated character string stored in the associated `pam_response`'s `resp`.

PAM_PROMPT_ECHO_ON

> Print text specified in `msg` as informational text (for example, on the standard output file descriptor), ask user for a response while echoing the characters typed (as for a user name), and return the text in a newly allocated character string stored in the associated `pam_response`'s `resp`.

PAM_ERROR_MSG

> Print text specified in `msg` as error text (for example, on the standard error file descriptor), set the associated `pam_response`'s `resp` to NULL.

PAM_TEXT_INFO

> Print text specified in `msg` as informational text (for example, on the standard output file descriptor), set the associated `pam_response`'s `resp` to NULL.

Other values may be defined as extensions to the standard; your conversation function should ignore them if it is not written to handle them, and should merely provide a NULL response for them. PAM (more specifically, the PAM module making the request) is responsible for freeing every non-NULL resp string, as well as the pam_message and pam_response structure arrays.

The appdata_ptr member that is set in the conversation structure is passed to the conversation function. This is useful if you are using one conversation function in multiple contexts, or if you wish to pass context information into the conversation function. This information might include an X display specification, an internal data structure storing file descriptors for a connection, or any other data that your application finds useful. It is not interpreted by the PAM library in any way.

The conversation function should return PAM_CONV_ERR if an error is encountered during execution, and PAM_SUCCESS otherwise.

28.2.2 PAM Actions

PAM does not hold any static information in the library between calls, and instead stores all persistent information using an opaque data structure that is passed to all calls. This opaque object, pam_handle_t, is maintained by PAM but held by the calling application. It is initialized with the pam_start() function and deallocated by the pam_end() function:

```
#include <security/pam_appl.h>
int pam_start(const char *service_name, const char *user,
              const struct pam_conv *pam_conversation,
              pam_handle_t **pamh);
int pam_end(pam_handle_t *pamh, int pam_status);
```

The service_name argument is intended to be a unique name for your application. This unique name allows the system administrator to configure security specifically for your application; two applications using the same service_name necessarily share the same configuration. The user argument is the user name being authenticated. The pam_conversation argument is the conversation structure already discussed. The pamh argument is the opaque object that tracks internal state. pam_start() is demonstrated on line 97 of pamexample.c.

The pam_end() function, demonstrated on line 137 of pamexample.c, cleans up all state stored in the opaque object pamh, and informs the modules referenced by it of the final status of the actions; if the application was successful in its use of PAM, it should provide a pam_status of PAM_SUCCESS; otherwise, it should provide the most recent error returned by PAM.

There are cases in which PAM modules can make use of extra information when deciding whether to authenticate a user; information provided by the system and not by the user. In addition, there are times that PAM modules may need to alert the application of a change. The mechanism for passing this extra information around is the *PAM item*. An item's value is set with the pam_set_item() function, and queried with the pam_get_item() function:

```
#include <security/pam_appl.h>
extern int pam_set_item(pam_handle_t *pamh, int item_type,
                        const void *item);
extern int pam_get_item(const pam_handle_t *pamh, int item_type,
                        const void **item);
```

The item_type argument determines the identity and semantics of the item. We cover only the commonly used values of item_type here:

PAM_TTY

> item is a pointer to a string containing the name of the TTY device that the authentication request is associated with. This might be ttyS0 for the first serial port on a standard system, or pts/0 for the first pseudo-tty, or tty1 for the first virtual console.

PAM_USER

> This is automatically set by pam_start() to the user argument passed to pam_start(). It is important to note that this name may change! If your application cares about the user name, it must check the value via pam_get_item() after calling into the PAM stack and before making use of the name in other code.

PAM_RUSER

> For network protocols (such as rsh and ssh), this item should be used to provide the remote system user name to any PAM modules that use it. This allows the system administrator to determine whether rhost-style authentication is allowed.

PAM_RHOST

> Like PAM_RUSER, PAM_RHOST should be set for network protocols where the name of the remote host might be used as a component of authentication or account management.

The rest of the functions each take two arguments, the pamh opaque object and an integer that can either be zero or the flag PAM_SILENT. The PAM_SILENT flag requests that the PAM framework and modules not generate informational messages, but does not prevent prompting for passwords. Normal applications do not set PAM_SILENT.

The pam_authenticate() function, demonstrated on line 100 of pamexample.c, does whatever the system administrator has configured this application (as determined by the service_name argument to the pam_start() function) to do to authenticate the user. This might include asking for one or more passwords, checking that the current user name (as determined by the PAM_USER PAM item, *not* by the current uid; PAM modules do not consider uid because applications calling PAM are normally explicitly not running as the user being authenticated) is the current user of the console, checking that the current user (again, by name) has authenticated to an equivalent level of service recently, checking the PAM items PAM_RUSER and PAM_RHOST against local tables of equivalent remote users and hosts (for example, as the rsh daemon does), or something else. (Note that most systems use the "shadow password" system, in which case, in order to protect the passwords, only processes with root permissions may check arbitrary users' passwords; a process not running as root may check only that uid's own password. This is one of the only exceptions to the rule that PAM modules must not consider the uid.)

The pam_acct_mgmt() function, demonstrated on line 107, assumes that pam_authenticate() has already been called and has succeeded, and then checks to see whether the user (again, specified by name) is permitted to do the requested access. It may consider the PAM items PAM_USER, PAM_TTY, PAM_RUSER, and PAM_RHOST in determining whether the access is allowed. For example, one particular user may be allowed on certain ttys only during certain hours, or each user in some class may be allowed only a certain number of concurrent logins, or certain sets of remote users and hosts may be allowed only during certain hours.

The `pam_setcred()` function, demonstrated on line 118, assumes that authentication has succeeded, and then sets up credentials for the user. While the uid, gid, and supplemental groups are technically credentials, they are not managed by `pam_setcred()` because to do so would not fit the security model of most applications. Instead, it sets up additional credentials. A likely candidate for a credential is a Kerberos ticket—a file containing cryptographic data that gives the user permission to access certain resources.

The `pam_open_session()` function, demonstrated on line 113, opens a new session. If the process forks, `pam_open_session()` should be called after the fork because it may take actions such as setting rlimits (see pages 120–120), and if your process starts as the root user and then changes to the uid for the authenticated user, `pam_open_session()` should be called before dropping root privileges, because session modules may attempt system operations (such as mounting home directories) that are reserved for root.

The `pam_close_session()` function, demonstrated on line 128, closes the existing session. It can be called from a different process than the one that called `pam_open_session()`, as long as the same data is available to PAM—the same arguments given to PAM, the same PAM items used for opening the session. Note that because the `PAM_USER` item can be changed during authentication and account management, you need to make sure that you have taken into account any changes made to `PAM_USER` if you call it from a separate process than the one that set up the session. The `pam_close_session()` function may require root privileges to function:

```
 1: /* pamexample.c */
 2:
 3: /* The pamexample program demonstrates some simple PAM handling.
 4:  * You will either have to use the --service command line option
 5:  * to choose a service name that is already installed ("system-auth"
 6:  * may work, check for /etc/pam.d/system-auth on your system), or
 7:  * install a system file * /etc/pam.d/pamexample with the following
 8:  * four lines (ignoring leading "*" characters):
 9:  * #%PAM-1.0
10:  * auth          required    /lib/security/pam_unix.so
11:  * account       required    /lib/security/pam_unix.so
12:  * session       required    /lib/security/pam_limits.so
13:  *
14:  * Note that if you run this program as a non-root user, there
15:  * may be system limitations on what you can do; account management
```

```
16:   * may fail, you may not be able to test other users' passwords,
17:   * and session management may fail, all depending on how the
18:   * service is configured.
19:   */
20:
21: #include <security/pam_appl.h>
22: #include <security/pam_misc.h>
23: #include <popt.h>
24: #include <pwd.h>
25: #include <sys/types.h>
26: #include <stdio.h>
27: #include <stdlib.h>
28: #include <unistd.h>
29:
30: /* This struct can be an automatic, but it must not go out
31:  * of scope between pam_start() and pam_end(), so it is
32:  * easier in simple programs to make it a static instead
33:  */
34: static struct pam_conv my_conv = {
35:     misc_conv, /* use TTY conversation function from libpam_misc */
36:     NULL       /* we have no special data to pass to misc_conf */
37: };
38:
39: void check_success(pam_handle_t *pamh, int return_code) {
40:     if (return_code != PAM_SUCCESS) {
41:         fprintf(stderr, "%s\n", pam_strerror(pamh, return_code));
42:         exit(1);
43:     }
44: }
45:
46: int main(int argc, const char **argv) {
47:     pam_handle_t *pamh;
48:     struct passwd *pw;
49:     char *username=NULL, *service=NULL;
50:     int account = 1, session = 0;
51:     int c;
52:     poptContext optCon;
53:     struct poptOption optionsTable[] = {
54:         { "username", 'u', POPT_ARG_STRING, &username, 0,
55:           "Name of user to authenticate", "<username>" },
56:         { "service", 'S', POPT_ARG_STRING, &service, 0,
```

```
57:                    "Name of service to initialize as (pamsample)",
58:                    "<service>" },
59:              { "account", 'a', POPT_ARG_NONE|POPT_ARGFLAG_XOR,
60:                &account, 0,
61:                    "toggle whether to do account management (on)", "" },
62:              { "session", 's', POPT_ARG_NONE|POPT_ARGFLAG_XOR,
63:                &session, 0,
64:                    "toggle whether to start a session (off)", "" },
65:            POPT_AUTOHELP
66:            POPT_TABLEEND
67:        };
68:
69:        optCon = poptGetContext("pamexample", argc, argv,
70:                                optionsTable, 0);
71:        if ((c = poptGetNextOpt(optCon)) < -1) {
72:            fprintf(stderr, "%s: %s\n",
73:                poptBadOption(optCon, POPT_BADOPTION_NOALIAS),
74:                poptStrerror(c));
75:            return 1;
76:        }
77:        poptFreeContext(optCon);
78:
79:        if (!service) {
80:            /* Note that a normal application must not give this
81:             * option to the user; it exists here to make it
82:             * possible to test this application without making
83:             * system changes requiring root access.
84:             */
85:            service = "pamexample";
86:        }
87:
88:        if (!username) {
89:            /* default to current user */
90:            if (!(pw = getpwuid(getuid()))) {
91:                fprintf(stderr, "Username does not exist");
92:                exit(1);
93:            }
94:            username = strdup(pw->pw_name);
95:        }
96:
97:        c = pam_start(service, username, &my_conv, &pamh);
```

```
 98:        check_success(pamh, c);
 99:
100:        c = pam_authenticate(pamh, 0);
101:        check_success(pamh, c);
102:
103:        if (account) {
104:            /* if authentication did not succeed, account management
105:             * is not defined
106:             */
107:            c = pam_acct_mgmt(pamh, 0);
108:            check_success(pamh, c);
109:        }
110:
111:        if (session) {
112:            /* We would fork here if we were going to fork */
113:            c = pam_open_session(pamh, 0);
114:            check_success(pamh, c);
115:
116:            /* Note that this will not set uid, gid, or supplemental
117:               groups */
118:            c = pam_setcred(pamh, 0);
119:
120:            /* We would drop permissions here if we were going to */
121:
122:            /* Call a shell that has been "authenticated" */
123:            printf("Running shell...\n");
124:            system("exec bash -");
125:
126:            /* We would wait4() here if we had forked instead of
127:               calling system() */
128:            c = pam_close_session(pamh, 0);
129:            check_success(pamh, c);
130:        }
131:
132:        /* Real applications would report failure instead of
133:         * bailing out as we do in check_success at each stage,
134:         * so c might be something other than PAM_SUCCESS in
135:         * those cases.
136:         */
137:        c = pam_end(pamh, c);
138:        check_success(pamh, c);
```

```
139:
140:     return 0;
141: }
```

Appendices

Header Files

This appendix includes all the local header files for the source code in *Linux Application Development*.

```
1: /* libhello.h */
2:
3: #ifndef LIBHELLO_H_
4: #define LIBHELLO_H_
5:
6: void print_hello(void);
7:
8: #endif /* LIBHELLO_H_ */
```

```
1: /* ptypair.h */
2:
3: #ifndef _PTYPAIR_H
4: #define _PTYPAIR_H
5: int get_master_pty(char **name);
6: int get_slave_pty(char *name);
7: #endif /* _PTYPAIR_H */
```

```
1: /* sockutil.h */
2:
3: void die(char * message);
4: void copyData(int from, int to);
5: #ifndef CMSG_DATA
6: #define CMSG_DATA(cmsg) ((cmsg)->cmsg_data)
7: #endif
```

ladsh *Source Code*

```
 1: /* ladsh4.c */
 2:
 3: #define _GNU_SOURCE
 4:
 5: #include <ctype.h>
 6: #include <errno.h>
 7: #include <fcntl.h>
 8: #include <glob.h>
 9: #include <signal.h>
10: #include <stdio.h>
11: #include <stdlib.h>
12: #include <string.h>
13: #include <sys/ioctl.h>
14: #include <sys/wait.h>
15: #include <unistd.h>
16:
17: #define MAX_COMMAND_LEN 250      /* max length of a single command
18:                                           string */
19: #define JOB_STATUS_FORMAT "[%d] %-22s %.40s\n"
20:
21: struct jobSet {
22:     struct job * head;        /* head of list of running jobs */
23:     struct job * fg;          /* current foreground job */
24: };
25:
26: enum redirectionType { REDIRECT_INPUT, REDIRECT_OVERWRITE,
27:                     REDIRECT_APPEND };
28:
29: struct redirectionSpecifier {
30:     enum redirectionType type;  /* type of redirection */
31:     int fd;                     /* fd being redirected */
32:     char * filename;            /* file to redirect fd to */
```

```
33: };
34:
35: struct childProgram {
36:     pid_t pid;                  /* 0 if exited */
37:     char ** argv;               /* program name and arguments */
38:     int numRedirections;        /* elements in redirection array */
39:     struct redirectionSpecifier * redirections;  /* I/O redirs */
40:     glob_t globResult;          /* result of parameter globbing */
41:     int freeGlob;               /* should we free globResult? */
42:     int isStopped;              /* is the program currently running? */
43: };
44:
45: struct job {
46:     int jobId;                  /* job number */
47:     int numProgs;               /* number of programs in job */
48:     int runningProgs;           /* number of programs running */
49:     char * text;                /* name of job */
50:     char * cmdBuf;              /* buffer various argv's point to */
51:     pid_t pgrp;                 /* process group ID for the job */
52:     struct childProgram * progs; /* array of programs in job */
53:     struct job * next;          /* to track background commands */
54:     int stoppedProgs;           /* num of programs alive, but stopped */
55: };
56:
57: void freeJob(struct job * cmd) {
58:     int i;
59:
60:     for (i = 0; i < cmd->numProgs; i++) {
61:         free(cmd->progs[i].argv);
62:         if (cmd->progs[i].redirections)
63:             free(cmd->progs[i].redirections);
64:         if (cmd->progs[i].freeGlob)
65:             globfree(&cmd->progs[i].globResult);
66:     }
67:     free(cmd->progs);
68:     if (cmd->text) free(cmd->text);
69:     free(cmd->cmdBuf);
70: }
71:
72: int getCommand(FILE * source, char * command) {
73:     if (source == stdin) {
```

```
 74:            printf("# ");
 75:            fflush(stdout);
 76:        }
 77:
 78:        if (!fgets(command, MAX_COMMAND_LEN, source)) {
 79:            if (source == stdin) printf("\n");
 80:            return 1;
 81:        }
 82:
 83:        /* remove trailing newline */
 84:        command[strlen(command) - 1] = '\0';
 85:
 86:        return 0;
 87: }
 88:
 89: void globLastArgument(struct childProgram * prog, int * argcPtr,
 90:                       int * argcAllocedPtr) {
 91:        int argc = *argcPtr;
 92:        int argcAlloced = *argcAllocedPtr;
 93:        int rc;
 94:        int flags;
 95:        int i;
 96:        char * src, * dst;
 97:
 98:        if (argc > 1) {        /* cmd->globResult already initialized */
 99:            flags = GLOB_APPEND;
100:            i = prog->globResult.gl_pathc;
101:        } else {
102:            prog->freeGlob = 1;
103:            flags = 0;
104:            i = 0;
105:        }
106:
107:        rc = glob(prog->argv[argc - 1], flags, NULL, &prog->globResult);
108:        if (rc == GLOB_NOSPACE) {
109:            fprintf(stderr, "out of space during glob operation\n");
110:            return;
111:        } else if (rc == GLOB_NOMATCH ||
112:                    (!rc && (prog->globResult.gl_pathc - i) == 1 &&
113:                    !strcmp(prog->argv[argc - 1],
114:                        prog->globResult.gl_pathv[i]))) {
```

```
115:            /* we need to remove whatever \ quoting is still present */
116:            src = dst = prog->argv[argc - 1];
117:            while (*src) {
118:                if (*src != '\\') *dst++ = *src;
119:                src++;
120:            }
121:            *dst = '\0';
122:        } else if (!rc) {
123:            argcAlloced += (prog->globResult.gl_pathc - i);
124:            prog->argv = realloc(prog->argv,
125:                            argcAlloced * sizeof(*prog->argv));
126:            memcpy(prog->argv + (argc - 1),
127:                    prog->globResult.gl_pathv + i,
128:                    sizeof(*(prog->argv)) *
129:                        (prog->globResult.gl_pathc - i));
130:            argc += (prog->globResult.gl_pathc - i - 1);
131:        }
132:
133:    *argcAllocedPtr = argcAlloced;
134:    *argcPtr = argc;
135: }
136:
137: /* Return cmd->numProgs as 0 if no command is present (e.g. an empty
138:    line). If a valid command is found, commandPtr is set to point to
139:    the beginning of the next command (if the original command had
140:    more than one job associated with it) or NULL if no more
141:    commands are present. */
142: int parseCommand(char ** commandPtr, struct job * job, int * isBg) {
143:    char * command;
144:    char * returnCommand = NULL;
145:    char * src, * buf, * chptr;
146:    int argc = 0;
147:    int done = 0;
148:    int argvAlloced;
149:    int i;
150:    char quote = '\0';
151:    int count;
152:    struct childProgram * prog;
153:
154:    /* skip leading white space */
155:    while (**commandPtr && isspace(**commandPtr)) (*commandPtr)++;
```

```
156:
157:       /* this handles empty lines and leading '#' characters */
158:           if (!**commandPtr || (**commandPtr=='#')) {
159:           job->numProgs = 0;
160:           *commandPtr = NULL;
161:           return 0;
162:       }
163:
164:       *isBg = 0;
165:       job->numProgs = 1;
166:       job->progs = malloc(sizeof(*job->progs));
167:
168:       /* We set the argv elements to point inside of this string. The
169:          memory is freed by freeJob().
170:
171:          Getting clean memory relieves us of the task of NULL
172:          terminating things and makes the rest of this look a bit
173:          cleaner (though it is, admittedly, a tad less efficient) */
174:       job->cmdBuf = command = calloc(1, strlen(*commandPtr) + 1);
175:       job->text = NULL;
176:
177:       prog = job->progs;
178:       prog->numRedirections = 0;
179:       prog->redirections = NULL;
180:       prog->freeGlob = 0;
181:       prog->isStopped = 0;
182:
183:       argvAlloced = 5;
184:       prog->argv = malloc(sizeof(*prog->argv) * argvAlloced);
185:       prog->argv[0] = job->cmdBuf;
186:
187:       buf = command;
188:       src = *commandPtr;
189:       while (*src && !done) {
190:           if (quote == *src) {
191:               quote = '\0';
192:           } else if (quote) {
193:               if (*src == '\\') {
194:                   src++;
195:                   if (!*src) {
196:                       fprintf(stderr,
```

```
197:                                    "character expected after \\\n");
198:                        freeJob(job);
199:                        return 1;
200:                    }
201:
202:                    /* in shell, "\'" should yield \' */
203:                    if (*src != quote) *buf++ = '\\';
204:                } else if (*src == '*' || *src == '?' || *src == '[' ||
205:                        *src == ']')
206:                    *buf++ = '\\';
207:                *buf++ = *src;
208:            } else if (isspace(*src)) {
209:                if (*prog->argv[argc]) {
210:                    buf++, argc++;
211:                    /* +1 here leaves room for the NULL which
212:                        ends argv */
213:                    if ((argc + 1) == argvAlloced) {
214:                        argvAlloced += 5;
215:                        prog->argv = realloc(prog->argv,
216:                                    sizeof(*prog->argv) * argvAlloced);
217:                    }
218:                    prog->argv[argc] = buf;
219:
220:                    globLastArgument(prog, &argc, &argvAlloced);
221:                }
222:            } else switch (*src) {
223:            case '"':
224:            case '\'':
225:                quote = *src;
226:                break;
227:
228:            case '#':                               /* comment */
229:                done = 1;
230:                break;
231:
232:            case '>':                               /* redirections */
233:            case '<':
234:                i = prog->numRedirections++;
235:                prog->redirections = realloc(prog->redirections,
236:                            sizeof(*prog->redirections) * (i + 1));
237:
```

```
238:                    prog->redirections[i].fd = -1;
239:                    if (buf != prog->argv[argc]) {
240:                        /* the stuff before this character may be
241:                           the file number being redirected */
242:                        prog->redirections[i].fd =
243:                            strtol(prog->argv[argc], &chptr, 10);
244:
245:                        if (*chptr && *prog->argv[argc]) {
246:                            buf++, argc++;
247:                            globLastArgument(prog, &argc, &argvAlloced);
248:                        }
249:                    }
250:
251:                    if (prog->redirections[i].fd == -1) {
252:                        if (*src == '>')
253:                            prog->redirections[i].fd = 1;
254:                        else
255:                            prog->redirections[i].fd = 0;
256:                    }
257:
258:                    if (*src++ == '>') {
259:                        if (*src == '>') {
260:                            prog->redirections[i].type = REDIRECT_APPEND;
261:                            src++;
262:                        } else {
263:                            prog->redirections[i].type = REDIRECT_OVERWRITE;
264:                        }
265:                    } else {
266:                        prog->redirections[i].type = REDIRECT_INPUT;
267:                    }
268:
269:                    /* This isn't POSIX sh compliant. Oh well. */
270:                    chptr = src;
271:                    while (isspace(*chptr)) chptr++;
272:
273:                    if (!*chptr) {
274:                        fprintf(stderr, "file name expected after %c\n",
275:                                *src);
276:                        freeJob(job);
277:                        return 1;
278:                    }
```

```
279:
280:                  prog->redirections[i].filename = buf;
281:                  while (*chptr && !isspace(*chptr))
282:                      *buf++ = *chptr++;
283:
284:                  src = chptr - 1;                    /* we src++ later */
285:                  prog->argv[argc] = ++buf;
286:                  break;
287:
288:              case '|':                              /* pipe */
289:                  /* finish this command */
290:                  if (*prog->argv[argc]) argc++;
291:                  if (!argc) {
292:                      fprintf(stderr, "empty command in pipe\n");
293:                      freeJob(job);
294:                      return 1;
295:                  }
296:                  prog->argv[argc] = NULL;
297:
298:                  /* and start the next */
299:                  job->numProgs++;
300:                  job->progs = realloc(job->progs,
301:                                  sizeof(*job->progs) *
302:                                      job->numProgs);
303:                  prog = job->progs + (job->numProgs - 1);
304:                  prog->numRedirections = 0;
305:                  prog->redirections = NULL;
306:                  prog->freeGlob = 0;
307:                  argc = 0;
308:
309:                  argvAlloced = 5;
310:                  prog->argv = malloc(sizeof(*prog->argv) *
311:                                  argvAlloced);
312:                  prog->argv[0] = ++buf;
313:
314:                  src++;
315:                  while (*src && isspace(*src)) src++;
316:
317:                  if (!*src) {
318:                      fprintf(stderr, "empty command in pipe\n");
319:                      return 1;
```

```
320:            }
321:            src--;        /* we'll ++ it at the end of the loop */
322:
323:            break;
324:
325:        case '&':                           /* background */
326:            *isBg = 1;
327:        case ';':                           /* multiple commands */
328:            done = 1;
329:            returnCommand = *commandPtr + (src - *commandPtr) + 1;
330:            break;
331:
332:        case '\\':
333:            src++;
334:            if (!*src) {
335:                freeJob(job);
336:                fprintf(stderr, "character expected after \\\n");
337:                return 1;
338:            }
339:            if (*src == '*' || *src == '[' || *src == ']'
340:                            || *src == '?')
341:                *buf++ = '\\';
342:            /* fallthrough */
343:        default:
344:            *buf++ = *src;
345:        }
346:
347:        src++;
348:    }
349:
350:    if (*prog->argv[argc]) {
351:        argc++;
352:        globLastArgument(prog, &argc, &argvAlloced);
353:    }
354:    if (!argc) {
355:        freeJob(job);
356:        return 0;
357:    }
358:    prog->argv[argc] = NULL;
359:
360:    if (!returnCommand) {
```

```
361:            job->text = malloc(strlen(*commandPtr) + 1);
362:            strcpy(job->text, *commandPtr);
363:        } else {
364:            /* This leaves any trailing spaces, which is a bit sloppy */
365:
366:            count = returnCommand - *commandPtr;
367:            job->text = malloc(count + 1);
368:            strncpy(job->text, *commandPtr, count);
369:            job->text[count] = '\0';
370:        }
371:
372:        *commandPtr = returnCommand;
373:
374:        return 0;
375: }
376:
377: int setupRedirections(struct childProgram * prog) {
378:        int i;
379:        int openfd;
380:        int mode;
381:        struct redirectionSpecifier * redir = prog->redirections;
382:
383:        for (i = 0; i < prog->numRedirections; i++, redir++) {
384:            switch (redir->type) {
385:            case REDIRECT_INPUT:
386:                mode = O_RDONLY;
387:                break;
388:            case REDIRECT_OVERWRITE:
389:                mode = O_RDWR | O_CREAT | O_TRUNC;
390:                break;
391:            case REDIRECT_APPEND:
392:                mode = O_RDWR | O_CREAT | O_APPEND;
393:                break;
394:            }
395:
396:            openfd = open(redir->filename, mode, 0666);
397:            if (openfd < 0) {
398:                /* this could get lost if stderr has been redirected,
399:                    but bash and ash both lose it as well (though zsh
400:                    doesn't!) */
401:                fprintf(stderr, "error opening %s: %s\n",
```

```
402:                        redir->filename, strerror(errno));
403:                return 1;
404:            }
405:
406:            if (openfd != redir->fd) {
407:                dup2(openfd, redir->fd);
408:                close(openfd);
409:            }
410:        }
411:
412:    return 0;
413: }
414:
415: int runCommand(struct job newJob, struct jobSet * jobList,
416:                int inBg) {
417:    struct job * job;
418:    char * newdir, * buf;
419:    int i, len;
420:    int nextin, nextout;
421:    int pipefds[2];                    /* pipefd[0] is for reading */
422:    char * statusString;
423:    int jobNum;
424:    int controlfds[2];                 /* a pipe to make the child pause */
425:
426:    /* handle built-ins here -- we don't fork() so we
427:       can't background these very easily */
428:    if (!strcmp(newJob.progs[0].argv[0], "exit")) {
429:        /* this should return a real exit code */
430:        exit(0);
431:    } else if (!strcmp(newJob.progs[0].argv[0], "pwd")) {
432:        len = 50;
433:        buf = malloc(len);
434:        while (!getcwd(buf, len) && errno == ERANGE) {
435:            len += 50;
436:            buf = realloc(buf, len);
437:        }
438:        printf("%s\n", buf);
439:        free(buf);
440:        return 0;
441:    } else if (!strcmp(newJob.progs[0].argv[0], "cd")) {
442:        if (!newJob.progs[0].argv[1] == 1)
```

```
443:                      newdir = getenv("HOME");
444:                  else
445:                      newdir = newJob.progs[0].argv[1];
446:                  if (chdir(newdir))
447:                      printf("failed to change current directory: %s\n",
448:                              strerror(errno));
449:                  return 0;
450:          } else if (!strcmp(newJob.progs[0].argv[0], "jobs")) {
451:              for (job = jobList->head; job; job = job->next) {
452:                  if (job->runningProgs == job->stoppedProgs)
453:                      statusString = "Stopped";
454:                  else
455:                      statusString = "Running";
456:
457:                  printf(JOB_STATUS_FORMAT, job->jobId, statusString,
458:                          job->text);
459:              }
460:              return 0;
461:          } else if (!strcmp(newJob.progs[0].argv[0], "fg") ||
462:                      !strcmp(newJob.progs[0].argv[0], "bg")) {
463:              if (!newJob.progs[0].argv[1] || newJob.progs[0].argv[2]) {
464:                  fprintf(stderr,
465:                          "%s: exactly one argument is expected\n",
466:                          newJob.progs[0].argv[0]);
467:                  return 1;
468:              }
469:
470:              if (sscanf(newJob.progs[0].argv[1], "%%%d", &jobNum) != 1) {
471:                  fprintf(stderr, "%s: bad argument '%s'\n",
472:                          newJob.progs[0].argv[0],
473:                          newJob.progs[0].argv[1]);
474:                  return 1;
475:              }
476:
477:              for (job = jobList->head; job; job = job->next)
478:                  if (job->jobId == jobNum) break;
479:
480:              if (!job) {
481:                  fprintf(stderr, "%s: unknown job %d\n",
482:                          newJob.progs[0].argv[0], jobNum);
483:                  return 1;
```

```
484:            }
485:
486:            if (*newJob.progs[0].argv[0] == 'f') {
487:                /* Make this job the foreground job */
488:
489:                if (tcsetpgrp(0, job->pgrp))
490:                    perror("tcsetpgrp");
491:                jobList->fg = job;
492:            }
493:
494:            /* Restart the processes in the job */
495:            for (i = 0; i < job->numProgs; i++)
496:                job->progs[i].isStopped = 0;
497:
498:            kill(-job->pgrp, SIGCONT);
499:
500:            job->stoppedProgs = 0;
501:
502:            return 0;
503:        }
504:
505:        nextin = 0, nextout = 1;
506:        for (i = 0; i < newJob.numProgs; i++) {
507:            if ((i + 1) < newJob.numProgs) {
508:                pipe(pipefds);
509:                nextout = pipefds[1];
510:            } else {
511:                nextout = 1;
512:            }
513:
514:            pipe(controlfds);
515:
516:            if (!(newJob.progs[i].pid = fork())) {
517:                signal(SIGTTOU, SIG_DFL);
518:
519:                close(controlfds[1]);
520:                /* this read will return 0 when the write side closes */
521:                read(controlfds[0], &len, 1);
522:                close(controlfds[0]);
523:
524:                if (nextin != 0) {
```

```
525:                    dup2(nextin, 0);
526:                    close(nextin);
527:                }
528:
529:                if (nextout != 1) {
530:                    dup2(nextout, 1);
531:                    close(nextout);
532:                }
533:
534:                /* explicit redirections override pipes */
535:                setupRedirections(newJob.progs + i);
536:
537:                execvp(newJob.progs[i].argv[0], newJob.progs[i].argv);
538:                fprintf(stderr, "exec() of %s failed: %s\n",
539:                        newJob.progs[i].argv[0],
540:                        strerror(errno));
541:                exit(1);
542:            }
543:
544:            /* put our child in the process group whose leader is the
545:               first process in this pipe */
546:            setpgid(newJob.progs[i].pid, newJob.progs[0].pid);
547:
548:            /* close the control pipe so the child can continue */
549:            close(controlfds[0]);
550:            close(controlfds[1]);
551:
552:            if (nextin != 0) close(nextin);
553:            if (nextout != 1) close(nextout);
554:
555:            /* If there isn't another process, nextin is garbage
556:               but it doesn't matter */
557:            nextin = pipefds[0];
558:        }
559:
560:        newJob.pgrp = newJob.progs[0].pid;
561:
562:        /* find the ID for the job to use */
563:        newJob.jobId = 1;
564:        for (job = jobList->head; job; job = job->next)
565:            if (job->jobId >= newJob.jobId)
```

```
566:              newJob.jobId = job->jobId + 1;
567:
568:      /* add the job to the list of running jobs */
569:      if (!jobList->head) {
570:          job = jobList->head = malloc(sizeof(*job));
571:      } else {
572:          for (job = jobList->head; job->next; job = job->next);
573:          job->next = malloc(sizeof(*job));
574:          job = job->next;
575:      }
576:
577:      *job = newJob;
578:      job->next = NULL;
579:      job->runningProgs = job->numProgs;
580:      job->stoppedProgs = 0;
581:
582:      if (inBg) {
583:          /* we don't wait for background jobs to return -- append it
584:             to the list of backgrounded jobs and leave it alone */
585:
586:          printf("[%d] %d\n", job->jobId,
587:                  newJob.progs[newJob.numProgs - 1].pid);
588:      } else {
589:          jobList->fg = job;
590:
591:          /* move the new process group into the foreground */
592:
593:          if (tcsetpgrp(0, newJob.pgrp))
594:              perror("tcsetpgrp");
595:      }
596:
597:      return 0;
598: }
599:
600: void removeJob(struct jobSet * jobList, struct job * job) {
601:      struct job * prevJob;
602:
603:      freeJob(job);
604:      if (job == jobList->head) {
605:          jobList->head = job->next;
606:      } else {
```

```
607:            prevJob = jobList->head;
608:            while (prevJob->next != job) prevJob = prevJob->next;
609:            prevJob->next = job->next;
610:        }
611:
612:        free(job);
613: }
614:
615: /* Checks to see if any background processes have exited -- if they
616:    have, figure out why and see if a job has completed */
617: void checkJobs(struct jobSet * jobList) {
618:        struct job * job;
619:        pid_t childpid;
620:        int status;
621:        int progNum;
622:        char * msg;
623:
624:        while ((childpid = waitpid(-1, &status,
625:                                   WNOHANG | WUNTRACED)) > 0) {
626:            for (job = jobList->head; job; job = job->next) {
627:                progNum = 0;
628:                while (progNum < job->numProgs &&
629:                           job->progs[progNum].pid != childpid)
630:                    progNum++;
631:                if (progNum < job->numProgs) break;
632:            }
633:
634:            if (WIFEXITED(status) || WIFSIGNALED(status)) {
635:                /* child exited */
636:                job->runningProgs--;
637:                job->progs[progNum].pid = 0;
638:
639:                if (!WIFSIGNALED(status))
640:                    msg = "Done";
641:                else
642:                    msg = strsignal(WTERMSIG(status));
643:
644:                if (!job->runningProgs) {
645:                    printf(JOB_STATUS_FORMAT, job->jobId,
646:                            msg, job->text);
647:                    removeJob(jobList, job);
```

```
648:                    }
649:               } else {
650:                   /* child stopped */
651:                   job->stoppedProgs++;
652:                   job->progs[progNum].isStopped = 1;
653:
654:                   if (job->stoppedProgs == job->numProgs) {
655:                       printf(JOB_STATUS_FORMAT, job->jobId, "Stopped",
656:                               job->text);
657:                   }
658:               }
659:          }
660:
661:      if (childpid == -1 && errno != ECHILD)
662:          perror("waitpid");
663: }
664:
665: int main(int argc, const char ** argv) {
666:      char command[MAX_COMMAND_LEN + 1];
667:      char * nextCommand = NULL;
668:      struct jobSet jobList = { NULL, NULL };
669:      struct job newJob;
670:      FILE * input = stdin;
671:      int i;
672:      int status;
673:      int inBg;
674:
675:      if (argc > 2) {
676:          fprintf(stderr, "unexpected arguments; usage: ladsh1 "
677:                          "<commands>\n");
678:          exit(1);
679:      } else if (argc == 2) {
680:          input = fopen(argv[1], "r");
681:          if (!input) {
682:              perror("fopen");
683:              exit(1);
684:          }
685:      }
686:
687:      /* don't pay any attention to this signal; it just confuses
688:          things and isn't really meant for shells anyway */
```

```
689:          signal(SIGTTOU, SIG_IGN);
690:
691:      while (1) {
692:          if (!jobList.fg) {
693:              /* no job is in the foreground */
694:
695:              /* see if any background processes have exited */
696:              checkJobs(&jobList);
697:
698:              if (!nextCommand) {
699:                  if (getCommand(input, command)) break;
700:                  nextCommand = command;
701:              }
702:
703:              if (!parseCommand(&nextCommand, &newJob, &inBg) &&
704:                              newJob.numProgs) {
705:                  runCommand(newJob, &jobList, inBg);
706:              }
707:          } else {
708:              /* a job is running in the foreground; wait for it */
709:              i = 0;
710:              while (!jobList.fg->progs[i].pid ||
711:                      jobList.fg->progs[i].isStopped) i++;
712:
713:              waitpid(jobList.fg->progs[i].pid, &status, WUNTRACED);
714:
715:              if (WIFSIGNALED(status) &&
716:                      (WTERMSIG(status) != SIGINT)) {
717:                  printf("%s\n", strsignal(status));
718:              }
719:
720:              if (WIFEXITED(status) || WIFSIGNALED(status)) {
721:                  /* the child exited */
722:                  jobList.fg->runningProgs--;
723:                  jobList.fg->progs[i].pid = 0;
724:
725:                  if (!jobList.fg->runningProgs) {
726:                      /* child exited */
727:
728:                      removeJob(&jobList, jobList.fg);
729:                      jobList.fg = NULL;
```

```
730:
731:                                /* move the shell to the foreground */
732:                                if (tcsetpgrp(0, getpid()))
733:                                    perror("tcsetpgrp");
734:                            }
735:                    } else {
736:                        /* the child was stopped */
737:                        jobList.fg->stoppedProgs++;
738:                        jobList.fg->progs[i].isStopped = 1;
739:
740:                        if (jobList.fg->stoppedProgs ==
741:                                        jobList.fg->runningProgs) {
742:                            printf("\n" JOB_STATUS_FORMAT,
743:                                    jobList.fg->jobId,
744:                                    "Stopped", jobList.fg->text);
745:                            jobList.fg = NULL;
746:                        }
747:                    }
748:
749:                    if (!jobList.fg) {
750:                        /* move the shell to the foreground */
751:                        if (tcsetpgrp(0, getpid()))
752:                            perror("tcsetpgrp");
753:                    }
754:                }
755:        }
756:
757:        return 0;
758: }
```

Glossary

advisory locking   Locking that is not enforced: All processes that manipulate the locked files must explicitly check for the existence of locks. (276)

anonymous mapping   A mapping of memory that is not associated with an inode in a file system, limited to private use within a process.   (269)

ar   The archiving utility used most often to create libraries.   (79)

basic regular expression (BRE)   The type of string-matching expression used by the `grep` utility.   (557)

big-endian   Multibyte values stored with the *most* significant byte in the lowest memory address or first byte transmitted, followed by the remainder of the bytes in order of significance.   (430)

blocked signals   Signals that a process is not prepared to accept. Usually, signals are blocked for a short time while the process is performing a sensitive task.   When a signal is sent to a process that is blocking that signal, the signal remains pending until the process unblocks the signal. (207)

break   A long stream of 0 bits on a serial interface.   (375)

buffer overflow   Writing data past the end of the memory location allocated for that data, which normally causes the program to fail in a seemingly random way and can also be the cause of security vulnerabilities. (59)

buffer underrun   Writing data before the beginning of the memory location allocated for that data.   (59)

canonical hostname   Hostname to which an IP address maps.   While many hostnames may map to a single IP address, that address maps only back to a single, canonical, hostname.   (438)

capability   Actions a terminal can take in response to received escape sequences.   (514)

catching a signal   Providing a function that gets executed when a particular signal is sent to the process.   (203)

Command Sequence Introduction (CSI)   A character that initiates a relatively complex escape sequence.   (517)

concurrent server   A server that can handle multiple requests (normally from multiple hosts) simultaneously.   (421)

connection-oriented protocol   A network protocol which provides communication between two endpoints by establishing a connection, communicating over that connection, and terminating the connection.   (409)

connectionless protocol   A network protocol that allows two endpoints to communicate without first creating a connection between them.   (409)

control character   A character in a data stream that provides control information to the processing program but does not change the processing mode.   (516)

copy-on-write   Marking as read-only a page meant to be writeable and private to multiple processes, producing a writeable version for each process as each process tries to write to it.   (128)

dangling link   A symbolic link that references a nonexistent file.   (192)

deadlocks   Cases in which at least two consumers of resources (such as processes) are waiting for a resource held by another of the consumers in the same set, ensuring that no progress can be made.   (133)

device files   Special files that represent physical or logical devices on the system. Representing these as files lets programs access them using the normal file system calls.   (156)

directories   Special files that contain lists of file names, and can include other files. Directories are widely used for arranging large number of files in a hierarchical manner.   (156)

dotted-decimal notation   The standard form for writing an IPv4 address as a decimal number for every byte in the address, with those bytes being separated by periods.   (431)

effective uid   The user ID used for most credential checks. Under Linux, the filesystem uid is used for file permission checks while the effective uid is used for all other credential checks.   (110)

environment variables   Name/value pairs, wherein each pair is represented as a single string of the form `NAME=VALUE`, and the set of these strings makes up the program's environment.   (115)

epoch   A point from which time is measured. Linux, like all Unix systems, defines its epoch as midnight, January 1, 1970 UTC.   (481)

error control   The characteristic of some network protocols that ensures the data which arrives is correct.   (410)

escape character   A character in a data stream that changes the data processing mode from *normal mode* to an *escape mode*, which usually involves reading some subsequent characters for control information.   (516)

escape sequence   A series of characters that is treated differently by the program reading it. The escape sequence often encodes control information in a stream of data.   (513)

Executable and Linking Format (ELF)   A generic file format for various kinds of binary files, including object files, libraries, shared libraries, and executables.   (81)

extended regular expression (ERE)   The type of string-matching expression used by the `egrep` utility.   (557)

file descriptor   A small positive integer, used by a process as a reference to an open file.   (165)

file mode   A 16-bit value that specifies a file's type and access permissions. (158)

file structure   The structure that is allocated each time a file is opened. File descriptors link a process to a file structure, and each file structure may be referenced by multiple descriptors in multiple processes.   (197)

filesystem uid   The user ID associated with a process that is used to verify permissions for file system accesses by that process.   (113)

glob   Expanding *, ?, and [ ] according to file name matching rules.   (300)

glyph   The shape used to represent a character.   (516)

heap   The dynamic memory pool from which the `malloc()` library call allocates memory during program execution.   (60)

init process   The first process on a Linux system. It is the only process started by the kernel and is responsible for starting every other process on the system. When processes are orphaned, the init process becomes the parent of the orphaned process and is responsible for preventing that process from becoming a zombie.   (107)

iterative server   A server that handles a single request at a time.   (421)

jiffies   Ticks of the underlying system clock, or a synthetic replica of a system clock.   (505)

job control   A feature that allows groups of related processes to be managed from a single terminal.   (325)

kernel mode   The unlimited, privileged execution environment in which the kernel runs, protected from programs running in user mode.   (92)

ld   The linker that combines object files into an executable.   (79)

little-endian   Multibyte values stored with the *least* significant byte in the lowest memory address or first byte transmitted, followed by the remainder of the bytes in order of significance.   (430)

locked memory   A memory region that is never swapped.   (275)

major fault   A fault caused by a process accessing memory that is not currently available, which forces the kernel to access the disk.   (118)

mandatory locking   Locking that is enforced; for example, processes attempting to write to an area on which another process has placed a write lock block until the write lock is removed.   (276)

memory leak   Allocating memory without deallocating it, usually including dropping all references to the allocated memory.   (59)

minor fault   A fault caused by a process accessing memory that is not currently available but that does not require a disk access for the kernel to satisfy.   (118)

modal   The method of control in which the response to input depends on the mode a program is in, which is generally determined by prior input.   (516)

network byte order   The order in which bytes in multibyte values are transmitted across a network.   For TCP/IP, the network byte order is big-endian.   (430)

origin   The first character of the first row of a character-matrix display.   (520)

orphan process   A process whose parent has died.   (107)

packet-based protocols   Network protocols that transmit data as groups of bytes; each group is delivered as a single unit and is neither merged with another group nor split up.   (410)

pending connections   Socket connections made to addresses that have been `listen()`ed to but have not yet been `accept()`ed.   (415)

pending signals   Signals that have been sent to a process but have not yet been delivered.   (204)

pid   A positive integer that uniquely identifies a process.   (107)

pipes   A simple mechanism of interprocess communication that lets processes write data to a file descriptor that appears as data to be read through another file descriptor.   (155)

process group   A set of processes logically related.   Process groups are moved between a terminal's foreground and background through job control, most commonly by shells.   (135)

real uid   The user ID that is actually responsible for running the process. This can be changed only by the root user, and allows setgid programs to know which user invoked them.   (110)

reentrant functions   Functions that can be interrupted by a signal and called again from the signal handler.   More generally, reentrancy is the ability for a code segment to be run simultaneously in multiple threads of execution.   (206)

regular files   Files that store normal data.   (155)

reliable signals   Signal implementations defined to allow consistent and correct signal handling.   (207)

reserved ports   The TCP port numbers from 0 to 1,024, which may be used only by processes running as root.   (432)

resident set size   The amount of RAM a process is currently using. The swapped-out portions of the process do not contribute to its resident set size.   (121)

reverse name lookup   The process of converting an IP address into the associated canonical hostname.   (438)

saved uid   The user ID that a process can make the effective uid even if they would not otherwise have sufficient permission to assume that uid. (110)

sequencing   The characteristic of some network protocols which guarantees that data arrives in the same order it was sent and that no data has been lost.   (409)

session   A set of process groups running on a single terminal.   (135)

shell   A program whose primary purpose is to run other programs and perform job control; popular Linux shells include the Bourne again shell (bash) and the enhanced C-shell tcsh.   (134)

shell script   A program that uses #! as the first two bytes of the file to specify a command interpreter used to execute the program.   (160)

sockets File-based abstraction for communication protocols. Sockets can communicate across a network or on a single machine. Unix Domain Sockets work only on a single machine and have entries in the file system that are used for accessing them. (157)

streaming protocols Network protocols that transmit data as a sequence of bytes without any boundaries between them. (410)

symbolic links Files that reference other files in the file system. This allows a single file to appear as if it exists in multiple directories, even if those directories are on separate devices (or even on separate network file systems). (156)

system call The mechanism used by user-mode processes to request kernel-mode services. (93)

termcap Original terminal capabilities database. (515)

terminfo New, improved terminal capabilities database. (515)

tty Bit-stream-oriented terminal interface. (335)

unreliable signals Signal implementations that make consistent signal handling impossible. Most unreliable signal implementations either deliver signals no matter what a process's execution state is, or they reset signal handlers to a default value when a signal is delivered. (206)

user mode The limited execution environment in which programs run. (92)

vcs A memory-oriented device for accessing and changing the contents of a virtual console. (528)

vcsa A memory-oriented device for accessing and changing the contents and attributes of a virtual console. (529)

well-known port A port number on which the Internet Assigned Numbers Authority has defined as being the primary port that a certain service is provided. For example, HTTP, the primary protocol for the Web, has the well-known port number of 80 and most Web servers provide HTTP access on that port. Well-known ports are normally, but not always, reserved ports. (431)

zombie   A process that has terminated, but whose parent has not collected its exit status, causing the terminated process to be left in the system's process table.   (107)

Bibliography

[Albitz, 1996] Albitz, Paul; and Liu, Cricket. *DNS and BIND (second edition)*. O'Reilly, 1996. ISBN 1-54592-236-0.

[Bach, 1986] Bach, Maurice J. *The Design of the UNIX Operating System*. Prentice Hall, 1986. ISBN 0-13-201799-7.

[Beck, 1996] Beck, Michael; Bohme, Harold; Dziadzka, Mirko; Kunitz, Ulrich; Magnus, Robert; and Verworner, Dirk. *LINUX Kernel Internals*. Addison-Wesley, 1996. ISBN 0-201-87741-4.

[Butenhof, 1997] Butenhof, David R. *Programming with POSIX*[R] *Threads*. Addison-Wesley, 1997. ISBN 0-201-63392-2.

[Cameron, 1996] Cameron, Debra; Rosenblatt, Bill; and Raymond, Eric. *Learning GNU Emacs*. O'Reilly, 1996. ISBN 1-56592-152-6.

[CSRG, 1994A] Computer Systems Research Group, UC Berkeley. *4.4BSD Programmer's Reference Manual*. O'Reilly, 1994. ISBN 1-56592-078-3.

[CSRG, 1994B] Computer Systems Research Group, UC Berkeley. *4.4BSD Programmer's Supplementary Documents*. O'Reilly, 1994. ISBN 1-56592-079-1.

[CSRG, 1994C] Computer Systems Research Group, UC Berkeley. *4.4BSD User's Reference Manual*. O'Reilly, 1994. ISBN 1-56592-075-9.

[CSRG, 1994D] Computer Systems Research Group, UC Berkeley. *4.4BSD User's Supplementary Documents*. O'Reilly, 1994. ISBN 1-56592-076-7.

[CSRG, 1994E] Computer Systems Research Group, UC Berkeley. *4.4BSD System Manager's Manual*. O'Reilly, 1994. ISBN 1-56592-080-5.

[Cormen, 1992] Cormen, Thomas H.; Leiserson, Charles E.; and Rivest, Ronald L. *Introduction to Algorithms*. McGraw-Hill, 1992. ISBN 0-07-013143-0.

[Gallmeister, 1995] Gallmeister, Bill O. *POSIX.4: Programming for the Real World*. O'Reilly, 1995. ISBN 1-56592-074-0.

[Garfinkel, 1996] Garfinkel, Simson; and Spafford, Gene. *Practical UNIX & Internet Security*. O'Reilly, 1996. ISBN 1-56592-148-8.

[IEEE, 1993] IEEE. *Portable Operating System Interface (POSIX) Part 2*. IEEE, 1993. ISBN 1-55937-255-9.

[Kernighan, 1988] Kernighan, Brian W.; and Ritchie, Dennis M. *The C Programming Language (second edition)*. Prentice Hall, 1988. ISBN 0-13-110362-8.

[Koenig, 1989] Koenig, Andrew. *C Traps and Pitfalls*. Addison-Wesley, 1989. ISBN 0-201-17928-8.

[Lamb, 1990] Lamb, Linda. *Learning the vi Editor*. O'Reilly, 1990. ISBN 0-937175-67-6.

[Lehey, 1995] Lehey, Greg. *Porting UNIX Software*. O'Reilly, 1995. ISBN 1-56592-126-7.

[Loukides, 1997] Loukides, Mike; and Oram, Andy. *Programming with GNU Software*. O'Reilly, 1997. ISBN 1-56592-112-7.

[McKusick, 1996] McKusick, Marshall Kirk; Bostic, Keith; Karels, Michael J.; and Quarterman, John S. *The Design and Implementation of the 4.4BSD Operating System*. Addison-Wesley, 1996. ISBN 0-201-54979-4.

[Murray, 1996] Murray, James D.; and van Ryper, William. *Encyclopedia of Graphics File Formats (second edition)*. O'Reilly, 1996. ISBN 1-56592-161-5.

[Newham, 1995] Newham, Cameron; and Rosenblatt, Bill. *Learning the bash Shell*. O'Reilly, 1995. ISBN 1-56592-147-X.

[Nichols, 1996] Nichols, Bradford; Buttlar, Dick; and Proulx Farrell, Jacqueline. *Pthreads Programming*. O'Reilly, 1996. ISBN 1-56592-115-1.

[Nohr, 1994] Nohr, Mary Lou. *Understanding ELF Object Files and Debugging Tools*. Prentice Hall, 1994. ISBN 0-13-091109-7.

[Open Group, 2002] The Open Group. *The Single UNIX^R Specification — Authorized Guide to Version 3*. The Open Group, 2002. ISBN 1-931624-13-5.

[Oram, 1993] Oram, Andrew; and Talbott, Steve. *Managing Projects with make*. O'Reilly, 1993. ISBN 0-93715-90-0.

[Oualline, 1993] Oualline, Steven. *Practical C Programming*. O'Reilly, 1993. ISBN 1-56592-03-5.

[Rubini, 1998] Rubini, Alessandro. *Linux Device Drivers*. O'Reilly, 1998. ISBN 1-56592-292-1.

[Salus, 1994] Salus, Peter H. *A Quarter Century of UNIX*. Addison-Wesley, 1994. ISBN 0-201-54777-5.

[Schneier, 1996] Schneier, Bruce. *Applied Cryptography*. John Wiley and Sons, 1996. ISBN 0-471-11709-9.

[Siever, 2003] Siever, Ellen; Weber, Aaron; and Figgens, Stephen P. *Linux in a Nutshell*. O'Reilly, 2003. ISBN 0-59600-482-6.

[Sobell, 2002] Sobell, Mark G. *A Practical Guide to Red Hat^R Linux^R 8*. Addison-Wesley, 2002. ISBN 0-201-70313-0.

[Stevens, 2004] Stevens, W. Richard; Fenner, Bill; and Rudoff, Andrew M.. *UNIX Network Programming, Volume 1*. Addison-Wesley, 2004. ISBN 0-13-141155-1.

[Stevens, 1994] Stevens, W. Richard. *TCP/IP Illustrated, Volume 1: The Protocols*. Addison-Wesley, 1994. ISBN 0-201-63346-9.

[Stevens, 1992] Stevens, W. Richard. *Advanced Programming in the UNIX^R Environment*. Addison-Wesley, 1992. ISBN 0-201-56317-7.

[Strang, 1991A] Strang, John. *Programming with curses*. O'Reilly, 1991. ISBN 0-937175-02-1.

[Strang, 1991B] Strang, John; Mui, Linda; and O'Reilly, Tim. *termcap & terminfo*. O'Reilly, 1991. ISBN 0-937175-22-6.

[Summit, 1996] Summit, Steve. *C Programming FAQs: Frequently Asked Questions*. Addison-Wesley, 1996. ISBN 0-201-84519-9.

[Tranter, 1996] Tranter, Jeff. *Linux Multimedia Guide*. O'Reilly, 1996. ISBN 1-56592-219-0.

[Vahalia, 1997] Vahalia, Uresh. *UNIX Internals: The New Frontiers*. Prentice Hall, 1997. ISBN 0-13-101902-2.

[Vaughan, 2000] Vaughan, Gary; Elliston, Ben; Tromey, Tom; and Taylor, Ian Lance. *GNU Autoconf, Automake, and Libtool*. New Riders, 2000. ISBN 1-57870-190-2.

[Welsh, 1996] Welsh, Matt and Kaufman, Lars. *Running Linux (second edition)*. O'Reilly, 1996. ISBN 1-565-92151-8.

Index

N